YOUTH AT RISK

*A Prevention Resource
for Counselors, Teachers,
and Parents*
Fourth Edition

Edited by

David Capuzzi
Douglas R. Gross

American Counseling Association
5999 Stevenson Avenue
Alexandria, VA 22304
www.counseling.org

Upper Saddle River, New Jersey
Columbus, Ohio

Youth at Risk: A Prevention Resource for Counselors, Teachers, and Parents
Fourth Edition

American Counseling Association
5999 Stevenson Avenue
Alexandria, VA 22304

Cover design by Brian Gallagher

Library of Congress Cataloging-in-Publication Data

Youth at risk : a prevention resource for counselors, teachers, and parents /
   [edited by] David Capuzzi, Douglas R. Gross. — 4th ed.
      p.   cm.
   ISBN 1-55620-230-X (alk. paper)
      1. Youth with social disabilities —United States.   2. Youth—
Counseling of—United States.   3. Deviant behavior.   4. Adolescent
psychopathology—United States.   5. Adolescent psychotherapy—United
States.   6. Dropout behavior, Prediction of.   I. Capuzzi, David.
II. Gross, Douglas R. III. Title.
HV1431.Y68   2004
362.74—dc21   2003002106

This special edition is published by Merrill/Prentice Hall, by arrangement with
the American Counseling Association.

Vice President and Executive Publisher: Jeffery W. Johnston
Executive Editor: Kevin M. Davis
Director of Marketing: Ann Castel Davis
Marketing Manager: Autumn Purdy
Marketing Coordinator: Brian Mounts

This book was printed and bound by Hamilton Printing. The cover was printed by
Phoenix Color Corp.

10 9 8 7 6 5 4 3 2 1
ISBN: 0-13-188248-1

DEDICATION

To: Kevin and Keith Capuzzi

> *Your supportiveness and quick wit made this book possible. You are wonderful role models, each in your own way, for other young people.*

To: Lola Gross

> *With love all is possible.*

CONTENTS

PREFACE

Youth at Risk: A Prevention Resource for Counselors, Teachers, and Parents is a revision of the 2000 third edition. In this fourth edition, major emphasis has again been placed on prevention efforts with at-risk populations as well as practical guidelines for successful intervention with behaviors most often identified as placing youth at risk. Selected chapters include case studies that explore prevention efforts from individual, family, school, and community perspectives. Every effort has been made to address the complexities of working with vulnerable youth in a way that provides professionals, as well as parents, with an information base and guidelines for working within the parameters of the prevention–intervention paradigm. This text differs from similar texts because of the attention placed on counseling and systems applications with youth at risk.

The text is developmental in orientation. Part One presents information dealing with population identification, definition, and behaviors and causal factors descriptive of youth at risk. Information is also included that serves as a foundation for understanding the prevention–intervention paradigm. An exciting feature of the fourth edition is a chapter in Part One that addresses prevention from the point of view of identification and promotion of resilience in our youth.

Part Two of the text deals with parameters that often serve as causal factors for the development of at-risk behaviors. Included in this section are chapters dealing with the effects of a dysfunctional family, low self-esteem, depression, and stress and trauma. Each chapter in this section not only identifies various aspects of the causal factor but also presents information related to prevention strategies designed to deal with these factors.

Part Three of the text addresses behaviors most often identified as placing youth at risk. These behaviors include those that lead to eating disorders, pregnancy, AIDS, suicide, gang membership, violence on school campuses, substance abuse, homelessness, and school dropout. This fourth edition contains a much needed new chapter focused on the counseling needs of queer youth. Each chapter in Part Three provides definitive information related to the specific behavior, includes a case study to illustrate the information presented, and provides approaches to prevention and intervention from individual, family, school, and community perspectives. Adaptations for diversity are also addressed because prevention and intervention efforts usually need to be modified to meet the needs of minority and disenfranchised youth served by school, community, and mental health practitioners.

Every effort has been made by the editors and contributors to provide the reader with current and relevant information in each of the 17 areas of focus. We hope that this new edition of *Youth at Risk: A Prevention Resource for Counselors, Teachers, and Parents* will prove to be an invaluable resource for individuals committed to assisting young people in the often difficult transition between adolescence and adulthood.

ACKNOWLEDGMENTS

We would like to thank the 22 authors who contributed their expertise, knowledge, and experience in the development of this text. We would also like to thank our families, who provided the freedom and encouragement to make this endeavor possible. Our thanks are also directed to American Counseling Association staff for their encouragement and assistance with copyediting and ultimately the production of the book. Thanks also to Mark Stauffer, graduate assistant for this project and a student in the couples, marriage, and family counseling specialization of the Counselor Education Program at Portland State University, who eased the burden of this task.

Special acknowledgment must be given to Dr. Cheryl Livneh and Dr. Ann Fullerton of the Graduate School of Education at Portland State University. Their support for the funding of the graduate assistantship made it possible to employ Mark Stauffer, an excellent scholar, research assistant, and manuscript reviewer.

MEET THE EDITORS

David Capuzzi, PhD, NCC, LPC, is a past president of the American Counseling Association (ACA; formerly the American Association for Counseling and Development) and is professor and coordinator of counselor education in the Graduate School of Education at Portland State University in Portland, Oregon.

From 1980 to 1984, Dr. Capuzzi was editor of *The School Counselor*. He has authored a number of textbook chapters and monographs on the topic of preventing adolescent suicide and is coeditor and author, with Dr. Larry Golden, of *Helping Families Help Children: Family Interventions With School-Related Problems* (1986) and *Preventing Adolescent Suicide* (1988). In 1989, 1996, and 2000, he coauthored and edited *Youth at Risk: A Prevention Resource for Counselors, Teachers, and Parents*; in 1991, 1997, and 2001, *Introduction to the Counseling Profession*; in 1992, 1998, and 2002, *Introduction to Group Counseling*; and in 1995, 1999, and 2003, *Counseling and Psychotherapy: Theories and Interventions* with Douglas R. Gross. His two latest texts are *Approaches to Group Work: A Handbook for Practitioners* (2003) and *Sexuality Issues in Counseling*, the latter coauthored and edited with Larry Burlew. He has authored or coauthored articles in a number of ACA-related journals.

A frequent speaker and keynoter at professional conferences and institutes, Dr. Capuzzi has also consulted with a variety of school districts and community agencies interested in initiating prevention and intervention strategies for adolescents at risk for suicide. He has facilitated the development of suicide prevention, crisis management, and postvention programs in communities throughout the United States; provides training on the topics of youth at risk and grief and loss; and serves as an invited adjunct faculty member at other universities as time permits. He is the first recipient of ACA's Kitty Cole Human Rights Award and also a recipient of the Leona Tyler Award in Oregon.

Douglas R. Gross, PhD, NCC, is a professor emeritus at Arizona State University, Tempe, where he served as a faculty member in counselor education for 29 years. His professional work history includes public school teaching, counseling, and administration. He is currently retired and living in Three Rivers, Michigan. He has been president of the Arizona Counselors Association, president of the Western Association for Counselor Education and Supervision, chairperson of the Western Regional Branch Assembly of the ACA, president of the Association for Humanistic Education and Development, and treasurer and parliamentarian of the ACA.

Dr. Gross has contributed chapters to seven texts: *Counseling and Psychotherapy: Theories and Interventions* (1995, 1999, 2003); *Youth at Risk: A Resource for Counselors, Teachers, and Parents* (1989, 1996, 2000); *Foundations of Mental Health Counseling* (1986, 1996);

Counseling: Theory, Process and Practice (1977); *The Counselor's Handbook* (1974); *Introduction to the Counseling Profession* (1991, 1997, 2001); and *Introduction to Group Counseling* (1992, 1998, 2002). His research has appeared in the *Journal of Counseling Psychology; Journal of Counseling & Development; Association for Counselor Education and Supervision Journal; Journal of Educational Research, Counseling and Human Development; Arizona Counselors Journal; Texas Counseling Journal;* and *AMHCA Journal.*

Dr. Gross provides national training for certification in the areas of bereavement, grief, and loss.

MEET THE AUTHORS

Valerie E. Appleton, EdD, MFCC, ATR, NCC, is associate dean of the College of Education and Human Development and professor and director of counselor education at Eastern Washington University. She is the author and principal investigator for a 5-year, U.S. Department of Education grant to develop a bilingual Counselor Education and School Support project. This project will define methods designed to impact the school climates and the approaches of school personnel and the inservice and preservice counselors who work with students who are migrant, immigrant, and English language learners. Over the past 20 years, Dr. Appleton has been a therapist on an intensive care burn unit, in private practice, in agencies, and in the public schools. Her numerous research publications are in the area of counselor education and supervision, the psychosocial aspects of trauma resolution, and art therapy.

Sonja C. Burnham, EdD, has been a counselor educator in Mississippi for the past 12 years. She began her professional life as a public school teacher in Louisiana and Mississippi and taught for 7 years. While working with students with disabilities at the university level, she implemented federal grants that promoted transition from school to work. Since that time, she has written and worked in the area of career counseling and supervision while educating and supervising school counselors. Her publications deal with issues related to school and school counseling. She was named Outstanding Teacher of the Year for 2002 and serves as program coordinator for counselor education in the Department of Leadership and Counselor Education at the University of Mississippi.

Jason J. Burrow-Sanchez is a doctoral candidate in the counseling psychology program at the University of Oregon. He received his master's degree in psychology from the University of the Pacific and his bachelor's degree in psychology from the University of California, Santa Barbara. His research and scholarship interests include examining the effects of depression in adolescent and young adult populations, improving the delivery of mental health services for underserved populations, and improving educational supports for first-generation college students.

Donna A. Champeau, PhD, CHES, is an assistant professor in the Department of Public Health at Oregon State University and director of the Oregon Program for HIV Education and Research. She earned a master's degree in school health from the University of Wisconsin–La Crosse and her PhD from Oregon State University. Her research interests include HIV prevention/intervention in underserved populations with an emphasis on the contributions of gender, power, and privilege.

Cass Dykeman, PhD, is an associate professor of counselor education at Oregon State University. He is a National Certified Counselor, Master Addictions Counselor, and National Certified School Counselor. Dr. Dykeman received a master's degree in counseling from the University of Washington and a doctorate in counselor education from the University of Virginia. He served as principal investigator for a $1.5 million federal school-to-work research project. In addition, he is the author of numerous books, book chapters, and scholarly journal articles. Dr. Dykeman is past president of both the Washington State Association for Counselor Education and Supervision and the Western Association for Counselor Education and Supervision. He is also past chair of the School Counseling Interest Network of the Association for Counselor Education and Supervision. His current research interests include school violence, addiction counseling, and brief counseling techniques.

Abbé Finn, PhD, has been a guest speaker at numerous national conferences and published book chapters and articles on the topic of school violence prevention over the past 4 years. She is an active member of a national crisis response team and went to New York City following the destruction of the World Trade Center. Dr. Finn is the incoming president of the Mississippi Association of Counselor Education and Supervision. She is an assistant professor of counselor education at the University of Mississippi and specializes in crisis intervention and response.

Camea J. Gagliardi, a doctoral student in counseling psychology at Arizona State University (ASU), has a bachelor of arts in English from the University of Colorado at Boulder and an MEd in counselor education from ASU. A licensed, professional secondary educator, she taught high school English in Highlands Ranch, Colorado, for 4 years before working as a curriculum coordinator and substance abuse counselor at an alternative educational facility for at-risk youth in Denver. She currently teaches educational psychology to future secondary teachers at ASU and serves as a research assistant and counselor on a longitudinal project for talented women in science, math, engineering, and technology, titled Gender Equity Options in Science, funded by the National Science Foundation.

Alberta M. Gloria, PhD, is an associate professor in the Department of Counseling Psychology at the University of Wisconsin–Madison. She has published and presented in areas related to educational issues for racial and ethnic minority students in higher education, in particular for Latino/Latina students, and professional practice issues for counselors in training. She is an active member of the American Psychological Association (APA) and the National Association for Chicana and Chicano Studies. She is currently a senior editor for the *Journal of Multicultural Counseling and Development*. She has served as secretary for APA's Division 17 (Counseling Psychology) Section on Ethnic and Racial Diversity. Some of her recent journal articles are published in *Cultural Diversity and Ethnic Minority Psychology, Professional Psychology: Research and Practice, The Career Development Quarterly*, and *Journal of Counseling & Development*.

Lizbeth A. Gray, PhD, taught at Oregon State University (OSU) in counselor education for 18 years and is currently part of an undergraduate Human Services Program in the OSU Department of Human Development and Family Sciences. She is a sex educator, therapist, and researcher with extensive experience working in developing countries. Her passion is social advocacy and addressing issues of oppression regarding women, sexual orientation, and people with HIV/AIDS.

Fernando J. Gutiérrez, EdD, JD, is a licensed psychologist, life coach, and attorney in inactive status in Santa Clara, California. He is coeditor of *Counseling Gay Men and Lesbians: Journey to the End of the Rainbow* (1992), published by the American Counseling Association (ACA), and a special issue of the *Journal of Counseling & Development* on lesbian, gay, and bisexual issues. In 1999, Dr. Gutiérrez received the Joe Norton Award from the Association for Gay, Lesbian, and Bisexual Issues in Counseling, a division of the ACA. Dr. Gutiérrez has presented at local, state, national, and international conferences on issues of lesbians, gays, and bisexuals; Hispanics and ethnic minorities; chemical dependency; and domestic violence. Additionally, Dr. Gutiérrez has taught courses in multicultural counseling, family dynamics of chemical dependency, and college student development.

Melinda Haley, MS, an Oregon Laurels Scholarship recipient for the years 2000–2002, is currently pursuing her PhD in counseling psychology at New Mexico State University. Ms. Haley was employed as a research assistant at Portland State University during the academic years of 2000–2002 and as an intern on the psychiatric dorm of Inverness Jail in Portland, Oregon, in 2001–2002. Her supervised responsibilities at the jail included assessment, diagnosis, treatment planning, and the provision of psychotherapeutic treatment to the inmates in her caseload. Ms. Haley's current research interests include, but are not limited to, personality disorders and personality development over the life span; criminology and the psychology of repeat offenders; multicultural issues, including racial bigotry and the psychology behind ethnic cleansing; and issues affecting single parenting and posttraumatic stress disorder and the efficacious factors in trauma counseling. Ms. Haley is author or coauthor of several textbook chapters covering the topics of group psychotherapy, Gestalt theory, and single parenting.

Mary A. Hermann, JD, PhD, is an assistant professor at Mississippi State University. She earned a PhD in counselor education from the University of New Orleans and a Juris Doctor from Loyola School of Law. She is a National Certified Counselor, a Licensed Professional Counselor in the state of Mississippi, and a Certified School Counselor in the state of Louisiana. Dr. Hermann's areas of specialization include legal and ethical issues in counseling, school counseling, adolescent female development, and school violence. In addition to teaching at Mississippi State University, she has taught school law and the law of higher education at the University of New Orleans.

Reese M. House, PhD, is a nationally recognized counselor educator. He is professor emeritus at Oregon State University, where he focused on preparing school counselors to be proactive change agents and advocates for social, economic, and political justice. He has experience as a school counselor, community activist, and HIV/AIDS educator. He currently works at the Education Trust in Washington, DC, as project director of the Transforming School Counseling Initiative.

Christina Lambert is a doctoral student in counseling psychology at Arizona State University. She has a bachelor of arts in communications from the University of California, San Diego and a master's degree in pastoral care and counseling from the University of San Diego. For 2 years she served as a full-time volunteer working with youth in Mexico and Central America. In addition, she worked for 4 years as a campus minister at the University of San Diego and trained for chaplaincy through San

Diego's Center for Urban Ministry. She currently teaches educational psychology at Arizona State University and provides counseling services to a diverse urban community at Good Samaritan Family Practice Clinic in Phoenix.

Rolla E. Lewis, EdD, is an associate professor of counselor education and school counseling coordinator at Portland State University (PSU). His research and scholarly interests include using structured narratives in counseling and supervision and creating university–community collaborations that place counselors-in-training in service to high-need youth and families. He has been recognized in his efforts to create local knowledge and community service; he received PSU's Civic Government Award for exemplary work in civic engagement and the Oregon Counseling Association Leona Tyler Award for outstanding contributions to professional counseling.

Benedict T. McWhirter, PhD, is an associate professor and director of training of the counseling psychology program at the University of Oregon. He received his PhD (1992) and his master's of counseling (1988) from Arizona State University and his bachelor of arts from the University of Notre Dame (1986). His areas of research scholarship include college student development, examining risk and resilience factors and the effectiveness of interventions for high-risk adolescents, and counseling training practices. Dr. McWhirter has published and presented extensively. With his spouse, Ellen Hawley McWhirter, he maintains an ongoing consultation project in Chile in which they train couples in conflict resolution and mediation skills in an impoverished neighborhood of Santiago. He has also consulted with two schools in Chile on developing and enhancing school-based universal drug/alcohol prevention programs. With members of his family, he has coauthored the book *At Risk Youth: A Comprehensive Response*, now in its third edition. He and Ellen have two daughters.

Sandra S. Meggert, PhD, NCC, president of Unfinished Business, is deeply involved in the areas of humor and career development. She has facilitated over 500 - Creative Humor at Work seminars throughout the United States and in Europe for counselors, educators, businesses, and various civic groups. She received her PhD in counselor education/counseling psychology from Arizona State University and has taught at counselor education programs, counseled, and consulted for several years. Dr. Meggert has written articles on career guidance and humor, and she has developed career guidance materials and the original chapter on self-esteem in this publication.

Russell D. Miars, PhD, is an associate professor in the counselor education program at Portland State University. Previously, Dr. Miars was director of the Counseling and Student Development Center and adjunct associate professor in clinical psychology at Indiana University of Pennsylvania. His research and scholarly interests include counselor supervision, legal and ethical issues, life span human development, career development, and assessment in counseling. An emphasis in all his work is translating theory and research into effective clinical practice.

Sharon E. Robinson Kurpius, PhD, received her doctoral degree in counseling and in education inquiry methodology from Indiana University in 1978. Since that time she has been a professor of counseling and counseling psychology at Arizona State University. She has a special interest in at-risk adolescents and has been the coprincipal investigator on several large grants focusing on working with talented, at-risk teenage girls. She has designed and taught specialized courses that examine the factors in the lives of adolescents that place them at risk. In addition, she has extensively researched these factors and published both conceptual and empirically based articles in this area.

Ardis Sherwood-Hawes, MS, is a mental health counselor in private practice and with a mental health agency. Her training includes a bachelor of science degree in psychology and a master of science in counselor education at Portland State University. She has worked extensively with women who experience economic, academic, and societal barriers at the community college level. She has published articles covering a wide range of topics, including counseling and therapy for children and adolescents, teenage pregnancy, and issues related to adolescent suicide.

Melissa Stormont, PhD, is currently an associate professor of special education at the University of Missouri–Columbia. In addition to her interest in at-risk youth, her other expertise areas are attention deficit hyperactivity disorder and the area of preschool contexts that create risk for behavior problems and implementing systems of positive behavioral support in schools. Dr. Stormont has published numerous articles for practitioners that review research literature and give feasible intervention options for the purpose of meeting the needs of children in the classroom.

Kimberly Wright, PhD, is a licensed psychologist who has worked with a full range of eating disordered clients at several universities. She earned her bachelor's and master's degrees from California State University, Long Beach and her doctorate in counseling psychology from Indiana State University. For the last 9 years she has served as the coordinator of eating disorder treatment at Arizona State University (ASU), coordinating a multidisciplinary team of counseling and health center providers. She is active in training and offers an eating disorder rotation for predoctoral interns at ASU's Counseling and Consultation. In addition, she serves as adjunct faculty for ASU'S Counselor Education Department.

PART ONE | INTRODUCING THE PROBLEM

Everyone who either works with or lives with youth has become increasingly aware of the potential that exists for the development of at-risk behaviors. This awareness is enhanced by media coverage, educational reform, mental health programming, governmental mandates, and law enforcement reporting. This ongoing bombardment of the vulnerability of youth provides a call to action for all persons involved with this population. Prior to taking such action, however, it is important to understand not only the demographics of this population but also current definitions of at-risk behaviors, generic causal factors, and preventive and interventive approaches to dealing with youth at risk. Part One of this text provides the reader with this foundational information. Chapter 1, Defining Youth at Risk, introduces the topic of *at-riskness* by providing the reader with foundational information related to definitions of at-risk behaviors and causal factors that enhance the development of at-risk behaviors. The chapter concludes with an introduction to the two approaches that are used to work with this population: prevention and intervention.

Building on this foundation, chapter 2, Prevention: An Overview, lays the groundwork for understanding the various strategies incorporated in the term *prevention*. This chapter reflects our belief that more emphasis needs to be placed on proactive prevention efforts so that individuals, families, schools, and communities can lessen the amount of time and energy directed toward remediation and containment of impairment and dysfunction. To meet the goals of the chapter, information presented includes a discussion of the defining qualities of prevention; primary, secondary, and tertiary concepts related to prevention; and program examples to illustrate prevention's place in the broad spectrum of helping. Some discussion of the schools' efforts to develop tragedy response plans is included. The chapter concludes with an explanation of how to plan prevention and intervention strategies.

Chapter 3, Resilience: Individual, Family, School, and Community Perspectives, adds a new dimension to the prevention paradigm by offering professionals an alternative view that sees youth at promise rather than at risk. As noted by the author of this chapter, "the resilience literature offers counselors, teachers, parents, and others an optimistic and hopeful developmental perspective that . . . see[s] people as having innate self-righting capacities for changing their life trajectories, a landscape that defines risks in ecosocial contexts rather than people, and an outlook that asks people

1

to slow down enough to listen deeply to the stories embedded in everyday lives" (p. 58). This chapter provides ideas for practices promoting resiliency that can guide counselors, teachers, and parents in their efforts to ensure possibilities for success for all youth.

These first three chapters provide a necessary foundation for all persons wishing to reduce the vulnerability of youth for the future development of at-risk behaviors.

1 | Defining Youth at Risk

Douglas R. Gross and David Capuzzi

As John Patron sat down at the large table in the conference room, he hoped that something positive could come from this meeting, perhaps something finally could be done to help some of the students in his classroom. He knew that he had been instrumental in forcing Ms. Callis, his principal, to call this meeting. He hoped that all of his colleagues attending shared his view on the urgency for taking some positive action.

This was John's third year of teaching, and each day he was confronted with problems in his classroom. The problems were not those of math, his subject area, but problems that he observed and that were reported to him by many of his students. The problems covered a wide range of areas, including pregnancy, gangs, drugs and alcohol, violence, eating disorders, and dropping out of school. Certainly, he was not the first to notice these problems or the only teacher in whom students confided. If these problems were so obvious to him, why hadn't something been done to deal with them? Most of his students were now juniors in high school, and he was sure that the problems did not have their origins in attaining junior status.

He did the best he could, but he was not trained to handle these issues. In seeking direction, he talked with the school counselor, the school psychologist, and Ms. Callis. Although all of the persons contacted wanted to help, they were also overwhelmed by the demands on their time. His questions for the most part went unanswered. If he was correct that these problems did not begin during the junior year in high school, why hadn't something been done earlier? Hadn't former school personnel recognized the difficulties these students were having? Hadn't parents asked for help with their children? Why hadn't something been done to prevent these problems from developing? John hoped that answers would be forthcoming at the meeting.

John sat in his classroom after the meeting and reflected on what had happened. He was very pleased that he was not alone in his concern about students and that his colleagues had raised many of the same questions that plagued him. He was also pleased that many of his colleagues saw a need for adding trained personnel to work with teachers, students, and parents in developing strategies to intervene in the disrupted lives of many of the students before it was too late. John felt that several helpful outcomes resulted from the meeting. The first of these was that of exploring the development of prevention strategies aimed at early identification of problem behaviors and establishing programs directed at impeding their development. This outcome generated much discussion centering around such questions as "What constitutes prevention?" "How does prevention differ from intervention?" "What have other schools tried and what has worked?" "Do we need to go beyond the school to build a prevention program?" and "What part will the community and parents play in the prevention program?"

The second outcome dealt with the identification of other at-risk issues such as suicide, increased sexual activity and the danger of sexually transmitted diseases including AIDS, and the impact of homelessness on a small percentage of the students. This outcome led to a discussion of the questions, "Are there community resources we can use to aid us in better dealing with these identified problems?" and "Where in the community can we find suicide prevention/intervention programs, AIDS education, and services to aid the homeless?"

A third outcome dealt with the concept of *resilience* and the related questions, "What makes some young people resilient to high-risk environments while others succumb to these same environments?" and "What are the characteristics of both the individual and his or her environment that make him or her resistant to these high risks?" John had not thought much about resilience and was excited over finding answers to these questions. He sensed that the questions came more easily than would the answers.

The major directives that came from the meeting were (a) the establishment of a committee to investigate what is currently being done by other schools to develop an approach to prevention, (b) the development of a list of community mental health services that could be utilized by the school to supplement the work currently being done by the school staff, and (c) the collection of data relating to the concept of resilience and how these data would impact the development of a prevention program. John had volunteered to serve as chairperson of the committee investigating current programs and to assist in gaining more information about the issue of resilience. He looked forward to the next meeting that was scheduled in 2 weeks.

This hypothetical situation has been repeated over and over in school districts across the United States as teachers, administrators, community leaders, and parents attempt to better understand what needs to be done to provide effective programs to help with the growing numbers of young people who are labeled *at risk* because of their involvement in certain destructive behaviors as well as to help prevent the development of these destructive behavioral patterns. The question these concerned citizens are striving to answer is "Do we continue to deal from a crisis-management perspective with the problem behaviors of youth, or do we take a preventive approach to attempt to stop these problem behaviors from developing?"

The answer to both parts of this complex question is yes. With the growing numbers of young people entering our educational systems identified as at risk, it is not possible to say no to continuing our crisis-management strategies. Because of these increasing numbers, however, most educational systems are not equipped to address this problem from a purely crisis-management perspective. Therefore, steps must be taken to attempt to stop its development. Such steps are usually described in terms of prevention modalities aimed at providing programs that will identify young people with the highest potential for developing at-risk behaviors, stop these destructive behaviors from developing, and work to identify individual and environmental characteristics that enhance the resilience of the individual and his or her environment. Thus, we must continue to intervene at the points of crisis and at the same time set into place prevention programs that will eventually reduce the need for crisis intervention.

This chapter first provides a foundational perspective on at-risk youth by presenting the definition, identifying the population, and describing the population's behavioral and causal characteristics. The chapter then introduces the concept of resilience and concludes with a discussion of a prevention and crisis-management paradigm.

A FOUNDATIONAL PERSPECTIVE

Many problems are encountered in attempting to understand the concepts and issues that surround the term *at-risk youth*. Such problems center on definition, cause and effect, calculating and determining the population, and developing and implementing both prevention and crisis-management programs that affect the various destructive behaviors that place youth at risk. According to Conrath (1988), "Principals and teachers have known at risk youth for a long time. They have recently been discovered by policy makers and budget sculptors" (p. 36). Simple answers and agreed-upon definitions do not currently exist. The best we have at this time are experimental programs; a host of opinions, definitions, and population descriptors; and a high motivation to find workable solutions. The concepts that surround the students at risk and the most effective ways to deal with this at-riskness are complex, filled with frustration for those who attempt to understand them, filled with despair for those who attempt to affect them, and often filled with tragedy for the individuals so labeled.

Overwhelming statistics place the concepts and issues surrounding at-risk youth high on the priority lists of educators, mental health workers, counselors, social workers, psychologists, parents, and community leaders. According to researchers Capuzzi and Gross (2000), Kronick (1997), Kushman, Sieber, and Heariold-Kinney (2000), J. J. McWhirter, McWhirter, McWhirter, and McWhirter (1998), the U.S. Department of Education (1997), and the U.S Department of Health and Human Services (2000), approximately

- 600,000 students drop out of high school each year
- 475,000 teenagers give birth each year
- 27,000,000 children live in poverty
- 14,000,000 children are being raised by a single parent
- 3,000,000 children are referred for some form of abuse each year
- 3,000,000 students and teachers are victims of crime each year
- 500,000 robberies, burglaries, assaults, and rapes are committed in schools each year
- 10,000 teenagers commit suicide each year.

It is important to keep in mind that each day steps are being taken to reduce these staggering numbers. Educational, psychological, sociological, governmental, and community-based entities are developing and applying prevention and crisis-management strategies directed toward a society at risk. This book's major purpose is to provide these entities with information and direction in meeting their difficult tasks.

The Definition

Tracing the exact origins of the term *at risk* as it applies to education and youth is impossible, but during the past 30 years, the term has appeared frequently in educational literature, federal reports, and legislative mandates from the individual states. In 1988, *Education Week* reported that three out of four states either have adopted or are preparing a definition of their populations determined to be at risk (Minga, 1988), and although current data are not available, it is assumed that all states have by now established legislative parameters for their at-risk populations. A review of the known definitions reveals not only a lack of clarity and consensus but also that the term is explained most often from an educational perspective and indicates individuals at risk of dropping out of the educational system. The characteristics of at-risk youth presented in these definitions include the well-known risk factors of tardiness, poor grades, low math and reading scores, and failing one or more grades (Kushman et al., 2000; Walker & Sprague, 1999).

A more interesting listing of characteristics was adopted by the Montana State Board of Education in April 1988. This definition (reported by Minga, 1988) is as follows:

At-risk youths are children who are not likely to finish high school or who are apt to graduate considerably below potential. At-risk factors include chemical dependence, teenage pregnancy, poverty, disaffection with school and society, high-mobility families, emotional and physical abuse, physical and emotional disabilities and learning disabilities that do not qualify students for special education but nevertheless impede their progress. (p. 14)

This definition speaks directly to the confusion that surrounds the issue of being at risk and somewhat indirectly addresses concerns regarding cause versus effect. From this definition, it could be concluded that behaviors such as tardiness, truancy, and low grades are the effects of identified causal factors, for example, chemical dependency, teenage pregnancy, and poverty (Aruffo, Gottlieb, Webb, & Neville, 1994; Donmoyer & Kos, 1993; Homebase, 1993).

If programs dealing with at-risk youth first attempt to deal with factors such as tardiness, truancy, and low grades, they may be placing the proverbial cart before the horse. If the desired effects are to reduce tardiness and truancy and to improve grades, with the ultimate aim of reducing the dropout rate, perhaps more attention needs to be directed toward such identified causal issues as are listed by the Montana State Board of Education. Underlying much of the confusion surrounding at-risk youth is the amount of emphasis placed on either cause or effect (behavior) or both. Whichever position is selected often determines both definition and strategies to operate within that definition. For example, if we approach this area from an effect (behavior) point of view, then what we need to do is identify the behaviors that place the individual at risk and develop strategies to change these behaviors. Or if we approach this area from a causal perspective, then we must try to determine what caused the development of the effect (behavior) and attempt to develop strategies that eliminate the causal factors, thereby stopping the development of the effect (behavior). But if we approach from both cause and effect perspectives, then we must develop strategies both to identify and eliminate the causal factors and at the same time put into motion programs that will change the behavior.

This latter approach—from both cause and effect perspectives—forms the basis for our definition of *at risk*. In this book, the term *at risk* encompasses a set of causal/effect (behavioral) dynamics that have the potential to place the individual in danger of a negative future event. This definition not only considers the effect (behavior) that may lead to a negative future event but also attempts to trace the causal factors that led to the development of the effect (behavior). For example, with school-age persons, one of these negative future events may be that of dropping out of school. The causal/behavioral approach identifies not only the behaviors that lead to this event but also the myriad of causal factors that aided in the development of this behavior. This definition speaks directly to the need for programs to change existing negative behaviors and for prevention programs to tackle the precipitating events that serve as causal factors in the development of the negative behavior. When viewed from the causal/effect (behavioral) perspective, the concept of being at risk broadens, and dropping out is only one of many possible outcomes. Other risks include, but are not limited to, graduating without an education, without goals and objectives, without direction for what comes next, without an understanding of potentials and possibilities, without appreciation for self, or without a knowledge of one's place in the larger society.

When viewed from this causal/effect (behavioral) perspective, the concept of being at risk takes on new dimensions and places the emphasis on individual and systemic dynamics that may or may not lead to a wide range of destructive outcomes. Such viewpoint emphasizes the vulnerability of all youth to be at risk and provides a stron rationale for the development of prevention programs directed toward stemming th negative impact of certain individual and systemic dynamics. This viewpoint directs attention to a set of causal issues and resultant behaviors that often have proved to be significantly related to the development of many personal and educational dilemmas faced by today's youth. Any one of these dilemmas could result in personal and educational impairment. In combination, the results could be both personally and educationally fatal. This book uses the causal/effect (behavioral) definition of being at risk and presents both information and strategies to deal with at-riskness from a preventive perspective.

The Population

One of the basic issues confronting those wishing to work in the area of at-risk youth centers on the identification of the population. Who are these persons identified as being at risk? Is it possible to identify young people who, by behavior or circumstance, are more at risk than others? Are not all young people, based on behaviors, environments, and developmental patterns, at risk? Specific answers to these questions are not readily available. The research literature in this area is as yet replete with more opinion and supposition than fact. Interest in this population is recent. Population identification may be possible only after the fact, as exemplified by the studies that deal with placing the label of at-risk youth on those who drop out of school, abuse alcohol and/or drugs, become involved in gangs, and attempt and/or complete suicide. In such studies, the population is identified by the specific behaviors manifested. Such an approach to identification, although interesting, limits the identification process of at-riskness to those who currently manifest the specified behaviors.

Another factor that may hinder gaining a comprehensive perspective on the population of at-risk youth is the fact that the terms *at-risk youth* and *adolescence* are used somewhat interchangeably. It seems that to be at risk is to be between the ages of 13 and 18. Such parameters are understandable when we realize that most of the behaviors that are used to describe at-risk youth are those that coincide with the turbulent and exploratory developmental period called adolescence. Factors such as sexual experimentation, first-time drug and alcohol use, ego and self-concept development, and peer inclusion or exclusion are descriptive both of adolescence and of the population labeled at-risk youth. Such age-specific parameters, however, are limiting and often rule out a large segment of youth, namely, those younger than 13, who also need to be a focus in any discussion of at-risk youth.

According to Stevens and Griffin (2001), it is alarming to realize the age at which youth begin to engage in at-risk behaviors. Large numbers of children ages 9 through 12 experiment with chemical substances. Stevens and Griffin reported that, based on a 1996 report, 32.4% of those who reported having had at least one drink in their lifetime were under 13, 7.6% had tried marijuana, and 9% had become sexually active. It is easy to see that such early behavior choices put young people at risk for poor outcomes in later life.

If we limit our identification process of at-risk youth to adolescence, we may also limit issues of cause and effect. From this perspective, both causal and behavioral dynamics are correlated with entrance into and exit from the developmental stage termed *adolescence*. On the basis of the definition of at-risk youth stated earlier and knowledge of human development, we take a somewhat different viewpoint in identifying this population and view adolescence as simply the emerging period for behaviors that have been developing over a much longer period of time.

In keeping with this definition and viewpoint, the population identified as at risk includes all youth regardless of age. All young people have the potential for the development of at-risk behaviors. The key words in this statement are *potential for*. All young people may move in and out of at-riskness depending on personal, social, educational, and family dynamics. No one can be excluded.

By expanding the at-risk population to include all youth, the doors are open to begin work with this population at a much earlier age, to identify causal factors in the individual's environment that may either encourage or impede the later development of at-risk behaviors, and to develop prevention programs for all youth regardless of age or circumstance. If all youth have the potential for the development of at-risk behaviors, preventive steps can be taken to see that the young person does not reach his or her at-risk potential. If this population also includes those who have achieved their at-risk potential, then crisis-management steps can be taken to reduce the level of at-riskness and return them to a level more descriptive of *potential for*.

Behaviors and Causal Factors

Based on the assumption that all youth have the potential for at-riskness, how then are we able to identify both behaviors and causal factors that make these behaviors reality? Is it possible to spell out a direct cause–effect relationship, or is this relationship much more indirect and circular in nature? The answers to these questions are at best speculative and perhaps best understood by looking at the developmental period that describes this population and then by identifying the behaviors and causal factors related to this population from school, mental health, and home perspectives.

The developmental period from childhood through adolescence is characterized by rapid physical change, striving for independence, exploration and implementation of new behaviors, strengthening peer relationships, sexual awakening and experimentation, and seeking clarity relating to self and one's place in the larger society. Pressures exerted by family, school, peers, and society to conform or not conform to established standards contribute to the highly charged environment in which this developmental process takes place and the degree of vulnerability that exists within it for the individual. Ingersoll and Orr (1988), in an article about adolescents at risk, discussed G. Stanley Hall's 1904 view of adolescence as a phase of "storm and stress" and painted a graphic picture of this developmental process in which adolescence is simply the emerging period for behaviors that have been developing over a much longer period of time:

> Still, for those who deal with adolescents in a therapeutic context, there remains a subgroup that does experience storm and stress, whose transition to adulthood is marked by turmoil and trial. Further, only a recluse could be unaware of the statistics that show an upsurge in adolescent suicide, pregnancy, and venereal disease, as well as continued patterns of drug and alcohol use and abuse, school dropouts, and delinquency. For some young people, adolescence is an extended period of struggle; for others the transition is marked by alternating periods of struggle and quiescence. During periods of stress and turmoil, the latter group's ability to draw on effective adaptive coping behaviors is taxed. The resulting maladaptive behavior risks compromising physical, psychological, and social health. These young people are at risk. (p. 1)

Terms such as *turmoil, trial, struggle, compromise,* and *stress* lend credence to the difficulty that surrounds this developmental period of youth. Research dealing with this developmental period includes but is not limited to such impacting factors as eating disorders (Brownell & Rodin, 1994; McLoyd, 1998; Wright, 2000), homelessness (Rafferty & Schinn, 1991; Stormont, 2000), sexual behaviors (Katz, Mills, Singh, & Best, 1995; Melchert & Burnett, 1990; Rounds, 1997), abuse (Dykeman & Appleton, 2000; Goldman & Galgino, 1990; Rencken, 1996), affective disorders (Capaldi & Stoolmiller, 1999; Lewinsohn, Rohde, Klein, & Seeley, 1999; Meggert, 2000; Pinto, Grapentine, Francis, & Picariello, 1996), substance use and abuse (Bryant, West, & Windle, 1997; Gloria & Robinson-Kurpius, 2000; Hawkins, Arthur, & Catalano, 1995), pregnancy (Alan Guttmacher Institute, 1994; Sherwood-Hawes, 2000), suicide and suicide ideation (Capuzzi & Gross, 2000; Durlak & Wells, 1997; Shaffer & Craft, 1999), and violence (Fernandez, 2000; Furlong & Morrison, 2000; Metropolitan Life Insurance Co., 1999; Wilson, 1997). Each of these factors is descriptive of either behaviors or causal factors that can be identified from the perspective of the school, the mental health community, and the home. The behaviors and causal factors are separated for purposes of discussion only. Many items could appear in each perspective's listing.

From a School Perspective

At-risk behaviors.   From an educational perspective, there seems to be a good deal of consistency regarding the behaviors of youth who fall within the parameters of the at-risk population. According to Brooks, Schiraldi, and Ziedenberg (2000), Kushman et al. (2000), Mayer and Leone (1999), and Walker and Sprague (1999), the following behaviors are red flags for those at risk:

- tardiness
- absenteeism
- poor grades
- truancy
- low math and reading scores
- failing one or more grades
- rebellious attitudes toward school authority
- verbal and language deficiency
- inability to tolerate structured activities
- dropping out of school
- aggressive behaviors–violence.

Causal factors.   Behaviors such as those just listed, viewed either individually or in combination, aid in the identification process. However, this type of identification focuses on existing behaviors that need crisis-management strategies to attempt to change them. A different approach, and one we support, identifies the causal factors that lead to these behaviors and suggests prevention programs that may keep these behaviors from developing.

Ekstrom, Goertz, Pollack, and Rock (1986) attempted to address these causal issues in their analysis of data from the U.S. Department of Education's High School and Beyond national sample of 30,000 high school sophomores and seniors. The researchers looked at sophomores in 1980 and 1982 and concentrated on the differences between graduates and nongraduates. Their findings indicated that behavior problems and low grades were major determinants of dropping out. Other determinants included family circumstances with few educational supports and parents uninvolved in the ongoing process of their child's education. Further, students who dropped out of school tended to have close friends whose attitudes and behaviors also indicated alienation from school.

In a study of a comprehensive high school in upper Manhattan, Fine (1986) concluded that the structural characteristics that may lead to dropping out include a school that has a disproportionate share of low-achieving students and insufficient resources to provide for this population; overcrowded classrooms; teachers who are predominantly White, leading to poor communication with minority students and a lack of understanding; and teaching styles based more on control than conversation, authority than autonomy, and competition than collaboration.

According to Kushman et al. (2000), studies of early warning signs have identified a variety of school and personal factors that aid in predicting dropping out. These factors are described by the following four categories: (a) poor academic performance (low grades, low test scores, behind in grade), (b) behavior problems (disruptive classroom behavior, acting out, truancy, suspension), (c) affective characteristics (poor self-concepts, alienation), and (d) personal circumstances (teen pregnancy, teen parenting, having to work, caring for family members).

Barber and McClellan (1987) and Paulu (1987) addressed the dropout problem from the students' perspective and reported that the reasons students gave for leaving school included personal reasons such as family problems, pregnancy, and academic problems. Other reasons that spoke directly to problems inherent in the educational structure included the absence of individual help, more challenging classes, smaller classes, more consistent discipline, and more understanding, support, and help by teachers as well as the presence of boredom and communication problems with teachers, counselors, and administrators.

From a Mental Health Perspective

At-risk behaviors. Today, more and more young people are seen by mental health agencies either in terms of clients who present for treatment or through the mental health agency's consulting relationships with schools. Regardless of the nature of the involvement, the following behaviors are most often presented:

- drug and alcohol use and abuse
- eating disorders
- gang membership
- pregnancy
- suicide or suicide ideation
- depression
- sexual acting out
- aggression
- withdrawal and isolation
- low self-esteem
- school-related problems.

Causal factors. On the basis of the behaviors identified, it is easy to realize that no single causal factor provides the answer as to why such behaviors develop, and that it may be better to answer in terms of combinations of causal factors leading to somewhat predictable behaviors. Often listed as causal factors for many of the behaviors just identified are dysfunctional family dynamics, peer group pressure for inclusion/exclusion, lack of positive adult models, an uninspired educational system, learning difficulties that go untreated, increased violence within the community and the school, homelessness and economic hardship, single-parent households, living in a highly stressed society, and physical, sexual, or psychological abuse (Cashwell,

Bloss, & McFarland, 1995; Dryfoos, 1990; Franklin, Grant, Corcoran, Miller, & Bultman, 1997; McCarthy, Brack, Lambert, Brack, & Orr, 1996; J. J. McWhirter et al., 1998; Zanarini et al., 1997).

From the Perspective of the Home
At-risk behaviors.   Parenting in today's society presents many challenges, not the least of which is attempting to understand children and the various factors that have an impact on them. Parents do not have the objective, somewhat clinical, viewpoint of at-risk behaviors as do either school personnel or members of the mental health profession. Because of their close relationship with their children, the following is descriptive of what parents might list if asked to identify behaviors that place their children at risk:

- failing to obey rules or directives
- avoiding taking part in family activities
- spending a great deal of time alone in their room
- being secretive about friends and activities
- not communicating with parents or siblings
- displaying values and attitudes different from family
- resisting going to school or discussing school activities
- arguing about everything
- staying away from home as much as possible.

Causal factors.   As the family and its dynamics are generally viewed as one of the major contributors (causal factors) to at-risk behaviors, what does the family identify as causal factors and where do they look for explanations? Families must look inside the family structure as well as to entities outside the family to arrive at causal factors. These include the educational system, the peer group, the media, the economic conditions that necessitate both parents working, the lack of time for family interaction, the absence of extended family, the availability of drugs and alcohol, the lack of funds or governmental support for child care, and the violence so common in the community, the school, and the society at large (Capuzzi & Gross, 2000; Dykeman & Appleton, 2000; B. T. McWhirter, McWhirter, Hart, & Gat, 2000; Nock & Kingston, 1991).

Origins of Causal Factors

The three perspectives illustrate not only the differing behaviors identified but also the differing opinions as to the origins of the causal factors that aid in the development of these behaviors. Is one more accurate than the other two? Does one provide a better answer than the other two? Are all three perspectives accurate? The answer to all three of these questions could be yes depending on the setting, the perspective of the person in the setting, and the individual under evaluation. No single factor can explain the development of at-riskness; only in combination are we able to understand the impact these factors have on the developmental process. For example, the young person growing up in a dysfunctional family often internalizes aspects of this dysfunction. Such internalization may stem from physical, sexual, or psychological abuse and result in low self-esteem, poor school performance, drug and alcohol use, or gang membership. The causal factors stem both from the degree of dysfunctionality within the family and how the young person reacts to that dysfunctionality. We know that not all young people who live in a dysfunctional family environment achieve at-risk status. We do know, however, that the potential for at-riskness in this type of environment is high.

This same situation exists when we move from the family environment to the school environment. The child who enters school for the first time may find this environment both frightening and difficult. So much depends on what is done to recognize these reactions in the child and to develop programs to aid the child in making the transition from home to school. First impressions can have a far-reaching impact on this person's movement through the educational system—an impact that has the potential for such future behaviors as poor grades, lack of interest in learning, disruptive behaviors, and eventually dropping out of the educational system.

Aligned closely with the school environment is the developing pressured environment of the peer group. Part of the developmental process from childhood through adolescence is the growing importance of the peer group and the need to conform or to belong. The peer group affects youth in areas such as self-identification, self-esteem and self-worth, interactive styles, attitudes, values, and beliefs. As youth develop, the peer group is like a magnet that continually pulls them away from family and often encourages behaviors that are decidedly different from those espoused by the family. Young people attempting to find their place in the world are faced with making choices, choices that for the most part place them at odds with one of two pulling forces: the family or the peer group. The ensuing stress demands the use of coping strategies and decision-making skills, both of which are often not part of the young person's behavioral repertoire. Unless something is done to relieve this pressure, the young person may develop a wide range of emotional reactions or behavioral dynamics in an attempt to relieve the stress, including depression, aggressiveness, use of alcohol and drugs, eating disorders, and suicide or suicide ideation. Any one of these classifies the young person as being at risk.

Society provides a further environment that has the potential for causing at-riskness in young people. One influencing element within today's society is conflicting standards for youth. On the one hand, through legislative actions, persons under the age of 18 have few rights. Decisions regarding many aspects of their life are made by parents or other adults. The message is clear: You are too young to make these important decisions. On the other hand, the media, which permeate so much of society, provide and promote all types of models that encourage youth to be more adult in terms of behaviors, clothes, physical appearance, and relationships. The pull that the media hold for youth is like that of the peer group. The only difference is that the pull may be even stronger and again may encourage youth to move away from the demands of the family, culture, racial/ethnic orientations, and religious teachings.

A second influencing element on youth in today's society is best summed up in the term *violence*. It is difficult to read a paper or view a newscast without being confronted with stories detailing robbery, rape, assault, murder, drive-by shootings, gang-related retaliations, and terrorism. In the late 1990s, schools in Pearl, Mississippi; Paducah, Kentucky; Jonesboro, Alabama; Edinboro, Pennsylvania; Springfield, Oregon; Green River, Wyoming; and Littleton, Colorado made national headlines as armed students killed or wounded both peers and school personnel. All of these involved young people and took place in environments generally thought of as safe: elementary and high school playgrounds and campuses. The terrorist attack of September 11, 2001, added yet another layer of violence, and again this took place in an environment generally viewed as safe: "America." Faced with vivid examples of such violent responses together with the death of family, friends, peers, and teachers, youth experience a great deal of uncertainty about their future. Such uncertainty creates stress, frustration, and often an attitude of hopelessness and helplessness. Any one of these enhances the at-riskness potential of youth; in combination, they almost assure it (U.S. Department of Education, 1997; Wilson, 1997). Because of the growing significance of violence in schools, we again devote an entire chapter (chapter 13) to a discussion of the issues surrounding violence in schools together with prevention information from an individual, family, school, and community perspective.

Within these four environments-the family, the school, the peer group, and society—are found most of the causal factors that lead to at-riskness in youth. However, the *internal environment* (what the individual brings to and takes from these environments) of the individual needs also to be considered in terms of its place in this causal paradigm. What part does the individual play in response to these various environments? Are youth simply the victims without recourse, or do they play an active role in determining their own at-riskness? Answers to these questions may be found in the growing body of research surrounding the concept of *resiliency*.

Resilience

The term *resilience*, when applied to at-risk youth, describes certain skills, abilities, personal qualities, or attributes that enable certain youth who are exposed to significant stress and adversity to cope and even thrive in spite of the stress and adversity. These youth, unlike many of their peer counterparts, do not succumb to the stresses and adversities present in their environment and in fact may develop strength and positive coping strategies from the exposure (Bernard, 1991, 1993, 1995; Garmezy, 1993; Rak & Patterson, 1996).

The research on resilience (Canino & Spurlock, 1994; Cosden, 2001; Krovetz, 1999; Sayger, 1996; Werner, 1992; Werner & Smith, 1992; Wolin & Wolin, 1993) identifies various sets of characteristics that, when present in youth, provide a screening device that allows them to adjust to and cope with the negative conditions within their environments. Such listings often include but are not limited to the following:

- approaching life's problems in an active way
- constructively perceiving pain, frustration, and negative experiences
- gaining positive attention from others
- having a view of life as both positive and meaningful
- possessing positive self-esteem
- comprehending, appreciating, and producing humor
- willing to risk and accept responsibility
- being proactive
- being adaptable
- being competent in the school, social, and cognitive dimensions.

There are no data to indicate what percentage of youth fit this profile. Based on the staggering figures presented earlier, it seems that the percentage is perhaps small. The research on resiliency, however, does provide direction for those working with at-risk youth (Bradley, Parr, & Gould, 1999; Brodsky, 1999; Mills, 1995; Parr, Montgomery, & DeBell, 1998; Sayger, 1996). On the basis of our view of its growing importance in prevention programming, we have devoted an entire chapter (chapter 3) to a discussion of resiliency and its application to prevention programs for at-risk youth.

PREVENTION AND CRISIS-MANAGEMENT PARADIGM

The descriptions of at-risk youth in terms of causal factors, behaviors, and factors of resilience provide a logical entry into a discussion of the prevention and crisis-management paradigm as this relates to developing programs that will assist in preventing the development of the problem behaviors, treating the problem behaviors that have developed, or enhancing resilience factors.

Prevention

Two basic criteria underlie the development of effective prevention programs for at-risk youth: the causal factors that lead to at-riskness can be enumerated, and the population of young people who are affected by these factors can be identified. Causal factors are enumerated for a variety of identified problems in this chapter and the chapters that follow, and there seems to be a good deal of similarity across these factors. The population of young people affected by these factors is also identified in this chapter: All young people have the potential for at-riskness. With these two basic criteria established, prevention programs can be developed to keep the identified population from achieving its at-risk potential.

Prevention programs can be and have been developed for a wide range of potential at-risk behaviors. The theory behind prevention is simply "stop certain behaviors from developing." Prevention programming for at-risk youth applies this theory but in a somewhat more comprehensive manner. Effective prevention programs directed at at-risk youth are generally viewed as multidisciplinary and are developed on the basis of the knowledge and expertise of several publics. For example, a prevention program directed at alcohol and drug abuse might involve not only school personnel (teachers, counselors, administrators) but also parents, students, community leaders, religious leaders, police, and representatives from various human service organizations. A multidisciplinary approach assures the widest range of expertise, involvement of those most likely to be affected by the program, and a commitment from the community in making the program work. It enhances the physical and financial resources of the proposed program and alerts young people to the fact that this is not just a school-based program but one that has the backing of both their parents and the community. Because the program has prevention as its purpose, as opposed to crisis management, information will be provided regarding alcohol and drug use, redesigning environments to remove the availability of alcohol and drugs, changing existing policies and procedures within the educational system to enhance the prevention of alcohol and drug use, changing parenting styles and rules and regulations within the home to better accommodate the needs of the young person, designing alternative activities for young people that do not include alcohol and drug use, and providing peer mentoring systems to allow young people to learn from each other. These are just examples. One of the key factors in prevention program development is individualizing the programs to better meet the unique needs of the targeted population, the school, and the community.

According to Conyne (1994), many of the identified problems of at-risk youth are preventable. What is needed are well-designed programs that take into consideration such factors as knowledge and understanding of the concepts that define prevention, local assessments to define target populations, information regarding existing programs both locally and nationally, and the selection of multiple strategies for implementation of the program. This is best done through a team composed of many individuals representing a broad spectrum of the community. This broadened base not only expands the knowledge and skill base of the program but also assures financial and personal commitment from the many publics affected by the program, including students, parents, school personnel, and members of the community (Keys, Bemak, Carpenter, & King-Sears, 1998; Keys, Bemak, & Lockhart, 1998; Shelley, 2001). Once the program is designed, it can be piloted and then restructured as needed. When the team is satisfied that the program is ready, formal implementation can take place. Evaluation is continual, and the program is revised as necessary. A more in-depth discussion of prevention is found in chapter 2, and each of the chapters that follow presents prevention programming with a problem-specific focus.

Crisis Management

Although crisis management is not the main thrust of this book, it is important to understand the basic differences between prevention and crisis management. Whereas prevention programs have as one of their basic goals reducing the at-risk potential for youth, crisis-management programs have as one of their basic goals eliminating existing at-risk behaviors and providing new behaviors, coping skills, and knowledge that will keep the at-risk behaviors from reoccurring. In the first, we attempt to stop something before it begins (primary prevention), and in the second, we attempt to stop something from continuing (secondary and tertiary prevention). Underlying the development of either secondary or tertiary prevention programs is the fact that many of the behaviors discussed in this chapter are currently present in a large percentage of youth and that steps need to be taken to change or remediate these behaviors. It is too late to prevent these behaviors from developing; they are present. Therefore, programs are designed to eliminate or reduce the behaviors that have placed the individual at risk. In so doing, programs that may be aimed at either individuals or groups of individuals identify the problematic behavior(s), identify the individual(s) operating within this behavioral pattern, design programs based on current knowledge or select existing programs that have proved effective, implement strategies, and then evaluate the results of the implementation. Similarities between programmatic aspects of primary prevention and secondary and tertiary prevention are obvious. Differences also exist. Secondary and tertiary prevention often occur in a structured setting such as a treatment center, mental health clinic, or school counseling office. In these settings, counseling/therapy is provided to address specific problem behaviors and varies according to identified problem behaviors, theoretical orientation of the counselor/therapist, institutional/organization policies, parameters of insurance reimbursement, and the willingness of the individual to take part in the process. Secondary and tertiary prevention are often of a more immediate nature than primary prevention because of the severity of the presenting at-risk behavior. Programs aimed at preventing youth from developing suicidal behaviors do not have the same immediacy as programs developed to deal with youth who have attempted suicide. Primary prevention programs tend to deal with healthy individuals or those with the potential for at-risk behaviors, whereas secondary and tertiary prevention programs tend to deal with individuals who have moved from healthy lifestyles to unhealthy lifestyles. A final difference is that primary prevention programs tend to be group or population based, whereas secondary and tertiary prevention programs focus more on the individual and his or her place in the larger group. Similarities and differences among these differing levels of prevention will become clearer in the chapters that follow.

SUMMARY

This chapter provides a working definition of at-risk youth, information pertaining to the causal factors and behaviors that are descriptive of this population, factors of resilience, and general information related to the similarities and differences between prevention and crisis management. Such information could have helped our hypothetical teacher, John Patron. It could have provided some foundational material to aid him in better understanding the various parameters that surround the students in his classroom. It could have provided him with directives as he began to seek out information regarding what is currently being done to develop approaches to prevention, community resources that could be utilized by the school, and insight into factors of resilience. If John had the opportunity to read this book, he could be in a much better place in terms of answering the many questions raised at the meeting. For those who share some of John's concerns, have questions similar to John's, and feel the need to know more about the areas of at-risk youth and prevention, this book can be of great assistance. The true benefit of the knowledge gained will be not only better service for those youth who have a potential for developing at-risk behavior but also better preparation for dealing with those youth whose behaviors currently place them at risk.

REFERENCES

Alan Guttmacher Institute. (1994). *Sex and America's teenagers*. New York: Author.

Aruffo, J., Gottlieb, A., Webb, R., & Neville, B. (1994). Adolescent psychiatric inpatients: Alcohol use and HIV risk-taking behavior. *Psychosocial Rehabilitation Journal, 17*, 150–156.

Barber, L. W., & McClellan, M. C. (1987). Looking at America's dropouts. *Phi Delta Kappan, 69*, 264–267.

Bernard, B. (1991). *Fostering resiliency in kids: Protective factors in the family, school and community*. Portland, OR: Western Center for Drug-Free Schools and Communities.

Bernard, B. (1993). Fostering resiliency in kids. *Educational Leadership, 51*(3), 44–48.

Bernard, B. (1995, August). Fostering resilience in children. *ERIC Digest*. Retrieved from http://www.ed.gove/databases/ERIC_Digests/ed386327.html

Bradley, L., Parr, G., & Gould, L. J. (1999). Counseling and psychotherapy: An integrative perspective. In D. Capuzzi & D. Gross (Eds.), *Counseling and psychotherapy: Theories and interventions* (2nd ed., pp. 459–480). Englewood Cliffs, NJ: Merrill.

Brodsky, A. E. (1999). Making it: The components and process of resilience among urban, African-American, single mothers. *American Journal of Orthopsychiatry, 69*, 148–160.

Brooks, K., Schiraldi, V., & Ziedenberg, J. (2000). *School house hype: Two years later*. Washington, DC: Justice Policy Institute.

Brownell, K. D., & Rodin, J. (1994). The dieting maelstrom: Is it possible and advisable to lose weight? *American Psychologist, 49*, 781–791.

Bryant, K. J., West, S. G., & Windle, M. (1997). Overview of new methodological developments in prevention research: Alcohol and substance abuse. In K. J. Bryant, S. G. West, & M. Windle (Eds.), *The science of prevention: Methodological advances from alcohol and substance abuse research* (pp. xvii–xxxii). Washington, DC: American Psychological Association.

Canino, I. A., & Spurlock, J. (1994). *Culturally diverse children and adolescents: Assessment, diagnosis, and treatment*. New York: Guilford Press.

Capaldi, D. M., & Stoolmiller, M. (1999). Co-occurrence of conduct problems and depressive symptoms in early adolescent boys: III. Prediction to young-adult adjustment. *Development and Psychopathology, 11*, 59–84.

Capuzzi, D., & Gross, D. (Eds.). (2000). *Youth at risk: A prevention resource for counselors, teachers, and parents* (3rd ed.). Alexandria, VA: American Counseling Association.

Cashwell, C. S., Bloss, K. K., & McFarland, J. E. (1995). From victim to client: The cycle of sexual reactivity. *The School Counselor, 42*, 233–238.

Conrath, J. (1988). A new deal for at-risk students. *NAASP Bulletin, 14*, 36–39.

Conyne, R. K. (1994). Preventive counseling. *Counseling and Human Development, 27*(1), 21–28.

Cosden, M. (2001). Risk and resilience for substance abuse among adolescents and adults with L.D. *Journal of Learning Disabilities, 34*, 352–359.

Donmoyer, R., & Kos, R. (1993). *At-risk students: Portraits, policies, programs, and practices.* Albany: State University of New York Press.

Dryfoos, I. C. (1990). *Adolescents at risk: Prevalence and prevention.* New York: Oxford University Press.

Durlak, J. A., & Wells, A. M. (1997). Primary prevention mental health programs for children and adolescents: A meta-analytic review. *American Journal of Community Psychology, 25*, 115–152.

Dykeman, C., & Appleton, V. (2000). The impact of dysfunctional family dynamics on children and adolescents. In D. Capuzzi & D. Gross (Eds.), *Youth at risk: A prevention resource for counselors, teachers, and parents* (3rd ed., pp. 81–108). Alexandria, VA: American Counseling Association.

Ekstrom, R. R., Goertz, M. E., Pollack, J. M., & Rock, D. A. (1986). Who drops out of school and why: Findings from a national study. *Teachers College Record, 87*, 356–373.

Fernandez, M. D. (2000). School violence: Implications for school counselor training programs. In D. S. Sandhu & C. B. Aspy (Eds.), *Violence in American schools: A practical guide for counselors* (pp. 371–386). Alexandria, VA: American Counseling Association.

Fine, M. (1986). Why urban adolescents drop into and out of public high school. *Teachers College Record, 87*, 393–409.

Franklin, C., Grant, D., Corcoran, J., Miller, P., & Bultman, L. (1997). Effectiveness of prevention programs for adolescent pregnancy: A meta-analysis. *Journal of Marriage and Family, 59*, 551–567.

Furlong, M., & Morrison, G. (2000). The school in school violence: Definitions and facts. *Journal of Emotional and Behavioral Disorders, 8*(2), 71–82.

Garmezy, N. (1993). Children in poverty: Resilience despite the risk. *Psychiatry, 56*, 127–136.

Gloria, A. M., & Robinson-Kurpius, S. E. (2000). I can't live without it: Adolescent substance abuse from a cultural and contextual framework. In D. Capuzzi & D. Gross (Eds.), *Youth at risk: A prevention resource for counselors, teachers, and parents* (3rd ed., pp. 409–439). Alexandria, VA: American Counseling Association.

Goldman, R., & Galgino, R. (1990). *Children at risk: An interdisciplinary approach to child abuse and neglect.* Austin, TX: PRO-ED.

Hawkins, J. D., Arthur, M. W., & Catalano, R. F. (1995). Preventing substance abuse. In M. Tonry & D. Farrington (Eds.), *Building a safer society: Strategic approaches to crime prevention* (pp. 124–186). Chicago: University of Chicago Press.

Homebase. (1993). *Reaching and teaching children without housing: Improving educational opportunities for homeless children and youth.* San Francisco: Author.

Ingersoll, G., & Orr, D. (1988). Adolescents at risk. *Counseling and Human Development, 20*, 1–8.

Katz, R., Mills, K., Singh, N., & Best, A. (1995). Knowledge and attitudes about AIDS: A comparison of public high school students, incarcerated delinquents, and emotionally disturbed adolescents. *Journal of Youth and Adolescence, 24*, 117–130.

Keys, S. G., Bemak, F., Carpenter, S. L., & King-Sears, M. E. (1998). Collaborative consultant: A new role for counselors serving at-risk youths. *Journal of Counseling & Development, 76*, 123–133.

Keys, S. G., Bemak, F., & Lockhart, E. J. (1998). Transforming school counseling to serve the mental health needs of at-risk youth. *Journal of Counseling & Development, 76*, 381–388.

Kronick, R. F. (1997). *At-risk youth: Theory, practice, reform.* New York: Garland.

Krovetz, M. L. (1999). Resiliency: A key element for supporting youth at-risk. *Clearing House, 73*, 121–124.

Kushman, J. W., Sieber, C., & Heariold-Kinney, P. (2000). This isn't the place for me: School dropout. In D. Capuzzi & D. Gross (Eds.), *Youth at risk: A prevention resource for counselors, teachers, and parents* (3rd ed., pp. 353–381). Alexandria, VA: American Counseling Association.

Lewinsohn, P. M., Rohde, P., Klein, D. N., & Seeley, J. R. (1999). Natural course of adolescent major depressive disorder: I. Continuity into young adulthood. *Journal of the American Academy of Child and Adolescent Psychiatry, 38*, 56–63.

Mayer, M. J., & Leone, P. E. (1999). A structural analysis of school violence and disruption: Implications for creating safer schools. *Education and Treatment of Children, 22*, 333–358.

McCarthy, C., Brack, C., Lambert, R., Brack, G., & Orr, D. (1996). Predicting emotional and behavioral risk factors in adolescents. *The School Counselor, 43*, 277–286.

McLoyd, V. C. (1998). Socioeconomic disadvantage and child development. *American Psychologist, 53*, 185–204.

McWhirter, B. T., McWhirter, J. J., Hart, R., & Gat, I. (2000). Depression in childhood and adolescence: Working to prevent despair. In D. Capuzzi & D. Gross (Eds.), *Youth at risk: A prevention resource for counselors, teachers, and parents* (3rd ed., pp. 137–165). Alexandria, VA: American Counseling Association.

McWhirter, J. J., McWhirter, B. T., McWhirter, A. M., & McWhirter, E. H. (1998). *At risk youth: A comprehensive response* (2nd ed.). Pacific Grove, CA: Brooks/Cole.

Meggert, S. S. (2000). Who cares what I think: Problems of low self-esteem. In D. Capuzzi & D. Gross (Eds.), *Youth at risk: A prevention resource for counselors, teachers, and parents* (3rd ed., pp. 109–136). Alexandria, VA: American Counseling Association.

Melchert, T., & Burnett, K. (1990). Attitudes, knowledge, and sexual behaviors of high risk adolescents: Implications for counseling and sexuality education. *Journal of Counseling & Development, 68*, 293–298.

Metropolitan Life Insurance Co. (1999). *Metropolitan Life survey of the American teacher, 1999: Violence in America's public schools.* New York: Author.

Mills, R. C. (1995). *Realizing mental health: Toward a new psychology of resiliency.* New York: Sulzburger & Graham.

Minga, T. (1988). States and the "at-risk" issues: Said aware but still "failing." *Education Week, 8*(3), 1–16.

Nock, S. L., & Kingston, P. W. (1991). Time with children: The impact of couples' worktime commitments. *Social Forces, 67*, 59–85.

Parr, G. D., Montgomery, M., & DeBell, C. (1998). Flow theory as a model for enhancing student resilience. *Professional School Counseling, 1*(5), 26–31.

Paulu, N. (1987). *Dealing with dropouts: The urban superintendents' call to action.* Washington, DC: Office of Educational Research and Improvement, U.S. Department of Education.

Pinto, A., Grapentine, W. L., Francis, G., & Picariello, C. M. (1996). Borderline personality disorder in adolescents: Affective and cognitive features. *Journal of the American Academy of Child and Adolescent Psychiatry, 34*, 1338–1343.

Rafferty, Y., & Schinn, M. (1991). The impact of homelessness on children. *American Psychologist, 46*, 1170–1179.

Rak, C. F., & Patterson, I. E. (1996). Promoting resilience in at-risk children. *Journal of Counseling & Development, 74*, 368–373.

Rencken, R. H. (1996). Body violation: Physical and sexual abuse. In D. Capuzzi & D. Gross (Eds.), *Youth at risk: A prevention resource for counselors, teachers, and parents* (2nd ed., pp. 59–80). Alexandria, VA: American Counseling Association.

Rounds, K. A. (1997). Preventing sexually transmitted infections among adolescents. In M. W. Fraser (Ed.), *Risk and resilience in childhood: An ecological perspective* (pp. 171–194). Washington, DC: NASW Press.

Sayger, T. V. (1996). Creating resilient children and empowering families using a multifamily group process. *Journal for Specialists in Group Work, 21*(2), 81–89.

Shaffer, D., & Craft, L. (1999). Methods of adolescent suicide prevention. *Journal of Clinical Psychiatry, 60*, 70–74.

Shelley, J. F. (2001). Controlling violence: What schools are doing. In S. G. Kellam, R. Prinz, & J. F. Shelley (Eds.), *Preventing school violence: Plenary papers for the 1999 Conference on Criminal Justice Research and Evaluation—Enhancing policy and practice through research* (Vol. 2, pp. 37–57). Washington, DC: U.S. Department of Justice, National Institute of Justice.

Sherwood-Hawes, A. (2000). Children having children: Teenage pregnancy and parenthood. In D. Capuzzi & D. Gross (Eds.), *Youth at risk: A prevention resource for counselors, teachers, and parents* (3rd ed., pp. 243–280). Alexandria, VA: American Counseling Association.

Stevens, P., & Griffin, J. (2001). Youth high-risk behaviors: Survey and results. *Journal of Addictions & Offender Counseling, 22*(1), 31–47.

Stormont, M. (2000). Nowhere to turn: Homeless youth. In D. Capuzzi & D. Gross (Eds.), *Youth at risk: A prevention resource for counselors, teachers, and parents* (3rd ed., pp. 335–352). Alexandria, VA: American Counseling Association.

U.S. Department of Education, National Center for Education Statistics, Fast Response Survey System. (1997). *Principal/school disciplinarian survey on school violence (FRSS 63).* Washington, DC: Author.

U.S. Department of Health and Human Services, Centers for Disease Control and Prevention. (2000). *Adolescent pregnancy.* Atlanta, GA: Author.

Walker, H. M., & Sprague, J. R. (1999). The path to school failure, delinquency, and violence: Causal factors and some potential solutions. *Intervention in School and Clinic, 35*(2), 67–73.

Werner, E. E. (1992). The children of Kauai: Resiliency and recovery in adolescence and adulthood. *Journal of Adolescent Health, 13,* 262–268.

Werner, E. E., & Smith, R. S. (1992). *Overcoming the odds: High risk children from birth to adulthood.* Ithaca, NY: Cornell University Press.

Wilson, K. J. (1997). *When violence begins at home.* Alameda, CA: Hunter House.

Wolin, S. J., & Wolin, S. (1993). *The resilient self: How survivors of troubled families overcome adversity.* New York: Villard Books.

Wright, K. S. (2000). The secret and all-consuming obsessions: Eating disorders. In D. Capuzzi & D. Gross (Eds.), *Youth at risk: A prevention resource for counselors, teachers, and parents* (3rd ed., pp. 197–242). Alexandria, VA: American Counseling Association.

Zanarini, M. C., Williams, A. A., Lewis, R. E., Reich, R. B., Vera, S. C., Marino, M. F., et al. (1997). Reported pathological childhood experiences associated with the development of borderline personality disorder. *American Journal of Psychiatry, 154,* 1101–1106.

2 | Prevention: An Overview

David Capuzzi and Douglas R. Gross

The number of children and adolescents who engage in behaviors (e.g., unprotected sex, substance use and abuse, abnormal eating patterns, suicide attempts) and are exposed to environmental factors (e.g., abuse, violence, homelessness) that place them at risk for adverse mental and physical health consequences is increasing at alarming rates (Hovell, Blumberg, Liles, Powell, & Morrison, 2001; Kazdin, 1993; Popenhagen & Qualley, 1998). In addition, many children and adolescents are experiencing serious psychological and emotional impairment. Because the impairments that youth experience can persist and increase in severity across the life span, the importance of early prevention and intervention efforts has increased in significance.

Conyne (1994) emphasized the significance and importance of early prevention efforts by offering examples of some of the problems that characterize contemporary residents of the United States:

- There are 20 million illiterate adults. This amounts to 13% of the U.S. population.
- Nineteen percent of the population (or 43 million adults) have been identified as experiencing some type of mental disturbance.
- The number of youth dropping out of school each year has reached 1 million or 25% of those enrolled in K–12 settings.
- AIDS has become one of the leading causes of death among the 15- to 24-year-old age group.
- Nearly 5,000 infants are born each year with fetal alcohol syndrome.
- Adolescent suicide ranks second or third in most reports of the leading causes of death in the 11- to 24-year-old age group.
- First marriages end in divorce 50% of the time, and 50% to 75% of child mental health referrals are for children affected by divorce.
- Almost 18.5 million Americans abuse alcohol, and over 100,000 alcohol-related deaths occur annually.
- Increasing numbers of women—3 to 4 million annually—are physically assaulted by intimate male partners.

Dryfoos (1997) summarized data supplied by the U.S. Bureau of the Census, the Centers for Disease Control, the U.S. Department of Justice, and the National Center for Education Statistics with respect to the prevalence of at-risk behaviors of the 14- to 17-year-old population. The data indicate that 25% of all the young people in this age range are behind in grade and that 5% have already dropped out. Between 18% and 48% are involved in some form of substance abuse, and 53% are sexually active. More than 9% have been adjudicated as delinquents, 22% carry some form of weapon, and

21% have frequently been truant. About 25% of this population report that they have been preoccupied with suicidal thoughts, and 9% report that they have made suicidal attempts. Similar data have been reported by Collins et al. (2002), Fetro, Coyle, and Pham (2001), and King (2001).

The cost associated with these examples in terms of economics is staggering; approximately $273 billion was spent in 1990 in treatment and social services associated with alcohol, drug abuse, and mental illness (Horner & McElhaney, 1993). These costs do not include those associated with teenage pregnancy, AIDS, eating disorders, suicide, homelessness, and school dropout. When these additional areas are taken into consideration, the estimated figure increases to incomprehensible levels. As significant as these dollar amounts are, however, they do not include the immeasurable costs associated with human loss and suffering and the concomitant issues related to grief and loss.

In the wake of the need for counseling and therapy created by conditions in the North American culture, the availability of counselors, social workers, psychiatric nurses, psychologists, and psychiatrists pales by contrast (Conyne, 1994). Mandates connected with managed care and the understaffing of social service agencies further compound the difficulties experienced by children, adolescents, and adults in need of assistance from the professionally prepared, licensed helper.

Prevention is based on a different approach to help giving than that associated with prevalent diagnostic/prescriptive approaches. Prevention is not focused on dysfunction and associated remediation; it is focused on a proactive approach designed to empower the individual, change systemic variables, and forestall the development of dysfunction. Prevention is also based on awareness of the risk factors that researchers have identified as the most common antecedents of at-risk behaviors (Dryfoos, 1997):

1. Parents' ability to provide nurturing and support is closely connected to a child's ability to mature and develop. Parents who are unable to parent in ways that convey a sense of nurturing and support provide barriers to optimal development.
2. The schooling experience is also a significant precursor to maturation and development. Poor grades, deficits in basic skills, low academic expectations, and repeated school discipline problems are predictors of involvement in at-risk behavior.
3. Peer influences are strong determinants of youth behavior during the middle school years and sometimes earlier. Youth who engage in high-risk behaviors lack ability to resist joining their friends in experimenting with drugs, sex, and other delinquent behavior.
4. Young people who are depressed or conduct disordered (engaging in multiple problem behaviors such as truancy, stealing, cheating, running away, arson, cruelty to animals, unusually early sexual intercourse, theft, and excessive fighting prior to the age of 15) are extremely vulnerable to making choices that are far from responsible and productive.
5. Life in a low-income family and an impoverished neighborhood also increases the probability of at-risk behavior because economically disadvantaged youth often lack access to quality education and safe environments.
6. Race and ethnicity are also factors affecting youth's vulnerability not because of race and ethnicity alone, but because African American, Hispanic, and Native American youth may be at a disadvantage economically and live in poorer, less safe neighborhoods.

DEFINING QUALITIES OF PREVENTION

As noted by Conyne (1994), Dryfoos (1997), Gilliland and James (1993), Janosik (1984), and Kadish, Glaser, Calhoun, and Ginter (2001), prevention efforts focus on averting human dysfunction and promoting healthy functioning. The emphasis in prevention is on enhancing optimal functioning or well-being in psychological and social domains and on developing competencies. This emphasis is in contrast to an emphasis on the identification and diagnosis of various disorders or maladaptive behavioral patterns in individuals and the provision of treatment to lessen impairment (Kazdin, 1993). Prevention efforts are characterized by a number of defining qualities:

1. *Prevention efforts are proactive.* Prevention initiatives address individual and systemic strengths and further develop those strengths so that dysfunction either does not develop or does not manifest itself to the point that impairment occurs. This contrasts with reactive approaches that are designed to intervene after problems have developed (King, 2001).

2. *Prevention efforts focus on functional people and those who are at risk.* As noted by Conyne (1994), prevention services (e.g., classroom guidance, individual or small-group counseling) focus on those who are healthy and coping well so that strengths may be identified and enhanced and additional skills can be learned. Prevention efforts are also directed to those known to be at risk, such as children of divorce, children of alcoholics, or the homeless. The purpose is to provide proactive intervention so that future difficulties are avoided (Bosworth, Espelage, DuBay, & Daytner, 2000).

3. *Prevention efforts are cumulative and transferable.* When professionals help others through prevention, every effort is made to point out relationships and to assist clients to master a hierarchy of skills. For example, elementary-age children who have participated in groups designed to enhance self-esteem may, at a later date, feel good enough about themselves to participate in assertiveness training. Ability to use assertiveness skills may be useful in the context of refusing drugs; these same skills may prevent a youth from being victimized in some other situation.

4. *Prevention efforts are used to reduce incidence.* Prevention activities are used before the fact so that problems do not develop. They might also be used to reduce the incidence of a new dysfunction (Conyne, 1994; King, 2001).

5. *Prevention efforts promote peer helping.* When elementary school, middle school, and high school youth learn to enhance communication, assertiveness, problem solving, and other related abilities, they are better able to help peers, encourage friends to seek professional assistance, and participate in supervised peer-helper programs. In many instances, the power of a member of the peer group outdistances that of a concerned adult in terms of providing encouragement, support, and straightforward feedback (Dryfoos, 1997; King, 2001).

6. *Prevention efforts can be population based, individually based, or group based.* Many prevention efforts are focused on at-risk populations (e.g., information and discussion about HIV or hepatitis B may be shared with sexually active adolescents, or victims of abuse may be assisted so that they do not develop lifelong dysfunctional patterns). Prevention may also be focused entirely on an individual so that suicidal preoccupation can be eliminated or depression can be overcome. When larger populations are reached through prevention programming, it is possible to impact the life space of large numbers of people (Conyne, 1994).

7. *Prevention efforts can be used early in the life span.* We know that children who are homeless or who have been physically or sexually abused may develop traits and self-concepts that put them at risk during adolescence and adulthood. Early prevention efforts can effect changes in self-esteem, behavior, feelings, and thinking so that these children are not at risk of substance abuse, prostitution, depression, and suicide at a later time (Buckley, 2000; Dryfoos, 1997).

8. *Prevention efforts target more than a single system.* Because each person must simultaneously interact in a variety of environments, practitioners do not emphasize one system to the exclusion of others. Healthy individuals must learn to cope with the demands of several systems on a daily basis (Dryfoos, 1997; King, 2001).

9. *Prevention efforts are sensitive to the needs of diverse populations.* No constellation of services or approach to prevention can make equal impact on all groups. Diverse populations present unique challenges; what one population finds acceptable may be totally incompatible with the needs of another. Practitioners must be sensitive to the traditions, needs, and differences presented by subcultures in North America (Brown & Simpson, 2000; Conyne, 1994; Dryfoos, 1997).

10. *Prevention efforts are collaborative.* As noted by Conyne (1994), prevention efforts can be complex and must be conducted in concert with professionals from a number of disciplines. For example, a counselor working with a depressed adolescent may need the assistance of a psychiatrist or nurse practitioner if medication is needed along with counseling to control a body-chemistry-related bipolar pattern of depression. Often the expertise needed to assist an individual, a family, or a larger population may require input and teaming among professionals from several disciplines.

11. *Prevention efforts are applicable in more than one context.* Faculty and staff in a school setting, for example, may seek the assistance of someone who can provide staff development, train a crisis team, and provide input in relation to a written crisis-management plan. Such efforts may be focused, initially, on substance use and abuse prevention or suicide prevention. After the adults connected with a particular school or school district have been prepared with respect to one particular at-risk population, they can usually apply the same principles and process to providing prevention services to another at-risk group.

12. *Prevention efforts are empowering.* Empowerment should be the primary goal of all prevention efforts (Conyne, 1994). This empowerment should apply not only to the recipients of prevention efforts but also to the providers of prevention services. When those receiving assistance build on strengths and learn new coping skills, they feel better about themselves and their ability to make responsible, healthy decisions. As professionals increase their ability to enrich the lives of others, they, too, feel productive, competent, and capable of impacting change.

13. *Prevention efforts involve parents.* Inviting parents to be in responsible roles in their children's schools, such as paid or volunteer classroom aides or voting members of school reorganization initiatives, results in more positive outcomes for children and adolescents. Establishment of parent centers in schools for parents and youth for whom English is a second language or for whom assistance with health and social services, transportation, child care, or meals is needed has been found to be effective (Dryfoos, 1997).

14. *Prevention efforts make connections to the world of work.* Many at-risk youth have little exposure to the world of work and may not have adult role models who are consistently employed. When these youth are exposed to curricula that provide career information, skills training, and opportunities for volunteer or paid work experience, their involvement in at-risk behaviors decreases (Dryfoos, 1997).

15. *Prevention efforts include social and life skills training.* Improving social, decision-making, and assertiveness skills leads to more positive outcomes. Research also demonstrates that consistency of participant involvement and opportunity for "booster" sessions are required to maintain long-term effects (Dryfoos, 1997).

16. *Prevention efforts include in-service training for both faculty and staff.* Prevention efforts rarely succeed unless time and money are committed to the in-service training necessary to provide the adults in the school with the insight, skills, and motivation needed to successfully implement initiatives aimed at aspects of systemic reform.

17. *Prevention efforts include the presence of dedicated adults.* Successful prevention programs are usually the result of the efforts of adult role models who have a great deal of empathy and provide high levels of support for young people who have risk factors in their lives that predispose them to engaging in at-risk behaviors. It is very difficult to implement new programs and policies in a school in which the faculty and staff are not receptive to new ways of enhancing the school climate and unreceptive to the needs of youth who may be quite different from themselves.

APPROACHES TO PREVENTION

A number of experts in contemporary prevention strategies (Buckley, 2000; Hadge, 1992; Janosik, 1984; King, 2001; McWhirter, McWhirter, McWhirter, & McWhirter, 1998; Roberts, 1991) identify prevention as primary, secondary, or tertiary. As practitioners consider prevention strategies for possible implementation with an individual, a family, a school, or a community, it is important to be able to assess needs and identify strategies in relation to whether these strategies can be categorized as primary, secondary, or tertiary.

Primary Prevention

Primary prevention involves proactive planning of strategies and activities to keep specific problems or crises from developing in the first place (Gilliland & James, 1993). In primary prevention, the purpose is to reduce the incidence of future problems by reinforcing internal coping ability, modifying external variables, or both. Primary prevention provides assistance prior to the development of problems through counseling, teaching, or other services that emphasize anticipatory planning. Through anticipatory planning, individuals of all ages are given the opportunity to select and practice behaviors that are helpful in both present and future circumstances.

Examples of primary prevention include parent education programs to prevent child neglect and abuse and educational programs on university campuses to prevent sexual harassment, date rape, or violation of affirmative action guidelines. School programs for teenage men and women regarding the consequences of teenage pregnancies, the impact of school dropout, or the importance of effective communication skills are additional examples of primary prevention. Entire communities might also benefit from primary prevention efforts. For example, a series of mental health education seminars might be offered, free of charge, to residents of a community and might be collaboratively planned by representatives from the local schools, mental health services, and business sectors. Television and radio journalists might provide coverage of the services offered by women's and children's shelters or local crisis hotlines. Whatever the emphasis, the focus is always on preventing future and, more often than not, long-term pain or impairment.

Chapter 3 presents valuable additional information on primary prevention from a resilience point of view. This provides an additional perspective that may prove helpful to those whose practice focus is working with children and adolescents.

Secondary Prevention

Secondary prevention consists of early intervention with people in crisis for the purpose of restoring equilibrium as soon as possible and reducing the impact of the distress. During periods of crisis, people are aware that the situation is out of control; they may feel helpless. Unless secondary prevention is made available, a crisis may escalate to the point at which it may be difficult to contain or consequences may be irreversible. For example, a suicidal adolescent who does not obtain assistance may attempt suicide, survive, and be left with lifelong physical impairment and emotional turmoil that overlay the traits and characteristics that precipitated the suicidal crisis in the first place. When individuals, families, schools, or communities recognize the parameters connected with a crisis situation, they may be quite motivated and extremely receptive to secondary prevention efforts.

Examples of secondary prevention include support groups for students who are experiencing the grief and loss associated with the unexpected death of a peer, school and community collaborative efforts to provide child care and alternative education opportunities for teenage parents, residential or outpatient treatment for teenagers who abuse alcohol, or counseling services established to stop battering or other violent behavior. During the secondary prevention process, emphasis should be placed on individual, family, school, and community resources and abilities. Preoccupation with defeat and negative consequences seldom results in the management of a particular crisis situation and the reestablishment of equilibrium.

It is important to note, at this juncture, that more and more school districts are writing "Tragedy Response Plans" for the purpose of planning and coordinating efforts of school personnel who are suddenly presented with a crisis situation. The reason for doing so is to prevent the systemic chaos and resultant negative impact on individuals and groups on a school campus at the time an unanticipated crisis occurs. These Tragedy Response Plans usually delineate not only the roles of members of the crisis team but also the roles of all other school personnel as well as the roles of individuals or groups in the community that the school may need to call on in the midst of a crisis. Developing plans in advance has a number of advantages that include the opportunity to have such plans evaluated by experts in crisis management and by the school or district's legal team in advance so that modifications and additions can be made.

Tragedy Response Plans usually outline crisis responses to natural disasters (earthquakes, tornados, release of airborne toxins, etc.), fire, death, accidents, child abduction, violence, and other events that need to be addressed immediately and may not have been anticipated. These plans are usually quite comprehensive and include guidelines for possible evacuation, transportation, contacting parents, responding to the inquiries of journalists, and working with police and disaster relief workers from the community. Many school districts are beginning to publish their plans on the World Wide Web, and we encourage school/community groups planning to commence work on Tragedy Response Plans to read what other school/community groups have developed and to contact representatives from schools that have experience in this realm. Making such contacts can provide opportunities for collaborative sharing and evaluation and can eliminate the necessity to "start from scratch."

Tertiary Prevention

Tertiary crisis prevention attempts to reduce the amount of residual impairment that follows the resolution of some crisis. Adolescents who complete residential or outpatient programs for substance abuse may benefit through participation in weekly support groups, facilitated by a professional, for the purpose of providing the reinforcement and support needed to prevent relapse. These same adolescents may need to participate, concurrently, in individual counseling or therapy to address the unmet needs that led to the use and abuse of a substance in the first place, because emotional development and coping skills are usually arrested about the time substance use begins. Victims of sexual abuse may participate in either group or individual (or both) counseling or therapy long after the abuse has ceased for the purpose of repairing damaged self-esteem and rebuilding the capacity to trust and share intimacy with significant others.

As emphasized by Janosik (1984), crisis in contemporary society is so prevalent that it is not possible for all those experiencing crisis to access the help of professionals. It is possible, however, to identify factors that place individuals, families, schools, and communities at risk. Thus, it is of paramount importance to reduce emotional pain, residual impairment, and cost to society as a whole through judicious use of prevention, whether primary, secondary, or tertiary in nature.

TYPES OF PRIMARY PREVENTION

The youth of today are faced with coping amidst a society that is more populated, more connected by advanced communication technology, and more complex with respect to a variety of psychosocial stressors. This edition of *Youth at Risk* places more emphasis on prevention with respect to causative factors (such as low self-esteem, stress, depression) and a number of at-risk behaviors (such as drug abuse, unprotected sex, eating disorders, suicidal preoccupation, gang membership). The chapters that follow chapter 3 highlight secondary and tertiary prevention efforts. This chapter provides information on primary prevention efforts based on the types described by McWhirter et al. (1998) and further addressed by Buckley (2000), Collins et al. (2002), Hovell et al. (2001), Kadish et al. (2001), and Watts (2000): developing life skills, enhancing interpersonal communication, learning strategies for cognitive change, achieving self-management and self-control, and coping with stress.

Developing Life Skills

Life skills can be defined as the ability to make use of personal resources for the purpose of expressing needs and positively influencing the environment. Such skills influence the formation of relationships and friendships, nonviolent methods of conflict resolution, and communication with adults (McWhirter et al., 1998). Developing life skills can be accomplished through education and training in life skills, school peer mediation, peer tutoring, and peer facilitation.

Education and training in life skills involve developing and incorporating instructional modules into the curriculum at elementary, middle, and high school levels. Also involved is the collaborative input of a variety of professionals (counselors, nurses, physicians, social workers, psychologists, physical educators, classroom teachers) for the purpose of teaching skills needed by most individuals on a day-to-day basis. The format for teaching any targeted skill should, ideally, contain the following components: teach, model, role-play, provide feedback, and assign homework. Almost any skill can be taught within this paradigm, and the fact that implementation is most often effected in the classroom means that entire populations can be accessed so that more and more young people can master skills that can help them avoid future problems.

School peer mediation, peer tutoring, and peer facilitation all involve training and supervising students to perform interpersonal helping tasks. School peer mediation requires trained peer mediators who work in partnerships with other students for the purpose of facilitating problem solving between disputing students. As noted by McWhirter et al. (1998), peer mediation ensures that both peer mediators and peer disputants increase experience with critical thinking, problem solving, and self-discipline.

Peer tutors are students who teach other students in both formal and informal learning situations. Peer tutoring can provide a cost-effective means of meeting individual needs, developing better ownership of the value of the educational experience, and enhancing self-esteem and motivation.

Peer facilitation, sometimes called peer helping, is a process in which students are trained to listen, paraphrase, support, and provide feedback to other students in the school. Peer facilitation is an effective way to empower children and adolescents and to provide adjunct support to the professional counselor or other human service specialist.

Enhancing Interpersonal Communication

Interpersonal communication skills are primary factors in the development of mutually beneficial relationships. Most programs designed to enhance interpersonal communication skills offer training in verbal and nonverbal communication, creation of constructive friendships, avoidance of misunderstanding, and the development of long-term relationships with significant others (McWhirter et al., 1998). Lack of ability to communicate well with others can lead to lowered self-esteem, isolation, and the development of future at-risk behaviors. Assertiveness training and resistance and refusal training are often important components of training in interpersonal communication.

Assertiveness training is most often accomplished in the context of small groups. It can include providing assistance with expressing positive and negative feelings; the ability to initiate, maintain, and end conversations; and practice on setting limits. Nonverbal communication is an important component of assertiveness training because the manner in which something is communicated—body language, eye contact, personal distancing—can influence the message as much as the context of the message itself.

Resistance and refusal training is provided to help children and adolescents resist peer pressure or other negative social influences. Students are taught to label and recognize various forms of pressure and develop behavior to resist such pressure and influence. Both assertiveness training and resistance and refusal training provide numerous modeling, role-play, feedback, and reinforcement opportunities during the process of acquiring such interpersonal communication skills so that new behaviors are more likely to be used in day-to-day interactions with peers.

Learning Strategies for Cognitive Change

Because cognition mediates both behavior and affect, cognitive restructuring can be an effective primary prevention strategy. Techniques used in problem solving and decision making, self-management and self-control, and cognitive restructuring are among the primary prevention strategies that can be taught to children and adolescents.

All young people have the potential to problem solve and make decisions. At times, however, the emotional components connected with a particular problem, the egocentric focus commonly associated with the early years of human growth and development, and the lack of experience with systematically approaching problem-solving situations provide barriers to effective problem solving and decision making (McWhirter et al., 1998). Instruction can be provided, however, in each step of the problem-solving and decision-making process. Teaching children and adolescents how to resolve problematic situations can help them enhance self-esteem, overcome feelings of being helpless, and promote a generalized sense of empowerment. McWhirter et al. (1998) suggested that the following components be taught:

1. *Define the problem.* The problem is defined as clearly as possible and is stated as a goal to be achieved. This goal is assessed: Does it meet the underlying needs? If it is attained, does it help the individual achieve satisfaction?
2. *Examine variables.* The specifics of the total situation are examined. Background issues and environmental factors are considered, so it may be necessary to gather and appraise additional information. It is particularly important to identify the feelings and thoughts of the youth at this step. Often earlier maladaptive responses must be modified. In both this step and Step 1, questions and suggestions from other students in the classroom or the group are useful.
3. *Consider alternatives.* Various means of solving the problem are considered. The strengths and weaknesses of each possibility are evaluated. Again, the teacher or counselor may call for brainstorming to generate ideas from other students about alternatives and strategies.
4. *Isolate a plan.* The alternatives are gradually narrowed down until what seems like the best response or solution remains. A plan for carrying out this alternative is prepared, and the potential consequences are considered in more detail.
5. *Do action steps.* After a plan is decided on, action must be taken to implement it. Thus, youngsters are systematically encouraged to follow through on the necessary steps to carry out their plan. They perform the behaviors that make up the solution plan.
6. *Evaluate effects.* Finally, youngsters need to evaluate the effectiveness of the solution. Teaching them to look for effects in their thoughts and feelings is important. They analyze and evaluate the outcome, review the decision, and, if necessary, develop another plan to achieve their goal.

McWhirter et al. (1998) called their model the DECIDE model and reported that it is an effective strategy for teaching problem solving and decision making.

Achieving Self-Management and Self-Control

Self-management means that self-control has been achieved. It implies that individuals can develop the ability to control, to a great extent, thoughts, feelings, and behaviors. Teaching children and adolescents the techniques of self-management and self-control can result in outcomes similar to those connected with teaching problem solving and decision making, enhanced self-esteem, overcoming feelings of being helpless, and a sense of empowerment. Teaching self-management and self-control involves teaching children and adolescents self-assessment, self-monitoring, and self-reinforcement (McWhirter et al., 1998). Self-assessment means that the individual learns to evaluate his or her own behaviors against a standard that has personal meaning to determine whether the behavior is adequate. Self-monitoring requires that the individual observes his or her own behavior and records it. Record keeping may involve notation of contingencies in the environment prior to and immediately following the behavior. Self-reinforcement involves supplying one's own consequences for a given behavior (e.g., self-praise, buying something of personal significance). Generally, children and adolescents who master the techniques of self-management and self-control feel energized, motivated, and positive about themselves.

Coping With Stress

The term *coping with stress* is particularly significant in contemporary society. There are so many potential stressors encountered by each of us on a day-to-day basis that it behooves the adults in society to teach children and adolescents as much as possible about stress and stress management. It is an important primary prevention strategy. Chapter 7, Stress and Trauma: Coping in Today's Society, addresses this topic fully through discussion and analysis of perspectives on stress, including stimulus-oriented views, response-oriented views, stress as a transaction between person and environment, life event stressors, daily stress, home and family stress, school stress, and developmental stress.

PLANNING PREVENTION PROGRAMS

Laudatory prevention efforts of schools and communities have failed because planning efforts have not included important steps or a group of concerned adults has moved to the implementation stage and short-changed the entire planning process. The following steps, which are based on our experience in a variety of school and community settings, will help assure success.

1. *Read the research on prevention programs.* There are excellent reviews and monographs on approaches to prevention (Collins et al., 2002; Dryfoos, 1997; Gager & Elias, 1997; Goldston, Yager, Heinicke, & Pynoos, 1990; Kadish et al., 2001; Romano, 1997; Weissberg, Caplan, & Harwood, 1991). Often practitioners who are anxious to implement programs and services do not take the time to learn about and build on the successes and failures of others. Based on numerous outcome studies, a number of generalizations can be made:

- Prevention programs directed to the early years (e.g., pre- and postnatal parents and children during preschool years) can reduce factors that increase risk for maladaptive behaviors. Most of these efforts are focused on primary prevention and reduce the incidence of dysfunction in childhood and adolescence (Lally, Mangione, & Honig, 1988).
- Prevention programs that involve parents, connect to the real world of work, incorporate social and life skills training, incorporate staff development, and involve dedicated role-model adults seem to have the most lasting and positive impact (Dryfoos, 1997).
- School-based programs targeting adolescents have improved prosocial competence and decreased at-risk behaviors (such as the behaviors discussed in Part Three of this book; Schinke, Botvin, & Orlandi, 1991; Schneider, Attili, Nadel, & Weissberg, 1989).
- Broad-based programs aimed at several causative factors or at-risk behaviors seem to be the most successful because youth at risk usually present with a number of conditions (Caplan & Weissberg, 1989).
- Occasionally, programs have not been effective or have made problems escalate (Bangert-Drowns, 1988). Finding out why could be extremely important to practitioners prior to implementing any prevention effort (Collins et al., 2002).

2. *Assess needs.* Sometimes the professional helper fails to target the right population, the best combination of causative factors, or the at-risk behaviors of most concern to children, adolescents, and their families. It is important to touch base with the population being served prior to doing much planning. Children and adolescents, families, school faculty and staff, and components of the community (e.g., hospitals, businesses, churches, social service agencies) should be asked about their view of factors creating risk, problematic behaviors, and skill deficits. Prevention programming should always be designed to address needs and concerns identified by recipients of future services.

3. *Meet with administrators, elected officials, and business owners.* Prevention efforts take time, commitment, and money to implement. Numerous prevention programs have met with failure because planners failed to obtain the input and support of those in positions to reinforce efforts and keep programs and services funded and in place on a long-term basis. This is a critical step in planning for program support.

4. *Establish a broad-based planning group.* Educators, parents, youth, administrators, mental health professionals, physicians, nurses, and police should all be included in planning efforts for prevention programming. The more interdisciplinary and representative the group, the richer the input. The best prevention efforts have been based on the collaborative teaming of members of the community to be served.

5. *Target the population, the causative factors, or the at-risk behaviors.* Often planning groups are too ambitious with respect to goals and expectations. There is always more to be accomplished than can be realized with respect to a given prevention program. It is important to use the results of a needs assessment to target initial efforts so that initiatives are well planned and supported by adequate resources. Once a focus has been established, findings of research conducted relative to similar populations, risk factors, or at-risk groups should be utilized so that problems can be circumvented and past successful practices can be used.

6. *Identify existing prevention programs and resources.* Sometimes planning groups re-create programs, services, or resources that already exist and could be built on or used as adjuncts to newly created programs. It is important to identify existing prevention programs and assess them in terms of whether they offer primary, secondary, or tertiary prevention. Planning groups can then determine how to focus new initiatives (i.e., primary, secondary, or tertiary) and do a better job of effectively utilizing newly committed funding and resources.

7. *Carefully describe policies and procedures.* Before implementing a new program, it is extremely important to draft a description of all policies and procedures to be followed. This ensures that everyone involved in the program can be clear about roles and responsibilities. A written description also provides opportunity for input, revision, and refinement. Program descriptions can (and should) be checked in advance of implementation for legal and ethical implications.

8. *Plan variations for diversity.* For many young people, minority status is associated with low socioeconomic status, poor living conditions, fragmented families, and a variety of critical cultural, ethnic, and racial differences. All human service specialists must be flexible about making adaptations in prevention programming in a way that shows sensitivity and respect for diversity. Variations for diversity are addressed throughout this edition of *Youth at Risk*.

9. *Plan staff development.* Whether prevention programming is centered in school or community settings, all staff need to be educated, supervised, and prepared in advance of program implementation. Adults working on behalf of children and adolescents need to be carefully prepared and provided with opportunities to have their questions answered and their concerns addressed.

10. *Make sure adjunct services and referral options have been identified.* Those working on behalf of children and adolescents often need the assistance of other medical and social service professionals. Identifying adjunct services and referral options and acting as a liaison with employees in those settings, in advance, should never be overlooked.

11. *Plan evaluation procedures prior to program implementation.* Practitioners often neglect the evaluative component of prevention programming efforts. Evaluation procedures should be preplanned, and data collection should be an integral part of efforts on behalf of youth. Data can be used to modify and improve the services offered and can provide justification for continued funding and commitment of other needed resources.

SUMMARY

Our overview of prevention has provided introductory material highlighting the problems that underscore the need for escalation of prevention efforts; defined the qualities of prevention programming; described the differences among primary, secondary, and tertiary prevention and noted the need for additional primary prevention programs; and suggested guidelines and steps for prevention programming. We hope that this information provides an enriched perspective with which to approach the material in the chapters that follow. The context of this chapter is reflective of our belief that more emphasis needs to be placed on proactive prevention efforts so that, as time passes, individuals, families, schools, and communities can lessen the amount of time and energy directed toward remediation and containment of impairment and dysfunction.

REFERENCES

Bangert-Drowns, R. L. (1988). The effects of school-based substance abuse education: A meta-analysis. *Journal of Drug Education, 18,* 243–264.

Bosworth, K., Espelage, D., DuBay, T., & Daytner, G. (2000). Preliminary evaluation of a multimedia violence prevention program for adolescents. *American Journal of Health Behavior, 24,* 268–280.

Brown, E. J., & Simpson, E. M. (2000). Comprehensive STD/HIV prevention education targeting US adolescents: Review of an ethical dilemma and proposed ethical framework. *Nursing Ethics, 7,* 339–349.

Buckley, M. A. (2000). Cognitive–developmental considerations in violence prevention and intervention. *Professional School Counseling, 4,* 60–70.

Caplan, M. Z., & Weissberg, R. P. (1989). Promoting social competence in early adolescence: Developmental considerations. In B. H. Schneider, G. Attili, J. Nadel, & R. P. Weissberg (Eds.), *Social competence in developmental perspective* (pp. 371–385). Norwell, MA: Kluwer Academic.

Collins, J., Robin, L., Wooley, S., Fenley, D., Hunt, P., Taylor, J., et al. (2002). Programs-that-work: CDC's guide to effective programs that reduce health-risk behaviors of youth. *Journal of School Health, 72,* 93–99.

Conyne, R. K. (1994). Preventative counseling. *Counseling and Human Development, 27*(1), 1–10.

Dryfoos, J. D. (1997). Adolescents at risk: Shaping programs to fit the need. *Journal of Negro Education, 66*(1), 5–18.

Fetro, J. V., Coyle, K. K., & Pham, P. (2001). Health-risk behaviors among middle school students in a large majority–minority school district. *Journal of School Health, 71,* 30–37.

Gager, P. J., & Elias, M. J. (1997). Implementing prevention programs in high-risk environments: Application of the resiliency paradigm. *American Journal of Orthopsychiatry, 67,* 363–373.

Gilliland, B. E., & James, R. K. (1993). *Crisis intervention strategies.* Pacific Grove, CA: Brooks/Cole.

Goldston, S. E., Yager, J., Heinicke, C. M., & Pynoos, R. S. (Eds.). (1990). *Preventing mental health disturbances in childhood.* Washington, DC: American Psychiatric Association.

Hadge, C. (1992). *School-based prevention and intervention program: Clearinghouse fact sheet* (Report No. CG 025 63 1). Piscataway, NJ: Rutgers University, Center of Alcohol Studies. (ERIC Document Reproduction Service No. ED 372 329)

Horner, J., & McElhaney, S. (1993). Building fences. *American Counselor, 2,* 17–21, 30.

Hovell, M. F., Blumberg, E. J., Liles, S., Powell, L., & Morrison, T. C. (2001). Training AIDS and anger prevention social skills in at-risk adolescents. *Journal of Counseling & Development, 79,* 347–355.

Janosik, E. H. (1984). *Crisis counseling: A contemporary approach.* Monterey, CA: Wadsworth Health Sciences.

Kadish, T. E., Glaser, B. A., Calhoun, G. B., & Ginter, E. J. (2001). Identifying the developmental strengths of juvenile offenders: Assessing four life-skills dimensions. *Journal of Addictions and Offender Counseling, 21,* 85–95.

Kazdin, A. E. (1993). Adolescent mental health: Prevention and treatment programs. *American Psychologist, 48,* 127–141.

King, K. A. (2001). Developing a comprehensive school suicide prevention program. *Journal of School Health, 71,* 132–137.

Lally, R., Mangione, P. L., & Honig, A. S. (1988). The Syracuse University Family Development Research Program: Long-range impact on an early intervention with low-income children and their families. In D. Powell (Ed.), *Parent education as early childhood intervention: Emerging directions in theory, research, and practice* (pp. 79–104). Norwood, NJ: Ablex.

McWhirter, J. J., McWhirter, B. T., McWhirter, A. M., & McWhirter, E. H. (1998). *At-risk youth: A comprehensive response* (2nd ed.). Pacific Grove, CA: Brooks/Cole.

Popenhagen, M. P., & Qualley, R. M. (1998). Adolescent suicide: Detection, intervention, and prevention. *Professional School Counseling, 1*(4), 30–36.

Roberts, A. R. (Ed.). (1991). *Contemporary perspectives on crisis intervention and prevention*. Englewood Cliffs, NJ: Rutgers University, Center of Alcohol Studies.

Romano, J. L. (1997). School personnel training for the prevention of tobacco, alcohol, and other drug use: Issues and outcomes. *Journal of Drug Education, 27,* 245–258.

Schinke, S. P., Botvin, G. J., & Orlandi, M. A. (1991). *Substance abuse in children and adolescents: Evaluation and intervention.* Newbury Park, CA: Sage.

Schneider, B. H., Attili, G., Nadel, J., & Weissberg, R. P. (Eds.). (1989). *Social competence in developmental perspective.* Norwell, MA: Kluwer Academic.

Watts, G. F., Sr. (2000). Attitude toward sexual intercourse and relationship with peer and parental communication. *American Journal of Health Studies, 16,* 156–163.

Weissberg, R. P., Caplan, M., & Harwood, L. (1991). Promoting competent young people in competence-enhancing environments: A systems-based perspective on primary prevention. *Journal of Consulting and Clinical Psychology, 55,* 542–549.

3 | Resilience: Individual, Family, School, and Community Perspectives

*Rolla E. Lewis**

The literature on resilience provides an alternative view that sees youth at promise rather than at risk and offers counselors, teachers, and parents positive and viable resources for promoting the well-being of youth. The models, methods, and data emerging from education, prevention, and counseling fields about resilience do not represent a single point of view, however. There is diversity that results in debate and controversies about resilience, but there is agreement that the family of phenomena referred to as resilience challenges the negative assumptions found in deficit-focused models. There is no denial that risk exists; resilience results from good outcomes in spite of exposure to risk, frequently when the individual exposed to risk has a connection to at least one caring adult. The issue becomes one of creating healthy systems that invite youth to participate in meaningful activities rather than repairing individuals who have been damaged by risks.

This chapter looks at resilience literature and practices not to synthesize but rather to call attention to pathways for the counseling and teaching professions to provide hopeful and rewarding service to youth by creating healthy systems and climates that support youth development. Additionally, this chapter calls for creating collaborative efforts between professionals and community members to help all youth grow toward their greatest potential in just and caring communities. The resilience literature cited in this chapter refers to the evolving multidisciplinary research and practices that have emerged from the prevention, counseling, education, social work, and youth development fields (Benard, 1991, 1996, 1997; Benard & Marshall, 2001a, 2001b; Gibbs, 2001; Henderson, Benard, & Sharp-Light, 1999, 2000a, 2000b; Luthar, Cicchetti, & Becker, 2000a, 2000b; Marshall, 1998; Masten, 2001; J. Pransky & Carpenos, 2000). Resilience literature moves primary prevention perspective and practices away from short-term, individual interventions and toward long-term, comprehensive interventions designed to foster positive youth development in and beyond the school and into the community (Benard, 1996, 1997; Benard & Marshall, 1997, 2001a, 2001b; Gibbs, 1994; Henderson & Milstein, 1996; Linquanti, 1992; Luthar et al., 2000a; Masten, 2001). The key difference between preventionists and resilience researchers should be noted. Preventionist efforts usually represent disease avoidance, whereas resilience researchers

*The author wishes to thank Kathy Marshall for her review of an early draft and clarification regarding "Tapping Resilience: A Framework for Practice." The author would also like to thank Jeanne Slingluff for sharing her expertise and knowledge about her work in the schools and Linda Hennessey for review of the chapter and her dialogue about ecology and careers.

concentrate on "wellness in addition to the absence of dysfunction" (Luthar et al., 2000b, p. 574). In many ways, the resilience literature offers school counselors one pathway back to and forward from the counseling profession's roots in human development and education, back to and forward from the assumption that growth and development are human imperatives. In following that pathway, this chapter is guided by key research, effective practices, and professional possibilities.

1. *Key research.* Key resilience research and prevention efforts acknowledge and recognize resilience as a dynamic process that leads to positive adaptation and as the inborn, self-righting capacity of people (Benard, 1991, 1993, 1996, 1997; Benard & Marshall, 2001a, 2001b; Luthar et al., 2000a, 2000b; Marshall, 1998, 2001; Masten, 2001; Werner, 1989, 1996, 1998; Werner & Smith, 1982, 1992, 2001). A notable body of resilience research and practice has at its heart the radical notion that "resilience is innate in all of us—our innate wisdom, mental health, common sense, etc." (B. Benard, personal communication, October 23, 1998). Such a view shifts the professional perspective to see youth as having the developmental resources and self-righting capacities they need to navigate through life. Counselors, teachers, and parents are in a position to help youth realize this, but core providers must perceive their own self-righting capacities if they are going to help youth understand their own health. In other words, to promote the health of youth at risk, helpers are advised to begin recognizing their own resilience and health.

   Most of the practices found in this chapter begin with the assumption that resilience is a self-righting capacity fostered transactionally in the presence of certain environmental variables. Resilience is an end product of buffering processes that do not eliminate risk (Werner & Smith, 2001). As such, risk should be considered in broader socially constructed and ecologically embedded contexts where poverty, racism, and injustice are embedded in social practices. Resilience can then be viewed as a dynamic process associated with global factors such as affiliation with caring adults. Metaphorically, youth are like diverse seeds with great potential, like acorns with the capacity to become oak trees but dependent on adequate ecological variables such as soil, water, and sun. Resilience practices can guide school counselors, teachers, and parents to appreciate the true meaning of education (*e-ducare* means to lead out rather than put in) by advocating for environments where students draw out their own self-righting capacities under the mentorship of caring adults.

2. *Effective practices.* What makes counseling practice effective? Four common factors have been proposed as the principal elements accounting for effective change in clients: (a) client/extratherapeutic factors account for 40% of successful outcomes, (b) relationship factors account for 30% of outcomes, (c) placebo/hope and expectancy account for 15%, and (d) model/technique accounts for 15% (Hubble, Duncan, & Miller, 1999).

   Client/extratherapeutic factors are those factors attributed within the client or the client's life circumstances (i.e., what the client brings to therapy and what influences the client outside of therapy), pointing, perhaps, to their self-righting capacities growing out of community support. Relationship factors are such qualities as caring, empathy, and acceptance, found in any effective family, classroom, or community. Hope and expectancy deal with both the counselor's and the client's belief in the possibility of change and are found in any meaningful, goal-oriented activity (Snyder, Feldman, Shorey, & Rand, 2002).

Model/technique refers to those interventions that counselors use to motivate clients to take actions to help themselves; these are the skills such as the "miracle question" that counselors learn in graduate school. De Shazer (1988, p. 5) described the classic miracle question, "Suppose that one night there is a miracle and while you were sleeping the problem that brought you into therapy is solved: How would you know? What would be different?"

The effective practices fostering resilience described in this chapter point to creating supportive systems, helping clients tap the qualities within themselves, and recognizing alternative stories within their experiences (Benard & Marshall, 1997; Bertolino & O'Hanlon, 2002; Monk, Winslade, Crocket, & Epston, 1997). In a narrow sense, effective practices fostering resilience draw on extratherapeutic factors, relationship factors, hope and expectancy factors, and finally technique factors. Fostering resilience has less to do with technique and more with taking a positive and affirming stance with others. Coupled with taking a positive and affirming stance, it is vital for counselors, especially those working in the schools, to develop research agendas, to determine what works in their schools, and to use the results to help all students (Whiston, 2002).

3. *Professional possibilities.* Practices promoting resilience can guide school counselors and teachers in their efforts to foster success for all students' personal/social, academic, and career development. As Masten (1994) pointed out, "Fostering resilience is an attempt to deflect a developmental pathway in a more positive direction" (p. 21). Schools and communities offer numerous possibilities for helping youth recognize their self-righting capacities and for shifting school systems to support youth in defining their life trajectories along positive pathways. Pathways that include instilling a sense of hope and recognizing self-righting capabilities are fundamental. As Werner and Smith (1992) concluded in their longitudinal study, "The central component in the lives of the resilient individuals . . . which contributed to their effective coping in adulthood appeared to be a confidence that the odds can be surmounted. Some of the luckier ones developed such hopefulness early in their lives, in contact with caring adults" (p. 207).

Begin by being an ally to youth. Allies see youth as resources, and professional efforts open pathways for youth to perceive their own ability to spring back from adversity, to realize their own self-righting capacities, to understand their own ability to learn, and to fulfill their own power to engage passionately in meaningful activities. Teachers and counselors model these capacities by showing how part of learning to live has to do with individuals' ability to get up after they have been knocked down, to have heart, gumption, determination, and compassion. Youth and adults experience the world in different ways; life can be rocky at any developmental or life stage; life demands participation and engagement. As such, life offers opportunities for adults to explore and join with youth to grasp the role of thought in interpreting experience (Mills, 1995; G. S. Pransky, 1998). Learning to learn is related to individuals' ability to learn from difficulties and failures, and from their capacity to struggle with uncertainty and let solutions and deeper wisdom emerge (Bruner, 1986, 1990; Claxton, 1997, 1999; Clinchy, 1996; Langer, 1997). Learning to learn is also concerned with helping all students develop competencies and access to adults who will nurture those competencies in meaningful contexts (Brooks, 1994, 1997; Masten & Coatsworth, 1998). Learning to work is connected to individuals' ability to adjust to the ongoing and continual changes in their livelihoods as students and adults. More importantly, learning to work is connected to finding our capacity to be passionate about the work we choose to do and doing things we find meaningful (Quattrociocchi & Peterson, 1997). Promoting resilience begins with wellness and seeing youth as having resources and providing opportunities for youth and adults to find healthy pathways to learn to live, learn to learn, and learn to work.

RESILIENCE DEFINED

Given the diversity within the resilience literature, this chapter defines *resilience* as a dynamic developmental process (Luthar et al., 2000a) of healthy human development growing out of nurturing relationships that support social, academic, and vocational competence and the self-righting capacity to spring back from exposure to adversity and other environmental stressors. The self-righting capacity does not occur in a social vacuum, may emerge at different developmental stages, and frequently entails having a caring teacher or an adult mentor available (Werner & Smith, 2001). Global factors associated with resilience include possessing cognitive and self-regulation skills, having positive views of self and the motivation to be effective, and connecting with competent and caring adults (Masten, 2001). Luthar et al. (2000a) pointed out that although resilience is a dynamic process, it is frequently misrepresented as a narrow trait that makes some youth "have what it takes" to overcome the odds and others not have those special qualities. According to Masten (2001), "Resilience does not come from rare and special qualities, but from the everyday magic of the ordinary, normative human resources in the minds, brains, and bodies of children, in their families and relationships, and in their communities" (p. 235). Resilience is not extraordinary; it is the "power of the ordinary." Tapping this power of the ordinary is the challenge.

Benard and Marshall (1997) argued that it is easier to teach health if it is known or embodied in our own lives. To foster the self-righting capacity for healthy human development in youth, counselors, teachers, parents, and others must recognize their own resilience. They pointed to the power inherent in this realization: "Resilience is an inside-out process that begins with one person's belief and emanates outward to transform whole families, classrooms, schools and communities. . . . It means we shift from a focus on fixing individuals to creating healthy systems" (Benard & Marshall, 1997, p. 1). Teachers, counselors, and parents who begin with their own well-being foster resilience.

Because diverse professional fields contribute to the evolving resilience literature, there are a variety of perspectives about resilience that lead to misunderstandings. On the one hand, as Masten (1994) pointed out, "Studies of resilience suggest that nature has provided powerful protective mechanisms for human development. . . . When adversity is relieved and basic human needs are restored, then resilience has a chance to emerge. Rekindling hope may be an important spark for resilience processes to begin their restorative work" (pp. 20–21). On the other hand, one of McWhirter, McWhirter, McWhirter, and McWhirter's (1998) concerns is that "the justice system has used the term resiliency to help punish offenders—contending that a violent and abrasive upbringing provides no explanation for violent behavior because some youth who grow up in the same type of environment do not engage in violence" (p. 80). Such practices by those in the justice system totally misunderstand the research and practices emerging from the resilience literature. As made clear by Werner (1998), "As long as the balance between stressful events and protective factors is favorable, successful adaptation is possible even for youngsters who live in 'high risk' conditions. However, when stressful life events outweigh the protective factors in a child's life, even the most resilient individual can develop problems" (p. 8).

As diverse as it is, the resilience literature does not support institutionalizing ways to blame individuals in need of help, creating policies that fail to support children and families, and spending more money on trying to fix serious coping problems rather than promoting prevention (Werner & Smith, 2001). Such practices are contrary to the assumptions guiding resilience practices cited in this chapter; the imperative for growth and development unfolds naturally when certain environmental attributes are present.

"Resilience is not the cheerful disregard of one's difficult and traumatic life experiences; neither is it the naive discounting of life's pains. It is rather the ability to bear up in spite of these ordeals" (Saleebey, 1997, p. 9). Blum (1998) offered a perspective regarding what should be done in response to the positive findings in the resilience research:

> Rather than viewing the findings from resiliency research as a rationale for inaction, we should redouble our efforts. The good news is that for those reared in adversity, the outcomes are not necessarily bleak. . . . It is likewise clear that, as the African proverb states, "it takes a community to rear a child." (p. 374)

To embody this proverb, individuals can learn to draw on their own resilience, foster resilience in others, and work within their schools and communities to encourage collaborative and systemic approaches that foster resilience in youth.

RESILIENCE: FACTORS, PERSPECTIVES, AND PRACTICES

There are multiple factors influencing the developmental trajectories of youth and many explanations for the difficulties they face (Benard & Marshall, 2001a, 2001b; Durlak, 1998; Luthar et al., 2000a, 2000b; Masten & Coatsworth, 1998). Merely identifying risks and causal factors does not always work. Benard's (1991) and Benard and Marshall's (2001a, 2001b) research synthesis is still useful in showing that identifying risks does not translate into strategies for reducing those risks. This section explores how resilience promotion efforts viewed in the broader social contexts shift how we view why some children are not damaged or spring back from deprivation and adversity. Rather than attempting to capture the scope of the literature and prevention efforts, this section highlights key longitudinal resilience research that reveals the self-righting capacity in people and the need to create structures to support those people. Research spanning over 40 years conducted by Werner and her colleagues that describes protective factors within youth, within the family, and within the community is discussed (Werner, 1989, 1996, 1998; Werner & Smith, 1982, 1992, 2001); then additional research that profiles qualities of resilient youth and three protective factors that enhance student resilience in the schools are examined (Benard, 1991, 1993, 1997; Benard & Marshall, 1997, 2001a, 2001b).

Werner: The Mother of Resilience

The life span, cross-cultural studies, such as those exemplified in the longitudinal studies of Werner and her colleagues, have concluded that resilience is the natural human capacity for self-righting (Werner, 1996; Werner & Smith, 1982, 1992, 2001). Their theory and research support the view that the human organism has an imperative for growth and development. Werner and Smith (1992) were guided by a transactional–ecological model of human development that posits people are active, self-righting organisms continuously adapting to their environment.

Their influential resilience research used a prospective, developmental, and longitudinal design to assess how youth, at various stages of development growing into high-risk conditions, respond to risk factors (Werner, 1989, 1996, 1998; Werner & Smith, 1982, 1992, 2001). Werner and Smith (1982) stated, "Prospective longitudinal studies have fairly consistently shown that even among children exposed to potent risk factors it is unusual for more than half to develop serious disabilities or persistent problems" (p. 4). Essentially, the longitudinal perspective has resulted in a change in what researchers find, including that most delinquent youth do not develop into career criminals (Werner, 1996, 1998; Werner & Smith, 1992, 2001). The observation that their research design changed how they discerned the individuals being studied over time and in their findings deserves explanation. The prospective design is different from the retrospective design. Researchers using prospective designs study groups of youth over time, whereas researchers using retrospective designs are more likely to investigate risk factors linked to the history of a person with identified difficulties. Prospective designs offer researchers different possibilities in describing youth who grow up in high-risk environments, whereas retrospective designs focus on events that lead to or interventions that are devised to diminish pathology. Longitudinal research offers an alternative way of understanding and learning about human self-righting capacities.

This hopeful and optimistic view needs to be explained in the context of research, commentary, and life stories supporting inborn, self-righting capacities. Werner and her colleagues' study (Werner, 1989; Werner, Bierman, & French, 1971; Werner & Smith, 1977, 1982, 1992, 2001) has extended more than 40 years and has found there are protective factors within youth, the family, and the community. Beginning with the entire population of 698 youth born in 1955, the study on Kauai, Hawaii, has followed 505 individuals from the prenatal stage to the adult stage of development. Data have been collected from cohort members in the prenatal period, at birth, and at ages 1, 2, 10, 18, 32, and 40 years. By birth, one third of the group was considered at risk because of four or more factors: significant poverty, being reared by parents with little formal education, moderate to severe perinatal stress, family discord, divorce, alcoholism, or mental retardation. One third of these high-risk youth did not develop difficulties as a result of the exposure to risk, and another one third rebounded as they reached adulthood to become competent adults (Werner, 1998; Werner & Smith, 1992, 2001). Werner and her colleagues broke down their study into the following areas:

- *Children of Kauai* (Werner et al., 1971), which documented the development from birth to age 10 and the cumulative effects of poverty, perinatal stress, and disorganized caretaking;
- *Kauai's Children Come of Age* (Werner & Smith, 1977), which analyzed the likelihood of persistent problems into childhood by examining learning disorders, mental health problems, and antisocial behavior of high-risk youth in their teens;
- *Vulnerable but Invincible* (Werner & Smith, 1982), which documented vulnerable and stress-resistant youth up to the transitional phase when they were about to leave high school;
- *Overcoming the Odds* (Werner & Smith, 1992), which traced the long-term effects of childhood adversity and examined the protective factors that led most of the youth to adapt successfully as adults;

- *Journeys From Childhood to Midlife* (Werner & Smith, 2001), which continued documenting the stability of resilience from childhood to adulthood and the ability of high-risk individuals to bounce back later in life.

Werner and Smith (1992) found that resilience is not something that is fixed and concrete but a quality that is enhanced by protective buffers that appear to transcend ethnic, social class, and geographical boundaries. Individual variability had to be taken into account, but the majority of resilient youth in the Kauai study had a variety of internal or external protective factors (Werner, 1996). Those youth who overcame the odds were described as resilient, and as Werner and Smith (1992) pointed out, "They began to perceive themselves as movers of their destiny rather than as pawns in a power game played by outsiders" (p. 21).

The vast majority of delinquent youth in the study did not become adult career criminals. The majority of chronic criminals from the study cohort consisted of a small group who had averaged four or more arrests before the age of 18. Those who did become persistent offenders needed remedial educational help (usually reading) prior to age 10, were considered troublemakers by their fifth-grade teachers and parents, and had grown up in homes where significant caregivers were absent for extended periods of time during adolescence (Werner & Smith, 1992). Youth "exposed to adversities in early childhood are not predestined to grow into adults with failed marriages, criminal records, or psychiatric disorders. At each developmental stage, there is an opportunity for protective factors (personal competencies and sources of support) to counterbalance the negative weight exerted by adverse experiences" (Werner & Smith, 1992, p. 171).

"Second-chance" opportunities were usually found at major life transitions. Such opportunities enabled high-risk individuals to rebound and are frequently found in adult education programs, military service, active participation in a church community, or a supportive friend or spouse.

Werner and Smith (1992) asserted that the protective factors within the individual, family, and community have a more profound impact on the lives of youth than risk factors. Key protective factors pointed out by Werner and Smith (1992) and expanded by Werner (1998) are worthy of note for professionals working with youth.

1. *Within the individual.* Resilient individuals were characterized by their caregivers as:
   - being active, affectionate, cuddly, good-natured, and easy to deal with in infancy
   - having effective reading skills by age 10 or Grade 4
   - having communication and reasoning skills
   - being responsible and achievement oriented and having competence and self-efficacy as general hallmarks
   - being more nurturant, compassionate, and socially perceptive
   - being more socially mature and possessing an internalized set of values
   - having a special interest or hobby
   - being liked by peers and adults
   - being reflective rather than having an impulsive dominant cognitive style
   - having an internal locus of control—believing that they can influence the environment around them
   - being flexible in coping strategies when dealing with adversity
   - setting career and job success as high priorities as adults
2. *Within the family.* Resilience is enhanced when:

- There are different child-rearing practices for boys and girls. Resilience is fostered in households with male role models who encourage the expression of emotion for boys and in households with an emphasis on risk-taking and independence for girls, with a tendency not to overprotect and reliable emotional support from another woman, such as a mother, grandmother, older sister, or aunt.
- There are affectional ties with alternate caregivers. Caring, nonjudgmental adults who are not necessarily family members are crucial in fostering resiliency.
- Youth from chaotic families have an association with friends and other individuals from stable households.
- There is an emphasis on youth being helpful. Chores and domestic responsibilities prove to be sources of competence and strength.
- There is faith that provides a sense of coherence and rootedness that give youth a sense of meaning and compassion.

3. *Within the community.* Resilience is enhanced when:
   - Youth are able to make and keep friends. Resilient youth keep friends into adulthood and look to them for emotional support.
   - There is a favorable attitude toward school.
   - There is structure and clear limits for boys, and the opportunity to take independent action for girls.
   - There is positive mentoring at school. Those remembering one or more teachers are more resilient (the most frequently identified role models are favorite teachers). The impact of positive mentoring may last a lifetime.

Werner and Smith (1992) concluded that the protective factors

> appear to transcend ethnic, social class, geographical, and historical boundaries. Most of all, they offer a more optimistic outlook than the perspective that can be gleaned from the literature on the negative consequences of perinatal trauma, caregiving deficits, and chronic poverty. They provide us with a corrective lens—an awareness of the self-righting tendencies that move children toward normal adult development under all but the most persistent adverse circumstances. (p. 202)

Counselors, teachers, parents, and other core providers can foster the protective buffers that support positive life trajectories for youth in which competence, confidence, and ability to care for others will flourish, but those helpers must believe in youth if this is going to happen. According to Werner and Smith (1992), "The life stories of the resilient youngsters now grown into adulthood teach us that competence, confidence, and caring can flourish, even under adverse circumstances, if children encounter persons who provide them with the secure basis for the development of trust, autonomy, and initiative" (p. 209).

Kitashima (1997), a youth from the Kauai study, has embodied this point in sharing what made a difference in her life growing up in a high-risk household. Kitashima found caring and supportive people in school significant contributors to her success. At the same time, she found some professionals in the school made her a target of racism and put-downs. She described a time when her fifth-grade math teacher told her, "You are a good-for-nothing Hawaiian and will never amount to anything." In contrast, her school principal told her, "You are Hawaiian, and you can be anything you choose to be" (Kitashima, 1997, p. 34). At age 16, when she got pregnant and had a child, another school principal supported her desire to stay in school. Like many youth from the Kauai study, the protective factors counterbalanced the risks, and Kitashima went on to become a successful adult.

One factor having a profound impact on her resilience was her faith in something greater than herself. Her faith in something greater led Kitashima (1997) to conclude, "Treasures exist in each one of our children—be they our own or somebody else's—and we need to be patient until they realize their promise. . . . Never give up on kids" (p. 36). Kitashima's guiding beliefs and comments open a larger question: the growing discussion about spirituality in public education.

Palmer (1998/1999) wrote,

> I advocate any way we can find to explore the spiritual dimension of teaching, learning, and living. By "spiritual" I do not mean the creedal formulation of any faith tradition. . . . I mean the ancient and abiding human quest for connectedness with something larger and more trustworthy than our egos—with our own souls, with one another, with the worlds of history and nature, with the invisible winds of the spirit, with the mystery of being alive. (p. 6)

Such discussion should cause counselors and teachers to pause because they place professionals in a position where they must wrestle with complex issues regarding "the spirit of education" in which educators can "neither ignore religion nor proselytize a particular belief" (Scherer, 1998/1999, p. 5). Ultimately, as Kitashima's experience and beliefs show, the act of believing in youth "becomes a concern of the spirit" (Wesley, 1998/1999, p. 42). Counselors and teachers thinking about spiritual issues are forced to recognize and appreciate the issues raised and how beliefs foster resilience.

Changing Perspectives and Practices

Early research regarding resilience concentrated on understanding the personal qualities found in resilient individuals. As research evolved, resilience has been acknowledged to derive from factors outside of the youth and to be the result of underlying protective processes rather than protective factors (Luthar et al., 2000a, 2000b). There is an interplay between the self-righting qualities inherent in the individual and the protective processes fostering resilience. Benard's (1991) review of the resilience research described personal and environmental sources of healthy development. Her review and subsequent work stand as a synthesis of the resilience literature that identifies major factors contributing to the enhancement of youth resilience. Benard's synthesis and practice continue to inform prevention efforts that balance the self-righting qualities inherent in the individual and the need to create systems that support protective processes fostering resilience (Benard, 1991, 1993, 1994, 1996, 1997; Benard & Marshall, 1997, 2001a, 2001b).

Drawing on the transactional–ecological model of human development, Benard (1997) stated, "Personality and individual outcomes are the result of a transactional process between self, agency, and environmental influences. To be successful, prevention interventions must focus on enhancing and creating positive environmental contexts—families, schools, and communities that, in turn, reinforce positive behaviors" (p. 16).

The individual traits include social competence, problem-solving skills, autonomy, and a sense of purpose and belief in a bright future. These resilience traits and protective factors support the self-righting tendencies within the person (Benard, 1994, 1996). Youth with a positive sense of well-being demonstrate the following (Benard, 1991):

- *Social competence:* responsiveness, flexibility, empathy and caring, communication skills, and a sense of humor
- *Problem-solving skills:* thinking abstractly and reflectively, planning skills, and flexibility
- *Autonomy:* internal locus of control, sense of power, self-discipline, and adaptive distancing
- *Sense of purpose and future:* healthy expectations, goal-directedness, success orientation, educational aspirations, persistence, hopefulness, hardiness, belief in bright or compelling future, and a sense of coherence or meaning.

Protective factors are also needed. Environmental characteristics or protective factors that support positive youth development include the following:

- *Caring and support:* Having a connection with at least one caring person is the single most important factor in fostering resilience in youth. Relationships noted for stable care, affection, attention, intergenerational social networks, and a basic sense of trust foster climates of care and support.
- *High expectations:* These imply that adults see strengths and assets more than problems and deficits, and they recognize the potential for maturity, responsibility, self-discipline, and common sense in youth. Providing structure, order, clear expectations, and cultural traditions; being valued; and promoting social and academic success foster resilience in youth.
- *Opportunities for participation:* These grow nationally from "high expectations for youth [and] for viewing youth as resources and not problems" (Benard, 1991, p. 17). Participation connects youth to other people, to interests, and to valuing life itself. Being valued participants, having socially and economically useful tasks, being responsible for decision making, planning, and helping others are the essence of meaningful participation.

Benard (1994) indicated that human development is a fluid process and that prevention efforts must focus on transactional processes that foster resilience traits and protective factors. Resilience research "promises to move the prevention, education, and youth development fields beyond their focus on program and what we do, to emphasis on process and how we do what we do; to move beyond our fixation with content to a focus on context" (Benard, 1996, pp. 9–10).

This shift requires invitations for all youth to connect with adults who offer them hope by providing care and support, high expectations, and opportunities for participation. Benard (1993) summed up the hope for all youth inherent in the resilience literature: "Solutions do not come from looking at what is missing; solutions will come by building on strengths" (p. 28). To assess student, school, and community strengths, Benard has been involved in developing the California Healthy Kids Survey (CHKS; see http://www.wested.org/hks/). The CHKS instrument enables local school leaders to assess their own systems, to develop plans for helping all students to become more connected with their schools, and to generate ongoing developmental plans for fostering resilience within school communities.

Like solution-focused, narrative, and other competency-based counseling approaches, resilience practices build on strengths. Professionals, such as school counselors, are challenged to create supportive systems and work as partners in collaborating with people to draw on the power to help themselves (Benard, 1991, 1993, 1994, 1996; Bertolino & O'Hanlon, 2002; De Jong & Berg, 2002; Monk et al., 1997; Parry &

Doan, 1994; Saleebey, 1997; White & Epston, 1990; Winslade & Monk, 1999, 2000). Seeing people as inherently possessing power shifts the professional role away from authority, expert, and director to that of collaborator working with others who have resources, expertise in their own lives, and the capacity to recognize their own well-being. Problems are defined as external to the person. Both Benard (1991, 1993) and narrative counselors (White & Epston, 1990) have stated that the person is not the problem; the problem is the problem. To begin solving problems, professionals are challenged to enter into dialogues with individuals, families, and communities who are seeking assistance in wrestling with problems. The next section explores problems influencing professional and personal discourses, developing dialogues, and how understanding resilience as transactional processes informs professional discourses related to risk, racism, poverty, and career development.

DISCOURSES OF RISK, RACISM, POVERTY, AND CAREERS

Like fish in water, people and cultures exist in language. We are biological, social, and psychological beings embedded in discourses that describe our ecosocial experience, understanding, and actions. Such discourses are culturally and ecologically embedded and define the taken-for-granted world in which we exist. Those being helped and those helping exist in complex ecosocial networks found in multiple bioregional, community, cultural, familial, and personal contexts that are described in various discourses, including a "discourse of disorder" (Bowers, 1997, 2000, 2001; Gergen & McNamee, 2000). As such, professionals are challenged to critically reflect on the discourses that shape their own taken-for-granted assumptions about the world, education, social situations, and their professional roles (Atkinson & Claxton, 2000; Hertz, 2001; Lott, 2002; Payne, 2001; Winslade & Monk, 2000). Reflecting on discourses defining the taken-for-granted world forces professionals to recognize a need to come as equals into dialogues shaping courses of action taken in systems such as schools or as helpers working with others who may exist in separate cultural discourses.

Looking at discourse patterns allows a number of professional possibilities, but, for the purposes of this chapter, we look at two things. First, exploring discourse patterns enables counselors to understand how both clients and professionals are shaped by a variety of discourses in their lives. Numerous discourses shape the way they experience the world and the language registers they use at home, school, and work to describe that experience to multiple audiences. For instance, Payne (2001) pointed out that middle-class people use formal-register discourse patterns that go straight to the point, whereas among many poor and underrepresented people casual-register discourse patterns go around and around. The formal-register discourse pattern is valued more in school and in middle-class venues and leads to the categorization of groups of people into upper and lower strata, thus allowing those using the valued discourse patterns to maintain their power and ability to "maneuver in the society they control" (Lott, 2002, p. 101). "Power, defined as access to resources, enables the group with greatest access to set the rules, frame the discourse, and name and describe those with less power" (Lott, 2002, p. 101).

Second, understanding discourses opens the opportunity for teachers and counselors to launch themselves out beyond their taken-for-granted world by listening to learn and by hearing people as experts of their own experiences. Moreover, understanding multiple discourses opens opportunities to develop collaborative dialogues between and among people in specific contexts at specific points in time. We all see, experience, and tell stories about the world from certain perspectives and use language in different ways, and counselors and teachers are challenged to enter into collaborative dialogues, to describe power, and to invite the less powerful to access tools to fully participate. Such a stance moves the image of helping from having an expert above the client and removing the problem from the person toward placing two people side by side viewing the problem together, knocking the problem out of the way, or working together to dissolve it.

Risk Discourse

The discourse that troubled families, schools, and communities perpetrate harm on youth binds problems to individuals composing those families, schools, and communities that are at risk. An alternative discourse would not place the problem in people; rather, problems would be described as interactive processes constructed in specific ecosocial locations. Benard (1994) pointed out, "Labeling youths, their families, and their communities as at risk means we are acting on stereotypes, on unquestioned assumptions about who people really are. . . . In contrast, resilience research focuses on learning . . . individual stories and truths, on studying the individual variation within groups having risk status" (p. 4). Fostering resilience means recognizing social ecology and the discourses that we participate in as people and professionals.

Swadener and Lubeck (1995), who seemed unfamiliar with the resilience literature, stated that describing youth as "at risk" creates an "ideology of risk, which has embedded in it interpretations of children's deficiencies or likelihood of failure due to environmental, as well as individual variables. The problem of locating pathology in the victim is the most objectionable tenet of much of the dominant rhetoric of risk" (p. 18). In other words, describing youth as at risk creates political consequences that result in the victims of social injustice being blamed for the results of that injustice. For Swadener and Lubeck, the need to confront structural injustices is lost when professional conversations and actions focus on fixing youth at risk. According to Fine (1995),

> "Youth at risk" is an ideological and historical construction. While numbers and their skewed class and racial distributions are intolerable, and the academic and economic consequences are severe, we must remember that today more students graduate from high school than was true fifteen years ago. . . . Fundamentally, the notion of "risk" keeps us from being broadly, radically, and structurally creative about transforming schools and social conditions for all of today and tomorrow's youth. (p. 90)

Although Swadener and Lubeck (1995) and Fine (1995) did not locate themselves in the counseling profession or even in prevention work, such perspectives should prompt counselors, teachers, parents, and others to pause and think. By taking advantage of the deconstruction of the at-risk construct, counselors and teachers can critically reflect on their own practice and open up possibilities for different kinds of professional practice.

Doing something about it. Counselors can offer alternative discourses. On the one hand, as Saleebey (1997) wrote, we might be a

> culture obsessed with, and fascinated by, psychopathology, victimization, abnormality, and moral and interpersonal aberrations. A swelling conglomerate of businesses and pro-

fessions, institutions and agencies, from medicine to pharmaceuticals, from the insurance industry to the mass media turn handsome profits by assuring us that we are in the clutch (or soon will be) of any number of emotional, physical, or behavioral maladies. (p. 4)

On the other hand, counselors can participate in discourses that build on the traditions that foster resilience, emphasize health and competence, and communicate hope to and faith in youth.

Racism Discourse

A special issue of the *Journal of Counseling & Development* on racism (Robinson & Ginter, 1999) captured how our lives are woven into stories that illustrate racism's toxic effects in counselors' personal and professional lives. Professionals and those they serve are woven into a racist social fabric. Euro American counselors and African American counselors experience the world in different ways; one might walk down the street sensing that there is no racism in the United States, whereas the other might experience racist remarks or more subtle forms of marginalization while walking down the same street. As Kitashima's (1997) earlier account demonstrates, racism infects both individual and environmental attributes fostering resilience; most counselors and teachers recognize that not every youth has the personal and environmental attributes Kitashima had when faced with racism at school. Youth need allies to advocate for safe space and equity.

Counselors, teachers, parents, and other core providers are challenged to understand how dominant discourses affect how their clients' stories are heard, understood, and responded to. Robinson (1999) stated, "Counselors must avoid attributing certain occupations, attitudes, and experiences to their clients due to the visibility of their race, gender, and other identities. Making judgments about people's humanity and its quality due to established criteria is to rely on tried but extremely powerful discourse steeped in oppression" (p. 78). Counselors have to know stereotypes, themselves, their privilege, and the cultural context in which they meet others, and they need to be able to listen deeply to the story of others without judgment if they are to engage in profoundly human conversations. Robinson argued that if counselors' practice takes a constructionist perspective, they do not assume a preferred position in any dialogue; a constructionist perspective allows for a plurality of ways for viewing the world and shows how power, privilege, and disadvantage do not have to be deemed as absolute and fixed.

Doing something about it. In the above example of the two counseling professionals, if the African American described feeling marginalized by some experience on the street or at a conference, the Euro American might be curious about the colleague's experience and listen to learn from the experience being described. There are separate realities that open themselves up to being shared and experiences that simply have to be understood. A Chinese American graduate student described an incident in Portland, Oregon, where he was told, "Why don't you go back to where you came from." Having been born in the United States, he was where he came from—a country where racism is woven into the social fabric. When he conveyed his story to the predominantly Euro American class, the group recognized that such comments are not part of their day-to-day experience; their White privilege shields them from such day-to-day hostility, but their responsibility is to make their community safe for all. Rather than merely saying "thanks for sharing," the Euro American students were challenged to describe ways they could take hold of the loom and weave stories that recognize and appreciate diversity, as well as the need to advocate for the basic right for all people to be able to walk safely in their communities. A diverse community is a resilient community.

Poverty Discourse

While recognizing there are multiple dimensions to poverty besides having financial need, the poverty discourse reveals social distancing (Lott, 2002; Payne, 2001). Look at poverty and children. In the United States, 16.2% of all children are poor; by race, 9.4% (over 4.2 million) of White non-Hispanic children, 30.9% (over 3.5 million) of Black children, and 28.0% (over 3.3 million) of Hispanic children are poor (Children's Defense Fund, 2001). All poor children experience various forms of social distancing, and all need multiple resources for overcoming poverty.

The nonpoor distance themselves from the poor in a variety of ways that result in exclusion, separation, devaluing, discounting, and classist discrimination (Lott, 2002). Such discrimination allows for the conscious and unconscious marginalization of the poor as expendable and undeserving individuals who are viewed as uneducated, unmotivated, lazy, unpleasant, angry, and stupid. As an individual problem, poverty can be described as resulting from behaviors rather than from the social and economic structures perpetuating poverty. For instance, schools perpetuate classism; the most profound memories a group of low-income women could recall about school were those of being treated with distain and not being encouraged by teachers and school officials (Lott, 2002). Lott asserted that the middle-class discourse blames the poor for their position and perpetuates social policies that maintain distance from the poor. Class distancing includes within-race status groupings as well. For instance, upper-strata Whites distance themselves from poor Whites by referring to them as White trash, crackers, okies, hillbillies, and so on.

Doing something about it. As important as financial resources are, poverty involves more than mere financial resources. Other resources include emotional, mental, spiritual, and physical support systems; relationship/role models; and knowledge of hidden rules (Payne, 2001). Understanding the hidden rules is one area that helps professionals foster collaborative dialogues with children, parents, and families. As mentioned earlier, middle-class formal-register discourse patterns are different from casual-register discourse patterns frequently used by the poor. In accounting for events, students, families, and communities using casual-register discourse patterns tell their stories in different, less direct ways. Listen, learn, and appreciate the richness found in the casual-register discourse patterns. At the same time, formal-register discourse patterns are given status by those in power in such settings as schools and some places of employment. For counselors and teachers, understanding the formal-register discourse pattern is privileged. This means entering collaborative dialogues with students, parents, and the community who use casual-register discourse patterns to let them in on a secret; learning the formal-register discourse pattern is one pathway for access to education and entrance into certain careers. This does not mean imposing middle-class values and forcing formal-register discourse patterns on all students; it means respectfully providing access to the resources necessary to enter into contexts that require a certain way of speaking. Fostering resilience requires flexibility and working with individuals, families, and communities to make choices, as well as helping them to access and develop multiple resources to address their poverty.

Careers Discourse

A meaningful careers dialogue begins with hopes and dreams. Quattrociocchi and Peterson (1997) pointed to the need for parents, counselors, and teachers to see that hope emerges from finding passion for work and meanings embedded in those activities we choose to do. Encouraging passion and meaningful participation can serve as guides when teachers, counselors, and parents collaborate their efforts in designing developmental, comprehensive counseling and guidance programs that focus on helping youth to become aware, explore, and make decisions about possible career pathways (Herring, 1998; Zunker, 2002).

Yet, it is crucial for teachers, counselors, and parents to recognize that embedded in any careers discourse are assumptions about the nature of work, career opportunities, corporate power, political power, social comparisons, material accumulation, consumerism, leisure, and so on (Bowers, 2000, 2001; Hertz, 2001; Schor, 1992, 1998). For instance, consider consumerism. Bowers (2001) pointed out,

> The more people rely on consumerism, the more they have to work in order to pay for their expanding dependencies: food preparation, entertainment, transportation, clothes, leisure time, health care, and so forth. And the more people have to work, the less time they have for parenting and involvement in activities that strengthen the reciprocal networks within the community. (p. 10)

Youth are developing career pathways in a historic period when the world and its diverse nations grapple with finite resources such as oil, communities face business upheaval such as jobs being exported to developing countries, and individuals confront career uncertainty such as being laid off when businesses downsize. Given the changing nature of the world we live in, fostering passion, hope, and career resilience is crucial to offer alternative discourses that empower youth with a sense of their competence and capacity to make it in an uncertain world (Brooks, 1994; Quattrociocchi & Peterson, 1997).

Doing something about it. Maintaining hope and passion is a challenge facing both adults and youth, and youth need models for finding passion and meaning in the activities in which they engage. First, start with fundamental questions: Why are we doing this? What are we trying to accomplish? Second, find role models who can show students how they maintain passion and find meaning in what they do. One model is the Edible Schoolyard concept that found root at Martin Luther King Jr. Middle School in Berkeley, California—a project growing out of a relationship between a nationally recognized chef, Alice Waters of Chez Panisse Restaurant, and the principal of the school, Neil Smith (Capra, 1998; Lappe & Lappe, 2002). The project also involves the Berkeley-based Center for Ecoliteracy and its cofounder, Fritof Capra (1996, 1998), who argued that resilient communities are ecologically and socially diverse communities that extend learning beyond the classroom. Those involved with the Edible Schoolyard see the project as an opportunity to integrate natural and human systems, as well as for youth to learn that life is about social and ecological connections, changes, and challenges (see http://www.edibleschoolyard.org or http://www.ecoliteracy.org/index.html or http://www.nwrel.org/msec/resource).

The Edible Schoolyard integrates middle school classroom learning and competence, relationships developed among students and adults, and processes involved in growing and preparing food they will eat at school; in other words, the project is guided by a tradition that teaches the head, the heart, and the hand. If the plants get eaten by pests, students must use their heads to find out what happened, have heart not to be discouraged, and use their hands for replanting and maintaining viable solutions for controlling the pests. Thus, the students learn to work together to get up after they are knocked down and to find the resources necessary to overcome real-life problems. Students also learn that work is related to community practices that foster passion and hope. Obviously, when it comes to weeding, there might not be much passion, but when it comes to learning how to grow, prepare, serve, and share food, there is the hope that the results will taste good and be appreciated by others in the school community. By taking on a number of roles and responsibilities that result from participating in processes that range from mulching the soil to planting the seed, to clearing the table in projects like the Edible Schoolyard, middle school students are taught fundamental skills related to career and life success. Fostering resilience means exposing youth to different career discourses, providing youth with the resources and opportunities to make connections, helping them to get back up after getting knocked down, experiencing competence in context, and making work-related adjustments in an ever-changing world.

APPROACHES TO FOSTERING RESILIENCE

Overview

This section discusses approaches that exemplify practices and connections within the resilience literature. The approaches were selected because they illustrate how resilience practices support processes that begin with believing in individuals, families, schools, and communities. Each approach shows how fostering resilience is a collaborative process, respectful of multicultural perspectives, and hopeful about engaging youth as resources. Each approach shows that significant relationships develop over time and include just hanging around, listening to another person's story, struggling with difficult tasks, and being alive in the moment with another person. Because a caring adult is the single consistent known factor fostering resilience found across the resilience literature (Benard, 1991, 1993, 1996; Benard & Marshall, 1997, 2001a, 2001b; Gregg, 1996; Resnick et al., 1998; Reynolds, 1998; Werner, 1996; Werner & Smith, 1982, 1992), these approaches describe ways caring adults can foster relationships with youth.

Structured Narrative

Youth have abundant opportunities to create stories of success or stories of woe. Because schools are one of those places where youth create stories regarding their abilities to learn to live, learn, and work, much of this section focuses on a written counseling intervention that can be adapted in different school contexts. The structured narrative intervention described here was developed in an effort to address the cold efficiencies necessitated from school counselor-to-student ratios that had been as high as 600:1 in the school in which the study took place.

The writing intervention was designed to help individual students cultivate positive stories about their possibilities for renewal and redirection and to provide normally anonymous students with voices during the critical transition into high school (Berliner, 1993; Lewis, 1995). Students had space to tell their stories and knew someone would take time to "listen" to every story by reading them. As a written approach, structured narrative prompts help students to clarify or redefine personal narratives and to see possibilities for living with greater hope and power (Lewis, 1999, 2002).

As an intervention, the structured narrative grows out of a tradition that uses narrative and writing in counseling (Bruner, 1986, 1990; Desetta & Wolin, 1998; L'Abate, 1992, 1994; Lewis, 1999, 2002; Lifton, 1993; Monk, 1997; Monk et al., 1997; Pennebaker, 1997; Riordan, 1996; Sarbin, 1986; White & Epston, 1990; Winslade & Monk, 1999, 2000). The nature of narrative is nonnormative and can be optimistic because every person has numerous possibilities for describing any experience. Structured narrative lessons may be used in a number of ways, from lessons designed to enhance transition into high school to lessons created to enhance the mindful practice required by graduate students in the teaching and counseling professions. Such lessons orient individuals to requirements defined by organizations, such as schools, or prompt individuals to explore narrative possibilities that entering the teaching and counseling professions provide. The lessons may also be used to assess individuals who might need additional help in developing their writing skills, making connections with caring adults, or reaching personal and professional goals.

"A Write Way," consisting of six structured narrative lessons, was used to help youth during their transition into high school (Lewis, 1995, 1996, 1999). The prompts are formatted on a page to limit the length of responses, to make responding more attractive to reluctant writers, and to focus respondents on time-limited tasks (see the Appendix). The prompts must be adapted to local needs and range from closed-ended questions to short essays that provide opportunities for creative responses. For instance, in a study focusing on youth transitioning into high school, youth were asked the closed-ended question: "Do you plan to graduate from high school? Yes or No." They were also given the prompt: "Describe a time when you were a positive leader or participant at home, school, or elsewhere" (Lewis, 1995). The study concluded that creating structures helps students understand high expectations, but caring and supportive face-to-face relationships are equally important (Lewis, 1995, 1999).

One purpose of the lessons of "A Write Way" was to help youth see possibilities for viewing or rewriting their school story in a positive way by assisting youth to become oriented to the organizational demands of the school, document their own perspective about learning, and open them up to see more possibilities for living and learning in themselves. Prompts were designed to help students explore developmental possibilities and not leap to conclusions about themselves as learners or as people because drawing conclusions too quickly might close off possibilities for discovering the world and themselves anew (Claxton, 1997; Langer, 1997).

Structured narratives assist individuals in seeing that their life trajectories are not set by the stars or fate: People can change their life stories by discovering the possibilities inherent in coexisting alternative stories, and the vast majority of youth do become successful adults. Structured narratives attempt to give youth greater agency in describing their lives and are especially useful when youth see their life stories in the context of other life stories. In the end, stories supporting positive relationships or overcoming the odds are critical to children, and they encourage students to take action in constructing more satisfying personal stories about their experiences. Resilience is fostered by taking action developing one's own ever-changing story and by listening to the success stories of others. At the same time, as Parry and Doan (1994) stated, "No one ever fully becomes the author of her/his own story; any such assumption can only lead back to the illusions of control, individual autonomy, isolated selfhood, and single truth. The person goes forth instead to join with others in the universal human action of multiple authorship" (p. 43). The structured narrative and other active approaches facilitate youth in becoming agents in their own life narratives, and reflective approaches like bibliotherapy facilitate youth in valuing the stories of others (Brooks, 1997; Fredericks, 1997; Gladding, 1997, 1998; Rockwell, 1998). Stories can focus on individual youth in organizational contexts, but what is frequently called for is to change the beliefs guiding the organization.

Tapping Resilience: A Framework for Practice

Tapping resilience is an "inside-out process" according to Benard and Marshall (1997), who posited that individual change can be encouraged and successfully tapped with systems change and education rather than risk-focused therapeutic interventions. Benard, senior associate for program development at WestEd, a nonprofit research, development, and service agency based in California, and Marshall, executive director at the University of Minnesota National Resilience Resource Center, have developed a tool for guiding school community systems change initiatives designed to foster resilience in children, youth, adults, and organizations. Successful systemic interventions, according to Benard and Marshall, are not quick fixes but require 3 to 5 years to implement. The framework is only one part of their comprehensive approach to establishing a resilience-operating philosophy in major systems, like school districts. Ultimately, the purpose is to help adults foster the resilience of individuals by first learning to discover and tap their own resilience.

The planning framework encourages planners to focus on four areas: (a) beliefs planners hold about the natural resilience and promise of human beings, (b) conditions for empowerment revealed in research and best practice, (c) program strategies to create these conditions that tap resilience, and (d) individual and societal outcomes to be evaluated as part of the process.

This framework cuts new ground. It directs planners to explore their fundamental beliefs about human functioning and how it is fully realized. Traditional prevention planning guides, for example, have primarily focused on needs assessment and community assets and deficits as precursors to poor youth outcomes. Staff development and technical assistance services offered by the National Resilience Resource Center use the framework for tapping resilience to shift the local focus from "at risk" to "at promise." Benard and Marshall suggested that our beliefs about the capacity of youth determine the degree to which youth are ultimately able to realize their own potential.

Belief is the foundation of the planning framework. Adults must "see how conditioned thoughts prevent us from recognizing students' natural strengths" (Benard & Marshall, 1997, p. 2). Understanding the power of conditioned, limiting beliefs and learning how to tap one's own resilience—the health of the helper—are of paramount importance. The key questions in the early planning phase are What do we believe about the capacity for resilience in all people? Is it natural and inborn in all human beings even though it is not always realized or manifested in behaviors, skills, and characteristics? If we look through behaviors, can we discern health? Is it there waiting to be tapped?

With the framework, planners also study resilience research and best practices. What creates the conditions of empowerment? What taps resilience? What evidence supports our beliefs about human resilience? This phase of program development unites common sense, research, and program evaluation. What do we know works? Where is more study needed?

In simplest terms, Benard (1991) categorized the conditions of empowerment as three major protective factors: caring and support, high encouraging expectations, and meaningful opportunities for participation. The challenge is how to prepare adults to provide these critical protective factors: to be caring, to believe youth can succeed, and to invite genuine participation, even when behavior is highly problematic, past performance meager, and social behavior completely obnoxious or even personally threatening.

Based on an understanding of both beliefs and evidence, planners are guided to develop or select strategies that will tap resilience. After an exhaustive search for effective prevention and youth development strategies, Benard and Marshall (1997) settled on the health realization approach as one of the most efficient and effective ways school and community representatives could be taught to foster resilience. The experiences of a district student assistance director trained by the National Resilience Resource Center using this system's change approach in fostering resilience are described later.

The framework also pushes planners to think about evaluation from the very beginning. Key questions to address include the following:

- What will it look like if a young person realizes his or her resilience?
- How will it look in adults?
- How does resilience look in a school, family, neighborhood, and community?
- Do we know what we are looking for and trying to make happen?
- Will we know healthy human functioning when we see it?

Resilience is not about labels. "To label a child, family, community or culture resilient—or not resilient—misses the mark. Labeling one child resilient implies another is not and contradicts the resilience paradigm in which resilience is part of the human condition and the birthright of all human beings" (Benard & Marshall, 1997, p. 4).

Benard and Marshall (1997) called for a systems change that shakes traditional prevention, special education, and mental health services at the very core. Are human beings capable by nature? As professionals, can we teach healthy functioning and in an organized fashion tap resilience? Can school counselors be most effective if they point students to their health rather than cementing student, parent, and professional thoughts about diagnosis, labels, problems, risks, and looming danger and failure? The framework for tapping resilience can assist counselors, teachers, and parents in encouraging school leaders to begin a systematic paradigm shift to health rather than dysfunction. The next section builds on the approach that has reported success in challenging environmental contexts such as inner-city housing projects and other environments like public schools.

Health Realization: The Psychology of Resilience

Health realization begins with the assumption that every person has the innate capacity for mental health, common sense, and living in a mature and responsible manner regardless of his or her past and current circumstances (Mills, 1995). As a prevention and education approach, health realization focuses on inside-out change and innate resilience (Health Realization Institute, 2001; Mills, 1995; G. S. Pransky, 1998; J. Pransky & Carpenos, 2000; Sedgeman, 2002). This section shares the principles and the impact the health realization approach had on a high-risk public housing site in Miami, Florida, and concludes with stories from a district student assistance director from St. Cloud, Minnesota, who uses health realization to guide her work with youth.

Health realization's three guiding principles—mind, thought, and consciousness—are described as providing a basis for the renaissance of psychology (G. S. Pransky, 1998) and are described as the source of human experience and psychological functioning (Mills, 1995; G. S. Pransky, 1998; Sedgeman, 2002). *Mind* is defined as the source of thought and consciousness (G. S. Pransky, 1998). Like physicists' use of terms like *energy* or *life force*, mind is the power that makes thought and consciousness possible. "Thought as a function originates beyond our individual psychological personage just as the life force originates beyond our individual physical personage" (G. S. Pransky, 1998, p. 38). The brain processes thoughts moment to moment, giving each person a different experience of reality. "The function of thinking, the ability to think is universal, but the content of that thinking is determined by each person" (G. S. Pransky, 1998, p. 38). *Consciousness* is the process of experiencing our thinking through our senses. "If you mistakenly thought you were in extreme danger, you would have a sensory experience of being in danger" (G. S. Pransky, 1998, p. 39).

Mills (1995) and G. S. Pransky (1998) saw individual problems as emerging from the way people think about themselves, and well-meaning efforts that focus on symptom reduction usually fail to point people toward the principle of thought. Because individuals construct their personal realities, health realization focuses on those qualities of thought that elicit a sense of well-being in the moment and do not explore the psychic damage resulting from past trauma. Mills (1995) found that "people's ability to change their outlook, and the quality of their lives, varied directly in relation to their understanding of thought" (p. 61). The counseling process is approached as educational (Mills, 1995, 1996; G. S. Pransky, 1998). "We concluded that we could help people much more by teaching them to elicit their own intrinsic health, rather than encouraging them to explore their dysfunctions" (Mills, 1995, p. 53). Psychological difficulties were approached as products of thoughts rather than as existing independently and having a life of their own. The intervention shifted to eliciting and teaching people to understand the source of their mental health. Individuals were helped to understand moment-to-moment thought.

"People who understand what mental health is . . . live effortlessly in mental well-being" (G. S. Pransky, Mills, Sedgeman, & Bleven, 1997, p. 412). Innate resilience is accessed when individuals recognize that reality is formed from moment-to-moment thought and that the trajectory of a life story can be changed by recognizing the role of thought in creating that story (Mills & Spittle, 1998, 2001). Teaching individuals about thought, coupled with community-building activities, has resulted in impressive preliminary results.

The model was used as a community intervention at the Modello-Homestead Gardens Project in Metro-Dade County, Florida. Staff were initially trained in health realization prior to conducting outreach activities. Outreach activities for project residents included initiating PTA meetings, parenting classes, and individual and family counseling sessions. Residents were taught about how their thinking formed their outlook and behavior and to recognize the difference between their learned, conditioned, or processing thinking from the past and their more free-flowing, here-and-now, commonsense thinking. All staff contact with the residents was respectful, and residents were viewed as being resilient and healthy.

After 3 years, the program served 142 families and 600 youth. Resident surveys after 3 years revealed the following (Mills, 1997, p. 2):

- 87% of parents reported that their children were more cooperative and they also reported significantly less frustration with or hostility toward their children.
- Over 60% of residents involved in programs became employed, from a baseline of 85% on public assistance.

- School discipline referrals and suspensions decreased by 75% from baseline at the middle school level.
- Attendance improved and school truancy rates improved around 80%.
- Parent involvement in schools improved by 500%.
- School failure dropped from 50% to 10%.
- Middle school teen pregnancy dropped 80%.
- The Homestead Police reported that they had not had any calls for drug trafficking or criminal activities such as stolen cars or burglaries for almost a year.

In addition, parents reported they stopped hitting their children, they got more involved with schools, and the children improved their school performance. The community became a better place to live for both adults and youth. With communities typically defined as at risk, the health realization approach has been helpful in promoting positive individual and community outcomes. Other communities and programs reporting successes using health realization range from the South Bronx, New York to the Avalon Gardens in South Central Los Angeles (Mills, 1995). The work is not merely directed toward high-risk communities.

Jeanne Slingluff, the district student assistance director in St. Cloud, Minnesota, was trained in health realization by the National Resilience Resource Center to improve the performance of student assistance teams, committees of teachers, principals, social workers, counselors, and others who focus on improving the performance of at-risk youth. Slingluff initially found that some teams met and others did not on a regular basis and that their success could be improved. Two pilot schools with staffs of 15–20 were selected for health realization training.

Staff were taught to talk about innate resilience and to teach youth the source of thought. One teacher used peanut M&Ms to move youth along; there were many different colors but a common interior. Youth were taught about the "busy mind" during a group exercise designed to help them "get quiet" and "clear their minds" on their own. The exercise used the following steps:

- Students were told they had been given a call slip to the office to talk to the principal and to write down their thoughts on a half sheet of paper.
- After writing, the students broke into groups and summarized their thoughts on post-its.
- Then, individually and in small groups they were asked to put their post-its on their teacher's glasses as she sat in front of the class. It was only moments before the teacher's glasses were covered with post-its, and soon her nose and other parts of her face were covered as well. The teacher said, "When you have a busy mind, you can't see." A busy mind can lead to problems.
- Next, the teacher posed some questions: "What would happen if this student had to go to a test after meeting with the principal? How would the student perform?"
- Finally, the teacher asked, "What can you do to clear your thoughts?" The students offered suggestions and strategies for getting quiet. Some suggestions were as simple as close your eyes or picture something relaxing.

Once the students have the concept, they know how to quiet their minds. According to Slingluff, when the class starts to get overly busy, the teacher can simply tell the class in a respectful way, "Put your heads down just for a minute to clear your heads." The students stop and clear their minds.

According to Slingluff, this occurs because teachers, counselors, and administrators believe in students' innate capacities. To illustrate her point, she shared the story of a young man who was sent to her after he expanded a one-paragraph assignment about conflict into a five-page catharsis that described his experience of being sexually abused and having substance-abusing parents. The teacher was concerned that the student was suicidal; Slingluff said she normally would think in terms of getting an ambulance but that this time she decided to clear her own mind before meeting the young man and to listen deeply to him without letting her mind get busy. She listened to the student as he told his story. He brought in a friend when they met, and the three of them talked about strengths that could be found in the story he told. From there, he generated options and a plan for taking care of himself.

The data and the stories point to a variety of possibilities for the health realization model. As more schools experiment with the approach and more research studies are conducted, there will be more opportunities to assess the impact the approach has on individuals and organizations. The Sydney Banks Institute for Innate Health, housed in the Robert C. Byrd Health Sciences Center at West Virginia University, has initiated a research program led by James Shumway (www.sbiih.org). The next section discusses how practices that foster resilience have been directed toward youth with special needs.

RESILIENCE AND YOUTH WITH DISABILITIES

Youth with disabilities may require specific interventions in addition to enhancing schoolwide protective processes, such as designing multidisciplinary and multimodal teams to address the needs of the whole person. Counselors may be designated on those teams as strengths advocates and define an important role for looking for strengths. In fact, individualized educational programs can identify and maximize strengths without eliminating the need to detect and accommodate weaknesses that add to risk, and remediation efforts can be directed toward building up youth competence (Gregg, 1996).

"Children with ADHD [attention deficit hyperactivity disorder] exhibit many characteristics attributed to creativity and giftedness," according to Gregg (1996, p. 6). These children need help with their social skills, but more importantly, they need the unconditional support of at least one "prosocial adult who believes in the child" (Gregg, 1996, p. 6). Three conditions must be present to help foster resilience in disabled youth: (a) giving opportunity for bonding to take place; (b) increasing academic skills, social skills, and self-esteem to assist youth in successful bonding; and (c) recognizing and reinforcing accomplishments in a consistent and systematic manner (Gregg, 1996).

One responsible and caring adult—teacher, counselor, administrator, relative, or other core provider—can help youth with disabilities become more prosocial. Providing disabled youth with coaches or mentors is one way to help them initiate the bonding relationship. Supporting all facets of each youth's education from art, to athletics, to reading helps them to find and express possible talents and encourages them to work effectively with others. Developing creative "alternatives to suspension and expulsion—like community service—for all but the most serious offences, to keep from further isolating and alienating" youth enables them to remain attached to the school culture (Gregg, 1996, p. 9). Helping youth find something meaningful to do at school is critical to their future success. Besides the critical skill of reading (there is a high correlation between reading and income), youth must be encouraged to develop a passion for what they do.

In a similar vein, according to Brooks (1997), it is vital to identify and reinforce youth's strengths because "every person possesses at least one small 'island of competence,' one that is, or has the potential to be, a source of pride and accomplishment" (p. 391). Teachers who are taught to show personal interest in youth by spending a few extra moments or writing words of encouragement on papers or in notes foster resilience in youth. Brooks (1997) stated, "Adults must constantly walk a tightrope when discipline is concerned, maintaining a delicate balance between rigidity and permissiveness, striving to blend warmth, nurturance, acceptance, and humor with realistic expectations, clearcut regulations, and logical and natural consequences" (p. 393). To foster resilience, schools must be made places where youth experience a growing sense of competence and resulting self-esteem (Brooks, 1994; Brooks & Goldstein, 2001).

ADAPTATIONS FOR DIVERSITY

Diversity is integral to resilience theory and practice because listening deeply to the experience of others opens up possibilities for relationships grounded in understanding and compassion. Each section in this chapter has raised concerns that call on counselors, teachers, parents, and others to become aware of their personal and professional discourse, to wrestle with the scourge of racism, and to listen deeply to the stories of their clients. Illustrated below, in an intervention integrating special needs and culturally appropriate practice, is an approach that sees the strengths in clients, that recognizes the self-righting capacities in all people, and that understands that resilience approaches are ultimately about empowerment.

Macfarlane (1998) developed an approach for Maori special education students in New Zealand that used culturally appropriate practice. "In New Zealand it is the dominant culture that provides the guidelines for conventional and special education, as well as the majority of professionals determining 'who is the problem'" (Macfarlane, 1998, p. 2). Like underrepresented youth in the United States, Maori youth frequently find themselves alienated from school. Macfarlane's (1998) bicultural approach begins with a meeting, or what the Maori refer to as *hui*, during which school officials and Maori youth could "speak with each other about difficult things in a way that avoids sliding back into the dynamics that gave rise to the problems in the first place" (p. 3). By moving away from punitive and judgmental discourse, the hui was designed to promote culturally appropriate alternatives to suspension-based community partnerships with the school. The conference was embedded in a culturally appropriate discourse that drew on Maori culture and values, such as the four principles of consensus, reconciliation, examination, and harmony. The conference started by saying in Maori and English, "I am who I am. You are who you are. Let us move together in tandem" (Macfarlane, 1998, p. 11). The youth were introduced to a new school discourse that placed their values and culture central to finding solutions to the problems being faced at school. The youth experienced discourse in school that embedded Maori students' success and well-being. It is an approach that does not leave youth out on their own but calls on adults and youth to move together in tandem. To foster resilience within all youth, we need to create systems that support the well-being of all youth.

SUMMARY

The resilience literature offers counselors, teachers, parents, and other core providers a path back to their roots in education and development. Resilience research supports an optimistic, longitudinal view of the person and offers a proactive approach for enhancing human development. Benard (1996) stated, "The astounding finding from these long term studies was that at least 50%—and often closer to 70%—of youth growing up in these high-risk conditions did develop social competence despite exposure to severe stress and did overcome the odds to lead successful lives" (p. 7). The resilience literature offers counselors, teachers, parents, and others an optimistic and hopeful developmental perspective that takes into account ecosocial contexts. Most radically, resilience adherents see people as having innate self-righting capacities for changing their life trajectories, a landscape that defines risks in ecosocial contexts rather than people, and an outlook that asks people to slow down enough to listen deeply to the stories embedded in everyday lives. Benard (1996) asserted that the shift to resilience has the power to "recreate a social covenant grounded in social and economic justice" (p. 11). Resilience-promoting interventions are primarily systemic and link individual, family, school, and community and require counselors, teachers, parents, and others to consider the ground they stand on.

At the very least, fostering resilience in the schools is vital to the well-being of youth. Counselors, teachers, parents, and others can look to prevention and practices designed to foster resilience to help youth learn to live, learn to learn, and learn to work (Gibbs, 2001; Henderson et al., 1999, 2000a, 2000b; Henderson & Milstein, 1996). Benard and Marshall (1997), Mills (1995), G. S. Pransky (1998), and J. Pransky and Carpenos (2000) have offered powerful approaches for teaching students to recognize their healthy thinking. Lewis (1996, 1999) has offered a tool for helping students make successful transitions at predictable developmental points, such as the move from middle to high school, as well as for developing more empowering learning stories. Gregg (1996) and Brooks (1997) have reminded counselors, teachers, parents, and others that every youth has a gift or an "island of competence" that can be tapped if we look. Indeed, the resilience literature calls on counselors, teachers, parents, and others to see that all people have the innate capacity for self-righting and well-being and they need support to tap it.

REFERENCES

Atkinson, T., & Claxton, G. (2000). *The intuitive practitioner: On the value of not always knowing what one is doing.* Philadelphia: Open University Press.

Benard, B. (1991). *Fostering resiliency in kids: Protective factors in the family, school, and community.* Portland, OR: Northwest Regional Educational Laboratory.

Benard, B. (1993). *Turning the corner: From risk to resiliency.* Portland, OR: Northwest Regional Educational Laboratory.

Benard, B. (1994, December). *Applications of resilience: Possibilities and promise.* Paper presented at the Conference of the Role of Resilience in Drug Abuse, Alcohol Abuse, and Mental Illness, Washington, DC.

Benard, B. (1996). From research to practice: The foundations of the resiliency paradigm. *Resiliency in Action, 1*(1), 7–11.

Benard, B. (1997). Changing the condition, place, and view of young people in society: An interview with youth development pioneer Bill Lofquist. *Resiliency in Action, 2*(1), 7–18.

Benard, B., & Marshall, K. (1997). *A framework for practice: Tapping innate resiliency.* Minneapolis: University of Minnesota, Center for Applied Research and Educational Improvement, College of Education and Human Development. Retrieved from http://education.umn.edu/carei/Reports/Rpractice/Spring 97/framework.htm

Benard, B., & Marshall, K. (2001a). *Competence and resilience research: Lessons for prevention.* Minneapolis: University of Minnesota, National Resilience Resource Center and the Center for the Application of Prevention Technologies. Retrieved August 20, 2002, from http://www.cce.umn.edu/nrrc/research.shtml

Benard, B., & Marshall, K. (2001b). *Protective factors in individuals, families, and schools: National longitudinal study on adolescent health.* Minneapolis: University of Minnesota, National Resilience Resource Center and the Center for the Application of Prevention Technologies. Retrieved August 20, 2002, from http://www.cce.umn.edu/nrrc/research.shtml

Berliner, B. A. (1993). *Adolescence, school transitions and prevention: A research-based primer.* San Francisco: Far West Regional Educational Laboratory.

Bertolino, B., & O'Hanlon, B. (2002). *Collaborative, competency-based counseling and therapy.* Boston: Allyn & Bacon.

Blum, R. W. (1998). Healthy youth development as a model for youth health promotion. *Journal of Adolescent Health, 22,* 368–375.

Bowers, C. A. (1997). *The culture of denial: Why the environmental movement needs a strategy for reforming universities and public schools.* Albany: State University of New York Press.

Bowers, C. A. (2000). *Let them eat data: How computers affect education, cultural diversity, and the prospects of ecological sustainability.* Athens: University of Georgia Press.

Bowers, C. A. (2001). *Educating for eco-justice and community.* Athens: University of Georgia Press.

Brooks, R. B. (1994). Children at risk: Fostering resilience and hope. *American Journal of Orthopsychiatry, 64,* 545–553.

Brooks, R. B. (1997). A personal journey: From pessimism and accusation to hope and resilience. *Journal of Child Neurology, 12,* 387–396.

Brooks, R., & Goldstein, S. (2001). *Raising resilient children.* Lincolnwood, IL: Contemporary Books.

Bruner, J. (1986). *Actual minds, possible worlds.* Cambridge, MA: Harvard University Press.

Bruner, J. (1990). *Acts of meaning.* Cambridge, MA: Harvard University Press.

Capra, F. (1996). *The web of life: A new scientific understanding of living systems.* New York: Anchor Books.

Capra, F. (1998, November). *Ecoliteracy: Connecting theory to practice.* Paper presented at the Northwest Regional Educational Laboratory Work Now and in the Future Conference, Portland, OR.

Children's Defense Fund. (2001, October). *Child poverty: Characteristics of poor children in America 2000.* Retrieved August 7, 2002, from http://childrensdefense.org/fs_cptb_child00.php

Claxton, G. (1997). *Hare brain, tortoise mind: Why intelligence increases when you think less.* London: Fourth Estate.

Claxton, G. (1999). *Wise up: The challenge of lifelong learning.* New York: Bloomsbury.

Clinchy, B. M. (1996). Connected and separate knowing. In N. R. Goldberger, J. M. Tarule, B. M. Clinchy, & M. F. Belenky (Eds.), *Knowledge, difference, and power: Essays inspired by women's ways of knowing* (pp. 205–247). New York: Basic Books.

De Jong, P., & Berg, I. K. (2002). *Interviewing for solutions* (2nd ed.). Pacific Grove, CA: Brooks/Cole.

Desetta, A., & Wolin, S. (1998). Youth communication: A model program for fostering resilience through the art of writing. *Resiliency in Action, 3*(1), 19–23.

De Shazer, S. (1988). *Clues: Investigating solutions in brief therapy.* New York: Norton.

Durlak, J. A. (1998). Common risk and protective factors in successful prevention programs. *American Journal of Orthopsychiatry, 68,* 512–521.

Fine, M. (1995). The politics of who's "at risk." In B. B. Swadener & S. Lubeck (Eds.), *Children and families "at promise": Deconstructing the discourse of risk* (pp. 76–94). Albany: State University of New York Press.

Fredericks, L. (1997). Why children need stories: Storytelling and resiliency. *Resiliency in Action, 2*(3), 26–29.

Gergen, K. J., & McNamee, S. (2000). From disordering discourse to transformative dialogue. In R. A. Neimeyer & J. D. Raskin (Eds.), *Constructions of disorder: Meaning-making frameworks for psychotherapy* (pp. 333–349). Washington, DC: American Psychological Association.

Gibbs, J. (1994). *Tribes: A new way of learning.* Santa Rosa, CA: Center Source.

Gibbs, J. (2001). *Tribes: A new way of learning and being together.* Windsor, CA: Center Source.

Gladding, S. T. (1997). Stories and the art of counseling. *Journal of Humanistic Education and Development, 36,* 68–73.

Gladding, S. T. (1998). *Counseling as an art: The creative arts in counseling* (2nd ed.). Alexandria, VA: American Counseling Association.

Gregg, S. (1996). *Preventing antisocial behavior in disabled and at-risk students: Policy briefs.* Charleston, WV: Appalachia Educational Laboratory.

Health Realization Institute. (2001, July). *The understanding behind health realization, a principle-based psychology: Summary of clinical, prevention, and community empowerment applications. Documented outcomes.* Saratoga, CA: Author.

Henderson, N., Benard, B., & Sharp-Light, N. (Eds.). (1999). *Resiliency in action: Practical ideas for overcoming risks and building strengths in youth, families, and communities.* Rio Rancho, NM: Resiliency in Action.

Henderson, N., Benard, B., & Sharp-Light, N. (Eds.). (2000a). *Mentoring for resiliency: Setting up programs for moving youth from stressed to success.* Rio Rancho, NM: Resiliency in Action.

Henderson, N., Benard, B., & Sharp-Light, N. (Eds.). (2000b). *Schoolwide approaches for fostering resiliency.* Rio Rancho, NM: Resiliency in Action.

Henderson, N., & Milstein, M. M. (1996). *Resiliency in schools: Making it happen for students and educators.* Thousand Oaks, CA: Corwin Press.

Herring, R. D. (1998). *Career counseling in schools: Multicultural and developmental perspectives.* Alexandria, VA: American Counseling Association.

Hertz, N. (2001). *The silent takeover: Global capitalism and the death of democracy.* New York: Free Press.

Hubble, M. A., Duncan, B. L., & Miller, S. D. (1999). *The heart and soul of change: What works in therapy.* Washington, DC: American Psychological Association.

Kitashima, M. (1997). Lessons from my life: No more "children at risk". . . all children are "at promise." *Resiliency in Action, 2*(3), 30–36.

L'Abate, L. (1992). *Programmed writing: A paratherapeutic approach for intervention with individuals, couples, and families.* Pacific Grove, CA: Brooks/Cole.

L'Abate, L. (1994). *A theory of personality development.* New York: Wiley.

Langer, E. J. (1997). *The power of mindful learning.* Reading, MA: Addison-Wesley.

Lappe, F. M., & Lappe, A. (2002). *Hope's edge: The next diet for a small planet.* New York: Jeremy P. Tarcher/Putman.

Lewis, R. E. (1995). *A Write Way: Programmed writing effects on high school math students' attendance, homework, grades, and attributions.* Unpublished doctoral dissertation, University of California, San Francisco.

Lewis, R. E. (1996). Writing changes lives: Counselors and English teachers working together. *Oregon English Journal, 18,* 8–12.

Lewis, R. E. (1999). A Write Way: Fostering resiliency during transitions. *Journal of Humanistic Education and Development, 37,* 200–211.

Lewis, R. E. (2002). The structured narrative exercise. In G. McAuliffe & K. Eriksen (Eds.), *Teaching strategies for constructivist and developmental counselor education* (pp. 55–58). Westport, CT: Bergin & Garvey.

Lifton, R. J. (1993). *The protean self: Human resilience in an age of fragmentation.* New York: Basic Books.

Linquanti, R. (1992). *Using community-wide collaboration to foster resiliency in kids: A conceptual framework.* Portland, OR: Northwest Regional Educational Laboratory.

Lott, B. (2002). Cognitive and behavioral distancing from the poor. *American Psychologist, 57,* 100–110.

Luthar, S. S., Cicchetti, D., & Becker, B. (2000a). The construct of resilience: A critical evaluation and guidelines for future work. *Child Development, 71,* 543–562.

Luthar, S. S., Cicchetti, D., & Becker, B. (2000b). Research on resilience: Response to commentaries. *Child Development, 71*, 573–575.

Macfarlane, A. H. (1998, November). *Hui: A process for conferencing in schools.* Paper presented at the Western Association for Counselor Education and Supervision Conference, Seattle, WA.

Marshall, K. (1998). Reculturing systems with resilience/health realization. In *Promoting positive and healthy behaviors in children: Fourteenth Annual Rosalyn Carter Symposium on Mental Health Policy* (pp. 48–58). Atlanta, GA: The Carter Center.

Marshall, K. (2001). *Bridging the resilience gap: Research to practice.* Minneapolis: University of Minnesota, National Resilience Resource Center and the Center for the Application of Prevention Technologies. Retrieved August 20, 2002, from http://www.cce.umn.edu/nrrc/research.shtml

Masten, A. S. (1994). Resilience in individual development: Successful adaptation despite risk and adversity. In M. C. Wang & E. W. Gordon (Eds.), *Educational resilience in inner-city America: Challenges and prospects* (pp. 3–25). Hillsdale, NJ: Erlbaum.

Masten, A. S. (2001). Ordinary magic: Resilience processes in development. *American Psychologist, 56*, 227–238.

Masten, A. S., & Coatsworth, J. D. (1998). The development of competence in favorable and unfavorable environments. *American Psychologist, 53*, 205–220.

McWhirter, J. J., McWhirter, B. T., McWhirter, A. M., & McWhirter, E. H. (1998). *At-risk youth: A comprehensive response: For counselors, teachers, psychologists, and human service professionals.* Pacific Grove, CA: Brooks/Cole.

Mills, R. C. (1995). *Realizing mental health: Toward a new psychology of resiliency.* New York: Sulzburger & Graham.

Mills, R. C. (1996, August). *Empowering individuals and communities through health realization; psychology of mind in prevention and community revitalization.* Paper presented at the 104th Annual Convention of the American Psychological Association, Toronto, Ontario, Canada.

Mills, R. C. (1997). *Comprehensive health realization community empowerment projects: List of completed and current projects.* Long Beach, CA: R. C. Mills & Associates.

Mills, R. C., & Spittle, E. B. (1998). *A community empowerment primer.* Long Beach, CA: R. C. Mills & Associates.

Mills, R. C., & Spittle, E. B. (2001). *The wisdom within.* Renton, WA: Lone Pine.

Monk, G. (1997). How narrative therapy works. In G. Monk, J. Winslade, K. Crocket, & D. Epston (Eds.), *Narrative therapy in practice: The archaeology of hope* (pp. 3–31). San Francisco: Jossey-Bass.

Monk, G., Winslade, J., Crocket, K., & Epston, D. (Eds.). (1997). *Narrative therapy in practice: The archaeology of hope.* San Francisco: Jossey-Bass.

Palmer, P. J. (December 1998/January 1999). Evoking the spirit in public education. *Educational Leadership, 56*, 6–11.

Parry, A., & Doan, R. E. (1994). *Story re-visions: Narrative therapy in the postmodern world.* New York: Guilford Press.

Payne, R. K. (2001). *A framework for understanding poverty* (2nd ed.). Highlands, TX: aha! Process.

Pennebaker, J. W. (1997). *Opening up: The healing power of confiding in others.* New York: Guilford Press.

Pransky, G. S. (1998). *The renaissance of psychology.* New York: Sulzburger & Graham.

Pransky, G. S., Mills, R. C., Sedgeman, J. A., & Bleven, J. K. (1997). An emerging paradigm for brief treatment. In L. Vandecreek, S. Knapp, & T. L. Jackson (Eds.), *Innovations in clinical practice: A source book* (Vol. 15, pp. 401–420). Sarasota, FL: Professional Resource Press.

Pransky, J., & Carpenos, L. (2000). *Healthy thinking/feeling/doing from the inside out: A middle school curriculum and guide for the prevention of violence, abuse and other problem behaviors.* Brandon, VT: Safer Society Press.

Quattrociocchi, S. M., & Peterson, B. (1997). *Giving children hope and skills for the 21st century.* Olympia, WA: WOIS/The Career Information System.

Resnick, M.D., Bearman, P. S., Blum, R. W., Bauman, K. E., Harris, K. M., Jones, J., et al. (1998). Protecting adolescents from harm: Findings from the national longitudinal study on adolescent health. *Journal of the American Medical Association, 278*, 823–832.

Reynolds, A. J. (1998). Resilience among Black urban youth: Prevalence, intervention effects, and mechanisms of influence. *American Journal of Orthopsychiatry, 68*, 84–100.

Riordan, R. J. (1996). Scriptotherapy: Therapeutic writing as a counseling adjunct. *Journal of Counseling & Development, 74*, 263–269.

Robinson, T. L. (1999). The intersections of dominant discourses across, race, gender, and other identities. *Journal of Counseling & Development, 77*, 73–79.

Robinson, T. L., & Ginter, E. J. (1999). Introduction to the *Journal of Counseling & Development's* special issue on racism. *Journal of Counseling & Development, 77*, 3.

Rockwell, S. (1998). Overcoming four myths that prevent fostering resilience. *Reaching Today's Youth, 2*(3), 14–17.

Saleebey, D. (Ed.). (1997). *The strengths perspective in social work practice* (2nd ed.). White Plains, NY: Longman.

Sarbin, T. R. (Ed.). (1986). *Narrative psychology: The storied nature of human conduct.* New York: Praeger.

Scherer, M. (1998, December/1999, January). Linking education with the spiritual. *Educational Leadership, 56*, 5.

Schor, J. B. (1992). *The overworked American: The unexpected decline of leisure.* New York: Basic Books.

Schor, J. B. (1998). *The overspent American: Why we want what we don't need.* New York: Harper Perennial.

Sedgeman, J. A. (2002). *The principles underlying life experience: The beauty of simplicity.* Morgantown: West Virginia University, Robert C. Byrd Health Sciences Center, Sydney Banks Institute for Innate Health. Retrieved August 17, 2002, from http://www.hsc.wvu.edu/sbi/

Snyder, C. R., Feldman, D. B., Shorey, H. S., & Rand, K. L. (2002). Hopeful choices: A school counselor's guide to hope theory. *Professional School Counseling, 5*, 298–307.

Swadener, B. B., & Lubeck, S. (Eds.). (1995). *Children and families "at promise": Deconstructing the discourse of risk.* Albany: State University of New York Press.

Werner, E. E. (1989). Children of the garden island. *Scientific American, 260*, 106–111.

Werner, E. E. (1996). How children become resilient: Observations and cautions. *Resiliency in Action, 1*(1), 18–28.

Werner, E. E. (1998). Resilience and the life-span perspective: What we have learned—so far. *Resiliency in Action, 3*(4), 1, 3, 7–9.

Werner, E. E., Bierman, J. M., & French, F. E. (1971). *The children of Kauai.* Honolulu: University of Hawaii Press.

Werner, E. E., & Smith, R. S. (1977). *Kauai's children come of age.* Honolulu: University of Hawaii Press.

Werner, E. E., & Smith, R. S. (1982). *Vulnerable but invincible: A longitudinal study of resilient children and youth.* New York: McGraw Hill.

Werner, E. E., & Smith, R. S. (1992). *Overcoming the odds: High risk children from birth to adulthood.* Ithaca, NY: Cornell University Press.

Werner, E. E., & Smith, R. S. (2001). *Journeys from childhood to midlife: Risk, resilience, and recovery.* Ithaca, NY: Cornell University Press.

Wesley, D. C. (1998, December/1999, January). Believing in our students. *Educational Leadership, 56*, 42–45.

Whiston, S. C. (2002). Response to the past, present and future of school counseling: Raising some issues. *Professional School Counseling, 5*, 148–155.

White, M., & Epston, D. (1990). *Narrative means to therapeutic ends.* New York: Norton.

Winslade, J., & Monk, G. (1999). *Narrative counseling in schools: Powerful and brief.* Thousand Oaks, CA: Corwin Press.

Winslade, J., & Monk, G. (2000). *Narrative mediation: A new approach to conflict resolution.* San Francisco: Jossey-Bass.

Zunker, V. G. (2002). *Career counseling: Applied concepts of life planning* (6th ed.). Pacific Grove, CA: Brooks/Cole.

APPENDIX

Name _____   Date _____

LESSON: THE STORY OF SCHOOL

We all have stories about school. Some of them are good, some of them are not. In fact, some stories about school can be painful, even when we say they were not. This lesson's goal is to help you look at your own school story and to take steps toward strengthening it.

This lesson will ask a series of questions related to your school story.

TIME

Stories exist in time and space. Let's begin first by looking at your past, then by looking at your future.

Four years ago, you were probably in the fifth grade. Now you are in the ninth. By meeting the requirements, you will graduate in four years.

1. Who were important people to you back in grade school? _____

2. What did you like about school? _____

3. What did you not like about school? _____

4. Where did you go when you needed help with school or problems?

_____

5. Who helped you the most? _____

6. Think back four years, describe two important things you learned or experienced since the 5th grade.

   1. _____

   2. _____

7. Describe your best or most powerful moment in the last four years.

_____

_____

Look forward four years: What will you be able to say about what you have learned or experienced at Resilience High? Write a few lines for Resilience's school newspaper about what a great student you have been at Resilience. Remember, this is a story. Make it up.

_____

_____

SUBJECTS

We are better in some classes than others.

Which subject has been your favorite? Why?_____

_____

Which subject have you not liked or avoided? Why?_____

_____

TEACHERS

Who is the best teacher you ever had? (Maybe that teacher is really your mother, father, uncle, aunt, friend, etc.)

Name _____

What did this person do to help you learn?

_____

Who is the worst teacher you ever had? What did this other teacher do to make you feel bad about yourself as a learner?

_____

Write a make-believe letter to this person about the following:

1. How you view what happened.
2. Why it was a problem for you.
3. How it hurt or got you angry.
4. How you are going to get the most from your education.

Note: You can use any language or words you want to.

Dear _____ :

_____

_____

_____

MATH, TEACHERS, AND PRACTICING APPROACH

Many people avoid math because it is difficult. For many people, it is easier to avoid some things than face them. Math is frequently one of those things that students avoid. At Resilience High, given the two required math proficiency exams and the 30-credit requirement, it is impossible to avoid math if you want to graduate.

What do you like most or least about math? _____

Running away from any problem does not always help, and it does take some courage to approach problems.

Describe two problems that you face every day (for instance, getting to class on time, finishing homework, helping the family, or even math).

_____

_____

Give an example of a time you tackled a problem _____

Would things have been better or worse if you avoided the problem?

_____

_____

Finish this sentence: The problem with math is_____

Let's look at approaching math. During the time between this lesson and the next one, practice asking your math teacher at least one question per day. If too many other students in math ask, practice asking one of your other teachers questions.

Here's the trick. Start with what you know, then ask about what you do not know. For instance, I know 2 + 2 = 4 but I do not know what 2 + −2 equals.

Here are three basic question stems to use with your teacher:

Could you tell me how to _____?

Could you show me how to _____?

What have I done right?_____

Now, could you tell me how Lesson Two helps? _____

_____

_____

Thank you for your efforts.

PART TWO	**EXAMINING THE CAUSES**

Building on the foundational information in Part One, the four chapters that compose Part Two provide the reader with current and comprehensive information regarding the factors generally considered to be causal to the development of at-risk behaviors. It is important to keep in mind that it is impossible to draw a direct cause–effect relationship between any one of the four factors identified and any of the specific behaviors identified in Part Three of this volume. Authors in Part Two understand this and caution their readers to view these causal factors as both cumulative and cyclical. This perspective enhances the awareness that, taken separately, any one of these causal dimensions enhances the likelihood of at-riskness in youth. When viewed from a cumulative and cyclical perspective, the development of at-risk behaviors is almost inevitable.

Chapter 4, The Impact of Dysfunctional Family Dynamics on Children and Adolescents, spells out the various gradations of family dysfunctionality and couples this with case examples to enhance the readers' understanding. The authors elaborate on five causal factors within the family dynamic that enhance the possibility of at-riskness in youth: at-risk adults parenting, parental conflict, family denial, parentification of children, and serious illness and disability within the family. Again, case examples highlight these explanations. After presenting some invaluable information on the incidence and impact of abuse and neglect, the chapter ends with a discussion of prevention approaches aimed at ameliorating the identified causal factors.

Chapter 5, "Who Cares What I Think": Problems of Low Self-Esteem, touches on a causal factor that permeates any discussion of at-risk behaviors. The information in this chapter includes not only definitions and indicators of low self-esteem but also causal factors from parental, individual, social, psychological, physical, environmental, and cultural perspectives. Prevention approaches are presented from individual, family, school, community, and global perspectives. After a discussion of adaptations for diversity, a case study provides a realistic application of the approaches described.

Chapter 6, Preventing and Treating Depression and Bipolar Disorders in Children and Adolescents, approaches the topic by illuminating the complex issues of both definition and diagnosis. The case study of Esteban provides a central theme around which the authors present information dealing with causal factors from biological, psychodynamic, behavioral, cognitive, and family perspectives. Individual, family, school, and community-based prevention and treatment programs are presented. The chapter ends with the presentation of the authors' approach to comprehensive intervention and adaptations for multicultural sensitivity.

Chapter 7, Stress and Trauma: Coping in Today's Society, begins by presenting the confusion surrounding the definition of stress and delineates the following perspectives on stress and traumatic stress: stimulus-oriented views, response-oriented views, stress as a transaction between the person and the environment, and trauma and post-traumatic stress. From this foundation, the author presents 10 factors that may have a causal relationship to the development of at-risk behaviors. Approaches to prevention from individual, family, school, and community perspectives, followed by a discussion of coping from an ethnocultural perspective, conclude the chapter.

4 | The Impact of Dysfunctional Family Dynamics on Children and Adolescents

Valerie E. Appleton and Cass Dykeman

In their influential work on high-risk youth in schools, Pianta and Walsh (1996) defined the term *at-risk status* as the likelihood that a given youth will attain a specific outcome, given certain conditions. The specific outcomes of concern for this book were presented in chapter 1. This chapter explores dysfunctional family dynamics as the certain condition. In addition, the chapter also provides readers with some practical ways to prevent at-risk status in youth.

The level of dysfunction in families can vary widely. Moreover, severity of at-risk status runs parallel to severity of family dysfunction. Thus, in this chapter we first define the multileveled nature of family dysfunction and then examine the causal factors, that is, the specific family situations that both precede and fuel at-risk behaviors. The final section considers prevention at the individual, family, school, and community levels.

DEFINITIONS OF FAMILY DYSFUNCTION LEVELS

When examining the level of dysfunction in family dynamics, it is possible to classify families at either the moderate dysfunction level or the severe dysfunction level. This classification is important because severity level suggests the appropriate interventions to be used. This section defines the distinctions between the moderate and severe levels of dysfunction to enable the reader to better understand family dynamics when planning work with youth and parents.

Moderate Dysfunction

In families at the moderate dysfunction level, each parent presents an appropriate image to the outside world. Hence, it is difficult to believe that there may be severe problems with one of the children. However, below the surface and hidden from the community views are problems that the family is not willing to reveal. The at-risk youth becomes the not-so-popular messenger, letting the community know that the family has secrets and is not perfect. The advantage of working with families at the moderate dysfunctional level is that the adults are competent in dealing with the basic aspects of life (i.e., working, providing food, etc.). The following case study fleshes out how a family at this level of dysfunction may present itself:

CASE STUDY

Derek Jones was a high school junior who was failing several classes. In addition, he appeared quite depressed at times. Mr. and Mrs. Jones were college-educated professionals who were well known in the local community. In terms of family dynamics, Mr. Jones had a very bad temper and engaged in frequent arguments with Derek. When these arguments happened, Mrs. Jones always sided with Derek against his father. Mrs. Jones's consistent siding with Derek caused significant problems between Mr. Jones and Mrs. Jones. The tension in the Jones family came to a head when Derek's failing quarter grades were posted. After these grades were posted, Derek's counselor, Mr. Dykeman, called together Derek, his parents, and his teachers for a before-school conference.

At the start of the conference, Mr. and Mrs. Jones voiced their concern and willingness to do what was necessary to have Derek be more successful and happy. However, as the conference proceeded, the dysfunctional patterns of communication noted above appeared. In the middle of the conference, an intense argument on TV privileges broke out between Mr. Jones and Derek. After a few minutes of arguing, Derek broke down in tears. Derek's sadness led Mrs. Jones to put her arm around him and cry as well. At this point, the school bell rang, signaling 5 minutes until the start of first period for Derek and his teachers. The teachers immediately got up and headed for their classes. After his tears had stopped, Derek was given a hall pass and left for first period.

With Derek gone, Mr. Jones expressed his remorse for fighting with Derek and his frustration that Mrs. Jones did not enforce the TV rules when he was gone. Mr. Dykeman first empathized with Mr. Jones's remorse and frustration as well as Mrs. Jones's sadness. Then he noted that the Joneses had problems that were common to parents of teenagers and that were fixable. Mr. Dykeman referred the Joneses to Ms. Macintosh, a local family counselor known for brief and effective treatment of families with communication problems. Because Mr. Dykeman couched his description of the Joneses' difficulties as both normative and fixable, the Joneses were able to consider his advice without further loss to their self-esteem or self-efficacy. Indeed, the Joneses appeared grateful for Mr. Dykeman's suggestions as well as his confidence in their ability to heal their family.

In family therapy, Mr. and Mrs. Jones began to understand the need for cooperation between them if there was to be any change in Derek. After a few weeks, Mr. Jones began to simply talk with Derek rather than yell. Mrs. Jones no longer took Derek's side during arguments and did not undercut Mr. Jones's attempts to enforce appropriate rules. Derek eventually quit using one parent against the other to get his way. Moreover, Derek and his father were able to establish a satisfying relationship with each other.

Severe Dysfunction

In the family at the severe dysfunction level, one or more adults may exhibit many at-risk behaviors such as substance abuse. In work with severely dysfunctional families, adults may often be found to be functioning at a less capable level than their children. This collapse of adult–child differentiation in functioning limits the extent to which one can effectively intervene in the life of an at-risk child. The following case study illuminates this difficulty:

CASE STUDY

Susan Smith was a high school junior with a long history of school attendance problems. She lived with her mother, Ms. Baker, and her mother's new live-in boyfriend, Mr. Green. Susan has never met her biological father. Both Ms. Baker and Mr. Green currently abuse alcohol and marijuana. On more than one occasion, Susan and her mother smoked marijuana together. Ms. Baker and Mr. Green are both currently unemployed and live on public assistance. The relationship between Ms. Baker and Mr. Green has been conflictual since he moved in 6 months ago. The two have frequent battles over money, friends, and drugs.

In the summer between her sophomore and junior year, Susan lived with her Aunt Joan and her older cousin Katie in a town on the other side of the state. Susan was impressed by how Katie seemed to have her life all together. When Susan moved back home at the end of the summer, she vowed to get her act together. In contrast to previous years, Susan's attendance during the first quarter of her junior year was excellent. She was well liked by both teachers and peers and maintained a B average. Susan dreamed of going to the local community college to study fashion merchandising like her older cousin Katie. However, as winter quarter began, the fighting at home between Ms. Baker and Mr. Green worsened exponentially. As Susan sought to escape this fighting by smoking marijuana, her attendance began to slide.

Concerned about the slip in attendance of a talented fashion design student, Susan's consumer and family life teacher asked if the school counselor, Mr. Dykeman, would talk to Susan. Mr. Dykeman called Susan into his office and expressed the concern everyone at school had about Susan's sliding attendance. Susan claimed that she had been feeling ill lately and that other than that, everything was fine. She rebuffed all of Mr. Dykeman's gentle invitations to talk about the issues that concerned her. After the conference with Susan, Mr. Dykeman attempted to call Ms. Baker. However, Ms. Baker's phone had been disconnected. Mr. Dykeman sent a letter to Ms. Baker asking her to contact him. However, she never responded to that letter. By the middle of winter quarter, Susan had stopped coming to school completely.

CAUSAL FACTORS

Before working with at-risk youth, one must understand how dysfunctional family dynamics can lead to specific destructive behavioral patterns in youth. Dysfunctional family dynamics create an invidious emotional atmosphere for at-risk youth. Such an atmosphere produces severe personal stress and emotional upheaval. Moreover, this highly charged emotional atmosphere causes the at-risk youth to accommodate his or her behavior in such a way as to reduce the internal stress and upheaval. Accommodating the stress and upheaval creates problem behaviors such as poor school performance, depression, anorexia, loss of control, and a myriad of other at-risk behaviors. This section first examines specific family factors that lead to these problem behaviors and then the incidence and impact of abuse, neglect, and poverty.

Specific Family Factors

Several specific family factors contribute to youth at-riskness. These factors include at-risk adults who become parents, parental conflict, family denial, parentification of children, and serious illness and disability.

At-Risk Adults Parenting

We can gain critical insight on the direction and depth of the problems exhibited by an at-risk youth through cultivating an awareness of the problems of the youth's parents. The problematic behaviors of the at-risk youth and his or her at-risk parents may differ, but the end goal of these separate behaviors typically runs parallel. The following case study illustrates this point:

CASE STUDY

Bob Adams was a 45-year-old father of two who had been married for 24 years to Terri. Both were professional people with highly responsible jobs. Bob had a severe drinking problem that had affected the family for years. In addition, Bob has been consistently impervious to suggestions that he address his problem. Bob and Terri's two daughters, ages 17 and 19, were both high achievers in high school. Despite Bob's problems, the Adamses appeared as a "picture-perfect" family to other members of the community. However, the family's underlying dysfunction emerged when the oldest daughter Mary left for college.

Although initially excited to go off to college, Mary soon found herself consumed with worries about her family; she had always been the one to smooth over conflicts between mom and dad. She found that these worries left her little time for peers or academics. She returned home after passing only one course during the fall quarter. After being home for the entire year, she applied to another college and went off to school once again. Needless to say, she could not stay at the new college either, returning home after only a few weeks. At about this time, Bob had a severe alcoholic episode, having to be brought home in a taxi one evening because of his drunkenness. He fought with his wife and destroyed the house before being hospitalized for several days. He checked out of the hospital before treatment was completed and against medical advice.

Mary's reaction to all of the confusion in her life was to take a bottle of pills. Her attempt at suicide was a cry for help—one that almost cost Mary her life. In trying to fix her parents and their marriage, she became unable to manage her own life.

This case demonstrates several important points. First, the father's severe drinking problem both produced and directed his daughter's at-risk behavior. Second, by never getting her life together, Mary avoids leaving home and abandoning her parents for whom and to whom she feels responsible. As many family counselors would conclude, Mary rescued the marriage and family by putting herself at risk. Thus, if a counselor attempted to work with Mary's suicidal feelings independent of her family role as the rescuer, the counseling would be doomed to fail.

One final note of importance needs to be mentioned. The transmission of at-risk tendencies from parent to child is much easier to see in families at the severe dysfunction level. Families at the moderate level generally possess the skills to hide problems. The at-risk behaviors in youth from families at this level can appear to exist without cause. However, rarely does an at-risk youth emerge sui generis (i.e., self-generated). While keeping mindful that exceptions do exist, one should always seek to understand the underlying family aspects of a youth's at-risk behavior. Otherwise, work with at-risk youth may never amount to more than the bandaging of symptoms.

Parental Conflict

If parents are having difficulty processing conflict between them, the situation is likely to deteriorate into communication problems between the parents. This problem also extends to communication problems between parents and children. Secrets begin to exist between the parents. In the conflict between parents, children often become the emotional pawns in the intensified atmosphere of the home. Moreover, a direct relationship exists between both verbal and nonverbal parent conflict and at-risk behavior in children (Amato, 2001; De Arth-Pendley & Cummings, 2002).

Conflict between parents also leads to power struggles in parenting children. Each parent attempts to structure his or her relationship with the child as an individual instead of as a member of the marital unit. Loyalty issues are pressed onto the child. For example, a teenager comes home after curfew and is grounded for a week by the father. However, after 2 days the mother allows the teenager to visit friends but says, "Don't tell Dad!" This pattern of deceit between parents empowers the at-risk youth in two ways. First, the youth learns not to follow rules, and second, the youth learns to be deceitful. As family functioning begins to deteriorate, the youth will begin to demonstrate increasingly maladaptive behavior (Cumsille & Epstein, 1994). The following case study concretizes this process:

CASE STUDY

James Cooper was a 10-year-old fourth grader who was in frequent difficulties at school and in the community. His teacher reported him to be an aggressive, high-energy boy with a low attention span. However, his level of inappropriate conduct was never very severe until the day he assaulted another student on the playground during recess. The student he assaulted had to go to the emergency room for four stitches. At that time, James's parents were forced to enter counseling to assist him with his anger management program. Completion of this anger management program was the main prerequisite for the school district's lifting of James's suspension. In the family counseling part of the anger management program, it was immediately evident that Mr. and Mrs. Cooper had a very long history of marital and parental discord. Mr. Cooper was upset with Mrs. Cooper over numerous issues. These included an affair, overspending, poor discipline of the children, and meddling in-laws. Both Mr. and Mrs. Cooper reported that their fighting had escalated recently. Given the Coopers marital trauma, the assault can be viewed as the inevitable act of a high-energy, aggressive boy who needed to create a major problem in order to bring his parents back together.

This brief example demonstrates several important points about the struggles faced by at-risk youth. First, it is difficult to discipline a youth having severe difficulties without complete cooperation between the parents. One parent undercutting the effectiveness of the other makes it impossible to bring about change in the family and creates a situation in which the youth can become at risk. Second, loyalty issues between family members can create severe problems if the loyalty lines are inappropriately drawn (Visher & Visher, 1996). A youth who is dependent on one parent can become angry with the other parent and attempt various at-risk behaviors. In other words, Parent A will fight Parent B through the at-risk behavior of their children.

Third, a youth's temperament will shape the at-risk behaviors the youth uses to heal family trauma. For example, an aggressive youth may choose fighting, whereas a depressed youth may choose a self-destructive act such as a suicide attempt. Finally, parental conflict can lead to divorce. To oversimplify a difficult and complex problem, let us say that a divorce happens when two people fail to communicate and resolve conflicts. Following divorce, if a youth exhibits at-risk behaviors, it usually takes a significant problem to force the parents to face the gravity of the issues. Amato (2001) reported that parental conflict after divorce is a significant problem for children—a problem because youth give voice to their concerns over parental conflict through at-risk behaviors.

Family Denial

Denial is the defense mechanism whereby problems and their intensity are ignored or redirected. Denial is acted out in two ways within families. The first way denial is enacted is by burying one's head in the sand, that is, ignoring the reality of the situation. The second way denial is enacted is by finger pointing, that is, blaming other persons or events for one's problems. Both methods of using denial lead to youth becoming at risk. The following case study illustrates the effect of denial on the development of at-risk youth:

CASE STUDY

Kathy was a 17-year-old senior who had become increasingly defiant with her parents. The parents attributed the defiance to Kathy's boyfriend of the past 8 months. She began to stay out beyond her assigned curfew, her grades at school declined, and her attitude at home became progressively negative. At various times over the end of her junior year and the beginning of her senior year, Kathy would become ill and was unable to work or attend school. Her parents suspected that she was pregnant, but Kathy denied that she was. Throughout this period of time, the parents were concerned about Kathy's relationship with her 20-year-old boyfriend. They had frequent violent arguments with Kathy about her need to see him less or break off the relationship.

During the 2nd month of her senior year, Kathy had a baby. The parents never knew she was pregnant until the night Kathy's water broke at home. After being rushed to the hospital, Kathy gave birth to a baby with numerous disabilities who lived only several months. During this time, the parents and Kathy continued to battle over the relationship with the baby's father.

This tragic case study presents the ultimate example of denial of a major problem while focusing on a serious but tangential problem. Kathy's parents ignored the issue of the pregnancy even though they strongly suspected something was physically wrong with their daughter. Rather than having their daughter examined by a physician, the parents went along with Kathy's denial. Instead of directly confronting issues with children, parents tend to allow them to have the power over major decisions in their life. Kathy's parents wanted to believe that she was fine but knew in their own minds she was not. Therefore, not wanting to risk a battle with Kathy, they denied that anything was wrong and placed their daughter in the at-risk category.

If Kathy's parents had become involved earlier in the process, a tragedy could have been avoided. Because the parents could only focus on Kathy's relationship, they could not see the larger picture. Kathy's relationship with her boyfriend was symbolic of the gap in the relationship between herself and her parents. Specifically, Kathy's parents had lost control of their relationship with Kathy, and they could not face their responsibility in having let this loss occur. Kathy's parents used denial to avoid examining the problems they had and affixed all the blame to the boyfriend. Because of their strong denial, they placed Kathy at risk.

Parentification of Children

One dysfunctional pattern of family dynamics that begins in the early years of childhood is parentification of children. This pattern occurs when parents give responsibilities and privileges to younger children that would be more appropriate for older children or adults. Young children, by their actions and requests, maintain the control of the household and frequently dictate the mood of the entire family. Parents, fearful of disrupting the family calm, refrain from effective discipline techniques. Thus, the children gain control of the family.

Parentified children are placed in situations in which they are given the power to make decisions that belong with the parents. The parents, by giving the power to the child, abdicate their responsibility for protecting the child from potentially dangerous situations. The following case study helps demonstrate this parentification process:

CASE STUDY

Ray, a 10th grader, was referred by a student to Mrs. Wall, an English teacher and the Natural Helpers adviser. Ray was referred by the student because he was overheard saying that he wanted to die. After talking with Ray, his school counselor assessed that Ray was at moderate risk for suicide and thus immediately contacted Ray's parents. The school counselor referred Ray's parents to three private practice counselors known for their strong skills with adolescents. Ray objected to the counseling and said he would not go to see anyone. The parents contacted one of the referred counselors and asked for a suggestion as to how they could get him into counseling. The counselor told them to tell Ray that he had no choice in the matter and that he had to go to counseling. This approach worked, and Ray and his family appeared at the counselor's office for help.

Ray was seen for three sessions alone and for one family session. After these sessions, the counselor provided the family with his feedback, suggesting that Ray remain in counseling to deal with his depression, mood swings, and suicidal tendencies. The parents were told that some family counseling would help them to deal more effectively with Ray. After the feedback session, the mother and father said they would let Ray decide because the counseling was for him! Even though they were told about Ray's depression and suicidal ideation, they felt Ray had to make the decision because they did not want to have to "fight" with him to get him to attend counseling sessions.

In this instance, the parents left the well-being of the child with the child rather than taking control of the situation. By permitting the child to make such decisions, the at-risk status increases significantly. The parentification process not only impacts dramatic issues such as suicide but also accelerates the at-risk status of youth confronting common teenage problems such as academic failure or alcohol use.

This parentification is a common by-product of divorce. As the conflict between divorcing parents escalates, more and more self-care is left with the child. In addition, some very young children are even expected to carry the burden for maintaining the well-being of the parents during the separation and divorce process. Life is fine as long as the child is behaving, giving attention to the parents, and causing no apparent difficulty. The burden can become intense as the child grows and matures. It is very tiring to always be happy, provide love for a parent, care for other children, and be adultlike. In these cases, the parents often report that the child has never been a difficulty but the ideal child who always took care of everything.

Children and youth want to be in control of the decisions that affect their lives and will take every opportunity to gather more power. Parents must be encouraged to involve their children in the decision-making process but be reminded that involvement is different from making a final decision. Final decisions belong to the parents, not the children. When the child makes the choices alone, at-risk status is inevitable.

Serious Illness and Disability Within the Family

Serious illness and disability can catapult a family into a trauma response and affect their ability to maintain healthy coping. Consider an example in which the father has a newly diagnosed heart condition but denies his symptoms to his family. He might fear his role as the provider would be questioned. If the parents are unable to discuss the issue with each other, or with the children, the family members are left more vulnerable to fears and fantasies about how bad the situation is. As secrecy or even dishonesty or deceit increases, these families become more at risk and sensitive at home, work, or school.

Kazak, Christakis, Alderfer, and Coiro (1994) discussed the impact of illness in families. They suggested that (a) family members tend to overreact to simple problems, (b) parents are protective of the children, and (c) in general, the entire family is acutely sensitive. In an attempt to cope with this sensitivity, the family will focus on less serious problems and concerns. Thus, denial becomes a major risk aspect. This denial can be considered dysfunctional. However, it can also be understood as an expected part of the reaction to trauma (Aguilera & Messick, 1986).

Typically, families will go through a series of stages in coping with the shock of the diagnosis of an illness, disability, hospitalizations, and treatment. There is a movement from defensive coping strategies such as denial or anger toward more functional ways of coping. The families at greatest risk are those unable to move toward the last stage. They remain mired in defensive coping patterns that affect all members in negative ways. The following case study illustrates the high at-risk status of families unable to address a child's suffering:

CASE STUDY

Jeff Stone was a 7-year-old brought to the Riverbend Pediatric Hospital for rehabilitation surgery. The surgery was for a hand deformed at birth that left it shrunken and twisted. All Stone family members referred to this appendage as the "paw." When Jeff experienced anxiety about reconstructive surgery, the Stones were unable to discuss the hand with him, because this issue had been avoided from the time of Jeff's birth. Mr. and Mrs. Stone felt tremendous guilt over their boy's disability. The consulting counselor to the surgery unit, Mrs. Appleton, supervised a counseling intern to develop an initial assessment of the boy's view of the situation. Because it is often easier to draw a problem than to discuss it, using art materials is an effective method for assessment and offers a rich symbolic view of the patient's experience of hospitalization and trauma (Appleton, 2001). The counseling intern suggested that the boy draw a person. Jeff drew an image of a teddy bear with a deformed paw. During the family interactions, Mrs. Appleton also observed the defensive nature of the family coping.

After the initial assessment, Mrs. Appleton worked with the counseling intern to create a plan that would increase family communications and address denial. In supervision, they invented a game called "Secrets." In this game, the family members examined the names they gave things that bothered them at home, school, or work. While playing the game, Mrs. Stone was able to disclose that the "paw" was her way to avoid discussing the boy's disability or embarrassing him or the other family members. Mrs. Stone hoped that the reference to a "paw" was easier on Jeff and the family. When this issue arose, the father and siblings spoke of the "paw" despairingly. With the intern's assistance, Jeff was able to share his feelings of inferiority in the family and of feeling like a nonperson (or stuffed bear). Through these disclosures, it was clear no one in the family was comfortable with the term *the paw*.

In follow-up counseling, medical staff members were accessed for a discussion about the diagnosis and plans for rehabilitation of the boy's weak hand. Mrs. Appleton and the intern discussed the ways the hospital team might help the family to discuss the disability openly during medical and counseling interventions. In this way, the multidisciplinary team of doctors, nurses, physical therapists, counselor, and intern shared methods to encourage the family to practice an exploration of more open communication during and after the surgery process. This support proved effective, and the Stones began to learn a new way to cope with difficult issues by discussing them together and with others.

As the case example demonstrates, the family faced with an illness or disability must handle many emotionally charged issues. Because there is relatively little support in the medical setting for such issues, multidisciplinary teams that include counselors and appropriate referral are critical. In most instances, problematic family issues that existed before the medical crisis are exaggerated during the trauma of illness, loss of function, surgery, and other medical interventions. Fortunately, diagnosis and medical intervention also provide an opportunity for change. In states of crisis and trauma, otherwise rigid or resistant families may be responsive to psychosocial resources. In this way, the danger of the illness can provide new opportunities for change in the communication and coping systems within the family.

The Incidence and Impact of Abuse and Neglect

Atrocities of violence against children are among the most difficult to discuss. However, abuse is a historical problem that does not go away. In fact, as professionals are trained to understand and report abuse, the number of reported cases has risen dramatically. A consideration of the incidence of abuse and neglect will help us recognize those children who are at the highest risk for maltreatment.

In 1973, the Child Abuse Prevention and Treatment Act (Public Law 93-247) defined the legal responsibilities of health care providers encountering child abuse or neglect. Intervention is defined as social, legal, medical, or any combination of the aforementioned. Congress declared that child abuse and neglect means the physical and mental injury, sexual abuse, negligent treatment, or maltreatment of a child under age 18 by a person who is responsible for the child's welfare under circumstances that indicate the child's health or welfare is thereby harmed or threatened. Every state now has within its statutes a legal definition of abuse.

Incidence

The United States Congress mandated a report documenting the incidence of child abuse and neglect in this country. This report is called the National Incidence Study of Child Abuse and Neglect (NIS). Professionals across a spectrum of schools and agencies act as sentinels and gather data about abuse incidences. In this way, the NIS estimates provide a more complete measure of the scope of child abuse and neglect known to community professionals that may not be included in official statistics. The most recent NIS study is NIS-3 (Sedlak & Broadhurst, 1996).

NIS-3, which covered a 7-year period, reported an alarming increase in the incidence of child abuse and neglect. This report revealed that the number of abused and neglected children had nearly doubled. An estimated 1.5 million children in the United States were abused or neglected. Physical abuse had almost doubled, and sexual abuse more than doubled. The number of children seriously injured and endangered had quadrupled.

The NIS-3 study also discovered there were specific characteristics of the abused and neglected children and families in which these behaviors occurred most often. The factors that contributed to the highest incidence of abuse included the child's gender and age, family's income, and family's size. Race was not a significant factor in the incidence of maltreatment or injury.

Child's age. There is little reporting of sexual abuse in children from age 1 to 3, but the number of children vulnerable to sexual abuse is consistent from age 3 onward, with reports of sexual abuse distributed evenly across these children. This flattening of the age differences is provocative and suggests a broad range of vulnerability for sexual abuse starting in preschool. In terms of neglect, there is a near linear comparison between the child's age and risk for maltreatment. However, the lower incidence of reported abuse in young children might reflect undercoverage of these children. As children mature, they are involved with an increasing number of community professionals who can observe them and make appropriate investigations. They may also be better able to escape, retaliate, or ask for help.

Child's gender. Girls are most vulnerable to sexual abuse, at a rate three times higher than boys. Because serious injury can accompany sexual abuse, this accounts for higher incidence rates for injury among girls. Boys are at greater risk for other forms of maltreatment and are 24% more likely than girls to be emotionally neglected and to suffer serious injury resulting in death.

Child's family. The demographics of the family are also linked to incidences of child maltreatment (Sedlak & Broadhurst, 1996). Children of single parents have a 77% greater risk of being harmed by physical abuse and an 87% higher risk of physical neglect than children living with both parents. Children in the largest families are physically neglected at about three times the rate of those who are single children. Children in poverty (annual family income of less than $15,000) are 25 times more likely to suffer some form of maltreatment than children in families who earn more than $30,000 per year. Moreover, poverty is directly linked with the incidence of sexual abuse and serious harm. Children in the lowest income families are more likely to be sexually abused and suffer serious injury from maltreatment.

Impact

Abuse is an issue of control and power, whether it is perpetrated within or outside of the family. The impact of physical and sexual abuse is directly related to intensity, the amount of coercion, and level of conflict involved. Webb and Terr (1999) distinguished between two kinds of trauma. A single traumatic event in an otherwise normal life is called Type I trauma, and the effects of prolonged and repeated trauma are called Type II trauma. Within families, children are more likely to suffer Type II trauma and endure repeated and anticipated pain, violence, and chaos. The Type II syndrome, according to Webb and Terr, includes coping mechanisms of denial, psychological numbing, self-hypnosis, dissociation, and extreme shifts between rage and passivity.

When observing children suspected of being maltreated, it is helpful to understand the form their trauma and symptoms take. According to Gil (1996), children will exhibit the impact of abuse and neglect through either internalized or externalized behaviors. Children who cope through internalized behavior negotiate the pain by themselves. They are likely to avoid interaction and appear depressed, joyless, phobic, hypervigilant, and regressed. Given the stress of coping without help, these children manifest physical symptoms including sleep disorders and somatic problems (e.g., headaches and stomachaches). Additionally, they withdraw emotionally and may appear overcompliant. In more severe cases they disassociate, self-mutilate, and may become suicidal. They are also likely to use drugs to numb both the physical and emotional pain of abuse.

Conversely, children who cope through externalized behavior direct their pain outwardly and toward others. They express emotions that are often hostile, provocative, and violent. They may kill or torture animals, destroy property through fire settings, and exhibit sexualized behaviors. However, the effects are not, for the most part, multigenerational.

Physical abuse effects. Physically abused children have deficits in gross motor development, speech, and language. The impact of physical abuse includes psychic trauma, chaos, rejection, deprivation, distorted parental perceptions, and unrealistic expectations. Further disruptions of family life occur with hospitalizations, separation, foster placement, and frequent home changes.

At a minimum, children hurt by others suffer an impaired capacity to enjoy life. When the abuse is more extreme, psychiatric symptoms will appear (e.g., enuresis, hyperactivity, and bizarre behavior). In school, abused children who exhibit more internalized behaviors will present learning problems, compulsiveness, hypervigilance, and suicidal tendencies. Children who cope with abuse through more externalized behaviors are oppositional. Typically, these children have problems managing aggressive behavior and cannot establish relationships with other children (Shields & Cicchetti, 2001).

Sexual abuse effects. The impact of child sexual abuse can be measured along a continuum from neutral to very negative (Friedrich, 2002). At its extreme, the effects of sexual abuse manifest in dissociation. The term *dissociation* refers to a disturbance in the normal functions of identity, memory, and consciousness (American Psychiatric Association, 2000). Dissociation occurs when the child is exposed to overwhelming events that result in extreme feelings of helplessness. In the traumatic situation, the child attempts to cope by dissociating the self from the act being perpetrated. This dissociation becomes part of the child's development and results in long-term difficulties. In this way, internalized behaviors such as eating disturbances, substance abuse, and depression can be understood as behavioral readouts of dissociation. Externalized behaviors accompanying sexual abuse include school difficulties, anger, running away, delinquency, and sexualized behaviors.

Sexualized behavior is an externalized behavior that is shaped by sexual experiences, feelings, and attitudes that occur in the abuse process (Finkelhor, 1984). Early and manipulated exposure to sex may result in a child's excessive or preoccupying interest in it. There is a difference between normal sexual curiosity and sexualization. Unlike other children, the sexualized child (a) completes intercourse without coercion, (b) is not inhibited about masturbating, and (c) exhibits focused sexual behavior in front of others. This lack of inhibition can extend to play, art, or conversation that is imitative of adult sexual relationships.

The sexualized child is clearly at risk for developmentally inappropriate sexual behavior as well as pregnancy, sexually transmitted diseases, and prostitution. Thus, it is critical for the professional to understand and differentiate what is normal sexual development in children from behaviors that indicate trauma.

Neglect effects. The dynamics of neglect differ markedly from those of physical or sexual abuse. The main difference is the attention received by the parents. The attention associated with abuse is inappropriate, excessive, harsh, and damaging, but the parent is still involved with the child. Neglecting parents do the opposite. For example, they fail to stimulate or interact on an emotional or a physical level. In extreme cases, it is as though the parent does not know the child exists.

The effects of child neglect and deprivation occur across all levels of development, including social, affective, physical, emotional, behavioral, and cognitive. We can expect to see internalized behaviors, including a lack of affect (feelings), social detachment, and impaired empathy, as well as externalized behaviors, including violence and delinquency. Neglected youth can be identified by behaviors that convey low self-esteem, a negative worldview, and internalized or externalized anxieties or aggressions. Because of the lack of nurturance, there is typically poor intellectual development, developmental disabilities, and developmental delays. In addition, neglected children are seriously bereft of personal or family resources for care.

Stress resistance. Some abused and neglected children appear relatively less traumatized than others do. Garbarino, Guttman, and Seeley (1986) proposed the concept of "stress-resistant children" who become prosocial and competent despite harsh or even hostile upbringing. It is speculated that these children receive compensatory psychological nurturance and sustenance. This nurturance may come from home, school professionals, neighbors, or family friends. Perhaps the experience of even minimal care enables the child to cope better and to develop social competence. With a basis of social competence, the child's view of the world and his or her role within it remain more positive. In a time when counseling is reduced to a bare minimum of contact with at-risk youth, school professionals might examine what is the good-enough intervention to promote the natural adaptability of young people. For a further examination of methods that are designed to increase the natural adaptability and resilience of children, see chapter 3 in this volume.

Continuing effects/youthful offenders. It is important to recognize that the majority of abuse victims do not become perpetrators. Further, the great majority of abuse survivors protect their children from enduring the fate they lived (Kaufman & Zigler, 1987). In this way, the concept of multigenerational abuse cycles is confounded.

According to Herman (1997), the small minority of survivors who take on the role of the perpetrator may be literally reenacting their childhood experiences. In the literature on this issue, youthful offenders are described as those who rape, initiate intrafamilial sexual contact between an adolescent and a prepubertal child, or exploit young children through sex or coercion (Okami, 1992). They may engage also in pseudosexual behaviors such as genital touching, exhibitionism, and voyeurism with a younger child who knows them (Higgs, Canavan, & Meyer, 1992).

Despite the aggressiveness of the young offenders' behavior, they are observed to be more asocial than antisocial. These adolescents suffer isolation, alienation, and lack of intimacy. Further, the young offender may be rather compliant, withdrawn, and isolated from peers. This inability to form successful relationships with peers is marked by feelings of low self-esteem and inadequacy. There may also be a generalized preference for nonsexual contact with younger children. School adjustment difficulties are to be expected.

APPROACHES TO PREVENTION

The preceding section has reviewed a number of dysfunctional family situations and some of the youth at-risk behaviors that could flow from such family situations. The impact of physical and sexual abuse on youth was also explored. However, when faced with at-risk youth, professionals need more than knowledge; they need to be armed with practical ways to help these youth. Such arming is the goal of this section.

Forms of Prevention

Pianta and Walsh (1996) posited that three forms of prevention operate in work with at-risk youth: primary prevention, secondary prevention, and tertiary prevention. We have placed the focus and timing aspects of all three forms for review in Table 4–1.

An example of primary prevention is Washington State's Elementary School HIV/AIDS Education Law. This law mandates that all students in Grades K–6 receive HIV/AIDS prevention education each year. The law represents primary prevention because it is directed to all students before the period when at-risk behaviors (e.g., IV drug use) begin. A transition-to-middle-school support group for students with low grades is an example of secondary prevention because it is directed at a specific population before it obtains at-risk status (e.g., school dropout). An example of tertiary prevention is a school-based aftercare group for students who have recently returned from a stay at a drug rehabilitation center. The goal of tertiary prevention is to remediate students who have already obtained an at-risk status.

With the forms of prevention defined, attention now turns to the levels of prevention: individual, family, school, and community.

Prevention at the Individual Level

Counseling

Individual counseling can be a secondary or tertiary prevention activity. Counselors who work with at-risk youth must exemplify the importance of well-defined rules and responsibilities. In working with the at-risk youth, the counselor must be sure to follow the rules of the counseling process. Just as the at-risk youth attempts to alter the rules in other settings for personal gain, the youth will attempt to have the professional alter and ignore the rules of the counseling process.

For example, the youth may have a simple request, such as asking the counselor to write an excuse that would allow him or her to miss a class at school or be permitted to miss detention. Other, more critical violations of the rules may be requests for emergency appointments late at night or over the weekend. One counselor from a rural district spent 6 hours with a youth along a country road following a phone call requesting her help. It was considerate of the counselor but also very risky and ethically questionable. The youth did not follow the rules of counseling—attending the counseling session—in the appropriate location. One way to decrease the at-risk behavior is to define upfront the role of the counselor and the rules of the counseling process.

Another aspect of prevention within the individual counseling process is the determination of the severity of the at-risk youth's actions and interactions. Whether the youth is abusing alcohol, is pregnant, or is a runaway, the counselor needs to determine the extent of danger to the well-being of the youth. The prudent counselor takes

Table 4–1 | Form, Focus, and Timing of Prevention Activities

Focus and Timing	Form		
	Primary	Secondary	Tertiary
All students	•		
Potential at-risk students		•	
At-risk students			•
Before at-risk status is obtained	•	•	
After at-risk status is obtained			•

few chances with at-risk youth. Risk taking on the part of the counselor is ill advised because these youth tend to be impulsive in their actions and prone to hurting themselves physically.

In determining severity, the counselor needs to be highly aware of the concept of duty to warn. This is prevention of the highest order. At the initiation of counseling, both the at-risk youth and the family are informed that any suspicious or questionable behaviors will be reported. Both confidentiality and at-risk status are clearly defined early in the process, reinforcing the professional's responsibility to follow the rules.

If there are questions about the level of severity of the behavior the youth exhibits, professionals need to follow a very cautious route and involve the parents. Following the rules may mean having a crisis team available to give the youth the appropriate treatment, including the possibility of hospitalization. If the youth is suicidal, a coordinated professional effort may need to be utilized to resolve the problem. The sooner the at-risk youth is involved in treatment, the greater the opportunity for successful resolution and prevention of problems.

In principle, the counselor should always involve a family in at-risk prevention planning. However, there are situations in which individual counseling with an at-risk student should be emphasized over family counseling. These situations include (a) when the relationship between the parents is questionable, (b) the parenting skills are almost nonexistent, (c) one parent is an alcoholic, and (d) the parents are frequently absent from the home.

An emphasis on individual counseling places even more responsibility on the counselor to follow the rules. To treat effectively the myriad of difficulties of at-risk youth, the professional must maintain a high level of confidence. Treating the at-risk youth can be a substantial test of a counselor's self-confidence. Thus, appropriate attention to the counselor's own self-care against stress and anxiety is warranted. This self-care is the best antidote to counselor burnout.

Abuse Prevention

Providing care.   It is critical that professionals who work with the difficult issues of child abuse and neglect are trained in the specifics of these issues. Hurt children evoke complex responses in caregivers. At some point, the most skilled practitioner wants to rescue the child from trauma. Therefore, a support system and professional contact base are essential in this work. Also, specific resources for reporting, legal issues, safe housing, and community support services are necessary for effective interventions to occur.

Clarification of roles, empowerment, and the stages of intervention.   Given the issues of control and coercion in child abuse, it is particularly important for the counselor to define his or her role with the young person. For example, Herman (1997) suggested that at the outset of working together, the counselor and the client must be able to name the problem. To debate the story or the existence of an abuse report undermines the potential for recovery from it. By acknowledging the story, the professional and the client begin to form an alliance. This alliance is critical because abused and neglected children have poor and often brutalized experiences with trust and intimacy. When hearing the story, the young person must understand that he or she is the survivor, not merely a victim. Further, the young person will need to know that he or she carries no responsibility for the abuse.

At the first stages of intervention, the counselor can work to develop small steps of self-care, plans for safety, and other support resources. The young person must be told at the outset that the counselor must report the threat of harm to self or others.

Depending on the severity of the abuse or neglect, the later stages of counseling will help the young person toward self-care and independence. In this way, the counselor can help the young person toward the future. This process cannot be rushed and will depend on the young person's internal, familial, and other support resources. As gains are made in a transfer of learning to the world outside counseling, prevention and education become important. When intention is delayed, group counseling is a valuable approach. Mutual support is critical and can reinforce affective awareness and empowerment.

Empowerment also occurs through mastery. As seen in other developmental sequences, children develop a sense of mastery by practicing. Nonverbal processes give an outlet for raw emotion and a place to practice or work through the trauma impact. The following case study of a child's abuse reflects the complexity of issues surrounding at-risk families:

CASE STUDY

Janet Firwood, age 13, was brought to the intensive care burn unit of a local pediatric hospital for reconstructive surgery. This surgery was for burns sustained when she was age 3. She had been burned while jumping over a candlestick, igniting her nightgown. Janet lived with her mother. Her father was the mother's boyfriend. This man had an intact family with a wife and several children and lived separately from Janet and her mother. Her mother was molested by this man when she was babysitting for him at age 17, and their relationship had continued since then.

The hospital's counselor began the assessment by talking with the medical staff and school personnel. A nurse reported seeing Janet holding hands with a 22-year-old patient during movie night. The hospital's schoolteacher also reported provocative behavior in class. In fact, Janet had shown other children her burn scars, including removing her underpants, if they gave her money. This pattern of premature sexual behavior, such as flirting with an older man and exhibitionism, is an indicator of sexual abuse.

The counseling intervention started at the first step by naming the problem. Janet did not see herself as having a problem. However, she was happy to have attention from the counselor. Eventually, through artwork, Janet portrayed her feelings of powerlessness and of being divided by her loyalties to her mother and father, who fought with one another. Before discharge, she revealed that her father sexually abused her. The referral to the local child abuse agency resulted in investigation and incarceration of the father. Unfortunately, Janet's case is one in which serious identity and role confusion for the survivor resulted. This confusion was the product of delayed identification of abuse and the lack of social services. Besides identity and role confusion, Janet also exhibited characteristics of the youthful offender discussed earlier in this chapter. These characteristics included exhibitionism and peer coercion. Intensive counseling and support services were necessary to help Janet and her mother begin to resolve the chaos of their lives.

Prevention at the Family Level

The Family Role of the At-Risk Youth
When an at-risk youth is identified, much attention is often given directly to the youth without commensurate attention to the entire family. This inattention is unfortunate

because at-risk behavior is simply a behavioral readout of family dysfunction. In other words, the youth's at-risk behavior is not sui generis, but rather the acting out of a script provided by the family system.

One common script is that of the identified patient. The family of at-risk youth asserts that all in the family is well except for the at-risk youth. In truth, the at-risk youth's behaviors are merely the symptoms of family dysfunction. The greater the difficulties demonstrated by the youth, the larger the number of issues that need attention within the family. It is inappropriate to assume that the identified problem child is the only family member with mental health needs or the only family member who may be at risk. The case of Justin illustrates the identified-problem role:

CASE STUDY

Justin, a 14-year-old high school freshman, was referred for counseling by his school counselor following the interception of a suicide note. Two of Justin's friends found a letter describing how he planned to shoot himself. Justin, along with his mother and father, came to counseling. It was apparent in the initial session that Justin did not want to be there. He was rude, obnoxious, and embarrassing to his parents. His mother was tearful, while his father remained stoic. Both parents were obviously shaken by Justin's recent behaviors. The counselor attempted to understand the relationship between the issues Justin expressed and the problems that the family faced, but no clear correlation emerged. Justin's behaviors were so disruptive that it was difficult to have his parents in the counseling session. Although several more counseling appointments were set up, the mother called the next day and canceled them. Two weeks later, the counselor received a call from the mother asking for help. Her husband had been placed in the psychiatric unit of the local hospital. She explained that her husband had been laid off from work for the last 6 months and was becoming increasingly withdrawn. He seemed devastated by the problems with Justin. In despair, he pulled out his shotgun and threatened to kill himself. Justin's mother called the police, and eventually her husband was placed in inpatient psychiatric care.

Impact of Malevolent Family Dynamics
Once a youth demonstrates at-risk behaviors, family dynamics play a significant role in whether the at-risk behaviors will escalate or decline. If the dysfunctional aspects of the family dynamics are not identified, discussed, and changed, the behaviors of the at-risk youth will continue to escalate. Moreover, parental conflict has a compounding effect for the at-risk youth (Wasserman, Miller, Pinner, & Jaramillo, 1996). Thus, involvement of the family is vital to preventing at-risk behaviors from escalating.

Families and Change of At-Risk Behavior
The involvement of the family of the at-risk youth in assessment, diagnosis, and treatment planning is essential. The counselor provides a model of behavior to the parents, and the parents provide a wealth of information, spoken or unspoken, to the counselor. Many counselors wonder which family members should be involved in the counseling process. It is important to consider all members of the household as potential participants in the work with at-risk youth.

Frequently, one of the most effective treatment modalities to bring about change in youth is parents' counseling. If the parents can commit to working on their relationship, along with being willing to learn different parenting approaches with their children, the chances of successfully assisting an at-risk youth increase significantly. However, as demonstrated throughout the case studies, there frequently is much disarray in the relationship between the parents. Such disarray makes it understandable why the youth may be having emotional difficulty. Also, parents provide an inappropriate model for the developing youth when they work too much, drink too much, or allow their lives to be out of control (Fincham, 1994). Once parents can be taught to reorient and redirect some of their energies, the positive changes in youth are absolutely astounding. Therefore, parents' counseling along with family counseling can produce remarkable changes in dysfunctional family structures.

Thus, family counseling must be part of the intervention and prevention plan for at-risk youth. In working with the family, the counselor must maintain a neutral position and avoid a position of being on someone's side. The youth and the parents will attempt to enlist the counselor's support in their efforts to maintain the dysfunctional family system. Phone calls by the youth or a parent, bringing damaging evidence to the session to demonstrate someone's problems, or asking for additional sessions are all situations that represent some of the influence peddling family members try. It is important to remember that the goal is not to fix the at-risk youth but rather to support the development of a new and functional family interaction system.

Postabuse Family Intervention

The critical issue for children not removed from their families is monitoring the risk factors for the child and his or her parents. Any postabuse plan must assess and ensure a safe environment by evaluating parental abuse proneness, the vulnerability of the child, and environmental stresses that trigger abuse (Green, 1988). The counselor will also need to assess the family's level of coping and complexity. At-risk families are typically ones with multiple problems, poor ability to cope with stress, and few resources for help internally or in the community. Therefore, it is important for the counselor to devise realistic goals. Postabuse counseling will be a process of mediating the need for the family members to express their feelings and safety from punishment or retaliation for this behavior at home. Self-help groups such as Daughters & Sons United, Parents Anonymous, and Parents United may be helpful to families as well.

Prevention at the School Level

Preservice/In-service Needs

School counselors and teachers are the frontline soldiers in the war against at-risk behaviors. To be capable soldiers, school counselors and teachers need to possess adequate knowledge in the following areas: parent consultation, referral and networking, and professional comportment.

Parent consultation. All school professionals need to be comfortable with the principle of parent consultation. If a school professional does not contact parents regarding at-risk behaviors, the professional is maintaining too much responsibility for the at-risk youth. Parents need to be encouraged to take responsibility for their at-risk children and to become actively involved in the prevention process as soon as possible.

Providing an effective consultation with the parents will assist the family in understanding the necessary steps of the helping process. It is very important for the school professional making the initial contact with the family to understand the critical nature of his or her role. It is essential to provide the family with a clear understanding of the helping process. The initial consultation should be used to encourage and assist the family in receiving the most effective services possible. If the initial consultation is a positive experience, more than likely the family will be ready to pursue the necessary steps of the treatment process.

Referral and networking. Another necessary knowledge area for school counselors and teachers is referral and networking. If school professionals cannot provide the at-risk youth with appropriate services, they must refer the at-risk youth and the family to an appropriate agency, institution, or private practitioner. Frequently, the at-risk youth is identified by school professionals, but the services required for treatment are offered elsewhere. Thus, schools must link their efforts for at-risk youth with the efforts of local agencies, practitioners, and hospitals.

Maintaining a comprehensive referral network of helping professionals is probably one of the most important aspects of prevention as well as a major responsibility for school professionals treating at-risk youth. The network should include both medical and nonmedical mental health service providers. Specifically, referral sources need to include psychiatrists, drug and alcohol counselors, mental health counselors, clinical psychologists, marriage and family specialists, and clergy. School professionals treating at-risk youth must have a thorough knowledge of the variability and comprehensiveness of various services in the community.

Professional comportment. Critical to proper professional comportment is knowledge on how to act in an ethical and legal manner when working with at-risk youth. One key ethical and legal concern in work with at-risk youth is the issue of confidentiality. Too often school professionals maintain confidentiality without considering the ramifications to the youth as well as to themselves. Being direct and upfront with the youth about the types of information and behavior that are treated in a confidential manner versus those to be reported to the parents helps avoid potential problems later.

School counselors and teachers often serve as the primary connection between at-risk youth and their families. Thus, it is essential for school professionals to possess knowledge of parental consultation, referral and networking, and proper professional comportment. Using professional colleagues for support and consultation, making effective and necessary referrals of particularly difficult cases, and seeking personal counseling when the stress becomes too great are some ways a school counselor or teacher can maintain a high level of self-confidence and effectiveness.

Curriculum-Based Interventions

When people think of school counselors working with at-risk youth, they usually think of school counselors performing secondary and tertiary prevention activities, for example, school counselors facilitating support groups or conducting individual counseling. However, school counselors have an important role to play with the primary prevention of at-risk status in youth.

In 1997, the American School Counselor Association published national standards for school counseling programs. The model program contained K–12 guidance curriculum goals in three areas: personal/social development, career development, and academic development. Lapan, Gysbers, and Sun (1997) have found that full implementation of a guidance program serves as a powerful antidote to at-risk status. Students in schools with a more fully implemented guidance program reported that (a) they earned higher grades, (b) their education was better preparing them for the future, (c) their school made more career information available to them, and (d) their school had a more positive climate. School guidance programs are not the sole domain of school counselors. In fact, because of their small numbers, the main role of the school counselor in the guidance program is that of facilitator. The key deliverer of the curricular parts of the guidance program is the teacher. Thus, the student outcomes just noted are possible only if school counselors and teachers work in concert.

School counselors are not the only education professionals with a curriculum that serves as an at-risk primary prevention activity. Family and consumer sciences teachers have also published a national curriculum. This curriculum aims to help young people develop the social skills and decision-making skills that can serve as a protection against at-risk behaviors. In addition, this curriculum contains standards on parent training for youth. There is no better example of primary prevention activity than giving people parenting skills before they become parents! Thus, national curricula exist in this country that directly address the skill deficits that can lead to an at-risk status for youth. Such curricula have been shown scientifically to be efficacious. Unfortunately, none of these curricula are universal in America's schools.

Mentoring Programs
To prevent the development of at-risk behaviors may mean that the child needs to find other role models and mentors in his or her own day-to-day experiences. At-risk youth sometimes find 3their own ability to develop appropriate roles and responsibilities from interactions with peers, schoolteachers, neighbors, and other community leaders. For at-risk youth to change their pattern of behavior means that they need to see an alternative way to life.

Physical and Sexual Abuse Education for Children
The NIS-3 report (Sedlak & Broadhurst, 1996) stressed that schools play a central role in identifying and helping abused and neglected young people. School professionals are the frontline observers who form relationships of care with young people. Rencken (1989) has advocated three axes of prevention for abuse that are useful at the school and community levels: empowerment, sex education, and gender equity. The first axis includes teaching assertiveness and the ability to say "no" from a foundation of self-esteem, responsibility, and age-appropriate control. The second axis is sex education to remediate ignorance for young people and their families. The third axis is a discussion of gender role differences between males and females in our society and the development of equitable power arrangements.

It is clear that physically abused and neglected children are not always helped even with reporting. Child protection agencies and the court system are already seriously overworked. Often they are unable to follow up on cases except where there is threat of fatality. To address this problem, grassroots support systems are being developed. Schools and mental health agencies are teaming together to develop individualized and tailored care that uses the natural support systems in communities to help protect children. These support systems include safe places for children to go after school, neighborhood police stations, child mentorship, and after-school activities such as tutoring and gym nights. Schools can become a place to provide support to at-risk youth and their families. Grants and donations of time and money are typically used by schools and agencies to development these support resources.

Prevention at the Community Level

Parent Education
A powerful prevention activity is parent education. Both schools and community agencies can sponsor such an activity for minimal cost. If only one activity could be

selected to prevent at-risk status in youth, it should be parent education. Nothing provides more bang for the buck.

Two parent education activities that have solid research support are STEP and parent monitoring. It is important to note that these activities can be easily sponsored and led not only by school personnel but also by local community agencies or churches. Neither is the kind of fancy, complex activity that garners media attention. Rather, they are doable, proven at-risk prevention activities that can make a difference in the lives of youth and their parents. As such, they merit the considerations of anyone looking for ways to address the at-risk youth problems they encounter in their workplace or in their community.

STEP. Systematic Training for Effective Parenting, or STEP, is a widely used parent education program. The STEP program curriculum presents practical ideas for parents based on Adlerian psychology. There are a wide variety of STEP modules, including those for parents of young children, parents of teens, Christian parents, and Latino parents. Although designed for the average parent, there is even evidence of STEP's effectiveness with parents who have previously abused their children (Fennell & Fishel, 1998).

The STEP program is well laid out with clear lesson plans and appropriate participant activities. There is also a training facilitator's handbook for support (Dinkmeyer, 1997). A person who has had some previous training in developmental psychology and in communication skills would do an excellent job of facilitating STEP training.

Parent monitoring.   Although it may sound like an incredibly simplistic solution, extensive research supports the idea that at-risk behaviors can be substantially decreased by increasing parental monitoring of youth. Murray, Kelder, Parcel, and Orpinas (1998) developed a parent education program that taught parents practical monitoring skills of middle school students. They identified four skills that are essential in building competent monitoring in parents:

1. Parents will ask their child where he or she is going.
2. Parents will obtain a list of telephone numbers of their child's friends.
3. Parents will call parents of their child's friends.
4. Parents will visit their child's school.

Learning objectives are identified for each skill. For example, one of the learning objectives for the second skill is "parents will be able to recognize most of their child's friends on the street and know their names" (Murray et al., 1998, p. 50).

Community Capacity Building

At-risk behaviors of youth do not wreak havoc in just families and schools. The social and economic costs of such behaviors affect every community. As such, building the capacity of communities to prevent at-risk behaviors benefits all citizens. Given the central role of schools in most communities, school personnel can be key instigators of a community's focusing on at-risk prevention. In terms of communitywide prevention efforts, school personnel should work toward two goals: education on family dynamics and communitywide networking.

Education on family dynamics.   One key community prevention goal is educating the general public about the variation in family structures and individual differences. It is still difficult for many local institutions such as churches, hospitals, and other community organizations to make allowances for the various family structures such as blended families, single-parent families, interracial families, and dual-career families. Moreover, if at-risk youth are to find surrogate role models in the community, it is important for the potential role models to understand the dysfunctional and nontraditional aspects of family life in the current culture.

Community-wide networking. Another key community prevention goal is the successful networking of school personnel with other professionals in the community who serve at-risk youth. These professionals include private practice counselors, community agency counselors, probation officers, law enforcement officers, and pediatricians. This networking is necessary given the multifaceted nature of youth at-risk status. For example, substance abuse may lead to both academic and health problems. Given this multifacetedness, school professionals must have an effective network of other professionals to offer the youth and the family the best services possible. The network should include knowledge of runaway shelters, crisis intervention teams, support groups, hospitals, and outpatient services.

ADAPTATIONS FOR DIVERSITY

Poverty among minority families is an underrecognized and poorly addressed factor that leads to family dysfunction and the development of at-risk behaviors in youth. For example, two thirds of African American children in the United States are born to single, unwed mothers who live below the poverty level (Kilgore & Snyder, 2000). For a single parent with no money, the effect of the chronic stressors often overwhelms efforts to cope with the demands of raising children. Single parents carry the greatest load of pressure in our society, often raising their children without economic or social resources to provide for basic needs and safety. A counseling approach that supports single parents understands that these parents often feel they should not ask for assistance, believing that they alone are responsible for their families. Reaching out in a nonjudgmental way is a critical first step toward changing the family dysfunction and at-risk behaviors of the children who live in poverty.

The American Psychological Association created a Minority Fellowship Program to support doctoral students in research that increases the knowledge of and studies about ways to improve the quality of mental health and substance abuse services delivered to ethnic minority populations. Their mission is consistent with Health People 2010, the Surgeon General's Report on Mental Health, and other federal initiatives to reduce health disparities. Outcomes from this program include the examination of an innovative approach known as *multidimensional family therapy* (MDFT). MDFT has been shown empirically to provide an effective treatment for single-parent families with youth who have drug and alcohol behavior problems (Becker & Liddle, 2001; Liddle, 2001). The strategy of MDFT is strengths based, wherein the counselor listens to and validates the parent's and the child's stories about the family while working to bring the parent and the youth into an increasing amount of involvement with one another. Additionally, the counselor must earn the trust of the parent by acknowledging the stereotypes of being representative of the system and find ways to nurture the nurturer.

As noted earlier in this chapter, the causes of at-risk behavior are directly linked to the parent's view of the child, the level of communication established in the family, and the ability to build positive relationships of support within the family. Among multiethnic families with delinquent inner-city youth, parents often believed that the cause of their family problems and at-risk youth behaviors was due to the level of discipline (Madden-Derdich, Leonard, & Gunnell, 2002). These parents saw themselves as needing to continually monitor their children's behavior and for their children to comply with their wishes or face harsh consequences. This parenting style has been associated with the development of antisocial behavior. In contrast, the children believed that poor communication, interpersonal conflict, lack of parental concern, and drug use were the factors that interfered with positive change in the family and their own behaviors. The youth saw the real problem. The counseling approach of choice in this situation is structural family therapy. Structural family therapy encourages the family to stop blaming the member who is in the identified-problem role (i.e., the child) and assists parents to gain control by taking responsibility for creating positive family communication and interactions. Acknowledging the rich heritage of ethnicity is critical to the success of this counseling intervention.

SUMMARY

This chapter provides an overview of how dysfunctional family dynamics both precede and fuel at-risk behavior. In addition, the chapter provides some ideas about how to best provide a program of prevention to assist at-risk youth and their families. Several points need to be emphasized for those charged with working with at-risk youth.

First, there is no more difficult population to serve than at-risk youth. They tend to be more professionally demanding, emotionally draining, and behaviorally unpredictable than youth as a whole. Professionals assigned to work with this population must learn to be direct and honest with the youth as well as his or her family. As mentioned in the discussion of prevention, these same professionals must learn to follow the rules in serving these youth.

Second, the at-risk family is a very special entity and needs tremendous amounts of attention to keep it functioning without tragedy. A professional working with an at-risk individual has to always be aware of the remaining family members to make sure that another member does not manifest a severe behavioral difficulty. Consultation with other important adults surrounding the family members is necessary to effectively work with the at-risk family. This is a responsible approach for counselors working with any family and is particularly important when these community persons reflect the culture of the family that is different from the counselor's own cultural background or identity.

Finally, treating at-risk youth mandates that professionals be involved with families and community agencies. There is no place in work with at-risk youth for the professional Lone Ranger. The biggest mistake made by caring professionals is to assume too much individual responsibility for the at-risk youth and his or her family. Find a support system to assist in the treatment process and be sure to have a support system available for you. Maintaining physical energy and emotional balance is as important as any decision the professional can make.

REFERENCES

Aguilera, D. C., & Messick, J. M. (1986). *Crisis intervention: Theory and methodology.* St. Louis, MO: Mosby.

Amato, P. R. (2001). Children of divorce in the 1990s: An update of the Amato and Keith (1991) meta-analysis. *Journal of Family Psychology, 15,* 355–369.

American Psychiatric Association. (2000). *Diagnostic and statistical manual of mental disorders* (4th ed., text revision). Washington, DC: Author.

Appleton, V. E. (2001). Avenues of hope: Art therapy and the resolution of trauma. *Art Therapy: Journal of the American Art Therapy Association, 18*(1), 6–13.

Becker, D., & Liddle, H. A. (2001). Family therapy with unmarried African American mothers and their adolescents. *Family Process, 40,* 413–427.

Cumsille, P. E., & Epstein, N. (1994). Family cohesion, family adaptability, social support, and adolescent depressive symptoms in outpatient clinic families. *Journal of Family Psychology, 8,* 202–214.

De Arth-Pendley, G., & Cummings, E. M. (2002). Children's emotional reactivity to interadult nonverbal conflict expressions. *Journal of Genetic Psychology, 163,* 97–103.

Dinkmeyer, D. (1997). *Systematic training for effective parenting: Leaders resource binder.* Circle Pines, MN: American Guidance Service.

Fennell, D. C., & Fishel, A. H. (1998). Parent education: An evaluation of STEP on abusive parents' perceptions and potential abuse. *Journal of Child and Adolescent Psychiatric Nursing, 11,* 107–121.

Fincham, F. D. (1994). Understanding the association between marital conflict and child adjustment: Overview. *Journal of Family Psychology, 8,* 123–127.

Finkelhor, D. (1984). *Child sexual abuse.* New York: Free Press.

Friedrich, W. M. (2002). *Psychological assessment of sexually abused children and their families.* New York: Sage.

Garbarino, J., Guttman, E., & Seeley, J. W. (1986). *The psychologically battered child.* San Francisco, CA: Jossey-Bass.

Gil, E. (1996). *Treating abused adolescents.* New York: Guilford Press.

Green, A. H. (1988). The abused child and adolescent. In C. J. Kestenbaum & D. J. Williams (Eds.), *Handbook of clinical assessment of children and adolescents* (Vol. 2, pp. 841–863). New York: New York University Press.

Herman, J. L. (1997). *Trauma and recovery.* New York: Basic Books.

Higgs, D. C., Canavan, M. M., & Meyer, W. J. (1992). Moving from defense to offense: The development of an adolescent female sex offender. *Journal of Sex Research, 29,* 131–139.

Kaufman, J., & Zigler, E. (1987). Do abused children become abusive parents? *American Journal of Orthopsychiatry, 57,* 186–192.

Kazak, A. E., Christakis, D., Alderfer, M., & Coiro, M. J. (1994). Young adolescent cancer survivors and their parents: Adjustment, learning problems, gender. *Journal of Family Psychology, 8,* 74–84.

Kilgore, K., & Snyder, J. (2000). The contribution of parental discipline, parental monitoring, and school risk to early-onset conduct problems in African American boys and girls. *Developmental Psychology, 36,* 835–847.

Lapan, R., Gysbers, N. C., & Sun, Y. (1997). The impact of more fully implemented guidance programs on the school experiences of high school students: A statewide evaluation study. *Journal of Counseling & Development, 75,* 292–302.

Liddle, H. A. (2001). *Multidimensional family therapy treatment (MDFT) for adolescent cannabis users* (Volume 5 of the Cannabis Youth Treatment, Substance Abuse and Mental Health Service Administration). Retrieved September 1, 2002, from http://www.samsha.gov/csat.html

Madden-Derdich, D. S., Leonard, S. A., & Gunnell, G. A. (2002). Parents' and children's perceptions of family processes in inner-city families with delinquent youths: A qualitative investigation. *Journal of Marital and Family Therapy, 28,* 355–369.

Murray, N., Kelder, S., Parcel, G., & Orpinas, P. (1998). Development of an intervention map for a parent education intervention to prevent violence among Hispanic middle school parents. *Journal of School Health, 68,* 46–53.

Okami, P. (1992). Child perpetrators of sexual abuse: The emergence of a problematic deviant category. *Journal of Sex Research, 29,* 109–130.

Pianta, R. C., & Walsh, D. J. (1996). *High-risk children in schools.* New York: Routledge.

Rencken, R. H. (1989). *Intervention strategies for sexual abuse.* Alexandria, VA: American Counseling Association.

Sedlak, A., & Broadhurst, D. (1996). *Third national incidence study of child abuse and neglect: Final report*. Washington, DC: U.S. Department of Health and Human Services, Administration of Children and Family.

Shields, A., & Cicchetti, D. (2001). Parental maltreatment and emotion dysregulation as risk factors for bullying and victimization in middle childhood. *Journal of Clinical Child Psychology, 30*, 349–364.

Visher, E. B., & Visher, J. S. (1996). *Therapy with stepfamilies*. New York: Brunner/Mazel.

Wasserman, G. A., Miller, L. S., Pinner, E., & Jaramillo, B. (1996). Parenting predictors of early conduct problems in urban, high-risk boys. *Journal of the American Academy of Child and Adolescent Psychology, 35*, 1227–1237.

Webb, N. B., & Terr, L. (1999). *Play therapy with children in crisis*. New York: Guilford Press.

5 | "Who Cares What I Think": Problems of Low Self-Esteem

Sandra S. Meggert

We observe many adolescents in pain. We see many with negative attitudes or low self-esteem and suspect there are many more. Many researchers believe that one of the major causes of deviant or potentially destructive behavior is low self-esteem (Kaplan, 1975; Leung & Drasgow, 1986; Maternal and Child Health Branch, Hawaii State Department of Health, 1991; Yanish & Battle, 1985). A review of the literature supports the belief that negative self-esteem affects behavior in negative or destructive ways (Aronson & Mettee, 1968; Graf, 1971; Kaplan, 1975; Kaplan, Martin, & Johnson, 1986; Lorr & Wunderlich, 1986; Yanish & Battle, 1985). Kaplan (1976) stated that poor self-esteem or "negative self-attitudes increase the probability of later adoption of each of a range of different types of deviant responses" (p. 788). Low self-esteem is a critical factor in at-risk behavior. Eskilson, Wiley, Meuhlbauer, and Dodder (1986) reported that adolescents who feel excessive demands to succeed academically are apt to disclose involvement in deviant activities, to have low self-esteem, and to feel inadequate and unable to fulfill their families' aspirations for them. Aronson and Mettee (1968) used college students as participants in a study of dishonesty. They hypothesized that students with "low self-esteem are more likely to engage in immoral behavior" (p. 123). Results showed that 87% of the students with induced low self-esteem cheated on a test as compared with 60% of the neutral group and 40% of the induced high self-esteem group. In a similar study, Graf (1971) reported that 40% of those with induced low self-esteem, 17% of the neutral group, and 14% of the group with induced high self-esteem engaged in dishonest behavior.

Kaplan's (1976) theory suggests that low self-esteem influences a person to adopt delinquent or other behaviors that are deviant from the norm. The theory identifies two routes that negative self-attitudes may take to influence deviant behavior. One is that these attitudes make conformity to membership group patterns painful or distressing; the other is "by influencing the person's need to seek alternatives to the disvalued normative patterns in order to satisfy the self-esteem motive" (Kaplan, 1976, p. 788). The Maternal and Child Health Branch of the Hawaii State Department of Health (1991) collected data on adolescent health in Hawaii and found that adolescents with low self-esteem were more likely to exhibit high-risk behaviors than their peers with high self-esteem.

The results of a study of adolescents at risk for compulsive overeating (Marston, Jacobs, Singer, Widaman, & Little, 1988) showed that students designated as being at risk perceived their life quality as poor, and Marston et al. hypothesized that this meant they were getting along poorly with the person to whom they felt closest. Because esteem is closely tied to perceived evaluations from significant others, the quality of significant relationships is a crucial ingredient of self-esteem. The research findings of Yanish and Battle (1985) supported the importance of significant others to the adolescent. They found depression in adolescents to be more strongly affected by the relationship with parents than with peers. Masche's (2000) longitudinal study of 54 intact families tentatively concluded that the self-concept of adolescents was influenced by the quality of both the parent–adolescent and marital relationships. A longitudinal study by Cohen, Burt, and Bjorck (1987) indicated that low self-esteem and depression, an indicator of low self-esteem, were positive predictors of controllable negative events, for example, expulsion from school. Portes and Zady (2000) studied cultural differences in self-esteem and adaptation of Spanish-speaking second-generation adolescents. They concluded that parent–child conflicts and depression were common predictors of self-esteem for this population and noted that this was similar to samples from the dominant culture labeled "mainstream."

Simmons, Burgeson, Carlton-Ford, and Blyth (1987) stated that young people who encounter several important life events at the same time they are adjusting to the changes of adolescence are expected to be at greater risk than those who have longer periods of time to adjust to adolescence. Findings in this study showed that girls suffer loss of self-esteem and that both boys and girls show declines in grade point average and participation in extracurricular activities. For girls, each subsequent life change brings more difficulty with coping. Simmons et al. suggested that, in terms of self-esteem, this group of young adolescents does better if one aspect of their life is comfortable. If this is accomplished, then the timing and pacing of major changes are of primary importance. Low self-esteem and family dysfunction in adolescent girls diagnosed with at least one mental disorder were found to be predictors of suicidal ideations by Kelly, Lynch, Donovan, and Clark (2001).

As discussed in the many preceding examples, adolescents who exhibit signs of low self-esteem may be considered at risk for adopting or experimenting with deviant or potentially destructive behaviors. These young people may or may not currently be responding to life situations with deviant behaviors (McCready, 1997). However, when the signs indicate low self-esteem, interventions designed to improve self-esteem are important to help these youth avoid at-risk behaviors.

This chapter examines low self-esteem as one of the primary causes of the at-risk behaviors just described and delineates strategies and programs to prevent low levels of self-esteem. Self-esteem is defined in relation to at-risk youth, and behavioral descriptions frequently linked to low self-esteem are discussed. The chapter then presents causal factors that influence the development of self-esteem, as well as prevention strategies that can be used by the individual, parents, schools, and communities to make young people feel valued and like significant participants in making their environment a satisfying, safe, and rewarding place. A case study describes a successful experimental program with at-risk students that has brought about changes that reflect improved levels of self-esteem.

DEFINITIONS OF SELF-ESTEEM

Self-esteem refers to subjective evaluations of worth. These value judgments develop through personal success or failure experiences, interactions with others, maturation, heredity, and social learning and are formulated from an individual's perspective. Kaplan (1975) discussed the self-esteem motive as being an individual's need to optimize positive feelings about self while reducing negative feelings. It is the process of increasing feelings of self-respect, approval, worth, and esteem. When the balance is on the negative side, a person is said to feel self-rejection, self-derogation, and, in many cases, self-hate.

Self-esteem is also a function of perceived evaluation by significant others. Mack and Ablon (1983) believed that no human is ever totally independent of the evaluation of others and that everyone retains "to some degree, a dependence upon connectedness with others for validation of our worth" (p. 10). A person's self-evaluation is referred to as self-esteem (Robison-Awana, Kehle, & Jenson, 1986). It is influenced by the individual's feelings of competence and efficacy. Carlock (1999) summed up various definitions compiled from Cantor and Bernay (1992) and McDowell (1984) and described self-esteem as

> how you feel about yourself, how highly you regard yourself. That degree of regard is based on your sense of how lovable and special you believe you are, how wanted you feel and your sense of belonging, how special or unique you believe you are, how competent you feel and how well you fulfill your potential, how willing you are to take risks and face challenges and how able you are to set goals, make choices, and fulfill your goals and dreams. (p. 5)

Two other terms are sometimes used interchangeably with self-esteem: self-concept and self-acceptance. *Self-concept* refers to the perception individuals have about their personal attributes and the roles they fulfill. Some of these perceptions are accurate, and some are not. According to Beane and Lipka (1980), we receive feedback about the roles we play and internalize information about the character and quality of our role performance, and "self-concept refers to the valuative assessment of those descriptions" (p. 3). For example, individuals have an academic self-concept, a social self-concept, or a physical appearance self-concept. Elliott (1988) maintained that anyone with low self-esteem has an unstable self-concept. The term *self-acceptance* pertains to the degree to which people are comfortable with their self-concept (Frey & Carlock, 1984).

For purposes of this discussion, *self-esteem* is defined as the pattern of beliefs an individual has about self-worth. It is the subjective part of self-concept, the evaluation of self and behaviors based on an individual's perceptions of personal experiences and feedback from significant others. It is expressed in feelings of power or helplessness, called efficacy, or in beliefs about personal control.

INDICATORS OF LOW SELF-ESTEEM

Beliefs about self develop as a result of perceptions and evaluations of success and failure experiences. In this process, an individual forms some beliefs about personal control (internal vs. external) and personal effectiveness (self-efficacy).

Locus of control refers to a person's belief about outcomes. Locus of control is the conviction that success or failure at a task is internally determined by one's own actions or ability, or that the outcome is due to external influences such as luck, fate, or chance. According to D. S. Johnson (1981), "internal attributions for success are associated with higher levels of self-esteem," and low self-concept "was predicted independently and significantly by internal attribution for failure and external attribution for success" (p. 174). Abramson, Seligman, and Teasdale (1978) suggested that low-achieving students ascribe any failures to internal causes and all successes to external causes.

Personal effectiveness, or *self-efficacy*, as defined by Benoit and Mitchell (1987), has four essential elements: awareness of required behavior to bring about success, expectation that this behavior will be successful, belief that there is a relationship between behavior and outcome and that this behavior will have an impact, and belief that the outcome will provide something valued.

Evidence supports the fact that an individual with low self-esteem does most likely believe in luck (external control) rather than ability (internal control) to achieve success. However, failure is attributed to personal shortcomings (internal control). Because self-esteem judges whether such an individual can, in fact, succeed at a given task, the lack of belief in self makes it likely that someone with low self-esteem will also exhibit feelings of helplessness or powerlessness, in other words, low levels of self-efficacy. In this case, a possible defense might be to deny that the outcome of the behavior has any value and to withdraw or drop out.

Individuals with low self-esteem often find it necessary to develop defenses. People who have low self-esteem hurt. To avoid this hurt, people with low self-esteem have a tendency either to shun experiences they believe will bring additional pain or to change these experiences in some way. They erect barriers or defenses. At times the individual might be hostile, critical, suspicious of others, or lack identification with others. Sometimes retreating defenses are exhibited when a person avoids coming to grips with problems or denies reality (Kaplan, 1975). A person might retreat into an "I don't care" stance or simply resist trying. It is too much of a risk for someone with feelings of poor self-worth to be exposed to additional hurt or situations in which failure is expected.

People with low self-esteem may be distractible, timid, shy, withdrawn, inhibited, anxious, and less academically able (Domino & Blumberg, 1987) and have a narrow range of interests. They are more likely to daydream and to want to find jobs in which they have little or no supervision and in which there is minimal amount of competition. From their perspectives, an ideal situation is one in which they have no supervision because then no one can confirm their failure. Generally, they express the idea that they do not really want to get ahead in life. This could be because they will not place themselves in a position where they expect to fail. This too is a defense.

Individuals with low self-esteem have few coping strategies. They often feel a lack of control over life events. They do not feel connected and have few, if any, expectations of future success. They lack a sense of belonging. Possibly, dropping out is a defensive way of demonstrating some power, self-defeating though it may be. Chapman and Mullis (1999) studied the connection between coping strategies and self-esteem in adolescents. Their data showed that boys had lower self-esteem and used more avoidance coping strategies than girls, who typically used spiritual and social support.

Low self-esteem can cause emotional distress as well. Many individuals who question their own worth are sad, lethargic, tense, anxious, and angry. Some of these feelings stem from concurrent feelings of helplessness and powerlessness. Physically they may exhibit sleeplessness, headaches, or nightmares. McGee and Williams (2000) found that levels of global self-esteem predicted reports of suicidal ideation, problem eating, and multiple compromising behaviors by adolescents in New Zealand.

Those who have low self-esteem are generally dissatisfied with themselves and their lives, are contemptuous of self, and have low levels of self-respect. Typically, they are fearful of new experiences and have a poor physical appearance and a low energy level. Apologizing, criticizing others, showing an interest in material things, and bragging are all indicators of low self-esteem.

CAUSAL FACTORS

Parental, social, psychological, physical, environmental, individual, and cultural influences affect self-esteem. They all contribute to the development of self-esteem to the extent that each or all of these are valued or devalued by significant others who provide feedback. This feedback is both verbal and nonverbal, overt and covert, and dramatically affects how adolescents see themselves.

Parental Influences on Self-Esteem

Frey and Carlock (1984) identified a representative list of "psychological pathogens" to self-esteem (pp. 25–31). Many of these are associated with parental influences. These pathogens may persist throughout life and, if so, may consistently keep self-esteem low unless someone or something intervenes. Among the pathogens they identified and the problems that might arise when these are present during childhood are the following:

- *Expecting perfection.* Nobody has achieved this state yet, but many people try. Carrying a burden of always trying to be perfect out of childhood guarantees failure. Those who have learned to set idealistic or unrealistic goals for themselves are constantly frustrated, critical, and impatient with themselves and others, always trying harder and never quite feeling successful. Negative self-evaluations, which are formulated by the individual from perceptions of adult reactions, deeply affect his or her feelings about self. Unless a person learns to set realistic goals and acknowledge small steps along the way, self-esteem remains low because the person never feels adequate.
- *Inconsistency and failure to set limits.* Though some people believe consistency is a myth, children often search for consistency and limits, apparently seeking the security that structure and predictability provide. When that is missing, the result is anger, insecurity, and hostility.
- *Failure to give positive feedback.* Many parents and significant others assume that children know that positive behavior is appreciated and only respond to negative or improper behavior. Being constantly reminded or punished when behavior is inappropriate, and seldom being appreciated when behavior is appropriate, creates feelings of inadequacy and inferiority.
- *Failure to listen.* Failing to listen to a child indicates a lack of respect and communicates that the child or what the child is trying to communicate is not important. When this feeling is carried through childhood, it fosters additional feelings of inferiority and inadequacy that are sometimes expressed in anger or hostility.
- *Rejection.* Consistent rejection critically impacts an individual's self-esteem. The rejected child's basic needs are not being met, in some cases deliberately. Death, divorce, severe illness, or ignoring the child can all be viewed as rejection by a child with the ensuing feelings of inadequacy, guilt, self-hate, or self-rejection.
- *Being a maladjusted role model.* Children who model their behavior after an adult who is maladjusted often end up disliking themselves because of those behaviors. Their self-esteem is greatly diminished in such cases.
- *Failure to help children adapt.* Societal and cultural values are being questioned more now than ever before. It is difficult for children to feel adequate in a society where values are shifting or unclear. It becomes even more difficult when children try to adapt to a different culture and values conflict.

- *Forcing children into a pattern.* Sometimes parents try to fit children into certain behaviors or patterns that may restrict their unique development or be beyond their capacity. This is sometimes called living vicariously and creates frustration, feelings of worthlessness, and inadequacy in both parent and child.
- *Allowing and supporting procrastination.* Believing that one does not have the self-discipline necessary to complete a task contributes to poor self-esteem. The longer the child procrastinates, the more the feelings of inadequacy and worthlessness multiply. Concurrently, there is a loss of self-respect.

Frey and Carlock (1984) listed several additional pathogens and observed that "one can be the recipient of several of these dynamics" (p. 31). Each of these, or a combination of several, is detrimental to a child's self-esteem.

Parents have a significant impact on the self-esteem of their children (Emler, 2001). Parental attitudes and behaviors have been shown to affect children (Buri & Kircher, 1993; Lord, Eccles, & McCarthy, 1994; Ohannesian, Lerner, Lerner, & Von Eye, 1994). The number of divorces and remarriages and the child's subsequent adjustment were the focus of a study that found some evidence of a "negative linear relationship" between these variables (Lord et al., 1994, p. 28). Buri and Dickinson (1994) reported that although parental authority was predictive of self-esteem, these behaviors were less important than overgeneralization, particularly in girls. The authors described overgeneralization as the inclination for a person to view a failure as an indication of his or her general inadequacy.

A consequence of the dynamics just described is that young people today feel unimportant or even irrelevant in their families (Glenn & Nelson, 1989). Many believe that they are important only when they are doing what someone else wants them to do. Glenn and Nelson speculated that this is one impetus for early sexual involvement. Sex becomes a strategy to make the individuals involved believe themselves to be significant in the eyes of someone else. For girls, the irony is that if she has a child, she is automatically treated as an adult when, in fact, there are now two children.

The need to feel significant is also a powerful motivator to become a gang member. News stories report daily regarding the initiation rites to join a gang. Some young people want so badly to belong that they lose their lives during the entry process.

Note that many of the pathogens identified are behaviors found in extremely inexperienced parents who may use the child to satisfy personal needs not previously filled. The child will not feel valued, may be confused, and, most likely, will develop low self-esteem. The cycle will remain unbroken unless there is some type of intervention.

Sim (2000) studied the role of parental regard on Singapore adolescents' psychosocial competence. He used self-esteem and psychosocial competence as indicators. Results indicated that adolescents' regard for parents was positively related to self-esteem and negatively associated with antisocial susceptibility. Regard for parents was also found to mediate the relationship between parental monitoring and antisocial susceptibility.

Individual Influences on Self-Esteem

We learn about ourselves as we interact with our environment and receive feedback on how well or how poorly we do things. Small children learn about their capabilities and their limits or strengths from others and form beliefs about their own competence. If a child receives negative feedback consistently, he or she will learn to believe in his or her own inferiority. This, in turn, could impact attitudes and outlook on life and leave the individual with a sense of not "fitting in" or not belonging and being powerless. In addition, poor peer relationships can lead to rejection by desirable peers, thus impacting self-esteem (Kashani, Jones, Bumby, & Thomas, 1999).

These beliefs about self are powerful and form a lens through which a person views the world. This view will have an influence on the experiences the individual chooses to undertake and probably on the outcomes as well. Building self-esteem includes a measure of being realistic about our abilities. When most feedback is negative, a person's view of his or her competence often becomes unrealistic, and the individual makes choices based on what he or she believes to be true about self. Carlock (1999) believed "it is important for young children not just to learn specific skills and behaviors but to acquire an overall belief in their ability to affect their world" (p. 291).

Social Influences on Self-Esteem

A basic assumption in social psychology is that self-concepts are heavily influenced by social contexts (Bachman & O'Malley, 1986). Each of us has a long history of dependency during infancy and childhood during which we need to receive positive responses from adults. We are motivated to behave in ways that increase the likelihood of receiving these positive responses. As children we internalize adult standards in this manner, and we attempt to regulate our own behavior and react with positive or negative self-feelings at the perceived evaluations and reactions of significant adults (Kaplan, 1976).

Kaplan (1976) further noted that low self-esteem is thought to be caused by self-perceptions that either our behavior or our characteristics do not meet personal standards valued by the social system, by self-perceptions that significant others do not value us positively or perhaps even negatively, or by self-perceptions that we might not have developed "normatively acceptable coping mechanisms" that could protect us from the effect of "self-perceptions of failure or rejection by others" (p. 790). Someone with a history of being devalued is most likely to have low self-esteem. This can be said to evolve from two sources: an individual's history of negative self-evaluation and perception, and perceptions of highly valued others in the environment responding to the individual with less than positive attitudes (Kaplan, 1975). An individual is more likely to value the attitudes of those persons "who were associated with need gratification or deprivation" (p. 37).

Society imposes strong gender-based role behaviors that continue their impact on self-esteem long after adolescence. A study has demonstrated that masculine bias is still strong in the United States (Burnett, Anderson, & Heppner, 1995). Masculinity, defined as having high levels of traditional masculine behaviors (such as competitiveness, decisiveness, and independence) as opposed to feminine characteristics (such as focus on relationships and nurturing), has been shown to be "significantly correlated with self-esteem for both men and women, but individual femininity was not significantly related to self-esteem in either sex" (Burnett et al., 1995, p. 325).

Even though masculine behaviors are clearly valued in the United States, they are not generally characteristic of at-risk youth. If they are evident in some, they are not generally evident in socially acceptable ways. For example, aggressiveness and rebelliousness might substitute for independence and competitiveness. Enns (1992) stated that "there is some evidence that the socialization process is even more stringent for men than it is for women, and that boys and men experience higher costs for straying from traditional gender roles than do girls and women" (p. 11). There is the possibility that absence of masculine skills in boys, and to some extent girls, has the potential of contributing to low self-esteem. Bower (1993) reported that development of self-esteem in males and females is different because of societal pressures that dictate male and female role behaviors. Some research has also indicated that teenage girls have lower self-esteem than teenage boys (Dwyer, 1993). A *U.S. News & World Report* article (Saltzman, 1994) surveyed research regarding self-esteem of adolescent girls. After examining several research studies, Saltzman concluded that social science has no conclusive answers and that parents have to assess and address the needs of their daughters individually.

Many of the social changes are high-risk changes. As young people are alienated from society and practice more violent methods to feel significant and powerful, many die or become incapacitated. Wars are fought on TV, and children feel threatened. Technology has changed the world of work, and many parents or parental figures are unemployed. Divorce is common, and homes are broken. Values are lost. Young people hear of people their own age dying from the variety of perils to which they are exposed. Many of them believe that they will live short lives. No one has prepared them for the choices they have to make.

Psychological Influences on Self-Esteem

It is "questionable, indeed, whether human beings can deeply experience positive self-worth except as the result of a relationship" (Mack & Ablon, 1983, p. 9). Everyone knows two basic truths about the self. One is that the self is alone and private, and the other is "that one is a real self only to the extent that caring and reaching beyond the self continue" (Yankelovich, 1981, p. 240). Therefore, an important psychological determinant of self-esteem is the individual's feelings about the level of success within relationships.

The whole notion of connectedness or belonging to someone is central to the development of self-esteem. Belonging to a family, a culture, a community, or a school provides a connection to aid in sustaining a sense of worth. Lacking such a feeling, a person is likely to feel not valued, or not of value, and retreat into a defensive posture to protect the self from the pain of feeling isolated, hopeless, worthless, and unconnected. "Virtually all maladaptive defensive patterns in childhood, adolescence, and adult life have as at least one major purpose, protection of the pain associated with lowered self-esteem" (Mack & Ablon, 1983, p. 38).

Television has become a psychological determinant of self-esteem (Glenn & Nelson, 1989). Young people receive messages about the society in which they live in a passive manner. They do not have to participate to learn. In the past, people learned about functioning in society while they were actively involved in living and working. The learning might be trial and error, role modeling, or direct teaching, but individuals were active. The authors referred to this as "on-the-job training." Today, with the use of television, children's reality becomes distorted. Within a short time, they see problems solved through miracles, violence, various medications, sex, and drinking. According to Glenn and Nelson (1989, pp. 42–43), children learn the following:

1. In productive and desirable social interactions drinking or substance abuse is necessary.
2. Pain, fatigue, listlessness, and boredom are all dispelled through self-medication.
3. Indiscriminate or uninvolved sexual encounters are appropriate ways to communicate.

4. Problems can be resolved instantly through manipulation, violence, and breaking the law.
5. Deferred gratification, hard work, and personal initiative are unacceptable, and drinking and self-medication can help a person avoid these stresses. Any stressful situation can be alleviated by using specific products and/or services.

These "truisms" are further complicated by parents who foster the belief that most material possessions can be obtained in ways other than hard work. So because things come easy, there is no respect for possessions and no positive messages about the purpose of life. It is easy to speculate that if no active role modeling or teaching of healthier, more productive attitudes disputes these claims, young people may feel alienated, angry, and confused. When they use these same behaviors that work on television to solve their problems, they get into trouble. The nonacceptance of their behaviors confirms their sense of worthlessness and insignificance. The only way they can feel any sense of worth is when they are with others who feel and think as they do.

Physical Influences on Self-Esteem

Inherited physical characteristics, such as physique, appearance, and disabilities, also may influence self-esteem. The physical attributes that an individual has inherited can affect others' perceptions and behavior. Others may respond negatively to an individual's disabled condition or physical appearance, thus affecting that individual's self-esteem, even though the individual's initial self-perception may not have been negative.

Others' reactions are also influenced by maturational rates. Adults treat children differently at differing maturation levels. Early-maturing children are quite often treated as adults and develop positive self-esteem. But those who mature later and continue to be treated as children tend to develop low self-esteem. Even when this latter group matures, they often maintain old self-perceptions and the corresponding low self-esteem. Maturation also affects mastery of developmental tasks. Social disapproval, maladjustment, and increased difficulty in mastering higher level developmental tasks are all possible results of delayed maturation (Frey & Carlock, 1984).

Environmental Influences on Self-Esteem

It is difficult to define the effect environment plays in the development of low self-esteem. A person learns values and has needs satisfied within the environment through social interaction with significant others, and if needs are not met and the expressions of beliefs and values meet with disapproval within the environment, self-esteem is likely to be damaged.

An additional aspect of environment has to do with the groups within the environment with which the person identifies. Each member of a group is evaluated by every other member. If the group is significant to an individual, these evaluations affect self-esteem. For example, if a person's perception is one of not being valued by the group, low self-esteem is probable. Esteem is related to one's rank in a group rather than rank of the group when compared with other groups (Rosenberg, 1965).

As the U.S. population has moved from rural to city areas, the environment in which children had built-in networks and role models has diminished and, in many cases, been lost. In the past, grandparents, aunts, uncles, cousins, neighbors, and friends were available to help educate and advise young people, and that was a given. In the absence of such an array of support in urban areas, young people have turned to their peers for guidance and approval. In doing so, they use peer norms, created out of lack of experience, to evaluate behavior rather than the collective experience and wisdom of a network of adult role models (Glenn & Nelson, 1989).

Parents have also suffered a loss of support. In most cases, the parents have no network of relatives nearby to assist in parenting, and they have to depend on themselves to make the right choices. And they have no experience being parents. Because both parents usually work, they parent part time. In single-parent families, even part-time parenting is shared with other stresses involved in survival. So now we have time factors as well as inexperienced parents as well as the challenges presented to children in today's world. It becomes easier to see why parents use the same stress reducers as their children.

APPROACHES TO PREVENTION

The pervasive distress and too frequent demise of our young people seem to be out of control. Jason et al. (1993) reported that in Chicago schools, "more than 40% of children do not graduate [from] high school" (p. 69), and they believed that the problems leading to dropping out often begin in the elementary schools. It is clear that some interventions and low self-esteem prevention strategies must be integrated into every level of the community. In this section specific approaches for parents, individuals, schools, and communities are discussed. No one segment of the population is solely responsible for providing prevention. All groups should overlap, and building and maintaining high levels of self-esteem should become an integral part of the total community structure. Although parents are charged with the initial environment for the child, they too are part of a community and have need of resources from the community. A global approach that could be utilized by the entire community is described at the end of this section.

Prevention at the Individual Level

Self-esteem develops as a result of interaction with and feedback from others. It is doubtful whether an individual can build self-esteem in a vacuum. If the feedback is negative, either verbal or nonverbal, the individual internalizes negative feelings about self and has poor feelings of worth. If feedback is positive and the individual feels successful, self-esteem is enhanced. An individual who feels valued and worthwhile has high self-esteem and responds to others in a manner that communicates this level of self-esteem.

It is difficult, perhaps impossible, for someone suffering from low self-esteem to undertake a prevention program alone. Most of the feedback that builds or destroys self-esteem comes either directly or indirectly from others. An individual is influenced by role models and can be encouraged to learn skills and attitudes that will lead to successful experiences. As self-esteem is raised, a person may seek out avenues that will bring more success.

Volunteering, learning to be assertive, learning to cope with anger and conflict constructively, attending workshops and special classes to learn life skills, and entering programs that are specifically designed for young people are all ways an individual can build self-esteem. In each of these possibilities, external guidance is often necessary for a person with low self-esteem.

Prevention at the Family Level

The environment in which a child is raised has a significant impact on the individual's self-esteem (Barber, Chadwick, & Orter, 1992; Blake & Slate, 1993; Cerezo & Frias, 1994; M. Harvey & Byrd, 1998; Shek, 1997). Historically, children were born into an intact family, and that was the primary environment in which the child learned about being an adult. Today, families vary in structure. Households in which both parents work outside the home are common. Single parenting, stepparenting, joint parenting, parenting by someone other than the biological parent, and homelessness have altered family structures and added to the pressures young people face as they grow into adulthood. Many who find themselves in parenting roles have no idea how to accomplish this and fall back on personal experience. They feel the loss of assistance and experience that an extended family provides, so they parent as they were parented, as best as they can remember. They may have low self-esteem as a result of their own childhood experiences and perpetuate their own feelings of worth in their children. Their own parental role models may not have had the wisdom of the extended family experience either, and lack of parenting skills continues from one generation to the next.

In terms of prevention, steps must be taken to teach parents how to parent. Recognizing and admitting the need to learn parenting is a primary step in the process of building self-esteem. Today's parents have access to parenting classes and special support groups to help them learn to work with their children. These groups are sponsored by school specialists as well as churches and agencies in the community. Joining a class or support group serves a dual purpose. The parents learn skills at the same time that they are increasing their network of support. Getting to know neighbors is another excellent way to extend their support network and can serve as a means to check perceptions of neighborhood situations.

Parents must understand their own needs for success, status, and control as these needs relate to their child-rearing practices. They must be able to put these needs aside and respond to each child as a unique person and to recognize and accept the contributions their children make in the family. There may have to be conscious efforts made to include each child and to discover ways in which each child can successfully contribute to the well-being of the family. Taking out the garbage can become significant if a child understands that his or her contribution is important to the family. When a parent asks a child for assistance with a task or project, one that cannot be done alone, the child learns that his or her contribution is an integral part in the task completion. In this case, it is essential that the child understands his or her help is not gratuitous but essential. For example, if the family pet has a thorn in a paw, it is difficult for one person to hold the animal, examine or probe the paw, and extract the thorn. It is much easier if someone else holds the animal. Asking for the child's assistance, and pointing out that this task is difficult or impossible for one person to do alone, will validate the value of the child's contribution.

Another way to prevent low self-esteem is to allow children to do what they can do and not do it for them. Often adults, who can do it faster or better, become impatient and complete tasks for the children. This indicates a lack of respect for the child and gives negative messages about the child's abilities and worth. These negative messages are both overt and covert and have a powerful effect on self-esteem. Though it may be difficult, allowing a child to complete a task more slowly and in a different manner or to make a mistake brings greater opportunities for learning. Using the mistake as a teachable moment is of greater value than scolding, punishing, or doing it for them.

Spending time with the child, talking or playing, gives positive messages about the child's importance. Letting children know that they are valued is critical in building self-esteem. Ironically, this is often the most difficult prevention technique; it takes time and is the first date to be canceled when schedules get tight. During regularly scheduled time together, bonds are cemented, relationships are nurtured, and both parent and child feel important. In using this strategy, parents must listen carefully, suspend judgment, and be accepting of the child's point of view. Children will discuss serious topics if they believe what they say will be heard and valued. They also learn from the role modeling.

Many families hold regularly scheduled meetings to discuss family matters. These meetings are used to resolve conflicts, plan outings, make decisions about the household, test out new ideas, and involve the whole family in a variety of discussions. Again, these should not be canceled except with solid reasons. If meetings are canceled too often, their usefulness diminishes. The interesting effect of using preventative measures is that the parents' or parental figures' self-esteem grows as well. When parent–child interactions are positive and productive, both participants feel valued.

Prevention at the School Level

Because every child has the opportunity to attend school, this is an ideal place to continue the low self-esteem prevention programs. Hamachek (1995) noted that school performance and "self-attitudes" (i.e., self-esteem) are interactive. D. W. Johnson, Johnson, and Taylor (1993) reported higher levels of self-esteem, achievement, and cohesion in fifth graders who participated in cooperative learning environments. Strategies for improving school performance cannot be developed without attending to using interventions to help individuals feel more positive about themselves. Educators have long been aware of the need for students to feel good about themselves and what they can do. Many schools have peer-tutoring or lower-grade-tutoring programs, peer helpers, and student aides. In such tutoring programs students are paired with students for teaching or coaching. The tutored students are either peers or, in many cases, younger students in elementary schools. Peer helper programs train selected young people in listening skills and have them talk with and listen to their peers. Student aides assist teachers and office staff. Some of these programs tend to exclude the high-risk populations.

Reasoner (1994) described several programs that have been successful in improving self-esteem and reducing crime and violence. A Florida high school program focused on positive adviser–advisee relationships and reported that within 3 weeks grade point averages and attendance, both indicators of levels of self-esteem, improved (Testerman, 1996). Still another study (McCormick & Wold, 1993) found positive changes in self-concept of gifted and talented females who had exhibited underachievement in science and math after exposure to a program describing nontraditional career choices.

Hains (1994) reported on the effectiveness of a cognitive stress management program that showed high school participants made significant improvement in anxiety, self-esteem, depression, and anger. In another cognitive restructuring program, participants were exposed either to a computer-based program that targeted irrational beliefs or a relaxation training program. Those participating in the computer-based program improved self-esteem (Horan, 1996).

A mediation intervention program was piloted at a middle school in Georgia, where results indicated a decrease in suspensions, a school morale improvement, and an increase in requests for peer mediation and the belief that it works (Thompson, 1996). Edmondson and White (1998) found significant improvement in the self-esteem of students who participated in both a tutorial and a counseling program. Conclusions drawn from a 3-year longitudinal study of urban children in Georgia stress the importance of both early and developmentally specific interventions (Spencer, 1991). Kraizer (1990) discussed skills children need to master the stresses of development. She identified a list of life skills essential to successful passage into adolescence and advocated early and continuing intervention to prevent development of inappropriate behaviors.

Because schools are community institutions and have the most contact with children, and because many services were available to families but delivery was fragmented or crisis oriented, the West Virginia Education Association and Appalachia Educational Laboratory (1993) surveyed the existing school and community partnerships in that state. In this survey process, the researchers gathered information about problems inherent in school-linked services and about additional school-linked service possibilities. With these data, the research team developed profiles for each of these social service programs and made recommendations for changes at the school, district, and policy-making levels.

School and district-level recommendations
- The responsibilities of schools should include serving as a focal point to connect families with health and social service providers.
- The mission of the school should include health and social services provision.
- Educational focus should be on prevention and early intervention.
- Schools should provide training to staff to teach them to work effectively with health and social service problems of students.
- Research and evaluation should be undertaken regularly to assess program success and recommend any needed improvements.
- Districts should establish foundations whose funds would be used to develop programs to benefit children and families. Independent sources would donate these funds. (p. 36)

Policy recommendations
- Funding for programs for at-risk populations should be provided for in the budget, which would serve to standardize school-linked programs. These programs should be protected from budget cuts.
- Early intervention and prevention programs should be given priority.
- Operational procedures of schools and service providers should be examined and changed if these procedures interfere with effective delivery of services. (p. 37)

These recommendations reflect the belief that no one group or institution is totally responsible for bringing health and social services to those community members who need them. The philosophy is that the entire community must work as a team, with the school being the common link between service providers and families.

Bernard Haldane (1989) developed the Dependable Strengths Articulation Process (DSAP) in 1948, initially for use with returning military personnel who wanted to change careers after World War II. The program has evolved and is currently being used with high school students in the state of Washington (Forster, in press). The DSAP encourages students "to articulate their strengths and use those strengths when making their most important plans." In a recent DSAP training workshop (conducted in June 2002), there were participants who have successfully used the DSAP with middle school, junior, and senior high school students. Using a prescribed set of activities, student are directed to identify strengths, get feedback from peers about strengths, prioritize them, test them for reliability, and use them when making plans. Although there were no formal data gathered from these experiences, users indicated students were more positive and more successful in school. (Meggert, 2002).

Jones and Watson (1990) studied high-risk students in higher education. Several of their findings can be considered for earlier educational experiences as well. Recommended prevention programs and strategies include the following:

- Market benefits of persistent, positive student behaviors.
- Provide career information beginning at an early age. Encourage goal identification.
- Use low-achieving college students to tutor students K–12. This raises self-esteem of each participant.
- Encourage and market counseling services as part of the curriculum. Involve teachers in the referral process.
- Provide in-class programs designed to teach positive attitudes and skills that would include acceptance of others, for example, high-risk students.
- Use peer advisers.
- Enlist school organizations to develop programs to assist fellow students.
- Provide educational programs to teach teachers how to teach. Provide opportunities for teachers to learn alternative teaching techniques and ways to empower students.
- Evaluate testing materials to see that needs of high-risk students are being assessed effectively.
- Develop orientation programs addressing the needs of high-risk populations.
- Acknowledge school personnel who work with high-risk students by reducing class loads.
- Develop methods to assure high-risk students an in-school support system. Using local businesses, provide opportunities for high-risk students to do visits, internships, or part-time work in the community. Many schools invite business people into the classroom to work with students.
- Provide programs for teachers and school personnel to examine their attitudes toward minorities, women, and other high-risk populations. (pp. 85–88)

Prevention at the Community Level

If we accept the philosophy that at-risk students, families, and the school are all part of the total community, any of the just listed strategies can be offered throughout the community and sponsored by any business or agency. Specific programs located in a major metropolitan area that may be similar to programs available in other areas are as follows:

YMCA Teen Services (1994)
- *County Youth Initiative* provides opportunities for leadership training, public speaking, project planning and delivery of community services, and employment.
- *Earth Service Corps* provides opportunities for environmental education and action, leadership development, and project planning and implementation.
- *The Manifesto Newspaper* provides an opportunity, through a youth-produced countywide newspaper, for teenagers to share their ideas and creativity with members of the community.

- *Y-Zone* provides a safe, alternative environment for youth to participate in activities and special events on a weekend night. This has expanded in adjacent communities to being available both weekend nights.
- *Youth Employment* sponsors a youth-run espresso cart at a local YMCA. The youth are hired and trained before they begin working this cart.

Central Area Youth Association (CAYA) (1992)

- *TeenPATH (Teen Parent Assistance and Transitional Housing Program)* provides assistance to homeless or near-homeless teen parents under the age of 18. The program's goal is to provide assistance to teen parents in breaking out of the poverty cycle. Through TeenPATH, stable, safe housing is found. In return, the teen parents are required to complete high school, get work training and/or employment, and be responsible parents.
- *Mentorship* assigns role models who offer companionship, guidance, and support and help empower participants to be free of gang and drug involvement.
- *STARS (Special Tutor for At-Risk Students)* provides one-on-one tutorial services to at-risk students in Grades K–8. Tutors are available both in school and after school in churches, libraries, and community centers.
- *Sports Program* provides adult role models who focus on team work, mental health, physical health, and individual and group responsibilities.
- *4-H Challenge* teaches participants, particularly minority males, coping skills, communication skills, problem-solving skills, and decision-making skills.
- *Introduction to Challenge* places youth in support groups and introduces rules, concepts, and benefits of the Challenge program.
- *Boot Camp/National Guard* introduces youth to orderly, disciplined environments and provides opportunities for building self-esteem.
- *Job Power* allows youth to explore assets and liabilities in regard to employment.
- Ropes Course provides outdoor activities to help adult and youth participants learn and develop problem-solving, goal-setting, and communication skills while experiencing total commitment.
- *I'll Take Charge* provides opportunities for youth to take responsibility for their choices.
- *Self-Determined Projects* allow members to determine, with guidance, their own projects that might not be available otherwise.
- *Multimedia* teaches students techniques and technology involved in video production while exposing them to drama, music, and arts.
- *Job Readiness* helps youth create contacts without turn-downs, teaches them job interviewing skills, and brings the community together to help youth become productive, responsible members of society.
- *Elite Boxing* provides a meaningful outlet for physically aggressive youth in a positive, acceptable manner.
- *BALANCE (Beautiful, Ambitious Ladies Able to Negotiate With Commitment to Self-Esteem and Excellence)* provides weekly support groups for young women, through which substance abuse education and services are provided (CAYA, 1992).

Nassar-McMillan and Cashwell (1997) offered adventure-based counseling as an intervention to foster self-esteem. Kennison (1996) described a similar wilderness program for youth with diagnosed attention deficit hyperactivity disorder in which activities are built to address the characteristic behaviors of this population. Another special population program, Camp Elsewhere, provided a program for adolescent girls with eating disorders, who reported the program had a positive impact on them (Tonkin, 1997). According to participants, a university-sponsored, 2-week residential leadership education program for adolescent girls had a positive impact on self-confidence (Taylor & Rosselli, 1997).

The HAWK federation focuses on issues unique to Black adolescent males and is rooted in African traditions. Initial reports indicate those who are involved have improved their academic achievement (Nobles, 1989). Delgado (1997) described a substance abuse program for Puerto Rican teenagers. Another program with a cultural focus is MAAT Center for Human and Organizational Enhancement Inc., a rites-of-passage program for Egyptian adolescents (A. R. Harvey & Coleman, 1997). (*Maat* is an Egyptian word meaning virtuous or moral life.)

Additional community programs include volunteer chore services; training to become volunteers; volunteer opportunities in social service agencies, churches, and community agencies; and community projects sponsored by individual clubs and organizations, for example, Junior Chamber of Commerce and Boys and Girls Clubs. Many of these offer training and provide built-in support and networking sources.

A Global Approach to Prevention

Seven tools that are critical to the parenting process and building of self-esteem have been identified by Glenn and Nelson (1989). These tools can also be used in schools, in the community, and by individuals. Glenn and Nelson noted that they discovered these tools, which are basic to survival in times of change, while they were studying failure, not success.

The Significant Seven
- perceptions of personal capabilities
- perceptions of personal significance
- perceptions of personal power or influence over life
- intrapersonal skills
- interpersonal skills
- systemic skills
- judgmental skills (pp. 48–49)

Perception, as described by Glenn and Nelson (1989), is "the conclusion we reach after we have had time to reflect on that experience" (p. 51). Perception guides our attitudes and behaviors, and as we mature, we become more and more creatures of perception. Perceptions include four components: "the experience, what we interpret as significant about the experience, why it is important, and how we generalize the experience" (p. 55). Because perceptions change as we mature and because they are unique to each individual, it is important that the four components reflect the perceiver's point of view. Even if an experience is shared, perceptions of the experience differ for each participant. It is significant to each person in different ways and important to each person for different reasons, and the experience is generalized individually. In terms of building self-esteem, the learner must see the personal importance and value of an experience for himself or herself. As teachers or role models, we have to suspend our own perceptions, judgments, and beliefs and genuinely and respectfully listen to the learner's perspective.

In teaching the first tool and helping young people develop a strong idea about their personal capabilities, there are some critical behaviors we have to give up (Glenn

& Nelson, 1989). We must give up assuming that we know how someone else will react in situations and acting as if that were true. We no longer need to rescue or explain, expect attainment of perfection, or dominate and control. Instead, we must learn to listen and hear individual perceptions; check out assumptions; be open to, accepting of, and respectful of a young person's thoughts and feelings; and be encouraging and celebrate successes. These changes in adult behaviors will help young people begin to feel valued and respected in the community.

As noted earlier, in the past, each family member used to feel that his or her contributions were essential to the family's maintenance and survival. For the most part, this reality has been lost. What has not been lost is the need to be needed. The individual's perception of personal significance is of primary importance. To develop this second tool, we must find ways to acknowledge each individual's personal worth, to help the individual see that the family is richer because this person is contributing his or her uniqueness. This can be done by listening, understanding, and accepting another's perspective; by soliciting ideas and perceptions from young people; by having frequent personal contact; and by providing a loving, warm family climate.

The third tool, the individual's belief in his or her ability to influence life, refers to the earlier discussion of internal versus external locus of control. Adults can help children build this internal power by establishing firm boundaries for behavior. One of the purposes for maladaptive behavior is to see if limits are real. If an adult cares enough to set limits and adhere to them, the child learns that he or she is valued and loved and knows the parameters within which to make decisions about behavior. At the same time, he or she also learns about the natural or logical consequences of stepping outside of these parameters. Children will learn from their mistakes if allowed to do so. They will build a belief system that says they have influence over their world. As already noted, adults have to be good listeners so there can be continued discussions with the child as he or she matures and encounters new decision-making opportunities.

Intrapersonal skills, the fourth tool, refer to an individual being able to understand and express feelings, to exercise self-control and self-discipline (Glenn & Nelson, 1989). As a child learns to make decisions within established boundaries, in new situations he or she can consider available responses and choose appropriately. The parent who does not allow the child to make a decision, and does it for him or her, is a primary interference here. A better intervention is to provide a list of alternatives, discuss with the child the consequences of each action (from the child's perspective), and allow the child to decide.

Interpersonal skills, the fifth tool, refer to those skills that allow people to communicate with each other. The extent to which a young person learns these skills is closely related to how well he or she gets along with others. Adults can teach these skills through modeling and talking with children.

The systemic and judgmental skills, identified by Glenn and Nelson (1989) as the sixth and seventh tools, are not always specifically taught. They are based on, composed of, and the result of earlier lessons learned. Understanding how the system in which we live works is to become aware of the connection between what we do and the result of our actions. By becoming aware of cause and effect, we learn to predict outcomes and are able to set attainable, realistic goals. We learn to be flexible and to take responsibility for our actions because we know the possible outcomes or consequences. In order for children to learn and increase these skills, adults must provide information about behavior in a caring, respectful climate. Helping an individual to develop good judgment skills requires adults to allow the person most affected by the decision to make it, to provide opportunities for young people to make decisions and experience the consequences, and to collaborate with them during the process. As part of the learning process, adults also need to help children evaluate their decisions.

ADAPTATIONS FOR DIVERSITY

Self-esteem develops within the cultural environment in which an individual lives (Hales, 1990). Culture defines how roles will be played by members. One's success or failure in fulfilling cultural role expectations influences self-esteem. Success brings with it a feeling of belonging to a group, of being an important contributing member of that culture, and of feeling good about self. Failure, of course, brings the opposite.

A problem occurs when at-risk youth belong to a nondominant culture and are faced with living in another culture, one with new or different expectations. Conflict is inevitable. A person who is respected for specific behaviors in one culture and chastised or punished for the same behavior in another could easily develop lowered self-esteem. We see evidence of this in at-risk youth today. Brendtro (1990) suggested a feeling of competence is one aspect essential to the development of self-esteem, and in the above scenario an individual may not feel competent.

Phinney (1992) suggested that continuing to identify with one's own culture as well as with the main culture is an important component of high self-esteem. Problems arise if the cultural or national group is not viewed as esteemed by other cultures/nations. Those identifying with the original culture/group may suffer low self-esteem. It becomes difficult when minorities identify with their own culture, are accepted and develop positive feelings of worth and belonging within that culture, and do not receive the same positive responses in the new culture. Ishiyama (1995) referred to this phenomenon as *cultural dislocation*. This is particularly painful when the culture of origin does not appear to be valued in the new culture, and the beliefs and values of the two cultures are divergent. We see this occurring with minorities when they experience difficulty assimilating another culture's values.

Another issue was highlighted in a recent discussion with immigrants in the State of Washington. Conflicts have emerged between those children who were born and lived in another country and culture before emigrating with their parents and those who were born in the United States after the move. Members of the same family are conflicted, some wanting to retain what is known and familiar and some wanting to "fit in" and not be associated with the "old" culture. Whatever the resolution of the conflict, it will be a direct threat to self-esteem.

Sheets (1995) and Washington (1989) discussed the impact of school culture on self-esteem. Describing different ethnic cultures, they both agreed that teaching and programs that are culturally appropriate can help minorities maintain a positive level of self-esteem and self-validation.

To add to any existing conflicts between dual cultures, norms, and values, Kumamoto (1997) explained that people's views of self and culture are changing because of the massive changes in the world today. The changing, or perhaps conflicting, guidelines for roles for everyone, regardless of culture, impact members of both the dominant and the minority cultures. With the resulting confusion, the success or failure in adapting to new ways of acting and interacting creates an additional assault on self-esteem.

In previous generations, young people had roles to play that confirmed their value as important contributors to the welfare of the family and community. This gave them a meaningful role in their community and ensured the transfer of cultural beliefs and values (Glenn & Nelson, 1989). In contemporary society, with single-parent families and population mobility, that is less likely to occur. Changes in society have provided more passive ways for values to be transmitted to the young. Roles that are depicted in the media often do not reflect appropriate cultural beliefs and values, and many young people do not have multiple adult role models who can correct inappropriate perceptions of behaviors and beliefs illustrated in the media.

CASE STUDY: PROJECT REACH

Project Reach is an alternative program for at-risk students in the Socorro School District in Texas (Heger, 1992). Students in this program were in serious trouble in school and had reached the stage at which the next step was expulsion. Health education, drama, group therapy, and computer-assisted instruction were blended in a program designed to prevent dropouts or expulsions and to assist in the reintegration of these at-risk students into the mainstream.

The curriculum was a traditional curriculum delivered in a nontraditional way, through computers. In the remaining time during the school day, students participated in health and drug education, drama, and personal log writing. The psychological part of the program is described as similar to "Tough Love" and "Boot Camp," which are highly structured programs that leave no doubt as to limits and consequences of misbehavior.

The school day started at 11 a.m. and continued into early evening, and admission was for an undetermined length of time. Students had levels of tasks to complete, and when these stages were accomplished, they were readmitted into the mainstream. The pace of progress was individualized.

Evaluators found dramatic results. Attrition rates went from 84% in 1990–1991 to 2.9% in 1992–1993. At the same time, 76% of the students reported better grades. Students were surveyed periodically, and 86% believed the program was helpful to them. The longer they were in the program, the more helpful they reported it to be.

Success of this program is attributed to the design, the staff, and the execution. Staff members were from nontraditional backgrounds, and many had turned to teaching after trying other occupations. Some were not fully certified, but all had prior experience in helping people in nontraditional curricula.

SUMMARY

In our society, young people daily exhibit deviant behaviors. There is evidence every day that there are many more adolescents demonstrating characteristics that are understood to be at risk. These young people are considered at risk because unless they are helped to succeed, they will become part of the deviant subculture. Research has shown that there is a connection between how a person feels about himself or herself and how that person acts (Kaplan, 1975; Kaplan et al., 1986; Marston et al., 1988). Self-esteem is an issue that must be confronted as a cause of at-risk behaviors.

This chapter identifies specific symptoms of low self-esteem, factors that influence self-esteem and prevention programs, and strategies for parents, individuals, schools, and communities. The activities and programs designed to be used with at-risk youth are not extensive. We must look within our own communities to discover available and successful youth programs. Additional information and resources may also be found in popular magazines (Corbett in *Essence*, 1995; Cordes in *Parenting*, 1994; Herman in *Utne Reader*, 1992; McMahon in *Cosmopolitan*, 1994; McMillan, Singh, & Simonetta in *Education Digest*, 1995; Tafel in *McCalls*, 1992). Carlock's book, *Enhancing Self-Esteem* (1999), identifies many books and educational audio and video cassettes that focus on building self-esteem. The goal is to reach all adolescents, particularly those at risk, and give them a chance to succeed and feel worthwhile.

REFERENCES

Abramson, L. Y., Seligman, M. E. P., & Teasdale, J. D. (1978). Learned helplessness in humans. Critique and reformulation. *Journal of Abnormal Psychology, 87*, 49–74.

Aronson, M., & Mettee, S. (1968). Dishonest behavior as a function of differential levels of induced self-esteem. *Journal of Personality and Social Psychology, 9*, 121–127.

Bachman, J. G., & O'Malley, P. M. (1986). The frog's pond revisited (again). *Journal of Personality and Social Psychology, 50*, 35–46.

Barber, B. K., Chadwick, B. A., & Orter, R. (1992). Parental behaviors and adolescent self-esteem in the United States and Germany. *Journal of Marriage and Family Therapy, 54*, 128–141.

Beane, J. A., & Lipka, R. P. (1980). Self-concept and self-esteem: A construct differentiation. *Child Study Journal, 10*, 1–6.

Benoit, R. B., & Mitchell L. K. (1987). Self-efficacy: Its nature and promise as an approach to dealing with high school dropout among minorities. *CACD Journal, 8*, 31–38.

Blake, P. C., & Slate, J. R. (1993). A preliminary investigation into the relationship between adolescent self-esteem and parental verbal interaction. *The School Counselor, 41*(2), 81–85.

Bower, B. (1993). Gender paths wind toward self-esteem: Gender differences in self-esteem development. *Science News, 143*(20), 308.

Brendtro, L. K. (1990). *Reclaiming youth at-risk: Our hope for the future.* Bloomington, IN: National Education Service.

Buri, J. R., & Dickinson, K. A. (1994, May). *Comparison of familial and cognitive factors associated with male and female self-esteem.* Paper presented at the annual meeting of the Midwestern Psychological Association, Chicago.

Buri, J. R., & Kircher, A. (1993, April). *Parental hostility, adolescent high standards, and self-esteem.* Paper presented at the annual meeting of the Midwestern Psychological Association, Chicago.

Burnett, J. W., Anderson, W. P., & Heppner, P. P. (1995). Gender roles and self-esteem: A consideration of environmental factors. *Journal of Counseling & Development, 73*, 323-326.

Cantor, D., & Bernay, T. (1992) *Women in power: The secrets of leadership.* Boston: Houghton Mifflin.

Carlock, J. (Ed.). (1999). *Enhancing self-esteem.* Philadelphia: Accelerated Development.

Central Area Youth Association (CAYA). (1992). *A history and overview* [Paper and brochures]. (Available from CAYA, 119 23rd Ave., Seattle, WA 98122)

Cerezo, M., & Frias, D. (1994, November). Emotional and cognitive adjustment in abused children. *Child Abuse and Neglect: The International Journal, 18*, 23–32.

Chapman, P. L., & Mullis, R. L. (1999). Adolescent coping strategies and self-esteem. *Child Study Journal, 29*, 69–77.

Cohen, L. H., Burt, C. E., & Bjorck, J. P. (1987). Life stress and adjustment: Effect on life events experienced by young adolescents and their parents. *Developmental Psychology, 23*, 583–592.

Corbett, C. (1995). The winner within: A hands-on guide to healthy self-esteem. *Essence, 26*(2), 56–70.

Cordes, H. (1994). Resources: Groups, books, magazines, and other tools for building girls' self-esteem. *Parenting, 8*(3), 96.

Delgado, M. (1997). Strengths-based practice with Puerto Rican adolescents: Lessons from a substance abuse prevention project. *Social Work in Education, 19*(2), 101–112.

Domino, G., & Blumberg, E. (1987). An application of Gough's conceptual model to a measure of adolescent self-esteem. *Journal of Youth and Adolescence, 16*(2), 87–90.

Dwyer, V. (1993). Eye of the beholder: Young women have self-image problems. *Maclean's, 106*(8), 46-47.

Edmondson, J. H., & White, J. (1998). A tutorial and counseling program: Helping students at risk of dropping out of school. *Professional School Counseling, 1*(4), 43–47.

Elliott, G. C. (1988). Gender differences in self-consistency: Evidence from an investigation of self-concept structure. *Journal of Youth and Adolescence, 17*(1), 41–57.

Emler, N. (2001). *Self-esteem: The costs and causes of low self-esteem.* York, UK: York Publishing Services.

Enns, C. (1992). Self-esteem groups: A synthesis of consciousness-raising and assertiveness training. *Journal of Counseling & Development, 71*, 7–13.

Eskilson, A., Wiley, G., Meuhlbauer, G., & Dodder, L. (1986). Parental pressure, self-esteem, and adolescent reported deviance: Bending the twig too far. *Adolescence, 21*(83), 501–515.

Forster, J. R. (in press). Your best plans must use your best strengths. In S. Wakefield (Ed.), *Unfocused kids: Innovative practices to help students focus on their plans after high school; a resource for educators.* Greensboro: University of North Carolina, ERIC/Cass.

Frey, D., & Carlock, C. J. (1984). *Enhancing self-esteem.* Muncie, IN: Accelerated Development.

Glenn, H. S., & Nelson, J. (1989). *Raising self-reliant children in a self-indulgent world.* Rocklin, CA: Prima.

Graf, R. C. (1971). Induced self-esteem as a determinant of behavior. *Journal of Social Psychology, 85*, 213–217.

Hains, A. A. (1994). The effectiveness of a school-based, cognitive–behavioral stress management program with adolescents reporting high and low levels of emotional arousal. *School Counselor, 42*(2), 114–125.

Haldane, B. (1989, March). *The Dependable Strengths Articulation Process: How it works.* Paper presented at the annual convention of the American Association for Counseling and Development, Boston.

Hales, S. (1990, Winter). Valuing the self: Understanding the nature of self-esteem. *The Saybrook Perspective,* 3–17.

Hamachek, D. (1995). Self-concept and school achievement: Interaction dynamics and a tool for assessing the self-concept component. *Journal of Counseling & Development, 73*, 419–423.

Harvey, A. R., & Coleman, A. A. (1997). An Afrocentric program for African American males in the juvenile justice system. *Child Welfare, 76*(1), 197–211.

Harvey, M., & Byrd, M. (1998). The relationship between perceptions of self-esteem, patterns of familial attachment and family environment during early and late phases of adolescence. *International Journal of Adolescence and Youth, 7*(2), 93–111.

Heger, H. K. (1992, October). *Retaining Hispanic youth in school: An evaluation of a counseling-based alternative school program.* Paper presented at the annual conference of the Rocky Mountain Educational Research Association, Stillwater, OK.

Herman, E. (1992, January/February). Are politics and therapy compatible? A lesson from the self-esteem movement. *Utne Reader,* 97–100.

Horan, J. J. (1996). Effects of computer-based cognitive restructuring on rationally mediated self-esteem. *Journal of Counseling Psychology, 43*, 371–375.

Ishiyama, F. I. (1995). Culturally dislocated clients: Self-validation and cultural conflict issues and counseling implications. *Canadian Journal of Counseling, 29*, 262–273.

Jason, L. A., Weine, A. M., Johnson, J. H., Danner, K. E., Kurasaki, K. S., & Warren-Sohlberg, L. (1993). The school transition project: A comprehensive preventative intervention. *Journal of Emotional and Behavioral Disorders, 1*, 65–70.

Johnson, D. S. (1981). Naturally acquired learned helplessness: The relationship of school failure to achievement behavior, attributions, and self-concept. *Journal of Educational Psychology, 73*, 174–180.

Johnson, D. W., Johnson, R. T., & Taylor, B. (1993). Impact of cooperative and individualistic learning on high-ability students' achievement, self-esteem, and social acceptance. *Journal of Social Psychology, 133*, 839–844.

Jones, D. J., & Watson, B. C. (1990). *High-risk students and higher education.* Washington, DC: George Washington University, Clearinghouse on Higher Education.

Kaplan, H. B. (1975). *Self-attitudes and deviant behavior.* Pacific Palisades, CA: Goodyear.

Kaplan, H. B. (1976). Self-attitude and deviant response. *Social Forces, 54,* 788–801.

Kaplan, H. B., Martin, S. S., & Johnson, R. J. (1986). Self-rejection and the explanation of deviance: Specification of the structure among latent constructs. *American Journal of Sociology, 92,* 384–411.

Kashani, J. H., Jones, M. R., Bumby, K. M., & Thomas, L. A. (1999). Youth violence: Psychosocial risk factors, treatment, prevention, and recommendations. *Journal of Emotional and Behavioral Disorders, 7,* 200–210.

Kelly, T. M., Lynch, K. G., Donovan, J. E., & Clark, D. B. (2001). Alcohol use disorders and risk factor interactions for adolescent suicidal ideation and attempts. *Suicide and Life-Threatening Behavior, 32,* 181–193.

Kennison, J. A. (1996). Therapy in the mountains. *Proceedings of the 1995 International Conference on Outdoor Recreation and Education.*

Kraizer, S. (1990). Skills for living: The requirement of the 90s. In *Critical issues in prevention of child abuse and neglect: Adolescent parenting life skills for children* (pp. 131–139). Austin: Children's Trust Fund of Texas.

Kumamoto, C. C. (1997, March). *Unison in variety, congeniality in difference: Sifting beyond the multicultural sieve.* Paper presented at the annual meeting of the Conference on College Composition and Communication, Phoenix, AZ.

Leung, K., & Drasgow, F. (1986, June). Relation between self-esteem and delinquent behavior in three ethnic groups. *Journal of Cross-Cultural Psychology, 17,* 151–167.

Lord, S., EccIes, J. S., & McCarthy, K. A. (1994). Surviving junior high school transition: Family processes and self-perceptions as protective and risk factors. *Journal of Early Adolescence, 14,* 162–199.

Lorr, M., & Wunderlich, R. A. (1986). Two objective measures of self-esteem. *Journal of Personality Assessment, 50,* 18–23.

Mack, J. E., & Ablon, S. L. (Eds.). (1983). *The development and sustenance of self-esteem in childhood.* New York: International Universities Press.

Marston, A. R., Jacobs, D. F., Singer, R. D., Widaman, K. F., & Little, T. D. (1988). Characteristics of adolescents at risk for compulsive overeating on a brief screening test. *Adolescence, 23*(89), 59–72.

Masche, J. G. (2000, March). *Does a happy marriage make positive parent–adolescent relationships and self-satisfied children?* Paper presented at the biennial meeting of the Society for Research on Adolescence, Chicago.

Maternal and Child Health Branch, Hawaii State Department of Health. (1991). *Adolescent health in Hawaii: The Adolescent Health Network's teen health advisor report.* Rockville, MD: Health Resources and Services Administration.

McCormick, M. E., & Wold, J. S. (1993). Programs for gifted girls. *Roeper Review, 16*(2), 85-88.

McCready, K. (1997, Spring). At-risk youth and leisure: An ecological perspective. *Journal of Leisurability, 24*(2). Retrieved from www.lin.ca/resource/html/Vol24/v24n2a5.htm

McDowell, J. (1984). *Building your self-image.* Wheaton, IL: Living Books.

McGee, R., & Williams, S. (2000). Does low self-esteem predict health compromising behaviours among adolescents? *Journal of Adolescence, 23,* 569–582.

McMahon, S. (1994). Let us now praise me. *Cosmopolitan, 217*(2), 6–70.

McMillan, J. H., Singh, J., & Simonetta, L. G. (1995). Self-oriented self-esteem self-destructs. *Education Digest, 60*(7), 9–12.

Meggert, S. S. (2002, June). [Communications at Dependable Strengths Articulation Process training, University of Washington, Seattle, WA].

Nassar-McMillan, S. C., & Cashwell, C. S. (1997). Building self-esteem of children and adolescents through adventure based counseling. *Journal of Humanistic Education and Development, 36*(2), 59–67.

Nobles, W. W. (1989, July). *The HAWK Federation and the development of Black adolescent males: Toward a solution to the crises of America's young Black men.* Testimony before the Select Committee on Children, Youth, and Families in the Congressional Hearings on America's Young Black Men: Isolated and in Trouble, Washington, DC.

Ohannesian, C., Lerner, R., Lerner, J.V., & Von Eye, A. (1994). A longitudinal study of perceived family adjustment and emotional adjustment in early adolescents. *Journal of Early Adolescence, 14*, 370–390.

Phinney, J. S. (1992). Acculturation attitudes and self-esteem among high school and college students. *Youth and Society, 23*, 299–312.

Portes, P. R., & Zady, M. F. (2000, April) *Cultural differences in the self-esteem and adaptation of Spanish-speaking second generation adolescents.* Paper presented at the annual meeting of the American Educational Research Association, New Orleans, LA.

Reasoner, R. W. (1994). *Self-esteem as an antidote to crime and violence.* Paper prepared for the National Council for Self-Esteem.

Robison-Awana, P., Kehle, T. J., & Jenson, W. R. (1986). But what about smart girls? Adolescent self-esteem and sex role perceptions as a function of academic achievement. *Journal of Educational Psychology, 78*, 179–183.

Rosenberg, M. (1965). *Society and the adolescent self-image.* Princeton, NJ: Princeton University Press.

Saltzman, A. (1994, November 7). Schooled in failure? Fact or myth—teachers favor boys; girls respond by withdrawing. *U.S. News & World Report*, 88–93.

Sheets, R. H. (1995). From remedial to gifted: Effects of culturally centered pedagogy. *Theory Into Practice, 34*, 186–193.

Shek, D. T. L. (1997). Family environment and adolescent psychological well-being, school adjustment and problem behavior: A pioneer study in a Chinese contest. *Journal of Genetic Psychology, 153*(1), 113–128.

Sim, T. N. (2000). Adolescent psychosocial competence: The importance and role of regard for parents. *Journal of Research on Adolescence, 10*, 49–64.

Simmons, R. C., Burgeson, R., Carlton-Ford, S., & Blyth, D. A. (1987). Impact of cumulative change in early adolescence. *Child Development, 58*, 1220–1234.

Spencer, M. B. (1991). *Adolescent African American male self-esteem: Suggestions for mentoring program content* (Mentoring program structures for young minority males conference paper series). Washington, DC: Urban Institute.

Tafel, R. (1992). How your self-esteem affects your child's. *McCalls, 119*(6), 40–42.

Taylor, E. L., & Rosselli, H. (1997, March). *The effect of a single gender leadership program on young women.* Paper presented at the annual meeting of the American Educational Research Association, Chicago.

Testerman, J. (1996). Holding at-risk students. *Phi Delta Kappan, 77*(5), 364–365.

Thompson, S. M. (1996). Peer mediation: A peaceful solution. *School Counselor, 44*(2), 151–154.

Tonkin, R. S. (1997). Evaluation of a summer camp for adolescents with eating disorders. *Journal of Adolescent Health, 20*, 412–413.

Washington, E. D. (1989). A componential theory of culture and its implications for African-American identify. *Equity and Excellence, 24*(2), 24–30.

West Virginia Education Association and Appalachia Educational Laboratory. (1993). *Schools as community social-service centers: West Virginia programs and possibilities.* (Available from Appalachia Educational Laboratory, PO Box 1348, Charleston, WV 25325)

Yanish, D. L., & Battle, J. (1985). Relationship between self-esteem, depression, and alcohol consumption among adolescents. *Psychological Reports, 57*, 331–334.

Yankelovich, Y. D. (1981). *New rules: Search for self-fulfillment in a world turned upside down.* New York: Random House.

YMCA. (1994). *YMCA teen services* [Flyer]. Seattle, WA: Author.

6 | Preventing and Treating Depression and Bipolar Disorders in Children and Adolescents

Benedict T. McWhirter and Jason J. Burrow-Sanchez

The incidence, nature, and treatment of depression and bipolar disorders during childhood and adolescence have been a topic of extensive research in recent years (Birmaher, Ryan, Williamson, Brent, & Kaufman, 1996; Kovacs & Devlin, 1998; Lewinsohn, Rohde, & Seeley, 1998; Michael & Crowley, 2002; Wagner & Ambrosini, 2001). Currently, depression in youth is viewed as a significant problem that affects approximately 30% of the adolescent population (Lewinsohn, Hops, Roberts, Seeley, & Andrew, 1993) and between 2% and 5% of younger children (Milling & Martin, 1992). In fact, one in five youth reports a minimum of one episode of major depression by the age of 18 (Lewinsohn et al., 1993). The incidence of childhood bipolar disorder, or early-onset bipolar disorder, is less clear because of common problems of misdiagnosis, but it is estimated that one out of every three children diagnosed with attention deficit hyperactivity disorder (ADHD) is actually bipolar, which suggests that over 1 million children in the United States suffer from this problem (Papolos & Papolos, 1999). Furthermore, the prevention of depression and bipolar disorders in childhood and adolescence is critical to reducing the high cost of treating these disorders among adults (King, 1991). Therefore, child and adolescent depression and bipolar disorders are major phenomena and deserve the full attention of mental health and educational professionals.

In this chapter, we focus on the problem of child and adolescent depression and bipolar disorders. First, we present some definitional and diagnostic issues associated with these disorders. For brevity, we refer to *mood disorders* in this chapter when we are discussing both childhood and adolescent depression and bipolar or early-onset bipolar disorders. We use each of these terms separately when we discuss etiology, treatment, and other issues that are unique to depression and to early-onset bipolar disorders as appropriate to do so. Next, we describe the story of Esteban, a Latino adolescent who is struggling with depression, as one way to illustrate some of its causes and interventions. We then discuss some of the causal factors associated with mood disorders and present prevention and treatment strategies that have been found to be effective for children and adolescents suffering from mood disorders. The strategies that we discuss include interventions at the individual, family, school, and community levels. We conclude this chapter with an exploration of how the various prevention and treatment strategies discussed can be combined to form a comprehensive response to young people experiencing these difficult problems.

PROBLEM DEFINITION AND DIAGNOSTIC ISSUES

Until recently, depression in childhood and adolescence was not well addressed in the psychological literature. Early concepts such as "adolescent turmoil" and the "masked depression" model either led practitioners to discount depression or hindered their understanding of depression in childhood and adolescence. For instance, adolescent turmoil suggests that all adolescents go through a period of turmoil that may appear to be pathological (Garrison, Shoenbach, & Kaplan, 1985). But the symptoms of inner unrest and deviant behavior that characterize adolescent turmoil were thought to be a normal part of adolescence and, therefore, clinically unimportant (Garrison et al., 1985). The notion of masked depression also confused, rather than clarified, this clinical problem. This model suggested that although depression is experienced in childhood and adolescence, it is not manifested as such. Instead, it is masked by other behaviors associated with depression. These include anxiety, aggressiveness, delinquency, somatic complaints, substance use, poor peer relationships, negative body image, poor school performance, school phobia, loss of initiative, social withdrawal, and sleep difficulties (Aseltine, Gore, & Colten, 1998; Lewinsohn, Clarke, Rohde, Hops, & Seeley, 1996; Miller-Johnson, Lochman, Coie, Terry, & Hyman, 1998; Windle & Windle, 1997).

Current research, however, has refuted those ideas, and experts agree that depression in childhood and adolescence is a valid psychological disorder. In fact, adolescents seen in mental health centers are most frequently diagnosed with an affective disorder, of which depression is one example (Marcotte, 1997). Extensive research efforts to understand the course of depression in children and adolescents, and to find efficacious treatment, have more recently been undertaken. It is now known that youth who have had depression are likely to have another episode within a few years (Birmaher, Ryan, Williamson, Brent, Kaufman, Dahl, et al., 1996; Kovacs & Devlin, 1998; Lewinsohn et al., 1998). So, addressing mood disorders among children and adolescents is critical, and the first step toward this end is to clarify procedures for diagnosis.

For the last four decades, the most widely used diagnosis and classification system has been the *Diagnostic and Statistical Manual of Mental Disorders (DSM)*, published by the American Psychiatric Association. The revised, third edition, *DSM–III–R* (1987), began the clarification and classification of depression in children and adolescents by providing symptom descriptions. The next versions, *DSM–IV* (1994) and most recent *DSM–IV–TR* (2000), added precision to the diagnosis of depression and bipolar disorders in childhood and adolescence. For instance, the *DSM–IV–TR* has addressed differential aspects of adolescent depressive symptomatology as opposed to common symptoms experienced by adults. The *DSM–IV–TR* also attends more to population-specific differences. For example, it reports that in childhood the rates of depression are relatively equal between boys and girls, but during adolescence girls begin to demonstrate increased rates of depression that more closely parallel the gender differences found in adulthood (Birmaher, Ryan, Williamson, Brent, Kaufman, Dahl, et al., 1996; Kazdin, 1994; Lewinsohn et al., 1998). There is further symptom delineation between prepubescent children and adolescents. For example, children commonly display irritable mood rather than depressed mood, somatic complaints, and social withdrawal, whereas depressed adolescents typically display psychomotor retardation and hypersomnia. Furthermore, depression is comorbid in childhood and adolescence more often than in adulthood (Rohde, Lewinsohn, & Seeley, 1991). Prepubertal children typically display major depressive episodes in conjunction with disruptive behavior disorders, attention deficit disorders, and anxiety disorders (American Psychiatric Association, 2000; Kovacs & Devlin, 1998). Adolescent depression is more commonly associated with anxiety, disruptive behavior disorders, attention deficit disorders, substance-related disorders, and eating disorders (American Psychiatric Association, 2000; Birmaher, Ryan, Williamson, Brent, Kaufman, Dahl, et al., 1996; Lewinsohn et al., 1996). In addition, the depressed adolescent is likely to have a depressotypic cognitive style, negative body image, less social support (peer and familial), and more conflictual family interactions than their nondepressed peers.

In the *DSM–IV–TR* (American Psychiatric Association, 2000), mood disorders are divided into three major categories: depressive disorders, bipolar disorders, and mood disorders due to a general medical condition. The depressive disorders include major depressive disorder, characterized by one or more depressive episodes without history of mania, and dysthymic disorder, characterized by conditions indicating mood disturbance that has been chronic or intermittent for at least 2 years but without the degree of severity to warrant a diagnosis of major depressive disorder. Bipolar disorders include Bipolar I disorder, Bipolar II disorder, and cyclothymic disorder. The bipolar disorders are distinguished by the presence of a manic episode. Cyclothymia, of course, is a milder form of bipolar disorder. The final category includes mood disturbances judged to be of medical etiology. This condition is found with increasing frequency among younger populations. The *DSM–IV–TR* also includes specifiers such as seasonal pattern indicators (i.e., seasonal affective disorder) in which people become more depressed during certain times of the year. Practitioners should also pay attention to adjustment disorders that may be accompanied by depressed mood as another important diagnostic category.

Although we primarily focus on depressive disorders in this chapter, it is also important to briefly consider the nature of bipolar disorders. Specifically, bipolar disorder is a serious mental condition that can negatively affect the normal functioning of children and adolescents. Young people suffering from this disorder may experience extreme episodes of mania and depression that switch very frequently and on a much shorter time interval than commonly found in adults. Based on the limited epidemiological data available, it appears that bipolar disorder is more prevalent in children after puberty (James & Javaloyes, 2001; Lewinsohn, Klein, & Seeley, 1995) but occurs as early-onset bipolar disorder with some frequency. Available evidence suggests that the rates of mania in adolescence are similar to the rates in adulthood (i.e., approximately 1%; Lewinsohn et al., 1995). Reported prevalence rates also vary depending on how strictly *DSM* criteria were applied in research studies (Carlson & Kashani, 1988).

Much of the current information on bipolar disorders in childhood and adolescence has been extrapolated from the adult literature. For example, this disorder is diagnosed for young people using the same *DSM* criteria as used for adults. Both types of bipolar disorder (i.e., Bipolar I and II) can be experienced in a rapid cycling fashion (i.e., rapidly changing episodes of manic and depressive symptoms). Research findings suggest that young children and adolescents with bipolar disorder initially experience a depressive episode, and then subsequent episodes (either manic, depressive, or both) occur in a rapid cycle manner (Geller & Luby, 1997; Papolos & Papolos, 1999). In one study of young depressed children, between 20% and 30% of the sample later experienced manic symptoms, suggesting that the earlier diagnosis of depression was probably incorrect (Geller, Fox, & Clark, 1994).

Bipolar disorders are often misdiagnosed in children and adolescents. Sanchez, Hagino, Weller, and Ronald (1999) suggested that misdiagnosis partially stems from

(a) a low rate of occurrence of the disorder in child and adolescent populations and (b) the fact that many symptoms overlap with other common childhood disorders such as ADHD and conduct disorder. Additional differential diagnostic issues and comorbid conditions for the practitioner to consider include language disorders, oppositional defiant disorder, sexual abuse, schizophrenia, and substance abuse (Geller & Luby, 1997). At a minimum, James and Javaloyes (2001) suggested that an accurate diagnosis will include clinical interviews with relevant individuals from the child's family and school environments. In addition, they suggested complete physical and biochemical examinations for the child or adolescent because certain medical conditions such as neurological diseases, Cushing's syndrome, use of antidepressants, and substance abuse can produce symptoms of mania (James & Javaloyes, 2001).

The clinical presentation of bipolar disorder varies depending on the age of the child. For example, younger children may present with disruptive behaviors, impulsivity, inattention, and overall moodiness (Sanchez et al., 1999). To complicate matters, periods of manic and depressive symptoms may cycle so rapidly that discrete episodes can be difficult to determine in children. In contrast, adolescents present with symptoms that are more similar to the adult presentation of the disorder. Specifically, some adolescents may experience psychotic features (e.g., hallucinations, delusions, thought disorders) that are associated with adult bipolar disorder. Children additionally experience horrible nightmares, massive carbohydrate cravings, and sleep and digestive system disturbances. (See Geller et al., 1995, for a more complete review of the clinical presentation of early-onset bipolar disorders in children and adolescents.)

In summary, the *DSM–IV–TR* (American Psychiatric Association, 2000) can be a useful tool for the clarification and diagnosis of childhood and adolescent mood disorders including depression and bipolar disorder. For example, practitioners can use the diagnostic criteria sets in the *DSM–IV–TR* as a way to identify the presence or absence of specific depressive or bipolar symptoms in young individuals. It certainly can be helpful for assisting the young man in the following story.

CASE STUDY

Esteban was a 15-year-old Mexican American high school sophomore who was referred to counseling at a community mental health center by his mother after he threatened to kill her with a kitchen knife. He had straight black hair, which was long on top and shaved from one inch above his ears on down. He had an earring in his left ear, crooked teeth, jeans that were fashionably oversized and hanging below his waistline, and an untucked flannel shirt. Esteban attended a school where the majority of students were European American from middle-class backgrounds. In our first session, Esteban sat silently and played with his hands while his mother provided information about the family and described her concerns.

Esteban had two sisters, Reynalda ("Reina"), age 16, and Catalina, age 13. His mother, Irma, and his father, Reynaldo, were married when they were 18 and 20, respectively. According to Irma, Reynaldo began a series of extramarital affairs shortly after Esteban was born. He had always been a heavy drinker and lost his job with the mining company after "too many Monday flus." The family environment described by Irma included harsh and inconsistent discipline by Reynaldo and guilt-induced permissiveness by Irma, in a context of poverty, frequent moves, and anxiety regarding Reynaldo's next binge. On several occasions, Reynaldo hit Irma in front of the children and was frequently verbally abusive toward her. Irma had finally divorced Reynaldo

3 years ago, and within 2 months he was remarried to an 18-year-old. Currently, Irma was working the 3–11 p.m. shift at a factory. Reynaldo has had intermittent contact with his children since the divorce. Reina and Esteban "hated" their father's new wife, Tina, and Reynaldo refused to spend time with them apart from Tina.

Irma described Esteban as a sweet little boy who had grown into a monster like his father. When he entered high school last year, his grade point average began slipping, he started to smoke, and he skipped classes. Whenever Irma confronted him, she reported that Esteban would use the same verbally abusive language that his father used, such as "It's none of your business, you dirty whore." He refused to help out around the house and spent most of his time locked in his room listening to rap and hip-hop CDs with "a girl who dresses like a boy." When asked whether she had concerns about sexual activity between Esteban and this young woman, Irma said scornfully, "Even if she did want it—and that girl don't want it—he wouldn't know what to do." Esteban visibly flinched as she said this—his first overt reaction since arriving in the office.

Irma made the appointment for Esteban after an argument in which he shouted, "If you don't leave me alone I'm going to come after you with that big ol' fuckin' knife! Everybody hates you, and if I killed you they would laugh." Irma said that although she didn't think Esteban would kill her or even attempt to hurt her, she was frightened by the hatred in his voice. When asked what she hoped counseling would accomplish, she said, "Find my sweet little boy and bring him back to me."

The remainder of that first session was spent alone with Esteban. As soon as his mother left he asked if he could smoke. That was his only question and his only spontaneous communication. It quickly became obvious that he was painfully shy, embarrassed, and very nervous. His brief answers to questions did not seem to convey hostility or resentment but a profound sense of frustration and inadequacy. Additional information slowly emerged in the one-on-one meeting. His mother had a string of boyfriends, none of whom he liked; he communicated very little with his siblings and knew nothing of how they felt; and he had only one friend—the aforementioned "girl who don't want it"—who did, in fact, "want it" but so far had only permitted him to lie in bed naked with her. This they did regularly while listening to CDs and smoking cigarettes. When asked how he felt toward others—his mother, teachers, people at school—he stated, unconvincingly, that he hated them. He frequently stated, more convincingly, that he didn't care or didn't know about much of what was going on around him most of the time.

In subsequent sessions, Esteban began to communicate more openly, using longer sentences and asking more questions. It was clear that Esteban lacked many basic social skills. He spent much of his time at home while his mother worked. Often, her current boyfriend would hang out there while she worked. Esteban didn't like this, but it was the only time that he would talk with his sisters—they would hang out in his room to avoid their mother's boyfriends. There were no indications of any attempted sexual contact between any of the boyfriends and the three children. Esteban indicated that he was embarrassed to ask his teachers for help and so he never tried to talk to them. He also reported that he felt responsible for his father's behavior—that if he wasn't the way that he was, his father would not have been a drunk and been so violent.

Esteban seemed to hate himself as much, if not more, than others around him. He was clearly experiencing a great deal of pain, frustration, guilt, and depression. Although he did not want to feel so isolated from others, he felt "stuck" and had never been taught the skills to move forward.

CAUSAL FACTORS

Esteban's depression could have been caused by any number of factors. In this section, we describe some of the more central causal and conceptual models of mood disorders—biological, psychodynamic, behavioral, cognitive, and family systems—and how each of these models might apply to Esteban. In the next section, we discuss how these causal models might flow into effective prevention and treatment for Esteban and young people struggling like him.

Biological Models of Mood Disorders

Biological models of mood disorders can be divided into two main categories: those that focus on the role of genetic factors and those that emphasize biochemical aspects of depression. There is a strong genetic component in the risk of depression (Kovacs & Devlin, 1998). Based on adult twin and adoption research, genetic factors account for approximately 50% of the variance in the transmission of mood disorders (Birmaher, Ryan, Williamson, Brent, Kaufman, Dahl, et al., 1996). These studies also report that children of depressed parents are three times more likely to have a major depressive episode at some point during their lives; this likelihood increases when the parent has had multiple depressive episodes (Garber & Robinson, 1997). Moreover, in studies of depressed children, 25% to 54% of first-degree relatives and approximately 15% of second-degree relatives have major depression (Kovacs & Devlin, 1998). The genetic links for bipolar disorder are typically much stronger than for depressive disorders (Papolos & Papolos, 1999). The specific nature of genetic transmission has not been determined, and further studies using children and adolescents may help to clarify the genetic contributions to the onset and maintenance of mood disorders.

Another biological model of depression focuses on biochemical processes such as growth hormones, serotonergic systems, hypothalamus-pituitary-adrenal axis, and so forth (Birmaher, Ryan, Williamson, Brent, Kaufman, Dahl, et al., 1996). Neurotransmitter actions and their interactions with antidepressant medications have been the focus of much biochemical research on depression. Whether a primary cause of depression or a secondary component, some evidence suggests that abnormalities in the metabolism of neurotransmitters are present in people who experience mood disorders and can be counteracted with antidepressant drugs. Research indicates more success in treating depressed adults with antidepressant medication, but studies with children and adolescents continue to focus on pharmacological interventions with youth (Ambrosini, 2000; Birmaher, Ryan, Williamson, Brent, & Kaufman, 1996; Wagner & Ambrosini, 2001; Ziervogel, 2000).

Although psychopharmacological interventions are commonly and successfully used with adults, the results with youth have not been as promising (Ambrosini, 2000; Birmaher, Ryan, Williamson, Brent, & Kaufman, 1996; Michael & Crowley, 2002; Wagner & Ambrosini, 2001; Ziervogel, 2000). To date, most medication trials have used tricyclic antidepressants (TCAs; e.g., amitriptyline, imipramine) and have failed to demonstrate significant differences between the active medications and the placebos (Ambrosini, 2000; Emslie & Mayes, 2001; Michael & Crowley, 2002). For example, Michael and Crowley (2002) reviewed 11 studies using TCAs and 2 studies using selective serotonin reuptake inhibitors (SSRIs) for depressed youth. They found TCAs to have serious side effects and did not perform significantly better than a placebo. Studies with SSRIs have found less negative side effects and the results have been more promising in treating depression, but limited research exists in this area for young populations (Ambrosini, 2000; Michael & Crowley, 2002; Wagner & Ambrosini, 2001; Ziervogel, 2000). One must interpret the results of the pharmacotherapy findings for children and adolescents with caution. Specifically, many of the trials had small or heterogeneous sample sizes, used the medications for a short duration, or did not obtain self-report information on the participants' perceived mood in addition to the doctors' reports. In addition, there has not been enough controlled research conducted with SSRIs with adults or with adolescents to draw firm conclusions at this point (Ambrosini, 2000; Michael & Crowley, 2002; Wagner & Ambrosini, 2001). It is clear that biological and chemical functioning of the developing child or adolescent reacts differently to traditional antidepressants that have been efficacious with adults; further investigation is warranted to determine appropriate use of antidepressants with children and adolescents (Ambrosini, 2000; Birmaher, Ryan, Williamson, Brent, & Kaufman, 1996; Michael & Crowley, 2002; Wagner & Ambrosini, 2001).

In Esteban's case, evidence suggests that both of his parents may have experienced some form of mood disorder. Both his mother's pattern of developing relationships and his father's alcoholism and abusiveness support the notion that they suffered from a lack of coping skills and poor self-esteem, which is almost always a concomitant of depression. The weakness of this model in explaining Esteban's depression is that it does not attend to the profound impact of Esteban's environment in contributing to his behavior and feelings about himself and others.

Psychodynamic Models of Depression

Psychodynamic models of depression focus on the loss of meaning or satisfaction in one's life and its effect on self-esteem regulation (Bemporad, 1988; Wolf, 1988). Depression is generally expressed in one of two ways: anger turned inward or feelings of emptiness and loss.

Heightened self-blame and rejection, often linked with the failure to live up to an idealized view of oneself, are viewed as reflections of anger turned inward (Wolf, 1988). Low self-esteem develops because it is impossible to meet the standards of this idealized view of self. In contrast, the latter expression of depression—feelings of emptiness or loss—relates to the loss of something important in one's life (e.g., relationship, job, academic achievement) without which one feels worthless or empty (Bemporad, 1988). This type of depression is viewed as a result of never being valued or accepted when young, so one's positive self-esteem does not develop. In this person, self-esteem is dependent on external sources rather than an internal sense of worth, so when the external source is lost the person is unable to maintain his or her self-worth. The reliance of these theories on untestable, intrapsychic constructs has prevented their validation, but these perspectives provide important conceptualizations of depression that can be useful for practitioners.

In Esteban's case, for example, it is likely that he did not feel valued while younger, so he did not learn to value himself. After the loss of his father, he may feel no one will ever love him because he is unworthy of being loved. He may also believe that if only he was perfect, his father would not have left. His realization that he will never be perfect then becomes anger that is directed inward because he is unable to achieve perfection. Over time, these feelings have severely damaged Esteban's self-esteem. In order for Esteban to resolve his depression, he must learn to value himself and accept realistic expectations for himself instead of trying to live up to an unachievable ideal.

Behavioral Models of Depression

Behaviorists view depression as a result of significant loss (Kovacs & Beck, 1977; Schwartz & Johnson, 1985) and the consequence of inadequate or insufficient reinforcement (Ferster, 1973, 1974). Lewinsohn's social learning theory provides a concise behavioral model of depression. This theory suggests that depressive behaviors are determined by the presence or absence of reinforcers and maintained through the reduction of response-contingent reinforcing events (Lewinsohn & Hoberman, 1985). Depression may be the result of limited positive reinforcement for the individual, which is determined by the number of potentially reinforcing events, the number of these events available in the environment, and the individual's social skills to elicit accessible reinforcers (Levitt, Lubin, & Brooks, 1983). Depression may also result from excessive punishment, especially when it occurs at high rates, when the individual is highly sensitive to punishment, and when necessary coping skills to terminate punishment are limited (Lewinsohn & Hoberman, 1985). Unfortunately, the depressive behaviors stimulated by inadequate reinforcement are further reinforced by the concern or sympathy expressed by significant others. Eventually though, others avoid the depressed person because of the nature of his or her depressive behaviors, which minimizes positive reinforcement and further exacerbates the depression (Lewinsohn & Hoberman, 1985).

To illustrate this model, Esteban receives almost no positive reinforcement, except perhaps from his female friend. Further, his lack of social skills does nothing to elicit positive reactions from others. On the contrary, his surly manner elicits negative reactions from others so that he never receives the social reinforcement that he so desperately needs to help lift his feelings of depression. He feels more and more isolated, less liked by others, and subsequently more depressed.

Cognitive Models of Depression

Research has also supported the role of cognition in depression (Beck, 1967; Rehm, 1977; Seligman, 1974, 1975). The following cognitive models of depression are helpful in understanding this perspective.

The first model, proposed by Beck (1967), suggests that cognition and affect are interactive and that the prior occurrence of cognition will determine a person's affective response to an event. If cognitions are distorted or inaccurate, the individual's emotional response will be inappropriate. Dysphoria may be the affective response of one's tendency to interpret experiences and events as negative or self-devaluative, indicating a cognitive role in the experience of depression.

Beck, Rush, Shaw, and Emery (1979) pointed to three cognitive components central to depression: the cognitive triad, schemas, and cognitive errors. The *cognitive triad* includes three negative thought patterns: a negative view of self, of the world, and of the future. *Schemas*, like personality traits, represent a stable cognitive pattern that individuals create to organize and evaluate information and events. People who experience depression develop schemas that distort environmental stimuli to coincide with a derogatory self-image. These dysfunctional or negative schemas are often created and exacerbated by faulty information processing or consistent errors in logic, called *cognitive errors*. The person suffering from depression uses these automatic cognitive errors to evaluate events, often leading to negativistic, categorical, absolute, and judgmental thinking (Levitt et al., 1983; Lewinsohn & Hoberman, 1985).

The second model of depression, Seligman's (1974, 1975) *learned helplessness* model, contends that depression exists in people who perceive that they have no control over their environment. They develop self-defeating attributions. They make internal (feeling responsible for an event), stable (the causes of an event remain constant), and global (event outcomes impact all areas of life) attributions for failure. In contrast, they attribute successful outcomes to external (caused by others), unstable (causes of events are transitory), and specific (situation-specific) causes (Kaslow & Rehm, 1983). According to this model, this self-defeating attributional style results in the lowered motivation and reduced self-esteem common in depressed clients (Kaslow & Rehm, 1983). Self-defeating attributional style has been correlated with depression (Garber & Robinson, 1997; Lewinsohn & Hoberman, 1985).

Cole, Martin, and Powers (1997) proposed a similar, competency-based model of depression. Their model links a child's perceived helplessness, pessimism, and depression to a negative self-construct based on a lack of competence across five important domains within his or her life (school, attractiveness, social, conduct, and athleticism). Thus, if the child is unable to master tasks in one or more of these domains, he or she forms negative self-constructs leading to depression and helplessness.

Rehm's (1977) self-control theory represents the third cognitive model of depression. Problems of self-control are manifested through deficits in three cognitive processes: self-monitoring, self-reinforcement, and self-evaluation. Depressed clients fail to view situations with an orientation to the future and tend to concentrate on immediate consequences of events (Gilbert, 1984). They selectively attend to negative outcomes and focus on immediate reinforcements, a negative view of the self, the environment, and the future results. Similarly, depressed individuals tend to have negative attribution styles in which events are seen as being due either to external causes beyond their control or to internal, unchangeable skill deficits. They tend to set high standards for positive self-evaluation while at the same time have low standards for negative self-evaluation (Lewinsohn et al., 1996; Stark, Swearer, Kurowski, Sommer, & Bowen, 1996). They are likely to take credit for failures but not successes.

In accord with these models, cognitions play a key role in Esteban's depression. For example, Esteban maintains the faulty belief that he is responsible for his father's behavior and for the demise of his family. Likewise, he attributes negative outcomes to deficiencies in himself (a negative internal attribution) instead of to the dysfunctional family and unstable economic environment around him.

Family Models of Mood Disorders

Finally, a family systems approach to understanding the development of childhood and adolescent depression attends to family dynamics and the family environment. These dynamics are of considerable importance. Proponents of this perspective suggest that young people who experience depression are "symptoms" of family malfunction. The homeostasis of a maladaptive family system is maintained when a child or adolescent performs the role of the "sick" family member. This person is often referred to as the identified patient. In accord with this model, other family members often resist any positive change in the adolescent because it risks upsetting the homeostasis of the family. This reality necessitates the involvement of the entire family system in treatment interventions (Guttman, 1983; Nichols & Schwartz, 1995). Regarding bipolar disorders more specifically, children have high needs for family clarity, structure, and consistency in order to learn how to respond effectively to the cognitive and behavioral consequences of their disorder (Basco & Rush, 1996), and so families that are marked by chaos, confusion, and arbitrariness contribute enormously to the problem their child experiences and can make the symptoms worse.

An approach that considers this model requires Esteban's entire family to be involved in the treatment process. Although Esteban's concerns may be more acute right now, his sisters are at risk for a variety of behavioral problems as well. Family intervention may help to not only resolve his issues but also prevent future problems from being expressed by his siblings. Furthermore, the behaviors and messages of Esteban's mother and father must be explored for each family member to recognize the resulting consequences. Clearly, the ideal is for Esteban's mother and father to be involved in treatment and to make changes. But if his father is no longer involved with the core family, then at least Esteban's mother needs to understand and modify her patterns of communication and behavior. It is also important that the entire family receive support and validation in treatment, especially given the economic marginalization and racial victimization they experience. According to this model, if family members are unwilling to be involved in treatment, any individual intervention focused solely on Esteban is likely to be ineffective.

In the next section, we discuss how these causal models of mood disorders flow into effective prevention and treatment. We begin by presenting a conceptual framework for discussing intervention. As before, we follow Esteban's treatment as a way of highlighting the practical aspects of the prevention and treatment strategies that we present.

APPROACHES TO PREVENTION AND TREATMENT

A conceptual model for understanding and intervening with at-risk youth has been articulated by J. J. McWhirter, McWhirter, McWhirter, and McWhirter (2004). This model is based on two key assumptions: (a) Being at risk for problematic behavior reflects not only a current condition but also an element of prediction for future problems, and (b) at-riskness must be viewed not so much as a discrete and unitary condition but rather as a step or placement along a continuum. This continuum begins with youth who are at *minimal risk* for problematic behavior; proceeds through *remote risk*, *high risk*, and *imminent risk*; and ends with those already engaged in *category activity*. Category activity refers to participation in one or more destructive behaviors such as drug use, delinquent activity, sexual promiscuity, and so forth, and by its nature also includes at-riskness for other problem behaviors. A child or adolescent's placement along the at-risk continuum is mediated by demographics, family and school environments, psychosocial stressors, and personal characteristics of the youth (e.g., critical school competencies, concept of self, connectedness with others that is enhanced by his or her communication skills, coping ability, and control; J. J. McWhirter et al., 2004). This model also proposes that prevention, early intervention, and treatment must involve the family, school, and community. In short, interventions must attend to current problems, to the potential for future difficulty, and to multiple aspects and levels of the ecology of a young person's life.

In J. J. McWhirter et al.'s (2004) model, for example, Esteban would be considered at imminent risk. He has a very negative family environment, comes from a poor socioeconomic background, experiences a great deal of psychosocial stressors including subtle and direct racial discrimination, and does not have effective coping skills or clear goals for his future. Further, he has already developed gateway behaviors such as smoking, being sexually explorative, and having violent outbursts, which highly predict future category behavior.

In accord with this model, practitioners should (a) use generic skills training programs for children in early elementary grades to prevent mood disorders and other problems, (b) move into more focused and topic-specific prevention/intervention efforts for youth around middle school age or earlier if risk factors demand it, and (c) use more topic-specific treatments and "second-chance" programs for older youth or for young people already engaged in category activity. At the prevention end of the continuum, efforts are focused on the building of general skills, such as assertiveness, communication, recognizing feelings, resolving conflict, and so forth. At the treatment end of the continuum, interventions are focused on resolving specific problems that have already developed, such as depression, drug use, or delinquency, as well as on techniques that enhance a broad range of skills to prevent more serious problems from developing as adolescents become young adults.

For instance, Esteban needs treatment focused specifically on his depression and on its root causes, as well as treatment focused on helping him develop skills for dealing with future problems across a wide range of areas. He could be helped by interventions for the entire family, by cognitive and behavioral strategies focused on him individually, by school intervention programs to help him connect more with others in school and perform better, and by community-based treatment approaches. Bronfenbrenner's (1979) ecological model is one way to conceptualize treatments across a variety of domains. He described four systems within a person's life: the micro-, meso-, exo-, and macrosystems. Each system represents a level of interaction of the person within his or her multiple contexts—from the immediate family and school environments (microsystems) to the political structures that organize society (macrosystems). We refer to this model as well when discussing subsequent interventions.

In the following sections we discuss how the core components of prevention as well as more specific treatment strategies might be applied to youth at risk for depression and bipolar disorders. We describe these prevention and treatment strategies with a focus on the individual, family, school, and community, and we conclude by discussing a comprehensive intervention that reaches across all of these domains.

Individual Approaches to Prevention and Treatment

Individual approaches vary, and practitioners should follow their own orientation in attending to child and adolescent mood disorders. Frequently, individual approaches involve both individual and family sessions with the focus remaining on the child or adolescent. Approaches that we discuss here include individual cognitive–behavioral interventions, interpersonal therapy, and pharmacological treatment.

Cognitive–Behavioral Interventions

We focus on cognitive–behavioral approaches that can be used to prevent and treat depression because they have demonstrated proven effectiveness. For instance, Reinecke, Ryan, and DuBois (1998) conducted a meta-analysis of cognitive–behavioral therapy for depression and dysphoria. All of the 24 studies they included demonstrated positive results in the treatment and alleviation of depression in adolescents as a result of the cognitive–behavioral interventions used. Similarly, Rosselló and Bernal (1996) modified a cognitive–behavioral treatment for depressed Puerto Rican adolescents, and their preliminary findings showed positive results for its use with this population. At the same time, we caution that in young children a cognitive focus in therapy may not be as effective because higher order thinking may not have developed yet. So, we suggest that professionals use these interventions in a manner that is consistent with their young client's level of development.

Cognitive–behavioral treatments for depression flow directly from the cognitive and behavioral models described earlier. For example, Beck et al. (1979) developed a therapy with both behavioral and cognitive components designed to reduce automatic negative cognition with the goal of challenging the assumptions that maintain these faulty cognitions. Because clients often have difficulty utilizing cognitive tasks, behavioral strategies should be used first in the therapeutic process. These strategies include scheduling pleasant activities, relaxation training, graduated task assignments, social skills training, role-plays, and behavioral rehearsal (Lewinsohn et al., 1996; Reinecke et al., 1998). Behavioral strategies increase an individual's activity level and, therefore, the frequency of potentially rewarding activities, which may also increase the level of response-contingent reinforcement. During the experience of depression and bipolar disorder, young people tend to withdraw from activities and interactions with others. Behavioral strategies directly address withdrawal behaviors and encourage children and adolescents to be active, which in turn lessens the attention to and perseverance of depressogenic cognitions. Behavioral interventions appear appropriate for Esteban. Unless he becomes more involved in more positive peer interactions and in pleasant activities, he may have great difficulty in improving his depressed mood and in learning more positive cognitions about himself and his environment.

After these strategies are successfully utilized, emphasis is moved to cognitive interventions that emphasize identifying, testing, and modifying cognitive distortions. Strategies that have been successfully used include (a) recognizing the connection between cognition, affect, and behavior; (b) monitoring negative automatic thoughts; (c) examining evidence related to distorted automatic cognition; (d) substituting more realistic interpretations for distorted cognitions; (e) learning to identify and modify irrational beliefs; (f) altering biased attentional processes; (g) affect regulation; and (h) impulse control (Brent et al., 1996; Ellis, 1962; Ellis & Bernard, 1983; Marcotte, 1997; Reinecke et al., 1998).

Such strategies could be implemented with Esteban as part of individual treatment to address his distorted cognitions and their relation to his mood and behavior. Of course, these strategies could be used as part of a prevention program in the school setting as well, which we discuss later.

Another cognitive–behavioral approach for depression is based on Rehm's (1977) self-control model. This intervention has been described as a primary prevention method, useful in teaching the skills necessary to avoid depression (Kaslow & Rehm, 1983). Kolko (1987) recommended that treatment in self-control involve specific training in monitoring positive events and self-statements, engaging in positive behaviors and cognitions, emphasizing long-term positive consequences, developing more realistic and achievable goals, making more legitimate attributions, and creating more frequent self-reinforcements.

Consistent with these models, we have found two cognitive–behavioral techniques to be particularly helpful. First, ask the child or adolescent to repeat a standard, positive phrase, such as "I am a good person," every time the child takes out a pen from his or her backpack. Second, ask the child or adolescent to write down on three-by-five cards a positive, affirming self-statement (e.g., "I am an honest and decent person" or "I am attractive and caring"). When three or four cards are completed, add one blank card and place them inside the child's or adolescent's class notebook. Each time the notebook is used, the child or adolescent silently reads one of the cards. When the blank card turns up, the client must spontaneously make up a new positive sentence. These types of interventions may prove helpful to Esteban, who clearly needs to augment his positive self-statements.

Interpersonal Therapy

Another individual approach that has received significant research attention and demonstrated positive results in alleviating depression in children and adolescents is interpersonal therapy. Preliminary results indicate that, after appropriate cultural modifications, interpersonal psychotherapy had moderate success in treating depressed Puerto Rican adolescents (Rosselló & Bernal, 1996). Interpersonal therapy conceptualizes depression as conflict taking place in the context of interpersonal relationships (Mufson, Moreau, & Weissman, 1996). There are five areas that form the problem areas and treatment goals in interpersonal therapy: (a) grief, (b) interpersonal role disputes, (c) role transitions, (d) interpersonal deficits, and (e) single-parent families (this is a modification for use with adolescents).

Goals in interpersonal therapy are to reduce depression and address the underlying conflict that was associated with the depression. Examples of techniques used in this approach include exploratory questioning, linking affect and events, clarifying conflicts and communication patterns, and behavior modification strategies. This approach has received promising empirical support (Mufson & Fairbanks, 1996; Rosselló & Bernal, 1996). In the case of Esteban, interpersonal psychotherapy would focus on his grief over his parents' divorce, as well as interpersonal deficits (poor social skills) and coping in a single-parent family. Role transitions around adolescence and increasing independence may also be areas on which to focus.

Pharmacological Treatment

Pharmacological interventions are, in some cases, required with young clients suffering from mood disorders. Medication usage for depressed youth has followed the trend of adult research. Since the 1960s, TCAs (e.g., imipramine) have been prescribed for young patients (Hodgman, 1985), although research clearly indicates no significant differences between active medication and placebo (Ambrosini, 2000; Emslie & Mayes, 2001; Michael & Crowley, 2002). More recently, SSRIs (e.g., Fluoxetine or Prozac) have been prescribed with more frequency for depressed youth (Ambrosini, 2000; Ziervogel, 2000) and have been found to have less severe side effects than TCAs (e.g., less dry mouth, sedation) and less risk of overdose. However, there has been limited research demonstrating the efficacy for SSRIs with depressed youth (Ambrosini, 2000; Wagner & Ambrosini, 2001; Ziervogel, 2000). Although frequently used in the clinical setting, the effectiveness of antidepressant medication for children and adolescents has not yet been firmly established through controlled research (Ambrosini, 2000; Brent et al., 1996; Michael & Crowley, 2002; Wagner & Ambrosini, 2001). Nevertheless, case studies, adult research, and informal clinical lore consider pharmacological interventions as useful in the treatment of depression, especially severe and chronic depression.

In the case of bipolar disorders, medication is probably essential because it is important to change a child's behavioral and cognition patterns early so that these dysfunctional and self-destructive patterns do not become entrenched. Controlled psychopharmacological studies for the treatment of bipolar disorder have received much less attention with child and adolescent samples than with adult samples (Geller & Luby, 1997; James & Javaloyes, 2001). In fact, much of the information known about drug treatments for bipolar disorders comes from the adult literature. However, the limited research findings in this area indicate that mood stabilizers such as lithium salts (e.g., Lithobid), valproic acid (e.g., Valproate, Depakote), and carbamazepine (Tegretol) may be effective in managing this disorder in young samples (James & Javaloyes, 2001; Kowatch et al., 2000; Sanchez et al., 1999). In addition, benzodiazepine has been used for agitation, and atypical antipsychotics (such as Thorazine [low potency] and Prolixin, Haldol, and Risperidal [high potency]) have also been used when indicated for psychotic features (James & Javaloyes, 2001). In only the most severe and treatment-resistant bipolar cases are methods such as electroconvulsive treatment utilized (James & Javaloyes, 2001). Of course, during a severe manic episode the behavior often causes problems that result in hospitalization. With children and adolescents, counselors and other practitioners need to be attentive to less severe mood swings or problems with more rapid cycling of moods and be open to early referral to and collaboration with medical and psychiatric professionals.

Pharmacotherapy has shown some promise in reducing symptoms of bipolar disorder among children and adolescents, but finding the correct and helpful medication balance can take time and be enormously frustrating for the child and for his or her parents and caregivers (James & Javaloyes, 2001). As such, James and Javaloyes (2001) recommended the use of individual and family psychoeducational approaches along with drug treatment, and they indicated that little empirical research exists on the efficacy of such treatments for this disorder in young populations. Given the severity of this disorder, it is clear that possible treatment approaches could be implemented on many levels, and individual and family psychoeducation approaches should always be used to assist the family in dealing with this disorder. In addition, comorbid disorders (e.g., ADHD, substance abuse) must be accurately identified and effectively treated for intervention to be effective with children suffering from bipolar disorder. While the existence of these other concerns and a bipolar disorder does not seem probable in Esteban's situation, a medical referral for his depression may still be important.

Family Approaches to Prevention and Treatment

The role of the family in the successful treatment of the depressed child or adolescent is crucial. Family counseling has been shown to be even more important in the effective treatment of childhood disorders, in part due to the extensive influence families have over young children compared with adolescents (Nichols & Schwartz, 1995). Counselors using only an individually based intervention strategy may be doomed to failure and may even exacerbate the problem because from a family systems view and from an ecological model the entire family system needs to change for the problem to be resolved. As such, to be successful, clinicians must be prepared to work with all family members, especially parents who may also suffer from a mood disorder or have marital conflict. Therefore, in Esteban's family, if his mother and sisters are not engaged in treatment, he will likely continue to suffer from the same environmental conditions that contributed to his depression in the first place.

In many circumstances parent training and education can benefit the family and help prevent depression and other problems. Workshops for parents can be particularly useful and cost-effective, especially those that focus on developing communication skills, enhancing family interactions, parent training, and sharing information about issues (such as birth control, signs of drug use, and so forth). Workshops also offer parents a forum for discussing fears, concerns, and frustrations with other parents and with a professional facilitator, which may increase parental confidence and comfort with discussing issues with their children. In families with greater dysfunction, therapeutic programs attending to child abuse and neglect, parental dysfunction, and family violence may also be required and extremely beneficial.

Parent training may also be utilized as prevention as well as treatment for many problems, including childhood and adolescent mood disorders. Examples of parent training include parent effectiveness training (PET), family effectiveness training (FET), and systematic–behavioral family therapy (SBFT).

PET (Gordon, 1975, 1977) combines lectures, role-playing, and homework exercises to train parents in healthy confrontation, conflict resolution, and active listening skills. FET (Szapocznik, Santisteban, Rio, Perez-Vidal, & Kurtines, 1986b, 1989) is a preventative training model for Latino families of preadolescents at-risk for future drug abuse. FET is designed to address three problems that often serve as antecedents to adolescent behavior problems: maladaptive family interactions, intergenerational conflict, and intercultural conflict. It is one of few empirically tested programs that directly address cultural differences. The model has three components.

The first component, family development, helps the family to negotiate the childhood-to-adolescence transition. All family members learn constructive communication skills and take increased responsibility for their own behaviors. Parents become educated about drugs so that they can teach their children; they also learn the skills to become democratic rather than authoritarian leaders.

The second component, bicultural effectiveness training (BET; Szapocznik, Santisteban, Kurtines, Perez-Vidal, & Hervis, 1984; Szapocznik, Santisteban, Rio, Perez-Vidal, & Kurtines, 1986a), is designed to bring about family change by (a) temporarily placing the blame for the family's problems on the cultural conflict within the family and (b) establishing alliances between family members through the development of bicultural skills and mutual appreciation of the values of both cultures. The family learns to handle cultural conflicts more effectively and reduces the likelihood that such conflicts will occur. BET represents an excellent parent training program in and of itself. This program would be particularly helpful for Esteban's family, which contends with acculturation issues as well as overt and covert racism on a daily basis.

The third component of FET is the implementation of brief strategic family therapy. Based on the work of Minuchin (1974), this component involves a series of family therapy sessions and is the most experiential aspect of this didactic/experiential model. The entire training consists of 13 sessions that last from $1\frac{1}{2}$ to 2 hours; the entire family is present for each session. Finally, FET can be modified to deal specifically with other child and adolescent behavior problems.

SBFT (Brent et al., 1996) is a combination of functional family therapy (Alexander & Parsons, 1973, as cited in Brent et al., 1996) and a behavior component developed by Robin and Foster (1989, as cited in Brent et al., 1996). In this approach the counselor joins with each family member and obtains commitment and engaged participation from each person. Then the problem is clarified and goals are set. Deficient communication and problem-solving skills, as well as structural difficulties (parent–child alliances), are conceptualized as the focus of the difficulty. Interventions include family tasks, self-monitoring, and positive practice. Although the study by Brent and colleagues is still in progress, early results indicated that this treatment remitted depression in approximately two thirds of the adolescent participants (Brent et al., 1996).

These programs represent some of the effective parent training programs that are useful for preventing depression and bipolar disorders. Other extensive, empirically based parent training programs have been developed for working with families in the home and school environments. For example, Carolyn Webster-Stratton and colleagues have developed and evaluated parent training programs that primarily target children with conduct disorders (see Reid & Webster-Stratton, 2001; Webster-Stratton & Hancock, 1998; Webster-Stratton, Reid, & Hammond, 2001). Others have developed additional parent training models (see Dinkmeyer & McKay, 1989), and, often, parenting resources are available at local community counseling centers on a variety of topics, including behavior management and discipline, nutrition, family budgeting, and preventing drug use.

Parent training programs could help Esteban, but because he already shows clear signs of depression, direct therapeutic intervention with the whole family is indicated. Helping Irma and her children communicate more effectively with each other and clarify roles and boundaries has the potential of creating a great deal of change in the family. In addition, helping the children to see their value and importance in the family is important. The family can become a primary source of support and encouragement if family members can share their needs, wants, and feelings more effectively.

School-Based Approaches to Prevention and Treatment

The occurrence of mood disorders among children and adolescents has increased in recent years and is likely due, in part, to both better diagnosis and increased environmental stressors (Birmaher, Ryan, Williamson, Brent, Kaufman, Dahl, et al., 1996). The presence of increased environmental stressors supports the need for environmental and microsystemic intervention, such as early prevention and treatment in the school setting. For example, school personnel can improve the early identification of depressed and bipolar children, whose mood disorder is sometimes overlooked because of the presence of acting-out and other overt problem behaviors (Hart, 1991). The following discussion on school prevention is quite extensive because schools are an ideal setting for prevention. Most children and adolescents can be reached in schools, and most can be taught critical life skills as an integral part of a school-based curriculum.

In responding to depression, school-based prevention programs may utilize multiple strategies. School counselors could more actively use instruments to assess mood disorders. To be effective, assessment should consider the young person's cognitive and affective characteristics, environment, life stressors, and relationships with others (Hart, 1991; Vernon, 1993). School prevention and treatment could include a mixture of affective, cognitive, and behavioral strategies that enhance self-acceptance, problem-solving and decision-making strategies, and social skills to improve interpersonal relationships (Vernon, 1989a, 1989b). Group interventions are one important modality for delivering school-based prevention because they help to reach a large number of children, can be adapted to the classroom format, and allow skills to be taught and learned in a social, peer context.

Early prevention in schools can take the form of educational programs focused on forming friendships (social skills), nonviolent conflict resolution, assertiveness training, and skills for relating to adults, dealing with peer pressure, and improving critical school competencies such as basic academic skills and academic survival skills (J. J. McWhirter et al., 2004). Broad-based skills training programs such as these not only prevent depression but also help to prevent other critical problems, such as teenage pregnancy and drug use. Schools are important focal points in building these prevention programs because they provide access to both families and communities. In Esteban's case, such programs might have provided the social skills training that he did not receive at home as well as assistance in mastering academic survival skills that he may have missed because of his frequent moves.

The core components of most effective social skills or life skills prevention programs include (a) interpersonal communication, (b) strategies for cognitive change, (c) coping with stress, and (d) managing health (J. J. McWhirter et al., 2004). Life skills are those that involve behaviors and attitudes necessary for coping with academic challenges, communicating with others, forming healthy and stable relationships, and making good decisions. Life skills training programs emphasize the acquisition of generic social and cognitive skills. The theoretical foundation of life skills training includes Bandura's (1977) social learning theory and Jessor and Jessor's (1977) problem behavior theory. In accord with these perspectives, children and adolescents are not blamed for causing their problems but are viewed as capable of learning new ways to behave that reduce the likelihood of future problems.

Counselors and other mental health professionals can all be involved in teaching life skills. Procedures for teaching life skills resemble those used in the teaching of any other skill. Overall tasks are broken down into smaller stages or component parts and taught systematically, moving from simple to more complex skills. Effective life skills training sessions follow a five-step model: (a) instruction (teach); (b) modeling (show); (c) role-play (practice); (d) feedback (reinforce); and (e) homework (apply). Within this general framework, steps may be modified in accord with the needs of the classroom or group. Three broad skill categories are usually included in basic life skills programs:

- *Interpersonal communication skills*, including assertiveness and refusal skills
- *Cognitive change strategies*, including problem-solving, decision-making, self-control, and self-management skills, and cognitive–behavioral restructuring approaches
- *Anxiety coping approaches*, including relaxation, imagery training, and exercise.

Learning effective social skills is core to life skills training because it improves the positive feedback and reinforcement that young people receive from others (Lewinsohn, Biglan, & Zeiss, 1976). Treatment here focuses on the improvement of interpersonal style and on the development of skills, such as peer etiquette and group entry (Frankel, Cantwell, & Myatt, 1996). Modeling, feedback, role-playing, instruction, situation logs, and homework practice are all utilized to help augment social skills and minimize the depression caused by an inability to elicit positive responses from others. The prevalence of social skills deficits and the results of social skills training among children and adolescents have received limited attention; generalizability from group to external environments has had mixed results (Frankel et al., 1996). Nevertheless, such approaches seem especially appropriate for young people like Esteban. Given the fact that Esteban has had relatively little peer group interaction and prefers to be alone, it appears that he has not developed effective social skills. Indeed, he seems unable to cope with the responses of his classmates and family. Thus, social skills training would appear to be a very useful strategy to help lift his depression.

Life skills training can also be achieved through leadership training programs. For example, students provided with leadership opportunities exercise decision-making skills and learn the importance of self-control. Some researchers have found very positive effects from improving adolescents' leadership skills through increasing problem-solving and decision-making skills (Beyth-Marom, Fischhoff, Jacobs, & Furby, 1989). Specifically, for example, schools have reported marked reduction in disruptive behaviors after teaching students to mediate disputes on their own (Lane & McWhirter, 1992). The ability of students to solve their own problems and peacefully settle disputes directly and positively impacts student climate and reduces the likelihood of violence and other problems. Equally important, these types of programs help enhance the self-efficacy for problem solving among the children and adolescents who are involved with them.

Exercise, nutrition, and additional self-care habits are often ignored in prevention efforts but may be very helpful to children and youth. In a study by Brown, Welsh, Labbe, Vitulli, and Kulkarni (1992), a group of psychiatrically institutionalized adolescent boys and girls was assigned to a 9-week aerobic exercise program. The treated girls showed lower incidence of depression, anxiety, hostility, confused thinking, and fatigue, and both the adolescent boys and girls in the aerobics program showed improved vigor and self-efficacy. The added benefits of using exercise and nutritional strategies with youth are multifold because forming healthy habits early in life is easier than changing habits later in life. Similarly, utilizing stress reduction techniques in school, such as relaxation training, biofeedback, meditation, and guided visual imagery, may also be helpful in preventing or reducing mood disorders among children and adolescents.

Group interventions are central to many school-based prevention programs because of their ability to reach a large number of children, cost-effectiveness, adaptability to the classroom, and their usefulness for training skills. Unfortunately, small-group intervention programs for depression and other psychosocial problems have not often been rigorously evaluated in school settings, but existing outcome studies indicate positive results. For example, Vernon (1989a, 1989b) developed an effective emotional education curriculum based on rational emotive therapy by Albert Ellis. This program targets thoughts, affect, and behavior and has specific grade-level interventions targeted to the young person's developmental level. Topics such as self-acceptance, feelings, behaviors, problem solving, decision making, and interpersonal relationships are addressed.

Lewinsohn et al. (1996) described an 8-week cognitive–behavioral group intervention titled Adolescent Coping With Depression Course (CWD-A). This structured intervention incorporates cognitive–behavioral techniques such as skill development, mood enhancement, problem solving, and role-playing (Lewinsohn et al., 1996). The groups are facilitated by therapists over 8 weeks with approximately 10 or fewer adolescents. In addition, there is a parallel parent group that meets with a therapist to teach parents how to support their adolescents in treatment. The CWD-A has been empirically evaluated over a number of studies and has been demonstrated to be effective for adolescents experiencing depression (Lewinsohn, Clarke, Hops, & Andrews, 1990; Lewinsohn et al., 1996, 1998). While success for the CWD-A group intervention has been demonstrated in clinical settings (see Lewinsohn et al., 1996., 1998), its individual sessions are presented in a classlike manner, and, thus, it may be adaptable to school settings.

Community Approaches to Prevention and Treatment

Thus far we have reviewed individual, family, and school approaches for the prevention and treatment of childhood and adolescent mood disorders. Many of the interventions discussed in this chapter could easily be used by counselors, psychologists, social workers, and other mental health professionals who work in community agencies. But approaches that specifically involve the larger community acknowledge the role of the larger context in which depression and other problems of childhood and adolescence emerge. Thus, we focus on a larger community program in this section. Given the high correlation between delinquency and depression (J. J. McWhirter et al., 2004), the community program described below can be seen as both a treatment and a prevention measure for depression and other concerns.

Teencourt (E. H. McWhirter, 1994; J. J. McWhirter et al., 2004) is an example of a community program that is used in many counties in many states throughout the United States for first-time juvenile offenders between the ages of 8 and 17 who have committed a misdemeanor offense, status offense, or minor traffic violation. The Teencourt program incorporates leadership skills, critical thinking, career exploration, taking responsibility, and influencing peer norms. Youth referred to Teencourt have a choice of (a) pleading guilty, participating in the program, and keeping their record clean or (b) going through the traditional juvenile justice court system. Teencourt sentencing is designed to fit the offense and usually includes community service, tutoring, attending workshops, and/or traffic survival school.

Each session of Teencourt lasts 4 months and involves six attorneys, 20 jurists, one court clerk, and three bailiffs, all of whom are trained high school students. Thus, offenders passing through Teencourt are tried and judged by their peers; the judge is the only adult representative of the legal system. All defendants are required to serve a term of jury duty after their own sentencing. This is consistent with the goals of Teencourt, which include preventing repeat offenses among those who are tried; preventing first-time offenses among the many students who voluntarily participate as attorneys, bailiffs, jurists, and clerks; educating adolescents about the legal system; and utilizing peer pressure to evoke conformity to positive behaviors. The recidivism rate for Teencourt participants is well below both state and national averages (J. J. McWhirter, McWhirter, McWhirter, & McWhirter, 1994). This program models an empowerment philosophy as defined by E. H. McWhirter (1994) because it not only prevents future problems but also helps young people develop skills for helping others and for changing their communities.

Thus far, Esteban has not been accused of any legal violation, although he does smoke before the legal age. However, he is at high risk for involvement in some form of offense. Participation in a program such as Teencourt as an offender and then a jury member could have a considerable positive effect on Esteban. Teencourt's philosophy of empowerment is manifested in a variety of ways: by increasing adolescents' awareness of the legal system, providing specific skills training as well as the broader experience of leadership and citizenship, utilizing peers—of equal power status—rather than adults, involving adolescents with community organizations, tailoring sentences to individual offenses, and emphasizing responsibility for behavior (J. J. McWhirter et al., 1994). In the context of Seligman's (1974, 1975) model of learned helplessness, the Teencourt program addresses many of the deficiencies and apathetic responses from which Esteban suffers.

ADAPTATIONS FOR DIVERSITY

We have discussed the issues of individual, family, school, and community interventions, but we are still confronted with a very depressed 15-year-old who needs support. The comprehensive model we propose here is built on the foundation of a solid interpersonal relationship between the depressed or bipolar child or adolescent and the helpers in his or her environment: counselors, teachers, and parents. This relationship, although necessary and yet not sufficient for fully treating a mood disorder, must incorporate the basic conditions of empathy, genuineness, warmth, and respect for differences. It must also incorporate multicultural awareness and sensitivity. In this case, multicultural sensitivity involves more than knowledge of Mexican American cultural norms; it must include awareness of the effects of societal influences such as racism, oppression, and economic marginalization on people of color and on their communities.

Bronfenbrenner's (1979) ecological model describes the dynamic interaction of four basic systems within an individual's life and provides a framework for a comprehensive intervention. As we have defined it, the most basic level of the ecological model is the *microsystem*, which is composed of the individual and his or her interactions within small contexts such as the family, classroom, and friends. Esteban's microsystems include his sibling relationships, relationship with his mother, family interactions, his classes, and his peers. Next is the *mesosystem*, in which interactions become more complex; this system involves the interactions of the individual and significant others across microsystems, such as a conference with Esteban, Irma, and one of his teachers. The *exosystem* is the even larger systems that indirectly influence the child but in which the child or adolescent need not be present. For example, this could refer to a school in-service training that the child's teacher attends that may indirectly affect the child. Finally, the *macrosystem* represents the larger societal influences that distantly relate to the individual. Government educational policies, race relations, and economic barriers within a person's community are all examples. Using this model helps counselors and others to examine the direct and indirect influences on a youth's depression and bipolar disorder and can illuminate possible ways to prevent or intervene.

Given the complexity of Esteban's present problems and the threat of future overtly violent behaviors, we recommend the use of a comprehensive treatment strategy that addresses Esteban's different contexts (micro- and mesosystems), his cognitions, behaviors, and affect (individual level), as well as attending to larger environmental issues (exo- and macrosystems). The nature and severity of his depression should be assessed thoroughly, by means of a family intake with measures of anxiety, depression, anger, and self-esteem. Vernon (1993) suggested that counselors and other helping professionals use the HELPING model developed by Keat (1979, as cited in Vernon, 1993), who adapted it from multimodal therapy (Lazarus, 1976, as cited in Vernon, 1993) as a comprehensive assessment strategy. Each letter stands for a domain within the child's life: Health, Emotions, Learning, Personal relationships, Imagery, Need to know, Guidance of actions, behaviors, and consequences. In sum, to be accurate and clinically useful, Esteban's comprehensive assessment needs to include individual factors as well as contextual and interpersonal ones such as family dynamics, poor school performance, fear of interaction with others, peer rejection, and overt and covert racism that he experiences regularly within the multiple contexts of his life.

After the assessment, an intervention should be collaboratively developed with Esteban and his family. This plan should be responsive to Esteban's degree of risk along the continuum that we presented earlier and should include as many levels of the ecology of Esteban's life as possible. Effective intervention for Esteban should include the following components:

- behavioral interventions of life skills training and increasing age-appropriate pleasurable activities
- cognitive interventions designed to identify, test, and modify his dysfunctional beliefs about himself, his family, and his future
- family interventions designed to improve the communication within the family, to improve his mother's parenting consistency, and to examine and build family communication around potential intrafamilial cultural differences and conflicts that may be impeding their relationships
- school interventions designed to attend to Esteban's poor performance and relationships with peers

- interventions that encourage Esteban to choose to become active in Mexican American groups at school or within his community.

Finally, some understanding and potential use of pharmacological interventions may be necessary if Esteban's depression does not remit or he does not respond well to treatment. Fundamentally, Esteban is currently depressed, but a comprehensive intervention, like the one described here, can prevent future depressive episodes and other problems for which Esteban is at imminent risk.

SUMMARY

Depression and bipolar disorders are significant and complicated mental health problems among children and adolescents. Their manifestation in childhood varies but in adolescence is more similar to patterns found in adulthood. Mood disorders have also been linked to other at-risk factors such as suicide, school attrition, substance use, and behavior problems, further augmenting the difficulty in making appropriate diagnosis and establishing effective treatment interventions. Current research supports several treatment approaches as being equally successful in remitting depression. Future research should continue to examine the active ingredients in depression and bipolar disorder intervention to improve efficacy and to further our understanding of mood disorders among children and adolescents. Although we have better knowledge about medications for adult mood disorders, we have much less knowledge about pharmacological interventions for young people, so pharmacological research for these problems among young people is clearly warranted.

What is very clear is that depression and bipolar disorders can have catastrophic effects on young people and on those around them. This is true for young Esteban. The interventions described in this chapter that involve the individual, family, school, and community could all be used in a comprehensive way to help tackle the depression that Esteban, and many young people experience. Parents, counselors, teachers, and other school personnel who play primary roles in the lives of children and adolescents must be especially aware of and responsive to the symptoms, causes, and problems associated with mood disorders. Recognizing and responding quickly to these problems and to their root causes are especially important in avoiding the potentially devastating effects of these disorders on the young people with whom we live and work.

REFERENCES

Ambrosini, P. J. (2000). A review of pharmacotherapy of major depression in children and adolescents. *Psychiatric Services, 51,* 627–633.

American Psychiatric Association. (1987). *Diagnostic and statistical manual of mental disorders* (3rd ed., rev.). Washington, DC: Author.

American Psychiatric Association. (1994). *Diagnostic and statistical manual of mental disorders* (4th ed.). Washington, DC: Author.

American Psychiatric Association. (2000). *Diagnostic and statistical manual of mental disorders* (4th ed., text revision). Washington, DC: Author.

Aseltine, R. H., Jr., Gore, S., & Colten, M. E. (1998). The co-occurrence of depression and substance abuse in late adolescence. *Development & Psychopathology, 10,* 549–570.

Bandura, A. (1977). Self-efficacy: Toward a unifying theory of behavioral change. *Psychological Review, 84,* 191–215.

Basco, M. R., & Rush, A. J. (1996). *Cognitive–behavioral therapy for bipolar disorder*. New York: Guilford Press.

Beck, A. T. (1967). *Depression: Causes and treatment*. Philadelphia: University of Pennsylvania Press.

Beck, A. T., Rush, A. G., Shaw, B. F., & Emery, G. (1979). *Cognitive therapy of depression*. New York: Guilford Press.

Bemporad, J. R. (1988). Psychodynamic treatment of depressed adolescents. *Journal of Clinical Psychiatry, 49*(Suppl. 9), 26–31.

Beyth-Marom, R., Fischhoff, B., Jacobs, M., & Furby, L. (1989). *Teaching decision making to adolescents: A critical review*. Washington, DC: Carnegie Council on Adolescent Development.

Birmaher, B., Ryan, N. D., Williamson, D. E., Brent, D. A., & Kaufman, J. (1996). Childhood and adolescent depression: Part II. A review of the past 10 years. *Journal of the American Academy of Child and Adolescent Psychiatry, 35*, 1575–1583.

Birmaher, B., Ryan, N. D., Williamson, D. E., Brent, D. A., Kaufman, J., Dahl, R. E., et al. (1996). Childhood and adolescent depression: Part I. A review of the past 10 years. *Journal of the American Academy of Child and Adolescent Psychiatry, 35*, 1427–1439.

Brent, D. A., Roth, C. M., Holder, D. P., Kolko, D. J., Birmaher, B., Johnson, B. A., & Schweers, J. A. (1996). Psychosocial interventions for treating adolescent suicidal depression: A comparison of three psychosocial interventions. In E. D. Hibbs & P. S. Jensen (Eds.), *Psychosocial treatments for child and adolescent disorders: Empirically based strategies for clinical practice* (pp. 187–206). Washington, DC: American Psychological Association.

Bronfenbrenner, U. (1979). *The ecology of human development: Experiments by nature and design*. Cambridge, MA: Harvard University Press.

Brown, S. W., Welsh, M. C., Labbe, E. E., Vitulli, W. F., & Kulkarni, P. (1992). Aerobic exercise in the psychological treatment of adolescents. *Perceptual and Motor Skills, 74*, 555–560.

Carlson, G. A., & Kashani, J. H. (1988). Manic symptoms in a non-referred adolescent population. *Journal of Affective Disorders, 15*, 219–226.

Cole, D. A., Martin, J. M., & Powers, B. (1997). A competency-based model of child depression: A longitudinal study of peer, parent, teacher, and self-evaluations. *Journal of Child Psychology and Psychiatry, 38*, 505–514.

Dinkmeyer, D., & McKay, G. D. (1989). *Systematic training for effective parenting* (3rd ed.). Circle Pines, MN: American Guidance Service.

Ellis, A. (1962). *Reason and emotion in psychotherapy*. New York: Stuart.

Ellis, A., & Bernard, M. E. (Eds.). (1983). *Rational–emotive approaches to the problems of childhood*. New York: Plenum.

Emslie, G. J., & Mayes, T. L. (2001). Mood disorders in children and adolescents: Psychopharmacological treatment. *Biological Psychiatry, 49*, 1082–1090.

Ferster, C. B. (1973). A functional analysis of depression. *American Psychologist, 28*, 857–870.

Ferster, C. B. (1974). Behavioral approaches to depression. In R. J. Friedman & M. M. Katz (Eds.), *The psychology of depression: Contemporary theory and research* (pp. 29–53). New York: Winston-Wiley.

Frankel, F., Cantwell, D. P., & Myatt, R. (1996). Helping ostracized children: Social skills training and parent support for socially rejected children. In E. D. Hibbs & P. S. Jensen (Eds.), *Psychosocial treatments for child and adolescent disorders: Empirically based strategies for clinical practice* (pp. 595–618). Washington, DC: American Psychological Association.

Garber, J., & Robinson, N. S. (1997). Cognitive vulnerability in children at risk for depression. *Cognition & Emotion, 11*, 619–635.

Garrison, C. Z., Shoenbach, V. J., & Kaplan, B. H. (1985). Depressive symptoms in early adolescence. In A. Dean (Ed.), *Depression in multidisciplinary perspective* (pp. 60–82). New York: Brunner/Mazel.

Geller, B., Fox, L. W., & Clark, K. A. (1994). Rate and predictors of prepubertal bipolarity during follow-up of 6 to 12 year old depressed children. *Journal of the American Academy of Child and Adolescent Psychiatry, 33*, 461–468.

Geller, B., & Luby, J. (1997). Child and adolescent bipolar disorder: A review of the past 10 years. *Journal of the American Academy of Child and Adolescent Psychiatry, 36*, 1168–1176.

Geller, B., Sun, K., Zimerman, B., Luby, J., Frasier, J., & Williams, M. (1995). Complex and rapid-cycling in bipolar children and adolescents: A preliminary study. *Journal of Affective Disorders, 34*, 259–268.

Gilbert, P. (1984). *Depression: From psychology to brain state*. London: Erlbaum.

Gordon, T. (1975). *PET: Parent effectiveness training*. New York: American Library.

Gordon, T. (1977). Parent effectiveness training: A preventive program and its delivery system. In G. W. Albee & J. M. Joffe (Eds.), *Primary prevention of psychopathology* (pp. 175–186). Hanover, NH: University Press of New England.

Guttman, H. A. (1983). Family therapy in the treatment of mood disturbance in adolescence. In H. Golombek & B. Garfinkel (Eds.), *The adolescent and mood disturbance* (pp. 263–272). New York: International Universities Press.

Hart, S. L. (1991). Childhood depression: Implications and options for school counselors. *Elementary School Guidance and Counseling, 25*, 277–289.

Hodgman, C. H. (1985). Recent findings in adolescent depression and suicide. *Developmental and Behavioral Pediatrics, 6*, 162–170.

James, A. C. D., & Javaloyes, A. M. (2001). The treatment of bipolar disorder in children and adolescents. *Journal of Child Psychology and Psychiatry and Allied Disciplines, 42*, 439–449.

Jessor, L. C., & Jessor, S. L. (1977). *Problem behavior and psychosocial development: A longitudinal study of youth*. New York: Academic Press.

Kaslow, N. J., & Rehm, L. P. (1983). Child depression. In R. J. Morris & T. R. Kratochwill (Eds.), *The practice of child therapy* (pp. 27–51). New York: Pergamon.

Kazdin, A. E. (1994). Psychotherapy for children and adolescents. In A. E. Bergin & S. L. Garfield (Eds.), *Handbook of psychotherapy and behavior change* (4th ed., pp. 543–594). New York: Wiley.

King, S. R. (1991). Recognizing and responding to adolescent depression. *Journal of Health Care for the Poor and Underserved, 2*, 122–129.

Kolko, D. J. (1987). Depression. In M. Herson & V. Van Hassalt (Eds.), *Behavior therapy with children and adolescents: A clinical approach* (pp. 137–183). New York: Wiley.

Kovacs, M., & Beck, A. T. (1977). An empirical–clinical approach toward a definition of childhood depression. In J. G. Schulterbrandt & A. Raskin (Eds.), *Depression in childhood: Diagnosis, treatment, and conceptual models* (pp. 1–25). New York: Raven Press.

Kovacs, M., & Devlin, B. (1998). Internalizing disorders in childhood. *Journal of Child Psychology and Psychiatry, 39*, 47–63.

Kowatch, R. A., Suppes, T., Carmody, T. J., Bucci, J. P., Hume, J. H., Kromelis, M., et al. (2000). Effect size of lithium, divalproex sodium, and carbamazepine in children and adolescents with bipolar disorder. *Journal of the American Academy of Child and Adolescent Psychiatry, 39*, 713–720.

Lane, P. S., & McWhirter, J. J. (1992). A peer mediation model: Conflict resolution for elementary and middle school children. *Elementary School Guidance and Counseling, 27*, 15–23.

Levitt, E. E., Lubin, B., & Brooks, J. M. (1983). *Depression: Concepts, controversies, and some new facts*. Hillsdale, NJ: Erlbaum.

Lewinsohn, P. M., Biglan, A., & Zeiss, A. M. (1976). Behavioral treatment of depression. In P. O. Davidson (Ed.), *The behavioral management of anxiety, depression and pain* (pp. 91–146). New York: Brunner/Mazel.

Lewinsohn, P. M., Clarke, G. N., Hops, H., & Andrews, J. (1990). Cognitive–behavioral treatment for depressed adolescents. *Behavior Therapy, 21*, 385–401.

Lewinsohn, P. M., Clarke, G. N., Rohde, P., Hops, H., & Seeley, J. R. (1996). A course in coping: A cognitive–behavioral approach to the treatment of adolescent depression. In E. D. Hibbs & P. S. Jensen (Eds.), *Psychosocial treatments for child and adolescent disorders: Empirically based strategies for clinical practice* (pp. 109–135). Washington, DC: American Psychological Association.

Lewinsohn, P. M., & Hoberman, H. M. (1985). Depression. In A. S. Bellack, M. Herson, & A. E. Kazdin (Eds.), *International handbook of behavior modification and therapy* (Student ed., pp. 173–207). New York: Plenum Press.

Lewinsohn, P. M., Hops, H., Roberts, R., Seeley, J. R., & Andrew, J. (1993). Adolescent psychopathology: I. Prevalence and incidence of depression and other *DSM–III–R* disorders in high school students. *Journal of Abnormal Psychology, 102*, 183–204.

Lewinsohn, P. M., Klein, D. N., & Seeley, J. R. (1995). Bipolar disorders in a community sample of older adolescents: Prevalence, phenomenology, comorbidity, and course. *Journal of the American Academy of Child and Adolescent Psychiatry, 34,* 454–463.

Lewinsohn, P. M., Rohde, P., & Seeley, J. R. (1998). Major depressive disorder in older adolescents: Prevalence, risk factors, and clinical implications. *Clinical Psychology Review, 18,* 765–794.

Marcotte, D. (1997). Treating depression in adolescence: A review of the effectiveness of cognitive–behavioral treatments. *Journal of Youth and Adolescence, 26,* 273–283.

McWhirter, E. H. (1994). *Counseling for empowerment.* Alexandria, VA: American Counseling Association.

McWhirter, J. J., McWhirter, B. T., McWhirter, A. M., & McWhirter, E. H. (1994). High- and low-risk characteristics of youth: The five Cs of competency. *Elementary School Guidance and Counseling, 28,* 188–196.

McWhirter, J. J., McWhirter, B. T., McWhirter, E. H., & McWhirter, R. J. (2004). *At risk youth: A comprehensive response* (3rd ed.). Pacific Grove, CA: Brooks/Cole.

Michael, K. D., & Crowley, S. L. (2002). How effective are treatments for child and adolescent depression? A meta-analytic review. *Clinical Psychology Review, 22,* 247–269.

Miller-Johnson, S., Lochman, J. E., Coie, J. D., Terry, R., & Hyman, C. (1998). Comorbidity of conduct and depressive problems at sixth grade: Substance use outcomes across adolescence. *Journal of Abnormal Child Psychology, 26,* 221–232.

Milling, L., & Martin, B. (1992). Depression and suicidal behavior in preadolescent children. In C. E. Walker & M. C. Roberts (Eds.), *Handbook of clinical child psychology* (2nd ed., pp. 319–339). New York: Wiley.

Minuchin, S. (1974). *Families and family therapy.* Cambridge, MA: Harvard University Press.

Mufson, L., & Fairbanks, J. (1996). Interpersonal psychotherapy for depressed adolescents: A one-year naturalistic follow-up study. *Journal of the American Academy of Child and Adolescent Psychiatry, 35,* 1145–1155.

Mufson, L., Moreau, D., & Weissman, M. M. (1996). Focus on relationships: Interpersonal psychotherapy for adolescent depression. In E. D. Hibbs & P. S. Jensen (Eds.), *Psychosocial treatments for child and adolescent disorders: Empirically based strategies for clinical practice* (pp. 137–156). Washington, DC: American Psychological Association.

Nichols, M. P., & Schwartz, R. C. (1995). *Family therapy: Concepts and methods* (3rd ed.). Boston: Allyn & Bacon.

Papolos, D., & Papolos, J. (1999). *The bipolar child.* New York: Broadway Books.

Rehm, L. P. (1977). A self-control model of depression. *Behavior Therapy, 8,* 787–804.

Reid, M. J., & Webster-Stratton, C. (2001). The incredible years parent, teacher, and child intervention: Targeting multiple areas of risk for a young child with pervasive conduct problems using a flexible, manualized treatment program. *Cognitive & Behavioral Practice, 8,* 377–386.

Reinecke, M. A., Ryan, N. E., & DuBois, D. L. (1998). Cognitive–behavioral therapy of depression and depressive symptoms during adolescence: A review and meta-analysis. *Journal of the American Academy of Child and Adolescent Psychiatry, 37,* 26–34.

Rohde, P., Lewinsohn, P. M., & Seeley, J. R. (1991). Comorbidity with unipolar depression: II. Comorbidity with other mental disorders in adolescents and adults. *Journal of Abnormal Psychology, 100,* 214–222.

Rosselló, J., & Bernal, G. (1996). Adapting cognitive–behavioral and interpersonal treatments for depressed Puerto Rican adolescents. In E. D. Hibbs & P. S. Jensen (Eds.), *Psychosocial treatments for child and adolescent disorders: Empirically based strategies for clinical practice* (pp. 157–186). Washington, DC: American Psychological Association.

Sanchez, L., Hagino, O., Weller, E., & Ronald, W. (1999). Bipolarity in children. *Psychiatric Clinics of North America, 22,* 629–648.

Schwartz, S., & Johnson, J. H. (1985). *Psychopathology of childhood* (2nd ed.). New York: Pergamon Press.

Seligman, M. E. (1974). Depression and learned helplessness. In R. J. Friedman & M. M. Katz (Eds.), *The psychology of depression: Contemporary theory and research* (pp. 83–125). New York: Wiley.

Seligman, M. E. (1975). *Helplessness: On depression, development, and death.* San Francisco: Freeman.

Stark, K. D., Swearer, S., Kurowski, C., Sommer, D., & Bowen, B. (1996). Targeting the child and family: A holistic approach to treating child and adolescent depressive disorders. In E. D. Hibbs & P. S. Jensen (Eds.), *Psychosocial treatments for child and adolescent disorders: Empirically based strategies for clinical practice* (pp. 207–238). Washington, DC: American Psychological Association.

Szapocznik, J., Santisteban, D., Kurtines, W. M., Perez-Vidal, A., & Hervis, O. (1984). Bicultural effectiveness training: A treatment intervention for enhancing intercultural adjustment in Cuban-American families. *Hispanic Journal of Behavioral Sciences, 6,* 317–344.

Szapocznik, J., Santisteban, D., Rio, A., Perez-Vidal, A., & Kurtines, W. M. (1986a). Bicultural effectiveness training (BET): An experimental test of an intervention modality for families experiencing intergenerational/intercultural conflict. *Hispanic Journal of Behavioral Sciences, 8,* 303–330.

Szapocznik, J., Santisteban, D., Rio, A., Perez-Vidal, A., & Kurtines, W. M. (1986b). Family effectiveness training (FET) for Hispanic families. In H. P. Lefley & P. B. Pedersen (Eds.), *Cross-cultural training for mental health professionals* (pp. 245–261). Springfield, IL: Charles C Thomas.

Szapocznik, J., Santisteban, D., Rio, A., Perez-Vidal, A., & Kurtines, W. M. (1989). Family effectiveness training: An intervention to prevent drug abuse and problem behaviors in Hispanic adolescents. *Hispanic Journal of Behavioral Sciences, 11,* 4–27.

Vernon, A. (1989a). *Thinking, feeling, behaving: An emotional education curriculum for adolescents: Grades 7–12.* Champaign, IL: Research Press.

Vernon, A. (1989b). *Thinking, feeling, behaving: An emotional education curriculum for children: Grades 1–6.* Champaign, IL: Research Press.

Vernon, A. (1993). *Developmental assessment and intervention with children and adolescents.* Alexandria, VA: American Counseling Association.

Wagner, K. D., & Ambrosini, P. J. (2001). Childhood depression: Pharmacological therapy/treatment (pharmacotherapy of childhood depression). *Journal of Clinical Child Psychology, 30,* 88–97.

Webster-Stratton, C., & Hancock, L. (1998). Training for parents of young children with conduct problems: Content, methods, and therapeutic processes. In J. M. Briesmeister & C. Schaefer (Eds.), *Handbook of parent training: Parents as co-therapists for children's behavior problems* (2nd ed., pp. 98–152). New York: Wiley.

Webster-Stratton, C., Reid, M. J., & Hammond, M. (2001). Preventing conduct problems, promoting social competence: A parent and teacher training partnership in Head Start. *Journal of Clinical Child Psychology, 30,* 283–302.

Windle, R. C., & Windle, M. (1997). An investigation of adolescents' substance use behaviors, depressed affect, and suicidal behaviors. *Journal of Child Psychology and Psychiatry, 38,* 921–929.

Wolf, E. S. (1988). *Treating the self: Elements of clinical self-psychology.* New York: Guilford Press.

Ziervogel, C. F. (2000). Selective serotonin re-uptake inhibitors for children and adolescents. *European Child & Adolescent Psychiatry, 9*(Suppl. 15), 120–126.

7 | Stress and Trauma: Coping in Today's Society

Russell D. Miars

Multiple, conflicting time demands; social, economic, and political competition; and the complex and ever-changing nature of technology and the world of work characterize the society in which we live. As popularized in numerous self-help guides (e.g., Davis, Eshelman, & McKay, 1988; Girdano, Everly, & Dusek, 1990; Williams & Pojula, 2002), coping with stress has become synonymous with modern adult life. It is interesting, however, that the image of a carefree childhood void of stress and trauma has dominated our cultural view of youth for most of the 20th century. Since the mid-1980s, however, there has been an increasing awareness not only that children and adolescents do experience stress and trauma (Dinicola, 1996; Humphrey, 1988; Youngs, 1985) but also that in complex fashions yet to be understood, the numerous stresses and trauma youth actually do experience are linked to the alarming rise in at-risk behavioral difficulties many youth display (Gottlieb, 1991). In addition, there is increasing interest in the role trauma (extreme stress) and posttraumatic stress play in at-risk behaviors and mental health problems of youth (Kilpatrick & Williams, 1998; Lahad, Shacham, & Niv, 2000; Parson, 1995).

PROBLEM DEFINITION

Paradoxically, while youth and adults alike seem to know what it means to be stressed (e.g., being under pressure; being tense or anxious about problems at work, at school, or in the family), there has yet to emerge a uniformly agreed-on definition of the stress concept by researchers. This problem of definition in the literature complicates any discussion of stress and coping in youth. Until recently, an additional complication in understanding stress in youth has been that most research has been conducted exclusively with adults (J. H. Johnson, 1986; Lazarus, 1991, 1999). This results in a temptation to extrapolate and apply our understanding of stress and coping in adults to youth (Ryan-Wenger, 1992). It is doubtful, however, that stress and coping in adults are the same as, or directly similar to, stress and coping in youth (J. H. Johnson, 1986). In fact, several authors (Dise-Lewis, 1988; Humphrey, 1988; Sandler, Wolchik, MacKinnon, Ayers, & Roosa, 1997; Youngs, 1985) are quite clear that stress in youth must be regarded as distinct. Yet, the research evidence to support this claim is preliminary and only now beginning to appear in the literature (Aneshensel & Gore, 1991; Colten & Gore, 1991; Ryan-Wenger, 1992; Salmon & Bryant, 2002; Wertlieb, 1991; Wolchik & Sandler, 1997; Yule, 2001).

This chapter examines what is currently known about human stress, trauma, and coping processes in general, giving special attention to causes and prevention of stress in youth. The chapter first reviews the predominant ways stress and trauma have been conceptualized over the past three decades and then concentrates on causal factors (the sources of stress and trauma) with consideration of how developmental stages interact with the experience of stress and the coping strategies used by youth when faced with stress and trauma. The chapter next addresses approaches to prevention of stress and trauma from individual, family, school, and community perspectives. It concludes with a brief consideration of stress and trauma from a cultural perspective.

In this chapter the term *children* refers to youth preschool to age 10, whereas the term *adolescents* refers to youth ages 11 to 19. This is a useful convention (see Petersen, Kennedy, & Sullivan, 1991) because of the key developmental transition from childhood to adolescence broadly represented by the start of the second decade of life at age 10, with individual variation in the starting of adolescence occurring with the timing of puberty. As used here, the term *youth* is inclusive of preschool to age 19.

PERSPECTIVES ON STRESS AND TRAUMATIC STRESS

As noted above, researchers and theorists have had difficulty agreeing on a consistent definition of stress (J. H. Johnson, 1986). *Trauma* is more consistently defined in the literature as a form of stress that is extreme, overwhelming, and subjectively experienced as uncontrollable or unpredictable (Allen, 1995). Stress research historically has focused more on the consequences of stress for organismic functioning (Selye, 1993) than on how stress is aroused (Pearlin, 1993) and subsequently coped with at the emotional and behavioral level (Moos & Schaefer, 1993; Sandler et al., 1997).

Although acknowledging that a complete and uniform definition of stress has yet to emerge in the literature, J. H. Johnson (1986) asserted that the stress concept has been conceptualized from only three major perspectives: stimulus-oriented views, response-oriented views, and stress as a transaction between person and environment. These three perspectives, however, do not include the special attention that is given in the research literature to trauma and posttraumatic stress as forms of debilitating stress (e.g., Shalev, Yehuda, & McFarlane, 2000; van der Kolk, McFarlane, & Weisaeth, 1996). For this reason, trauma and posttraumatic stress are included below as a fourth perspective on the stress concept.

Stimulus-Oriented Views

From this perspective, the focus is on stress as a specific stimulus: "Stress is seen as resulting from experiencing any of a number of situations that are noxious or threatening or that place excessive demands on the individual" (J. H. Johnson, 1986, p. 16). Research that has defined stress from a life events perspective (e.g., divorce, death in the family) falls under this view. Although useful, particularly when relating stress to the onset of physical disease (e.g., Creed, 1993; Holmes & Rahe, 1967), this perspective alone is significantly limiting in that it cannot account for why some individuals experience potential stressors negatively whereas others experience the same stressor as a positive challenge (J. H. Johnson, 1986; Undergraff & Taylor, 2000).

Response-Oriented Views

Up until the 1960s, stress was almost exclusively defined from a stimulus perspective, meaning the effects of destructive environmental demands (Lazarus, 1993b). Embedded in this framework was an engineering analogy of stress in which an external force created a strain on the object and deformed it in proportion to the pressure of the stressor (Lazarus, 1993b). After several decades of work around the stress concept, Selye (1974) asserted that stress is the organism's physiological response to external stressors. Selye's work popularized a physiological version of the engineering analogy by conceiving of stress as having three distinct phases: alarm, resistance, and exhaustion. This sequence was termed the *general adaptation syndrome* (GAS) and refers to the "manifestations of stress in the whole body" (Selye, 1974, p. 139).

In the *alarm reaction* phase, considered to be the most important element of the GAS, the organism responds with a series of complex biochemical alterations. Numerous bodily systems speed up (breathing, blood sugar release) through the discharge of hormones preparing the body for fight or flight (Selye, 1993).

Because a state of alarm cannot be maintained continuously, a second phase, the *stage of resistance*, ensues. If the stressor continues to impinge on the organism, its limited adaptational energy is focused more singularly on resisting further the threat presented by the stressor. Unfortunately, when the organism's adaptational energy is focused on selected stressors in an ongoing fashion, it leaves itself vulnerable to other ensuing stressors (Ivancevich & Matteson, 1980). This biological stress syndrome (Selye, 1974) is how numerous stress studies have successfully linked various stressors with the onset of psychiatric (Rabkin, 1993) and somatic disease processes (Creed, 1993; Holmes & Rahe, 1967; Selye, 1993).

The final and third phase of the GAS is the *stage of exhaustion*. Selye (1993) emphasized that the body is limited in adaptability, or the amount of adaptational energy available to withstand stress. Once the adaptational energy has been expended, significant efforts at restoration must follow, and even then there is some wear and tear on the body's total reserve of adaptational energy. If the body cannot engage in replenishment and restore itself to the level of resistance, a phase of burnout (Pines, 1993) may ensue. Most adults have had some experience with burnout in terms of their involvement with work, career, or other prolonged life stress events. We tend to forget, however, that because of the incredible energy that youngsters expend in multiple spheres of activity, they too, by their very developmental nature, are equally vulnerable to burnout (Youngs, 1985).

Two limitations of the response-oriented perspective are that some individuals do not show the stressful response even in the face of a presumably stressful stimulus and that a stressful stimulus cannot be specified independent of a person's stressful response to it (J. H. Johnson, 1986; Lazarus, 1999).

Stress as a Transaction Between Person and Environment

Because of the limitations of the stimulus-oriented and response-oriented views, an additional model has emerged in the literature that not only incorporates many aspects of the stimulus and response perspectives but also considers the interaction between the person and the environment in accounting for stress and coping. This view has been most fully developed by Lazarus (Lazarus & Folkman, 1984). Of critical significance from this perspective is how the person views (appraises) the stressfulness of the environmental event; whether the event is seen as threatening or nonthreatening, desirable or undesirable, controllable or uncontrollable; and whether the person believes coping resources are readily available for dealing with the events. Out of this perspective, Lazarus and Folkman (1984, p. 19) offered their definition of stress: "Psychological stress is a particular relationship between the person and the environment that is appraised by the person as taxing or exceeding his or her resources and endangering his or her well-being." The emphasis in this definition is on the psychological processes (cognitive and mediational variables) in the person's experience of stress. As Lazarus has developed his theory from the mid-1960s to the present, he has argued that stress should be seen as a subset of emotion (Lazarus, 1993b, 1999). This view is adopted for two reasons. First, knowing that a person is experiencing "emotions resulting from harms, losses and threats" (anger, anxiety, fear) or from "emotions resulting from benefits" (joy, pride) in response to stress is very useful and says a lot more about how a troubled "person–environment" relationship is being coped with than when the subjective experience of emotion is omitted (p. 24). As Houston (1987) has noted, "An event cannot be regarded as a stressor without reference to the affective response it elicits" (p. 379). Second, the more striking issue in understanding stress is the person's various coping responses to stressors, not just the body's physiological response and adaptation to stress.

Although it is beyond the scope of this chapter to present a full discussion of Lazarus's theoretical model (see Lazarus, 1991, 1993a, 1999; Lazarus & Folkman, 1984), it is useful to highlight here that a significant portion of stress research has shifted from an emphasis on the physiological response aspects of stress (although that is an inseparable aspect of stress; Arnold, 1990b) to an examination of the psychological experience of stress and the ways in which the organism copes with or buffers (is resilient to) stress (Houston, 1987; Lazarus, 1993a, 1999). This is particularly true of research on stress and coping in youth.

Trauma and Posttraumatic Stress

Trauma is the extreme stress reaction that results from the experience of a threatening and overwhelming (traumatic) life event (Allen, 1995). The American Psychiatric Association (2000) defined a traumatic stress event as including both the witnessing of and/or involvement in a threatening (to self or others) situation (including death or serious injury) and the person's psychological response of intense fear, helplessness, or horror. Posttraumatic stress includes the "generalized reaction pattern to traumatic events, which is predetermined by the limited response range of affective, cognitive and behavioral responses that humans have to overwhelming stress" (McFarlane & de Girolamo, 1996, pp. 129–130). Only since the 1980s has it been acknowledged that exposure to trauma, over and beyond stress in general, is a widespread human experience, being reported as high as 40% in the population of young adults in one study (Breslau, Davis, & Andreski, 1991). Like adults, youth are exposed to traumas of various types (Costello, Erkanli, Fairbank, & Angold, 2002) and are vulnerable to posttraumatic stress reactions including the most severe form, posttraumatic stress disorder (PTSD). PTSD is a syndrome that includes three clusters of symptoms: hyperarousal, reexperiencing the trauma, and avoidance or numbing (Allen, 1995). Although PTSD can be construed (paradoxically) as a form of adaptation to trauma (Allen, 1995), its dysfunctional and self-damaging nature causes maladaptive functioning in the person's present life experience (including coping with common life stressors). PTSD symptoms may be acute (less than 3 months duration) or chronic (more than 3 months), and for some traumas (e.g., war related, rape) the disorder can occur or recur weeks, months, or even years after exposure to the traumatic event (Freedy & Donkervoet, 1995). Children and youth frequently show posttraumatic stress symptoms and PTSD from such traumas as child sexual/physical abuse, domestic violence, criminal violence, and any number of natural or man-made (caused) disasters.

The traumatic stress field has become a major subspecialty within the larger stress and coping field. The area of traumatic stress research includes youth, and adults as youth, who have experienced trauma and show posttraumatic effects including PTSD (Freedy & Donkervoet, 1995), as well as those who do not show such symptomatic responses and who are somehow resilient to the effects of the traumatic event(s) and show no or minimal posttraumatic reaction. Preventive factors that appear to buffer the effects of trauma in some youth as well as facilitate faster recovery from posttraumatic stress are noted in the Approaches to Prevention section below. Because the research literature on traumatic stress has burgeoned over the past several decades, it is not possible to provide a complete review of the many important aspects of traumatic stress and PTSD. For more comprehensive presentations, refer to Allen (1995), Freedy and Hobfoll (1995), Harvey and Miller (2000), Marsella, Friedman, Gerrity, and Scurfield (1996), Shalev et al. (2000), or van der Kolk et al. (1996).

CAUSAL FACTORS

Exact causal factors relating stress to certain emotional or behavioral outcomes are exceedingly difficult to show in the stress field, and researchers may never be able to make many exact causal inferences from the available data (J. H. Johnson, 1986). Part of the difficulty is that it is now known that the experiences of stress and traumatic stress are multiply determined by personality characteristics and contextual factors (Allen, 1995; Petersen et al., 1991) compounded even further by a large range of individual response variation around any one given source of stress (Lazarus, 1991, 1993b). This is particularly true for children and adolescents because developmental age changes interact with stressors to produce varied outcomes in coping responses (Compas & Phares, 1991). Thus, the identified sources of stress highlighted in this section do not prove a causal relationship between the identified source and a stress outcome, especially when applied to an individual case.

Because whole volumes have been compiled on current research and theory on stress and coping in youth and the effects of traumatic stress, what follows are selected highlights of what is currently known about the sources of stress and traumatic stress in childhood and adolescence. For more complete presentations on these topics, numerous excellent sources are available, including Allen (1995), Arnold (1990a), Colten and Gore (1991), Goldberger and Breznitz (1993), Humphrey (1988), Marsella et al. (1996), van der Kolk et al. (1996), and Wolchik and Sandler (1997).

Life Event Stressors

Life event scales have been developed for children (Coddington, 1972) similar to those originally developed for adults (Holmes & Rahe, 1967). The key feature of these scales is that they index *the source* and the *amount of change* demanded by the occurrence of specific events that are common across the developmental age range of youth. For example, the death of a parent is regarded uniformly as a very major life change (and stress) across preschool, elementary, junior, and senior high, whereas change to a different school is regarded as a minor change for preschoolers and progresses to a moderately challenging change for high school students (J. H. Johnson, 1986). Each stress event has its own rated level of life change units that varies across the preschool to senior high age range. There are 41 life events listed in Coddington's (1972) scale, including such events as divorce or remarriage of parents, increase in arguments between parents, arguments with parents, and death of brother or sister (see J. H. Johnson, 1986, p. 34, for the complete life events list).

Two problems arise with the life events approach to the causes of stress in children and adolescents. One is that the external view of raters such as parents, teachers, and other adults is questionable in terms of whether the ratings would actually correspond well with children's self-ratings of the same events (J. H. Johnson, 1986). The other is that life events are regarded as stressful (i.e., negative) without consideration of their desirability (e.g., getting married). An alternative approach to address these issues, and one that may be more useful in practice settings, is to ask the child to indicate events as either *good* or *bad* and then provide self-ratings of the extent of impact of the event (e.g., from *none* to *great*) in the child's life (see the Life Events Checklist in J. H. Johnson, 1986). The child's or adolescent's evaluation and subjective perspective are thus preserved and may be a more valid indicator of childhood stress. J. H. Johnson summarized a number of studies that show that child/adolescent adjustment and life stress scores, using either measurement approach, have shown a significant relationship between increased levels of life stress and difficulties with self-esteem, delinquent behavior, poor school performance, and overall level of psychiatric symptomatology. This includes such specific psychological problems as suicidal tendencies and anorexia nervosa. The implication of these studies was that the accumulation of unchecked stressful life events may set the stage for vulnerability to, and possible development of, at-risk emotional (e.g., depression) and behavioral (e.g., conduct disorder) problems in youth. Further, when the coping resources of youth are strained or depleted, they are particularly vulnerable to traumatic stress reactions when faced with trauma (Hobfoll, Dunahoo, & Monnier, 1995).

Daily Stress

A source of stress that has been identified over and beyond the occurrence of specific life events is the stress-inducing potential of mundane, chronic daily events, or what has been called *daily hassles* (Vingerhoets & Marcelissen, 1988). In adults, Delongis, Coyne, Dakoff, Folkman, and Lazarus (1982) have shown that daily hassles not only have the potential to induce stress but also may play an even stronger role in a person's physical health status than traditional life event stressors.

With respect to children, Youngs (1985) has suggested that the abundance of choices in modern society (especially in urban environments) and the increased cultural emphasis placed on self-fulfillment create a chronic underlying current of stress in children. In the adolescent years, a similar stress may exist stemming from so many choices around forming interpersonal relationships (Compas & Wagner, 1991) and pursuing career/vocational options (Youngs, 1985). In both of these areas, however, choice also means the stress of relinquishment: Not all desired peer relationships are possible, and career/vocational aspirations may be frustrated by today's economic environment of low growth and diminishing expectations in the rapidly changing world of work (Zunker, 2002).

Traumatic Stress

The most extreme and disruptive stressors youth face are traumatic events that result from some human action, such as violence, or a natural disaster, such as an earthquake. The defining characteristics of trauma are that the event is perceived as a potential threat to survival and that on a subjective level the event is experienced as uncontrollable or unpredictable (Friedman & Marsella, 1996). Many traumas are possible from man-made and natural sources, but those affecting youth the most are likely to be violence or violent crimes, domestic violence, physical abuse, sexual abuse (incest or rape), life-threatening illness or severe accidental injury, or one of numerous natural disasters. Traumatic stress from any of these sources differs from challenging or painful stress in that an acute or chronic posttraumatic stress condition results as normal coping resources are ineffective or depleted (Hobfoll et al., 1995).

The key to whether a traumatic event leads to a posttraumatic stress condition is based on a complex matrix of preexisting genetic factors (proneness to anxiety), developmental factors (disruption of attachment), and coping style (resilience) that interact with length of exposure to the traumatic experience, the subjective intensity of the traumatic experience, and posttrauma factors such as quickness of treatment intervention, strength of the person's social support (especially family), and overall coping resources. When extreme or negative levels of these factors converge in one person's experience and coping fails, the clinical syndrome of PTSD is the likely outcome. PTSD can be acute or chronic, and as a diagnosable psychiatric condition includes symptoms of intrusive recollection (flashbacks), emotional numbing to avoid the trauma-based memories, and hyperarousal (generalized anxiety, insomnia, irritability; American Psychiatric Association, 2000). PTSD requires clinical diagnosis and intervention at the individual and family levels, as the condition rarely resolves on its own (Allen, 1995) and may actually induce secondary traumatic stress in spouses, children, and other family members (Steinberg, 1998).

Home and Family Stress

Home and family are important contexts for understanding stress in children and adolescents and represent a large portion of the types of stressors youth experience (Humphrey, 1988). Numerous studies have identified significant relationships between the extent of parental stress and levels of child distress (Compas & Phares, 1991; Steinberg, 1998). Most, but not all, of these studies show that as one or both parents' stress and maladjustment increase so does the level of stress and maladjustment in the child or adolescent. Discussions of child abuse, divorce and marital dissolution, family economic problems, and adolescent–parent conflict are considered to illustrate how home and family stress can be strong sources of stress for many youth.

Child Abuse

Physical, sexual, emotional, and negligent abuse of children is of enormous concern in our society, and despite the increased effort to combat child abuse over the past half century, the true incidence and damaging consequences of abuse (including later posttraumatic reactions in adults) are still not fully known or understood (C. F. Johnson & Cohn, 1990). Relevant for a discussion of abuse and family stress is that parental stress is considered to be the major cause of child abuse (Straus, 1980), with child abuse being a major family stressor in the lives of those youth who are abused. Typically, the stress the child or adolescent experiences from the abuse is not expressed as such but rather is expressed through a wide range of posttraumatic-linked emotional and behavior difficulties such as anger, apathy, delinquency (Widom, 1991), school problems, shame, or eating disorders. C. F. Johnson and Cohn (1990) have provided a comprehensive list of reported effects. Interestingly, the typical runaway is likely to have come from an abusive family and may regard life on the street as less stressful than the home environment (Farber, Kinast, McCoard, & Falkner, 1984). This is just one example of how the ongoing effects of the stress of child abuse can be displaced in the form of other at-risk coping strategies in youth.

Divorce and Marital Dissolution

From a life events perspective, parental divorce is ranked second only to death of a parent as the most stressful life event a child or adolescent might experience (Coddington, 1972). Statistics have indicated that as many as 60% of youth will spend a portion of childhood or adolescence in a single-parent situation (Norton & Glick, 1986). Because of the high incidence of divorce, researchers have expanded their concern about the effects of divorce from a more singular life event readjustment to the chronic effects of divorce on children's mental, emotional, social, and academic development (Kalter, 1987; Wertlieb, 1991). The antecedents (emotional conflict and diminished support) and aftermath (divorce wars) of divorce are now considered as more inclusive aspects of the actual stress youth experience from marital dissolution (Arnold & Carnahan, 1990). These researchers have also summarized a number of studies that showed an interaction among sex, age, time of divorce in the youth's life, and the stress of readjustment. In general, boys appear to experience the stress of divorce more intensely at the elementary level, whereas girls at this age fair about as well as those in intact families. Later, however, adolescent girls of divorcing parents show significantly increasing problems with self-esteem and, later still, in heterosexual relationships. Overall, one of the better ways to understand divorce as a source of stress for youth is to recognize the significant loss/change in access to parents the experience usually represents. Diminished access to parents can significantly reduce the felt social support youth receive from parents at times when they may critically need it (e.g., around the stress of school). As noted further in the section on prevention approaches, for a variety of life events and chronic stressors, social support plays a critical role in buffering the negative effects of stress (Gottlieb & Wagner, 1991).

Economic Stress

No discussion of home and family stress is complete without mentioning the chronic and often devastating effects of economic stress in the family (Committee for Economic Development, 2002). Poverty creates an overall psychological environment in the family that is stressful for parents and youth alike, and it is linked to the incidence of numerous mental health adjustment issues of children, such as child abuse and its associated stresses. But economic stress is not limited to those families struggling to make ends meet. Occupational stress in adults has been associated with a number of health and psychological adjustment variables (Holt, 1993), contributing to the overall level of stress in the family. The dual roles of career and parent, especially for women, but increasingly for men as well (Zunker, 2002), create stress in the form of daily hassles, such as child-care arrangements, and strain in the parenting role. Finally, job loss, career change, and being a displaced worker are all stresses derived from economic change/uncertainty and the stress inherent in the rapid change to a technology and service-based economy (Zunker, 2002). Whether directly through financial strain or indirectly through parent job/career stress, economic stressors are a significant source of stress for today's youth.

School Stress

All aspects of the school experience challenge youth to adapt to the stresses of the educative process. Sears and Milburn (1990, p. 225) listed 25 common school-age stressors. These include anxiety about going to school, changing schools, competitiveness (including fear of failure and fear of success), conflict with teachers, failing an exam, worrying about taking tests, and peer teasing.

Paradoxically, although for some youth school is a major source of stress, for others school can be a source of motivational challenge and stress relief (Elias, 1989). Thus, when assessing the stress experienced by a child or adolescent, the nature and impact of the stress can be ascertained only in the context of the child's whole life space—background, home life, school life, age, and gender (Humphrey, 1988).

For many youth, and possibly increasing numbers of youth, the school experience is not the benign academic learning experience it was once regarded to be (Elias, 1989; Skinner & Wellborn, 1997). School reform pressures, which overemphasize academic success at the expense of psychosocial learning/development, may be contributing to "debilitating student stress" in up to 30% of the student population (Elias, 1989, p. 394). Rather than providing a balance between academics and preparation of students for adult citizenship, social competence, and the world of work, schools are under tremendous pressure from parents who are "looking to the schools to guarantee their children's future success" (Elias, 1989, p. 395). As this singular pressure for academic success and test score performance has increased, so has the stress level of students, to the point that for some the stress is debilitating. Students display the effects of this debilitating stress through physical symptoms of fatigue, headaches, and nausea; a sense of alienation from satisfaction gained through effectiveness and success; and delinquent and antisocial behavior, such as substance abuse or gang involvement, as a means of coping with the stress of thwarted expectations for a positive future (Elias, 1989). Elias's recommendations for addressing the pervasive and debilitating effects of school stress are included in the section on approaches to prevention.

Developmental Stress

The biological, cognitive, and emotional changes in youth from childhood to adolescence are complex and numerous. They also interact with the perception of and response to other life stress (Peterson et al., 1991; Trad & Greenblatt, 1990). Some of these additional as well as interactive sources of stress in youth—biological, cognitive–emotional, gender, and interpersonal—are briefly discussed here. For a comprehensive review of the literature on these complex interactions, see Arnold (1990a, 1990b) and Colten and Gore (1991).

Biological Changes

Puberty is the most dramatic of all the developmental transitions in the human life span (Petersen et al., 1991; Sigelman & Rider, 2003). Biological changes in early adolescence leading to adult appearance and size, reproductive capacity, and internal endocrine changes produce challenges and stresses in the intrapersonal and social adaptation spheres of adolescent functioning. Issues of sexuality and sexual behavior emerge as a result of these biological changes and can be very stressful for early adolescents and their parents. Further, sex has become an issue for more young people at an earlier age than in previous generations (Youngs, 1985). This observation supports the belief that there is a downward age trend for today's youth in the timing of the stress of emerging sexuality.

Cognitive–Emotional Changes

The increase in cognitive and emotional complexity required for expanding from a concrete and certain experience of the world to a capacity for abstract and relativistic thinking and emotion (Piaget & Inhelder, 1969) is a developmental stressor of enormous implications in the transition from childhood to adolescence. Larson and Asmussen (1991) reported data that show there is an increase in the experience of negative emotion (anger, worry, hurt) from preadolescence to adolescence. In a certain sense, maturing cognitive and emotional capacities set the stage for adolescence to be the first major confrontation with the existential issues of choice, responsibility, and freedom in the life span (Bugental, 1981; Sigelman & Rider, 2003). As is commonly recognized, the inherent stress of this developmental transition can be overwhelming for many youth. What is less commonly recognized is the adolescent's critical need for parent and peer support (Petersen & Ebata, 1987) as a means of navigating through this challenging transitional period of life.

Gender Differences

Gender socialization has emerged as a significant moderator variable in the experience of stress in youth (Gore & Colten, 1991). Some of the conclusions emerging from the literature in this area are extremely relevant to our understanding of the sources of stress in youth, particularly in older adolescents. For example, Petersen et al. (1991) concluded from a number of studies that although in early adolescence there is only one gender divergence (for body image with girls showing a decline), by late adolescence there is marked gender divergence across all measures of self and negative affect, with girls becoming markedly more depressed as adolescence proceeds. The available evidence suggests that girls "amplify" negative moods as a form of coping with developmental stressors, whereas boys are "more likely to distract themselves from a depressed mood" (Petersen et al., 1991, p. 105). Thus, girls' coping responses to stress change along gender lines during adolescence (suggesting they become more vulnerable to various stressors), but boys' coping responses appear to remain the same. Paradoxically, girls' coping responses to developmental stress in adolescence may set a life-long pattern of coping with stress with depressive affect. Similarly, the pattern of boys' coping may be protective for gender-based functioning in instrumental and achievement spheres, but it may also be quite maladaptive for future interpersonal relationships requiring emotional intimacy (Petersen et al., 1991).

Interpersonal Stress

Interpersonal relationships increasingly become a source of stress for youth as they progress from childhood to early adolescence and through late adolescence. This appears to be true for both girls and boys, but adolescent girls report greater interpersonal stress than boys (Compas & Wagner, 1991). Further, Compas and Wagner (1991) noted that when stressful life events occur in an adolescent's life they are likely to be *"directly* related to others in their social networks, especially their parents" (p. 75). In a study that directly examined adolescent–parent conflict, Smetana, Yau, Restrepo, and Braeges (1991) found that conflict, although stressful, provides a context for debates over the extent of adolescents' developing autonomy and thus serves an adaptive function. However, when the interaction style between parent and adolescent is negative (i.e., when the interaction is constraining, devaluing, or judging), adolescent development is inhibited (causing further intrapersonal stress and interpersonal conflict). Another significant finding was that adolescent–parent conflict is greater in married than divorced families and that children and adolescents who have had to deal with the stress of parental divorce may actually increase their coping competence and resilience to future life stress (Smetana et al., 1991). Finally, Compas and Wagner (1991) have noted that interpersonal stress shows a reliable developmental variation: In junior high, negative family interaction is the predominant source of interpersonal stress, whereas by senior high conformity and concerns about acceptance by the peer group are the dominant interpersonal stressors. Stress arising from dependency on the peer group subsides by later adolescence, and with entry into college, academic events become the predominant source of stress.

APPROACHES TO PREVENTION

Both primary and secondary prevention strategies are important in reducing stress in youth. Primary prevention consists of attempts to minimize youths' vulnerability to stress or actually prevent its occurrence, whereas secondary prevention consists of teaching vulnerable youth the therapeutic coping skills they need to know (Lazarus, 1991). Tertiary prevention consists of clinical treatment of stress and posttraumatic stress after the damage has occurred, and although not preventive in an absolute sense, such intervention can prevent the exacerbation of traumatic stress as well as lessen the secondary traumatic stress of family members of the traumatized individual (Steinberg, 1998).

Because so many stressors of youth (especially in children) are outside of their control and related to situations with parents, other family members, teachers, or socioeconomic conditions (Ryan-Wenger, 1992), it is particularly relevant to approach the prevention of stress in youth from a systemic perspective. At the same time, many life and traumatic stressors are unavoidable for youth or stem from normal developmental challenges. Given this, an additional prevention strategy becomes maximizing the coping resources of youth so that the negative effects of stress are buffered to the greatest extent possible (Gottlieb, 1991; Sandler et al., 1997). This latter strategy reflects the current research emphasis on understanding individual coping processes (Lazarus, 1991, 1993a, 1993b, 1999) and psychosocial protective factors (Kimchi & Schaffner, 1990; Roosa, Wolchik, & Sandler, 1997) when the person is under stress. In this overview of approaches to prevention in the individual, family, school, and community, consideration is given to possible systemic prevention of stress as well as various coping and protective factors that appear to buffer the effects of stress and trauma in youth.

Individual Approaches to Prevention

As already noted, secondary prevention of stress consists of teaching therapeutic stress and coping skills to the individual in hopes that the negative effects of stress will not escalate. This may be done in a remedial fashion once stress reduction has been identified to be needed, or more broadly and in advance through coping skills training (Elias, 1989; Sandler et al., 1997). Because children, and to a certain extent adolescents, are less able to identify the sources of stress or know how to cope with a variety of stressors (Ryan-Wenger, 1992), the adults in their lives must facilitate the referral of youth for remedial stress reduction and anticipate the need for and benefits of coping training (Folkman, Chesney, McKusick, Ironson, & Coates, 1991). Stress reduction strategies and techniques that rely on progressive muscle relaxation, visual imagery, and biofeedback have been shown to be effective for both adults (Girdano et al., 1990) and children (Humphrey, 1988; Humphrey & Humphrey, 1981; Romano, 1997; Youngs, 1985). Stress reduction in children might best focus on the aspects of body relaxation, nutrition, and exercise to counter the effects of stress (Humphrey, 1988), while, as cognitive development increases, cognitive, emotional, and social support coping skills training are additional forms of preventive intervention for adolescents (Folkman et al., 1991). Interestingly, however, Romano (1997) found that cognitive coping strategies were being used in the school environment by children as early as the fourth and fifth grades.

With respect to coping, researchers have identified three conceptual frameworks that relate to the present discussion of coping effectiveness in the individual as a preventive measure against stress (Ebata & Moos, 1991). The first is identified as the approach/avoidance coping model (Lazarus & Folkman, 1984) and distinguishes between active approach-oriented coping (toward threat) and passive or avoidance-oriented (away from threat) coping. Approach coping includes efforts to change ways of thinking about a problem (stressor) as well as behavioral attempts to resolve or address the problem. Avoidant coping includes cognitive attempts to deny or minimize threat and behavioral attempts to avoid or get away from the problem. Research has shown that adolescents who use more approach coping than avoidance coping are better adjusted and less distressed (Ebata & Moos, 1991). Further, Ebata and Moos concluded that adolescents who show a pattern of avoidance coping may be at greater risk for poorer adjustment to subsequent life stressors and crises. Through coping skills training, adolescents can be shown the positive value of approach coping and be encouraged to engage in approach coping behavior when faced with life events and developmental stressors.

A second useful way to think about stress prevention for the individual from a coping perspective is highlighted by the problem-focused/emotion-focused distinction (Lazarus, 1993a, 1999). In this framework, coping efforts can be focused on modifying the stressor itself (problem-focused coping) or on attempts to regulate the emotional responses that accompany the stressor (emotion-focused coping). Ebata and Moos (1991) reported research suggesting that adolescents who used more problem-focused coping with interpersonal stressors (i.e., talking with the other person) reported fewer stressful emotional and behavioral reactions than those who used emotion-focused strategies, such as ignoring the situation or yelling at the other person. It should be noted, however, that although problem-focused coping is a more effective coping strategy in general, emotion-focused coping may be more effective for certain types of stressors over which the person can exercise no useful action (Lazarus, 1993b).

The third framework for understanding and facilitating positive coping in the individual is related to the role of seeking social support as a coping response. Ebata and Moos (1991) summarized several studies that examined the relationship among family and peer support, active coping strategies, and substance use in adolescents. In general, adolescents who used active behavioral and cognitive coping as well as the seeking of adult support showed less substance use, whereas those adolescents who relied more on peers and acting out to cope showed more substance use (Ebata & Moos, 1991). Other authors (e.g., Gottlieb, 1991; Hendron, 1990) have also noted that attachment, support, and guidance from at least one adult figure (teacher, coach, parent, school counselor) in an adolescent's life can buffer the effects of stress and facilitate approach and problem-focused coping.

The prevention of traumatic stress can take two additional forms. First, preliminary research has shown that when trauma occurs, immediate crisis intervention and critical incident stress debriefing can minimize the risk of posttraumatic stress reactions in many individuals (Saylor, Belter, & Stokes, 1997). This type of prevention applies more to singular events (natural disasters, catastrophic accidents, violent crime) than it does to repeated or more hidden traumas (child sexual abuse, domestic violence). In the latter case, posttraumatic symptoms or PTSD often shows a delayed onset in the individual and requires corrective therapy in the form of psychological or pharmacological therapies (Allen, 1995). In all cases of traumatic stress in the individual, crisis intervention is likely to be preventive of an intensification of posttraumatic stress reactions (Sorenson, 2000). Thus, community efforts to have services in place in advance of trauma, whether in disaster agencies, hospitals, schools, or clinics, are the best prevention when traumatic events inevitably occur in the lives of youth (Saylor et al., 1997).

Family Approaches to Prevention

From a larger systems perspective, those services that reduce stress in family life can directly prevent the stress in children that can interfere with normal development (Wagner, 1994) or cause secondary traumatic stress reactions in children (Steinberg, 1998). Petersen et al. (1991) observed that when such a strategy can be implemented from childhood to early adolescence, and through adolescence, a positive trajectory of coping with the stress of developmental transitions is set in motion. The earlier and the more consistent the support is from parents in this process, the more positive is the overall mental health trajectory of the child. Petersen et al. also noted that positive mental health in children and adolescents (higher self-esteem) is related to greater internal coping resources when youth are faced with unexpected life event stressors. Given this overall picture, school-based health clinics (Sleek, 1994) that can provide family support (Gottlieb, 1991) in the form of integrated social, health, and mental health services may be one of the most effective means of ameliorating family stress and, by extension, preventing stress in youth. In addition, the school context can be a good intervention and referral point for youth needing therapeutic services for posttraumatic stress reactions or PTSD.

A more direct way in which the family plays a role in the prevention of stress in youth is through the family's function as an informal social support network (Sandler et al., 1997; Willis, 1987). Willis (1987) believed the extent to which the family functions as an "informal help-seeking" support system is the extent to which such "informal support may serve to reduce the stressful impact of adverse events" (p. 34). This idea has also been advanced for posttraumatic stress reactions (Dinicola, 1996), although the caregivers of traumatized youth may also be at risk for developing secondary traumatic stress reactions (Steinberg, 1998). Dimensions of parent/family support, which appear to make a real difference in buffering the negative effects of stress, are esteem support (e.g., emotional and confidant support), informational support (e.g., problem-solving steps), motivational support (e.g., encouragement), and instrumental support (e.g., material aid such as money). In contrast, one of the reasons child abuse is so likely to have posttraumatic stress features is that the various forms of family support are so lacking in the abusive family. Other family factors that appear to be protective of stress in youth are noted by Kimchi and Schaffner (1990) and include such dimensions as adequate rule setting and structure, family cohesion, lower parental conflicts, open communication, warmth toward the child, and being patient in parenting style. As noted earlier, the family can be a powerful source of stress in youth; likewise, it can be a powerful buffer to stress when functioning effectively.

School Approaches to Prevention

Elias (1989) has outlined a number of recommendations that reflect both primary (systemic) and secondary (coping skills) stress prevention strategies in the schools. Basing his perspective on the assumption that school stress does interfere with both academic and social growth in youth, which in turn diminish the coping resources available to youth, he asserted that "it is . . . logical and necessary to rethink our view of 'academic time' and incorporate the teaching of coping and learning-to-learn skills into the mainstream of educational programming" (p. 400). Skinner and Wellborn (1997) corroborated this idea and suggested that interventions promoting academic coping are both preventive and developmental in nature. Using this general perspective, Elias (1989) made the following recommendations to reduce school stress:

- *promote accomplishment* by expanding opportunities for children to feel connected to schools as well as feel efficacious in all learning contexts of the school
- *teach coping skills and learning-to-learn skills* as part of the mainstream educational programming
- *adjust the culture of classrooms and schools* to reflect an integrated approach to social and coping skills development rather than the isolated clinical approach to intervention that is common
- *ensure that schools are physically safe* because safety is paramount to managing stress
- *increase the value placed on long-term educational planning* to address complex issues rather than favor a tendency to seek short-term "program in place" solutions that eventually fade
- *use action research* as "a procedure in which new programs are tried, monitored, evaluated, refined, and tried again" (p. 402)
- *shift the emphasis of current training programs for teachers* so that debilitating stress in schools is recognized and addressed through social development education of the child and changes in the learning environment.

As another means of countering the stress adolescents experience in school, Gottlieb (1991) emphasized the benefits of social support interventions. Because inclusion, acceptance, and approval from one's peer group are so important in adolescence, peer counseling programs in schools can increase the social support adolescents feel. With such added peer/social support, the stressful aspects of school and the challenges of developmental changes can be minimized.

Further, Humphrey (1988) has suggested that stress from academic competition needs to be offset by an increased emphasis on cooperative learning experiences. For example, the stress of math anxiety is centrally based on the way in which math is often taught—in a context of time pressure to finish first, humiliation when being called on to perform in front of the class, and an emphasis on one right answer (only the end product). All three of these elements are negative and stressful for many youth and reveal a child's weakness rather than his or her competence (Humphrey, 1988). By altering this approach to learning math, teachers can significantly reduce stress in the classroom and produce more confident and capable students.

Community Approaches to Prevention

Wagner (1994) observed that the povertization of childhood is the single largest threat to the welfare of children today. It is clear that poverty is stressful for parents and families and plays a large role in the chronic stress that many youth experience in the family, school, and community. In addition, poverty may also be associated with more frequent witnessing of violent crime by many youth, serving as a source of traumatic stress and its associated risks (Parson, 1995). There are no simple or direct ways to prevent poverty, but communities can advocate for changes in public policy that empower children, protect their rights, and facilitate access to social and mental health services to reduce stress (Stern & Newland, 1994). Such efforts, when successful, can go a long way in preventing stress in youth while benefiting all children as a social group.

The stress associated with violence in the schools can be another important target of community prevention. The threat of violence in schools affects nearly all students, and the fear that results can inhibit a sense of industry, achievement, and self-confidence (Christie & Toomey, 1990). Further, posttraumatic reactions and PTSD are likely for those in immediate proximity to a violent crime at school or a school shooting. Given that schools are embedded in the larger community, the stress of violence must be prevented by community-based programs. Because much of the violence in schools may be related to the problems of drugs and gangs in and around schools (in the inner city and suburbs alike), school and community prevention strategies that address these issues (see chapters 12, 14, and 15) reduce an aspect of chronic stress in youth.

In addition, the community can play a preventive role in reducing stress in youth by publicly supporting the continuing efforts of schools to integrate psychosocial education and other at-risk intervention programs into the schools (see Elias, 1989). McWhirter, McWhirter, McWhirter, and McWhirter (1994) have identified "five C's of competency" that distinguish high- and low-risk youth: critical school (academic) competencies; concept of self and self-esteem; communication with others; coping ability; and control—over decision making, delay of gratification, and purpose in life. Parents, teachers, clergy and all adults in the community can help prevent stress in youth by teaching and valuing these coping competencies that are so necessary to deal with a rapidly changing world.

ADAPTATIONS FOR DIVERSITY

Considering stress, traumatic stress, and coping from an ethnocultural perspective is the most recent development in the stress field (de Vries, 1996; Marsella et al., 1996; Nader, Dubrow, & Stamm, 1999). Cross-cultural applicability is an important question and begins with whether the stress concept (including posttraumatic stress) validly applies to children, adolescents, and adults from other cultures (de Vries, 1996). On the basis of the available research, Marsella et al. (1996) concluded that PTSD is a valid and clinically meaningful diagnosis in non-Western cultures. They cautioned, however, that in most cases there are culture-specific responses to trauma not captured in the universal aspects of the diagnosis. Similarly, de Vries (1996) and Perren-Klinger (2000) supported the concept that traumatic stress is valid cross-culturally, but they added that a person's unique culture or ethnic subculture may offer protective responses to stress that are integrated into the culture's existing framework for holding problems and illnesses, including stress and traumatic stress. For example, fatalistic cultures may assign external (unalterable) causation to stress and trauma and, therefore, have cultural rituals in place to accept and support traumatized individuals, but other cultures may medicalize trauma and expect curative solutions to it from expert treatment providers. Clearly, subtle cultural factors do exist beyond the apparent universality of the trauma construct, and, therefore, sensitivity to and inclusion of unique ethno-cultural definitions and experiences of stress and trauma are required in treatment and prevention efforts (Dinicola, 1996; Dragnus, 1996; Dubrow & Nader, 1999).

From the same perspective, Gonzales and Kim (1997) indicated that the available literature on stress, coping, and overall mental health of youth also requires specific consideration of cultural factors. In addition to all the life stress and coping adaptation concepts outlined in the literature, working with ethnic minority youth requires consideration of their cultural ecology, which includes the stress-related variables of socioeconomic status, neighborhood context, migration/acculturation, and ethnic/racial discrimination. Although beyond the scope of the present discussion, Gonzales and Kim's cultural ecological process model for ethnic minority children provides a comprehensive picture of how ethnicity and cultural protective factors interact to produce varied stress and coping outcomes.

SUMMARY

In this chapter, stress is discussed from three perspectives: stimulus-oriented view, response-oriented view, and person–environment transaction view. In addition, trauma and posttraumatic stress are considered as extreme stress and significant challenges to coping. Recent research and theory emphasize the person–environment transactional model in which both the perception of stress and coping responses to stress play an active role in the stress phenomenon (including traumatic stress). Only since the mid-1980s has research focused specifically on stress and coping in youth, and only in the past two decades has a fuller appreciation of trauma and posttraumatic stress in youth, especially ethnocultural considerations, emerged in the literature. Causal factors for stress and trauma in youth are multiple and varied and are complexly interwoven with the developmental challenges of childhood and adolescence. Life events, daily hassles, traumatic stress, family stress, child abuse, divorce, economic factors, school stress, and developmental challenges are high-lighted as causal factors for stress in youth. Approaches to prevention are considered across individual, family, school, and community from a larger systems perspective as well as from individual coping skills and social support factors that are preventive of stress in youth. Important ethnocultural factors are also highlighted as they relate to the cross-cultural validity of posttraumatic stress and stress and coping in ethnic minority youth.

REFERENCES

Allen, J. G. (1995). *Coping with trauma: A guide to self-understanding*. Washington, DC: American Psychiatric Press.

American Psychiatric Association. (2000). *Diagnostic and statistical manual of mental disorders* (4th ed., text revision). Washington, DC: Author.

Aneshensel, C. S., & Gore, S. (1991). Development, stress, and role structuring: Social transitions of adolescence. In J. Eckenrode (Ed.), *The social context of coping* (pp. 55–77). New York: Plenum Press.

Arnold, L. E. (Ed.). (1990a). *Childhood stress*. New York: Wiley.

Arnold, L. E. (1990b). Stress in children and adolescents: Introduction and summary. In L. E. Arnold (Ed.), *Childhood stress* (pp. 1–19). New York: Wiley.

Arnold, L. E., & Carnahan, J. A. (1990). Child divorce stress. In L. E. Arnold (Ed.), *Childhood stress* (pp. 373–403). New York: Wiley.

Breslau, N. D., Davis, G. C., & Andreski, P. (1991). Traumatic events and posttraumatic stress disorder in an urban population of young adults. *Archives of General Psychiatry, 48*, 216–222.

Bugental, J. F. T. (1981). *The search for authenticity* (Enlarged ed.). New York: Irvington.

Christie, D. J., & Toomey, B. G. (1990). The stress of violence: School, community, and world. In L. E. Arnold (Ed.), *Childhood stress* (pp. 297–323). New York: Wiley.

Coddington, R. D. (1972). The significance of life events as etiological factors in the diseases of children: A study of a normal population. *Journal of Psychosomatic Research, 16*, 205–213.

Colten, M. E., & Gore, S. (Eds.). (1991). *Adolescent stress: Causes and consequences.* New York: Aldine de Gruyter.

Committee for Economic Development. (2002). *Preschool for all: Investing in a productive and just society.* New York: Author.

Compas, B. E., & Phares, V. (1991). Stress during childhood and adolescence: Sources of risk and vulnerability. In E. M. Cummings, A. L. Greene, & K. H. Karraker (Eds.), *Life-span developmental psychology: Perspectives on stress and coping* (pp. 111–129). Hillsdale, NJ: Erlbaum.

Compas, B. E., & Wagner, B. M. (1991). Psychosocial stress during adolescence: Intrapersonal and interpersonal processes. In M. E. Colten & S. Gore (Eds.), *Adolescent stress: Causes and consequences* (pp. 67–85). New York: Aldine de Gruyter.

Costello, J. E., Erkanli, A., Fairbank, J. A., & Angold, A. (2002). The prevalence of potentially traumatic events in childhood and adolescence. *Journal of Traumatic Stress, 15*, 99–112.

Creed, F. (1993). Stress and psychosomatic disorders. In L. Goldberger & S. Breznitz (Eds.), *Handbook of stress: Theoretical and clinical aspects* (pp. 496–510). New York: Free Press.

Davis, D., Eshelman, E. R., & McKay, M. (1988). *The relaxation and stress reduction workbook* (3rd ed.). Oakland, CA: New Harbinger.

Delongis, A., Coyne, J. C., Dakoff, G., Folkman, S., & Lazarus, R. A. (1982). Relationship of daily hassles, uplifts, and major life events to health status. *Health Psychology, 1*, 119–136.

de Vries, M. W. (1996). Trauma in cultural perspective. In B. A. van der Kolk, A. C. McFarlane, & L. Weisaeth (Eds.), *Traumatic stress: The effects of overwhelming experience on mind, body, and society* (pp. 398–413). New York: Guilford Press.

Dinicola, V. F. (1996). Ethnocultural aspects of PTSD and related disorders among children and adolescents. In A. J. Marsella, M. J. Friedman, E. T. Gerrity, & R. M. Scurfield (Eds.), *Ethnocultural aspects of posttraumatic stress disorder: Issues, research, and clinical applications* (pp. 389–414). Washington, DC: American Psychological Association.

Dise-Lewis, J. E. (1988). The Life Events and Coping Inventory: An assessment of stress in children. *Psychosomatic Medicine, 50*, 484–489.

Dragnus, J. G. (1996). Ethnocultural considerations in the treatment of PTSD: Therapy service considerations. In A. J. Marsella, M. J. Friedman, E. T. Gerrity, & R. M. Scurfield (Eds.), *Ethnocultural aspects of posttraumatic stress disorder: Issues, research, and clinical applications* (pp. 459–482). Washington, DC: American Psychological Association.

Dubrow, N., & Nader, K. (1999). Consultations amidst trauma and loss: Recognizing and honoring differences among cultures. In K. Nader, N. Dubrow, & B. H. Stamm (Eds.), *Honoring differences: Cultural issues in the treatment of trauma and loss.* Philadelphia: Brunner/Mazel.

Ebata, A. T., & Moos, R. H. (1991). Coping and adjustment in distressed and healthy adolescents. *Journal of Applied Developmental Psychology, 12*, 33–54.

Elias, M. J. (1989). Schools as a source of stress to children: An analysis of causal and ameliorative influences. *Journal of School Psychology, 27*, 393–407.

Farber, E. D., Kinast, C., McCoard, W. D., & Falkner, D. (1984). Violence in families of adolescent runaways. *Child Abuse and Neglect, 18*, 295–299.

Folkman, S., Chesney, M., McKusick, L., Ironson, D. S., & Coates, T. J. (1991). Translating coping theory into an intervention. In J. Eckenrode (Ed.), *The social context of coping* (pp. 239–260). New York: Plenum Press.

Freedy, J. R., & Donkervoet, J. C. (1995). Traumatic stress: An overview of the field. In J. R. Freedy & S. E. Hobfoll (Eds.), *Traumatic stress: From theory to practice* (pp. 3–28). New York: Plenum Press.

Freedy, J. R., & Hobfoll, S. E. (Eds.). (1995). *Traumatic stress: From theory to practice.* New York: Plenum Press.

Friedman, M. J., & Marsella, A. J. (1996). Posttraumatic stress disorder: An overview of the concept. In A. J. Marsella, M. J. Friedman, E. T. Gerrity, & R. M. Scurfield (Eds.), *Ethnocultural aspects of posttraumatic stress disorder: Issues, research, and clinical applications* (pp. 11–32). Washington, DC: American Psychological Association.

Girdano, D., Everly, G., & Dusek, D. (1990). *Controlling stress and tension: A holistic approach* (3rd ed.). Englewood Cliffs, NJ: Prentice-Hall.

Goldberger, L., & Breznitz, S. (Eds.) (1993). *Handbook of stress: Theoretical and clinical aspects.* New York: Free Press.

Gonzales, N. A., & Kim, L. S. (1997). Stress and coping in an ethnic minority context: Children's cultural ecologies. In S. A. Wolchik & I. N. Sandler (Eds.), *Handbook of children's coping: Linking theory and intervention* (pp. 481–511). New York: Plenum Press.

Gore, S., & Colten, M. E. (1991). Adolescent stress, social relationships, and mental health. In M. E. Colten & S. Gore (Eds.), *Adolescent stress: Causes and consequences* (pp. 1–14). New York: Aldine de Gruyter.

Gottlieb, B. H. (1991). Social support in adolescence. In M. E. Colten & S. Gore (Eds.), *Adolescent stress: Causes and consequences* (pp. 281–306). New York: Aldine de Gruyter.

Gottlieb, B. H., & Wagner, F. (1991). Stress and support processes in close relationships. In J. Eckenrode (Ed.), *The social context of coping* (pp. 165–188). New York: Plenum Press.

Harvey, J. H., & Miller, E. D. (Eds.). (2000). *Loss and trauma: General and close relationship perspectives.* Philadelphia: Brunner-Routledge.

Hendron, R. L. (1990). Stress in adolescence. In L. E. Arnold (Ed.), *Childhood stress* (pp. 247–264). New York: Wiley.

Hobfoll, S. E., Dunahoo, C. A., & Monnier, J. (1995). Conservation of resources and traumatic stress. In J. R. Freedy & S. E. Hobfoll (Eds.), *Traumatic stress: From theory to practice* (pp. 49–72). New York: Plenum Press.

Holmes, T. H., & Rahe, R. H. (1967). The social readjustment rating scale. *Journal of Psychosomatic Research, 11,* 213–218.

Holt, R. R. (1993). Occupational stress. In L. Goldberger & S. Breznitz (Eds.), *Handbook of stress: Theoretical and clinical aspects* (pp. 342–367). New York: Free Press.

Houston, K. B. (1987). Stress and coping. In C. R. Snyder & C. E. Ford (Eds.), *Coping with negative life events* (pp. 373–399). New York: Plenum Press.

Humphrey, J. H. (1988). *Children and stress.* New York: AMS Press.

Humphrey, J. H., & Humphrey, J. N. (1981). *Reducing stress in children through creative relaxation.* Springfield, IL: Charles C Thomas.

Ivancevich, J. M., & Matteson, M. T. (1980). *Stress and work: A managerial perspective.* Glenview, IL: Scott, Foresman.

Johnson, C. F., & Cohn, D. S. (1990). The stress of child abuse and other family violence. In L. E. Arnold (Ed.), *Childhood stress* (pp. 267–295). New York: Wiley.

Johnson, J. H. (1986). *Life events as stressors in childhood and adolescence.* Beverly Hills, CA: Sage.

Kalter, N. (1987). Long-term effects of divorce on children: A developmental vulnerability model. *American Journal of Orthopsychiatry, 57,* 587–599.

Kilpatrick, K. L., & Williams, L. M. (1998). Potential mediators of posttraumatic stress disorder in child witnesses to domestic violence. *Child Abuse and Neglect, 22,* 310–330.

Kimchi, J., & Schaffner, B. (1990). Childhood protective factors and stress risk. In L. E. Arnold (Ed.), *Childhood stress* (pp. 475–500). New York: Wiley.

Lahad, S., Shacham, Y., & Niv, S. (2000). Coping and community resources in children facing disaster. In A. Shalev, R. Yelhuda, & A. C. McFarlane (Eds.), *International handbook of human response to trauma* (pp. 389–395). New York: Plenum Press.

Larson, R., & Asmussen, L. (1991). Anger, worry, and hurt in early adolescence: An enlarging world of negative emotions. In M. E. Colten & S. Gore (Eds.), *Adolescent stress: Causes and consequences* (pp. 21–41). New York: Aldine de Gruyter.

Lazarus, R. S. (1991). *Emotion and adaptation.* New York: Oxford University Press.

Lazarus, R. S. (1993a). Coping theory and research: Past, present, and future. *Psychosomatic Medicine, 55,* 234–247.

Lazarus, R. S. (1993b). Why we should think of stress as a subset of emotion. In L. Goldberger & S. Breznitz (Eds.), *Handbook of stress: Theoretical and clinical aspects* (pp. 21–39). New York: Free Press.

Lazarus, R. S. (1999). *Stress and emotion: A new synthesis*. New York: Springer.

Lazarus, R. S., & Folkman, S. (1984). *Stress, appraisal, and coping*. New York: Springer.

Marsella, A. J., Friedman, M. J., Gerrity, E. T., & Scurfield, R. M. (1996). Ethnocultural aspects of PTSD: Some closing thoughts. In A. J. Marsella, M. J. Friedman, E. T. Gerrity, & R. M. Scurfield (Eds.), *Ethnocultural aspects of posttraumatic stress disorder: Issues, research, and clinical applications* (pp. 529–538). Washington, DC: American Psychological Association.

McFarlane, A. C., & de Girolamo, G. (1996). The nature of traumatic stress and the epidemiology of posttraumatic reactions. In B. A. van der Kolk, A. C. McFarlane, & L. Weisaeth (Eds.), *Traumatic stress: The effects of overwhelming experience on mind, body, and society* (pp. 129–154). New York: Guilford Press.

McWhirter, J. J., McWhirter, B. T., McWhirter, A. M., & McWhirter, E. H. (1994). High- and low-risk characteristics of youth: The five Cs of competency. *Elementary School Guidance and Counseling, 28*, 188–196.

Moos, R. H., & Schaefer, J. A. (1993). Coping resources and processes: Current concepts and measures. In L. Goldberger & S. Breznitz (Eds.), *Handbook of stress: Theoretical and clinical aspects* (pp. 234–257). New York: Free Press.

Nader, K., Dubrow, N., & Stamm, B. H. (Eds.). (1999). *Honoring differences: Cultural issues in the treatment of trauma and loss*. Philadelphia: Brunner/Mazel.

Norton, A., & Glick, P. (1986). One parent families: A social and economic profile. *Family Relations, 35*, 9–17.

Parson, E. R. (1995). Post-traumatic stress and coping in an inner-city child: Traumatic witnessing of interparental violence and murder. *Psychoanalytic Study of the Child, 50*, 135–147.

Pearlin, L. I. (1993). The social context of stress. In L. Goldberger & S. Breznitz (Eds.), *Handbook of stress: Theoretical and clinical aspects* (pp. 303–315). New York: Free Press.

Perren-Klinger, G. (2000). The integration of traumatic experiences: Culture and resources. In J. M. Violnati & D. Patton (Eds.), *Posttraumatic stress intervention: Challenges, issues, and perspectives* (pp. 43–64). Springfield, IL: Charles C Thomas.

Petersen, A. C., & Ebata, A. T. (1987). Developmental transitions and adolescent problem behavior: Implications for prevention and intervention. In K. Hurrelmann, F. X. Kaufmann, & F. Losel (Eds.), *Social intervention: Potential and constraints* (pp. 167–184). New York: Walter de Gruter.

Petersen, A. C., Kennedy, R. E., & Sullivan, P. (1991). Coping with adolescence. In M. E. Colten & S. Gore (Eds.), *Adolescent stress: Causes and consequences* (pp. 93–110). New York: Aldine de Gruyter.

Piaget, J., & Inhelder, B. (1969). *The psychology of the child*. New York: Basic Books.

Pines, A. M. (1993). Burnout. In L. Goldberger & S. Breznitz (Eds.), *Handbook of stress: Theoretical and clinical aspects* (pp. 386–402). New York: Free Press.

Rabkin, J. G. (1993). Stress and psychiatric disorders. In L. Goldberger & S. Breznitz (Eds.), *Handbook of stress: Theoretical and clinical aspects* (pp. 477–495). New York: Free Press.

Romano, J. L. (1997). Stress and coping: A qualitative study of 4th and 5th graders. *Elementary School Guidance and Counseling, 31*, 273–282.

Roosa, M. W., Wolchik, S. A., & Sandler, I. N. (1997). Preventing the negative effects of common stressors: Current status and future directions. In S. A. Wolchik & I. N. Sandler (Eds.), *Handbook of children's coping: Linking theory and intervention* (pp. 515–533). New York: Plenum Press.

Ryan-Wenger, N. M. (1992). A taxonomy of children's coping strategies: A step toward theory development. *American Journal of Orthopsychiatry, 62*, 256–263.

Salmon, K., & Bryant, R. A. (2002). Posttraumatic stress disorder in children: The influence of developmental factors. *Clinical Psychology Review, 22*, 163–188.

Sandler, I. N., Wolchik, S. A., MacKinnon, D., Ayers, T. S., & Roosa, M. W. (1997). Developing linkages between theory and intervention in stress and coping processes. In S. A. Wolchik & I. N. Sandler (Eds.), *Handbook of children's coping: Linking theory and intervention* (pp. 3–40). New York: Plenum Press

Saylor, C. F., Belter, R., & Stokes, S. J. (1997). Children and families coping with disaster. In S. A. Wolchik & I. N. Sandler (Eds.), *Handbook of children's coping: Linking theory and intervention* (pp. 361–383). New York: Plenum Press.

Sears, S. J., & Milburn, J. (1990). School age stress. In L. E. Arnold (Ed.), *Childhood stress* (pp. 223–246). New York: Wiley.

Selye, H. (1974). *Stress without distress.* New York: Lippincott.

Selye, H. (1993). History of the stress concept. In L. Goldberger & S. Breznitz (Eds.), *Handbook of stress: Theoretical and clinical aspects* (pp. 7–17). New York: Free Press.

Shalev, A. Y., Yehuda, R., & McFarlane, A. C. (Eds.). (2000). *International handbook of human response to trauma.* New York: Plenum Press.

Sigelman, C. K., & Rider, E. A. (2003). *Life-span human development* (4th ed.). Belmont, CA: Wadsworth/Thomas Learning.

Skinner, E. A., & Wellborn, J. G. (1997). Children's coping in the academic domain. In S. A. Wolchik & I. N. Sandler (Eds.), *Handbook of children's coping: Linking theory and intervention* (pp. 387–422). New York: Plenum Press.

Sleek, S. (1994, September). Psychology is finding a home in school-based health clinics. *APA Monitor,* pp. 1, 34.

Smetana, J. G., Yau, J., Restrepo, A., & Braeges, J. L. (1991). Conflict and adaptation in adolescence: Adolescent–parent conflict. In M. E. Colten & S. Gore (Eds.), *Adolescent stress: Causes and consequences* (pp. 43–65). New York: Aldine de Gruyter.

Sorenson, S. B. (2000). Preventing traumatic stress. *Journal of Traumatic Stress, 15,* 3–7.

Steinberg, A. (1998). Understanding the secondary traumatic stress of children. In C. R. Figley (Ed.), *Burnout in families: The systemic costs of caring* (pp. 29–46). New York: CRC Press.

Stern, M., & Newland, L. M. (1994). Working with children. *The Counseling Psychologist, 22,* 402–425.

Straus, M. A. (1980). Stress and physical child abuse. *Child Abuse and Neglect, 4,* 75–88.

Trad, P. V., & Greenblatt, E. (1990). Psychological aspects of child stress: Development and the spectrum of coping responses. In L. E. Arnold (Ed.), *Childhood stress* (pp. 23–49). New York: Wiley.

Undergraff, J. A., & Taylor, S. E. (2000). From vulnerability to growth: Positive and negative effects of stressful life events. In J. H. Harvey & E. D. Miller (Eds.), *Loss and trauma: General and close relationship perspectives* (pp. 3–28). Philadelphia: Brunner-Routledge.

van der Kolk, B. A., McFarlane, A. C., & Weisaeth, L. (Eds.). (1996). *Traumatic stress: The effects of overwhelming experience on mind, body, and society.* New York: Guilford Press.

Vingerhoets, A. J., & Marcelissen, F. H. (1988). Stress research: Its present status and issues for future developments. *Social Sciences in Medicine, 26,* 279–291.

Wagner, W. G. (1994). Counseling with children. *The Counseling Psychologist, 22,* 381–401.

Wertlieb, D. (1991). Children and divorce: Stress and coping in developmental perspective. In J. Eckenrode (Ed.), *The social context of coping* (pp. 31–54). New York: Plenum Press.

Widom, C. S. (1991). Childhood victimization: Risk factors for delinquency. In M. E. Colten & S. Gore (Eds.), *Adolescent stress: Causes and consequences* (pp. 201–221). New York: Aldine de Gruyter.

Williams, M. B., & Pojula, S. (2002). *The PTSD workbook: Effective techniques for overcoming traumatic stress symptoms.* Oakland, CA: New Harbinger.

Willis, T. A. (1987). Help-seeking as a coping mechanism. In C. R. Snyder & C. E. Ford (Eds.), *Coping with negative life events* (pp. 19–50). New York: Plenum Press.

Wolchik, S. A., & Sandler, I. N. (Eds.). (1997). *Handbook of children's coping: Linking theory and intervention.* New York: Plenum Press.

Youngs, B. (1985). *Stress in children.* New York: Arbor House.

Yule, W. (2001). Posttraumatic stress disorder in the general population and in children. *Journal of Clinical Psychiatry, 62,* 23–28.

Zunker, V. G. (2002). *Career counseling: Applied concepts of life planning.* Pacific Grove, CA: Brooks/Cole.

PART THREE

WORKING WITH YOUTH AT RISK: PREVENTION AND INTERVENTION

In the previous two sections, the topic of youth at risk was introduced and the causes were examined. In Part Three, the text addresses behaviors most often identified as placing youth at risk. Each of the chapters in this part of the text contains the following subtopics: an introduction, problem identification, a case study, approaches to prevention, intervention strategies, adaptations for diversity, and a summary. Authors discuss both prevention and intervention from individual, family, school, and community perspectives. In this way the reader is able to obtain a comprehensive and comparative overview of the material in each chapter.

Chapter 8, The Secret and All-Consuming Obsessions: Eating Disorders, provides excellent introductory material with respect to the impact of the media, gender socialization, and body image on youth at risk for eating disorders. Risk factors such as gender, age, race, socioeconomic status, family characteristics, and identification with socialized norms are also discussed. Such background information, along with a thorough discussion of definitions, symptoms, and etiology, creates the context for the case study and subsequent presentation of approaches to prevention and intervention. The chapter includes an extremely current and well-done subsection on diversity issues, including those faced by men, gay and lesbian individuals, and athletes.

It is estimated that over 1 million adolescent women become pregnant each year. Thousands of these infants are raised by children under the age of 14; likewise, thousands will be the second child born to a 16-year-old mother. When children rear children, the repercussions for the young parents, their children, and our society are enormous. Chapter 9, Children Having Children: Teenage Pregnancy and Parenthood, is based on the assumption that universal remedies are necessary for the successful reduction of adolescent pregnancy and childbearing. Traditional sex education, life management skills training, the impact of the Adolescent Family Life Act, school-based clinics, community family planning services, residential programs, and life options programs are just a few of the possibilities discussed in this comprehensive treatment of the topic.

Chapter 10, A Future in Jeopardy: Adolescents and AIDS, provides an indispensable resource for those working with this at-risk population. As noted by the authors of this chapter, researchers are currently struggling to acquire the information and medical technology needed to develop a cure for HIV/AIDS. The outlook for a cure, however, is not optimistic; some say we must learn to live with some form of HIV as long as there are human beings on this planet. Others say that even with a cure, elements such as poverty, racism, sexism, and homophobia will continue to contribute to the far-reaching consequences of HIV/AIDS. In addition to the introduction, case study, prevention, and intervention material in this chapter, an Appendix of national AIDS resources is also provided.

The adolescent at risk for suicide has become an increasing concern for schools and communities throughout the United States. Between 1960 and 1988 the adolescent suicide rate rose by 200% compared with an increase in the general population of approximately 17%. According to some experts, one teenager attempts suicide every 90 seconds, and one completes the act of suicide every 90 minutes. Chapter 11, "I Don't Want to Live": The Adolescent At Risk for Suicidal Behavior, discusses information all professionals and all parents should know if prevention and intervention efforts are to succeed. Discussions of ethnic and gender differences, methods, risk factors, precipitants, myths, and profiles provide the groundwork for the subsequent case study, prevention, intervention, and diversity material. An adolescent who is suicidal is communicating the fact that he or she is experiencing difficulty with problem solving, self-esteem, managing stress, and expressing feelings. It is important for all of us to respond in constructive, safe, informed ways when working with this very vulnerable adolescent population.

Chapter 12, "I Am Somebody": Gang Membership, examines the youth gang phenomenon. Robin Hood and his Merry Men are perhaps the most celebrated gang in literature. Not unlike some gangs operating today, Robin Hood's gang was believed to be helpful by some people in the communities in which it operated. Often modern street gangs first present themselves as "protectors" of the community. Yet Robin Hood's Merry Men carried weapons, and even though they robbed from the rich to give to the poor, their behavior was illegal under existing criminal codes of the era.

Setting the modern youth gang within the context of history and literature, the discussion in chapter 12 includes an examination of views as to why gangs form, risk factors for gang involvement, and statistics that set the stage for understanding gangs and their impact on society. A case study profiles a young man involved in gangs as a way of understanding the reality of those factors shaping the choices and lives of our youth. From the information about gang organization, risks, and statistics, the focus shifts to an understanding of diversity and gang involvement, prevention approaches, and strategies for intervention.

Chapter 13, Counseling Queer Youth: Preventing Another Matthew Shepard Story, is new to the fourth edition of this book and reclaims the use of the term *queer* youth in the process of discussing the public's lack of scientific knowledge, the heterosexist assumptions, and the homophobia that ironically still pervade the increasingly pluralistic society in the United States. This chapter discusses the many stressors that queer youth face, such as invisibility, isolation, victimization, suicide potential, substance abuse, and exposure to sexually transmitted diseases. The chapter makes the important point that, although queer youth must address these stressors, counselors need to shift much of the focus of their efforts to the community at large to transform the cultural context in which queer youth live.

Chapter 14, Death in the Classroom: Violence in Schools, is an excellent chapter and addresses the recent escalation of violence in schools. This is a particularly timely chapter given the fact we are hearing more and more about school violence and its consequences. Readers will find this chapter to be an important component of our text and will find merit in learning about the prevention and intervention programs that seem to be the most effective in addressing this problem.

Adolescent substance abuse often results in harm to youth, their families, communities, and society as a whole. According to recent U.S. Department of Health and Human Services statistics, drug and alcohol abuse contributes to the death of more than 120,000 Americans and costs taxpayers more than $143 billion every year in preventable health care costs, lost productivity, automobile crashes, law enforcement, and crime. More specifically, alcohol use is associated with over half of all murders and rapes in the United States and is a factor in 40% of all violent crimes as about 20,000 crimes involve alcohol or other drugs. Most recently, President Bush allocated $4.4 billion to provide treatment and services for substance abuse for the 2003 fiscal year. Although the yearly estimated costs of health care, lost productivity, and legal and social support systems are extreme, monetary amounts do not describe the emotional, social, and psychological costs to families and communities. Chapter 15, "I Can't Live Without It": Adolescent Substance Abuse, focuses on why teens turn to drugs, the physiological mechanisms of drug use, and the roles that individuals, families, schools, and the community have in both prevention and intervention.

Chapter 16, Nowhere to Turn: Homeless Youth, tackles the topic of homelessness. At least half a million youth in the United States are homeless. From the most recent statistics available, it is clear that the faces of the homeless have changed drastically since the days of the White, male alcoholic or "skid row bum." Forty-three percent of the homeless are families with small children. Homeless children's differences in appearance, behavior, and ability demand tolerance and flexibility from teachers and school administrators. The purpose of this chapter is to describe homelessness both demographically and more descriptively using a case example. Next, the chapter discusses preventive measures society must take to avoid the problem of homelessness. Finally, the chapter offers several interventions to help increase the numbers of homeless youth in the classroom and address their educational needs.

The text concludes with chapter 17, "This Isn't the Place for Me": School Dropout. The placement of this chapter at the end of the book is fitting because the problem of the school dropout involves many of the personal, family, and social issues discussed in previous chapters. Demographic correlates, early warning signs, underlying causes, a case study, clinical and systemic approaches to prevention and intervention, and adaptations for diversity form the basis for this informative and cutting-edge chapter.

8 | The Secret and All-Consuming Obsessions: Eating Disorders

Kimberly Wright

The standard for body size and weight is socially determined. It is a cultural phenomenon that demands that the current ideal physique is slim. Countries that commonly experience the threat of famine have historically had virtually no cases of anorexia or bulimia, and obesity has been considered desirable (Bruch, 1973; Nasser, 1988). In previous eras in the United States, larger bodies were associated with prosperity, in contrast with current mores that associate thinness with affluence. Obesity is now considered a correlate of the lower class. Continuous images indoctrinate the public with the message that, to be considered successful, masterful, and acceptable, one must display a thin physique (Vandereycken, 1993). This image is one that emphasizes self-control and discipline over self-indulgence. For women, this message is especially strong. Since Twiggy reigned as a premier fashion model in the late 1960s, America has promoted a thinner and thinner standard for the female ideal (Garner, Garfinkel, Schwartz, & Thompson, 1980; Stice, 2002). It is within this context that the current escalation of eating disorders in the United States is occurring.

This chapter provides a review of the literature in the area of eating disorders, including identifying the differences between the various eating disorders, the etiology of these disorders, and prevention and intervention strategies. The chapter places a special emphasis on the power of the media in a consumer economy, as well as the impact of gender, ethnicity, and culture on eating disorder prevalence and maintenance. A clinical case example illustrates how these disorders can manifest.

Among the most powerful transmitters of social standards is the media. According to Garner et al. (1980), "the potential impact of the media in establishing identificatory role models cannot be overemphasized" (p. 652). Newspapers, television, movies, magazines, and billboards bombard the public with images and messages about appropriate behavior, dress, food, entertainment, appearance, and beliefs. Avoiding the overt and covert messages of society portrayed through the media would be virtually impossible. For men, the standards portrayed include fitness, power, and independence. For women, the standards portrayed include thinness, femininity, and beauty.

The female ideal as defined by the culture fluctuates. The extent of these fluctuations is revealed by a classic study (Garner et al., 1980) comparing the weights and measurements of *Playboy* centerfolds and Miss America Pageant contestants from 1959 to 1978. There was a significant decrease in body weight and body measurements for both groups, despite an increase in height. Additionally, the Miss America Pageant winners were significantly slimmer than the average contestant in the same pageant.

This trend occurred while the average woman under age 30 was becoming heavier during the same time period. The ideal female figure has continued to become thinner, despite the increase in the size of the average woman (Wiseman, Gray, Mosimann, & Ahrens, 1992).

The trend toward a slim female ideal is also illustrated by the changes in diet advertisements over the last 30 years. Between 1973 and 1991, the United States witnessed a consistent increase in television commercials featuring diet products (Wiseman, Gunning, & Gray, 1993). Another study of media messages compared food and diet advertisements from 48 women's magazines and 48 men's magazines (Silverstein, Perdue, Peterson, & Kelly, 1986). It is interesting to note that 1,179 different food and diet advertisements appeared in the women's magazines, compared with 10 in the men's magazines. Anderson and DiDomenico (1992) found that women's magazines contain over 10 times the number of diet advertisements and articles than do men's magazines. The inherent double message is that women need to indulge in various foods and that they need to diet to avoid weight gain.

Few would argue that men and women are socialized in different ways. The female and male socialization experiences can be viewed as representative of different cultures. Women are socialized to draw their self-esteem from their physical appearance rather than from what they do (Beattie, 1988). For men, self-esteem tends to be more frequently related to success. This discrepancy, combined with the ideal standards for female appearance, increases a woman's vulnerability to eating disorders but does not rule out the vulnerability among men.

Body image is the perception of one's own shape and size. Those who compare themselves with models or other "ideals" often distort their own body image negatively (Kalodner, 1997). The body is perceived to be inadequate if it fails to meet ideal criteria. Currently, nearly 25% of the female models in some magazines satisfy the weight criteria for anorexia nervosa (Stice, 2002). This provides the standard against which many women measure themselves. It is not unusual to hear women or even young girls state, "I feel so fat," even when their weight is normal. Body dissatisfaction has been found to increase the risk of eating disturbances (Killen et al., 1996). Research indicates that increased exposure to these ultra-thin ideals increases the risk of developing eating pathology among vulnerable adolescent girls who already have internalized a thin ideal (Stice, Spangler, & Agras, 2001).

Among women, it is now the norm to diet. While it may not be healthy, Polivy and Herman (1987) found that the majority of women are dissatisfied with their bodies and have dieted. This dynamic is highlighted by the concept of "malnutrition of affluence" (Hill, 2002). Malnutrition is no longer the plight of poverty. Thirty-nine percent of women and 21% of men report trying to lose weight. Dieting among adolescents has increased and is occurring at younger ages. Twenty-five percent of 11-year-old girls report at least one dieting attempt (Stice, 2002). This same trend is occurring outside of the United States, most notably in Asian countries such as China and Japan where there is already a low rate of obesity (S. Lee & Katzman, 2002).

Body image distortions are more prevalent among women than among men. In a sample of 340 college men, 65% reported that they weighed within 5 percentage points of their ideal weight (Franco, Tamburrino, Carroll, & Bernal, 1988), in contrast to the typical body dissatisfaction of their female peers. Women tend to exhibit greater body dissatisfaction and body image distortion than do men (Connor-Greene, 1988). Even among men with bulimia, the desired ideal weight has been found to be more realistic than the desired ideal weight of women with bulimia (Schneider & Agras, 1987). Although the current trend indicates that body image distortions among men are on the rise, men still view themselves as thin when they are 105% of their ideal weight.

Women, in comparison, do not see themselves as thin unless they are 90% or below their ideal weight. Men are more likely to be dissatisfied with their shape, rather than their weight, and desire a more muscular physique (Anderson, 2002).

PROBLEM DEFINITION

The prevalence of eating disorders has consistently increased in the United States across the last 30 years. Increasing emphasis on thinness and physical fitness has altered the standard for appearance for women and men. The "fitness movement" is misleading. Many individuals flock to gyms and fitness classes under the guise of cardiovascular health and physical fitness, seeking instead to achieve the physical ideal of attractiveness. This is further fueled by recent reports of the health benefits of strength training, which has become an obsession among some, especially men. The current trends are not in danger of reversing, which leaves the social climate primed for a continuing increase in eating pathology.

Risk Factors

Gender
Although anorexia, bulimia, and, to a lesser extent, binge eating disorder are typically characterized as female afflictions, they cross gender lines. While both bulimia and binge eating disorder feature consuming large quantities of food in a sitting, those with binge eating disorder do not purge or use other compensatory behaviors such as excessive exercise or laxative abuse. Although anorexia and bulimia do appear more frequently among females, males can develop these disorders. It is likely that many cases of anorexia or bulimia among males go unreported for several reasons: (a) the reluctance of men to admit symptoms of a "female disorder," (b) eating large quantities of food is not considered abnormal by adolescent boys and young men, and (c) clinicians are less likely to explore eating disorder symptoms among males. Even considering the potential underreporting among men, women are at higher risk for developing anorexia or bulimia because of the value placed on their appearance by the culture. (The gender differences will be reflected by the primary use of the female pronoun throughout, unless specifically referring to males.) Binge eating, typically associated with obesity, is less gender specific but also occurs more frequently in women than in men (American Psychiatric Association, 2000; Bruce & Agras, 1992; Grilo, 2002). It is important to note, however, that *binge eating* and *obesity* are not comparable terms, although they are often used interchangeably. Binge eating refers to a behavior, whereas obesity (excessive weight) refers to the likely consequences of the behavior. Only 25% of obese persons are estimated to be binge eaters, as weight is regulated by a variety of biological and behavioral factors.

Age
Adolescence is a high-risk period for the development of eating disorders. The most frequent period for the emergence of anorexia and bulimia is between the ages 14 and 18; however, atypical onset patterns exist. Late adolescence is also the most likely period for the development of binge eating disorder, with 18 being the modal age of onset (Striegel-Moore, 1993). The developmental tasks of adolescence interact with the physical and social demands of maturation to create a vulnerability to developing eating disorders during adolescence or early adulthood. Binge eating disorder may develop, however, in adulthood, and it is not unusual for the disorder to be diagnosed once bulimia is in remission. This common clinical observation has recently been chal-

lenged, however, by evidence that suggests that this is a rare development (Fairburn, Cooper, Doll, Norman, & O'Connor, 2000).

Race
Anorexia and bulimia have historically been more frequently associated with upper-middle-class White populations, and the greatest risk for these disorders continues to be in this group. However, recent evidence suggests that the risk and prevalence are increasing for minority groups (Sanders & Heiss, 1998; Striegel-Moore & Smolak, 2002). In addition, binge eating and obesity are more common among some minority populations such as African American and some Native American groups (Klesges, DeBon, & Meyers, 1996).

Socioeconomic Status Level
Women with anorexia and bulimia have most frequently come from the middle- to upper-middle socioeconomic class (Anderson & Hay, 1985), whereas obesity (and by extension, binge eating) tends to be associated with lower socioeconomic status (SES). This pattern is not consistent, however, especially among youth with upwardly mobile aspirations, such as first-generation college students and recent U.S. immigrants. Upward social comparison that leaves individuals feeling inadequate has been noted as one dynamic that might promote eating disorders across sociocultural class lines.

Family Characteristics
The families of those with eating disorders are described as chaotic and conflicted, in the case of the bulimic (Humphrey, 1994; Schwartz, Barrett, & Saba, 1985), or over-controlling and rigid, in the case of the anorexic (Humphrey, 1994; Sargent, Liebman, & Silver, 1985). Those with binge eating disorder report being neglected or overlooked as children, as well as having experienced overinvolvement or lack of structure around meals (Pike & Wilfley, 1996). Although these are simplified, stereotypical portrayals, family problems are common among the eating disordered population. It is also common for another family member to have struggled with weight problems or an eating disorder. Eating disturbances among women have been found to be related to weight concerns expressed by parents (Keel, Heatherton, Harnden, & Hornig, 1997). Previous research and a review of the literature indicate convergent evidence that the families of eating disordered individuals have a higher rate of affective disorders, alcoholism, and conflictual and controlling family relationships (Kog & Vandereycken, 1985; Pike & Wilfley, 1996; Vandereycken, 2002).

Identification With Socialized Norms

Among a sample of 682 college students, Mintz and Betz (1988) reported that disordered eating similar to that found in anorexia and bulimia was strongly related to the endorsement of sociocultural norms that regard female thinness and attractiveness as an indication of worth. Those women who hold beliefs similar to the traditional gender expectations are at greater risk for these eating disorders. One aspect of the social norms for women has been to strive for the ideal of thinness. It has been reported that persistent weight and shape concerns (Killen et al., 1996) and the internalization of the thinness ideal (K. J. Thompson & Stice, 2001) pose a risk for the development of eating pathology among young women. Certainly, this is related to the continuing phenomenon of women's subordinate position in a society in which women's value is significantly determined by appearance.

Although many of the risk factors prominent in eating disorders are featured in other disturbances of youth, such as alcohol and drug abuse or depression, the socio-cultural and gender pressures are the distinguishing features of anorexia nervosa and bulimia. Risk factors for binge eating disorder have been less clearly identified. The anticipated risk factors of childhood obesity and parental obesity have been found to be more predictive of bulimia than binge eating disorder (Grilo, 2002).

Definitions, Symptoms, and Etiology

Anorexia Nervosa

The prevalence of anorexia nervosa (typically referred to as anorexia) among the general population is reported to be between 0.5% and 1.0% (American Psychiatric Association, 2000) but is believed to be higher among high school and college populations (Mintz & Betz, 1988). Approximately 90% of the cases of anorexia nervosa are female. Cases with eating disturbances that do not meet all of the criteria for anorexia nervosa are more common. The onset is most likely to occur in adolescence and early adulthood, but cases of earlier and later onset have been reported, with a later onset more common among ethnic minorities (Anderson & Hay, 1985).

Anorexia nervosa is a constellation of symptoms in which an extreme drive for thinness, a fear of becoming fat, and a restriction of food intake are central. Anorexia nervosa is actually a misnomer. Literally translated, anorexia nervosa means "nervous lack of appetite." Although there is a denial of hunger, actual hunger loss does not occur until the very advanced stages of the disorder.

The most recent diagnostic criteria presented in the *Diagnostic and Statistical Manual of Mental Disorders* (4th ed., text revision [*DSM–IV–TR*]; American Psychiatric Association, 2000) allow for specificity in diagnosis and highlight the similarity of some symptoms common to both anorexia nervosa and bulimia nervosa. The critical elements of anorexia include the following:

- Refusal to maintain body weight at or above a minimally normal weight for age and height (e.g., weight loss leading to maintenance of body weight less than 85% of that expected, or failure to make expected weight gain during period of growth, leading to body weight less than 85% of that expected).
- Intense fear of gaining weight or becoming fat, even though underweight.
- Disturbance in the way in which one's body weight or shape is experienced, undue influence of body weight or shape on self-evaluation, or denial of the seriousness of the current low body weight.
- In postmenarcheal females, amenorrhea, that is, the absence of at least three consecutive menstrual cycles. (A woman is considered to have amenorrhea if her periods occur only following hormone, e.g., estrogen, administration.)

Further, the *DSM–IV–TR* specifies two types of anorexia:

- *Restricting type*: During the current episode of anorexia nervosa, the person has not regularly engaged in binge eating or purging behavior (i.e., self-induced vomiting or the misuse of laxatives, diuretics, or enemas).
- *Binge eating/purging type*: During the current episode of anorexia nervosa, the person has regularly engaged in binge eating or purging behavior (i.e., self-induced vomiting or the misuse of laxatives diuretics, or enemas).

One of the first noticeable symptoms of anorexia is a preoccupation with food, particularly a focus on the fat and calorie content of food. The woman with anorexia may begin by restricting herself to a "healthy" diet or may begin exercising more than usual. She may slowly add to her list of "forbidden foods" until the list of foods she will allow herself to consume becomes scant. The most striking feature is the determination she evidences. As the disorder progresses, she may begin removing herself from social dining situations. She may claim to be too busy to eat lunch with friends or will excuse herself from an invitation by claiming to have already eaten. As her weight begins to drop, she may conceal herself with loose-fitting clothes or wear warmer clothing than would be necessary. She may become compulsive with list-making, being sure that no free time exists in her schedule. As her work or activities begin to consume all of her day, she may stay up late at night in an effort to burn more calories. As others begin to notice the change in her appearance or behavior, she is likely to become defensive and isolate herself further. She will take any comment regarding her weight loss as a compliment and a sign of success. As the disorder progresses, her cognitive functions become less sharp, decisions are more difficult, and her obsession with food becomes unrelenting.

Throughout the process, she becomes more and more entrenched in her behavior. She will appear rigid, will react with denial if confronted, and will become more secretive in her eating rituals. Thoughts of food, calories, and weight will consume her daily, and she will develop rules that dictate her food intake and exercise behavior. She will become more depressed and anxious, and mood swings will be frequent. She may develop comorbid obsessive-compulsive symptoms unrelated to her weight and food obsessions, such as ensuring her room is orderly, frequent checking behavior, compulsive list-making, or repetitive counting. Her sense of self-worth will become intimately linked with her control of food, largely as a mask for her pervasive feeling of ineffectiveness and inadequacy. True emotional intimacy will be difficult for her to bear, yet she will strive to please others in a process that completely ignores her own needs or identity development. She will strive for extreme achievement and perfection in her endeavors and may believe that she does not deserve to eat, as if eating were a right that had to be earned. Her emotional development and social interactions will be less mature than those of her peers.

A single etiology of anorexia has yet to be determined. It is currently accepted that the disorder is of a multidimensional nature. Although the anorexic female appears to the world to be a "perfect child" who is a high achiever, is compassionate toward others, and is respectful toward authority, it is believed that personality deficits precede the onset of the illness (Steiger & Houle, 1991). She is compliant, socially inhibited, emotionally restrained, and highly perfectionistic (Wonderlich, 2002). The extreme control exhibited in the young woman with anorexia becomes a compensation for poor coping skills and feelings of instability (Beaumont, 2002; Bruch, 1973). (See Table 8–1 for the symptoms of anorexia nervosa.)

Psychoanalytic theory postulates that anorexia serves as a defense against maturation. Fears about becoming a woman and developing sexually inspire attempts to control the body. The maintenance of a childlike physique is seen as an unconscious strategy to forestall adult relationships and sexuality. Developmentalists view anorexia as an adaptive tool used to combat great anxiety about developmental crises, such as increased expectations and responsibilities associated with maturation. Sociocultural theorists claim that it is the striving for perfection in appearance as a visible hallmark of success that motivates the woman with anorexia. Learning theory is related to this sociocultural explanation in that initial weight loss is met with praise

Table 8–1 | Symptoms of Anorexia Nervosa

Psychological

Perfectionism	Denial of problem
Depression	Anxiety
Distorted body image	Thoughts of suicide
Intense fear of food and weight gain	High need for control
	Mood lability
Inflexibility in thought and behavior	Poor self-esteem
	Compliance
Feelings of guilt about eating	

Behavioral

Extreme food restriction	Preoccupation with food and eating
Isolation from friends and family	
Fatigue and irritability	Compulsive exercise
Extreme physical activity	Vomiting meals
Eating alone	Abuse of laxatives, diet pills, or diuretics
Adoption of loose clothing	
High caffeine intake	

Physical

Noticeable weight loss—15% or more of total body weight	Lanugo—growth of fine facial and body hair
Absent or erratic menses	Exhaustion
Cognitive disturbances	Cardiac disturbances
Electrolyte imbalance	Malnutrition
Distortion of hunger and satiety	Tooth decay/gum disease
	Lowered metabolism
Hypersensitivity to cold	

and positive reinforcement. As the anorexic becomes emaciated, the initial attention received from others turns to concern that may be positively reinforcing as well. Internal reinforcement operates simultaneously as the anorexic prides herself on her self-control. The control issue escalates as she resists others' attempts to feed her and refuses external intervention. Negative reinforcement maintains the pattern as the fears of food and fat provide the incentive for the avoidance of food. Family theorists hypothesize that the behavior is a means of gaining control and independence from a critical and overcontrolling parent. Food and the body become the areas in which the anorexic can exert control. Biological theories suggest that some individuals have a biological predisposition to developing anorexia. This vulnerability can then be triggered by environmental or developmental stressors. It is most reasonable to propose a multietiological perspective that incorporates several theoretical considerations while recognizing that no single etiological course can apply to each case.

Bulimia Nervosa

Prevalence estimates for bulimia nervosa vary from 1%–3% for women and 0.3% for men (American Psychiatric Association, 2000) to 11%–13% in college populations (Coric & Murstein, 1993; Gray & Ford, 1985). Despite these considerable statistics, a great number of people exhibit bulimic symptoms without meeting the complete diagnostic criteria. As with anorexia, the typical onset of bulimia nervosa is during adolescence and early adulthood.

Bulimia nervosa is commonly known as bulimia. Roughly translated from the ancient Greek, bulimia means "ravenous or ox-like hunger" (Stunkard, 1993) and is a disorder characterized by cyclical periods of binge eating, typically followed by purging behavior (vomiting, laxative use, diuretic use, or excessive exercising). Many individuals engage in purging behavior without a binge precursor. This behavior would be classified in *DSM–IV–TR* as eating disorder not otherwise specified (ED NOS) and often takes the form of purging small or normal meals or purging a forbidden food eaten in a small quantity. The latest diagnostic criteria (American Psychiatric Association, 2000) have specified two types of bulimia, although in practice the occasional overlap of symptoms with those of anorexia makes the distinctions less clear. The diagnostic criteria for bulimia nervosa are as follows:

- Recurrent episodes of binge eating in which an episode is characterized by both of the following:
    —eating, in a discrete period of time (e.g., within any 2-hour period), an amount of food that is definitely larger than most people would eat during a similar period of time and under similar circumstances, and
    —a sense of lack of control over eating during the episode (e.g., a feeling that one cannot stop eating or control how much one is eating).
- Recurrent inappropriate compensatory behavior to prevent weight gain, such as self-induced vomiting; misuse of laxatives, diuretics, enemas, or other medications; fasting; or excessive exercise.
- The binge eating and inappropriate compensatory behavior occur, on average, at least twice a week for 3 months.
- Self-evaluation is unduly influenced by body shape and weight.
- The disturbance does not occur exclusively during episodes of anorexia nervosa.

Further, the *DSM–IV–TR* specifies two types of bulimia nervosa:

- *Purging type:* During the current episode of bulimia nervosa, the person has regularly engaged in self-induced vomiting or the misuse of laxatives, diuretics, or enemas.
- *Nonpurging type:* During the current episode of bulimia nervosa, the person has used other inappropriate compensatory behaviors, such as fasting or excessive exercise, but has not regularly engaged in self-induced vomiting or the misuse of laxatives, diuretics, or enemas.

Perhaps the first identifiable symptom of bulimia is an occasional binge eating episode. The episode may be in response to feeling a need to nurture oneself with food or to indulge oneself following a period of dieting or restricted food intake. The reinforcement of the binge (feeling soothed, reducing anxiety) leads to repeated binges. The fear of weight gain is often the impetus for later purging behavior, but the relief the purge provides can also be an accidental discovery (as when spontaneous vomiting following a large meal affords physical relief). As with addictive behaviors, the cycle escalates from an occasional episode to a daily habit.

Binges most commonly occur in the late afternoon or late evening, often after a day of food restriction, but they may begin in the early morning. It is not unusual for bingeing to occur on a daily basis and for normal meals during the day to be vomited as well. Binges are frequently planned, and time alone must be negotiated. Social activities become limited as activities are scheduled with bingeing and purging episodes in mind. The woman with bulimia may withdraw most noticeably from meals in which she will be observed and will become very anxious if prevented from purging (either by interruption or situational factors). Mood swings are common. As the disorder progresses, the bulimic's body image becomes more distorted, and her sense of being out of control is less tolerable. As she exerts more effort into controlling her food intake, she increases her sense of deprivation and sets the scenario for future binges. She may steal food from roommates or shoplift in grocery stores when the food requirements for the binges are not readily available. Increasingly, the binge/purge cycle becomes a means of managing all painful emotions, and her awareness of her feelings becomes muted. Although her weight will likely remain stable, fluctuating within 5 pounds, she will begin to look less physically well. Her face and neck may appear swollen, and she may develop a burst blood vessel in the eye from the force of vomiting.

The woman with bulimia is susceptible to depression and typically has low self-esteem and poor impulse control. She may abuse drugs or alcohol in the way that she abuses food. Her body image is invariably distorted, and she is highly self-critical. She may become sexually impulsive as a result of being unable to set limits, abusing alcohol, or in hopes of seeking male approval. Like the woman with anorexia, she may define herself as a "people pleaser" and be fearful of confrontation, conflict, or anger. Frequently, she will identify as feeling lonely, despite the fact that her isolation is often self-imposed. (See Table 8–2 for the symptoms of bulimia nervosa and Table 8–3 for a comparison between anorexia and bulimia nervosa.)

The etiology of bulimia is not agreed on, and it appears that there may be many avenues to onset. Some women develop bulimic symptoms following a diet. Childhood obesity and parental obsessions with weight have been identified as risk factors for the development of bulimia (Grilo, 2002). A developmental transition or move may trigger bulimic behavior or intensify existing symptoms (as in the transition to high school or a move away to college; Smolak & Levine, 1996). Losses (such as deaths, parental separations) have been particularly painful and difficult for the woman with bulimia to manage (Armstrong & Roth, 1989; Schmidt, 2002).

Increasingly, the etiology of bulimia nervosa is being viewed as multidimensional. A risk factor model has been proposed that posits an interaction among biological,

Table 8–2 | Symptoms of Bulimia Nervosa

Psychological

Low self-esteem	Feeling out of control
Depression	Anxiety
Suicidal thoughts/feelings	Feelings of worthlessness
Overconcern with weight and body image	High need for approval

Behavioral

Cyclical bingeing and purging	Preoccupation with food and body image
Bingeing on high-calorie foods (carbohydrates/fats)	Eating in secret
Increasing time spent on bingeing/purging	Hoarding food
Abuse of laxatives, diet pills, diuretics, or exercise	Isolating from friends and family
	Abusing alcohol or drugs
Poor impulse control	Restroom visits after meals

Physical

Normal weight	Occasional burst blood vessel in the eye
Dehydration	
Irritability and fatigue	Tooth decay/gum disease
Chronic sore throat	Chronic illness
Esophageal erosion	Swollen neck glands
Gastrointestinal problems	Cardiac irregularities
Electrolyte imbalance	

Table 8–3 | Distinguishing Features Between Anorexia Nervosa and Bulimia Nervosa

Anorexia	Bulimia
Great weight loss	Minor weight fluctuations
More introverted	More extroverted
Pride in weight and food control	Shame in bulimic behavior
Less sexually active	More sexually active
Feels in control with food	Feels out of control with food
Emaciation itself is the goal	Happiness (as a result of thinness) is the goal

family, developmental, personality, and sociocultural factors (Johnson, Tobin, & Steinberg, 1989). Investigations of the biological factors in eating disorders have found that eating disorders tend to be more common among biological relatives, and there is an increased concordance in monozygotic twins than in dizyotic twins (Strober & Bulik, 2002). Another biological factor implicated is the correlation between bulimia and affective disorders, particularly depression. The affective instability typically appears prior to the onset of bulimia and suggests a biological vulnerability to bulimic symptoms. Although the disorder may begin with restrictive dieting, the biological urge for food preempts a binge episode. A binge eating episode is followed by guilt and disgust over the binge, which leads to purging. The purging itself serves to reduce tension and guilt (Beaumont, 2002). This cycle is maintained by the physical need for food and the soothing emotional benefits of the binge (Lacey, Coker, & Birtchnell, 1986).

Research has supported the position of family theorists that eating disorders are a response or adaptation to coping with a dysfunctional family (Lundholm & Waters, 1991; Vandereycken, 2002). The family factors that tend to be related to bulimia include a family environment that is chaotic, conflicted, and neglectful, resulting in children who feel insecure, anxious, and disorganized. The inability of the woman with bulimia to identify internal states is seen as a developmental deficit resulting from the parents' inability to respond to the child in a manner that allowed the child to internalize her own awareness. Contributing personality factors are low self-esteem, feelings of ineffectiveness, sensitivity to rejection, and compliance with others. These women have persistent shame and guilt about not meeting their idealized goals. Sociocultural factors include the changing gender roles in the dominant culture, the increased pressure for thinness, and the use of the pursuit of thinness as a means of adaptation and social acceptability.

Binge Eating Disorder

Binge eating disorder is a more recently recognized eating disorder that afflicts approximately 5%–10% of the general population (Grilo, 2002; Yanovski, Nelson, Dubbert, & Spitzer, 1993). Currently, binge eating disorder falls under the diagnostic criteria of ED NOS but has been proposed as a disorder of its own (American Psychiatric Association, 2000). Binge eating disorder is characterized by binge eating (eating a large amount of food in a short period of time) without compensatory behavior and feeling out of control during the binge episode. The disorder may develop in the absence of a history with anorexia or bulimia or may result when the purging aspects of bulimia have been discontinued. Recent evidence suggests, however, that binge eating disorder has a separate course and rarely evolves from bulimic behaviors (Fairburn et al., 2000). The disorder is somewhat more common among women (ratio of 3:2) and is equally common among White and African American women. The modal age of onset is 18, but many experience some episodes of overeating behavior at earlier ages.

The diagnostic category of ED NOS includes other types of eating pathology that do not meet criteria for anorexia or bulimia. The following are examples of ED NOS:

- For females, all of the criteria for anorexia nervosa are met except that the individual has regular menses.
- All of the criteria for anorexia nervosa are met except that, despite significant weight loss, the individual's current weight is in the normal range.
- All of the criteria for bulimia nervosa are met except that the binge eating and inappropriate compensatory mechanisms occur at a frequency of less than twice a week or for a duration of less than 3 months.
- The regular use of inappropriate compensatory behavior by an individual of normal body weight after eating small amounts of food (e.g., self-induced vomiting after the consumption of two cookies).
- Repeatedly chewing and spitting out, but not swallowing, large amounts of food.
- Binge eating disorder: recurrent episodes of binge eating in the absence of the regular use of inappropriate compensatory behaviors characteristic of bulimia nervosa.

The proposed criteria for binge eating disorder (American Psychiatric Association, 2000) include the following:

- Recurrent episodes of binge eating in which an episode is characterized by both of the following:
  —eating, in a discrete period of time (e.g., within any 2-hour period), an amount of food that is definitely larger than most people would eat in a similar period of time under similar circumstances, and
  —a sense of lack of control over eating during the episode (e.g., a feeling that one cannot stop eating or control what or how much one is eating).
- The binge eating episodes are associated with three (or more) of the following:
  —eating much more rapidly than usual
  —eating until feeling uncomfortably full
  —eating large amounts of food when not feeling physically hungry
  —eating alone because of being embarrassed by how much one is eating
  —feeling disgusted with oneself, depressed, or very guilty after overeating.
- Marked distress regarding binge eating is present.
- The binge eating occurs, on average, at least 2 days a week for 6 months.
- The binge eating is not associated with the regular use of inappropriate compensatory behaviors (e.g., purging, fasting, excessive exercise) and does not occur exclusively during the course of anorexia nervosa or bulimia nervosa.

Although there are many consistencies among those with binge eating disorder, a typical progression is difficult to describe because binge eating disorder develops in more varied ways. It is common, but not invariable, for the seeds of binge eating to be germinating in childhood and the symptoms to develop slowly throughout adolescence and adulthood. Binge eaters may begin as larger children who develop an over-reliance on food for comfort to assuage hurt feelings or to disconnect from painful events of childhood. They may experience a period of chubbiness during which they are teased or are made to feel self-conscious about weight. Parental concern may take the form of restricting snacks allowed for other children in the family, criticizing or mocking size or weight, or encouraging the child to become more physically active to slim down. During this time the children may begin to hoard food without the family's awareness and hide it for later consumption in private. They may be sent to special summer camp programs for overweight children and later refer to it as "fat camp." They may seem undisturbed by the remarks about their weight or robust appetite and may even develop a self-deprecating sense of humor. They may begin to isolate to spare themselves from critical remarks or the harsh judgments of peers. As they enter adolescence, they may become less socially engaged and find greater solace in food rather than take the social risks required of adolescent socialization. As they become more lonely, their use of food for managing distressing feelings increases their overconsumption of food. Bingeing becomes more frequent, and loss of control is more common. A numbness is experienced during the binge episodes that is almost dissociative. This begins a cycle of bingeing in response to negative affective states that leads to increased weight, to further guilt and isolation, and to increasingly recurrent binges. Feelings of depression may also escalate simultaneously. Their sense of shame (about their inability to control their eating and increasing weight) is pervasive and hinders the development of interpersonal relationships. Once their binge eating produces considerable weight gain, medical complications may arise, such as hypertension and diabetes. (See Table 8–4 for the symptoms of binge eating disorder.)

As with anorexia and bulimia, there is disagreement about the etiology of binge eating disorder. There is some similarity in the etiology of binge eating disorder with that of bulimia. Developmentalists note that the passage through adolescence into adulthood stresses coping skills beyond their capacity. This is the time when female sex role socialization promotes an excessive emphasis on appearance and the value of thinness (Striegel-Moore, 1993). The mechanisms operating for men during this time have been less defined, but it is reasonable to assume that the sex role expectations of boys during adolescence are also challenging. Biological factors are also implicated in the development of binge eating disorder. While 50%–60% of those with binge eating disorder are estimated to also suffer from a depressive disorder, men especially are also prone to anxiety and alcohol abuse (Grilo, 2002). A restraint model posits that binge eating develops in response to a period of dieting, but there is sufficient evidence that this is not always the case. A significant number (approximately half) of binge eaters develop the disorder without a history of intake restriction or body dissatisfaction

Table 8–4 | Symptoms of Binge Eating Disorder

Psychological

Low self-esteem	Feeling out of control
Depression	Preoccupation with food
Anxiety	Shame about bingeing and weight

Behavioral

Frequent, recurrent bingeing	Avoidance of emotional or sexual
Eating alone in private	intimacy
Hoarding food	Social isolation

Physical

Higher than normal weight or obesity	Sexual impairment
High blood pressure	Fatigue
Risk of diabetes	Difficulty with physical activity
Joint strain	Lack of hunger or satiety awareness
Edema of the lower extremities	Renal disease
Coronary disease	Osteoarthritis

(Wilson, Nonas, & Rosenblum, 1993). A conditioning model, based on learning theory, suggests that the comfort derived from food gradually reinforces a pattern of self-soothing that relies on food. An addictions model contends that the processes for binge eating are similar to those of an alcohol or drug addiction, and some treatment programs and self-help groups (Overeaters Anonymous) have been based on the 12-step model of recovery (Westphal & Smith, 1996).

The high rate of comorbidity of binge eating disorder with depression has led to the proposition that binge eating is a variant of affective disorders and that the binge eating serves to regulate negative emotional states. Some contend, however, that the most promising model of binge eating disorders is a biopsychosocial model that takes into account biological vulnerability as well as the cognitive, behavioral, and social determinants of binge eating (Polivy & Herman, 1996). The difficulty with this type of model is that it does not account for the various factors operating at different stages of the disorder. Polivy and Herman suggested that identifying the phases of the disorder would lend valuable information to the research and treatment of binge eating disorder.

CASE STUDY

Carrie is a 19-year-old female of White/Latina heritage. She is in the second semester of her freshman year at a large university. She originally sought counseling to deal with her increasing sense of depression. During her first session with the psychologist, she presented as bright and cheerful, in contrast to her reported feelings of sadness and hopelessness. She was immaculately groomed, of normal weight, and casually dressed.

As Carrie described her current situation, her pain was evident even as she smiled through the tears she fought to keep from falling. She just didn't understand why she couldn't control herself. She had been bingeing and purging (via vomiting) since her junior year of high school and was feeling increasing shame and powerlessness. Although there had been periods when she binged and purged less often (such as during the football season when she was busy with cheerleading and had less time alone), the transition to college escalated the pattern from occasionally to daily. She was also now taking laxatives several times a week and would go for an entire day without eating in order to pay for having binged the day before. Her hunger would eventually lead to another late-night binge, after which she would vomit, and the cycle would begin again. However, even these efforts in conjunction with 2 hours of daily aerobic exercise did little to conquer her intense fear that she would gain an enormous amount of weight.

She had begun by self-inducing vomiting when she had overeaten or had been drinking alcohol. She had been an unpopular child, and once she had made the cheerleading squad in high school she feared that she would gain weight and lose her newfound social status. She lived in terror that she would be discovered to be as inadequate as she felt.

She described her parents as "perfect" and her younger sister as the "baby" of the family. Mom was a perfectionist who was hardworking and demanded the same from her oldest daughter. Dad worked long hours and was not as involved with the family. Carrie did not mention until a later session that her mother was generally quite critical, especially of Carrie's appearance; had chronically dieted; and had very high expectations. Dad was later reported to drink frequently on the occasions when he was home with the family and had paid little attention to Carrie since she entered junior high school.

During the first session Carrie described the painful pattern of her daily life:

Carrie: I just can't seem to control anything. It feels like this is never going to end.

Dr. W: That sounds pretty hopeless.

Carrie: It is hopeless. I've been depressed since I first got here. At first, I thought it was just homesickness, but everything seems to be falling apart. I can barely get out of bed, except to eat, and I can't have another semester with the grades as bad as last semester. Everything seems dark, like there's no escape.

Dr. W: Can you tell me what feels so overwhelming?

Carrie: Every day feels overwhelming. It starts out with my planning not to eat at all. As long as I don't eat, I feel okay and pretty happy. If I could just control myself I know I could be happy. But once I start eating I know it's all over.

Dr. W: All over?

Carrie: Yeah, I'll start to eat and I won't be able to stop. When I finally realize how much I've eaten, it's too late and my stomach is huge and I have to get rid of it.

Dr. W: It sounds like you aren't aware of your behavior when you're in the middle of a binge.

Carrie: I'm not. It's like I just go numb. Then I feel horrible at what I've done and I get sick.

Dr. W: Does that mean that you intentionally vomit?

Carrie: I don't call it that but that's the only way I will truly feel better. If I can get rid of it, then maybe I'm not so bad and maybe I don't have to feel too guilty.

Dr. W: It doesn't feel like you deserve to eat?

Carrie: Not when I can't control myself. And I usually end up eating bad food anyway.

Dr. W: Bad food?

Carrie: You know, crackers and cookies and ice cream and bread and pizza.

Dr. W: And how are those bad?

Carrie: Do you know the calories and fat in that stuff? I don't allow myself to eat that kind of food. If I can just make it through the day without eating, everything will be okay. But even when I make it through the day, I can never seem to have the willpower at night. That's the most dangerous time.

Dr. W: So, the food you don't feel you deserve is the food you end up craving. Can you tell me what happens right before you binge?

Carrie: Nothing happens. I just start eating and don't stop.

Dr. W: Are you aware of the circumstances or what you are feeling?

Carrie: Just stressed out.

Dr. W: What does "stressed out" mean to you?

Carrie: I've never thought about it, but I guess I'm nervous a lot. And I'm scared and lonely, which I feel all the time, but mostly at night.

Dr. W: And what makes you frightened?

Carrie: I'm afraid I'll get fat.

Dr. W: What else?

Carrie: I'm afraid that I won't make it at college, that I'll never be good enough.

Dr. W: Good enough for what?

Carrie: Good enough to make everyone happy, good enough to succeed.

Dr. W: Tell me about when you get angry.

Carrie: I never get angry, but I cry a lot.

Dr. W: You never get angry? Could it be that you know when you're scared, or sad, or hurt but not when you're angry?

Carrie: No, I just don't get angry.

Dr. W: You don't let yourself get angry?

Carrie: No. Except at myself when I eat a bunch of bad stuff. I get mad when I don't do what I should.

Dr. W: When would that be?

Carrie: Like when I don't study enough, or call my mom enough, or work out enough, or when I eat too much.

Dr. W: Sounds like you're pretty hard on yourself and your expectations are pretty high. I wonder if anyone could expect to live up to those expectations? It doesn't seem like you give yourself much room to make mistakes or have any emotions.

Carrie: I'm supposed to be better than that. I shouldn't get angry at anyone and I shouldn't have to make mistakes. I shouldn't have to eat.

APPROACHES TO PREVENTION

Prevention in the area of eating disorders has recently come under greater scrutiny. Primary prevention has been aimed at preventing the development of eating disorders in unafflicted individuals. The goal of secondary prevention has been to detect early warning signs of eating disorders and encourage treatment for those in the early stages of the disorders. The effectiveness of prevention efforts has recently been called into question, however. Although many school and college programs are designed and administered in an attempt to prevent disturbed eating and the associated psychological problems, there is some evidence that such programs are ineffective or detrimental (Carter, Stewart, Dunn, & Fairburn, 1997; Mann et al., 1997). Research has suggested that psychoeducational interventions intended to reduce the risk and incidence of eating pathology may, in fact, increase the likelihood that a participant will develop disturbed eating symptomatology (Carter et al., 1997). It has been further considered that using the same psychoeducational strategy to accomplish both primary and secondary prevention goals may be ill-advised. Mann et al. (1997) contended that primary prevention efforts that stress the severity of the disorders and secondary prevention programs that tend to normalize the disorders in order to encourage those in need to seek help have conflicted goals. Their study of the effects of prevention programs on female college freshmen revealed that the participants had more symptoms of eating disorders at follow-up than did the control group. Prevention interventions may have an unintentional effect of reducing the stigma and normalizing eating disorders, thereby increasing the likelihood that individuals will engage in such behaviors. Mann et al. recommended that prevention programs may be more effective if they do not attempt to address both primary and secondary prevention goals simultaneously. The conclusions drawn in these studies have been challenged (Cohn & Maine, 1998). It has been suggested that the methodology of these studies in assessing the effectiveness of prevention programs was faulty and that prevention must be viewed as a developmental process rather than a single effort.

Although abandoning prevention programs based on limited data would not be prudent, more investigation of the impact of prevention programs is necessary. One prevention study with 11- and 12-year-old girls concluded that prevention programs will be most effective with high-risk groups rather than the general population (Killen, 1996). A study of self-selected college women reported positive outcomes from an 8-week prevention program (Franko, 1998). Although eating patterns were not altered as a result, body image concerns and the importance of appearance were reduced. Some authors recommend ongoing prevention programs that emphasize health promotion along with opportunities for girls and women to develop attributes beyond attractiveness (Huon, 1996) and the introduction of feminist processes to fully validate the female experience (Piran, 1996). Others suggest that teaching girls and women to be media literate and educated consumers of the media images that permeate our culture will allow them to evaluate the media more critically (Berel & Irving, 1998). This may be especially important for those with some eating disorder symptomatology given the finding that those with disordered eating are more significantly influenced by the body ideals presented in the media (Murray, Touyz, & Beumont, 1996; Stice et al., 2001).

A promising model of prevention strategy based on dissonance theory has recently been investigated (Stice & Ragan, 2002). Dissonance theory contends that attitudes and behaviors change when individuals adopt a position contrary to their current behaviors, creating cognitive dissonance. Attitudes and behaviors change to resolve the internal conflict between these two sets of beliefs. These researchers designed a program in which at-risk female college students were asked to critique the societal standard of the thin ideal and develop a program for helping younger girls avoid internalizing such an ideal. The three-session experiment resulted in reduced thin-ideal internalization, body dissatisfaction, dieting, negative affect, and bulimic symptoms at both termination of the study and at 4-week follow-up. Given that many prevention programs have struggled to demonstrate effectiveness, this line of research is encouraging. The most notable result is the reduction in bulimic symptoms reported by the participants, because this dimension of eating disturbance has not been shown to be affected by other prevention programs. Given the health risk of eating disorders and their complex etiology, prevention alone cannot extinguish eating disorders (Levine, Smolak, & Striegel-Moore, 1996). However, innovative programs such as this may improve the effectiveness of eating disorder prevention in the future.

Individual

Approaches to prevention at the individual level are typically identified as educational programming, especially among groups of high-risk individuals, and early detection of symptoms. In the case of Carrie, high-risk factors were prominent. Her low self-esteem was not ameliorated by her acceptance to a popular peer group and her cheerleading status (a high-risk group in itself). In addition, her family situation compounded her low self-esteem and depression. Never feeling adequate for her mother's standards and feeling alienated from her father left her with no sense of safety or acceptance, making her acceptance within her peer group that much more significant.

Programs aimed at high-risk groups might have helped Carrie to identify her problems earlier. One important task might be to assist young, developing women in maintaining self-esteem through adolescence when their sense of self-esteem is most tenuous. One program aimed at junior high school girls (Friedman, 1998) reported some success in helping girls to cope with the demands of adolescence and maturation, including respecting their bodies' development and then challenging the societal pressure for women's appearance. As has been noted by Huon (1996), girls need opportunities to develop and demonstrate their own sense of power and competence. In addition to programming, secondary prevention efforts at the individual level also require that friends and family members take an active role in identifying the warning signs and confronting the behavior of the person in jeopardy.

Family

The role of the family in the prevention of eating disorders is rarely discussed. Although the stereotypical dysfunctional characteristics of the family with an eating disordered member have been identified, intervention at the family level is more common than prevention. The family can, however, be significant in deterring the development of these disorders.

Avoiding the dysfunctional dynamics that contribute to eating pathology would be prudent for family members. Family environments that foster an eating disorder tend to be overcontrolling, emotionally neglectful, and conflictual, but members typically do not express their feelings. Families should be encouraged to keep communication open, including discussing unpleasant feelings such as anger and disappointment. Further, parents should be instructed to nurture developmental maturation and separation, as is appropriate throughout the adolescent years. With each year, the child is learning to take on new levels of independence and responsibility. This task is impeded when the parents are critical or doubtful, or foster dependence, refusing to allow the child the freedom to grow.

The family can also model an acceptance of making mistakes. This includes a tolerance of human mistakes made by others, themselves, and their children. Tolerance is also warranted with regard to appearance. Families who place a strong emphasis on appearance (how each member looks) and on appearances (how they are judged by others) tend to imbue these values in their children. It is the lack of tolerance with imperfection that characterizes the unrealistically high self-standards and shame of the eating disordered adolescent. Removing the value of appearance from the family environment would also require a reduced emphasis on food and weight. Even learning to manage such concerns by family activity or exercise would be an improvement over the diet-obsessed family.

Some authors have recommended that parents can play a key role in the prevention of eating disorders (Graber & Brooks-Gunn, 1996). They recommend that parents be educated about the normal progression of puberty, the importance of staying involved in the meal practices of adolescents, and the negative impact of parental comments about appearance. They emphasize the need to address the changing relationship between parent and child throughout adolescence.

Secondary prevention can take the form of early symptom identification. Because pathological eating is so common (Betz & Fitzgerald, 1993; Polivy & Herman, 1987) and eating disorders are difficult to understand, many families do not acknowledge the problem until the illness is in the advanced stages. In their study of 14 European exchange students diagnosed with eating disorders while in the United States, Van den Broucke and Vandereycken (1986) noted that most of the students had evidence of disturbed eating or weight preoccupation prior to their departure from home. These disturbances were ignored by the parents and were not identified in the medical examination required before leaving home. These authors recommended becoming aware of the more obvious risk factors and early detection of preliminary symptoms by family members and professionals (doctors, school nurses, and teachers).

Carrie's family would have been most helpful had they identified the dysfunctional family patterns that allowed Carrie's disorder to escalate without acknowledgment. Addressing the family conflicts, critical style, and withdrawal via alcohol would have likely prevented an extended course of her bulimia.

School

High school and junior high personnel are in an important position to assist with the prevention and early detection of eating disorders among adolescents, but it should also be noted that children, particularly girls, are showing evidence of weight preoccupation and disturbed body image at younger ages. It is not unusual to find elementary school age girls demonstrating concern about their weight and dieting. Some prevention programs have targeted this younger audience with minimal but positive results (Levine, Smolak, & Schermer, 1996). It is unknown if the effects of such programs could be enduring enough to buffer the challenges of adolescence.

With regard to secondary prevention, Omizo and Omizo (1992) suggested that a school counselor should be aware of the risk factors and be watchful of those in high-risk groups, such as cheerleaders, drill team members, wrestlers, track team members, gymnasts, and those in the performing arts. In addition to the emphasis on weight and appearance, these are highly competitive environments made more stressful by perfectionistic tendencies and the potential for failure. The first responsibility of the school counselor is recognizing the symptoms of anorexia, bulimia, and compulsive overeating. The counselor should be aware that some students will not admit eating problems or acknowledge their behavior as a problem. Much of the therapeutic work with eating disordered clients is developing enough trust in the relationship that the clients' defenses can recede and they can acknowledge their difficulties. Without the student's willingness to participate, treatment is likely to be ineffective.

Although some school counselors may be trained to work with eating disordered clients, a decision to undertake treatment in a high school setting should be made with caution. Despite the ethical consideration of counseling minors, especially those with serious disorders, the treatment is likely to be more involved than an overextended school counselor could manage.

Because of the setting and frequent contact with groups at high risk for eating disorders, school counselors might most profitably aim their energies toward education and prevention programs. Some programs that have incorporated eating disorder education and evaluation into the school curriculum have been successful in prevention and early detection efforts (Moriarty, Shore, & Maxim, 1990). Given some research challenging prevention programming (Carter et al., 1997; Mann et al., 1997), however, the impact of such programs may be most significant among at-risk groups (Killen, 1996; Killen et al., 1993), because most adolescents will not develop an eating disorder. Another recommendation is to include prevention efforts in other curricula rather than see prevention as a single-session event (Piran, 1999). Research has also indicated that eating disorder behaviors may develop in response to a crisis (Troop & Treasure, 1997). The researchers indicated that anorexic symptoms seem to be related to cognitive avoidance following a crisis, whereas bulimic symptoms seem to be related to cognitive rumination about the event or situation. In both groups, women who felt helpless were more likely than others to develop an eating disorder. The authors recommended that primary and relapse prevention of eating disorders focus on facilitating the development of coping skills. Such programs might have helped Carrie more quickly identify her dilemma, improve her coping strategies, and recognize that help was available.

Community

At present, community prevention has occurred primarily through the media by publicizing famous cases of anorexia. Perhaps because anorexia is considered more glamorous than bulimia or binge eating, less public attention has been given to the latter two. Primarily female actors, fashion models, and athletes who have struggled with anorexia have been highlighted through news programs and magazine articles. Talk shows have aired episodes that interview eating disordered individuals with less fame. Television movies have portrayed the consequences of the progression of eating disorders. We have yet to see public service announcements that warn of the dangers of extreme dieting. Given the heavy investment in thinness as the social ideal and the enormous profits generated by the diet industry, warnings against dieting are not likely to emerge soon.

The most important community intervention would be to address the larger societal issues. The strong influence of the media on the development and maintenance of eating disorders has led most authors to suggest that a change in the societal norms is necessary (Cohn & Maine, 1998; Jasper, 1993; Levine, Smolak, & Striegel-Moore, 1996; Polivy & Herman, 1987; Ussery & Prentice-Dunn, 1992). Without a reduced emphasis on the value of thinness within the society, prevention efforts will remain primarily early detection devices. The task of shifting societal standards, although seemingly monumental, is central to the prevention effort at the community level. It is less likely that Carrie would have developed an eating disorder as a means of managing her distress had the emphasis on women's appearance not been so prominent in our culture. One organization in particular, the National Eating Disorder Association (formerly Eating Disorders Awareness and Prevention), has as its central mission to educate the public about the dangers of dieting and eating disorders and to promote media literacy.

INTERVENTION STRATEGIES

Given the enormity of the challenge in preventing eating disorders, the majority of theorizing and research has been in the area of intervention and treatment of eating disorders.

Individual

Individual interventions vary depending on the theoretical approach used in conceptualization. Psychoanalytic, cognitive–behavioral, developmental, and feminist counselors may approach the treatment of eating disorders in different ways; however, there are some central unifying principles. Regardless of counseling orientation, an initial consideration is the medical stability of the client. Consultation with a physician is essential during the assessment phase. The medical complications arising from anorexia, bulimia, and binge eating are dangerous, and the need to monitor the client's physical condition is imperative.

A medical evaluation of blood pressure, heart rate, and body temperature will help determine the extent of the client's physical danger. Further laboratory tests are necessary to evaluate vulnerable physical conditions, including electrolyte levels, estrogen and cholesterol levels, liver and thyroid functioning, and cardiac functioning. Continued monitoring by a physician is appropriate when the medical condition of the client warrants close observation, but a medical evaluation should be a component of treatment with all eating disordered clients as a precaution.

A second consideration is the need for nutritional restabilization. Without adequate nutrition, counseling will be less effective because of the cognitive and affective disturbances that result from starvation or bingeing. For those with bulimia and those with anorexia, the quality of the nutritional state is highly compromised as a result of the eating pathology (Story, 1986). For the anorexic, the nutritional goal is a restoration of body weight. For the bulimic, the goal is a restabilization of the nutritional process. For the binge eater, the goal is regulation of the caloric intake. Consultation with a nutritionist skilled at nutritional restoration among an eating disordered population is a useful adjunct to treatment, but such interventions must be done skillfully, as these interventions can be fearful for the client, possibly resulting in an escalation of eating disordered behavior.

Counseling Approaches

Once a therapeutic relationship is built through support and trust, individual counseling will proceed on the basis of the therapeutic orientation. Cognitive–behavioral treatment protocols and interpersonal therapy have been the most frequently identified effective treatments of eating disorders (Agras, Walsh, Fairburn, Wilson, & Kraemer, 2000; Garner, Vitousek, & Pike, 1997; Marcus, 1997; Wilson, Fairburn, & Agras, 1997). Unfortunately, some therapeutic approaches are less amenable to research and have not been experimentally tested. An eclectic approach may be most suited to the multidimensional nature of eating disorders. Treatment should address the behavioral, cognitive, affective, and interpersonal disturbances as they apply to each client. Initial steps in counseling may include helping the client manage affect in more appropriate ways. Learning alternative means of expressing emotions and self-soothing can interrupt the dysfunctional behavioral patterns. By increasing the client's awareness of the distinction between physiological and emotional states, the client becomes more adept at managing denied feelings. Expressing affect, becoming more self-directed and autonomous, and tolerating ambiguity are reasonable goals for counseling. Behavioral strategies can give the client a sense of structure by introducing small behavior changes gradually. Cognitive interventions are intended to challenge the distorted thought processes that have served to maintain and support the disordered eating. Challenging the irrational beliefs inherent in eating disorder pathology can address issues of body image and self-esteem. Progress in these areas may lead to the exploration of interpersonal and intrapersonal conflicts that plague eating disordered clients. A necessary treatment goal is "helping individuals develop a more internalized sense of self-worth independent of the eating disorder" (Pike & Wilfley, 1996, p. 381).

When feasible, family counseling can be a powerful component of treatment for the adolescent or young adult client with anorexia or bulimia (Pelch, 1999; Sargent et al., 1985; Schwartz et al., 1985). In addition to addressing the distress created in the family by the eating disorder, family counseling can intervene in any dysfunctional interpersonal relationships. Common issues in these families are enmeshment, overprotection, hostility, and rigidity (Kog & Vandereycken, 1985; Vandereycken, 2002). The goals of family counseling might include expression of feelings, resolution of conflict, and fostering autonomy. Families are discouraged from monitoring the client's weight or food intake, however, and tend to be less involved if the client is an independent adult (Pike & Wilfley, 1996).

Family therapy has not been frequently described in the treatment of binge eating disorder, perhaps because binge eating disorder is more frequently treated in adulthood. It is more likely that family counseling will address issues in the client's current relationships, such as marital or parenting issues, in addition to attempting to resolve those in the family of origin (Pike & Wilfley, 1996).

Group counseling has been used successfully with eating disordered clients, although it has been less frequently recommended for those with anorexia (N. F. Lee & Rush, 1986; Polivy & Federoff, 1997). The use of group counseling in conjunction with individual counseling or for individuals at a more advanced stage of recovery allows clients to reduce the isolation and shame of their disorders. Groups can be effective venues for the development of interpersonal skills and challenging dysfunctional thoughts and behaviors. Clients with anorexia should be carefully screened for level of rigidity and weight competitiveness prior to admission in a counseling group (Hall, 1985).

Pharmacological treatment, especially for bulimia, has gained favor in recent years (American Psychiatric Association, 2000; Garfinkel & Walsh, 1997; Mitchell, 1988). The use of antidepressant medication may have some merit in treating the related depression and in reducing the compulsion to binge. A review of the literature suggests that antidepressant medication is most effective when combined with cognitive–behavioral counseling for bulimia (Garfinkel & Walsh, 1997). In the treatment of anorexia, the issue is more complicated. Although medications may assist the client with co-occurring depression, obsessional thinking, and compulsive behaviors, many of these symptoms remit without medication once weight stabilization has occurred. In addition, those with anorexia often do not respond to the medication when they are at a low weight. Antidepressant medication may also be helpful in the treatment of binge eating disorder, in treating co-occurring depression and helping to break the cycle between negative mood and bingeing (Marcus, 1997). Although controversial, treatments using a pharmacological component seem to be a reflection of the current trend toward a biological-based etiology.

Inpatient treatment is warranted in severe cases. Especially for clients with anorexia who have lost 25% of their expected body weight, inpatient treatment is considered necessary. Some bulimic clients, especially those who refuse or are unable to sustain any meals or who have severe depression associated with their disorder, are also recommended for inpatient treatment. Inpatient treatment is less often discussed for binge eating disorder but would follow a protocol similar to that for bulimia. Individuals with eating disorders may also be referred for inpatient treatment if they have not responded to outpatient treatment. Clients may be admitted by the family if they are under legal age or are in imminent medical danger, but involuntary hospitalization is complicated and is most therapeutically useful if the client voluntarily agrees to inpatient care. A program specifically designed for eating disorder treatment is more effective than a general psychiatric inpatient center.

The structured environment of an inpatient setting often helps to reduce the anxiety of the eating disordered client. The treatment protocol will differ, however, depending on the disorder. The focus for the treatment of anorexia is often weight restoration. For the treatment of bulimia, the focus is on a normalization of the eating process. Both of these strategies are used in combination with individual, group, and family therapy during the inpatient stay. Inpatient programs vary in length depending on the individual needs and financial resources of the client and can range from 1 week to several months. Close follow-up and extensive outpatient treatment are necessary for these clients because of the high rate of relapse.

Bibliotherapy or self-help books are becoming increasingly common and have carved a niche in this field. This medium can provide a useful adjunct to counseling or may be an introduction to the treatment process. Many individuals strive to avoid the stigma of psychological disorders and are reluctant to present for treatment. The shame that arises from eating disorders makes individuals in this population particularly likely candidates for self-help literature. There are books available on a variety of topics: anorexia, bulimia, binge eating, self-esteem, body image. Many of these books contain testimonials that sufferers find helpful in alleviating their sense of isolation and fears that they are alone in their distress. Many communities also offer self-help groups. A self-help approach may be less appropriate for more severe cases, however (Fairburn & Carter, 1997).

Prognosis of eating disorders has been related to type of disorder and body weight. Bulimia has a more positive prognosis than anorexia, and anorexic clients with lower body weights have the poorest prognosis (Herzog et al., 1993). Clinical observation indicates that anorexia is the more intractable disorder and requires longer term counseling. Research on binge eating disorder treatment indicates that although the relapse rate is high, approximately one third of those in short-term treatment will remain abstinent at follow-up (Agras, 1996).

Internet Resources

The rise of the Internet as a source of information, companionship, and therapy has brought the eating disorder community both questions and answers. There are over 27,000 Internet sites pertaining to eating disorders (Shafran, 2002). Many of these provide helpful information to individuals who might otherwise feel too shameful to seek help. However, the information on the Internet can vary in accuracy, and some sites actively promote unhealthy behavior (pro-anorexia sites). Ensuring the validity of the information is impossible; however, national association or governmental mental health sites are more likely to provide current and accurate information or referrals.

Treatment information is also available on the Internet, where many treatment programs and therapists now advertise. Therapy is now also conducted on the Internet, although this is a risky endeavor for all involved. The client is less able to validate the therapist's credentials, and the therapist is less able to fully evaluate a client with whom there has been no face-to-face contact.

One of the potentially beneficial aspects of the Internet is the ability for those with eating disorders to gain social support through chat rooms and self-help meetings online. For those unwilling to attend a live support group, these contacts can provide understanding and comfort. Some sites monitor the communications to ensure that unhealthy material is not exchanged, but other sites are less proactive and should be used with caution.

Family

Family therapy is considered by some to be among the most effective treatments for eating disorders, especially with adolescents, and at the very least should be considered as an adjunct to other treatment modalities (Pelch, 1999; Schwartz et al., 1985). The families of anorexic clients have been described as overcontrolling and rigid (Sargent et al., 1985), whereas the families of bulimic clients have been described as conflicted and chaotic (Schwartz et al., 1985). Despite these differences, some universal principles in family counseling for eating disordered clients have been prescribed.

Common issues to be addressed in family counseling often include strengthening boundaries between parents and children, dealing with family and parental conflict in more healthy ways, and openly dealing with other disorders such as depression or alcoholism of another family member (Schwartz et al., 1985). Reducing the family's focus on food, weight, and appearance is often an immediate goal of the process. The family members need to learn healthy expression of emotions to move beyond the past issues (Pelch, 1999). Teaching the family to allow appropriate development of adolescents (which includes allowing less reliance on the parents) is also necessary. Particularly for younger clients, family counseling is considered an important piece of the treatment process.

School

Although few school counselors are trained in the treatment of eating disorders, it may be the school personnel who first identify disturbed eating patterns. School personnel should be aware of the eating disorder symptomatology and be prepared to encourage youth suspected of such disturbances to seek counseling. Resources and referrals that are available to the students seeking treatment should be current.

Some school settings offer support groups for eating disorders, and this is reasonable if the counselor is skilled in group counseling with eating disordered clients and treatment consent can be obtained from parents. An assessment of the extent of the student's disorder is prudent prior to beginning any type of intervention at the school level.

Athletic coaches should be especially vigilant in identifying disturbed eating patterns. R. A. Thompson (1998) has warned that given the central role that coaches play in the lives of athletes, coaches must avoid encouraging, even tacitly, unhealthy eating practices. R. A. Thompson admonished those coaches who are aware of and allow dangerous weight-cutting practices by competitive wrestlers. This is emphasized in light of the recent deaths of three competitive wrestlers who died as a direct result of the common practice of trying to "make weight," which entails efforts to drop their weight rapidly to compete in a lighter weight class (R. A. Thompson, 1998).

Community

Community interventions are as yet minimal. Perhaps because of the perceived rarity of these disorders, wide-scale community interventions are not practiced. Another possibility for the lack of community-level intervention is the inherent challenge of the societal standard of beauty and appearance should such interventions be proposed. Changes at the community level would require a concerted effort toward abolishing the value placed on thinness and appearance. K. J. Thompson and Heinberg (1999) have called for greater social activism and media responsibility in deglamorizing eating disorders and in challenging the thin ideal. Currently, the fervor does not appear to exist to orchestrate such a rebellion.

ADAPTATIONS FOR DIVERSITY

Ethnicity

The cultural norms of the United States have historically been dominated by the values of the White middle class. Although the stereotypical picture of the eating disordered client is a young, White American, adolescent female, the recent increase of anorexia and bulimia among non-White women must be explored (Gordon, 2001;

Root, 1990). In addition, binge eating disorder and obesity have been commonly identified among people of color (Klesges et al., 1996). An important consideration, given the impact of the media on eating disorders, is that few non-White women are featured in the media, and those who do appear tend to have physical characteristics that are similar to the White standard of beauty (Osvold & Sodowsky, 1993). It is as yet unclear what impact these images have on women of color.

A further consideration is that because eating disorders have been related to SES, the increasing status of non-White populations in the United States may serve to increase their vulnerability to eating disorders (Anderson & Hay, 1985). Additionally, Hsu (1987) predicted that as African Americans became more upwardly mobile, they may be more likely to adopt traditional While middle-class values and the related disorders as well. For example, as African Americans more commonly live biculturally, an internalized devaluing of their own race can occur. This can result in greater acceptance of White standards, especially given the lack of African American role models. The typical help-seeking patterns and underutilization of mental health services by people of color may, however, continue to obscure the prevalence of the disorders among these groups (Root, 1990; Striegel-Moore & Smolak, 1996). The rise in eating pathology among people of color would tend to support these hypotheses.

The assumption that eating disorders are "culture-bound" syndromes has been challenged, however (Gordon, 2001). It has been suggested that eating disorders do not develop in response to the introduction of Western values but in response to industrialization and consumerism that change the social and economic structure of a culture. In such an environment, there are increased gender role confusion, emphasis on achievement, and increasingly fragmented family structures, all of which contribute to developmental challenges of adolescents. This change in social structure can be especially challenging for women, whose role will likely endure sweeping changes as society shifts from a traditional economic structure to a consumerism structure. Although Dolan (1991) has warned against using broad statements about racial groups, cultural considerations here will attempt to highlight the similarities and differences between cultures with respect to eating disorders.

One study compared eating and psychological pathology between White and minority women and found that there were no differences in eating disorder symptomatology between the two groups (le Grange, Telch, & Agras, 1997). Unfortunately, little can be gleaned from these findings given the considerable within-group differences among the minority group (Striegel-Moore & Smolak, 1996). Findings from one ethnic sample cannot necessarily be generalized to another, and non-Whites cannot be adequately investigated as if they were a single group.

Another difficulty in interpreting the eating disorder research with ethnic minorities is that the variety of measures and samples makes it challenging to draw firm conclusions. For example, some recent research with ethnically diverse samples has provided inconsistent evidence. A large survey of female subscribers (9,971 women) to *Consumer Reports* found that there were no differences among the White, African American, Hispanic, Native American, and Asian American women with respect to reported binge eating behavior (le Grange, Stone, & Brownell, 1998). Black women were reported to purge more than the other groups, and Asian American women more frequently endorsed exercise as weight control. This sample was identified as being above the median income level of the United States, which likely skewed the results, but may suggest that SES level remains an important variable.

A large study of 36,320 boys and girls from 7th to 12th grade found results both consistent and inconsistent with other literature (Story, French, Resnick, & Blum, 1995).

For both boys and girls, higher SES was related to greater weight satisfaction and fewer unhealthy weight control practices. Self-report indicated that, compared with White girls, African American girls vomited more often, Hispanic girls used diuretics more frequently, and Asian American girls reported more binge eating. Among this sample, Black and Native American girls had greater body satisfaction.

Robinson et al.'s (1996) investigation of White, Hispanic, and Asian American sixth- and seventh-grade schoolgirls identified higher rates of body dissatisfaction among the Asian American group than the White group, but not as high as the Hispanic group. The authors contended that body dissatisfaction may be more common among the Asian population than has been recognized. Similar results were obtained by Sanders and Heiss (1998), who found that female Asian immigrant college students reported similar eating attitudes and body dissatisfaction similar to their Caucasian counterparts but reported a greater fear of fat. It is not clear whether this translates to a higher prevalence of eating disorders as well, because others have found less body image dissatisfaction among Asian American men and women than among Whites or Hispanics in a sample of 315 college students (Altabe, 1998). Contradictory evidence may be related to sampling differences. It cannot be assumed that acculturated Asian Americans will be similar to recent Asian immigrants with respect to eating disorder behaviors, and this distinction tends to be overlooked.

Another study with a large ethnically diverse sample (17,159 White, Black, Asian American, Native American, and Hispanic adolescent females) found that among all ethnic groups body dissatisfaction and perceptions of being overweight were correlated with restricting, purging, and binge eating (French et al., 1997). The researchers concluded that overall, the non-White groups have lower prevalence of dieting and weight concerns but that the "ethnic subculture does not appear to protect against the broader sociocultural factors that foster body dissatisfaction among adolescent females" (p. 315). It may be, as these authors suggested, that the discrepancies between studies are due to the within-group cultural differences of the ethnic groups. Such inconsistencies make it difficult to draw conclusions about eating disorders within non-White groups. Pumariega (1997) has warned that the protective factors of the native culture of people of color are eroding as adolescents, hungry for acceptance by the mainstream culture, abandon their native values. He recommended continued investigations to address the cultural values, beliefs, and level of acculturation.

African American Women

Historically, African American women have not been at risk for developing anorexia or bulimia because of several protective factors. As a group, they have typically not identified with the standards of the White culture (including the standards for thinness), and they have displayed greater acceptance of their body sizes, despite being heavier than their White peers (Altabe, 1998; Gray, Ford, & Kelly, 1987). Eating disorders among this population tend to develop at a later age (Anderson & Hay, 1985). Even among the high-risk group of ballet dancers, Black females have reported lower rates of disturbed eating (Hamilton, Brooks-Gunn, & Warren, 1985). African American females have been seen as taking on more adult responsibilities at earlier ages, whereas Caucasian females may experience more of an extended adolescence that could result in an extended period of vulnerability. The socialization of many African American women has also been believed to differ from that of women in the White culture. African American women are expected to be independent and successful, in contrast to the White values for women to be attractive and feminine (Osvold & Sodowsky, 1993). African American women may be raised with a more pragmatic attitude with an emphasis on self- and community pride rather than on appearance.

A survey of 507 male and female undergraduate students at a Black university revealed that 3% of the sample fit the *DSM–III* (American Psychiatric Association, 1980) criteria for bulimia. When compared with a similar White sample, however, the African American students reported less emphasis on food and weight (Gray et al., 1987). A more recent study of 123 African American college women found rates of bulimia symptoms comparable with those found in similar White samples (Lester & Petrie, 1998). Among this sample, identification with White culture was not related to bulimic symptomatology. Having internalized societal standards of attractiveness was, however, found to be predictive of bulimic symptoms, suggesting a less direct path of influence. This finding confirmed a previous study that found higher levels of eating pathology to be identified among those African American women with greater assimilation to White culture (Abrams, Allen, & Gray, 1993).

Silber (1986) has suggested that the rarely seen case of anorexia among African Americans and Hispanics may be due more to misdiagnosis than to scarcity of the disorder in these populations. Although it has been concluded that the symptoms present themselves similarly in Caucasian and African American women (Anderson & Hay, 1985), Osvold and Sodowsky (1993) highlighted the importance of culture in the etiology of anorexia nervosa.

A recent study of 413 African American college women revealed that no participants met criteria for anorexia or bulimia, and 2% were classified with ED NOS. However, 23% reported some disturbed eating symptomatology within a range similar to that of White women. This confirms other research that found that African American women are more likely to have binge eating disorder than anorexia or bulimia, and they more often experience the resulting consequence of obesity (Klesges et al., 1996). In a study of 351 White, Hispanic, and Black women (Fitzgibbons et al., 1998), depression was found to be predictive of binge eating among Whites and depression and higher weight predictive among Hispanic women. Depression, higher weight, and body image were not found to predict binge eating in Black women in this sample, indicating that other variables need to be investigated.

With regard to body image, an earlier literature review revealed that African American adolescent girls typically identify a larger size as more ideal than do their Caucasian peers and are more likely to perceive that friends and family want them to be larger. African American adult women have reported some weight consciousness but little social pressure to be thin and a more positive body image than White women (Crago, Shisslak, & Estes, 1996; Klesges et al., 1996).

Counselors and researchers are urged to be conscious of the later age occurrence of anorexia and bulimia among African American women. Additionally, as acculturation to the dominant White culture increases, a higher incidence of eating disorder symptoms among African American women is likely.

A greater understanding of the factors believed to be protective against anorexia and bulimia might lend needed information to the prevention efforts for all groups. If messages sent to children in the Black community help these children guard against unrealistic appearance goals, these messages should be incorporated into the rearing of all children. It is unclear, however, if these messages place African American women at greater risk for binge eating disorder.

Latina Women

Studies of eating disorders among Latina women in the United States are quite limited. An earlier study compared the treatment outcomes of 10 Hispanic women

(6 Mexican Americans, 2 Colombians, and 2 Mexicans) and 20 White women with diagnoses of anorexia nervosa in San Diego, California (Heibert, Felice, Wingard, Munoz, & Ferguson, 1988). No differences between the two groups were reported with regard to clinical characteristics or treatment outcome. Another study (Smith & Krejci, 1991) with a larger male and female high school sample (327 Hispanic, 129 Native American, and 89 White) found considerable eating pathology among the Hispanic group. On most measures of disturbed eating (fasting, induced vomiting, binge-ing), the Hispanic group scored comparably with the White group but not as high as the Native American group. A recent review of the literature has echoed the conclusion that Native Americans have the highest rates of eating disturbance of any ethnic minority group (Crago et al., 1996).

A comparison of White, Hispanic, and African American women with regard to binge eating behavior found that Hispanics had the highest rate of binge eating behavior of the three groups (Fitzgibbons et al., 1998). Among the Hispanic women in this sample, binge eating was predicted by level of depression and current weight, whereas binge eating among the White women was predicted by depression alone.

Risk factors among minority populations have also begun to be investigated. One comparison of body dissatisfaction among White, Hispanic, and Asian American sixth- and seventh-grade girls (mean age = 12.4 years) found that the Hispanic girls had the highest level of body dissatisfaction, followed by Asian American and White girls, respectively (Robinson et al., 1996). If body dissatisfaction is indeed a precursor to eating disorder pathology, this finding suggests that these two groups are at greater risk than has previously been assumed. This was found to be the case in an investigation of 120 Mexican American, lower SES, adolescent women (Joiner & Kashubeck, 1996). Among this sample, body dissatisfaction was significantly related to anorexic and bulimic symptomatology. Reported eating disorder symptoms were not, however, related to acculturation level among this sample.

The prevalence of eating pathology among Latina women has likely been underestimated. It appears that Hispanic girls and women are engaging in disturbed eating behaviors at a rate that is similar to that among Whites. This disturbing trend suggests that the interaction of ethnicity, social environment, self-perception, and level of acculturation remains a rich direction for future clinical investigation.

Native American Women

Few data are available on the prevalence of eating disorders among Native American women, who are among the least researched ethnic group in the eating disorders literature. The data available suggest a very high risk for eating pathology among this group. One study found that among 85 Chippewa girls and women living on a reservation in Michigan, 74% reported dieting to lose weight, and of those, the majority had purged, used diet pills, and fasted (Rosen et al., 1988). Another investigation of Pueblo Indians and Hispanic girls in the rural Southwest found that 11% of the total sample met the diagnostic criteria for bulimia, over 80% in both groups worried about being too fat, and the majority either fasted extensively or reported binge eating episodes (Snow & Harris, 1989). Although generalizations cannot be made from these isolated samples, the prevalence of eating disorders among Native American women may have been previously miscalculated.

A similar conclusion has been drawn by Smith and Krejci (1991). In a comparison of disturbed eating patterns among Native American, Hispanic, and White high school students, the Native American group scored higher than the comparison groups on all measures of disturbed eating. The Native American group was heavier than the comparison group, and students who were heavier reported more body dissatisfaction, greater fear of weight gain, more frequent extreme dieting, and more frequent vomiting as a weight control technique. Crago et al. (1996) concluded that Native Americans have more eating disturbances than any other ethnic group or their White counterparts. The few studies to include Native Americans have had small samples, however, which limits generalizability. Further exploration is needed before any reasonable conclusions can be drawn about eating disorders among Native Americans.

Asian American Women

Although anorexia is well known in Japan (including a specially named binge episode related to anorexia), few studies of eating disorders among Asian American women have been reported in the literature. One study of eating pathology compared the responses of White and Asian American women on the Eating Attitudes Test and found that the White women were 5.5 times more likely to score in the highest range of clinical significance (Lucero, Hicks, Bramlette, Brassington, & Welter, 1992). This would suggest that Asian American women are less likely to experience severe eating disturbances. However, an examination of eating disturbances among 257 Asian American women (ages 18–30) indicated that prevalence rates for bulimia in this population are higher than had previously been reported (Tsai & Gray, 2000). Another study with a large sample (36,320 middle and high school students) found that Asian American middle and high school girls reported more binge eating than the White, African American, or Latina students (Story et al., 1995). In addition, other studies that have included Asian American women in their samples have found that Asian American middle school girls have reported a level of body dissatisfaction similar to the White girls in the samples (Robinson et al., 1996). Among a college sample, however, Asian American women reported a lower level of body dissatisfaction than the White or Latina participants (Altabe, 1998).

Few conclusions can be drawn about eating pathology among Asian American women. It may be that the typically thin body type of Asian American women creates less body dissatisfaction and, therefore, fewer unhealthy weight control methods. It may be that there are fewer cases of eating disorders among this population or that the cases are not detected through ordinary channels. Or it may be that the culture itself provides protective factors. The last hypothesis seems unlikely given the data on the rise of eating disorders in Asian populations outside the United States. Some studies have found that acculturation level is not associated with eating disturbances (Haudek, Rorty, & Henker, 1999; Yoshimura, 1995), whereas other studies have proposed a relationship between cultural identity conflict and eating disorders.

A component of the confusing and inconsistent findings may be that the within-group differences have been underestimated. In addition to acculturation level, ethnic and cultural identity, and body dissatisfaction, there are likely significant differences among Japanese Americans, Chinese Americans, and Korean Americans, for example. These differences may be reflected in the samples, especially when one considers that research samples are often samples of convenience, regionally determined, and may therefore capture a higher concentration of a particular subgroup. Asian Americans are often categorized as a single group, which may blur the research findings. This concern is also relevant to other ethnic minority groups. Asian American populations have received little research attention in the United States. Without adequate data, speculation about the prevalence or course of eating disorders within this population would be unwise.

Immigrant Women in the United States

There is mounting evidence that exposure to the standards of the dominant culture has increased the risk for eating disturbances among immigrant women. The assumption has been that as women enter the United States they are flooded with the expectations and messages of the dominant culture. This exposure has been believed to provide an unrealistic standard of the female form and negative self-comparison. Among women who are eager to assimilate, this can lead to disturbed eating practices. Although this may simplify the process, some evidence suggests that increased exposure and identification with the White standards increase the risk of developing an eating disorder. As noted earlier (Sanders & Heiss, 1998), female Asian immigrant college students were reported to have similar eating attitudes and body dissatisfaction as the White women but expressed an even greater fear of fat. This finding conflicts with other research that has found fewer weight concerns among Asian Americans, suggesting that the issue of immigration plays a key role.

Even Caucasians from different cultures have been susceptible to the influences of American, White, middle-class standards. Van den Broucke and Vandereycken (1986) studied 14 European exchange students in the United States who had been diagnosed with an eating disorder during their year-long stay. Although most evidenced at least minor eating disorder symptomatology prior to departing from home, the challenges of adolescence combined with the culture shock, separation from family, and the stress of academic and social adjustment served to exacerbate the disorders.

Non-Western Women

An increase in anorexia and bulimia has been reported in many countries outside the United States and Western societies, most notably in the Asian countries of Japan, Hong Kong, Taiwan, Singapore, China, and the Philippines. The early symptoms of these disorders have been identified at young ages. High rates of body image distortions and body dissatisfaction have been observed among school children and adolescents in Japan (Ohtahara, Ohzeki, Hanaki, Motozumi, & Shiraki, 1993).

The literature has begun to accumulate evidence suggesting that the risk for eating disorders among international women increases with the level of exposure to White standards. A revealing study in Fiji demonstrated a strong relationship between media exposure and disturbed eating (Becker, 1995). In the 36 months following the introduction of television to the island, eating pathology increased, suggesting that the media is a strong and rapid transmitter of societal norms.

Other countries are also reporting increasing eating pathology. Assuming a continuum of eating disorder symptomatology, Hooper and Garner (1986) compared Black, White, and mixed-race schoolgirls in Zimbabwe on eating disorder behaviors. The White group showed the greatest symptomatology, the Black group showed the lowest, and the mixed-race group had scores that fell between the comparison groups. The researchers concluded that the acculturation and adoption of Western ideals influence the development of eating disorders.

It has been suggested that eating disorders may present similarly in countries outside the United States but that cultural issues may also affect the presentation. A cross-cultural study of 132 American and Austrian college women found that the American group had higher rates of depression and alcohol and drug abuse (Mangweth, Pope, Hudson, & Biebl, 1996). This was true for both the bulimic group and the control group. This finding suggests that the depression and substance abuse associated with bulimia in the United States may be more a function of the culture than the eating disorder.

Some non-Western cultures do not seem to manifest eating disorders with the diagnostic criteria used in Western cultures. India, for example, tends to exhibit milder forms of eating disturbances and identifies a minor disorder known as *eating distress syndrome* (Srinivasan, Suresch, & Jayaram, 1998). It is noted that more eating disturbances are seen in the young female college students in India, indicating that as Western norms infiltrate the culture, greater severity of eating problems may be anticipated.

S. Lee and Katzman (2002) made a strong case for using culturally sensitive assessment measures in non-Western cultures. They contended that whereas bulimia presents similarly in Asian countries as in the United States, anorexia tends to manifest in a way that does not meet *DSM–IV–TR* criteria. Many Asian women with apparent anorexia do not report "fear of fat" among their symptoms. Instead they attribute their food refusal to stomach bloating or loss of appetite. This phenomenon may be due to (a) denial of their weight concerns, (b) the disorder being instead a form of somaticized depression, or (c) their genetic thinness making them less vulnerable to weight gain concerns. The authors contended that the Asian culture may not support fat phobia as a valid concern, whereas physical symptoms such as stomach bloating are more culturally valid. This description of symptoms from an Asian immigrant can baffle clinicians unfamiliar with the cultural differences in the disorder. Especially with anorexia, the criteria and interpretation of the disorder may vary with culture. Feminists have charged that viewing eating disorders as an appearance disorder is belittling and minimizes food refusal as a universal means of proclaiming self-control, which may be more apparent in Asian societies.

Recommendations for counseling women of color and of nondominant cultures include an awareness of the cultural aspect of the disorders. It may be necessary to assess the extent of identification a woman has with her own ethnic culture and that of the dominant White society, in addition to the eating disorder diagnostic criteria (Osvold & Sodowsky, 1993)—criteria that Root (1990) reminded were developed from observations of White clients. Although some researchers have found that acculturation and cultural identity conflict may be related to eating disturbances, others have found level of acculturation to be unrelated to eating disorder symptomatology (Joiner & Kashubeck, 1996). The relationship among body dissatisfaction, eating disorder symptomatology, and cultural background requires further research. Greater attention to the effects of racism is also warranted (Crago et al., 1996). Feelings of low self-esteem, social isolation, and attempting to be accepted by the dominant culture may make one vulnerable to developing eating disorder symptoms. In the meantime, mental health professionals should be cognizant of the socially sanctioned stereotypes of women of color and avoid such stereotypes from influencing the assessment process (Root, 1990).

Prevention efforts among ethnically diverse groups should address the previous lack of prevention involvement in communities of color. Outreach programs can be established with these communities only after allowing for time to build relationships with key leaders and showing genuine interest in the group (Root, 1990). Outreach and prevention programs need to take into account the norms of the community with regard to help-seeking patterns, beliefs about causation and healing, and meaning of the disorder. Ethnographic research is recommended by some authors to gain a better understanding of the particular population and improve the likelihood that any prevention efforts will be effective (Nichter, Vuckovic, & Parker, 1999). This strategy might allow for greater inclusion of people of color into research protocols and prevention/treatment programs. (For recommendations regarding inclusion of people of color in empirical studies, see Root, 1990.)

Males

Although females have been the most affected by eating disorders, the prevalence among males may be underestimated (Anderson, 2002; Lachenmeyer & Muni-Brander, 1988). Approximately half of those with binge eating disorder are men. Steiger and Houle (1991) have suggested that similar factors that make women vulnerable to anorexia and bulimia operate to make men vulnerable as well. One risk factor is that of athletic involvement, especially in sports that have a weight or physical appearance orientation, such as wrestling or body building (Anderson, 1999; Franco et al., 1988). A second risk factor for men is a history of obesity (Anderson, 1999; Franco et al., 1988). Males with bulimia were found to have relatively higher current weights and histories of higher past adolescent and prepubescent weights. A third risk factor for men is homosexuality. It appears that the heterosexual male population is more protected from standards that emphasize physical appearance, whereas gay men feel more pressure to be thin or attractive (Anderson, 1999; Schneider & Agras, 1987).

Although men tend to score lower on the Eating Disorders Inventory (EDI) drive for thinness scale and report less body dissatisfaction (Grogan, Williams, & Conner, 1996; Schneider & Agras, 1987), a correlate of the drive for thinness among women may be the drive for fitness (Ussery & Prentice-Dunn, 1992). Men with this disorder may see themselves as too thin, even when quite muscular, and may abuse anabolic steroids. Men with eating disorders also develop hormone irregularities as their testosterone levels drop, and they typically report less sexual interest. Despite prior assumptions, these men are at even greater risk than women for osteopenia and osteoporosis and, when compared with similar women, have lower bone density levels (Anderson, Watson, & Schlechte, 2000). Eating disorder symptoms among men may also take the form of excessive compulsive exercise, which is less likely to be identified as problematic.

Ussery and Prentice-Dunn (1992) found that the strongest predictors of bulimia among men were similar to the predictors of bulimia among women: restrained eating, lack of interoceptive awareness, and lack of confidence in identifying one's emotions that lead to underdeveloped coping skills. In a comparison of men and women with comparable bulimic histories, Schneider and Agras (1987) found some gender differences. Men with bulimia have been noted to differ from women with bulimia in that they are less likely to identify the intake of large amounts of food as a binge; are less likely to report laxative, diuretic, or diet pill use; and have been less likely to exercise excessively (although this may be changing). Men also report greater success with diet plans compared with women. Whereas women tend to binge in private, men tend to binge during mealtime with larger quantities of food, and they are less likely to report feeling guilty about eating in public. Of all the eating disorders, men are most likely to develop binge eating disorder (American Psychiatric Association, 2000).

An exception to the previous discussions of ethnicity is the report of an investigation of bulimia among African American college students, in which Black men were more likely than their Caucasian counterparts to report significantly more frequent bingeing, dieting, and fasting (Gray et al., 1987). A recent study of steroid use among adolescents found that among minority boys, Asian Americans were more likely to use steroids in an attempt to build a more muscular body (Irving, Wall, Neumark-Sztainer, & Story, 2002).

It has been suggested that men and women are differentially affected by the cultural pressure for weight and body shape. Social cues that determine appropriate or desired weight hold women to a more stringent standard (Schneider & Agras, 1987). Recent evidence suggests that men also may be influenced by media images (Grogan et al., 1996). Both men and women in this study experienced a drop in body esteem after viewing same-gender models' photographs. A similar investigation, however, found that only women were negatively affected by viewing slim, physically fit, same-gender models in the media (Kalodner, 1997).

In addition, males with bulimia may go undiagnosed. Men may experience greater embarrassment at acknowledging symptoms that have been characterized as a disorder of adolescent females (Schneider & Agras, 1987). Although eating disorders occur more rarely in men, and even more rarely in men of color, the disorders do exist in these populations (Anderson, 1999; Gray et al., 1987; Lawlor, Burket, & Hodgin, 1987), and assessing for risk factors alone may not alert the clinician. For example, eating disorders have been present in male clients who come from lower socioeconomic groups and do not fit the typical clinical picture. Clinicians should be cautious of dismissing this diagnosis among atypical populations.

Affectional Orientation

Homosexuality has been reported to be a risk factor for developing eating disorders among men but not women. Most samples of eating disordered females report very small percentages of identified lesbians (Herzog, Newman, Yeh, & Warshaw, 1992). For women, homosexuality may offer protection from a vulnerability to eating disorder symptomatology. Several factors have been cited as potential explanations for this phenomenon: increased body satisfaction, greater appreciation for the female form, and elevated feminist values that challenge the status quo.

Unlike heterosexual women, lesbian women are reported to be more satisfied with their bodies (Bergeron & Senn, 1998; Herzog et al., 1992). In a study of 64 heterosexual and 45 homosexual unmarried women, Herzog et al. (1992) found that significantly more heterosexual women wanted to lose weight, despite the fact that the lesbian women among the sample were heavier than the heterosexual women. Although both groups chose ideal weights below the appropriate life weight tables (Metropolitan Life Insurance Company, 1983), lesbian women were more likely to choose higher weights that were closer to the norm. The heterosexual women were more likely to diet and were more susceptible to the image society portrays as the female ideal. Similar conclusions were drawn by Bergeron and Senn (1998), who found that heterosexual women reported more negative attitudes toward their bodies than did lesbian women, even though there were no significant differences in their weights. Heterosexual women in this predominantly White sample also identified an ideal weight that was lower than that chosen by the lesbian women. It may be, as Brown (1987) has noted, that feminist ideology rejects the cultural standards of beauty and reduces the guilt associated with eating that is found in the majority of the traditional female culture. A more recent finding suggests that involvement in lesbian activities, rather than feminist activities, provided a protection against developing low body esteem (Heffernan, 1999). This sample of 263 lesbians, who were generally critical of the traditional social norms, did not differ from the heterosexual control group with regard to weight and appearance. Almost half were dissatisfied with their body, dieting was common, and self-esteem was strongly influenced by how these participants felt about their body.

Herzog et al. (1992) have concluded that the dissatisfaction with one's body that increases the risk of eating disorders among the heterosexual female population is less prominent among the lesbian population and may explain the lower incidence of eating disorders among lesbian women. Others contend that young lesbians may also value society's ideal of thinness but that sexual relationships with women promote greater acceptance of the female form (Beren, Hayden, Wilfley, & Striegel-Moore, 1997). Interviews with 26 lesbian college students yielded evidence of considerable internal conflict between feminist values and the social pressure toward female thinness.

Another dynamic not yet addressed in the literature is the incidence of eating disorder behaviors among those questioning their sexual orientation. The eating disorder behaviors can provide an effective, albeit unhealthy, distraction from the angst often associated with sexual orientation uncertainty. Caution is warranted in discarding the potential eating disorder diagnosis among lesbians. The incidence of anorexia and bulimia among lesbian women is low, but not absent, and the prevalence of binge eating disorder in this group has been virtually ignored in the literature.

Gay men have been reported to have eating disorder symptomatology (primarily anorexia and bulimia) at higher rates than are found among heterosexual men (Anderson, 1999; Yager, Kurtzman, Landsverk, & Wiesmeier, 1988). It is estimated that nearly 20% of men with eating disorders are gay men (Seiver, 1994). Compared with heterosexual men, gay men have been more likely to be underweight, to choose an ideal weight that is lower, and to believe that a thinner body type would be more attractive to potential partners (Herzog, Newman, & Warshaw, 1991).

When 48 nonclinical homosexual men were compared with 300 nonclinical heterosexual men, the gay male sample was reported to present past problems with binge eating, use of diuretics, feeling fat despite others' perceptions of them, and feeling terrified of becoming fat. Additionally, gay men scored higher than their heterosexual peers on the EDI scales of drive for thinness, interoceptive awareness, bulimia, body dissatisfaction, ineffectiveness, maturity fears, and the total overall score.

There has been speculation that findings of higher than would be expected rates of disordered eating among the gay male population may be related to the tendency toward the effeminate for at least some gay men (Yager et al., 1988). A more reasonable explanation might be that some gay men feel the same pressure that heterosexual women feel to be attractive to males and might be more conscious of the competition for partners. This explanation is further supported by the long tradition among men in general to seek attractive partners. Herzog et al. (1991) have noted that gay men may fear weight gain more than heterosexual men do because weight gain would surpass their ideal body weight and the weight they believe would be most attractive to a male partner.

The rise of AIDS among the gay male population may ameliorate the emphasis on thinness within this group. Some authors have noted that the physical deterioration associated with AIDS has fostered a slang for the disease, "slims," in some countries (Mickalide, 1990). This association may help to diminish the thin ideal.

Investigations of anorexic and bulimic pathology among the gay and lesbian culture remain in preliminary stages, and explanations of the increased prevalence in the gay male population can only be speculative. In addition, binge eating disorder has not been adequately studied among gay or lesbian groups.

Athletes

Despite anecdotal data, evidence suggests that athletes are not, as a group, at greater risk for developing eating disorders, particularly anorexia and bulimia (Kirk, Singh, & Getz, 2001). Certain sport groups may, however, produce an increased vulnerability for developing eating disorder symptoms (Stoutjesdyk & Jevne, 1993). Among a sample of 191 Canadian athletes, eating disorder prevalence was not higher for women than is found in the general and college populations. The prevalence of disturbed eating patterns for men was, however, higher than has been reported in college and general populations. For women, the risk factors included being involved in a sport that emphasized leanness or physical appearance (such as diving or gymnastics) or that had weight restrictions (such as judo or lightweight rowing). For both men and women, eating disorder symptomatology was related to the level of competition. Only those athletes who regularly competed on the national or international level showed elevated scores on a measure of disturbed eating behaviors and attitudes. It was concluded that the combination of high-level competition and weight or aesthetic considerations within the sport makes for a vulnerability to disturbed eating.

Similarly, Depalma et al. (1993) studied 131 lightweight college football players and found that 9.9% fit the criteria for an eating disorder and 42% evidenced disturbed eating patterns. Wrestlers and body builders are also at high risk for eating disorder pathology. Steen and Brownell (1990) found that 30% to 40% of high school and college wrestlers reported pathological eating, including food restriction, fasting, vomiting, using laxatives and diuretics, and bingeing after matches. Preoccupation with weight and food was common among this sample of 431 male wrestlers. Authors reviewing the literature on eating disturbances in body builders concluded that severe dieting, preoccupation with weight and shape, body image distortions, and diagnosable eating disorders are relatively common among serious recreational and competitive body builders (Goldfield, Harper, & Blouin, 1998). The eating disturbances combined with lower body fat than is considered healthy make this a particularly high-risk sport.

Among the female athletic community, two risk factors have been identified (Powers & Johnson, 1996). *Appearance thinness* refers to the belief that judges reward thinner competitors in sports like gymnastics and figure skating. *Performance thinness* refers to the belief that lower body fat enhances performance, particularly in sports like track and swimming in which endurance is required. Despite the lack of convincing evidence, this belief is so strongly held among coaches, trainers, and athletes that it has become an assumption of the culture of competition. In a study of elite athletes in Norway (Sundgot-Borgen, 1993), eating disorders were identified in 25% of those women in sports in which thinness is emphasized. Among Australian elite athletes, only the athletes in "thin" sports and dancers were at high risk for the development of eating disturbances (Byrne & McLean, 2002). These prevalence rates are higher than those found in American athletics by the National Collegiate Athletic Association (NCAA; Johnson, Powers, & Dick, 1999). These researchers reported no cases of anorexia and only 1% of the females with bulimia in a large sample of 1,445 student athletes. However, clinically significant (if not diagnosable) eating concerns were found among both the male and female athletes, with binge eating being the most common practice among men (13%) and women (10%). The conservative results may indicate that the criteria used were not sufficiently sensitive. Given the high-risk environment, any eating or body image disturbance among athletes is cause for concern.

Dancers have long been considered to be at high risk for the development of eating disorders; however, this generalization has been challenged. Hamilton, Brooks-Gunn, Warren, and Hamilton (1988) have contended that those ballet dancers who are most successful show similar rates of eating disorder pathology as is found in the general population. Those dancers who are struggling to gain recognition in a major dance company, however, are more likely to report eating pathology. This pattern held true for dancers in both American and Chinese ballet companies.

Johnson et al. (1989) have noted a steady increase in the use of exercise as a purging strategy, especially in recent years as the standard of thinness for women is being replaced with the standard of physical fitness or strength. Given this trend, they warned those involved in the supervision of athletics, such as athletic trainers, to be observant of suspicious behavior. Trainers may be the initial contact for someone struggling with an eating disorder, and they need to be informed and capable of providing a safe environment for the potential disclosure of psychological problems. The personality traits associated with eating disordered individuals (perfectionism, competitiveness, emphasis on achievement) are common in athletics (Byrne, 2002) but are less likely to be seen as problematic. Fostered by the athletic culture, these traits can be precursors to eating pathology that goes unrecognized because athletes seem to have a purpose for their efforts and tend to present with higher levels of self-esteem. This self-confidence may be tenuous, however, if based primarily on their athletic success.

Proposed prevention efforts are aimed at educating athletes and sports management personnel (coaches and trainers) in the dangers of disturbed eating (Grandjean, 1991; R. A. Thompson & Sherman, 1993). The female athlete triad (disturbed eating, amenorrhea, and osteoporosis) carries considerable health risks, has become more common, and is now attracting the attention of eating disorder prevention experts in athletics. Recent efforts of the USA Gymnastics governing board include increasing the age limit to 16 for gymnastics in the 2000 Olympics and providing sport psychology and nutrition consultants for the national teams. The NCAA has also undertaken a research and prevention program for eating disorders within college athletics (Powers & Johnson, 1996). In addition to increasing the awareness of warning signs of eating disorders, it has recommended that weight be de-emphasized and that group weigh-ins be eliminated. In sports in which weight is a determinant for competition, such as wrestling, unhealthy weight management strategies should not be condoned, even passively (R. A. Thompson, 1998).

SUMMARY

A clear conclusion is that eating disorders reflect an interaction of social, interpersonal, intrapersonal, and physical variables. The societal ideal for people, especially women, to be thin and attractive promotes greater pressure for women with regard to appearance and places them at greater risk for developing anorexia and bulimia. These disorders manifest during adolescence or young adulthood, usually as a means of coping with problems or life transitions. Other risk factors include higher SES, participation in some types of athletics, disturbed family dynamics, and low self-esteem. Binge eating disorder is a more recently acknowledged syndrome that threatens to afflict more individuals and often results in obesity and the associated health and social risks. Although a small proportion of the population may develop a clinical eating disorder, great numbers of individuals suffer with subclinical symptoms of disturbed eating and dieting patterns.

Treatment may include individual, group, and/or family counseling. A medical evaluation and nutritional counseling are also recommended. In severe cases, inpatient or pharmacological treatment may be warranted. Treating the eating disordered client requires patience and an understanding of the psychological depth of the disorder. Recovery from an eating disorder is often a slow process, and the relapse rate is high.

Prevention efforts at the individual, family, school, and community levels should be considered by those involved with adolescents or young adults, especially those youths in high-risk groups. Special attention should be paid to atypical groups such as people of color and men. These groups are least likely to be identified as at risk for an eating disorder and may be neglected in treatment and research of eating disorders.

The power of society and the media must not be overlooked. It is the responsibility of each individual to challenge the damaging and demeaning messages of our culture. It is equally important to teach our youth to challenge those same messages, whether the messages stem from the media, their peers, their families, or their own internalized belief systems.

REFERENCES

Abrams, K. K., Allen, L. R., & Gray, J. J. (1993). Disordered eating attitudes and behaviors, psychological adjustment, and ethnic identity: A comparison of Black and White female college students. *International Journal of Eating Disorders, 14*, 49–57.

Agras, W. S. (1996). Short-term psychological treatments for binge eating. In C. G. Fairburn & G. T. Wilson (Eds.), *Binge eating* (pp. 270–286). New York: Guilford Press.

Agras, W. S., Walsh, B. T., Fairburn, C. G., Wilson, G. T., & Kraemer, H. C. (2000). A multicenter comparison of cognitive–behavioral therapy and interpersonal psychotherapy for bulimia nervosa. *Archives of General Psychiatry, 57*, 459–466.

Altabe, M. (1998). Ethnicity and body image: Quantitative and qualitative analysis. *International Journal of Eating Disorders, 23*, 153–159.

American Psychiatric Association. (1980). *Diagnostic and statistical manual of mental disorders* (3rd ed.). Washington, DC: Author.

American Psychiatric Association. (2000). *Diagnostic and statistical manual of mental disorders* (4th ed., text revision). Washington, DC: Author.

Anderson, A. E. (1999). Eating disorders in males: Critical questions. In R. Lemberg (Ed.), *Eating disorders: A reference sourcebook* (pp. 73–78). Phoenix, AZ: Oryx Press.

Anderson, A. E. (2002). Eating disorders in males. In C. G. Fairburn & K. D. Brownell (Eds.), *Eating disorders and obesity* (pp. 188–192). New York: Guilford Press.

Anderson, A. E., & DiDomenico, L. (1992). Diet vs. shape content of popular male and female magazines: A dose–response relationship to the incidence of eating disorders? *International Journal of Eating Disorders, 11*, 283–287.

Anderson, A. E., & Hay, A. (1985). Racial and socioeconomic influences in anorexia nervosa and bulimia. *International Journal of Eating Disorders, 4*, 479–487.

Anderson, A. E., Watson, T., & Schlechte, J. (2000). Osteoporosis and osteopenia in men with eating disorders. *Lancet, 355*, 1967–1968.

Armstrong, J. G., & Roth, D. M. (1989). Attachment and separation difficulties in eating disorders: A preliminary investigation. *International Journal of Eating Disorders, 8*, 141–155.

Beattie, H. J. (1988). Eating disorders and the mother–daughter relationship. *International Journal of Eating Disorders, 7*, 453–460.

Beaumont, P. J. V. (2002). Clinical presentation of anorexia nervosa and bulimia nervosa. In C. G. Fairburn & K. D. Brownell (Eds.), *Eating disorders and obesity* (pp. 162–170). New York: Guilford Press.

Becker, A. E. (1995). *Body, self, and society: The view from Fiji.* Philadelphia: University of Pennsylvania Press.

Berel, S., & Irving, L. M. (1998). Media and disturbed eating: An analysis of media influence and implications for prevention. *Journal of Primary Prevention, 18*, 415–430.

Beren, S. E., Hayden, H. A., Wilfley, D. E., & Striegel-Moore, R. H. (1997). Body dissatisfaction among lesbian college students. *Psychology of Women Quarterly, 21*, 431–445.

Bergeron, S. M., & Senn, C. Y. (1998). Body image and sociocultural norms. *Psychology of Women Quarterly, 22*, 385–401.

Betz, N. E., & Fitzgerald, L. F. (1993). Individuality and diversity: Theory and research in counseling psychology. *Annual Review of Psychology, 44*, 343–381.

Brown, L. (1987). Lesbians, weight, and eating: New analyses and perspectives. In Boston Lesbian Psychologies Collective (Eds.), *Lesbian psychologies* (pp. 294–310). Chicago: University of Illinois Press.

Bruce, B., & Agras, W. S. (1992). Binge eating in females: A population-based investigation. *International Journal of Eating Disorders, 12,* 365–374.

Bruch, H. (1973). *Eating disorders.* New York: Basic Books.

Byrne, S. (2002). Sport, occupation, and eating disorders. In C. G. Fairburn & K. D. Brownell (Eds.), *Eating disorders and obesity* (pp. 256–259). New York: Guilford Press.

Byrne, S., & McLean, N. (2002). Elite athletes: Effects of the pressure to be thin. *Journal of Science and Medicine, 4,* 145–160.

Carter, J. C., Stewart, A., Dunn, V. J., & Fairburn, C. G. (1997). Primary prevention of eating disorders: Might it do more harm than good? *International Journal of Eating Disorders, 22,* 167–172.

Cohn, L., & Maine, M. (1998). More harm than good. *Eating Disorders, 6,* 93–95.

Connor-Greene, P. A. (1988). Gender differences in body weight perception and weight-loss strategies of college students. *Women and Health, 14,* 27–42.

Coric, C., & Murstein, B. I. (1993). Bulimia nervosa: Prevalence and psychological correlates in a college community. *Eating Disorders, 1,* 39–51.

Crago, M., Shisslak, C. M., & Estes, L. S. (1996). Eating disturbances among American minority groups: A review. *International Journal of Eating Disorders, 19,* 239–248.

Depalma, M. T., Koszewski, W. M., Case, J. G., Barile, R. J., Depalma, B. F., & Oliaro, S. M. (1993). Weight control practices of lightweight football players. *Medicine and Science in Sports and Exercise, 25,* 694–701.

Dolan, B. (1991). Cross-cultural aspects of anorexia nervosa and bulimia: A review. *International Journal of Eating Disorders, 10,* 67–78.

Fairburn, C. G., & Carter, J. C. (1997). Self-help and guided self-help for binge-eating problems. In D. M. Garner & P. E. Garfinkel (Eds.), *Handbook of treatment for eating disorders* (2nd ed., pp. 494–499). New York: Guilford Press.

Fairburn, C. G., Cooper, Z., Doll, H. A., Norman, P., & O'Connor, M. (2000). The natural course of bulimia nervosa and binge eating disorder in young women. *Archives of General Psychiatry, 57,* 659–665.

Fitzgibbons, M. L., Spring, B., Avellone, M. E., Blackman, L. R., Pingitore, R., & Stolley, M. R. (1998). Correlates of binge eating in Hispanic, Black, and White women. *International Journal of Eating Disorders, 24,* 43–52.

Franco, K. S. N., Tamburrino, M. B., Carroll, B. T., & Bernal, G. A. A. (1988). Eating attitudes in college males. *International Journal of Eating Disorders, 7,* 285–288.

Franko, D. L. (1998). Secondary prevention of eating disorders in college women at risk. *Eating Disorders, 6,* 29–40.

French, S. A., Story, M., Neumark-Sztainer, D., Downes, B., Resnick, M., & Blum, R. (1997). Ethnic differences in psychosocial and health behavior correlates of dieting, purging, and binge eating in a population-based sample of adolescent females. *International Journal of Eating Disorders, 22,* 315–322.

Friedman, S. S. (1998). Girls in the 90's: A gender-based model for eating disorder prevention. *Patient Education and Counseling, 33,* 217–224.

Garfinkel, P. E., & Walsh, B. T. (1997). Drug therapies. In D. M. Garner & P. E. Garfinkel (Eds.), *Handbook of treatment for eating disorders* (2nd ed., pp. 372–380). New York: Guilford Press.

Garner, D. M., Garfinkel, P. E., Schwartz, D., & Thompson, M. (1980). Cultural expectations of thinness in women. *Psychological Reports, 47,* 647–656.

Garner, D. M., Vitousek, K. M., & Pike, K. M. (1997). Cognitive–behavioral therapy for anorexia nervosa. In D. M. Garner & P. E. Garfinkel (Eds.), *Handbook of treatment for eating disorders* (pp. 94–144). New York: Guilford Press.

Goldfield, G. S., Harper, D. W., & Blouin, A. G. (1998). Are bodybuilders at risk for an eating disorder? *Eating Disorders, 6,* 133–157.

Gordon, R. A. (2001). Eating disorders East and West: A culture-bound syndrome unbound. In M. Nasser, M. A. Katzman, & R. A. Gordon (Eds.), *Eating disorders and cultures in transition* (pp. 1–16). New York: Taylor & Francis.

Graber, J. A., & Brooks-Gunn, J. (1996). Prevention of eating problems and disorders: Including parents. *Eating Disorders, 4*, 348–363.

Grandjean, A. C. (1991). Eating disorders: The role of the athletic trainer. *Athletic Training, 26*, 105–112.

Gray, J. J., & Ford, K. (1985). The incidence of bulimia in a college sample. *International Journal of Eating Disorders, 4*, 201–211.

Gray, J. J., Ford, K., & Kelly, L. M. (1987). The prevalence of bulimia in a Black college population. *International Journal of Eating Disorders, 6*, 733–740.

Grilo, C. M. (2002). Binge eating disorder. In C. G. Fairburn & K. D. Brownell (Eds.), *Eating disorders and obesity* (pp. 178–182). New York: Guilford Press.

Grogan, S., Williams, Z., & Conner, M. (1996). The effects of viewing same-gender photographic models on body-esteem. *Psychology of Women Quarterly, 20*, 569–575.

Hall, A. (1985). Group psychotherapy for anorexia nervosa. In D. M. Garner & P. E. Garfinkel (Eds.), *Handbook of psychotherapy for anorexia nervosa and bulimia* (pp. 462–475). New York: Guilford Press.

Hamilton, L. H., Brooks-Gunn, J., & Warren, M. P. (1985). Sociocultural influences on eating disorders in professional ballet dancers. *International Journal of Eating Disorders, 4*, 465–477.

Hamilton, L. H., Brooks-Gunn, J., Warren, M. P., & Hamilton, W. G. (1988). The role of selectivity in the pathogenesis of eating disorders in ballet dancers. *Medicine and Science in Sports and Exercise, 20*, 560–565.

Haudek, C., Rorty, M., & Henker, B. (1999). The role of ethnicity and parental bonding in the eating and weight concerns of Asian-American and Caucasian college women. *International Journal of Eating Disorders, 25*, 425–433.

Heffernan, K. (1999). Lesbians and the internalization of societal standards of weight and appearance. *Journal of Lesbian Studies, 3*, 121–127.

Heibert, K. A., Felice, M. A., Wingard, D. L., Munoz, R., & Ferguson, J. A. (1988). Comparison of outcome in Hispanic and Caucasian patients with anorexia nervosa. *International Journal of Eating Disorders, 7*, 693–696.

Herzog, D. B., Newman, K. L., & Warshaw, M. (1991). Body dissatisfaction in homosexual and heterosexual males. *Journal of Nervous and Mental Disease, 179*, 356–359.

Herzog, D. B., Newman, K. L., Yeh, C. J., & Warshaw, M. (1992). Body image satisfaction in homosexual and heterosexual women. *International Journal of Eating Disorders, 11*, 391–396.

Herzog, D. B., Sacks, N. R., Keller, M. B., Lavori, P. W., von Ranson, K. B., & Gray, H. M. (1993). Patterns and predictors of recovery in anorexia nervosa and bulimia nervosa. *Journal of the American Academy of Child and Adolescent Psychiatry, 32*, 835–842.

Hill, A. J. (2002). Prevalence and demographics of dieting. In C. G. Fairburn & K. D. Brownell (Eds.), *Eating disorders and obesity* (pp. 80–83). New York: Guilford Press.

Hooper, M. S., & Garner, D. M. (1986). Application of the Eating Disorders Inventory to a sample of Black, White, and mixed race schoolgirls in Zimbabwe. *International Journal of Eating Disorders, 5*, 161–168.

Hsu, L. K. G. (1987). Are eating disorders becoming more common in Blacks? *International Journal of Eating Disorders, 6*, 113–125.

Humphrey, L. L. (1994). Family relationships. In K. A. Halmi (Ed.), *Psychobiology and treatment of anorexia nervosa and bulimia nervosa* (pp. 263–282). Washington, DC: American Psychiatric Press.

Huon, G. F. (1996). Health promotion and the prevention of dieting-induced disorders. *Eating Disorders, 4*, 27–32.

Irving, L. M., Wall, M., Neumark-Sztainer, D., & Story, M. (2002). Steroid use among adolescents. *Journal of Adolescent Health, 30*, 243–252.

Jasper, K. (1993). Monitoring and responding to media messages. *Eating Disorders, 1*, 109–114.

Johnson, C., Powers, P. S., & Dick, R. (1999). Athletes and eating disorders: The National Collegiate Athletic Association Study. *International Journal of Eating Disorders, 26*, 179–188.

Johnson, C. L., Tobin, D. L., & Steinberg, S. L. (1989). Etiological, developmental and treatment considerations for bulimia. In L. C. Whitaker & W. N. Davis (Eds.), *The bulimic college student* (pp. 57–73). New York: Haworth Press.

Joiner, G. W., & Kashubeck, S. (1996). Acculturaltion, body image, self-esteem, and eating-disorder symptomology in adolescent Mexican-American women. *Psychology of Women Quarterly, 20*, 419–435.

Kalodner, C. R. (1997). Media influences on male and female non-eating disordered college students: A significant issue. *Eating Disorders, 5*, 47–57.

Keel, P. K., Heatherton, T. F., Harnden, J. L., & Hornig, C. D. (1997). Mothers, fathers, and daughters: Dieting and disordered eating. *Eating Disorders, 5*, 216–228.

Killen, J. D. (1996). The development and evaluation of a school-based eating disorder symptoms prevention program. In L. Smolak, M. Levine, & R. Striegel-Moore (Eds.), *The developmental psychopathology of eating disorders* (pp. 313–339). Mahwah, NJ: Erlbaum.

Killen, J. D., Taylor, C. B., Hammer, L. D., Litt, I., Wilson, D. M., Rich, T., et al. (1993). An attempt to modify unhealthful eating attitudes and weight regulation practices of young adolescent girls. *International Journal of Eating Disorders, 13*, 369–384.

Killen, J. D., Taylor, C. B., Hayward, C., Haydel, K. F., Wilson, D. M., Hammer, L., et al. (1996). Weight concerns influence the development of eating disorders: A 4-year prospective study. *Journal of Consulting and Clinical Psychology, 64*, 936–940.

Kirk, G., Singh, K., & Getz, H. (2001). Risk of eating disorders among female college athletes and nonathletes. *Journal of College Counseling, 4*, 122–132.

Klesges, R. C., DeBon, M., & Meyers, A. (1996). Obesity in African American women: Epidemiology, determinants, and treatment issues. In J. K. Thompson (Ed.), *Body image, eating disorders, and obesity* (pp. 461–478). Washington, DC: American Psychological Association.

Kog, E., & Vandereycken, W. (1985). Family characteristics of anorexia nervosa and bulimia: A review of the research literature. *Clinical Psychology Review, 5*, 159–180.

Lacey, J. H., Coker, S., & Birtchnell, S. A. (1986). Bulimia: Factors associated with its etiology and maintenance. *International Journal of Eating Disorders, 5*, 475–487.

Lachenmeyer, J. R., & Muni-Brander, P. (1988). Eating disorders in a nonclinical adolescent population: Implications for treatment. *Adolescence, 90*, 303–312.

Lawlor, B. A., Burket, R. C., & Hodgin, J. A. (1987). Eating disorders in American Black men. *Journal of the National Medical Association, 79*, 984–986.

Lee, N. F., & Rush, A. J. (1986). Cognitive–behavioral group therapy for bulimia. *International Journal of Eating Disorders, 5*, 599–615.

Lee, S., & Katzman, M. A. (2002). Cross cultural perspectives on eating disorders. In C. G. Fairburn & K. D. Brownell (Eds.), *Eating disorders and obesity* (pp. 260–264). New York: Guilford Press.

le Grange, D., Stone, A. A., & Brownell, K. D. (1998). Eating disturbances in White and minority female dieters. *International Journal of Eating Disorders, 24*, 395–403.

le Grange, D., Telch, C. F., & Agras, W. S. (1997). Eating and general psychopathology in a sample of Caucasian and ethnic minority subjects. *International Journal of Eating Disorders, 21*, 285–293.

Lester, R., & Petrie, T. A. (1998). Physical, psychological, and societal correlates of bulimic symptomalogy among African American college women. *Journal of Counseling Psychology, 45*, 315–321.

Levine, M., Smolak, L., & Schermer, F. (1996). Media analysis and resistance in elementary school children in the primary prevention of eating problems. *Eating Disorders, 4*, 310–322.

Levine, M., Smolak, L., & Striegel-Moore, R. (1996). Conclusion, implications, and future directions. In L. Smolak, M. Levine, & R. Striegel-Moore (Eds.), *The developmental psychopathology of eating disorders* (pp. 399–416). Mahwah, NJ: Erlbaum.

Lucero, K., Hicks, R. A., Bramlette, J., Brassington, G. S., & Welter, (1992). Frequency of eating problems among Asian and Caucasian college women. *Psychological Reports, 71*, 255–258.

Lundholm, J. K., & Waters, J. E. (1991). Dysfunctional family systems: Relationship to disordered eating behaviors among university women. *Journal of Substance Abuse, 3*, 97–106.

Mangweth, B., Pope, H. G., Jr., Hudson, J. I., & Biebl, W. (1996). Bulimia nervosa in Austria and the United States: A controlled cross-cultural study. *International Journal of Eating Disorders, 20*, 263–270.

Mann, T., Nolen-Hoeksema, S., Huang, K., Burgard, D., Wright, A., & Hanson, K. (1997). Are two interventions worse than none? Joint primary and secondary prevention of eating disorders in college females. *Health Psychology, 16*, 215–225.

Marcus, M. D. (1997). Adapting treatment for patients with binge-eating disorder. In D. M. Garner & P. E. Garfinkel (Eds.), *Handbook of treatment for eating disorders* (2nd ed., pp. 484–493). New York: Guilford Press.

Metropolitan Life Insurance Company. (1983). Metropolitan height and weight tables. *Statistical Bulletin of the Metropolitan Life Foundation, 64*, 2–9.

Mickalide, A. D. (1990). Sociocultural factors influencing weight among males. In A. M. Anderson (Ed.), *Males with eating disorders* (pp. 30–39). New York: Brunner/Mazel.

Mintz, L. B., & Betz, N. E. (1988). Prevalence and correlates of eating disordered behavior among college women. *Journal of Counseling Psychology, 35*, 463–471.

Mitchell, P. B. (1988). The pharmacological management of bulimia nervosa: A critical review. *International Journal of Eating Disorders, 7*, 29–41.

Moriarty, D., Shore, R., & Maxim, N. (1990). Evaluation of an eating disorder curriculum. *Evaluation and Program Planning, 13*, 407–413.

Murray, S. H., Touyz, S. W., & Beumont, P. J. (1996). Awareness and perceived influence of body ideals in the media: A comparison of eating disorder patients and the general community. *Eating Disorders, 4*, 33–46.

Nasser, M. (1988). Culture and weight consciousness. *Journal of Psychosomatic Research, 32*, 573–577.

Nichter, M., Vuckovic, N., & Parker, S. (1999). The looking good, feeling good program: A multiethnic intervention for healthy body image, nutrition, and physical activity. In N. Piran, M. P. Levine, & C. Steiner-Adair (Eds.), *Preventing eating disorders* (pp. 175–193). Philadelphia: Brunner/Mazel.

Ohtahara, H., Ohzeki, T., Hanaki, K., Motozumi, H., & Shiraki, K. (1993). Abnormal perception of body weight is not solely observed in pubertal girls: Incorrect body image in children and its relationship to body weight. *Acta Psychiatrica Scandinavica, 87*, 218–222.

Omizo, S. A., & Omizo, M. M. (1992). Eating disorders: The school counselor's role. *The School Counselor, 39*, 217–224.

Osvold, L. L., & Sodowsky, G. R. (1993). Eating disorders of White American, racial and ethnic minority American, and international women. *Journal of Multicultural Counseling and Development, 21*, 143–154.

Pelch, B. L. (1999). Eating-disordered families: Issues between generations. In R. Lemberg (Ed.), *Eating disorders: A reference sourcebook* (pp. 121–123). Phoenix, AZ: Oryx Press.

Pike, K. M., & Wilfley, D. E. (1996). The changing context of treatment. In L. Smolak, M. Levine, & R. Striegel-Moore (Eds.), *The developmental psychopathology of eating disorders* (pp. 365–397). Mahwah, NJ: Erlbaum.

Piran, N. (1996). The reduction of preoccupation body weight and shape in schools: A feminist approach. *Eating Disorders, 4*, 323–333.

Polivy, J., & Federoff, I. (1997). Group psychotherapy. In D. M. Garner & P. E. Garfinkel (Eds.), *Handbook of treatment for eating disorders* (2nd ed., pp. 462–475). New York: Guilford Press

Polivy, J., & Herman, C. P. (1987). Diagnosis and treatment of normal eating. *Journal of Consulting and Clinical Psychology, 55*, 635–644.

Polivy, J., & Herman, C. P. (1996). Etiology of binge eating: Psychological mechanisms. In C. G. Fairburn & G. T. Wilson (Eds.), *Binge eating: Nature, assessment, and treatment* (pp. 173–205). New York: Guilford Press.

Powers, P. S., & Johnson, C. (1996). Small victories: Prevention of eating disorders among athletes. *Eating Disorders, 4* 364–377.

Pumariega, A. J. (1997). Body dissatisfaction among Hispanic and Asian-American girls. *Journal of Adolescent Health, 21*, 1.

Robinson, T. N., Killen, J. D., Litt, I. F., Hammer, L. D., Wilson, D. M., Haydel, K. F., et al. (1996). Ethnicity and body dissatisfaction: Are Hispanic and Asian girls at increased risk for eating disorders? *Journal of Adolescent Health, 19*, 384–393.

Root, M. P. P. (1990). Disordered eating in women of color. *Sex Roles, 22*, 525–536.

Rosen, L. W., Shafer, C. L., Dummer, G. M., Cross, L. K., Deuman, G. W., & Malmberg, S. R. (1988). Prevalence of pathogenic weight-control behaviors among Native American women and girls. *International Journal of Eating Disorders, 7*, 807–811.

Sanders, N. M., & Heiss, C. J. (1998). Eating attitudes and body image of Asian and Caucasian college women. *Eating Disorders, 6*, 15–28.

Sargent, J., Liebman, R., & Silver, M. (1985). Family therapy for anorexia nervosa. In D. M. Garner & P. E. Garfinkel (Eds.), *Handbook of psychotherapy for anorexia nervosa and bulimia* (pp. 257–279). New York: Guilford Press.

Schmidt, U. (2002). Risk factors for eating disorders. In C. G. Fairburn & K. D. Brownell (Eds.), *Eating disorders and obesity* (pp. 247–250). New York: Guilford Press.

Schneider, J. A., & Agras, W. S. (1987). Bulimia in males: A matched comparison with females. *International Journal of Eating Disorders, 6*, 235–242.

Schwartz, R. C., Barrett, M. J., & Saba, G. (1985). Family therapy for bulimia. In D. M. Garner & P. E. Garfinkel (Eds.), *Handbook of psychotherapy for anorexia nervosa and bulimia* (pp. 280–307). New York: Guilford Press.

Seiver, M. (1994). Sexual orientation and gender as factors in socioculturally acquired vulnerability to body dissatisfaction and eating disorders. *Journal of Consulting and Clinical Psychology, 62*, 252–260.

Shafran, R. (2002). Eating disorders and the Internet. In C. G. Fairburn & K. D. Brownell (Eds.), *Eating disorders and obesity* (pp. 362–366). New York: Guilford Press.

Silber, T. J. (1986). Anorexia nervosa in Blacks and Hispanics. *International Journal of Eating Disorders, 5*, 121–128.

Silverstein, B., Perdue, L., Peterson, B., & Kelly, E. (1986). The role of the mass media in promoting a thin standard of bodily attractiveness for women. *Sex Roles, 14*, 519–532.

Smith, J. E., & Krejci, J. (1991). Minorities join the majority: Eating disturbances among Hispanic and Native American youth. *International Journal of Eating Disorders, 10*, 179–186.

Smolak, L., & Levine, M. P. (1996). Adolescent transitions and the development of eating disorders. In L. Smolak, M. P. Levine, & R. Striegel-Moore (Eds.), *The developmental psychopathology of eating disorders* (pp. 207–234). Mahwah, NJ: Erlbaum.

Snow, J. T., & Harris, M. B. (1989). Disordered eating in Southwestern Pueblo Indians and Hispanics. *Journal of Adolescence, 12*, 329–336.

Srinivasan, T. N., Suresch, T. R., & Jayaram, V. (1998). Emergence of eating disorders in India: Study of eating distress syndrome and development of a screening questionnaire. *International Journal of Social Psychiatry, 44*, 189–198.

Steen, S. N., & Brownell, K. D. (1990). Patterns of weight loss and regain in wrestlers: Has the tradition changed? *Medicine and Science in Sports and Exercise, 22*, 762–768.

Steiger, H., & Houle, L. (1991). Defense styles and object-relations disturbances among university women displaying varying degrees of "symptomatic" eating. *International Journal of Eating Disorders, 10*, 145–153.

Stice, E. (2002). Sociocultural influences on body image and eating disturbance. In C. G. Fairburn & K. D. Brownell (Eds.), *Eating disorders and obesity* (pp. 103–107). New York: Guilford Press.

Stice, E., & Ragan, J. (2002). A preliminary controlled evaluation of an eating disturbance psychoeducational intervention for college students. *International Journal of Eating Disorders, 31*, 159–171.

Stice, E., Spangler, D., & Agras, W. S. (2001). Exposure to media-portrayed thin-ideal images adversely affects vulnerable girls: A longitudinal experiment. *Journal of Social and Clinical Psychology, 20*, 270–288.

Story, M. (1986). Nutrition management and dietary treatment of bulimia. *Journal of the American Dietetic Association, 86*, 517–519.

Story, M., French, S. A., Resnick, M. D., & Blum, R. W. (1995). Ethnic/racial and socioeconomic differences in dieting behaviors and body image perceptions in adolescents. *International Journal of Eating Disorders, 18*, 173–179.

Stoutjesdyk, D., & Jevne, R. (1993). Eating disorders among high performance athletes. *Journal of Youth and Adolescence, 22*, 271–282.

Striegel-Moore, R. (1993). Etiology of binge eating: A developmental perspective. In C. G. Fairburn & G. T. Wilson (Eds.), *Binge eating: Nature, assessment and treatment* (pp. 144–172). New York: Guilford Press.

Streigel-Moore, R., & Smolak, L. (1996). The role of race in the development of eating disorders. In L. Smolak, M. P. Levine, & R. Striegel-Moore (Eds.), *The developmental psychopathology of eating disorders* (pp. 259–284). Mahwah, NJ: Erlbaum.

Striegel-Moore, R., & Smolak, L. (2002). Gender, ethnicity, and eating disorders. In C. G. Fairburn & K. D. Brownell (Eds.), *Eating disorders and obesity* (2nd ed., pp. 251–255). New York: Guilford Press.

Strober, M., & Bulik, C. M. (2002). Genetic epidemiology of eating disorders. In C. G. Fairburn & K. D. Brownell (Eds.), *Eating disorders and obesity* (2nd ed., pp. 238–242). New York: Guilford Press.

Stunkard, A. J. (1993). A history of binge eating. In C. G. Fairburn & G. T. Wilson (Eds.), *Binge eating: Nature, assessment and treatment* (pp. 15–34). New York: Guilford Press.

Sundgot-Borgen, J. (1993). Prevalence of eating disorders in elite female athletes. *International Journal of Sport Nutrition, 3*, 28–40.

Thompson, K. J., & Heinberg, L. J. (1999). The media's influence on body image disturbance and eating disorders: We've reviled them, now can we rehabilitate them? *Journal of Social Issues, 55*, 339–353.

Thompson, K. J., & Stice, E. (2001). Thin-ideal internalization: Mounting evidence for a new risk factor for body-image disturbance and eating pathology. *Current Directions in Psychological Science, 10*, 181–183.

Thompson, R. A. (1998). Wrestling with death. *Eating Disorders, 6*, 207–210.

Thompson, R. A., & Sherman, R. T. (1993). Reducing the risk of eating disorders in athletics. *Eating Disorders, 1*, 62–78.

Troop, N. A., & Treasure, J. L. (1997). Psychosocial factors in the onset of eating disorders: Responses to life-events and difficulties. *British Journal of Medical Psychology, 70*, 373–385.

Tsai, G., & Gray, J. (2000). The Eating Disorders Inventory among Asian-American college women. *Journal of Social Psychology, 140*, 527–529.

Ussery, L. W., & Prentice-Dunn, S. (1992). Personality predictors of bulimic behavior and attitudes in males. *Journal of Clinical Psychology, 48*, 722–729.

Van den Broucke, S., & Vandereycken, W. (1986). Risk factors for the development of eating disorders in adolescent exchange students: An exploratory survey. *Journal of Adolescence, 9*, 145–150.

Vandereycken, W. (1993). The sociocultural roots of the fight against fatness: Implications for eating disorders and obesity. *Eating Disorders, 1*, 7–16.

Vandereycken, W. (2002). Families of patients with eating disorders. In C. G. Fairburn & K. D. Brownell (Eds.), *Eating disorders and obesity* (pp. 215–220). New York: Guilford Press.

Westphal, V. K., & Smith, J. E. (1996). Overeaters Anonymous: Who goes and who succeeds? *Eating Disorders, 4*, 160–170.

Wilson, G. T., Fairburn, C. G., & Agras, W. S. (1997). Cognitive–behavioral therapy for bulimia nervosa. In D. M. Garner & P. E. Garfinkel (Eds.), *Handbook of treatment for eating disorders* (pp. 67–93). New York: Guilford Press.

Wilson, G. T., Nonas, C. A., & Rosenblum, G. D. (1993). Assessment of binge-eating in obese patients. *International Journal of Eating Disorders, 13*, 25–34.

Wiseman, C. V., Gray, J. J., Mosimann, J. E., & Ahrens, A. H. (1992). Cultural expectations of thinness in women: An update. *International Journal of Eating Disorders, 11*, 85–89.

Wiseman, C. V., Gunning, F. M., & Gray, J. J. (1993). Increasing pressure to be thin: 19 years of diet products in television commercials. *Eating Disorders, 1*, 52–64.

Wonderlich, S. A. (2002). Personality and eating disorders. In C. G. Fairburn & K. D. Brownell (Eds.), *Eating disorders and obesity* (pp. 204–209). New York: Guilford Press.

Yager, J., Kurtzman, F., Landsverk, J., & Wiesmeier, E. (1988). Behaviors and attitudes related to eating disorders in homosexual male college students. *American Journal of Psychiatry, 145,* 495–497.

Yanovski, S. Z., Nelson, J. E., Dubbert, B. K., & Spitzer, R. L. (1993). Association of binge eating disorder and psychiatric comorbidity in obese subjects. *American Journal of Psychiatry, 150,* 1472–1479.

Yoshimura, K. (1995). Acculturative and sociocultural influences on the development of eating disorders in Asian-American females. *Journal of Treatment and Prevention, 3,* 216–228.

9 | Children Having Children: Teenage Pregnancy and Parenthood

Melinda Haley and Ardis Sherwood-Hawes

The incidence of adolescent pregnancy and parenthood in the United States has remained at an alarmingly high level for the past 30 years and is higher than most other industrialized nations (Goodyear, 2002). During the 1970s, numerous studies indicated that one of the most profound trends among American adolescents was a significant increase in both pregnancy (Dryfoos & Heisler, 1978) and the subsequent rearing of offspring by single, school-age mothers (Ogg, 1976). A study by Ogg (1976) indicated that the number of one-parent families had increased seven times as rapidly as the number of two-parent families, and according to Nye (1976), school-age children between 14 and 16 years of age represented the most rapidly increasing group of single parents.

Although the size of the adolescent population in the United States has decreased considerably over the past 30 years (Voydanoff & Donnelly, 1990), birth rates of United States adolescents increased substantially during the 1980s, and rates accelerated sharply from 1986 to 1991, increasing 24% during this time period ("State Specific Birth Rates," 1997). Annually, approximately 1 million teenage women become pregnant (Kiselica, Stroud, Stroud, & Rotzien, 1992; Somers, Gleason, Johnson, & Fahlman, 2001; Wingert, 1998), and of those, 80% are not married (Blake & Bentov, 2001). Of these pregnancies, approximately 51% end with a live birth, 35% end because of abortion, and 14% end because of miscarriage (Blake & Bentov, 2001). Many of these teens began having sex before the age of 15 (O'Donnell, O'Donnell, & Stueve, 2001), and according to a study conducted by the Centers for Disease Control and Prevention (2002), 9.4% of male students and 4.5% of female students had initiated sex before the age of 13. The same study found that 48.4% of all students had sex during their teenage years, and of those students, 16.0% had sex with four or more partners.

Recent reports contradict earlier reports, however, and indicate there may be an encouraging decline in these dire statistics. Current studies show that between 1986 and 1996, even while the teen birth rate increased, teen pregnancy rates actually dropped by 9%, the teen abortion rate declined by 24%, and condom use increased significantly (Committee on Adolescence, 2001; Goodyear, 2002; Koshar, 2001). Although these decreases are nationwide and encompass all ages and racial and ethnic groups, some groups declined more than others. Percentage of decrease was greater for younger adolescents, ages 10–14 (14%), and for African American adolescents (20%), with the largest drop in pregnancy and childbearing rates occurring among married adolescents (Wingert, 1998). Hispanic American youth, who have the highest rate of pregnancy and childbearing among American adolescents, sustained the lowest birth rate decline, 6% between the years 1991 and 1996 (Koshar, 2001).

Nevertheless, despite the reduction in adolescent pregnancy and childbearing rates, the overall birth rate for United States adolescents is still as high or higher than rates 20 years ago (S. Smith & Ramirez, 1997). It is estimated that 8% of children age 14, 18% of children ages 15–17, and 22% of adolescents ages 19–20 become pregnant each year (Bell, 1997). The vast majority of these pregnancies are unintended (Bell, 1997; Mapanga, 1997; White & White, 1991), yet over 50% of these pregnancies result in live births ("State Specific Birth Rates," 1997). Thus, each year, a greater percentage of our nation's youth are bearing children before they complete their education or secure their economic future (Patterson, 1990). Over 9,000 of these infants are reared by children under the age of 14, and almost 5,000 of these infants are the second child born to 16-year-old mothers (McCullough & Scherman, 1991). Only 5% of the more than 500,000 infants born each year to American adolescents are placed for adoption (Cervera, 1993a; Voydanoff & Donnelly, 1990). In addition, 80% of adolescent parents do not marry, and the preponderance of these infants are reared by single mothers with meager assistance from fathers of the children (Bell, 1997; Mapanga, 1997; Wingert, 1998). Teenagers who are single parents have increased in number exponentially over the last five decades.

Even though the rates of adolescent pregnancy and childbearing in the United States are decreasing, the percentages of adolescent pregnancy, abortion, and childbirth in the United States are still significantly higher than in other industrialized nations (Allen-Meares, 1989; Bell, 1997; Christopher & Roosa, 1990; Meyer, 1991; "State Specific Birth Rates," 1997). American adolescents under the age of 15 are five times more likely to give birth than same-age adolescents in comparable countries (Allen-Meares, 1991). Conversely, the rates of sexual activity among adolescents in the United States are predominantly the same or lower than other analogous nations (Allen-Meares, 1989; Freeman, 1989). (Sexual activity denotes initiation of intercourse. Note that studies have rarely investigated alternative expressions of sexual behaviors among adolescents [Furstenberg, Brooks-Gunn, & Chase-Lansdale, 1989].)

Although adolescents in Sweden become sexually active at earlier ages than adolescents in the United States, the U.S. pregnancy rate is three times higher than that of Sweden (Alan Guttmacher Institute, 1994; Foster, Green, & Smith, 1990) and two times higher than rates in Canada or England (Bell, 1997). (Noteworthy is that Sweden has the highest, and Canada the lowest, percentage of sexually active adolescents [Foster et al., 1990].) In addition, the United States has the same percentage of sexually active adolescents as the Netherlands (Voydanoff & Donnelly, 1990) but a pregnancy rate nine times higher than the Netherlands (Bell, 1997). Most researchers attribute these disturbing statistics to higher levels of consistent and effective use of contraceptives among adolescents in other countries (Christopher & Roosa, 1990).

Sexual activity among adolescents has steadily increased over the past 30 years, and present-day adolescents are engaging in sexual intercourse at much younger ages. Surveys have revealed that 76% of women and 80% of men have experienced sexual intercourse before the age of 20, and only 56.8% of those sexually active students reported using a condom during last coitus (Blake & Bentov, 2001; Centers for Disease Control and Prevention, 2002). The results from another school-based survey of over 8,000 high school students documented that 59% of students experienced coitus and 40% of the sexually active students reported sexual intercourse with four or more partners (Koniak-Griffin & Brecht, 1997).

There are many interrelated social, economic, family, and biological factors that contribute to the current trend in adolescent sexuality patterns (Brewster, Billy, & Grady, 1993; Hofferth, 1991; White & White, 1991). For example, over the past century, young women in industrialized nations have been reaching menarche at younger ages. Menarche, or biological maturity, is caused by the increased production of sex hormones, and this increase is positively correlated with sexual activity (Allen-Meares, 1991; Voydanoff & Donnelly, 1990). Although the average age of menarche is currently slightly over 12 years, the number of children who reach biological maturity at age 9 or younger is rising. These young adolescents may be biologically equipped to produce children, but they rarely have the developmental maturity to cope with their emerging and often bewildering sexual urges or to understand and prevent pregnancy (Patterson, 1990).

Concurrently, societal changes have overtly and covertly affected the sexual behavior of young people. Contemporary adolescents experience much more social freedom than did adolescents in the first half of the 20th century. Television, automobiles, telephones, computers, and changes in family structure all contribute to the increased autonomy of today's young people. Families are typically smaller and no longer include extended family members such as grandparents or other relatives.

Children often live in single-parent families, and opportunity for adult supervision is reduced. Even in two-parent households, both parents typically work outside the home, and children have greater spans of time for unsupervised activity with their own peers. When adolescents have expanded periods of unsupervised free time, they become more susceptible to peer pressure and have increased opportunities to experiment with drugs, alcohol, and sexual activity. Research suggests that sexual intercourse among adolescents is more likely to occur in homes with little or no adult supervision (Blake & Bentov, 2001; McCullough & Scherman, 1991).

In addition, contemporary children have more exposure to external influences that shape the formation of their value systems. Mass media messages have a powerful impact on the belief systems of young people, and in recent years, media messages have consistently indicated that social attitudes are more permissive toward the expression of sexuality through premarital sexual activity. Our culture condones explicit sexual themes in advertising, the entertainment industry, and all forms of mass media, and these sexual messages convey information to our nation's youth about societal expectations toward the development of gender roles, sexuality, and male and female relationships.

Conversely, as we bombard our children with confusing sexual images and messages, our culture often denies realistic and complete sexuality information to our young people. Unfortunately, these skewed messages may be the primary source of sexual education for our children. Thus, adolescents may be engaging in sexual activity at younger ages, not only because of earlier physical maturation and the accompanying sexual feelings, but also because of permissive societal attitudes regarding premarital or extramarital sexual intercourse, media messages that promote and glamorize sexuality, unsupervised free time, and inadequate training on issues related to sexuality (Croft & Asmussen, 1992; Furstenberg et al., 1989; Plotnick, 1993). Self-report inventories show that 50% of both male and female adolescents report having sex during their teen years (Committee on Adolescence, 2001).

Although young people are becoming physically mature and progenitive at younger ages, they may lack the capacity or maturity to prevent pregnancy or protect themselves from sexually transmitted diseases (STDs) and HIV, the precursor of AIDS (Patterson, 1990). At present, adolescents are the population considered to be most vulnerable to HIV, and every day, because of spontaneous unprotected sexual activity, many of our nation's young people are being exposed to and possibly contracting HIV (Committee on Adolescence, 2001; Cervera, 1993b; O'Donnell et al., 2001). One in four new HIV infections occurs among people who are younger than age 20 (Azzarto, 1997), and adolescent parents are considered to be at even greater risk of contracting HIV than nonparenting adolescents (Koniak-Griffin & Brecht, 1997). Attempts to reduce these tragic numbers by instituting HIV/AIDS awareness and education are apparent in the following statistics: By 1997, 91.5% of students had been taught about HIV/AIDS in school, and 62.8% of students had discussed these issues with their parents (Centers for Disease Control and Prevention, 2002; Mcilhaney, 2002).

In addition to HIV/AIDS, approximately 3 million adolescents contract an STD annually, with 30% of females contracting chlamydia and 30%–50% of all sexually active adolescents becoming infected with the human papillomavirus. Sexually active adolescents between 15 and 19 years of age have the highest rates of gonorrhea. Cases of genital herpes have also increased among teens by more than 50% (Committee on Adolescence, 2001). Minority youth are especially at high risk for HIV and other STDs because proportionately they live in communities with higher levels of these diseases in the population, are more likely to initiate sex before the age of 15, and are the least likely to use condoms (O'Donnell et al., 2001).

Many professionals attribute the failure of the United States culture to adequately address issues of adolescent pregnancy and contraction of STDs during adolescence to a lack of specific definition of the problem. Should the primary focus of programs be on abstinence, or should pregnancy be prevented through the promotion of effective and regular use of contraception and use of condoms, which would also help lower the risk for STDs? Or would a multidimensional approach be more effective in preventing adolescent pregnancy and childbearing? The outcome of the solutions designed to reduce the rate of adolescent pregnancy depends on how our society defines the problem of adolescent childbearing (Croft & Asmussen, 1992).

PROBLEM DEFINITION

An enormous amount of research has been conducted to identify factors associated with rates of adolescent sexual activity, pregnancy, and childbirth. The majority of this research has investigated the characteristics of adolescent mothers to determine what type of female child is most likely to become pregnant and the childbearing consequences for these young mothers (Brooks-Gunn & Furstenberg, 1989; Christmon, 1990; Dearden, Hale, & Alvarez, 1992; Freeman, 1989; Meyer, 1991; Watson & Kelly, 1988). This research, which focuses predominantly on unmarried adolescents, seems to infer that adolescent pregnancy is acceptable if the female is married.

The recognition of cultural bias that places the responsibility of fertility control on the female has led to an increasing interest in investigative reports on adolescent fatherhood. Recent studies on adolescent fathers revealed that male and female adolescents who are at risk for early parenthood share many of the same characteristics. Recently, attention has focused on the male role in teen pregnancy and community interventions such as the one offered by the Office of Population Affairs/Office of Family Planning involving family planning, reproductive health education, human sexuality, life skills, and other services to men (P. B. Smith, Buzi, Weinman, & Mumford, 2001). In addition, males are the focus of current research regarding sexuality, contraception use, teen pregnancy, childbirth, and parenting (Marsiglio, Hutchinson, & Cohan, 2001). Therefore, this chapter primarily uses a gender-neutral approach for the discussion of variables related to adolescent pregnancy and childbearing.

Research has connected adolescent pregnancy and parenthood to a complex and interrelated combination of factors based on culture, economy, family, education, environment, and human development and behavior (Azzarto, 1997; Brewster et al., 1993; Hofferth, 1991; Kiselica et al., 1992). For example, a well-developed body of literature has demonstrated that use of chemical substances and early school withdrawal are substantially correlated with premature initiation of unprotected sexual behavior (Allen-Meares 1991; Brooks-Gunn & Furstenberg, 1989; Franklin & Corcoran, 2000). This empirical research suggested that use of drugs and alcohol is strongly indicative of future detrimental behavior. However, these studies do not clearly demonstrate whether chemical usage is a cause of deleterious conduct or an identifier of underlying issues that predispose at-risk behaviors in adolescence (Bayatpour, Wells, & Holford, 1992). Many professionals maintain that chemical substance use is a response to a combination of factors, none of which is causative. Perhaps adolescents, in part, use substances to cope with debilitating emotions (e.g., rage, depression) that emanate because of life stressors or previous traumatic occurrences (Adger, 1991).

When considering the link between noncompletion of education and alcohol abuse, professionals might ask, "Does alcohol abuse cause declines in academic performance, or do students begin to use alcohol as a method to cope with academic difficulties and their subsequent feelings of discouragement and failure?" These theories are further illustrated by studies indicating that the use of chemical substances is positively correlated to a history of physical or sexual abuse (Bayatpour et al., 1992; Berenson, San Miguel, & Wilkinson, 1992; Schamess, 1993).

Both Franklin and Corcoran (2000) and Kirby (2001) raised the issue that sexual abuse, as a factor, is involved in a high number of cases whereby females become sexually active at an early age. Franklin and Corcoran (2000) stated, "Approximately 50–75 percent of females whose first sexual experience happened before age 14 or 15 were forced into sexual relationships" (p. 51). Survivors of abuse, especially sexual abuse, often manifest feelings of low self-esteem, unresolved anger, helplessness, and hopelessness, and experience a sense of powerlessness in their relationships. These children may use alcohol and drugs to mask their painful emotions, or the chemical usage may be an unconscious attempt to gain assistance from outside authorities.

Research also suggests that childhood abuse is strongly linked to calamitous decisions about sexuality and sexual behavior. Recent studies have revealed that children who have survived or are being traumatized by sexual abuse are more likely to become sexually active at younger ages and are at heightened risk for adolescent pregnancy and parenthood (Bayatpour et al., 1992; Koshar, 2001; McCullough & Scherman, 1991; Plotnick, 1993; Rhodes, Fischer, Ebert, & Meyers, 1993; Schamess, 1993). In addition, research demonstrates a positive correlation between childhood emotional problems and high risk for contracting HIV and STDs (Azzarto, 1997; Koniak-Griffin & Brecht, 1997).

ANTECEDENTS FOR AT-RISK ADOLESCENT SEXUAL BEHAVIOR

Adolescent sexual activity, use of contraception, and responses to unplanned parenthood are dependent on many variables. Most adolescents do not intend to become pregnant. The initiation of sexual intercourse is often perceived as an unexpected and spontaneous event, as something that just "happened" (Brooks-Gunn & Furstenberg, 1989, p. 251). Generally, sexual intercourse is precipitated by a serious relationship, although younger adolescents are less likely to be engaged or involved in a steady relationship when they become sexually active. The risk of pregnancy and childbirth is linked to individual beliefs about contraception, decisions about usage, knowledge about effective methods of birth control, and attitudes toward adolescent parenthood (Voydanoff & Donnelly, 1990).

Many younger adolescents are sexually active for approximately 1 year prior to using contraception (Allen-Meares, 1989). The major reasons for this delay include procrastination, fear of parental reprisal, belief that pregnancy is impossible, and fear about the safety of methods of birth control (Zabin, Stark, & Emerson, 1991). However, studies show that over the past two decades, condom use has increased as much as 58% in some geographical areas and age ranges (Committee on Adolescence, 2001). Adolescents who clearly understand that pregnancy can result from even one unprotected sexual encounter are somewhat more inclined to use effective contraception than those who do not understand the risks of unprotected sex (Voydanoff & Donnelly, 1990). Moreover, complete and comprehensive information regarding the risks for AIDS has increased adolescent abstinence and use of protection during intercourse (Wingert, 1998). Studies also show a positive correlation between increased condom use and adolescents who have educated parents, come from two-parent intact families, and have good communication with their parents (Committee on Adolescence, 2001).

Many of the antecedents associated with adolescent pregnancy and childbearing echo conditions linked to disadvantaged socioeconomic status, so it is not surprising that researchers have found that adolescents from impoverished backgrounds tend to become sexually active at younger ages, are less inclined to use effective contraception, and are therefore more likely to become adolescent parents (Voydanoff & Donnelly, 1990). Poverty has been found to have one of the strongest correlations to unmarried teen pregnancy. Eighty-five percent of all unmarried teen pregnancies occur in families whose income is 200% below the poverty line, and 66% of families headed by a single parent are living in poverty (Blake & Bentov, 2001; Mcilhaney, 2002). These same adolescent parents and social agencies bear the $7 billion annual cost spent on adolescent childbearing (Koshar, 2001). Studies have consistently recapitulated that, regardless of racial or cultural background, all adolescents who experience socioeconomic advantage, family stability, and higher levels of religiosity are more likely to delay onset of sexual intercourse or use contraception at initial intercourse than adolescents from disadvantaged socioeconomic backgrounds or unstable family environments (Kirby, 2001). Some studies have indicated that White adolescents are more likely to use contraception than Black adolescents, but when socioeconomic status, family stability, and community milieu are considered, these differences decrease dramatically (Voydanoff & Donnelly, 1990). Likewise, adolescents who chose abortions over childbearing are more likely to live in higher socioeconomic environments, be successful in school, have parents and friends who have positive attitudes toward abortion, reside in communities that provide accessible public-funded abortions, and tend to have fewer friends or relations who are adolescent parents (Furstenberg et al., 1989). Less than 5% of all pregnant adolescents release their infants for formal adoption, and the vast majority of these adoptees are children born to White adolescents from advantaged socioeconomic backgrounds (Cervera, 1993a; Resnick, Blum, Bose, Smith, & Toogood, 1990). Formal adoption is rarely an accepted practice among families of African heritage, although frequently young children are informally adopted by relatives. These adoption customs may have evolved due to the generations of racial discrimination experienced by Black people in America (Brooks-Gunn & Furstenberg, 1989) and related fears of Black genocide.

Developmental Influences

Childhood development is a gradual, steady process that ranges from the dependency of infancy to the self-sufficiency of adulthood (Allen-Meares, 1991). The outcome of this maturation interval is dependent on an interaction between children's unique characteristics, capabilities, and their environment. Throughout this period, children need consistent attachments to adults who protect them and provide the nurture and structure necessary for healthy development. Under satisfactory conditions, as their cognitive processes mature, children are gradually encouraged and allowed to become more autonomous and responsible for their behaviors. When children experience adverse childhood conditions, such as neglect, emotional or physical abandonment, poverty, instability, or emotional, mental, or physical abuse, they may experience delays in their developmental growth and fail to form the skills necessary to cope with the challenges and stressors of adolescence and adulthood. Adolescents who come from impoverished family environments may be more at risk than those with stable environments. Kirby (2001) stated that adolescents who have greater attachment to peers rather than parents are associated with greater sexual risk taking and earlier onset of sexual activity.

Interpersonal Influences

Sexual activity and responses to pregnancy among adolescents are highly connected to the adolescents' observations and discernment about normative behavior in their families of origin and peer groups (Brooks-Gunn & Furstenberg, 1989; Kirby, 2001; Voydanoff & Donnelly, 1990). There is a significant probability that adolescents who anticipate a positive response to early parenthood from family or friends will become adolescent parents. This risk is increased when their families or peer group members have a history of adolescent pregnancy and childbearing (Kirby, 2001; Resnick et al., 1990). Conversely, adolescents who expect negative reactions from significant others are more likely to delay or avoid pregnancy through use of reliable contraception (Freeman, 1989; Kirby, 2001). Furthermore, there may be many other underlying multidimensional factors that influence adolescent sexual behavior. For example, pregnancy may be perceived as a method to identify with the value systems of families or peers, as a way to maintain relationships with the family or with sexual partners, or as a means to declare independence from the family. Childbearing may be perceived as an avenue to freedom and autonomy or as a way to escape from unsatisfactory or intolerable family conditions (Bell, 1997; Cervera, 1993b; Freeman, 1989; White & White, 1991).

Adolescents who are reared in families that have experienced separation or divorce, and families headed by single parents, are at elevated risk for early pregnancy (Blake & Bentov, 2001; P. B. Smith et al., 2001; Wu & Thomson, 2001). When parents divorce, the lines of communication between parents and children can become distorted and disrupted. Family income may become drastically reduced, and this economic hardship can create stress within the family and adversely affect the parents' ability to effectively nurture and structure their children. Children may be required to cope with reductions in emotional support and simultaneously deal with overwhelming changes, such as a different school, community, or residence. During these difficult times, adolescents may rely more on peers for emotional support and, subsequently, become more susceptible to at-risk behaviors (McCullough & Scherman, 1991; Voydanoff & Donnelly, 1990). Conversely, adolescents raised in two-parent homes have lower rates of sexual risk-taking behavior (Kirby, 2001).

Environmental Influences

Communities can have an impact on the sexual behavior of young people through educational standards, labor market conditions, attitudes about sexual education, and policies regarding abortion. Children growing up in economically depressed environments have reduced rates of high school completion and lowered expectations toward their future socioeconomic status. Academic performance is significantly connected to adolescent sexual behavior. Students who are academically successful and internalize aspirations for higher education are more likely to delay initiation of sexual intercourse or use effective measures to prevent pregnancy than students who experience difficulty in school, do not visualize themselves as successful students, and have diminished educational and vocational goals (Bloch, 1991; Brewster et al., 1993; Kiselica et al., 1992; Plotnick, 1993; Whitbeck, Hoyt, Miller, & Kao, 1992).

Career and educational aspirations may be tied to adolescents' perceptions of the opportunity structure of their communities. A high school diploma probably means less to adolescents who lack the resources to pay for college or those who live in communities with high rates of unemployment. These adolescents may have learned through observation that higher education and career achievement are unattainable goals, and they may perceive parenthood as the only route to independence and adulthood. These helpless, hopeless beliefs about future possibilities are exacerbated when parents have not completed high school or are unemployed. (Note that numerous studies have indicated that daughters are significantly influenced by their mother's educational achievement [Voydanoff & Donnelly, 1990].) Furthermore, unlike other adolescent at-risk behaviors, such as suicide, substance abuse, and violence, pregnancy and parenthood are customarily positive and valued occurrences.

In disadvantaged communities, vocational resources and job opportunities may be limited, and when the probability for adequate employment is low, the costs of early childbearing are also low (Patterson, 1990). Young women are particularly affected by community employment practices. Community values on women in the workforce affect opportunities, pay scales, and career advancement for women and contribute to decisions young women make about their pursuit of, and attainability of, career goals (Brewster et al., 1993). Adolescent women tend to prevent pregnancy through abstinence or birth control when they expect to achieve higher wages through career development (Martin & Hutchinson, 2001; Plotnick, 1993).

Federal, state, and local policies that regulate family planning education as well as accessibility and financial costs of abortion also affect rates of adolescent pregnancy and childbearing (Plotnick, 1993). Research consistently reveals that availability of abortion does not influence adolescent decisions on the initiation of sexual activity or their decisions regarding the use of contraception. However, abortion availability increases the probability that pregnant adolescents will terminate unintended pregnancies through abortion and, therefore, deceases the percentage of adolescent childbearing. Data have disclosed that communities with restricted availability to abortion have higher rates of adolescent childbirth, and birth rates are dramatically reduced when states adopt liberalized laws on abortion (Hofferth, 1991; Plotnick, 1993). In addition, adolescents who live in communities that tend to deny or hide factual sexual information from children may find it difficult to acknowledge, understand, and cope with their maturing sexuality and may become at greater risk for unplanned pregnancies (Brewster et al., 1993). For example, a community that prohibits the discussion of contraception in the public schools influences the availability of birth control information for adolescents who live in the community and reduces the likelihood that adolescents will effectively contracept if they choose to become sexually active.

In socioeconomically disadvantaged communities, adolescents, regardless of gender, race, or ethnicity, realistically may not be sacrificing much in income potential or future financial stability by not postponing parenthood. Studies show that teens who live in disadvantaged communities, who feel the future is bleak, also have higher rates of teen pregnancy (Kirby, 2001). Furthermore, childbearing may allow them to become accepted as adult members of the community (Plotnick, 1993). The literature invariably shows that when young people believe they have the opportunity to achieve educational and career goals, they are less apt to become pregnant and jeopardize the achievement of these goals (Brewster et al., 1993).

CONSEQUENCES

The human and economic consequences of adolescent childbirth are enormous. Whether married or unmarried, adolescent mothers are susceptible to numerous pregnancy-related complications, such as toxemia of pregnancy (eclampsia) and maternal mortality. The high percentage of negative outcomes of adolescent pregnancy is often associated with inadequate prenatal care, poor nutrition, and physical immaturity (White & White, 1991). Data have suggested that reproductive immaturity, pregnancy hormonal deficiencies, distress, and underdeveloped body size significantly contribute to the incidence of premature parturition among adolescents (Stevens-Simon, Kaplan, & McAnarney, 1993). Babies born to adolescent mothers are vulnerable to the adverse effects of premature birth, such as low birth weight, infant mortality, neurological disorders, intellectual impairment, and developmental delays (Allen-Meares, 1989). The risks are even greater among socioeconomically disadvantaged Black adolescents who face the additional distress of discrimination. Studies have indicated the mortality rate of infants born to young Black mothers is almost twice that of infants born to young White mothers (Rhodes et al., 1993).

Infants born to adolescents may be further jeopardized because of the socioeconomic circumstances of their parents. Adolescent parents are less likely to complete high school, less likely to find stable employment, and more likely to live in poverty and become dependent on some form of public assistance. The majority of these young families live in substandard, unsafe, or crowded housing; are nutritionally deprived; and have restricted access to adequate cultural and social advantages. Children of economically disadvantaged families are less healthy and have higher mortality rates than children of economically advantaged families. These children are vulnerable to the adverse conditions associated with poverty, and their quality of life is reduced at the onset of conception (Bloch, 1991; Cervera, 1993a; Combs-Orme, 1993; Foster et al., 1990; Mapanga, 1997).

The development of effective pregnancy prevention programs is essential to the welfare and prosperity of our society. Economically, it is far less costly to prevent adolescent pregnancies than it is to direct interventions toward the financial, emotional, and educational assistance of adolescent parents (Hofferth, 1991). The focus of this chapter is on prevention and is based on the assumption that universal remedies are necessary for the successful reduction of adolescent pregnancy and childbearing. Therefore, this chapter concentrates on a community-oriented approach to the prevention of adolescent pregnancy and childbearing.

CASE STUDY

Several years ago, Mary was referred to the women's program at a community college by the local Job Opportunities and Basic Skills (JOBS) training program. At that time, she was 32 and the single parent of three children, ages 15, 14, and 8. Her downcast demeanor conveyed a sense of desperation, and her facial expression reflected her feelings of distress and apprehension toward this initial contact. She wore no makeup, yet it was apparent she had made an effort to dress appropriately for this appointment. Despite her intense fear of speaking with a college counselor, Mary courageously began to communicate her feelings of despair, helplessness, and hopelessness about her life situation. Her disclosure revealed that she felt depressed and a sense of shame about her circumstances and that she possessed a drastically limited reservoir of effective life and social skills. Despite her dangerously low sense of self-esteem, Mary demonstrated high intelligence; a yearning for change; the ability to perceive, accept, and internalize encouragement; and a tremendous source of intrinsic strength. It was apparent that buried beneath the layers of abuse, neglect, and trauma was the spirit of a remarkable and talented young woman.

Mary was born when her mother, Sue, was 17 and her father, Jim, 19. She was the oldest of three children. Mary's childhood was chaotic and consisted of extended periods of abandonment and terror. Jim fluctuated between bouts of severe depression and violent rages. Sue was withdrawn and chronically depressed. During her early childhood, Mary's father periodically abused alcohol and began to batter her mother. Mary's earliest memories of police intervention began when she was about 5 years old, and she remembers a woman came to talk with her. She had been told to "keep her mouth shut," and she obediently refused to answer the woman's questions. The authorities did not pursue any further action. Mary's mother attempted to modify Jim's behavior by maintaining a perfect home environment (e.g., clean house, prompt meals, invisible children). Mary's job was to keep the younger children quiet and out of the way; thus, she and her mother "became responsible" for the control of Jim's behavior.

When Mary was 8, Jim lost his job and Sue began work as a swing shift waitress. Mary was given the adult responsibilities of child care, meal preparation, and other household chores. Her father's drinking escalated, and he either forced the children to spend the evening in their bedroom or went to the local bar. At this time, he began to physically abuse Mary. The children were often awakened in the middle of the night by violent arguments that culminated in the physical abuse of Sue. Neighbors periodically requested the police to intervene with this pattern of domestic violence, and the police would come and tell Jim to stop beating Sue and Sue to stop provoking Jim's anger.

During her first 2 years of school, Mary was the ideal student. She loved being at school and was bright, eager to learn, and a "model female" student (quiet, nondisruptive, compliant). During her 3rd and 4th years of elementary school, Mary's academic performance began to decline dramatically. She was frequently absent. By middle school, Mary was seriously struggling with her school work. She had difficulty concentrating, neglected her homework assignments, and was not involved in any extracurricular activities. She had few friends, rarely smiled, and quietly occupied a desk in the back of the classroom. By the time Mary entered high school, she believed she hated school.

Mary ran away from home when she was 13. The authorities brought her back to her parents. She ran away again at 14, was placed in juvenile detention for 3 days, and returned to her parents. At 15, she made friends with a group of young people who manifested serious at-risk behaviors and began regularly skipping school, using drugs and alcohol, and having unprotected sexual intercourse with her boyfriend, Allen. Mary was apprehensive about becoming sexually active but complied because of peer pressure and her desire to please Allen. The lack of adequate nurture and positive structure in Mary's childhood was directly correlated to the formation of her sense of low self-esteem and her inability to effectively and assertively care for herself. Mary does not remember learning about birth control at home or at school. She did know what condoms were, but Allen refused to use them. Mary was 16 and Allen 17 when their first child was conceived.

Mary lived in an academically disadvantaged community that had a high rate of unemployment. Jobs were particularly scarce for women. Mary can remember her parents telling her that college was impossible for "people like them." When she learned she was pregnant and would not be able to complete high school, Mary did not believe these events would make a big difference in the quality of her future life. The parents of both children considered marriage to be the only alternative. Mary and Allen quit school, and Allen got a job at a gas station.

Mary and Allen's marriage was quite similar to the marriage of Mary's parents. Allen continued to abuse drugs and alcohol, and after a few years, domestic violence became a regular part of their relationship. They divorced when Mary was 29. Since then, she and her children have relied on public assistance programs for survival.

APPROACHES TO PREVENTION

Individual

The normal course of adolescent development is filled with upheaval and over-whelming physical, emotional, mental, and social changes. During this passage from childhood to adulthood, adolescents experience myriad transformations, including an accelerated growth in cognitive abilities. This gradual transition from concrete opera-tional responses to more formal operational thinking generally begins during late childhood and early adolescence. The development of flexible and abstract thinking patterns enables most older adolescents to consider logically the possibilities and subsequent ramifications of certain behaviors, such as unprotected sexual activity or use of alcohol (Allen-Meares, 1991; Brooks-Gunn & Furstenberg, 1989). However, because of the heightened egocentrism and narcissism typical of adolescence, this exploration has a tendency to be self-directed, and adolescents may alternate between concrete and abstract modes of thinking. Consequently, adolescents often become fixated on the here and now, have difficulty determining long-term consequences of intentions, and make decisions solely based on immediate self-gratification (Blinn & Stenberg, 1993).

In addition to the cognitive, physical, emotional, and relational changes of adoles-cence, young people are faced with the simultaneous emergence of intensified feelings of sexuality and the need to develop a mature value system and formulate guidelines for social and intimate relationships. Social and romantic relationships are critical to the developmental process of adolescence. This process enables children to learn and practice the skills that are necessary for the formation of more permanent relations, such as marriage and parenthood.

While young people attempt to cope with the multitude of psychosocial stressors associated with adolescent development, they also strive to establish a unique sense of identity. Identity formation and emotional emancipation from parents are crucial tasks for adolescents (Allen-Meares, 1991; Croft & Asmussen, 1992). During this progressive and difficult process, adolescents struggle toward the achievement of emotional, financial, and functional independence. When differentiation of self from parents is not encouraged or permitted, the adolescent potential to become maturely responsible for self and others may become thwarted (Freeman, 1989).

Adolescents often need practical assistance in building self-esteem and developing life management skills (Goodyear, 2002; McCullough & Scherman, 1991). Advocates of the cognitive–behavioral approach to prevention of at-risk behaviors propose that adolescents engage in certain behaviors because they lack relevant information and the skills necessary to utilize that information effectively in life situations. Many proponents of this approach advocate a four-step model to facilitate responsible sexual behavior in adolescents. The first two steps involve comprehending and storing information on sexuality and reproduction as well as on the consequences of sexual experimentation and use of chemical substances. This knowledge is generally transmitted, integrated, and practiced in a small-group format. The second two steps are decision making and decision implementation. Adolescents learn to transform abstract information into everyday reality and how to investigate potential consequences of behaviors. Simulated role-plays and feedback help group members personalize knowledge about sexuality and drugs, practice newly acquired skills, and learn assertive behaviors (Allen-Meares, 1991).

Outcome measurements can be used to determine the changes in youth attitudes and knowledge about contraception, human sexuality, risk-taking behaviors, abstinence, decision making, communication and interpersonal skills, and of course reduction in teen pregnancy, in order to evaluate if primary prevention programs are effective. However, it has been noted that these changes are often obtained by self-report and, therefore, may not always be accurate (Franklin & Corcoran, 2000). Studies conducted have shown that the most effective programs for influencing teen sexual behavior were based in a clinical setting (Franklin & Corcoran, 2000).

How might Mary's life have been different if she had received training in assertiveness, self-esteem, and other life management skills? The coping and problem-solving skills Mary received from her parents were minimal and often dysfunctional. Her father repeatedly coped through alcoholism and abusive behavior, and her mother usually coped through depression and submissive behavior. She learned helpless and hopeless behaviors from both parents. The nonintervention of authorities (police, children's services, school professionals) reinforced her sense of powerlessness. Children have an intrinsic need for positive life-sustaining messages, and such interventions might have significantly altered the course of Mary's life.

Family

The quality of the relationship between parents and adolescents contributes to childhood manifestation of at-risk behaviors. Parental rejection or a lack of warmth and affection is related to emotional problems and developmental delays in moral reasoning, and adolescents who experience deficient communication with parents may become susceptible toward unsafe activities such as drug abuse or unprotected sexual experimentation (Brooks-Gunn & Furstenberg, 1989; Committee on Adolescence, 2001). Parental neglect, rejection, or abuse is much more predictive of at-risk behaviors in children than is family conflict (McCullough & Scherman, 1991). Studies have suggested that female adolescents from emotionally inadequate environments often become depressed and seek to compensate for this lack of love and support by establishing intimate relationships with nonfamily members. Young males are likely to counterbalance lack of nurture by abusing drugs and alcohol (Whitbeck et al., 1992). Additionally, research has indicated that adolescent sexual activity is highly associated with parental responses to structure. When parents provide structure with abuse, or fail to provide structure (e.g., rules, guidelines, instruction, discipline) and convey a sense of apathy or powerlessness toward parental responsibilities, their offspring have a propensity toward early initiation of sexual activity (Brooks-Gunn & Furstenberg, 1989; Voydanoff & Donnelly, 1990).

Many children are not nurtured by a stable and functional family atmosphere that promotes support and encouragement and teaches effective problem-solving and coping skills. When parents do not demonstrate or model adequate life skills, children may perceive their own situation as hopeless and fail to develop the necessary skills for survival and growth. In addition, adolescents and children who have not been exposed to self-sustaining skills may become overwhelmed by the natural yet stressful circumstances of maturation and development (e.g., academic achievement, formation and maintenance of relationships, peer pressure, sexual growth) and may perceive themselves as powerless. This sense of powerlessness is positively associated with early sexual activity (White & White, 1991).

The family milieu has a most powerful impact on the successful development of our society's children. Young people learn how to function as adults and how to parent their future children in their families of origin. Parents can optimally influence their children's sexual behaviors by (a) providing consistent nurture and structure, (b) limiting opportunities for sexual experimentation, (c) imparting concrete information about sexual intercourse and reproduction, and (d) sharing personal beliefs and values about sexuality (Franklin & Corcoran, 2000; Voydanoff & Donnelly, 1990). Research has revealed that children who are encouraged to discuss sexuality, pregnancy, and contraception openly with their parents generally use protection if they become sexually active (Barth, Fetro, Leland, & Volkan, 1992). Communities can promote favorable family interactions by offering parenting programs for adults who were not taught adequate life management skills in their own families of origin. In addition, parental involvement is vital to the efficacy of school- or community-based pregnancy prevention programs. Program facilitators can offer workshops on issues related to adolescent sexuality, provide parents with outlines of course curricula, and encourage family discussions so parents can integrate their value system into educational material (Croft & Asmussen, 1992).

How might Mary's life have been different if the authorities had mandated various interventions for this young family when the unstable conditions first became apparent? Might her life story have changed if her father had received early alcohol abuse and anger management counseling? Perhaps he had a condition that could have been ameliorated by medical treatment and mental health services. Could her parents have benefited from receiving parenting and life management training? Could mental health counseling have assisted her mother in her ability to more effectively care for herself and her children?

School

The three basic strategies for school-based pregnancy prevention programs can be organized according to the principal objectives of each approach: (a) abstention from or delay or reduction of sexual activity, (b) provision of information and methods to prevent pregnancy and childbearing, and (c) enhancement of self-esteem and instruction on meaningful alternatives to childbearing (Foster et al., 1990; Franklin & Corcoran, 2000; Hofferth, 1991; Plotnick, 1993).

Two major types of educational programs emphasize abstinence or delay of sexual activity. The first includes traditional sex education courses that provide information on sexuality, reproduction, and life management skills (e.g., decision making, problem solving, and goal setting). The second teaches assertiveness skills to facilitate a healthy response to sexual proclivity (Hofferth, 1991). The goal of 94% of these programs is to provide education so adolescents can make informed decisions about sexuality. Around 80% of these programs concentrate on education about reproduction, and 40% attempt to reduce adolescent childbearing through promotion of abstinence (Barth et al., 1992). One program, CAS (Children's Aid Society)—Carrera, was found to be more effective in delaying sex, increasing long-term contraceptive use, and reducing childbirth and pregnancy in adolescent women than any other program (Kirby, 2001). Components of the CAS—Carrera program include family life and sexuality education, academic support, employment, self-expression through the arts, sports, and health care. One effective aspect of this program is that adult staff bond with the adolescent, becoming a type of surrogate parent, thus increasing the adolescent's secure attachment with an adult that is so important for the adolescent to complete important developmental tasks (Kirby, 2001).

The U.S. government has funded abstinence-only programs in the schools at a cost of more than $440 million since 1996 (Cook, 2001). However, there is some controversy as to whether or not these programs, which are based on abstinence alone, without education about sexuality and contraception, have shown any decrease in the age of onset of intercourse, the frequency of intercourse, or number of sexual partners (Committee on Adolescence, 2001; Cook, 2001). However, studies have shown that preventative programs in schools targeting communication and problem-solving skills were most effective in reducing those variables, and programs that focused on building skills to help youth resist and affront social and peer pressure were more effective than those programs that simply educated about the risks and consequences of teen sexual behavior. It has also been found that sex education curricula are more effective when based on social learning theory and skills training than any other type (Franklin & Corcoran, 2000).

Programs that work in schools have the following factors: *awareness*, when basic information is provided to educators and educators have an interest in using it; *adoption*, when a district, school, or teacher selects the program for use; *implementation*, when the innovation is used; *wholeness*, when a complete program is used and not just portions of it (e.g., a video or guest speaker); and *continuity*, when the program is in place, becomes institutionalized, and is an ongoing part of the yearly curriculum (Collins et al., 2002). However, these effective preventions must be started earlier. Some studies are indicating that many school-based programs are being started too late to be effective because many adolescents are becoming sexually active while in middle school but prevention programs are not targeting youth until high school (O'Donnell et al., 2001).

Traditional Sex Education

Traditional sex education courses attempt to delay or reduce sexual activity by providing formal instruction about sexuality and reproduction. These programs may also offer training on life management skills and social action skills (e.g., sexual and social responsibility, conflict resolution, assertiveness training, interpersonal relationships, and communication skills) to encourage informed and healthy choices about potential sexual behaviors (Franklin & Corcoran, 2000; Plotnick, 1993).

Close to 90% of all large school districts offer some form of sexual education (Barth et al., 1992), but there are serious limitations connected with most school programs. School-based sexuality education is often noncomprehensive and restricted to topics of biology and reproduction. Educators often avoid the discussion of controversial or sensitive subjects, such as birth control or homosexuality, because of perceptions that this information is unacceptable to parents and other community members (Croft & Asmussen, 1992; Franklin, Grant, Corcoran, Miller, & Bultman, 1997). (Community members may be more receptive to school-based sexuality education if educators changed the title from sex education to sexuality education [Croft & Asmussen, 1992].) Consequently, less than half of school programs provide complete information on sexuality or how to use and where to obtain birth control (Barth et al., 1992). In addition, adults, not adolescents, determine the informational content of the courses.

Surveys have revealed that young people are less interested in learning the biological facts of reproduction than in receiving education on contraception and on social issues surrounding sexuality. Most adolescents want factual and complete information about sexuality, STDs, and HIV/AIDS, and they assert that concealing information interferes with their ability to make responsible decisions about future sexual intentions. They regard the tendency of adults to withhold information and to decide what children should and should not know about sexuality as an irresponsible action (Croft & Asmussen, 1992). Many professionals agree and maintain that children must be given detailed information on all the methods that will provide them protection from disease and prevention of pregnancy (abstinence through birth control) before they can make healthy choices about sexual activity (Allen-Meares, 1989; Barth et al., 1992; Committee on Adolescence, 2001).

Prevention of at-risk behaviors is a process that begins in early childhood and continues through the later stages of life. Unfortunately, the majority of traditional sexuality programs are severely time limited (Croft & Asmussen, 1992) and do not accommodate the developmental learning processes of children. Studies have indicated that this hasty, sporadic approach to sexuality education is not effective in reducing the rate of adolescent pregnancy. Moreover, prevention programs often target at-risk groups too late in the developmental cycle (Allen-Meares, 1991; O'Donnell et al., 2001).

Many professionals maintain that an effective prevention program for at-risk behaviors of children and adolescents needs to encompass Grades K–12 and include comprehensive, developmentally appropriate information that incorporates all aspects of human sexuality and sexual behavior. These programs are not designed to teach young people how to have sex but to help them better understand their emerging sexuality as well as to learn ways to cope with this mysterious, yet natural part of maturation. This learning process begins in early childhood and includes components other than sexual behaviors, such as self-esteem, respect for self and others, sexual responsibility, interpersonal relationship skills, and life management skills (Croft & Asmussen, 1992; Goodyear, 2002). The results from school programs that have integrated comprehensive sexuality education in class curricula for Grades K–12 have been highly favorable. Although abstinence is encouraged throughout the educational process, the programs also promote consistent use of effective contraception for young people who choose to become sexually active.[1] Evaluations of these programs reveal that this approach dramatically reduces the rate of premature sexual experimentation, pregnancy, and contraction of STDs (Christopher & Roosa, 1990; Kaplan, 2002; Mcilhaney, 2002).

---

[1] Research demonstrates that sexuality education that includes a contraception component does not increase sexual activity among adolescents, even when participants are 14 years and younger (Franklin et al., 1997; Sellers, McGraw, & McKinlay, 1994).

Research has consistently revealed that sex education and family life courses significantly increase student knowledge about reproduction and the biological aspects of sexuality but have little influence on adolescent sexual behavior or rates of pregnancy (Barth et al., 1992; Franklin & Corcoran, 2000; Hofferth, 1991; Voydanoff & Donnelly, 1990). The results of a meta-analysis of adolescent pregnancy by Franklin et al. (1997) indicated that pregnancy prevention programs had no effect on adolescent sexual activity across age, gender, and ethnicity, and programs that emphasized contraception knowledge building and distribution of birth control were successful in reducing rates of pregnancy and childbearing.

How might Mary's life have been different if her elementary school had included a prevention program for at-risk students? Could the existence of such a program have encouraged teachers to become more aware of her emotional difficulties? What if teachers had received training to help the students detect early signals of potential school withdrawal? What if they were given a convenient source for referral? Might early intervention have empowered Mary to complete her education and realize her full human potential?

Life Management Skills Training

Life skills educators maintain that analytical reasoning processes are necessary to make rational decisions about future sexual behavior. During life management skills training, adolescents are presented with factual information about reproduction and taught problem-solving, decision-making, and interpersonal communication skills. Research has suggested that interactions that provide nonjudgmental instruction and encourage self-determination have a more enduring impact on human growth and development. Consequently, many family life educators recommend that educators provide complete information and withhold value judgments on sexual or contraceptive behavior and that adolescents ultimately be allowed to determine their own sexual goals and objectives. This approach not only provides concrete birth control instruction but also encourages abstinence or delays in sexual activity. Adolescents learn how to anticipate and recognize at-risk situations and to problem solve ways to avoid engaging in unprotected intercourse while simultaneously forming and maintaining relationships with their peers (Hofferth, 1991). During this didactic process, it is important for educators to use language that facilitates adolescents' comprehension and internalization of proffered messages (Freeman, 1989). Studies have shown that students who participate in life skills programs have better problem-solving, negotiation, and communication skills; greater comprehension of reproduction and contraception; and more favorable attitudes toward regular and effective family planning than do nonparticipating students (Hofferth, 1991).

Adolescents learn best through action, and it is important to get them involved in their own learning processes. Role-plays provide a safe medium in which adolescents can experiment, practice, and become comfortable with healthy decisions regarding their sexuality. Drama and exercises are also excellent interventions for adolescents. For example, all middle school students in one innovative program are given the assignment of caring for an "infant" for 7 days. These infants are actually 10-pound sacks of kitty litter wrapped in pink or blue bags. Students must have these infants with them at all times and tote their children around school in infant carriers. After school or during the weekend, these students must arrange and pay (either through barter or money) for child care. This exercise is an excellent learning tool to help adolescents learn about how it feels to be responsible for a helpless infant. Most begin the week in high excitement, choosing names and dressing their babies in purloined baby clothes. Toward the end of the week, they are scrounging for baby-sitters, hoping to survive the weekend, and anticipating their impending freedom from parenthood.

Other pregnancy prevention programs offer a more technologically advanced method to teach adolescents about the responsibilities of parenthood. Students receive computerized life-sized dolls called the "Baby Think It Over" (BTIO), which are programmed to mimic the behaviors of a newly born infant. These dolls awaken and cry at random hours over a 24-hour period, demand to be fed every few hours, have crying cycles, and manifest typical behaviors of normal infants (Somers et al., 2001).

The decision tree is another exercise that assists adolescents in the realization that behaviors have consequences. This task helps adolescents carefully scrutinize a proposed action and the outgrowth of that contemplated behavior. The tree's branches sprout with decisions, possible consequences, and potential outcomes of each decision. For example, a heterosexual adolescent considering sexual intercourse looks beyond the decision of initiating sexual activity to the next option, the decision whether to contracept. If the adolescent elects to contracept, he or she next determines whether to obtain information about the effectiveness of various types of birth control and evaluate those potential methods. The decision tree now expands to include choices on whether to learn how to contracept effectively and where to obtain birth control. If the adolescent decides not to contracept, he or she plans for the possibility of a pregnancy or a sexually transmitted disease. If pregnancy occurs, further decisions include choices of abortion, marriage, child support, adoption, or single parenthood (Kriepe, 1983).

How might Mary's life have been different if she had been encouraged in self-determination and taught she had the right to make healthy decisions about her body, her emotions, and her future goals? Might she have avoided seeking affirmation through the relationship with Allen?

Adolescent Family Life Act

In response to the escalating rates of adolescent pregnancy and childbearing and the adverse outcomes associated with adolescent parenthood, Congress passed the Adolescent Family Life Act (AFLA) of 1981. This is the first federal program devoted exclusively to addressing concerns about adolescent pregnancy. Proponents of the AFLA assert that premature sexual activity is the main problem and that pregnancy, STDs, HIV/AIDS, and childbirth can all be avoided if sexual intercourse is postponed (Committee on Adolescence, 2001). AFLA programs promote abstinence as a primary prevention for all adolescents and secondary intervention strategies to ameliorate the negative outcomes of childbearing for adolescent parents and their infants. Programs for the AFLA are designed by the Office of Adolescent Pregnancy Programs, and planners assume that the development of internal controls (e.g., self-responsibility, self-determination) will enable adolescents to assertively resist social and personal influences, such as peer pressure, media messages, and natural sexual urges (Christopher & Roosa, 1990; White & White, 1991). These programs promote abstinence through developmentally appropriate skill-building exercises and activities and rely on the use of peer counselors as well as parental involvement and support (Hofferth, 1991).

The AFLA reports of positive results in interpersonal growth and decreases in sexual activity should be cautiously considered because detailed evaluations of AFLA programs are rare, unscientific, nontechnical, brief in content, and methodically unsound (White & White, 1991). The few scientific studies have indicated that abstinence programs do not influence sexual decisions of adolescents who are not yet sexually active and suggested that this strategy has little effect on the behavior of sexually active adolescents (Committee on Adolescence, 2001; Cook, 2001; Plotnick, 1993). Research by Christopher and Roosa (1990) disclosed that programs that rely exclusively on a premarital abstinence approach are not effective in reducing adolescent sexual activity or pregnancy rates. In fact, a study of Success Express, an AFLA program that targets midlevel school children, revealed an increase in sexual activity among participants, particularly male adolescents. In addition, the dropout rate for this program was very high, indicating that students at risk were not motivated to complete the program. Programs that focus on abstinence as the only alternative to pregnancy ignore young people who have already experienced coitus. This exclusion includes the many adolescents who have been forced to endure sexual intercourse through rape or sexual abuse (Franklin & Corcoran, 2000). Moreover, sexually active adolescents may resist courses that strictly promote abstinence because they may hear the message that they have done something bad or wrong and may feel defensive, ashamed, and immobilized (Christopher & Roosa, 1990). In addition, adolescents may discredit messages that emphasize the importance of preventing unwanted pregnancies through abstinence when they perceive having a child as a positive life experience (Ravert & Martin, 1997). Thus, Koniak-Griffin and Brecht (1997) maintained that the promotion of abstinence for every adolescent may create a situation that places adolescents who have experienced sexual exposure at increased risk for contracting STDs and HIV. Programs need to focus on reduction of risk-taking behaviors, emphasize the use of condoms as a protection from AIDS (not strictly pregnancy), and promote effective contraception and condom usage with every sexual encounter.

School-Based Clinics

Modern children are faced with learning how to handle multiple adverse environmental conditions, and when they have not been taught effective coping skills, they may respond to environmental deficiencies with behaviors such as suicide attempts, drug or alcohol abuse, and unprotected sexual experimentation. Comprehensive mental health services are vital to this population, and it is imperative that these services are accessible to targeted populations. School-based clinics (SBCs) can fulfill this need (Harold, 1988). SBCs are administered by the school system, located on site at the school or near school grounds, and are a convenient method to comprehensively serve the mental and physical health needs of students. However, although SBCs improve the health care received by students, they show little impact on sexual behavior, use of contraception, and adolescent rates of pregnancy and childbirth.

Research has indicated that community-based clinics located near, but not on, school grounds and not administered by the school system are more effective in reducing adolescent pregnancy rates (Franklin & Corcoran, 2000; Franklin et al., 1997). These statistics may be due to several factors. Although SBCs can serve a vast number of students, clinic schedules revolve around school hours and the school year, and the population served is restricted to registered students. In addition, family planning is generally not a major focus at these clinics. Even when family planning is stressed, students may feel apprehensive about obtaining contraception at the school clinic because of problems with confidentiality. Unfortunately, information from student files may be accessible to teachers, or clinic staff may divulge personal information to other school employees. Personnel may not be cognizant of the ethical, moral, and legal aspects or, more important, the realistic repercussions of these breaches of confidentiality. Fear of discovery is one of the major reasons adolescents practice unprotected sexual intercourse, and when they believe their privacy may be violated, they avoid using the SBCs' contraceptive services (Zabin et al., 1991). Studies have shown that effective programs that impact teen sexual practices are ones that provide clear norms with factual information to back them up, provide youth activities to personalize the norms, have adults who model the desired behaviors, and also engage youth in role-plays to practice the norms (Kirby, 2001). Clearly, most SBCs do not provide these kinds of services.

Community

Community members, parents, and educators are searching for strategies to reduce the escalating rates of adolescent pregnancies and the growing exposure of our nation's youth to STDs, HIV, and AIDS (Barth et al., 1992). Kirby (2001) stated that those communities that are more disorganized and disadvantaged have a higher rate of adolescents who engage in early sexual experimentation without protection. Allen-Meares (1991) proposed that, to be effective, prevention programs for at-risk behaviors must (a) target multiple systems (e.g., family, school, community) and use diverse strategies to transmit information, (b) direct intervention efforts toward the entire community, (c) encompass all adolescents and reject assumptions that subgroups are the only students at risk, and (d) focus efforts on encouragement, success, and advantage rather than on deviance or etiology of the problem. Brewster et al. (1993) and Kirby (2001) maintained that the community context and clearly stated norms are major influences on the sexual behavior of community youth. Brewster et al. (1993) suggested that three interwoven factors are crucial to the prevention of pregnancy among adolescents:

1. *Community and family attitude:* Adolescents need structured information about appropriate modes of behavior. It is the responsibility of adults to model and define social norms that proscribe, constrain, and delineate acceptable, healthy, and successful behaviors and clearly communicate the realistic consequences of at-risk behaviors.

2. *Provision of hope and possibilities:* Children who reside in communities that empower and encourage goal achievement as well as provide career-related opportunities have positive expectations toward successful accomplishment of educational and vocational goals.

3. *Access to contraception:* There needs to be a concerted community and parental effort toward the exposure of youth to knowledge of the reproductive system, complete and factual information about contraception, and accessible family planning clinics.

Family Planning Services

Contraceptive use among adolescents in recent decades has increased significantly (Committee on Adolescence, 2001). This trend may be due to an elevated societal concern over the possibility of exposure to AIDS and an impetus toward providing information on protection against this syndrome. However, the majority of sexually active adolescents either randomly use ineffective methods of birth control or completely avoid contraceptive use (Committee on Adolescence, 2001; Zabin et al., 1991). Studies have indicated that adolescents who experience sexual intercourse at younger ages are more likely to contracept inconsistently, choose ineffective methods of contraception, or engage in unprotected sexual intercourse. Thus, adolescents with meager understanding about their sexuality and how to protect themselves sexually are least likely to use contraception.

Simple awareness about sexuality and contraception rarely changes contraception behaviors. Concrete, practical instruction about birth control is positively correlated to contraception use at first intercourse, regular contraception use, and choice of more effective methods of sexual protection. Research has consistently shown that comprehensive knowledge of contraception, more than knowledge of reproduction, significantly lowers practices of unprotected sexual activity among sexually active adolescents. Unfortunately, information about contraception is usually gained from peers, and misinformation about availability, cost, effectiveness, safety, and proper utilization is prevalent (Barth et al., 1992).

Statistics have indicated that adolescents who do use some form of protection often choose methods that are inexpensive and easy to obtain. These methods are generally the least effective forms of birth control. The most effective modes of contraception (e.g., birth control pill, injections, diaphragm, cervical cap) require contact with medical personnel and instruction on usage. Many professionals maintain that the recent decline in rates of adolescent pregnancy and childbearing is positively correlated with the increased use of an injectable form of birth control called Depo-Provera. Depo-Provera is simple to use and requires one visit every 3 months to a clinic for an injection (Kluger, 1998; Wingert, 1998). Nonprescription methods of protection (e.g., foam, gel, condoms) are not as effective in preventing pregnancy, but condoms are imperative for protection against AIDS. Adolescents who use condoms rarely receive instruction on correct condom application and removal, and improper use of condoms further increases adolescent risk for pregnancy and AIDS (Committee on Adolescence, 2001; Voydanoff & Donnelly, 1990).

Family planning services promote sexually responsible behavior by concentrating on increasing regular and effective use of contraception among sexually active youth. It is well documented that family planning programs that distribute contraception and offer information and guidance on abortion and adoption are the most effective method for reducing adolescent birth rates. However, studies have not clearly shown whether these services decrease rates of adolescent pregnancy. Studies have also demonstrated that the effectiveness of family planning services is enhanced when combined with sexuality education, and sexuality education is more effective when combined with direct access to contraception. In addition, research has not indicated that these services encourage or increase sexual activity among adolescents (Franklin et al., 1997; Hofferth, 1991; Sellers et al., 1994). After reviewing the literature that examines the impact of social policies on adolescent pregnancy and childbearing and the effectiveness of various programs, Plotnick (1993) concluded that "policies that offer tangible family-planning services and that improve access to and affordability of abortion are more likely to succeed than those that focus on changing personal attitudes and values" (p. 327). He further stated that policies that improve educational and economic opportunities for adolescents will likely have an indirect, yet important, long-term impact on reducing future adolescent pregnancy and childbearing rates.

How might Mary's life have been different if she had received information that helped her understand her sexuality, her need for intimate relationships, and her emerging sexual desires? What if she (and Allen) had received concrete, complete information on human sexuality and use of contraception? Might they have avoided pregnancy?

Residential Programs

Prevention works best when it targets communities instead of families and individuals within society (Freeman, 1989) and is directed toward reshaping community climates. Comprehensive residential programs that provide multidimensional services for adolescents can help communities reach goals of reducing at-risk behaviors among children (Hofferth, 1991). These community-based centers can foster propitious changes in community characteristics that can positively impact community youth. Residential programs have several major advantages. The centers are open during periods of idle time, such as weekends, after school, and during vacations, and are available to all adolescents, including those who are withdrawn, suspended, or expelled from school. More important, when programs are situated in close proximity to families and the residential environment, family and community members become more involved, and programs are able to tailor strategies that accurately reflect and address conditions within the community (Foster et al., 1990; Freeman, 1989).

Needs Assessment

The development and strategic planning stages of a comprehensive community-based prevention center for adolescents require extensive cooperative efforts among educators, parents, and community members (Croft & Asmussen, 1992). Community involvement in the goal development stages of prevention programs is vital to the future success of proposed projects. Involvement not only cultivates the commitment necessary to project sustentation but also critically promotes the identification and resolution of potential areas of disagreement among community members (Foster et al., 1990).

During the planning stages, it is important to administer a systematic and accurate assessment of the specific needs of targeted communities. Communities are unique and have precise needs, and generalized programs may fail in certain communities because the needs of the community are not addressed. The needs assessment should focus on (a) identification of existing community resources, (b) limitations in necessary resources, (c) how available resources can be used advantageously, and (d) strategies to make resources available and accessible to community youth (Freeman, 1989). The needs assessment can be accomplished through written questionnaires, semi-structured interviews, and the use of focus groups (Croft & Asmussen, 1992; Nix, Pasteur, & Servance, 1988). Surveys should include a reliable sample of all community residents (e.g., all ages, economic and educational levels, racial and ethnic groups). After the initial contact that identifies the needs of the community, it may be necessary to gather additional information to further define requirements and specify priorities. In addition, although different groups may agree on certain needs, they may perceive these needs as requiring disparate solutions. For example, adults may devise solutions that do not accommodate the requisites of community youth and thus jeopardize the successfulness of programs (Freeman, 1989).

Spaha is a successful community program for adolescents that operates on a limited budget, with one paid director and adult volunteers. Adolescents are active in the needs assessment process, and their opinions are crucial in determining services offered by Spaha (Azzarto, 1997). One service requested by adolescents was a female support group, and Azzarto (1997) recommended this intervention as a strategy to prevent at-risk behaviors for young women. Research has indicated that low self-esteem, isolation, and lack of positive interactions with adults are related to at-risk behaviors (e.g., unprotected sexual intercourse and increased exposure to HIV/AIDS and STDs). Support groups can provide an unconditionally accepting environment in which young women can improve self-esteem through the (a) cultivation of healthy relationships with peers and nondidactic, nonjudgmental adults and (b) development of self-identity by sharing and exploring personal beliefs, behaviors, and feelings.

Life Options Programs

Evidence has strongly indicated that student employment opportunities are positively associated with delays in childbearing, and multidimensional programs that combine employment, sexuality and contraception instruction, and life options training significantly decrease rates of adolescent pregnancy and childbearing (Franklin & Corcoran, 2000; Martin & Hutchinson, 2001; Plotnick, 1993). The goals of life options programs are to help adolescents understand the consequences of early parenthood, motivate them to defer childbearing, teach life management and interpersonal skills, and provide social and economic alternatives to parenthood. Program strategies include personal counseling, career and vocational training, human development courses, and work opportunities.

High unemployment rates for adolescents within their immediate community can decrease opportunities for work experiences and prevent the acquisition of career-related knowledge. In economically depressed communities, it is difficult for adolescents to internalize an image of themselves as responsible, working adults. This frustration in the ability to visualize and develop career goals can negatively impact the self-worth of male and female adolescents. Furthermore, adults in economically disadvantaged communities are also affected by high rates of unemployment and may be less capable of modeling positive career-related behaviors and providing adequate guidance about career preparation (Freeman, 1989).

Hofferth's (1991) review of the effectiveness of programs for high-risk adolescents revealed some promising results for community-based prevention programs. Research data from Youth Incentive Entitlement Plot Projects (Olsen & Farkas, 1987) indicated that when adolescents are guaranteed a job (part time during school year and full time during summer vacation), they are more likely to delay childbearing. The program evaluations demonstrated that after 2 years, program participants, when compared with the control group, had substantially higher levels of knowledge about sexual reproduction and contraception, had a greater tendency to delay initiation of sexual activity, and were more likely to use contraception when sexually active. There was a 30% decrease in pregnancy rates for older adolescents compared with a 58% increase in nonparticipants.

A more comprehensive approach was developed in 1985 by public/private ventures. This experimental project, Summer Training and Education Program (STEP), was designed to reduce rates of early school withdrawal, school suspension, course failure, and pregnancy rates among adolescents from disadvantaged socioeconomic backgrounds. The randomly selected STEP participants were provided with remedial education (90 hours of reading and math tutoring), sexuality education and life skills training (18 hours of learning how to make responsible decisions about social and sexual behaviors), work experience (80 hours of part-time work provided by local youth jobs program), and a comprehensive support system throughout the entire year. The control group received full-time summer employment and no other special treatment. Program evaluations revealed that the experimental group showed increases in effective use of contraception when sexually active, and youth in the experimental group were more likely than the control group to delay initiation of sexual intercourse.

How might Mary's life have been different if, since childhood, she had carried an image of herself as a productive, worthy, self-empowered, and satisfied working adult? What if she had been encouraged to set goals and to visualize herself as capable of achieving these goals and could depend on obtaining the resources necessary for attaining these goals?

INTERVENTION

Individual

It is imperative that professionals consistently consider the individual developmental stages of the pregnant adolescent. "It is easy to forget that pregnant adolescents are still children, subject to the same cognitive and emotional limitations as any child" (Combs-Orme, 1993, p. 353). Ideally, adolescence is a time for children to define and establish self-identity and to learn and practice the skills of adulthood. Conversely, pregnancy is a time for adults to prepare for childbirth and learn to meet the impending needs of their unborn child. The conflict between these natural processes can manifest in intensified feelings of distress and instability in adolescents as they struggle to fulfill both developmental tasks (Christopher & Roosa, 1990). Professionals can facilitate healthy resolution of this dichotomy by focusing interventional efforts toward the needs of both parents (male and female) and their infant. When adolescents are assisted in fulfilling developmental goals and resolving their feelings about the pregnancy, they become more capable of nurturing and caring for their unborn or newborn infant (Combs-Orme, 1993).

The combination of the immature cognitive processes of adolescence and the trauma of pregnancy may distort young people's ability to make rational decisions on how to resolve the pregnancy. Thus, many adolescent parents may need crisis intervention counseling when they first admit they are pregnant. They may feel overwhelmed and immobilized, and they need strategies that can assist them in becoming calmer, less emotional, and more capable of solving problems and making crucial, life-consequential decisions (e.g., adoption, abortion, marriage, employment, education). It is important that health care workers assist adolescents in planning for their future and urge them not to lose sight of their long-term dreams. This encouragement needs to be directed toward both male and female adolescents.

A study by Softas-Nall, Baldo, and Williams (1997) demonstrated that intern counselors may be more likely to influence adolescent fathers to drop out of school and seek employment to provide financial support for their child. This study indicated that male adolescents who were of Hispanic descent were the population least encouraged to pursue high school completion and higher education. In addition, adolescents often experience instant gratification when they earn a minimum wage, and they may tend to discard long-term plans for education and career. Professionals can help adolescents problem solve, make long-range plans, and realize their former goals are not only accessible and attainable but also vital to their future quality of life (Combs-Orme, 1993; Kiselica et al., 1992). Belief that their goals are obtainable creates a greater likelihood that adolescent parents will remain educationally motivated, which will help limit family size and will increase financial independence (Koshar, 2001).

Programs and policies need to encourage single fathers to establish paternity legally for their children. Fathers who establish paternity legally have a basis for asserting their rights with regard to regular visitation (if the father is the noncustodial parent), adoption, parenting practices, and custody decisions (e.g., paternal, maternal, shared). Legal paternity permits children to have knowledge of the identity of their fathers, allows them access to Social Security or military benefits, provides them with the opportunity to seek important medical information about their fathers, and when followed by adequate child support, enhances their economic well-being. Paternity should be legally established as soon after the birth of the child as possible at a stage when the father is most motivated to become involved with prenatal and postnatal

care and decisions regarding the future well-being of the child. It has also been suggested that minors be approached differently than single fathers who are legal adults.
For example, with cases involving noncustodial unmarried fathers under 18, financial
obligations might be postponed until adulthood, with provisions for token financial
support and guidelines that specifically outline other paternal responsibilities toward
care of the child (e.g., regular visitation, transportation to day care, and medical services) might be developed.

Family

There are critical implications for intervention that must be integrated into adolescent
pregnancy and parenting program development. Successful intervention strategies
enable teens, both male and female, to avoid additional pregnancies and provide compelling reasons for them to do so. Intervention programs for pregnant or parenting adolescents focus predominantly on adolescent females[2] and are directed toward the
facilitation of healthy pregnancies for mother and infant, completion of education, resolution of immediate and long-term social and emotional difficulties, deferral of subsequent pregnancies, and acquirement of self-sufficiency skills, economic independence
(Hofferth, 1991), and parenting skills (Koshar, 2001). Pregnant and parenting adolescents frequently need preliminary subsistence assistance, and this support is typically
acquired from parents, public assistance, and nutritional programs such as food stamps
or the Special Supplemental Food Program for Women, Infants, and Children (WIC),
which provides nourishment for eligible pregnant and lactating women and children up
to 5 years of age. Evaluations of WIC show this program is successful in improving the
outcome of pregnancy for mother and infant and can have the strongest impact on at-
risk adolescent mothers (Allen-Meares, 1989). The two major public sources for assistance are Aid to Families With Dependent Children (AFDC) and Medicaid. Medicaid
has eliminated a previous connection with AFDC and is now expanded to provide
health care assistance to multifarious groups of women (Combs-Orme, 1993).

An important function of intervention programs is to provide information and
referrals to accessible resources. Thus, professionals who work with adolescent parents should be familiar with and understand the eligibility requirements and application procedures of all federal, state, and local services available to adolescent parents.
In addition to financial, medical, and nutritional assistance, referrals can include mental health and other support services, adoption/abortion clinics, child care, programs
that provide clothing and other basic needs, housing, educational options (e.g., alternative schools, high school equivalency programs, community colleges), vocational
training (Combs-Orme, 1993), and parent education classes. Mapanga (1997) promoted the services of midwives and community health nurses, either at health centers
or with community outreach programs, as a resource for adolescent parents and pregnancy prevention programs. Midwives and nurses can provide information about sexuality, contraception, and the prevention of HIV/AIDS and offer comprehensive
services with prenatal and postnatal care.

Adolescent mothers list transportation, child care, support groups, and counseling
services as top priorities for assistance programs. Support groups are an important

---

[2] It is important to note that intervention programs often neglect the needs of adolescent fathers, despite
data that indicate that fathers who participate in such programs are more involved with prenatal care and
that offspring of participating fathers have higher birth weights than do infants of nonparticipating fathers
(Softas-Nall et al., 1997).

intervention for pregnant and parenting adolescents. Approval and support from peer groups is an imperative need for most adolescents. Unfortunately, pregnant female adolescents are often rejected by their friends and classmates (Blinn & Stenberg, 1993). These young mothers feel comfortable with other young women who are experiencing similar situations and value the acceptance, nurture, encouragement, and constructive feedback the peer groups can provide. In addition, young mothers report that lack of transportation is a serious obstacle to completing education and obtaining medical assistance. Even when financial assistance is provided for child care, the use of public transportation to get their child to day care, go to school, and pick up the child after school is often perceived as an overwhelming barrier (McCullough & Scherman, 1991).

School

Many studies have indicated that postnatal services are effective in reducing subsequent pregnancies for adolescent mothers (Kirby, 2001). A longitudinal study conducted by Seitz and Apfel (1993) examined the effects of female adolescents' postnatal attendance at a public alternative school for pregnant adolescents.

This school adheres to the regular school calendar, schedule, and curriculum and provides students with medical services, prenatal and parenting classes, life management skills training, and mental health counseling. The goal of school personnel is to promote and encourage development of self-sufficiency skills. Usually pregnant adolescents remain at the alternative school until their infant is born and return to regular school the first quarter following the birth. However, students who deliver during the third quarter are allowed to complete the fourth quarter at the alternative school. Consequently, students who experience parturition January through April are permitted to remain at the school longer than students who deliver May through August.

Information gathered by Seitz and Apfel (1993) on 102 alternative school female students revealed that students who were allowed to remain at the alternative school for 7.1 weeks or longer were almost three times less likely to have a second child within a 2-year period than were students who returned to regular school in less than 7.1 weeks. After 5 years, over half of the single-child group had not delivered a second child. Adolescents who did not give birth to a second child within 2 years had significantly better educational outcomes (e.g., passing grades, high school diploma) than did students who delivered a second child. In addition, adolescent mothers who deliver a second child within 2 years are inclined to have larger families, abandon hope for educational and vocational achievement, and rely on public assistance to support their families.

Seitz and Apfel (1993) proposed that there is a critical interval during the second postnatal month in which adolescents make pivotal decisions about future sexual responsibilities and the consequences of their sexual behaviors. The availability of an effective support system during this time period promotes the probability that young mothers will make decisions that lead to more positive life outcomes. It appears "that intervention with economically disadvantaged women is especially effective when it begins during the pregnancy with the first-born child and continues postnatally" (Seitz & Apfel, 1993, p. 580).

Community

Studies show that early and regular prenatal and postnatal care significantly reduces the health risk to infants and their mothers, and utilization of programs that provide these services conjoined with one-on-one home visits has been shown to delay the onset of second births substantially (Kirby, 2001). However, utilization of available services by low-income pregnant and parenting women is extremely low. Research has indicated several factors that may contribute to the underutilization of prenatal and postnatal services for pregnant and parenting mothers who are economically disadvantaged. These include (a) reduction of services due to governmental cutbacks, (b) difficulties with child care and transportation, (c) programmatic barriers (e.g., inefficiencies, confusion about eligibility, application procedures, long lines, and extensive waiting periods), (d) inappropriate behavior of staff (e.g., judgmental attitude, intrusiveness, discrimination), and (e) treatment and assessment strategies that are biased toward the dominant segment of the population. Women who experience discrimination, depression, or other psychological difficulties or who feel disempowered are the population who will benefit most from these services, yet they typically do not initiate and sustain program assistance (Rhodes et al., 1993).

The tendency to defer prenatal care is further increased among disadvantaged adolescents, and the youngest adolescent group, whose babies are at the greatest risk, are the least likely to seek medical assistance (Combs-Orme, 1993). It is important that professionals consider the unique adolescent characteristics that can underlie adolescent disuse of medical care. Adolescents may fail to seek prenatal care because of immature cognitive processes and lack of knowledge. Their thinking processes are often concrete and existential, and the concept of a child developing within the body of a young female may be too abstract for them to understand (Christopher & Roosa, 1990). Younger adolescents may not be knowledgeable about the symptoms of pregnancy and may not initially realize they are pregnant. Sometimes adolescents delay the commencement of prenatal care during the critical first trimester because they are undecided on how to resolve the pregnancy or want to deny the fact they are pregnant. Denial can emanate from magical thinking processes (ignore it and it will go away) or as a way to cope with the perceived consequences of discovery. For example, adolescents may avoid acknowledging the pregnancy because they fear parental reactions or are anxious about medical tests and pelvic examinations (Combs-Orme, 1993).

Public nutritional resources are available to pregnant and lactating adolescents, yet many young women do not take advantage of these services (Combs-Orme, 1993). Typically, adolescents gain less weight during pregnancy, and their nutritional intake is often poor. Consequently, they are at heightened risk for being malnourished during gestation. Inadequate maternal weight gain in adolescents is positively correlated to the maternal and neonatal risks linked to adolescent childbearing (Stevens-Simon et al., 1993).

Many factors are associated with poor nutrition and insufficient weight gain among pregnant adolescent females. Adolescents frequently experience feelings of negativity about their body image. These feelings are especially intense during periods of rapid growth and extensive physical changes. Studies have indicated that when adolescent women are pregnant, their perceptions of self-image, self-esteem, and self-identity are further diminished. This may lead to an increased need to conform to the current societal message that only extremely thin women are attractive and thus create a conflict between complying with the societal mores of thinness and the need to gain weight during pregnancy (Blinn & Stenberg, 1993). Malnourishment is exacerbated by the combination of reduced nutritional consumption and an immature reproductive system that requires additional sustenance. Reduced nutritional intake could be due to typical teenage eating habits (e.g., skipping meals, eating junk food), may derive from conditions in which adolescents are unable to afford sufficient amounts of healthy food, or may result from supplemental food programs that do not meet the special nutritional needs of pregnant adolescent females. Finally, adolescent mothers are vulnerable to depression, and this affective disorder can precipitate a failure to thrive in children. Adolescents who fail to gain weight during gestation should be evaluated for depression (Combs-Orme, 1993). Pregnancy prevention and intervention programs for adolescents need to include information on nutritional requirements during pregnancy and emphasize how weight gain is necessary for the health of the mother and unborn child (Blinn & Stenberg, 1993).

ADAPTATIONS FOR DIVERSITY

Our society is failing to educate approximately one third of our population (Bloch, 1991). The risk for noncompletion of education is dramatically increased for adolescent parents, young people who live in urban areas, and members of certain ethnic and racial groups (Barber & McCellan, 1987). For example, high school noncompletion rates are dangerously high for students of Native American and Puerto Rican descent (Barber & McCellan, 1987). Research that investigated conditions leading to high rates of high school noncompletion has predominantly focused on the individual, family, and socioeconomic status as possible contributing factors. Despite the vast amount of research directed toward identifying students who are at high risk for early school withdrawal, not one component or a combination of circumstances has emerged that clearly predicts adolescent at-risk behavior (Bloch, 1991).

Some studies have seemed to indicate that lower economic status, limited educational background of parents, and being born to a certain ethnic or racial group are highly predictive of at-risk behaviors such as drug abuse, adolescent pregnancy, or high school noncompletion. Blake and Bentov (2001) found that the number of students living in poverty was 11% White, 37% Hispanic, and 43% Black. Meyer (1991) found a cultural bias in the majority of medical and social research in that minorities are invisible regardless of their socioeconomic status and Whites have a privileged status regardless of theirs.

Recent research continues to support a disparity between ethnicities, especially among Whites, Hispanics, and African Americans. During the early 1990s, it seemed the rate of sexual activity, STDs, and adolescent childbirth were on the decline for Black and Hispanic youth. In fact, at one time, the incidence of White adolescent childbirth was much greater than that of Black adolescents. Since the 1960s, the rate of pregnancy increased by more than 300% for White adolescents and by only 12% for Black adolescents (Meyer, 1991), and in the 1990s, the pregnancy rate for Black adolescents reduced more significantly than the rate for White adolescents. However, this trend may be reversing itself as more Hispanic and Black youth are becoming initiated into sexual intercourse at earlier ages than before. Some studies now indicate that Black males are three times more likely than Hispanic males and nearly seven times more likely than White males to have had sex before the age of 15, and the rates are nearly the same for females (O'Donnell et al., 2001). Although minority youth childbirth rates are still declining, they remain disproportionately high in the Hispanic and Black populations (O'Donnell et al., 2001). In addition, a study conducted by Wu and Thomson (2001) found that for White female adolescents, the number of family transitions was positively correlated to age of sexual initiation. This was not found to be true of Black female adolescents. However, for Black female adolescents, it was the amount of time spent in a single-parent home during adolescence that correlated to age of first sexual intercourse (Martin & Hutchinson, 2001; Wu & Thomson, 2001). Another study conducted by Martin and Hutchinson (2001) showed that Black adolescent females who showed high self-efficacy, self-responsibility, self-protection, believed in getting an education, and wanted financial independence were able to abstain from having sex while in their teens.

One answer to reducing the age of sexual initiation is to keep minority students in school and focused on a future. Studies need to be directed toward examining the behaviors students exhibit prior to withdrawing from school so educators can plan more effective strategies for prevention. Students may delay physical withdrawal from school until they are in junior high or high school, but they may begin to leave emotionally and mentally in much earlier grades. In addition, students who behave in ways that increase the possibility of suspension or expulsion from school may be surreptitiously withdrawing from school. When a student who has negative experiences in school is suspended, the suspension may be reinforcing for that student. Is it possible that our educational system discourages the participation of students who do not fit the norm of the average student and covertly or overtly attempts to remove these students from the system? The consequences to breaking rules in school seem to be irrevocably connected to subsequent denial of education. Does it make sense to suspend or expel a student for truancy?

The tendency of research to focus on factors unrelated to school responsibility for dropout behaviors may emanate from ideology that promotes the belief that it is easier to fix certain students so they can better function in the traditional educational setting than it is to change the education system to accommodate the diverse needs of students. When students feel culturally or racially isolated and when their style of learning does not conform to the traditional modes of education, they may feel discouraged, disempowered, and alienated and, thus, cease to pursue their education. All students have the right to feel involved and accepted in the classroom, and educators must examine their roles in the estrangement of certain students (Wehlage & Rutter, 1986). The focus of prevention must shift from attempting to mold students to adapt to standard educational criteria to determining how the school system can be restructured to recognize and respond to the diverse requirements of all students.

CASE STUDY: AFTERMATH

Mary enrolled in the community college and used various free services (e.g., personal counseling, group counseling, and human resource classes) to learn more effective life management skills and improve her emotional well-being. She received her associate degree in 1993 and her bachelor of arts in psychology in 1995. She completed her master's degree in 1998 and is currently fulfilling her vocational dream of counseling children from disadvantaged environments.

SUMMARY

The continued increase of pregnancy rates among adolescents in the United States implies that the strategies established by current programs to prevent adolescent pregnancy are not working. Many variables contribute to the effectiveness of intervention programs. For example, problem definition, setting, project design, curriculum, and execution of services are important determinants of program performance. However, even excellently designed pregnancy prevention programs may be unsuccessful when the target group is already engaging in risk-taking activity. Studies have suggested that pregnancy prevention programs may be more successful when they incorporate multiple systems (e.g., community, family, school) and when participants have not yet experienced sexual intercourse. Consequently, professionals recommend starting comprehensive sexuality education in elementary school because programs that target preadolescents have a greater likelihood of reaching young people before they become sexually active. However, many adults believe sexuality education promotes sexual activity and resist comprehensive sexuality programs, especially those that provide information about birth control or that encompass preadolescents. Although studies reveal sexuality education does not encourage or increase sexual experimentation, program developers often comply with societal preferences, modify middle school and high school curricula, and avoid offering sexuality education to elementary school students. Regardless of this attempt to deny sexuality education to our nation's children, more preadolescents are initiating sexual activity each year. Unfortunately, because of their lack of knowledge and immature thinking processes, American children are becoming increasingly vulnerable to the negative consequences of unprotected sexual activity (e.g., HIV/AIDS, STDs, pregnancy). Moreover, when children rear children, the repercussions for the young parents, their offspring, and our society are enormous. Thus, the development of responsible and effective pregnancy prevention programs is essential for the protection and preservation of our nation's future generations. (For additional information on related sources on the World Wide Web, see the Appendix.)

REFERENCES

Adger, H. (1991). Problems of alcohol and other drug use and abuse in adolescents. *Journal of Adolescent Health, 12*, 606–613.

Alan Guttmacher Institute. (1994). *Sex and America's teenagers*. New York: Author.

Allen-Meares, P. (1989). Adolescent sexuality and premature parenthood: Role of the Black church in prevention. *Journal of Social Work and Human Sexuality, 8*, 133–142.

Allen-Meares, P. (1991). Educating adolescents on the dangers of premature childbearing and drug use: A focus on prevention. *Child and Adolescent Social Work, 8*, 327–338.

Azzarto, J. (1997). A young women's support group: Prevention of a different kind. *Health and Social Work, 22*, 299–305.

Barber, L., & McCellan, M. (1987). Looking for America's dropouts: Who are they? *Phi Delta Kappan, 69*, 256–263.

Barth, R., Fetro, J., Leland, N., & Volkan, K. (1992). Preventing adolescent pregnancy with social and cognitive skills. *Journal of Adolescent Research, 7*, 208–232.

Bayatpour, M., Wells, R., & Holford, S. (1992). Physical and sexual abuse as predictors of substance use and suicide among pregnant teenagers. *Journal of Adolescent Health, 13*, 128–132.

Bell, A. (1997). Pregnant on purpose. *Teen Magazine, 41*(8), 106.

Berenson, A., San Miguel, V., & Wilkinson, G. (1992). Violence and its relationship to substance abuse in adolescent pregnancy. *Journal of Adolescent Health, 13*, 470–474.

Blake, B. J., & Bentov, L. (2001). Geographical mapping of unmarried teen births and selected sociodemographic variables. *Public Health Nursing, 18*, 33–39.

Blinn, L., & Stenberg, L. (1993). Feelings about self and body during adolescent pregnancy. *Families in Society: The Journal of Contemporary Human Services, 74*, 282–290.

Bloch, D. (1991). Missing measures of the who and why of school dropouts: Implications for policy and research. *The Career Quarterly, 40*, 36–47.

Brewster, K., Billy, J., & Grady, W. (1993). Social context and adolescent behavior. The impact of community on the transition to sexual activity. *Social Forces, 71*, 713–740.

Brooks-Gunn, J., & Furstenberg, F., Jr. (1989). Adolescent sexual behavior. *American Psychologist, 44*, 249–257.

Centers for Disease Control and Prevention. (2002). *Adolescent and school health: Sexual behaviors*. Retrieved April 30, 2000, from http://www.cdc.gov/nccdphp/dash/sexualbehaviors facctssheet.htm

Cervera, N. (1993a). Decision making for pregnant adolescents: Applying reasoned action theory to research and treatment. *Families in Society: The Journal of Contemporary Human Services, 74*, 355–365.

Cervera, N. (1993b). Serving pregnant and parenting teens. *Families in Society: The Journal of Contemporary Human Services, 74*, 323.

Christmon, K. (1990). Parental responsibility and self-image of African American fathers. *Families in Society: The Journal of Contemporary Human Services, 71*, 563–567.

Christopher, F., & Roosa, M. (1990). An evaluation of an adolescent pregnancy prevention program: Is "just say no" enough? *Family Relations, 39*, 68–72.

Collins, J., Robin, L., Wooley, S., Fenley, D., Hunt, P., Taylor, J., et al. (2002). Programs-That-Work: CDC's guide to effective programs that reduce health-risk behavior of youth. *Journal of School Health, 72*, 93–100.

Combs-Orme, T. (1993). Health effects of adolescent pregnancy: Implications for social workers. *Families in Society: The Journal of Contemporary Human Services, 74*, 344–354.

Committee on Adolescence, American Academy of Pediatrics. (2001). Condom use by adolescents. *Pediatrics, 107*, 1463–1470.

Cook, S. (2001, February 28). Deciding it's ok to wait. *Christian Science Monitor*, 15–19.

Croft, C., & Asmussen, L. (1992). Perceptions of mothers, youth, and educators: A path toward detente regarding sexuality education. *Family Relations, 41*, 452–459.

Dearden, K., Hale, C., & Alvarez, J. (1992). The education antecedents of teen fatherhood. *British Journal of Educational Psychology, 62*, 139–147.

Dryfoos, J., & Heisler, T. (1978). Contraceptive services for adolescents: An overview. *Family Planning Perspectives, 10*, 229–233.

Foster, H., Green, L., & Smith, M. (1990). A model for increasing access: Teenage pregnancy prevention. *Journal of Health Care for the Poor and Underserved, 1*, 136–146.

Franklin, C., & Corcoran, J. (2000). Preventing adolescent pregnancy: A review of programs and practices. *Social Work, 45*, 40–56.

Franklin, C., Grant, D., Corcoran, J., Miller, P., & Bultman, L. (1997). Effectiveness of prevention programs for adolescent pregnancy: A meta-analysis. *Journal of Marriage and the Family, 59*, 551–567.

Freeman, E. (1989). Adolescent fathers in urban communities: Exploring their needs and role in preventing pregnancy. *Journal of Social Work and Human Sexuality, 8*, 113–131.

Furstenberg, F., Jr., Brooks-Gunn, J., & Chase-Lansdale, L. (1989). Teenaged pregnancy and childbearing. *American Psychologist, 44*, 313–320.

Goodyear, R. K. (2002). A concept map of male partners in teenage pregnancy: Implications for school counselors. *Professional School Counseling, 5*, 186–194.

Harold, N. (1988). School-based clinics. *Health and Social Work, 13*, 303–305.

Hofferth, S. (1991). Programs for high-risk adolescents: What works? *Evaluation and Program Planning, 14*, 3–16.

Kaplan, D. (2002, April 23). *Abstinence education: Hearings before the Subcommittee on Health of the House Energy and Commerce Committee* (FDCH Congressional testimony).

Kirby, D. (2001). Understanding what works and what doesn't work in reducing adolescent sexual risk-taking. *Family Planning Perspective, 33*, 276–281.

Kiselica, M., Stroud, J., Stroud, J., & Rotzien, A. (1992). Counseling the forgotten client: The teen father. *Journal of Mental Health Counseling, 14*, 338–351.

Kluger, J. (1998, October 26). The hot shot. *Time*, 69.

Koniak-Griffin, D., & Brecht, M. (1997). AIDS risk behaviors, knowledge, and attitudes among pregnant adolescents and young mothers. *Health Education & Behavior, 24*, 613–623.

Koshar, J. H. (2001). Teen pregnancy 2001—Still no easy answers. *Pediatric Nursing, 27*, 505–509.

Kriepe, R. (1983). Prevention of adolescent pregnancy: A developmental approach. In E. R. McAnarney (Ed.), *Premature adolescent parenthood and pregnancy* (pp. 37–59). New York: Grune & Stratton.

Mapanga, K. (1997, March–April). The perils of adolescent pregnancy. *World Health, 50*(2), 16–18.

Marsiglio, W., Hutchinson, W., & Cohan, M. (2001). Young men's procreative identity: Becoming aware, being aware and being responsible. *Journal of Marriage and the Family, 63*, 123–136.

Martin, K. K., & Hutchinson, S. A. (2001). Low-income Africa American adolescents who avoid pregnancy: Touch girls who rewrite negative scripts. *Qualitative Health Research, 11*, 238–257.

McCullough, M., & Scherman, A. (1991). Adolescent pregnancy: Contributing factors and strategies for prevention. *Adolescence, 26*, 809–816.

Mcilhaney, J., Jr. (2002). *Abstinence education: Hearings before the Subcommittee on Health of the House Energy and Commerce Committee* (FDCH Congressional testimony).

Meyer, V. (1991). A critique of adolescent prevention research: The invisible White male. *Adolescence, 26*, 217–222.

Nix, L., Pasteur, A., & Servance, M. (1988). A focus group study of sexually active Black male teenagers. *Adolescence, 23*, 741–751.

Nye, F. (1976). *School-age parenthood: Consequences for babies, mothers, fathers, grandparents, and others*. Pullman: Washington State University, Cooperative Extension Service.

O'Donnell, L., O'Donnell, C. R., & Stueve, A. (2001). Early sexual initiation and subsequent sex-related risks among urban minority youth: The reach for health study. *Family Planning Perspectives, 33*, 268–275.

Ogg, E. (1976). *Unmarried teenagers and their children* (Public Affairs Pamphlet No. 537). New York: Public Affairs Press.

Olsen, R., & Farkas, G. (1987). *The effect of economic opportunity and family background on adolescent fertility among low-income Blacks* (Final report to the National Institute of Child Health and Human Development, Grant No. R01-HD-19153). Columbus: Ohio State University.

Patterson, D. (1990). Gaining access to community resources: Breaking the cycle of adolescent pregnancy. *Journal of Health Care for the Poor and Underserved, 1*, 147–149.

Plotnick, R. (1993). The effect of social policies on teenage pregnancy and childbearing. *Families in Society: The Journal of Contemporary Human Services, 74*, 324–328.

Ravert, A., & Martin, J. (1997). Family stress, perception of pregnancy and age of first menarche among pregnant adolescent adolescents. *Adolescence, 32*, 261–269.

Resnick, M., Blum, R., Bose, J., Smith, M., & Toogood, R. (1990). Characteristics of unmarried adolescent mothers: Determinants of child rearing versus adoption. *American Journal of Orthopsychiatry, 60*, 577–584.

Rhodes, J., Fischer, K., Ebert, L., & Meyers, A. (1993). Patterns of service utilization among pregnant and parenting African American adolescents. *Psychology of Women Quarterly, 17*, 257–274.

Schamess, S. (1993). The search for love: Unmarried adolescent mothers' views of, and relationships with, men. *Adolescence, 28*, 425–438.

Seitz, V., & Apfel, N. (1993). Adolescent mothers and repeated childbearing: Effects of a school-based intervention program. *American Journal of Orthopsychiatry, 63*, 572–581.

Sellers, D., McGraw, S., & McKinlay, J. (1994). Does the promotion and distribution of condoms increase teen sexual activity? *American Journal of Public Health, 84*, 1952–1959.

Smith, P. B., Buzi, R. S., Weinman, M. L., & Mumford, D. (2001). The use of focus groups to identify needs and expectations of young fathers in a male involvement program. *Journal of Sex Education and Therapy, 26*, 100–105.

Smith, S., & Ramirez, S. (1997, March–April). Teenage birthrates—variations by state. *Public Health Reports, 112*, 173.

Softas-Nall, B., Baldo, T., & Williams, S. (1997). Counselor trainee perception of Hispanic, Black, and White teenage expectant mothers and fathers. *Journal of Multicultural Counseling and Development, 25*, 234–243.

Somers, C. L., Gleason, J. H., Johnson, S. A., & Fahlman, M. M. (2001). Adolescents' and teachers' perceptions of a teen pregnancy prevention program. *American Secondary Education, 29*(3), 51–66.

State specific birth rates for teenagers: United States, 1990–1996. (1997). *Journal of the American Medical Association, 278*, 1143–1147.

Stevens-Simon, C., Kaplan, D., & McAnarney, E. (1993). Factors associated with pre-term delivery among pregnant adolescents. *Society for Adolescent Medicine, 14*, 340–342.

Voydanoff, P., & Donnelly, B. (1990). *Adolescent sexuality and pregnancy*. Newbury Park, CA: Sage.

Watson, F., & Kelly, M. (1988). Targeting the at-risk male: A strategy for adolescent pregnancy prevention. *Journal of the National Medical Association, 81*, 453–456.

Wehlage, G., & Rutter, R. (1986). Dropping out: How much do schools contribute to the problem? *Teachers College Record, 87*, 374–392.

Whitbeck, L., Hoyt, D., Miller, M., & Kao, M. (1992). Parental support, depressed affect, and sexual experience among adolescents. *Youth and Society, 24*, 166–177.

White, C., & White, M. (1991). The Adolescent Family Life Act: Content, findings, and policy recommendations for pregnancy prevention programs. *Journal of Clinical Child Psychology, 20*, 58–70.

Wingert, P. (1998, May 1). The battle over falling birthrates. *Newsweek, 131*, 40.

Wu, L. L., & Thomson, E. (2001). Race differences in family experience and early sexual initiation. *Journal of Marriage and the Family, 63*, 682–697.

Zabin, L., Stark, H., & Emerson, M. (1991). Reasons for delay in contraceptive clinic utilization. *Journal of Adolescent Health, 12*, 225–232.

APPENDIX

For additional information on the World Wide Web

The Alan Guttmacher Institute
http://www.agi-usa.org

Choosing the Best
http://www.choosingthebest.org

Friends First
http://friendsfirst.org

National Abstinence Clearing House
http://www.abstinence.net

National Campaign to Prevent Teen Pregnancy
http://www.teenpregnancy.org

Planned Parenthood
http://www.plannedparenthood.org

Resource Center for Adolescent Pregnancy Prevention
http://www.etr.org/recapp

Teen Health and the Media
http://depts.washington.edu/ecttp/index.html

Teen Sexuality in a Culture of Confusion
http://www.intac.com/~jdeck/habib

10 | A Future in Jeopardy: Adolescents and AIDS

Lizbeth A. Gray, Donna A. Champeau, and Reese M. House*

Jennifer is an 18-year-old American adolescent. She has just tested HIV-positive. She is fairly certain she contracted the virus through sexual contact, although she is not sure when or with whom. She frequented many parties in which alcohol was abundant, and she, along with many of her friends, drank to the point of passing out. A few times while she was drinking at these parties, she had sexual intercourse. She found it hard to say no to sexual advances when she was under the influence of alcohol. Because of her current HIV-positive status, her family has expressed mixed reactions including confusion, some of her friends have rejected her, she has been depressed, and she has had a difficult time talking about her illness.

Talking about high-risk behaviors for HIV/AIDS, projected numbers, causal agents, transmission processes, and prevention strategies in an intellectual and objective manner is relatively easy. Speaking of the possibility of Jennifer's illness progression is harder. To embrace the pain associated with these experiences is difficult, and to deal with institutions and communities that contribute to a family's pain through roadblocks erected from ignorance is frustrating. This chapter focuses on HIV/AIDS information that we need to know as counselors and other professionals working with adolescents. What we are asking readers to do is learn about HIV/AIDS, integrate the information, and open their hearts to the anguish that HIV/AIDS is continuing to cause in our society. We must begin to emphasize how to learn to live with this disease by incorporating hope and positive perspectives instead of only despair. We must learn to understand this disease with our minds and our hearts.

There is clear evidence that the human immunodeficiency virus (HIV), which causes AIDS, is spreading rapidly among adolescents in the United States. As of December 2001, 4,428 adolescents between the ages of 13 and 19 have been diagnosed with AIDS (Centers for Disease Control and Prevention [CDC], 2002c). This small number is misleading because HIV, without drug treatments, has an average latency of 10 years. The CDC reported in June 2001 that 27,880 Americans between the ages of 20 and 24 years had been diagnosed with AIDS. Because of the long latency period, virtually all of these young adults are believed to have contracted the virus while in their teens. Ramifications of this crisis are far-reaching, and there is no doubt that the health and welfare of today's adolescents are in jeopardy. The HIV/AIDS pandemic continues to have a tremendous social and psychological impact on individuals, families, schools, and communities.

*Special acknowledgment to Oregon State University graduate students Beth A. Hilberg and Amy M. Goodall for their invaluable assistance.

There is no cure for HIV disease and no vaccine; thus, adolescents will continue to be vulnerable to HIV infection and AIDS for the foreseeable future. Adolescents are at risk for HIV because they are sexually active, often do not use condoms, may have multiple sexual partners, and do not use precautions if they believe that their partner is safe. A small percentage of adolescents are also injection drug users. The antecedents for these behaviors are many. As adolescents continue to engage in unprotected sex and to use drugs intravenously, the risk escalates.

Adolescents have a hard time believing that contracting HIV is a possibility for them. Only a small number of the thousands of adolescents infected with HIV are aware of their seropositive status, and those who know they are positive often keep it secret to avoid rejection by friends or family. Because their peers do not manifest symptoms of the syndrome, it is easy to understand why adolescents in general do not see themselves at risk for HIV/AIDS. The image of AIDS as a disease of gay men and injection drug users has also allowed youth to feel invulnerable to HIV. Even adolescent boys who experiment with unprotected sex with other males may not see themselves at risk if they do not self-identify as gay. Others believe that they cannot get HIV/AIDS from someone with whom they are in love or with whom they engage in serial monogamy. It is difficult to counter these myths when messages from some parents, churches, and government agencies continue to put forth the idea that monogamy, marriage, and love are equated with health whereas promiscuity and drug addiction are the sole source of HIV/AIDS.

Adolescents take risks on a daily basis. No magic bullets have been found to prevent adolescents from becoming pregnant, help them refrain from drunk or dangerous driving, or stop drug abuse. Indeed, the only possible effective weapons in the fight against the spread of HIV are education, compassion, and reason. Prevention and intervention programs must be offered that are sensitive and take into consideration the multicultural needs of adolescents, families, schools, and communities. Contemporary and accessible services that address developmental needs must be designed for all adolescents. The role of the family must be targeted in all HIV/AIDS education efforts. States must include HIV/AIDS prevention programs as an integral part of comprehensive school health education for all public school students. There is a need to develop special educational outreach programs for hard-to-reach groups of adolescents engaging in behaviors that put them at risk of becoming HIV infected.

For those infected adolescents, we must help them continue to live their lives fully and in the ways they choose. Kain (1998) asked us to be mindful about understanding the difference between what it means to counsel HIV-positive clients in the 1980s and now. Instead of primarily helping HIV-positive adolescents face their diagnosis and death, we must now counsel people living with the disease without separating their illness from the rest of their lives.

PROBLEM DEFINITION

Factual Information About HIV/AIDS

The cause of AIDS is believed to be a retrovirus that targets and destroys certain white blood cells essential to the functioning of the body's immune system (CDC, 2001c). Once the immune system is severely depressed, opportunistic infections develop that typically cause death if there is no medical intervention. When an individual contracts the AIDS virus, he or she is infected for life. To date, there is no cure for HIV, but because treatment in recent years has been promising and mortality rates have dropped, there seems to be a false sense of security among the younger population. It is predicted that an effective vaccine may be available in 7–10 years (Makgoba, Solomon, & Tucker, 2002). It is still important to remember that although vaccines to prevent HIV infection are being developed, a vaccine will only prevent new infections, not offer a cure for those already infected.

HIV is not as contagious as other well-known viruses such as the common cold and is not transmissible through casual social contact such as coughing, sneezing, shaking hands, sharing eating utensils, or using the same telephone. The virus is actually quite fragile and is quickly killed on environmental surfaces when treated with disinfectants. Medical authorities repeatedly state that transmission occurs only through three modes: unprotected high-risk sexual contact, exposure to infected blood or blood products (e.g., sharing needles, blood transfusions), and passage of the virus from a woman to her fetus or newborn infant. HIV can be transmitted from the mother to the child during pregnancy or delivery or through breast milk. In addition to blood and semen, vaginal and cervical secretions are known to contain the virus and may account for female-to-male transmission. Body fluids that may transmit the virus are those surrounding the brain, spinal cord, bone joints, and an unborn baby (CDC, 2001c). It is thought that the vast majority of HIV-infected persons are carriers who are unaware that they have been exposed to the virus but are nevertheless capable of infecting others. Saliva, tears, urine, cerebrospinal fluid, and feces may also contain traces of the virus in infected persons but not in sufficient amounts to transmit the virus to another person (CDC, 2001a).

Since HIV/AIDS was first reported in the United States, those individuals diagnosed have been predominantly homosexual or bisexual males. In other areas of the world, however, heterosexual transmission of HIV accounts for the clear majority of cases. In the United States the percentage of heterosexual AIDS cases has increased each year. Of the total AIDS cases reported among adults and adolescents as of December 2001, 11% contracted the virus through unprotected heterosexual activity (CDC, 2002c). HIV/AIDS is a problem among all races, but a disproportionate number of African Americans and Hispanics are infected with the virus in the United States. Approximately 38% of AIDS cases in the United States are among African Americans, who constitute 12% of the U.S. population (CDC, 2002a), and 19% are among Hispanics, who constitute 13% (CDC, 2002b).

Many people infected with HIV have no symptoms when they are first infected, whereas others experience flulike symptoms 1 week to 1 month after infection. These symptoms may include tiredness, fever, swollen lymph glands, and headaches. Unlike the common cold, symptoms of the person with AIDS are ongoing and persistent. More persistent and severe symptoms may not occur for 10 or more years (National Institute of Allergy and Infectious Diseases, 2000). The virus frequently affects the brain and central nervous system, causing confusion or dementia. People living with AIDS frequently contract life-threatening infections such as Pneumocystis carinii pneumonia or a type of cancer known as Kaposi's sarcoma.

With the advent of improved medical practices, experimental drug treatment, and new drugs approved by the U.S. Food and Drug Administration, people are living longer with AIDS. The life expectancy for someone with an HIV-positive diagnosis has almost tripled in the last 20 years because of changes with earlier reporting practices and new, effective antiviral therapy. Age-adjusted death rates from HIV infection in the United States declined 42% from 1996 to 1997, and this has slowed considerably with a 10% decline in 1999–2000. HIV infection fell from 8th to 14th among leading causes of death in the United States. Furthermore, by December 2001, it was ranked as low as the 18th leading cause of death (CDC, 2002f). These figures mean that new treatments have been very effective in extending lives, but they do not mean that there has been a reduction in HIV transmission. From 1999 to 2000, the number of deaths among persons with AIDS fell only 11%, and the total number of people living with AIDS increased 7.9% (CDC, 2001b).

Adolescents Are at Risk

In 2001, AIDS was the sixth most frequent killer of youth 15–24 years of age (CDC, 2002e). HIV is primarily spread among adolescents through unprotected sexual contact with an infected person or by sharing a needle with an infected person in the course of intravenous drug use. A national survey of college undergraduates reported that 80% to 90% of all college students reported having engaged in sexual intercourse. And of those who were sexually active, 43% said they used a condom most of the time (Kellogg, 2002). These statistics along with the fact that adolescents are initiating sexual intercourse at younger ages indicate that many of the nation's younger people continue to be at considerable risk for HIV infection.

The 2001 Youth Risk Behavior Survey conducted by the CDC examined risk behaviors in high school students nationwide. The survey revealed that although 89% of students reported having some HIV/AIDS education in school, only 58% of the 33% of sexually active students used a condom during their last sexual intercourse (CDC, 2002f). There is still a gap between awareness and subsequent risk reduction behaviors. It is important that counselors, and other professionals who deal with youth, not take a back seat on these issues.

Increasing the adolescent's risk for HIV/AIDS is the high percentage of teens who have tried drugs or who use drugs and alcohol on a regular basis. Use of alcohol or drugs such as amphetamines (speed), amyl nitrate (poppers), cocaine, and marijuana impairs judgment and increases the chance of risky behaviors or the sharing of needles (Hsu, 2002). Surveillance data from 2000 across 34 states indicate that drug injection led to at least 6% of HIV diagnoses in those age 13–24 (CDC, 2002e).

Overall, because of the high frequency of sexual activity, failure to use condoms and spermicides, lack of access to good preventative health care, drug involvement, and sexual experimentation and injection drug use, adolescents are particularly vulnerable to contracting HIV/AIDS. The fact that they are not changing risky behavior supports the premise that it is very difficult to convince adolescents to believe in the dangers of HIV/AIDS. A decade ago, Bowler, Sheon, D'Angelo, and Vermund (1992) identified several factors that contribute to adolescent disbelief: (a) susceptibility to peer pressure; (b) propensity to take risks, including sexual and drug experimentation; (c) sense of invulnerability and immortality; and (d) difficulty grasping the long-term adverse consequences of current behavior.

Response of Adolescents

Panic and denial have been common responses to HIV/AIDS among adolescents. When examining these psychological reactions, it is critical to understand the way in which parental and community attitudes affect adolescents' thinking. Often public attitudes about HIV/AIDS, based in part on misinformation and fear of sexuality and AIDS, manifest themselves through adolescents.

Adolescents' anxiety of contracting a deadly disease through sexual activity is heightened by embarrassment about sexual intimacy that is common to the normal developmental processes of adolescents (Santrock, 2003). Many adolescents seem to have factual information about reproduction, birth control, and safer sex practices but lack the skills and maturity necessary to talk effectively about these issues with a partner.

Similarly, some adolescents exhibit a lack of concern or denial with respect to the AIDS epidemic, believing that they are invulnerable. This belief in personal invulnerability, particularly in relationship to health issues, is also an intrinsic developmental feature of adolescents and points to maturity as one key factor in developing a healthy sexuality (Santrock, 2003). Weinstein (1984) established that most adolescents judge their risk level by imagining a stereotype of who will be involved in a negative event (such as contracting HIV/AIDS). People continue to associate AIDS with gay men or injection drug users and intellectually distance themselves from the possibility of contracting AIDS (Henderson, 1998). Weinstein labeled this process as *unrealistic optimism.*

CASE STUDY

Jennifer is one of thousands of American adolescents who are HIV-positive. Although there will be similarities between her experiences and others, it is important to realize that her situation is unique only to her. Each adolescent is an intricate map of emotions, cognitions, personal experiences, physical needs, relationships, and genetic composition, and consequently, counselors and other professionals must expect that there will be no two cases exactly alike. We can learn from Jennifer. We must remember that the following situation does not offer a prescription response to all youth who are struggling with HIV/AIDS.

Identifying Characteristics
Jennifer is an 18-year-old White female who tested HIV-positive 6 months ago. She currently lives with her family.

Presenting Problem
Jennifer's presenting problem was, "Please help me. I am afraid I may get sick and die."

Family History
Jennifer is the oldest of five children. She has three brothers ages 15, 14, and 11 and one sister age 9. The family had been active in the Catholic Church, and the two younger children attend Catholic schools. Her father is 45 years old and works in middle management in a high-tech corporation. Her mother is 43 years old and works part-time as a librarian at the city library.

Jennifer describes a history of "happy family vacations" and frequent outings until her preteen years. In the last year, the family has experienced financial stress and subsequent withdrawal of the father due to a "need to make more money." The mother expresses that at the same time she has felt helpless about the family situation, she sees herself providing continuity to the family. In the absence of her father, Jennifer describes taking over the role of second parent to the two youngest children.

Educational History
Jennifer's grades in high school have ranged between C+ and A−. She is particularly gifted at computer science. Jennifer has always been a vocal student in the classroom, and she describes her senior year of high school as "pretty good."

Social History
Jennifer has always been a well-liked student and considers herself "a party girl." Since her diagnosis, some of her friends have acted cool and aloof toward her. She can-

not help thinking their distancing is because of her HIV-positive status. She no longer attends parties because she is not asked very often to go to them.

Employment History
Jennifer works in the public library and also has a part-time job at the local bakery. She is afraid to tell her employers of her HIV-positive status for fear that they may treat her differently.

Medical History
Jennifer has no significant medical history other than normal childhood illnesses prior to her HIV-positive diagnosis. Jennifer has had sex with approximately five young men. She remembers two experiences of sexual intercourse in which a condom was not used. Currently she shows no sign of a compromised immune system.

Mental Status
Jennifer appeared agitated, restless, and was able to make eye contact only for short periods of time. During the initial contact, she was teary-eyed, admitted great fear, and expressed confusion and helplessness. She struggled to maintain her composure throughout the session. She was reluctant to talk about her sexual history, although she seemed quite willing to relate other information about her past. She expressed bitterness toward her family and friends for "avoiding me like the plague." There was no evidence of tangential thinking or suicidal ideation.

APPROACHES TO PREVENTION

Counselors as Educators

In the absence of treatments or vaccines that are totally effective and available for everyone, we must still rely on risk and harm reduction prevention/education programs to reduce the incidence rate of HIV/AIDS in adolescents such as Jennifer. The goal of such programs is prevention of the spread of the virus through behavioral change. It is critical for counselors and other professionals to expand the definition of helping by accepting the responsibility to provide prevention education about HIV/AIDS. Education may be done with individuals, with families, in the schools, in community programs, or in whatever milieu adolescents are found.

To present effective prevention programming, counselors and other professionals need to be both knowledgeable about AIDS-related issues and comfortable talking about sexuality. In the only national survey of counselor education programs, 243 programs identified AIDS as high priority for inclusion in curricula, yet nearly 40% of the responding programs did not include any AIDS training in their curricula (Gray, House, & Eicken, 1996; House, Eicken, & Gray, 1995). Kain (1998) affirmed that such lack of training suggests that many counselors entering the profession may not be prepared to assist clients with AIDS-related issues. It is essential that counselors learn about HIV/AIDS through attending appropriate continuing education seminars and workshops.

Sexual comfort is the most important qualification of professionals who work with HIV/AIDS and adolescents. No matter how carefully organized HIV/AIDS curricula and outreach strategies are, embarrassed or fearful professionals can inadvertently sabotage HIV/AIDS prevention efforts. Counselors and other professionals are part of a larger American society that typically receives inaccurate information and powerful negative messages about sexuality that impede talking comfortably about this topic.

Communication about sexual issues is frequently made difficult by the profound emotional impact that sexual vocabulary carries. Confusion also arises because many sexual terms lack precision. Consequently, not only is effective communication with adolescents diminished, but also HIV/AIDS professionals may transfer negative emotional feelings to the youth with whom they work.

It is erroneous to assume that counselors have developed sexual comfort as part of their training. Over 10 years ago, a survey of counselor education programs indicated that only 42% offered courses in sexual counseling (Gray, House, & Eicken, 1996). The majority of programs did not require sexuality courses for master's programs in counseling, and no counselor education program surveyed indicated that sexual training for counselors was overemphasized. There is no current information about the status of sexuality training in counselor education so we can only guess that this trend continues.

Becoming sexually comfortable is an ongoing process that is circular and interactive in nature. The sexually uncomfortable person sets an awkward professional atmosphere that invites inhibition. Conversely, success as an HIV/AIDS educator may contribute to the development of a positive self-concept in youth. To work with adolescents at risk for HIV/AIDS, counselors and other professionals must consciously begin the process of increasing their own sexual comfort. This journey begins by actively addressing the following factors that are likely to contribute to physical, mental, or emotional constraint in the role of HIV/AIDS educator and prevention specialist:

- inaccurate sexual knowledge
- inaccurate knowledge about HIV/AIDS
- lack of an explicit sexual vocabulary
- limited practice in talking about sexuality and HIV/AIDS
- lack of identification and resolution of personal sexual issues
- sexual values and biases (e.g., homophobia) that interfere with openness to alternative lifestyles for others.

Prevention via Counseling Individuals

As counselors and other professionals work with adolescents in an HIV/AIDS prevention mode, they will find a range of responses. These include adolescents whose behavior is currently high risk but who are not concerned and those who may be anxious but whose behavior is not risky. This second population has been referred to as the "worried well."

Working with adolescents can take many forms. The individual counseling model is one model that counselors and other professionals might use. The key to the effectiveness of applying the model's concepts is the personal approach of the counselor. Creating a comfortable environment, as suggested earlier, is paramount. It is important to both understand developmental issues that adolescents face and respect adolescent culture. The individual counseling model applies the following nine guidelines:

1. Provide information about HIV/AIDS.
2. Address the difficulties of implementing safer sex plans.
3. Introduce assertiveness techniques and methods for resisting peer pressure.
4. Respond to the emotional and psychological confusion surrounding sexual behaviors and relationship dynamics.

5. Work to build self-esteem.
6. Incorporate exploration about sexual decision making.
7. Utilize active counseling techniques, such as role-plays, so that adolescent clients can rehearse discussing safer sexual behavior and asserting boundaries with prospective partners.
8. Assist the adolescent client in exploring personal values to come to terms with similarities and differences between values of self and family of origin.
9. Refer the adolescent client to community resources for assistance with medical, legal, and social service issues related to HIV/AIDS.

These guidelines are incorporated into a simulation of a counselor's responses to adolescents. The following are sections of dialogues between a school counselor and adolescents in the same high school as Jennifer.

1. *Information*
   Adolescent: I heard that Jennifer has AIDS. I thought only gays got AIDS.
   Counselor: I'm glad that you are concerned about Jennifer and about HIV/AIDS. However, HIV is not just a disease of the gay population. Anyone can get HIV if he or she puts himself or herself at risk. For example, if a person is sexually active, he or she needs to protect himself or herself by using condoms. (The counselor could provide a pamphlet with more information about HIV/AIDS and teens or refer to an appropriate community agency if providing direct information is not an option.)

2. *Safer sex plan*
   Adolescent: I heard that Jennifer didn't use condoms with those guys she slept with. But, forget it, I'm not using condoms . . . they are too stupid.
   Counselor: At first it is hard to use condoms. Can you tell me more about condoms being stupid? What do you mean? (The counselor and the adolescent could discuss safer sex practices [or where to get safer sex information] keeping in mind that the less behavior the counselor asks someone to change the more likely the behavior change will occur. The key concept is "What is the least amount of change that will protect you from being at risk for HIV/AIDS?")

3. *Assertiveness*
   Adolescent: Since hearing about Jennifer, I think I want Steven to use a condom. But he says, "No fucking way will I wear that raincoat on my dick."
   Counselor: It is sometimes hard to stand up for what you believe when people you care about think differently. How about practicing some ways to tell Steven you really mean it about wearing a condom? (Skills such as using "I" language, making eye contact, voice and tone level, and outcome clarification can be utilized when helping adolescents assert themselves.)

4. *Confusion*
   Adolescent: Pam doesn't want to sleep with me anymore. She's afraid she will get AIDS. But it feels so good to be with her.
   Counselor: If sexual intercourse is the source of Pam's concern, what other ways can you be close to her? (A discussion might follow regarding relationships, especially the confusion that often exists about emotional closeness and sexual intercourse.)

5. *Self-esteem*
   Adolescent: I think maybe I deserve to get AIDS like Jennifer. I've never been popular so I have to take who I can. Mary called me a royal slut the other day.

Counselor: Sounds like you don't like yourself very much. We all do things we don't feel good about and things we do feel good about. Let's talk about when you feel good about yourself and when you don't.

6. *Decision making*

Adolescent: Some of the guys only go out with girls who—you know—do it. I don't know what to do anymore because of Jennifer getting AIDS.

Counselor: Making these decisions is not easy. It would be great if there was a right answer that I could give you. What is most important is to help you decide which sexual activities feel right for you and how to be responsible with your choices. (The counselor might want to use the decision-making model [Table 10–4] or the listing of sexual activities model [Table 10–2] included later in this chapter. These models speak to safer sex activities and emphasize that sexuality includes a broad range of activities, including abstinence, and is not limited to penile–vaginal intercourse.)

7. *Communication about safer sex and relationship boundaries*

Adolescent: The speaker at the AIDS assembly said we are supposed to talk to our sexual partners about safer sex and other stuff. But what do you say? And what's this "other stuff"?

Counselor: It is hard to talk about sex. This county health brochure is a place to start. Let's go over it together. Then we can talk (or you can talk to the health clinic staff) about the other stuff like your values, birth control, your feelings about the relationship, and your and your partner's sexual needs.

8. *Values*

Adolescent: My mom thinks that I shouldn't be Jennifer's friend because she has AIDS. But I like her better than any of the other girls. At least she's not a fake.

Counselor: It sounds like you and your mom have a difference in values. Sometimes people whom we care about believe differently than we do. How can I help you talk to your mom about these differences? (This might lead into a discussion of personal and parental values and how we decide what is right for each of us.)

9. *Referral*

Adolescent: I don't know quite how to say this, but I'm worried that I might have AIDS like Jennifer. Last week I slept over at a friend's house, and we messed around. That guy was with Jennifer once.

Counselor: I appreciate your honesty. I have the name of a confidential community clinic that you can go to for information about HIV/AIDS and testing. Tell me more about your concerns.

Working Directly With Families as a Preventative Measure

Although the majority of parents agree it is their responsibility to provide sexuality education to their children, they frequently feel ill prepared to do so. Similarly, parents often struggle with the complexities and specifics regarding HIV/AIDS education even though they might want to be directly involved with their adolescents. It is important to recognize that working with parents, in order to help them effectively educate their own children, is an important role of the counselor and other professionals.

Parent–adolescent education courses about HIV/AIDS are an appropriate and useful prevention measure. For example, classes in which mothers and adolescent daughters participate are currently a popular and an effective way to enhance communication about sensitive issues like sexuality within families. This model has been extremely effective with younger children in that they need to have information about sexuality reinforced by their family members. Seemingly, the same holds true for HIV/AIDS education.

All formal AIDS education programs for adolescents, whether in the school, church, or community setting, should solicit parental input. Parents must be involved in not only the development of curricula but also the implementation. It is exciting to see school- and community-based AIDS educational programs in which parents observe and participate with the educational process. AIDS prevention measures that include homework assignments that encourage family communication are more likely to achieve the final goal: safer behavior that reduces HIV risk for adolescents.

Prevention in the Schools

Most schools have been directly impacted by HIV/AIDS. Some, like in the case of Jennifer, have a student who has been diagnosed HIV-positive; others have students whose family members or friends have HIV or AIDS. Some professionals believe that in the near future all school personnel will have direct or indirect contact with a student who is infected with or affected by HIV disease (Cobia, Carney, & Waggoner, 1998).

Counselors and other professionals need to take the lead in making sure that appropriate HIV/AIDS education is implemented in the schools. In addition to HIV/AIDS curricula, counselors and other professionals can help organize activities such as HIV/AIDS awareness programs, school fundraisers for local prevention programs, and a school health resource center. One specific strategy that many organizations have used is to have HIV-positive persons tell their personal stories. Another is large city schools incorporating health clinics into their campuses. Models for such endeavors can be found through contacting Advocates for Youth (listed in the Appendix at the end of this chapter).

More than 15 years ago the former United States Surgeon General Dr. C. Everett Koop (1988) specifically called for schools to start frank discussions about sexuality and teach children about HIV/AIDS and its dangers at the lowest grade possible. Many schools have answered this call. By 2001, 89% of students in Grades 9–12 reported being taught about AIDS or HIV (CDC, 2001d). Most state health departments have developed AIDS curricula for youth unique to the values and concerns of each geographical area. To achieve optimum effectiveness, HIV/AIDS curricula must include information that is age specific and viewed in terms of a larger health context. For example, in a school setting such information can be included in a communicable disease or health education unit that can be taught as part of a comprehensive K–12 health education curriculum. Such programs must be geared toward adolescents' own needs, perceptions, fears, and concerns and be sensitive to the contemporary youth culture.

Over recent years, Congress has supported abstinence-only education rather than comprehensive sexuality education. Funds for abstinence-only education increased in 2002, and a request has been made by President George W. Bush to increase these funds by another $33 million in 2003. However, research indicates that there is no evidence that abstinence-only education delays sexual initiation or rates of unplanned pregnancies and sexually transmitted diseases. Meanwhile, research does indicate the efficacy of comprehensive sexuality education resulting in positive behavior changes, reducing sexually transmitted infections without increasing the number of sexual partners or encouraging earlier initiation of sexual behavior (Collins, Alagiri, & Summers, 2002). The bottom line is that programs that are limited to an abstinence-only focus fail to address the reality that the majority of American young people engage in risky sexual behavior prior to high school graduation (Parker, 2001).

Comprehensive HIV/AIDS curricula may be viewed as five separate, yet interfacing, content areas that include medical information, risky and safer sexual behaviors, common myths and misinformation, effective sexual decision-making skills, and effective sexual communication skills. Tables 10–1 through 10–5 present examples of the content that can be included in these topical areas. Other curricula examples can be found by contacting the Sexuality Information and Education Council of the United States (SIECUS), which is listed in the Appendix.

Prevention in the Community

Building prevention programs in the community takes place by utilizing networker and advocacy processes. In the role of networker and advocate, one must be knowledgeable about the particular political issues the HIV/AIDS crisis poses. Typical political problems include lack of funding for research and social services, community values that prevent or thwart education about sexual issues, and religious and moral views that might reject some sexual behavior.

Some people believe that promotion of safer sexual behaviors encourages sexual activity among adolescents. Others say that sexuality education belongs in the home, school, and community. It is safe to say that opinions are polarized regarding HIV/AIDS prevention for adolescents. All too evident is that some individuals have an intense emotional investment in their value position about HIV/AIDS and sex education. When working in the community setting, it is realistic to expect opposition and to be prepared to counter it (Collison et al., 1998; Homan, 1999a, 1999b).

TABLE 10–1 | HIV/AIDS Curricula: Medical Information

The most recent medical information about HIV/AIDS includes four areas: cause, acquisition, treatment, and prevention. The questions delineated below are typical questions about the four areas that could be utilized when educating adolescents about HIV/AIDS.

- **What is HIV/AIDS?** HIV/AIDS is a disorder caused by the human immunodeficiency virus that contributes to weakening of the immune system to the point that it is unable to prevent life-threatening infections.

- **How is HIV/AIDS transmitted?** The AIDS virus is spread by unprotected high-risk sexual contact, needle sharing, passage of the virus from infected mother to fetus or newborn infant, exposure to infected blood products, and less commonly through HIV-infected transfused blood or its components. The virus may also be transmitted from infected mother to infant through breast-feeding.

- **How is HIV/AIDS not transmitted?** The AIDS virus is not spread by casual contact such as hugging, kissing, holding hands, touching objects handled by an infected person, toilet seats, dishes, or telephones.

- **Who can get HIV/AIDS?** Anyone who has unprotected high-risk sexual contact with an infected person or who shares needles is at risk for HIV. Having multiple sexual partners increases this risk.

- **Is there a test for HIV?** A blood test can usually identify the presence of antibodies to the AIDS virus. Consult your local AIDS project or state/county health division for the latest information.

- **Is there treatment for AIDS?** There is no cure for HIV/AIDS. However, treatments for AIDS-associated infections are improving, and thus people are living longer and healthier lives with HIV/AIDS.

TABLE 10–2 | HIV/AIDS Curricula: Risky and Safer Sexual Behavior

It is important to include the latest available information about risky and safer sexual behavior in HIV/AIDS curricula for adolescents. Please consult your local or state health agency for the latest updates. When educating adolescents about the risky to safe behaviors identified below, the use of straightforward language is necessary.

- **Risky behaviors** include vaginal and anal intercourse without a condom; oral–anal contact (rimming); putting a hand or fist into vagina or anus (fisting); fingers, tongue, or penis touching the vagina during menstruation; sharing sex toys (e.g., vibrators); oral sex without a condom; masturbation on open/broken skin.

- **Safer behaviors** include vaginal intercourse with a condom*, anal intercourse with a condom, oral sex on a man with a condom, oral sex on a woman with use of a dental dam.

- **Safe behaviors** include kissing if neither person has open cuts or sores, masturbation on healthy skin, touching, massage, fantasy, parallel masturbation, solitary masturbation, clothed body-to-body rubbing, consensual voyeurism, exhibitionism.

- **The safest** behavior is abstinence from sexual contact.

***Use of the condom:** It is only with the proper use of a condom that HIV transmission can be prevented. Condoms can break or slip off during sexual intercourse. There is a correct procedure for applying a condom. It is important to put the condom on the penis prior to any sexual contact. Applying the condom includes squeezing and holding the end of the condom while unrolling it over the entire erect penis. The man must withdraw the penis while still erect to prevent the condom from slipping off and leaking. Condoms must not be reused. Latex condoms are effective barriers against the virus; natural animal skin condoms are not effective. Currently, there is controversy regarding the use of nonoxynol-9 on latex condoms. If additional lubrication is used it is important to avoid oil-based lubricants such as Vaseline, mineral oil, or cold cream. Oil-based lubricants can erode and create holes in the condom. A recommended option is the water-based lubricating jelly K-Y.

For example, advocates must become familiar with the power structure of the community, as well as lines of decision making within specific agencies or programs. Effective community involvement can make a difference between success and failure in addressing HIV/AIDS issues. All points of view must be represented before and during the development of a prevention program. This can be done, in part, by seeking participation from select members of the community who represent diverse populations. These members may disagree about the need for HIV/AIDS education but at the same time may be willing to work toward common community goals. Including adolescents and parents is critical. Additionally, networking with other educators, regionally and nationally, who have successfully addressed controversy in their own communities provides a reference for strategic planning.

TABLE 10–3 | HIV/AIDS Curricula: Common Myths and Misinformation

It is critical for the educator to dispel common myths and misinformation about HIV/AIDS. The following six myths typically are found in the adolescent population:

1. Only gay men and lesbians get HIV/AIDS.
2. Only the sexually promiscuous get HIV/AIDS.
3. Donating and receiving blood in the United States is unsafe.
4. Casual contact such as touching, sneezing, having a meal with/sharing eating utensils with someone who has HIV/AIDS, sharing a bathroom, or going to the same school with a person with HIV/AIDS can transmit the virus.
5. HIV/AIDS can be transmitted through saliva, sweat, and tears.
6. Alcohol and drugs do not increase the risk of contracting HIV/AIDS.

TABLE 10–4 | HIV/AIDS Curricula: Sexual Decision-Making Model

Effective sexual decision-making skills need to be taught in terms of a larger frame of personal values. The exercise below is one example of a sexual decision-making model for adolescents.

Check any of the reasons listed below that you used in deciding to become involved in the following sexual behavior: _____
(Behavior)

_____ I wanted to find out what it felt like.
_____ I was sexually excited.
_____ I wanted to be as experienced as my friends are.
_____ I was talked into it.
_____ I didn't really decide—it just sort of happened.
_____ I felt it would make me feel more mature or adult.
_____ My partner and I decided we were ready for it.
_____ I felt it was about time I tried it.
_____ My parents said it would be okay.
_____ Other: _____

Check any of the reasons listed below that you used in deciding not to participate in the following sexual behavior: _____
(Behavior)

_____ I was scared.
_____ I didn't really like the person.
_____ My parents would disapprove.
_____ I wasn't sure how to do it.
_____ I don't believe people my age should be doing that.
_____ I wanted to wait until I was in love.
_____ I was afraid of getting caught.
_____ My partner wouldn't agree to it.
_____ I was afraid of getting a sexually transmitted disease.
_____ I was afraid of getting HIV/AIDS.
_____ I was afraid it would result in pregnancy.
_____ Other: _____

Possible sexual behaviors
- abstinence from all sexual activity
- holding hands
- hugging
- kissing
- French kissing
- cuddling and caressing
- breast fondling
- rubbing bodies to orgasm
- mutual masturbation
- parallel masturbation
- cunnilingus
- fellatio
- intercourse between the thighs
- intercourse between the breasts
- vaginal intercourse
- anal intercourse
- analingus (rimming)
- brachioproctic sex (fingers/fist in anus)
- use of sex toys
- use of sexual reading material
- use of pornography

continues

TABLE 10–4 | continued

- sex with strangers
- sex with more than one person at a time
- monogamy
- serial monogamy
- use of condoms during oral sex
- use of condoms during vaginal sex
- use of condoms during anal sex
- birth control

Note. From *About Your Sexuality* by D. Calderwood, 1983. Copyright 1983 by Beacon Press. Adapted with permission.

When talking with community members about building or expanding an HIV/AIDS prevention program, professionals must correct misunderstandings by providing the most current and accurate factual information about HIV/AIDS. Professionals can use statistics that speak specifically to their community. For example, in Jennifer's community many of the citizens appear to believe that HIV/AIDS is predominantly a disease afflicting gay men. However, Jennifer, like many other individuals, was infected via heterosexual contact. There are ample data indicating that heterosexual transmission, worldwide, is becoming the most common form of infection. Women, in particular, are becoming infected with HIV at an alarmingly rapid rate. From 1999 to 2000, AIDS incidence declined in most populations but increased in women and persons infected via heterosexual contact (CDC, 2001b). These data are important so parents with heterosexual children recognize the need to educate their children about HIV/AIDS.

Some education experts (ActionAid, 2002) specifically mention that cooperation from churches is essential for effective community educational programs. Although some religious organizations have taken positions opposing HIV/AIDS education on moral grounds, others are willing and eager to participate in educational efforts. For example, American Friends Service Committee, a Quaker organization, purports that withholding information about safer sexual behavior is immoral because of health implications.

Community members who are angry, confused, or anxious about HIV/AIDS deserve the help of professionals who are sensitive to local community concerns. Yet, the public must recognize that the goal of HIV/AIDS prevention programs is to focus on health issues, not to become blocked by differing views of morality. Over 10 years ago, Calamidas (1991) set an important tone for the future by advocating that:

TABLE 10–5 HIV/AIDS Curricula: Sexual Communication Skills

Effective sexual communication skills are critical for developing a healthy sexuality. Listed below are several areas that need to be talked about with a prospective partner prior to a sexual relationship. Counselors and other professionals can use many creative methods to operationalize communication about these issues. Role-plays, fishbowls, mock advertisements, and use of art, dance, music, video, drama, and popular film are only a few possibilities.

1. Feelings
2. Significance of the sexual encounter
3. Sexual preferences and needs
4. Birth control methods
5. Safer sex plans including abstinence

educators should not be intimidated into offering educational programs that are weakened in order to avoid controversy . . . educators must emphasize that they are compelled to discuss all aspects of controversial and ethical issues and it is imperative that they be allowed to freely answer all questions . . . if educators acknowledge that values and value positions are inherent to the educational program and that the primary value of concern is health, controversy can be reduced. (pp. 56–57)

INTERVENTION STRATEGIES

Working Systemically With HIV-Diagnosed Youth: An Integrated Individual, Family, School, and Community Model

Counselors and other professionals need to undertake multifaceted roles when working with an HIV-diagnosed youth. No singular intervention is effective. Different roles include, but are not limited to, intervening with HIV-positive adolescents individually and with families, schools, and communities. A systems approach to intervention is critical. However, it is important for the counselor or other professional to be aware of conflicting responsibilities inherent in these roles.

Working with the HIV/AIDS-diagnosed youth through one-on-one or group counseling takes sensitivity, skill, compassion, and affirmation. The adolescent who has HIV/AIDS is facing a life-threatening illness and probable stigmatization by some individuals in society. The adolescent might be confused about the medical aspects of the disease. He or she may feel extremely guilt-ridden and regretful about past sexual experiences or drug use. Or he or she may not. It is the counselors' responsibility to avoid making an adolescent's experience into what they want it to be, but instead to work hard at understanding what it is to their client (Kain, 1998). Helping the HIV-positive adolescent from a perspective of hope and respect is paramount.

The family of the HIV-positive adolescent is also struggling with its own set of issues. For example, Jennifer's family consists of three brothers, ages 15, 14, 11, and one sister, age 9. Jennifer's siblings have all felt some sense of stigmatization and ostracism since their sister's diagnosis became public. They are aware that Jennifer may die at a young age. This possibility overwhelms both parents, and they have responded through withdrawal and verbal helplessness. Each of the siblings has responded differently with his or her own unique issues.

Further, an adolescent's school community is affected by an HIV-positive diagnosis. From the case study of Jennifer, it is possible that several other adolescents may be directly linked to the original HIV carrier. These adolescents, like Jennifer, may have since had unprotected sexual experiences. Many of Jennifer's classmates and their parents are reacting to the information that Jennifer is HIV-positive with ignorance, others with hostility. Teachers and administrators from Jennifer's school are immobilized. There has been no organized response by the school to the concerns exhibited by students and parents. The teachers struggle, from lack of experience and education, with how best to address their own feelings and those of the student body.

The community at large in which the HIV-positive youth lives needs attention. Counselors and other professionals need to be proactive with local community agencies to ensure that Jennifer receives the care and treatment to which she is entitled. As in the landmark case of one teenager, Ryan White, Jennifer still may need social, political, and legal advocacy to help fight the social injustices that affect adolescents with HIV/AIDS. (Ryan White contracted AIDS as a child from blood transfusions. He lived in Kokomo, Indiana, and was not allowed to continue enrollment in his local school. Ryan died on April 8, 1990, at the age of 19.)

Table 10–6 is one model of how to work with the adolescent with HIV/AIDS by using a multidimensional and affirming framework integrating all components of the system. It is important to remember that the suggested steps are not linear, and emphasis is dependent on the relationship with a particular adolescent, his or her family, school, and community. Usually, therapeutic issues center around helping people find the personal strength and resources to cope with a positive diagnosis. The two most important aspects of counseling with a person who is HIV-positive and others affected by the illness are a willingness to be a compassionate listener and a commitment to advocate assertively for the rights of the individual with HIV/AIDS.

The following is an example of how the counselor or other professionals might begin to respond to Jennifer, the 18-year-old who is HIV-positive, from an affirming and integrated perspective. The guidelines from Table 10–6 are used as the framework for intervention.

Assessing

Jennifer currently feels well physically. Her psychological stress, however, is high; her core issues seem to be fear of death and abandonment as well as guilt about her sex-

---

TABLE 10–6 | Guidelines for Counseling the HIV/AIDS Diagnosed Youth: Utilizing a Multidimensional Framework Integrating All Components of the System

- **Assessing**
  1. Degree of medical illness
  2. Degree of psychological stress
  3. Degree of social isolation–support systems
  4. Significant others and family responses
  5. Impact of daily living
  6. Financial need

- **Educating**
  1. Effects of the virus
  2. Medical intervention
  3. Living with the virus
  4. Health care, insurance, and Social Security issues
  5. Transmission of the virus
  6. Sexual activity options

- **Assisting**
  1. Networking with social agencies
  2. Responding to employment, housing, and discrimination needs
  3. Developing support systems

- **Counseling**
  1. Providing an emotionally caring atmosphere
  2. Viewing the illness contextually and in relation to the rest of life
  3. Working with denial about the HIV/AIDS diagnosis
  4. Addressing rejection and stigma issues
  5. Addressing loss and grieving issues
  6. Acknowledging an individual's unique experience of being HIV-positive
  7. Supporting the lifestyle desired
  8. Teaching stress identification and reduction techniques
  9. Bridging communication with friends and family

- **Advocating**
  1. Social/cultural
  2. Political
  3. Legal

ual contact with several partners. She wonders about whether she can continue to have her "normal life" and for how long. Jennifer is afraid of not being able to go to the prom, stay the night with her friends, and take the car to the beach. Currently, her emotional support system is weak. However, the possibility of building support exists with parents, siblings, former friends, and teachers. Some of Jennifer's daily needs are being met. For example, her parents provide basic food and shelter. She is currently receiving consistent health care and medication from a family physician and infectious disease specialist. The family's financial situation prior to the illness was tenuous and is further stretched by the high medical costs associated with HIV/AIDS.

Educating

It is important that Jennifer, her family, and other individuals understand the life cycle of HIV/AIDS and its related infections. Information must be shared about learning to live hopefully and fully with the disease, and that focuses on quality of life rather than quantity. With accurate information about HIV, educated choices can be made. One reason for some of the emotional and relational distancing may be due to misinformation. In addition, Jennifer and her family need accurate information about the effects of medications Jennifer is taking so that they can distinguish between side effects and the symptoms of the infections associated with HIV/AIDS. If there is understanding about the course and the cyclical nature of the virus, Jennifer and her family will be able to make the most of times when she is feeling well. Because there is a connection between physiological responses of the body and health habits, it is imperative that Jennifer eats and sleeps well.

Assisting

It is essential to work with community agencies that can provide outside assistance for Jennifer. These include, but are not limited to, local HIV/AIDS projects and county and state health departments. Frequently, services are duplicated or ignored because of lack of coordination. It is especially critical to help facilitate the effective use of multiple helping systems. For example, support groups usually exist for persons with HIV/AIDS, and volunteers may be available to help with transportation and other practical needs. These kinds of intervention would give an HIV-positive person the opportunity to continue with his or her life as much as is possible and also relieve stress on the family as primary caregivers. The issues of medical expenses for the family also need to be addressed through linking with appropriate agencies, such as Social Security, home health care, and legal aid. The student body at large and the staff of the school may also have special needs due to public awareness of Jennifer's diagnosis. For example, an aggressive HIV/AIDS education program should be implemented in the school to reduce unnecessary fear and stigmatization.

It is critical to make efforts to help Jennifer live the kind of life she wants. This may include continuing all the activities she is currently involved in, including part-time employment at the library and bakery. If Jennifer's health deteriorates, then education and career modifications need to be planned. For example, the school may need to be contacted and a plan initiated so Jennifer can continue her high school education. If needed, special services of the high school should be identified.

Although not fully functioning, Jennifer's primary support system is her family. Family meetings should be held to work with the withdrawal patterns of her brothers and sister, the distancing of her father, and the helplessness of her mother. It might be important for the family to understand the caretaker role Jennifer plays as oldest sibling in the family and possible fears that family members associate with the prospect of losing such a caretaker's full energy. The family needs to come to terms with the stigma that they associate with having a child/sibling who has HIV/AIDS. Family members must be assisted to recognize the critical part they play in supporting Jennifer, and that their support is intrinsically connected to her continued physical and psychological well-being.

Another potential support system for Jennifer is her many female friends at school. These girls, and their parents, need special outreach efforts to reestablish positive relationships. Jennifer's teachers, especially ones such as the computer specialist whom she felt close to, also need to be utilized as potential support people.

Counseling: Individual and Family

When establishing a helping relationship with Jennifer, the counselor must be particularly emotionally supportive and affirming. Jennifer's values, culture, and developmental issues—her context—cannot be separated from the core of the counseling. It is also important for the counselor to commit to a long-term counseling relationship with Jennifer. The first step in the process is to assist Jennifer in expressing her emotions—whatever they may be—in a safe and nonjudgmental setting, whatever they may be. To work with Jennifer about issues, it is essential to create a trusting bond. The pain associated with her sense of some emotional abandonment by her family and some rejection by her friends must also be addressed. The counselor can help Jennifer begin to face her diagnosis by encouraging her to grieve and deal with her losses. As Kain (1998) put it, "Living with HIV disease often brings an end to old ways of thinking, old ways of acting, and old ways of living. Often hope is lost" (p. 1). The counselor can also support Jennifer in continuing to live her life the way she wants.

Because research has suggested that increases in stress levels exacerbate the rate of HIV-related infections, the counselor is obligated to teach Jennifer stress identification and stress reduction techniques or refer her to appropriate professionals (e.g., licensed masseuse, biofeedback technician, nutritionist). Participants in one study who learned coping strategies showed significant reduction in dysphoria, anxiety, and distress-related symptoms as well as improvement in positive reframing and acceptance of the disease (Schneiderman, Antoni, & Ironson, 2002).

Family members may benefit from counseling as well. As parents or siblings, family members may experience feelings of shock, embarrassment, hurt, and anger. Seemingly simplistic questions may be present: What should they say to other family members, friends, and neighbors? More complicated situations such as understanding medication regimens and interactive effects also are common for the family. The strain of a life-threatening illness is intense for everyone involved, and the strain frequently affects the family's other relationships.

Advocating

Advocacy is going beyond addressing issues that solely affect Jennifer to intervening with larger systemic components that oppress many individuals like Jennifer. Social/cultural advocacy is helping to shape a community climate so that acceptance and understanding of people with HIV/AIDS are apparent. This occurs through processes such as developing educational programs for community members about HIV/AIDS. Meeting with community leaders to create policy that supports health services for all youth regardless of HIV status is an example of political advocacy. Identifying allies and acknowledging the concerns of opponents is part of the political process. Legal intervention is demonstrated by using the law to battle discrimination and ensure the rights of all students like Jennifer to attend school, rent housing, and continue to be employed. Discrimination and injustice are often subtly displayed. The legal system is a tool with which to confront such difficult situations.

Ethical Issues in Counseling With the HIV/AIDS Adolescent

The development of HIV/AIDS and resulting deaths raise endless ethical questions for the counselor. Manuel et al. (1990) divided the literature surrounding HIV/AIDS and ethics into the following eight categories:

1. Quarantine and isolation of HIV patients
2. Discriminatory measures concerning specific population groups
3. Nonrespect of the confidential nature of medical information
4. Application of the penal code
5. Screening, compulsory notification, and registration
6. Protection of blood given for transfusion
7. Research on drugs and vaccines
8. Fundamental right of the person with HIV/AIDS.

One primary ethical concern is confidentiality limits with the HIV/AIDS client who continues to be sexually active without informing his or her partner. The question that continues to be debated asks, "At what point, if any, do counselors breach a confidential relationship with a client who has the AIDS virus to preserve society's goals of health and safety?" (Gray & Harding, 1988; Harding, Gray, & Neal, 1993; Stevenson & Kitchener, 2001). This ethical dilemma highlights the fine line between individual freedom and the health and welfare of society at large. As there is no dominant legal precedent to look to for guidance on this issue, it is likely that statutes will vary from state to state (Harding et al., 1993; Stevenson & Kitchener, 2001).

Limits of confidentiality in the counseling relationship have previously been defined in terms of "clear and imminent danger" (American Counseling Association [ACA], 1995) to self or others, ordinarily seen in the context of client suicide and homicide. However, ethical standards do not precisely define how clear and imminent danger relates to the sexually active and noninforming individual with HIV. Some professional associations, however, have delineated policy regarding this issue. The ACA (1995) addressed this issue, in part, when it stated,

> A counselor who receives information confirming that a client has a disease commonly known to be both communicable and fatal is justified in disclosing information to an identifiable third party who by his or her relationship with the client is at a high risk for contracting the disease. (Section B1.d)

ACA ethical standards obligate the counselor to consult with other professionals whenever possible. Counselors who struggle with the conflict that exists between confidentiality issues and clear and imminent danger guidelines should, at the least, consult with other professionals as a part of their decision-making process.

Counselors as Referral Agent

Referral can be used in a variety of circumstances surrounding HIV/AIDS and adolescents. The first may be when counselors recognize that their own biases and values are interfering with delivering appropriate services, whether working at the individual, family, school, or community level. At this time, it is critical for counselors to refer in a manner that does not negatively impact adolescents or their families. A second reason for referral may arise when a problem is so specialized that it requires unique assistance that the counselor cannot provide. A third reason is that working as a personal counselor with an HIV-positive adolescent, family, and significant others presents potential role conflicts.

It is important for counselors to be familiar with existing resources or how to find them. State, county, and community health departments have current information and services about HIV/AIDS and are considered a major information source. In addition, HIV/AIDS organizations that specifically focus on providing services, such as volunteer transportation and meals, are available in most large communities. Many national helping professional organizations, such as ACA, can provide guidance for locating appropriate resources. Advocates for Youth is one of the primary HIV/AIDS and adolescent resource centers with which counselors should link. The center provides bibliographies, curricular information, pamphlets, materials for parents, videos, and leader resources. The CDC provides updated statistics and medical information about HIV. The nonprofit organization, SIECUS, has the largest sexuality library in the United States and is rich with examples of HIV/AIDS curricula. These three organizations, and other resources, are listed in the Appendix at the end of this chapter.

ADAPTATIONS FOR DIVERSITY

Curricula and counseling services must be accessible to people from a wide variety of backgrounds. HIV/AIDS does not exclude any culture, ethnic, or economic group, and neither should HIV/AIDS prevention curricula and intervention programs. In many cases, however, HIV/AIDS programs are developed for European American middle-class adolescents and their families. We discuss in this section some specific considerations for working with youth of color and the harder-to-reach youth.

Working With Youth of Color

Youth of color are at higher risk for contracting HIV/AIDS, as indicated by the disproportionate percentage of African American and Hispanic people affected by HIV infection and AIDS since the beginning of the epidemic. Factors including income-related social inequalities and stigma in minority communities related to gay and bisexual behavior contribute to the higher rates of infection among these populations (Kates, Sorian, Crowley, & Summers, 2002). Further, minority adolescents have cultural or linguistic barriers that make it likely that standard educational programs will not work. Providing brochures and other written information in languages other than English may be a necessity for specific communities. Many state and local AIDS education organizations provide information in Spanish and other languages. If such written information is not available, then interpreters need to be provided for non-English-speaking teenagers who need access to information.

Sensitivity to cultural values, religious beliefs, and social customs increases the likelihood that adolescents will understand and incorporate information being conveyed to them (Jue & Lewis, 2001). Social networks are powerful forces in both the African American and Hispanic cultures. Counselors should use these networks in preventive education and intervention programs. Showing family, relatives, and peers specific ways they can help reduce risk-taking behaviors in adolescents is an important strategy. As early as 1993, Atwood proposed a systemic approach to behavior change with African American and Hispanic youth. Like the authors of this chapter, her approach views the adolescent as a member of a family, a school, a community, and also the larger social system. Messages that focus on the adolescent as a responsible member of a family and a social network may be more helpful than the individualistic message of "protect yourself."

Cross-age helping in which adolescents play an important role in the educational and social service enterprise as volunteer educators is another important strategy when working with high-risk adolescents from underrepresented populations. Older adolescents can teach younger ones in any prevention program. Peer counseling groups can be established to discuss reasons for having sexual relationships (see Table 10–4). Reasons initially identified in the 1980s and 1990s continue to be in effect now: wanting to be loved, wanting to be accepted, needing closeness and nurturance, proving masculinity or femininity, participating in the rites of passage into maturity, wishing to conform to peer group expectations, rebelling against parents, curiosity, experiencing readiness, and needing to know whether they are sexually attractive and acceptable to members of the opposite sex (Atwood, 1993; Calderwood, 1983; Santrock, 2003).

Working With the Special Needs of the Harder-to-Reach Youth

Although adolescents within the mainstream of the school system may benefit from traditional school-based HIV/AIDS education, adolescents outside the school system need to be reached through specially designed programs. The harder-to-reach adolescent often is the dropout, the homeless, the incarcerated youth, the runaway, the drug abuser, the gay and bisexual youth, and the poor adolescent. In fact, U.S. studies have reported that HIV infection occurs disproportionately and increasingly among the poor (Zierler et al., 2000). Many members of these adolescent groups are frequently kicked out of their homes because their families are unable to accept their behavior, do not have money to support them, or believe they cannot handle them. Every day 1.3 million runaway and homeless youth live on the streets, and 1 out of 7 American youth will run away from home by the time that they turn 18 (National Runaway Switchboard, 2001; http://www.nrscrisisline.org). These runaways are escaping stressful environments and often are victims of extremely dysfunctional families.

Street kids have been labeled *throwaways*. These adolescents frequently engage in "survival sex" to meet financial needs. It is clear from studies of homeless youth and from the risk behaviors that many are already HIV-positive.

Gay and bisexual males are currently and have always been the number one high-risk group for HIV/AIDS in the United States. It is generally thought that 10% of the adult population is gay; that means 1 out of every 10 children in a classroom will eventually identify themselves as gay. Gay youth are constantly pressured into a male–female lifestyle by a society that assumes everyone is heterosexual. It is not surprising that gay youth have become one of the biggest subgroups that make up the street kid phenomenon. The pain and fear of struggling with sexual identity create a lonely world not often shared with anyone. When adolescents identify as gay, they often lose their family and peer group support system. Over two decades into the epidemic, it is clear that preventive strategies among gay youth are failing, and a "second wave" of HIV-positive youth is emerging. Condom use is decreasing among gay adolescents (Kellogg, 2002). Numerous locations with confidential reporting attributed

59% of HIV cases among those age 13–19 and 53% among those age 20–24 to male-to-male sexual contact (CDC, 2002d). Counselors and other professionals must challenge their own heterosexual or homosexual assumptions. They must make a conscious effort to look for youth in classrooms and in community programs who are grappling with sexual identity issues. It is important to listen in a nonjudgmental fashion and help these youth find support in their struggle. Counselors and other professionals must help gay youth face at least two major issues: (a) isolation and possible rejection by family and (b) life-threatening illness as a result of unprotected high-risk sexual experiences. Through proactive and supportive interventions, it is possible to meet their needs. Consequently, this may prevent some of these youth from becoming runaways engaging in survival sex—and almost certainly contributing to the HIV/AIDS pandemic.

Abstaining from sexual experiences or participating in traditional sexuality education is not a realistic vision for the adolescents who are functioning in a survival mode. Emphasis needs to be placed on outreach programs that move outside of the classroom and into the streets. Counselors and other professionals must be creative and develop prevention programs using whatever methods work to meet the special needs of the harder-to-reach youth. If adolescents cannot come to counselors and other professionals, then the counselors and professionals must go to the adolescents with information about HIV, counseling, and testing (Clark, Brasseux, Richmond, Getson, & D'Angelo, 1998). Workers from programs for runaway children in New York City cruise the streets until 5:00 a.m. each morning offering hot chocolate, sandwiches, and condoms. The language that counselors and other professionals use may need to be changed. Terms such as *intercourse* and *oral sex* may need to be thrown out the window for *fucking* and *sucking* in order to clearly communicate. Along with concern for professionalism, counselors must also bring their own "street smarts" when talking to adolescents if high-risk behavior for HIV/AIDS is going to be changed.

Other youth groups that are difficult to reach include the physically disabled, developmentally delayed, or mentally ill. It is erroneous to assume that these adolescents are refraining from sexual activity or drug use. These groups are frequently neglected in HIV/AIDS education efforts. Recently, sexuality education organizations (e.g., SIECUS) have designed programs that include these populations. More efforts are needed in these areas.

SUMMARY

We have emphasized in this chapter the importance of counselors and other professionals working as prevention and intervention specialists with individuals, families, schools, and communities. Educational processes have been emphasized. It would be a grave mistake, however, to assume that effective educational intervention equals factual information and this, by itself, translates into behavioral change. Counselors and other professionals must be progressive, compassionate, and creative. More so, they must apply reason to their work. They need to break through resistance to behavioral change because of strong, misguided mindsets. Adolescents believe "this won't happen to me." Uninformed parents believe "only gay men and injection drug users contract HIV/AIDS." Bigots purport that "people with AIDS are our modern-day lepers." These beliefs must be confronted.

Researchers are currently struggling to acquire the information and medical technology needed to develop a cure for HIV/AIDS. The outlook for a cure in the near future is not optimistic; some say we must learn to live and live fully with some form of HIV as long as there are human beings on this planet. Others say that even with a cure, elements such as poverty, racism, sexism, and homophobia will continue to contribute to the far-reaching consequences of diseases like HIV/AIDS. But as deep-seated and seemingly intractable as these problems are, they are not excuses to remain stagnant in our efforts. As counselors, we must go forward with the best of our abilities. And we must continue our involvement in the social, psychological, political, legal, and ethical ramifications of HIV/AIDS. We are not powerless. We certainly have the skills and knowledge to impact the course of negative societal reactions. Most assuredly, we have the ability to help many adolescents rethink their behavior. Most of all, we can provide and foster compassion and affirmation for those youth diagnosed with HIV/AIDS. Assuming the responsibility of addressing HIV/AIDS would be a legacy of counselors and other professionals worth remembering.

REFERENCES

ActionAid. (2002, July). *Open to God: Priests challenge Africa's churches on HIV.* Retrieved August 28, 2002, from http://www.ActionAid.org/newsandmedia/churches.shtml

American Counseling Association. (1995). *Code of ethics and standards of practice.* Alexandria, VA: Author.

Atwood, J. D. (1993). AIDS in African American and Hispanic adolescents: A multisystemic approach. *American Journal of Family Therapy, 21,* 333–351.

Bowler, S., Sheon, A. R., D'Angelo, L. J., & Vermund, S. H. (1992). HIV and AIDS among adolescents in the United States: Increasing risk in the 1990s. *Journal of Adolescence, 15,* 345–371.

Calamidas, E. G. (1991). Reaching youth about AIDS: Challenges confronting health educators. *Health Values, 15,* 55–61.

Calderwood, D. (1983). *About your sexuality.* Boston: Beacon Press.

Centers for Disease Control and Prevention. (1998). *HIV/AIDS Surveillance Report, 10,* 1–40.

Centers for Disease Control and Prevention. (2001a, January 31). *HIV and its transmission.* Retrieved August 30, 2002 from http://www.cdc.gov/hiv/pubs/facts/transmission.htm

Centers for Disease Control and Prevention. (2001b). *HIV/AIDS Surveillance Report, 13,* 1–41.

Centers for Disease Control and Prevention. (2001c, February 6). *Questions and answers: HIV is the cause of AIDS.* Retrieved August 30, 2002, from http://www.cdc.gov/hiv/pubs/cause.htm

Centers for Disease Control and Prevention. (2001d). *Youth Risk Behavior Surveillance—United States 2001.* Retrieved August 13, 2002, from www.cdc.gov/mmwr/preview/mmwrhitml/ss5104al.htm

Centers for Disease Control and Prevention. (2002a, March 11). *HIV/AIDS among African Americans.* Retrieved August 22, 2002, from http://www.cdc.gov/hiv/pubs/facts/afam.htm

Centers for Disease Control and Prevention. (2002b, March 11). *HIV/AIDS among Hispanics in the United States.* Retrieved August 22, 2002, from http://www.cdc.gov/hiv/pubs/facts/hispanic.htm

Centers for Disease Control and Prevention. (2002c, March 11). *HIV/AIDS Surveillance Report.* Retrieved March 10, 2003, from http://www.cdc.gov/hiv/stats

Centers for Disease Control and Prevention. (2002d, March 11). *Need for sustained HIV prevention among men who have sex with men.* Retrieved August 30, 2002, from http://www.cdc.gov/hiv/pubs/facts/msm.htm

Centers for Disease Control and Prevention. (2002e, March 11). *Young people at risk: HIV/AIDS among America's youth.* Retrieved August 30, 2002, from http://www.cdc.gov/hiv/pubs/facts/youth.htm

Centers for Disease Control and Prevention. (2002f). Youth Risk Behavior Surveillance: United States, 2001 [Electronic version]. *Morbidity and Mortality Weekly Report, 51,* 15–18.

Centers for Disease Control and Prevention. (n.d.). *10 leading causes of death, United States 1999, all races, both sexes.* Retrieved August 22, 2002, from http://webapp.cdc.gov/cgi-bin/broker.exe

Clark, L. R., Brasseux, C., Richmond, D., Getson, P., & D'Angelo, L. J. (1998). Effect of HIV counseling and testing on sexually transmitted diseases and condom use in an urban adolescent population. *Archives of Pediatrics and Adolescent Medicine, 152*, 26.

Cobia, D. C., Carney, J. S., & Waggoner, I. M. (1998). Children and adolescents with HIV disease: Implications for school counselors. *Professional School Counseling, 1*(5), 41–45.

Collins, C., Alagiri, J. D., & Summers, T. (2002). *Abstinence only vs. comprehensive sex education: What are the arguments? What is the evidence?* San Francisco: University of California, San Francisco, Center for AIDS Prevention Studies. Retrieved August 27, 2002, from http://www.caps.ucsf.edu/index.html

Collison, B. B., Osborne, J. L., Gray, L. A., House, R. M., Firth, J., & Lou, M. (1998). Preparing counselors for social action. In C. C. Lee & G. R. Walz (Eds.), *Social action: A mandate for counselors* (pp. 263–277). Alexandria, VA: American Counseling Association.

Gray, L. A., & Harding, A. K. (1988). Confidentiality limits with clients who have the AIDS virus. *Journal of Counseling & Development, 66*, 219–223.

Gray, L. A., House, R. M., & Eicken, S. (1996). Human sexuality instruction: Implications for couple and family counselor educators. *The Family Journal, 4*, 208–216.

Harding, A. K., Gray, L. A., & Neal, M. (1993). Confidentiality limits with clients who have HIV: A review of ethical and legal guidelines and professional policies. *Journal of Counseling & Development, 71*, 297–305.

Henderson, C. W. (1998, January 15). Study reveals views of young people toward sex, health, AIDS. *AIDS Weekly Plus*, 18–19.

Homan, M. (1999a). *Promoting community change: Making it happen in the real world* (2nd ed.). Pacific Grove, CA: Brooks/Cole.

Homan, M. (1999b). *Rules of the game: Lessons from the field of community change.* Pacific Grove, CA: Brooks/Cole.

House, R. M., Eicken, S., & Gray, L. A. (1995). A national survey of counselor education programs regarding HIV/AIDS. *Journal of Counseling & Development, 74*, 5–11.

Hsu, J. H. (2002). Substance abuse and HIV. *The Johns Hopkins HIV Report.* Retrieved from http:/hopkins-aids.edu

Jue, S., & Lewis, S. Y. (2001). Cultural considerations in HIV ethical decision making: A guide for mental health practitioners. In J. R. Anderson & B. Barret (Eds.), *Ethics in HIV-related psychotherapy: Clinical decision making in complex cases* (pp. 60–82). Washington, DC: American Psychological Association

Kain, C. T. (1998). Counseling HIV-positive clients: The tenets of HIV affirmative counseling. *ACAeNews, 1*(9). Retrieved September 3, 2002, from www.counseling.org/enews/volume_1/0109a.htm

Kates, J., Sorian, R., Crowley, J. S., & Summers, T.A. (2002). Critical policy challenges in the third decade of the HIV/AIDS epidemic. *American Journal of Public Health, 92*, 1060–1063.

Kellogg, A. P. (2002). "Safe sex fatigue" grows among gay students. *Chronicle of Higher Education, 48*, 37–39.

Koop, C. E. (1988). *AIDS and the education of children.* Washington, DC: U.S. Department of Education.

Makgoba, M. W., Solomon, N., & Tucker, T. J. P. (2002). The search for an HIV vaccine. *British Medical Journal, 324*, 211–213.

Manuel, C., Enel, P., Charrel, J., Reviron, D., Larher, M. P., Thirion, X., & Sanmarco, J. L. (1990). The ethical approach to AIDS: A bibliographical review. *Journal of Medical Ethics, 16*, 14–27.

National Institute of Allergy and Infectious Diseases. (2000, July). *A primer: HIV infection and AIDS.* Retrieved August 29, 2002, from http://usinfo.state.gov/journals/itgic/0700/ijge/gj07.htm

Parker, J. T. (2001). *School-based sex education: A new millennium update* (Report No. EDO-SP-2001-10). East Lansing, MI: National Center for Research on Teacher Learning. (ERIC Document Reproduction Service No. ED460130)

Santrock, J. W. (2003). *Adolescence* (9th ed.). New York: McGraw-Hill.

Schneiderman, N., Antoni, M., & Ironson, G. (2002). Cognitive behavioral stress management and secondary prevention in HIV/AIDS. *APA Online.* Retrieved August 31, 2002, from www.apa.org/pi/aids/schneiderman.html

Stevenson, S. R., & Kitchener, K. S. (2001). Ethical issues in the practice of psychology with clients with HIV/AIDS. In J. R. Anderson & B. Barret (Eds.), *Ethics in HIV-related psychotherapy: Clinical decision making in complex cases* (pp. 19–41). Washington, DC: American Psychological Association.

Weinstein, N. D. (1984). Why it won't happen to me: Perceptions of risk factors and susceptibility. *Health Psychology, 3,* 431–457.

Zierler, S., Krieger, N., Tang, Y., Coady, W., Siegfried, E., DeMaria, A., & Auerbach, J. (2000). Economic deprivation and AIDS incidence in Massachusetts. *American Journal of Public Health, 90,* 1064–1074.

APPENDIX

NATIONAL AIDS RESOURCES

Advocates for Youth
1025 Vermont Avenue, NW, Suite 200
Washington, DC 20005
(202) 347-5700
E-mail: info@advocatesforyouth.org
Web site: www.advocatesforyouth.org

Advocates for Youth (formerly the Center for Population Options), a national education and advocacy organization, is dedicated to improving the quality of life of adolescents by preventing risk-taking behaviors and too-early childbearing. Advocates for Youth offers a variety of services, including training for youth services professionals, materials development and distribution, peer education, and technical assistance. The Advocates for Youth Resource Center maintains an extensive collection of materials, the focus of which is major journals, including back issues on adolescent sexuality issues. The center also houses books and newspaper articles, as well as a large video collection on topics such as HIV/AIDS, adolescents, pregnancy, and general family planning issues.

AIDS Information Network
1233 Locust Street, 5th Floor
Philadelphia, PA 19107
(215) 985-4851
E-mail: aidsinfo@cr.tpath.org
Web site: www.aidslibrary.org

The AIDS Information Network (AIN), formerly the AIDS Library of Philadelphia, provides comprehensive, current information on all aspects of HIV/AIDS. The library shares information with caregivers, AIDS service organizations, medical practitioners, case managers, hospitals, and families, partners, and friends of those with HIV/AIDS. The Web site offers resources for HIV information and services.

American Civil Liberties Union Foundation, AIDS Project
125 Broad Street, 18th Floor
New York, NY 10004-2400
(212) 576-2627
E-mail: aclu@aclu.org
Web site: www.aclu.org

The AIDS Project of the American Civil Liberties Union (ACLU) Foundation undertakes litigation, public policy advocacy, and public education on civil liberties issues raised by the AIDS crisis. The project is headquartered in New York, staffed by four attorneys and two support personnel, and supplemented by a legislative expert in Washington, DC, and five ACLU affiliate attorneys whose efforts focus on HIV/AIDS-related issues.

American Foundation for AIDS Research
120 Wall Street, 13th Floor
New York, NY 10005-3902
(212) 806-1600
(800) 392-6327
Web site: www.amfar.org/content.html

The American Foundation for AIDS Research (AmFAR) is the nation's leading non-profit organization dedicated to the support of HIV/AIDS research, education, prevention, and sound public policy. AmFAR identifies unmet needs in HIV/AIDS biomedical research (including clinical research), the social sciences, education for prevention, and public policy development. The foundation has provided nearly $58 million to innovative projects in these vital areas. In support of scientific research, AmFAR selects innovative proposals and approaches and awards grants in basic science, social research, clinical research, public policy, and education.

CDC National AIDS Clearinghouse
Prevention Information Network
P.O. Box 6003
Rockville, MD 20849-6003
(800) 458-5231
Web site: www.cdcnpin.org

The Centers for Disease Control and Prevention (CDC) National AIDS Clearinghouse (NAC) is a national reference, referral, and publication distribution service for AIDS and HIV information. CDC NAC is a comprehensive information service for public health professionals, educators, social service workers, attorneys, human resource managers, and employers. Information services are provided by telephone or mail. The clearinghouse maintains several computerized databases, which reference specialists with a broad knowledge of AIDS organizations and materials access to answer inquiries, make referrals, and help locate publications about HIV infection and AIDS.

CDC National STD and AIDS Hotline
P.O. Box 13827
Research Triangle Park, NC 27709
(800) 342-AIDS
Web site: www.ashastd.org/hotlines/index.html

The Centers for Disease Control and Prevention (CDC) National STD and AIDS Hotline provides current and accurate information about HIV infection and AIDS to the general public. Callers access the hotline anytime, day or night, to receive information. The hotline provides callers with descriptive information about HIV and AIDS; confidential information about preventing and reducing the risk of transmitting HIV infections; information about counseling, testing, and support services; referrals for local legal, financial, and treatment resources; and HIV/AIDS publications.

Center for AIDS Prevention Studies
74 New Montgomery, Suite 600
San Francisco, CA 94105
(415) 597-9100
E-mail: CAPSWeb@psg.ucsf.edu
Web site: www.caps.ucsf.edu

The Center for AIDS Prevention Studies at the University of California, San Francisco provides HIV/AIDS information regarding current research topics and prevention strategies. The Web site provides fact sheets, current research information, a prevention tool kit, and recent articles and press releases. Some information is also available in Spanish.

Center for Women Policy Studies, National Resource Center on Women and AIDS
1211 Connecticut Avenue, Suite 312
Washington, DC 20036
(202) 872-1770
E-mail: cwps@centerwomenpolicy.org
Web site: www.centerwomenpolicy.org

The Center for Women Policy Studies established the National Resource Center on Women and AIDS to fill the vacuum in public policy discussion of HIV/AIDS and to address, from women's perspectives, critical policy issues for women of color and low-income women related to the AIDS crisis. A centralized information resource for researchers, policymakers, advocates, and caregivers, the resource center annually publishes the *Guide to Resources on Women and AIDS*, with a state-by-state directory of programs serving women and case studies of exemplary programs. The center develops policy options to ensure that women's needs are met in biomedical and behavioral research, clinical trials of AIDS treatments, development of HIV prevention strategies and risk reduction education, and delivery of health care and social services.

Gay Men's Health Crisis
119 West 24th Street
New York, NY 10011-0022
(212) 807-6655
(800) 243-7692
Web site: www.gmhc.org

The Gay Men's Health Crisis (GMHC) is a community-based, volunteer AIDS service organization that pursues a threefold mission: services, education, and advocacy for people whose lives are affected by HIV. GMHC provides individual and group support, financial advocacy, recreational opportunities, and crisis intervention services. Legal services are provided to ensure that people with HIV infection can live full, productive lives in the face of possible legal difficulties. GMHC uses many avenues in addition to a hotline to reach its audiences: publications, videos, safer sex workshops, outreach into communities of color, information tables on city streets, distribution of condoms and safer sex guidelines to bars and clubs, and educational programs for mental health professionals and employers.

Multicultural AIDS Resource Center of California
390 4th Street
San Francisco, CA 94107
(415) 777-3229
(800) 871-6688 (for California only)
E-mail: information@marcconline.org
Web site: www.marcconline.org

The Multicultural AIDS Resource Center of California is a subsidiary of the Multicultural Training Resource Center (MTRC) of San Francisco, established in 1984 as the first national center to provide multicultural and culturally specific HIV/AIDS and substance abuse prevention services. MTRC views multiculturalism as a concept that celebrates culture and cultural differences without limiting its definition to race, ethnicity, and color, thereby including women, the elderly, lesbians, homosexuals, and the homeless.

National Association of People With AIDS
1413 K Street, NW
Washington, DC 20005
(202) 898-0414
E-mail: napwa@napwa.org
Web site: www.napwa.org

The National Association of People With AIDS (NAPWA) serves as a national voice for all those infected and affected by HIV/AIDS. Funded by the Centers for Disease Control and Prevention, private corporations, other donors, and membership fees, NAPWA achieves its mission through three mechanisms: (a) information dissemination, (b) public policy advocacy, and (c) technical assistance to organizations. NAPWA's primary requesters are people with HIV/AIDS and related AIDS service organizations, including NAPWA's affiliate people with AIDS coalitions.

National Coalition of Hispanic Health and Human Services Organizations
1501 16th Street, NW
Washington, DC 20036
(202) 387-5000
E-mail: alliance@hispanichealth.org
Web site: www.cossmho.org

The mission of the National Coalition of Hispanic Health and Human Services Organizations (COSSMHO) is to improve the health and well-being of all Hispanic communities in the United States by conducting national demonstration programs, coordinating research, and serving as a source of information, technical assistance, and policy analysis. COSSMHO addresses HIV/AIDS in the Hispanic community through the Community HIV and AIDS Technical Assistance Network (CHATAN), which provides technical assistance on the local, state, regional, and national levels by identifying, implementing, and assessing culturally appropriate intervention strategies.

National Minority AIDS Council
1931 13th Street, NW
Washington, DC 20009
(202) 483-6622
Web site: www.nmac.org

The National Minority AIDS Council (NMAC) is dedicated to developing leadership within communities of color to address the challenges of HIV/AIDS. NMAC provides technical assistance, public policy advocacy, conferences, research and treatment advocacy, and three newsletters: *CONNECTIONS* (technical assistance), *Update* (public policy), and *Treatment Alert* (research and treatment advocacy).

National Native American AIDS Prevention Center
436 14th Street, Suite 1020
Oakland, CA 94610
(510) 444-2051
E-mail: information@nnaapc.org
Web site: www.nnaapc.org

The National Native American AIDS Prevention Center (NNAAPC) is directed and managed by and for American Indians, Alaskan natives, and Hawaiian natives. NNAAPC operates a national, toll-free, Indian-specific, AIDS hotline and a clearinghouse for native-specific HIV/AIDS and sexually transmitted disease information. The center also publishes a yearly newsletter, *Seasons.*

National Pediatric and Family HIV Resource Center
University of Medicine and Dentistry of New Jersey
Francis-Xavier Bagnood Center
30 Bergen Street
ADM C #4
Newark, NJ 07103
(973) 972-0410
(800) 362-0071
Web site: www.pedhivaids.org

The National Pediatric and Family HIV Resource Center (NPHRC) serves professionals who care for children and families with HIV infection and AIDS. The center, funded in part by the Maternal and Child Health Bureau of the Health Resources and Services Administration, offers consultation, technical assistance, and training for medical, social service, and planning personnel. The center, which is staffed by professionals including a physician, nurse, psychologist, and social worker, receives numerous requests for assistance from providers working with HIV-infected children as well as the general public. Consultation is provided to organizations designing new programs and modifying existing ones to serve children, youth, and families with HIV. Technical assistance is provided in areas such as developing family education materials, conducting needs assessments, evaluating programs, and designing systems of care that are family-centered, community-based, and culturally competent. Training and clinical fellowships are available to physicians, nurses, social workers, mental health professionals, and other providers.

National School Boards Association, HIV/AIDS Education Project
1680 Duke Street
Alexandria, VA 22314
(703) 838-6722
Web site: www.nsba.org/schoolhealth

Funded by the Centers for Disease Control and Prevention, the HIV/AIDS Education Project of the National School Boards Association (NSBA) helps school board members, superintendents, and other school-affiliated personnel to deal effectively with the issues of HIV and AIDS in schools.

Planned Parenthood Federation of America
810 Seventh Avenue
New York, NY 10019
(212) 541-7800
Web site: www.plannedparenthood.org

The Planned Parenthood Federation of America (PPFA) is a federation of 132 non-profit affiliates operating 900 clinics in 49 states and the District of Columbia. The affiliates provide reproductive health care and sexuality education to nearly 5 million men and women each year. Services include contraception, abortion, sterilization, and infertility services. PPFA also sponsors and advocates biomedical, socioeconomic, and demographic research regarding reproductive health issues. PPFA produces educational materials, acts as a clearinghouse, and provides community education through the affiliates. Most PPFA affiliates offer anonymous or confidential HIV testing and counseling to clients. All affiliates provide HIV educational materials, safer sex counseling, and referral services.

Project Inform
205 13th Street, Suite 2001
San Francisco, CA 94103
(415) 558-8669
(800) 822-7422 (hotline; see last sentence)
Web site: www.projinf.org

The three main goals of Project Inform are (a) to inform those infected by HIV (or at risk of infection) of lifesaving strategies such as early diagnosis and early intervention, (b) to give people and their health care providers the means to make informed choices about the most promising treatment options, and (c) to change research and regulatory polices that delay or prevent access to treatment. Anyone can call the toll-free Treatment Hotline for up-to-date HIV treatment information.

Sexuality Information and Education Council of the United States
130 West 42nd Street, Suite 350
New York, NY 10036
(212) 819-9770
E-mail: siecus@siecus.org
Web site: www.siecus.org

The Sexuality Information and Education Council of the United States (SIECUS) was founded to provide health care professionals, educators, policymakers, students, and ethnic minorities with information and education on family life and related issues. SIECUS provides information to more than 12,000 people a year, serving all populations and racial and ethnic minorities. SIECUS's Mary S. Calderone Library provides library and information services by telephone or mail and in person at SIECUS headquarters in New York City. The library contains a unique collection of 5,000 sexuality-related resources, of which about 10% are related to HIV and AIDS. The AIDS collection comprises books, current journal articles, HIV/AIDS-related newsletters, and vertical files. The library is open by appointment for SIECUS members; information requests are accepted by telephone and mail.

World Health Organization HIV/AIDS Programme
20 Avenue Appia
CH-1211 Geneva 27
Switzerland
E-mail: hiv-aids@who.int
Web site: www.who.int/HIV_AIDS/first.html

The World Health Organization (WHO) is the United Nations' specialized agency for health. WHO's objective is the attainment of the highest level of health for all people. WHO's HIV/AIDS Programme provides up-to-date information in English, French, and Spanish concerning care for those with HIV/AIDS, prevention of HIV/AIDS, HIV/AIDS surveillance data, and information regarding other sexually transmitted infections.

11 | "I Don't Want to Live": The Adolescent at Risk for Suicidal Behavior

David Capuzzi and Douglas R. Gross

The adolescent at risk for suicidal preoccupation and behavior has become an increasing concern for schools and communities throughout the United States (King, 2001b). Between 1960 and 1988, the suicide rate among adolescents increased much more dramatically than it did in the general population. The adolescent suicide rate rose by 200% compared with an increase in the general population of approximately 17% (Garland & Zigler, 1993). Much of the current literature (Coy, 1995; Zenere & Lazarus, 1997) ranks suicide, following accidents, as the second leading cause of death for our nation's youth.

The topic of adolescent suicide has been a major focus for newspaper features, television specials, and legislative initiatives as the problem of adolescent suicide has reached epidemic proportions (Hafen & Frandsen, 1986). In 1999, U.S. Surgeon General David Satcher made urgent recommendations to the public regarding suicide, stating that "the country is facing an average of 85 suicides and 2,000 attempts per day" (p. 1). In 2000, there were nearly 4,000 adolescent suicides recorded, accounting for 15% of deaths between the ages of 15 and 24 (National Center for Health Statistics, 2002). Such data provide the basis for ranking suicide as the third leading cause of death among the 11–24 age group (National Institute of Mental Health, 2002). Centers for Disease Control and Prevention (2000) surveillance data from 1999 reported that 19.3% of high school students had seriously considered attempting suicide, 14.5% had made plans to attempt suicide, and 8.3% had made more than one suicide attempt during the 12-month period prior to the survey. Because teachers in typical U.S. high school classrooms can expect to have at least one young man and two young women who attempted suicide in the previous year (King, 2000), counselors, teachers, and parents are becoming more and more concerned about their responsibilities. Many states are requiring that schools include guidelines for suicide prevention, crisis management, and postvention in their written tragedy response plans.

PROBLEM DEFINITION

Ethnic and Gender Differences

The suicide rate is higher among adolescent males than among adolescent females (although adolescent women attempt three to four times as often as adolescent men). Caucasian adolescent males complete suicide more often than any other ethnic group

275

(Canetto & Sakinofsky, 1998; Metha, Weber, & Webb, 1998; Price, Dake, & Kucharewski, 2001). A number of explanations to account for the differences in rates between genders and races have been proposed, but no clear answers have been found. As early as 1954, Henry and Short provided an explanation based on a reciprocal model of suicide and homicide that suggested that some groups were seen as more likely to express frustration and aggression inwardly and others were more likely to express them outwardly. Empirical data, however, do not support this reciprocal relationship. Some models used to explain racial differences in suicide have suggested that the extreme stress and discrimination that African Americans in the United States confront help to create protective factors, such as extended networks of social support, that lower the risk and keep the suicide rates for African American adolescents lower than those of Caucasian adolescents (Borowsky, Ireland, & Resnick, 2001; Bush, 1976; Gibbs, 1988). It is important to note, however, that despite the overall pattern suggested by the data, during the period between 1980 and 1994, the suicide rates for African American adolescent males showed a 320% increase in the 10–14 age group and a 196% increase in the 15–19 age group (Lyon et al., 2000; Metha et al., 1998).

Native Americans have the highest adolescent suicide rates of any ethnic group in the United States (Committee on Adolescence, 2000). There is considerable variability across tribes; the Navajos, for example, have suicide rates close to the national average of 11 to 13 per 100,000 of the population, whereas some Apache groups have rates as high as 43 per 100,000 (Berlin, 1987). The high suicide rates in the Native American population have been associated with factors such as alcoholism and substance abuse, unemployment, availability of firearms, and child abuse and neglect (Berman & Jobes, 1991). In general, less traditional tribes have higher rates of suicide than do more traditional tribes (Wyche, Obolensky, & Glood, 1990). Suicide rates for both Asian American and Hispanic American adolescents continue to be lower than those for African American and Native American youth, even though the 1980–1994 time period bore witness to much higher rates than previously recorded (Metha et al., 1998).

Methods

The use of firearms outranks all other methods of completed suicides; firearms are now being used by both genders. Studies in the United States show that availability of guns increases the risk of adolescent suicide (Brent et al., 1993; Committee on Adolescence, 2000). The second most common method is hanging, and the third most common is gassing. Males use firearms and hanging more often than do females, but females use gassing and ingestion more often than do males for completed suicides (Berman & Jobes, 1991). The most common method used by suicide attempters is ingestion or overdose.

Risk Factors

As noted by Garland and Zigler (1993) and Shaffer and Craft (1999), the search for the etiology of suicide spans many areas of study (Orbach, 2001). Risk factors that have been studied include neurotransmitter imbalances and genetic predictors, psychiatric disorders, poor self-efficacy and problem-solving skills, sexual or physical abuse, concerns over sexual identity or orientation, availability of firearms, substance abuse, violent rock music, divorce in families, unemployment and labor strikes, loss, disability, giftedness, and phases of the moon. It is important to note that almost all adolescent suicide victims have experienced some form of psychiatric illness. The most prevalent psychiatric disorders among completed adolescent suicides appear to be affective disorders, conduct disorder or antisocial personality disorder, and substance abuse (Shaffer, 1988; Shaffer & Craft, 1999). Among affective disorders, particular attention should be paid to bipolar illness and depressive disorder with comorbidity such as attention deficit disorder, conduct disorder, or substance abuse (Rohde, Lewinsohn, & Seeley, 1991).

The suicide of a family member or a close friend of the family can also be a risk factor for adolescent suicide; prior attempts also escalate risk. An adolescent experiencing a physical illness that is chronic or terminal can also be at higher risk (Capuzzi, 1994). Many researchers have studied cognitive and coping style factors, such as generalized feelings of hopelessness and poor interpersonal problem-solving skills, as risk factors for adolescent suicide (Garland & Zigler, 1993). High neuroticism and low extraversion, high impulsiveness, low self-esteem, and an external locus of control have also been studied and can be used to predict risk (Beautrais, Joyce, & Mulder, 1999). Alcohol and drug abuse, the breakup of a relationship, school difficulties or failure, social isolation, a friend who committed suicide, chronic levels of community violence, and availability of lethal methods have also been studied and identified as risk factors (Price et al., 2001).

The best single predictor of death by suicide seems to be a previous suicide attempt (King, 2000; Shaffer, Garland, Gould, Fisher, & Trautman, 1988). Some studies indicate that as many as 40% of attempters will make additional suicide attempts, and as many as 10%–14% of these individuals will complete suicide (Diekstra, 1989).

Precipitants

Often, completed suicide is precipitated by what, to the adolescent, is interpreted as a shameful or humiliating experience (e.g., failure at school or work, interpersonal conflict with a romantic partner or parent). There is mounting evidence indicating that adolescents who do not cope well with major and minor life events and who do not have family and peer support are more likely to have suicidal ideation (Mazza & Reynolds, 1998; Stanard, 2000). The humiliation and frustration experienced by some adolescents struggling with conflicts connected with their sexual orientation may precipitate suicidal behavior (Harry, 1989), although being gay or lesbian, in and of itself, may not be a risk factor for suicide (Blumenthal, 1991; Russell & Joyner, 2001). Hoberman and Garfinkel (1988) found that the most common precipitant of suicide in a sample of 229 youth suicides was an argument with a boyfriend, a girlfriend, or a parent (19%) followed by school problems (14%). Other humiliating experiences such as corporal punishment and abuse also serve as precipitants; the experience of sexual or physical assault seems to be a particularly significant risk factor for adolescent women (Hoberman & Garfinkel, 1988).

Understanding the Myths

The biggest problem connected with the topic of adolescents at risk for suicide is the fact that parents, teachers, mental health professionals, and the adolescent population itself are not made aware of a variety of myths and misconceptions as well as the signs and symptoms associated with adolescent suicide. Because subsequent case study, prevention, and intervention information in this chapter is based on prior awareness of these areas, the following information about myths and the suicidal profile is pertinent.

It is important to disqualify myths and misconceptions surrounding the topic of adolescent suicide at the beginning of any initiative to provide prevention, crisis management, and postvention services. Some of the most commonly cited misconceptions include the following (Capuzzi, 1988, 1994; Capuzzi & Gross, 2000; King, 1999):

Adolescents who talk about suicide never attempt suicide. This is probably one of the most widely believed myths. All suicidal adolescents make attempts (either verbally or nonverbally) to let a friend, parent, or teacher know that life seems to be too difficult to bear. Because a suicide attempt is a cry for help to identify options, other than death, to decrease the pain of living, always take verbal or nonverbal threats seriously. Never assume such threats are only for the purpose of attracting attention or manipulating others. It is better to respond and enlist the aid of a professional than it is to risk the loss of a life.

Suicide happens with no warning. Suicidal adolescents leave numerous hints and warnings about their suicidal ideations and intentions. Clues can be verbal or in the form of suicidal gestures, such as taking a few sleeping pills, becoming accident prone, reading stories focused on death and violence, and so on. Quite often, the social support network of the suicidal adolescent is small. As stress escalates and options, other than suicide, seem few, suicidal adolescents may withdraw from an already small circle of friends, thus making it more difficult for others to notice warning signs.

Most adolescents who attempt suicide fully intend to die. Most suicidal adolescents do not want to end their lives. They feel desperate and ambivalent about whether it would be better to end their lives and, thus, their emotional pain or try to continue living. This confusion is usually communicated through behavior and verbal communication (both of which are discussed in a subsequent subsection of this chapter).

Adolescents from affluent families attempt or complete suicide more often than adolescents from poor families. This, too, is a myth. Suicide is evenly divided among socioeconomic groups.

Once an adolescent is suicidal, he or she is suicidal forever. Most adolescents are suicidal for a limited period of time. In our experience, the 24–72-hour period around the peak of the crisis is the most dangerous. If counselors and other mental health professionals can monitor such a crisis period and transition the adolescent into long-term counseling/therapy, there is a strong possibility there will never be another suicidal crisis. The more effort that is made to help an adolescent identify stressors and develop problem-solving skills during this postsuicidal crisis period and the more time that passes, the better the prognosis.

If an adolescent attempts suicide and survives, he or she will never make an additional attempt. There is a difference between an adolescent who experiences a suicidal crisis but does not attempt suicide and an adolescent who actually makes an attempt. An adolescent who carries through with an attempt has identified a plan, had access to the means, and maintained a high enough energy level to follow through. He or she may believe that a second or third attempt may be possible. If counseling/therapy has not taken place or has not been successful during the period following an attempt, additional attempts may be made. Most likely, each follow-up attempt will become more lethal.

Adolescents who attempt or complete suicide always leave notes. Only a small percentage of suicidal adolescents leave notes. This is a common myth and one of the reasons why many deaths are classified and reported as accidents by friends, family members, physicians, and investigating officers when suicide has actually taken place.

Most adolescent suicides happen late at night or during the predawn hours. This myth is not true for the simple reason that most suicidal adolescents actually want help. Mid to late morning and mid to late afternoon are the time periods when most attempts are made because a family member or friend is more likely to be around to intervene than would be the case late at night or very early in the morning.

Never use the word suicide *when talking to adolescents because using the word gives some adolescents the idea.* This is simply not true; you cannot put the idea of suicide into the mind of an adolescent who is not suicidal. If an adolescent is suicidal and you use the word, it can help an adolescent verbalize feelings of despair and assist with establishing rapport and trust. If a suicidal adolescent thinks you know he or she is suicidal and realizes you are afraid to approach the subject, it can bring the adolescent closer to the point of making an attempt by contributing to feelings of despair and helplessness.

The most common method for adolescent suicide completion involves drug overdose. Guns are the most frequently used method for completing suicide among adolescents, followed by hanging. The presence of a gun or guns in the home escalates the risk of adolescent suicide by approximately five times even if such firearms are kept locked in a cabinet or drawer. Restricting the presence of and access to guns significantly decreases the suicide rates among adolescents.

All adolescents who engage in suicidal behavior are mentally ill. Many adolescents have entertained the thought of suicide, but this does not indicate mental illness. Adolescents who attempt or complete suicide are usually not suffering from a mental disorder but are having a great deal of difficulty coping with life circumstances.

Every adolescent who attempts suicide is depressed. Depression is a common component of the profile of a suicidal adolescent, but depression is not always a component. Many adolescents simply want to escape their present set of circumstances and do not have the problem-solving skills to cope more effectively, lower stress, and work toward a more promising future.

Suicide is hereditary. Although suicide tends to run in families, just as physical and sexual abuse does, and has led to the development of this myth, suicide is not genetically inherited. Members of families do, however, share the same emotional climate because parents model coping and stress management skills as well as high or low levels of self-esteem. The suicide of one family member tends to increase the risk among other family members that suicide will be viewed as an appropriate way to solve a problem or set of problems.

In conjunction with this myth, it should be noted that some adolescents are predisposed, because of genetic factors, to depression as a response to life circumstances. Because of the connection between depression and suicide, many have mistakenly come to the belief that suicide can be genetically inherited.

If an adolescent is intent on attempting suicide, there is nothing anyone can do to prevent its occurrence. Two of the most important things a counselor, teacher, or parent can do are to know the risk factors and warning signs connected with adolescent suicide and to know how to respond. It is important for counselors to be prepared to provide preventive and crisis management services and for teachers and parents to know how to facilitate a referral to a qualified professional. Suicide can be prevented in most cases.

Recognizing the Profile

A number of experts (Beautrais et al., 1999; Capuzzi, 1994; Capuzzi & Golden, 1988; Cavaiola & Lavender, 1999; Cohen, 2000; Curran, 1987; Davis, 1983; Fernquist, 2000; Hafen & Frandsen, 1986; Hussain & Vandiver, 1984; Johnson & Maile, 1987; Mazza & Reynolds, 1998) believe that about 90% of the adolescents who complete suicide (and lethal first attempts can result in completions) give cues to those around them in advance. Whether these cues or hints are limited or numerous will depend on the adolescent because each adolescent has a unique familial and social history. It is important for adults (and young people as well) to recognize the signs and symptoms to facilitate intervention. A comment such as "I talked with her a few days ago and she was fine—I am so shocked to learn of her death" may mean that no one was aware of the warning signs. One of the essential components of any staff development effort is teaching the profile of the suicidal or potentially suicidal adolescent so that referral and intervention can take place. Behavioral cues, verbal cues, thinking patterns and motivations, and personality traits are the four areas that are described below.

Behavioral Cues

The following are some behavioral cues that can be possible warning signs of adolescents who are suicidal:

Lack of concern about personal welfare. Some adolescents who are suicidal may not be able to talk about their problems or give verbal hints that they are at risk for attempting suicide. Sometimes such adolescents become unconcerned with their personal safety in the hopes that someone will take notice. Experimenting with medication, accepting dares from friends, reckless driving, carving initials into the skin of forearms, and so on may all be ways of gesturing or letting others know "I am in pain and don't know how to continue through life if nothing changes."

Changes in social patterns. Relatively unusual or sudden changes in an adolescent's social behavior can provide strong cues that such a young person is feeling desperate. A cooperative teenager may suddenly start breaking the house rules that parents have never had to worry about enforcing. An involved adolescent may begin to withdraw from activities at school or end long-term friendships with school and community-related peers. A stable, easygoing teenager may start arguing with teachers, employers, or other significant adults with whom prior conflict was never experienced. Such pattern changes should be noted and talked about with an adolescent who does not seem to be behaving as he or she usually has in the past.

A decline in school achievement. Many times, adolescents who are becoming more and more depressed and preoccupied with suicidal thoughts are unable to devote the time required to complete homework assignments and maintain grades. If such an adolescent has a history of interest in the school experience and has maintained a certain grade point average, loss of interest in academic pursuits can be a strong indication that something is wrong. The key to assessing such a situation is the length of time the decline lasts.

Concentration and clear thinking difficulties. Suicidal adolescents usually experience marked changes in thinking and logic. As stress and discomfort escalate, logical problem solving and option generation become more difficult. It becomes easier and easier to stay focused on suicide as the only solution as reasoning and thinking become more confused and convoluted. "It may become more and more obvious that the adolescent's attention span is shorter and that verbal comments bear little relationship to the topic of a conversation" (Capuzzi, 1988, p. 6).

Altered patterns of eating and sleeping. Sudden increases or decreases in appetite and weight, difficulty with sleeping, or wanting to sleep all the time or all day can all be indicative of increasing preoccupation with suicidal thoughts. These altered patterns can offer strong evidence that something is wrong and that assistance is required.

Attempts to put personal affairs in order or to make amends. Often, once a suicide plan and decision have been reached, adolescents will make last minute efforts to put their personal affairs in order. These efforts may take a variety of directions: attempts to make amends in relation to a troubled relationship, final touches on a project, reinstatement of an old or neglected friendship, or the giving away of prized possessions (skis, jewelry, compact discs, collections, etc.).

Use or abuse of alcohol or drugs. Sometimes troubled adolescents use or abuse alcohol or other drugs to lessen their feelings of despair or discontent. Initially, they may feel that the drug enhances their ability to cope and to increase feelings of self-esteem. Unfortunately, the abuse of drugs decreases ability to communicate accurately and problem solve rationally. Thinking patterns become more skewed, impulse control lessens, and option identification decreases. Rapid onset of involvement with illicit or over-the-counter drugs is indicative of difficulty with relationships, problem solving, and ability to share feelings and communicate them to others.

Unusual interest in how others are feeling. Suicidal adolescents often express considerable interest in how others are feeling. Because they are in pain but may be unable to express their feelings and ask for help, they may reach out to peers (or adults) who seem to need help with the stresses of daily living. Such responsiveness may become a full-time pastime and serve to lessen preoccupation with self and to serve as a vehicle for communicating, "I wish you would ask me about my pain" or "Can't you see that I need help too?"

Preoccupation with death and violence themes. Reading books or poetry in which death, violence, or suicide is the predominating theme can become the major interest of an adolescent who is becoming increasingly preoccupied with the possibility of suicide. Such adolescents may be undecided about the possibility of choosing death over life and may be working through aspects of such a decision with such reading. Other examples of such preoccupation can include listening to music that is violent; playing violent video games; writing short stories focused on death, dying, and loss; drawing or sketching that emphasizes destruction; or watching movies or videos that emphasize destruction to self and others.

Sudden improvement after a period of depression. Suicidal adolescents often fool parents, teachers, and friends by appearing to be dramatically improved, after a period of prolonged depression, in a very short period of time. This improvement can sometimes take place overnight or during a 24-hour period and encourages friends and family to interpret such a change as a positive sign. It is not unusual for this type of change to be the result of a suicide decision and the formulation of a concrete suicide plan on the part of the adolescent at risk. It may mean that the suicide attempt (and the potential of completion) is imminent and that the danger and crisis are peaking. The important point for family and friends to remember is that it is not really logical for a depression to lessen that rapidly. It takes time, effort, and, at times, medical assistance to improve coping skills and lessen feelings of depression, just as it took time (months or years) to develop nonadaptive responses to people and circumstances and feelings of hopelessness.

Sudden or increased promiscuity. It is not unusual for an adolescent to experiment with sex during periods of suicidal preoccupation in an attempt to refocus attention or lessen feelings of isolation. Unfortunately, doing so sometimes complicates circumstances because of an unplanned pregnancy or an escalation of feelings of guilt.

Verbal Cues

As noted by Schneidman, Farberow, and Litman (1976), verbal statements can provide cues to self-destructive intentions. Such statements should be assessed and considered in relation to behavioral signs, changes in thinking patterns, motivations, personality traits, and so on. There is no universal language or style for communicating suicidal intention. Some adolescents will openly and directly say something like "I am going to commit suicide" or "I am thinking of taking my life." Others will be far less direct and make statements such as "I'm going home," "I wonder what death is like," "I'm tired," "She'll be sorry for how she has treated me," or "Someday I'll show everyone just how serious I am about some of the things I've said."

The important thing for counselors, parents, teachers, and friends to remember is that when someone says something that could be interpreted in a number of ways, it is always best to ask for clarification. It is not a good idea to make assumptions about what a statement means or to minimize the importance of what is being communicated. Suicidal adolescents often have a long-term history of difficulty with communicating feelings and asking for support. Indirect statements may be made in the hopes that someone will respond with support and interest and provide or facilitate a referral for professional assistance (Capuzzi & Gross, 2000).

Thinking Patterns and Motivations

In addition to the areas previously described, thinking patterns (Gust-Brey & Cross, 1999) and motivations of suicidal adolescents can also be assessed and evaluated. For such an assessment to occur, it is necessary to encourage self-disclosure to learn about changes in an adolescent's cognitive set and distortions of logic and problem-solving ability. As noted by Velkoff and Huberty (1988), the motivations of suicidal adolescents can be understood more readily when suicide is viewed as fulfilling one of three primary functions: (a) an avoidance function that protects the individual from the pain perceived to be associated with a relationship or set of circumstances; (b) a control function that enables an adolescent to believe he or she has gained control of someone or something thought to be out of control, hopeless, or disastrous; or (c) a communication function that lets others know that something is wrong or that too much pain or too many injuries have been accumulated.

Often suicidal adolescents distort their thinking patterns in conjunction with the three functions of avoidance, control, and communication so that suicide becomes the best or only problem-solving option. Such distortions can take a number of directions. All-or-nothing thinking, for example, can enable an adolescent to view a situation in such a polarized way that the only two options seem to be continuing to be miserable and depressed or carrying out a suicide plan; no problem-solving options to cope with or overcome problems may seem possible (Capuzzi, 1988; Capuzzi & Gross, 2000). Identification of a single event that is then applied to all events is another cognitive distortion, that of overgeneralization. Being left out of a party or trip to the mountains with friends may be used as "evidence" for being someone no one likes, a "loser," or someone who will always be forgotten or left out. "I can't seem to learn the material for this class very easily" becomes "I'm never going to make it through school" or "I'll probably have the same difficulties when I start working full time." Adolescents who are experiencing stress and pain and who are becoming preoccupied with suicidal thoughts often experience more and more cognitive distortions. Such distortions result in self-talk that becomes more and more negative and more and more supportive of one of the following motivations for carrying through with a suicide plan:

- wanting to escape from a situation that seems (or is) intolerable (e.g., sexual abuse, conflict with peers or teachers, pregnancy, etc.)
- wanting to join someone who has died
- wanting to attract the attention of family or friends
- wanting to manipulate someone else
- wanting to avoid punishment
- wanting to be punished
- wanting to control when or how death will occur (an adolescent with a chronic or terminal illness may be motivated in this way)
- wanting to end a conflict that seems unresolvable
- wanting to punish the survivors
- wanting revenge.

Personality Traits

As noted by Capuzzi (1988), it would be ideal if the research on the profile of the suicidal adolescent provided practitioners with such a succinct profile of personality traits that teenagers at risk for suicide could be identified far in advance of any suicidal risk. Adolescents who fit the profile could then be assisted through individual and group counseling and other means. Although no consensus has yet been reached on the usual, typical, or average constellation of personality traits of the suicidal adolescent, researchers have agreed on a number of characteristics that seem to be common to many suicidal adolescents (Orbach, 2001).

Low self-esteem. A number of studies (Beautrais et al., 1999; Cull & Gill, 1982; Faigel, 1966; Freese, 1979; King, 1999; Price et al., 2001; Stein & Davis, 1982; Stillion, McDowell, & Shamblin, 1984) have connected low self-esteem with suicide probability. Our counseling experience as well as the experience of other practitioners seems to substantiate the relationship between low self-esteem and suicide probability. Almost all such clients have issues focused on feelings of low self-worth, and almost all such adolescents have experienced these self-doubts for an extended time period.

Hopelessness/helplessness. Most suicidal adolescents report feeling hopeless and helpless in relation to their circumstances as well as their ability to cope with these circumstances. The research support (Beautrais et al., 1999; Cull & Gill, 1982; Jacobs, 1971; Kovacs, Beck, & Weissman, 1975; Peck, 1983; Stanard, 2000) for verification of what clinicians report is growing. Most practitioners can expect to address this issue with suicidal clients and to identify a long-term history of feeling hopeless and helpless on the part of most clients.

Isolation. Many, if not most, suicidal adolescents tend to develop a small network of social support. They may find it uncomfortable to make new friends and rely on a small number of friends for support and companionship. (This may be the reason why so often those around a suicide victim state they did not notice anything unusual. The suicidal adolescent may not be in the habit of getting close enough to others so that changes in behavior, outlook, and so on can be noted.) A number of authorities (Gust-Brey & Cross, 1999; Hafen, 1972; Kiev, 1977; Peck, 1983; Sommes, 1984; Stein & Davis, 1982) support this observation.

High stress. High stress coupled with poor stress management skills seem to be characteristic of the suicidal adolescent. A number of studies have addressed this trait in terms of low frustration tolerance (Cantor, 1976; Kiev, 1977; Stanard, 2000).

Need to act out. Behaviors such as truancy, running away, refusal to cooperate at home or at school, use or abuse of alcohol or other drugs, and experimentation with sex are frequently part of the pattern present in the life of a suicidal adolescent. Such behaviors may be manifestations of depression. Often, adults remain so focused on the troublesome behavior connected with an adolescent's need to act out that they may overlook underlying depressive episodes.

Need to achieve. Sometimes, adolescents who are suicidal exhibit a pattern of high achievement. This achievement may be focused on getting high grades, being the class clown, accepting the most dares, wearing the best clothes, or any one of numerous other possibilities. In our counseling experience, this emphasis on achievement often is a compensation for feelings of low self-esteem. Readers should be cautioned, however, about jumping to the conclusion that every adolescent who achieves at a high level is suicidal. This trait, along with all of the other traits and characteristics connected with the profile of the suicidal adolescent, must be assessed in the context of other observations.

Poor communication skills. Suicidal adolescents often have a history of experiencing difficulty with expression of thoughts and feelings. Such adolescents may have trouble with identifying and labeling what they are feeling; self-expression seems awkward if not stressful. It is not unusual to discover that adolescents who have become preoccupied with suicidal thoughts have experienced a series of losses or disappointments that they have never been able to discuss and, understandably, integrate or resolve.

Other-directedness. Most suicidal adolescents are "other-directed" rather than "inner-directed." They are what others have told them they are instead of what they want to be; they value what others have said they should be instead of what they deem to be of personal value and worth. This trait may also be linked to low self-esteem and may lead to feelings of helplessness or inability to control interactions or circumstances around them.

Guilt. Usually connected with feelings of low self-esteem and a need to be other-directed, the guilt experienced by many suicidal adolescents is bothersome and sometimes linked to a "wanting to be punished" motivation for suicide. Some statements common to the guilt-ridden suicidal adolescent might include "Nothing I do seems to be good enough," "I feel so bad because I disappointed them," or "I should not have made that decision and should have known better."

Depression. Depression is a major element (Mazza & Reynolds, 1998) in the total profile of the suicidal adolescent. Hafen and Frandsen (1986) pointed out that there are sometimes differences between depression in an adult and depression in an adolescent. Adults are often despondent, tearful, sad, or incapable of functioning as usual. Although adolescents sometimes exhibit these characteristics, they may also respond with anger, rebelliousness, truancy, running away, using and abusing drugs, and so on. Those adults and peers who associate depression only with feelings of sadness and despondency may not recognize depression in adolescents who mask the depression with behavior that creates discomfort in family and school environments.

As noted by Capuzzi (1988),

> Given the complexity of being an adolescent in the late 1980's, coupled with the normal ups and downs of the developmental stage of adolescence, it is normal for every adolescent to experience short periods of depression. But when depressive periods become more and more frequent, longer and longer, and of such intensity that the adolescent has difficulty functioning at school and at home, they could be a strong warning sign of suicide potential, especially if other aspects of behavior, verbalization, motivations and cognitive distortions have been observed. (p. 10)

It is extremely important for counselors and other professionals who may be working with suicidal adolescents to complete additional coursework or training experiences to learn about the different types of depression. Although familiarity with resources and guidelines such as those provided by McWhirter and Kigin (1988) and the *Diagnostic and Statistical Manual of Mental Disorders* (American Psychiatric Association, 2000) are readily available to mental health practitioners, case supervision and consultation may be needed to accurately determine the nature of a depressive episode. Frequently, well-meaning practitioners fail to discriminate between depression created by a constellation of factors (negative self-talk, poor problem-solving skills, high stress, etc.) and depression that is a result of the body chemistry an adolescent inherited at birth. Treatment or counseling plans are different based on the kind of depression being experienced. Counselors, therapists, and core or crisis team members need to liaison with nurse-practitioners and psychiatrists when medical assessment and subsequent medication are appropriate for depression.

Poor problem-solving skills. Most parents notice differences in the problem-solving ability of their children. Some children are more resourceful than others in identification of problem resolution options. Suicidal adolescents seem, in our experience, to have less ability to develop solutions to troublesome situations or uncomfortable relationships. This may be a reason why suicidal preoccupation can progress from a cognitive focus to an applied plan with little dissonance created by the formulation and consideration of other problem-solving options and decisions.

CASE STUDY

Jim was a 17-year-old high school junior and the son of affluent, well-educated parents. Jim's dad was a successful attorney, and his mom was an assistant superintendent for the local school district. Jim's sister, Janell, was 15, well liked, a cheerleader, and involved in a variety of school and community-related activities. Janell had a beautiful singing voice and frequently accepted prominent roles in school, church, and community musical productions.

Although Jim had a few close friends, he preferred to spend most of his time reading and studying and was a straight A student. He accepted an opportunity to spend most of his junior year traveling and studying in Europe and thought such an experience would provide an excellent educational option as well as time away from his parents. Jim resented the high expectations his parents placed on both he and Janell and felt that his father did not approve of an earlier decision not to participate in varsity sports. Both parents, Jim felt, pressured him to be involved in school and community civic and social organizations; Jim preferred more solitary and intellectual pursuits. Jim felt somewhat self-conscious and awkward in social situations and never felt that he could present himself as well as his sister or in a way acceptable to his parents. He felt directed and criticized by both parents and resented the fact that his parents always seemed too busy to listen to him talk about things of importance to him. He really resented his father's lack of approval and felt that no one in his family seemed to really understand his point of view.

Jim had experienced periodic episodes of depression, and because he had decided that it was best not to talk with family members about his feelings, he usually tried to keep his sister and his parents from knowing that he felt really down. Jim noticed that his depression was the worst when he was under a lot of stress with respect to completing class assignments and during times that his parents pressured him into social situations. Bob, Jim's best friend, got so concerned about Jim toward the end of the exam period in the spring of their sophomore year that he told Jim's parents. Jim's parents took him to a psychiatrist, who prescribed an antidepressant and recommended weekly therapy. Jim's parents were angry with their son, resented the additional expense, and demanded that Jim get better as soon as possible. Janell hoped her friends would not find out because she was in the midst of being nominated for Queen of the Rose Festival and had already been selected as a Rose Festival Princess. Jim did not like the psychiatrist and felt as criticized by him as he did by his parents. He disliked the side effects of the medication, often skipped his weekly therapy session, and could hardly wait to leave home in late August to attend the orientation session at Cambridge prior to initiation of his travel/study itinerary.

Shortly after Thanksgiving, Jim's parents received a call from Switzerland; Jim had nearly died after an overdose of his medication and was recovering in a hospital in Zurich. Jim was sent home during the first part of December.

APPROACHES TO PREVENTION

Individual

Individually focused preventive counseling with Jim could have been focused in several ways. Jim could have benefited from a therapeutic relationship that included self-esteem enhancement as part of the treatment plan. If counseling/therapy had been initiated during elementary school years, Jim might not have responded with depression and, to a great extent, isolation and withdrawal from all but a few friends who provided a limited network of social support. Jim might also have been encouraged to share feelings and communicate with his parents. He also would have benefited from assertiveness training to assist him with sending needed messages to his parents at times when his parents were more preoccupied with career-related responsibilities and interests. Jim's counselor/therapist would probably have worked with him to become more aware of stressors and more adept at managing stress and removing stressors from his environment. Possibly, the combination of efforts made by his parents in couples' counseling and by Jim in the context of his individual work would have resulted in outcomes very different from those described in the previous case description.

Family

Most suicidal adolescents have developed their at-risk profiles over time beginning during early childhood. In families in which there is more than one child, it is often easy for parents to identify differences in self-esteem, communication skills, stress management, problem-solving, and so on. By the time a child is in elementary school, there may be visible indicators or traits that, if no intervention takes place, will result in the child's involvement in one or several at-risk behaviors. It is our opinion that such a child, by the time the middle school or junior high transition occurs, will be vulnerable to becoming pregnant, contracting AIDS, abusing drugs, developing an eating disorder, dropping out of school, or attempting or completing suicide.

Jim's family could have noted Jim's low self-esteem, discomfort with respect to sharing feelings, depression, response to stress, poor stress-management skills, and his resentment toward them. They might have been able to detect changes in his thinking patterns or fluctuations in day-to-day behaviors had they developed a relationship with him that included more open lines of communication. Jim's parents did not real-ize that their son experienced even higher levels of stress in conjunction with the Euro-pean study program and felt compelled to succeed at all costs. Jim also did not anticipate the amount of interchange and collaboration required by the group living situations he found himself in as he and his peers and teachers traveled from one com-munity to another and had begun to feel less self-assured than ever. Ideally, Jim's par-ents should have sought counseling assistance for themselves and their son when Jim was in elementary school. A counselor might have done an assessment of possible risk factors connected with Jim's family of origin and the families of his grandparents so that counseling could have compensated for predisposing factors and included an educational component for Jim's parents.

School and Community

There are a number of steps that can be taken to involve both the school and the community in prevention efforts (King, 2001a). In general, it is easier to initiate efforts in the school setting than it is in the context of a mental health center be-cause schools can easily access young people, reach and prepare school faculty and staff, involve parents, and collaborate with mental health professionals from the sur-rounding community.

A number of steps must be taken to facilitate a successful school–community pre-vention effort. Collaboration with administrators, faculty/staff in-service, preparation of crisis teams, providing for individual and group counseling options, parent educa-tion, and classroom presentations are described in the following subsections.

Collaboration With Administrators

There is a compelling need for prevention, crisis management, and postvention pro-grams for the adolescent suicide problem to be put in place in elementary, middle, and high schools throughout the country (Metha et al., 1998; Speaker & Petersen, 2000; Zenere & Lazarus, 1997). Based on our experience in the process of working with school districts all over the United States, one of the biggest mistakes made by coun-selors, educators, and coordinators of counseling/student services is to initiate pro-grams and services in this area without first obtaining commitment and support of administrators and others in supervisory positions. Too often efforts are initiated and then canceled because little or no negotiation with those in decision-making positions has taken place (Adelman & Taylor, 2000). Building principals and superintendents must be supportive; otherwise all efforts are destined for failure. Developing under-standing of the parameters connected with suicide prevention and intervention must start with the building principal and extend to all faculty and staff in a given building (Adelman & Taylor, 2000; King, 2001a) so that advance understanding of why quick action must take place is developed. During a crisis, schedules must be rearranged, and faculty and staff may be called on to teach an extra class, assist with an initial assessment, and so on. Everyone connected with a given building must have advance preparation.

In addition to the groundwork that must be done on the building level, it is also important to effect advance communication and planning on the district level. The superintendent, assistant superintendent, curriculum director, staff development director, student services coordinator, research and program evaluation specialist, and others must all commit their support to intervention efforts. When administrators have the opportunity to listen to an overview of proposed efforts and ask questions, a higher level of commitment can be established, and efforts can be more easily expedited. The probability of extending proposed programming to all schools in a given district is also increased.

Faculty/Staff In-Service

Because teachers and other faculty and staff usually learn of a student's suicidal preoccupation prior to the situation being brought to the attention of the school counselor or another member of the core or crisis team (assuming such a team exists), *all* faculty and staff must be included in building- or district-level in-service on the topic of adolescent suicide. Teachers, aides, secretaries, administrators, custodians, bus drivers, food service personnel, librarians, and school social workers all come in contact with adolescents at risk for suicide. It is imperative that all such adults be educated about both adolescent suicide and building and district policies and programs for prevention, crisis management, and postvention. There are a growing number of publications that provide excellent guidelines for elements of prevention programming focused on school faculty and staff (Davidson & Range, 1999; Kirchner, Yoder, Kramer, Lindsey, & Thrush, 2000; Metha et al., 1998; Speaker & Petersen, 2000; Zenere & Lazarus, 1997). When a young person reaches out to a trusted adult, that adult must have a clear understanding and a considerable amount of self-confidence so he or she knows exactly what to say and do as well as what not to say and do.

Many schools and school districts have actually precipitated suicide attempts by not providing for faculty/staff in-service on the topic prior to introducing discussion among student groups. When middle and high school students participate in educational programs on the topic of adolescent suicide, they begin to realize that they, as well as some of their friends, are at risk and they approach admired adults for assistance. Adults in the school who have no knowledge of what to do and who have not had the opportunity to have their questions answered and their apprehension lowered may be threatened by what a student is sharing and fail to make appropriate comments and decisions. Highly stressed, depressed, suicidal adolescents do not have the perspective to realize that such responses are connected with discomfort on the part of the adult and have little to do with what could be interpreted as disapproval and lack of acceptance. Awkward and minimal responses to suicidal self-disclosure on the part of a trusted adult can be interpreted by the adolescent as the loss of the last link to society and provide additional reinforcement for finalizing a suicide plan.

It is unethical not to prepare school faculty and staff in advance of the presentation of information on suicide to the students in a school. To do so could also become the basis for legal action by parents and family members. Much of the content in this chapter can become the basis for necessary in-service efforts.

Preparation of Crisis Teams

Many schools have crisis or core teams composed of faculty, staff, and parents connected with a particular building. These teams often exist in conjunction with a program for the prevention and intervention efforts necessary to cope with the drug problem among the young people in today's schools. Such teams usually consist of some combination of teachers, counselors, parents, social workers, school psychologists, school nurses, and school administrators. Usually these teams have been educated about traits that place adolescents at risk for substance use and abuse and have had supervision and instruction on the use of appropriate communication, diagnostic, and intervention skills necessary to begin the long-term process of recovery from alcoholism and other addictions. With education beyond that which is provided during the faculty/staff in-service discussed previously, as well as additional supervision and evaluation of clinical skills, a core or crisis team can be taught how to facilitate prevention efforts in a school as well as how to respond to a student already experiencing a suicidal crisis or in need of postvention efforts. In addition, such a team can be expected to write a policy statement that covers all parameters connected with prevention, crisis management, and postvention efforts. Such a policy could be adopted in other schools; in reality, except for specifics connected with a given building, the same policy statement should be adopted and followed throughout a school district. It is important to realize that everyone who is called on to assist a suicidal adolescent must know what to do. Confusion or lack of certainty about a chain of command or notification of parents procedures can result in delays and interfere with efforts to save a young person's life.

Individual and Group Counseling Options

Prior to providing students with any information about suicide and suicide prevention efforts in a school, arrangements must be made for the individual and group counseling services that will be needed by those who seek assistance for themselves or their friends. Unless such counseling options are available, any effort at prevention, crisis management, or postvention will be doomed to failure. This may present a problem to school personnel, particularly on the secondary level, unless there is a commitment on the part of administrators to free counselors from scheduling, hall monitoring, and other duties not related to the emerging role of the counselor of the 21st century. Working with suicidal adolescents requires a long-term commitment on the part of those interested in intervening. No counselor, psychologist, or social worker can undo the life experiences and self-perceptions of a lifetime without providing consistent, intensive opportunities for counseling.

If the school district cannot make a commitment to providing counseling, then arrangements for referral to community agencies and private practitioners must be made. It is important to provide adolescents and their families with a variety of referral possibilities along with information on fee schedules. There may be some question about whether the school district will be liable for the cost of such counseling if the referral is made by the school. (This issue should be explored by whatever legal counsel is retained by the district.) The dilemma, of course, is that unless counseling takes place when a suicidal adolescent has been identified, the probability is high that an attempt or a completion will take place. If the school is aware of a teenager's suicidal preoccupation and does not act in the best interests of such a teenager, families may later bring suit against the district. Counselors in the school and members of the mental health network in the community must preplan to work in concert for the benefit and safety of adolescents at risk for suicide.

Parent Education

Parents of students in a school in which a suicide prevention program is to be initiated should be involved in the school's efforts to educate, identify, and assist young people in this respect. Parents have a right to understand why the school is taking such steps and what the components of a schoolwide effort will be. Evening or late afternoon parent education efforts can be constructive and engender additional support for a school or school district. Parents have the same information needs as faculty and staff with respect to the topic of adolescent suicide. They will be more likely to refer themselves and their children to the school for assistance if they know of the school's interest in adolescent suicide prevention, have had an opportunity to ask questions about their adolescent sons' and daughters' behavior, and have been reassured about the quality and safety of the school's efforts.

Classroom Presentations

There is continuing debate surrounding the safety of adolescent suicide prevention programs that contain an educational component that is presented to adolescents. This debate is similar to the one that emerged years ago when schools initiated staff development and classroom presentations on the topic of physical and sexual abuse. There are a number of advocates of education and discussion efforts that are focused on students in conjunction with a schoolwide suicide prevention effort (Capuzzi, 1988, 1994; Capuzzi & Golden, 1988; Curran, 1987; Ross, 1980; Sudak, Ford, & Rushforth, 1984; Zenere & Lazarus, 1997). Providing adolescents with an appropriate forum in which they can receive accurate information, ask questions, and learn about how to obtain help for themselves and their friends does not precipitate suicidal preoccupation or attempts (Capuzzi, 1988, 1994; Capuzzi & Gross, 2000). Because newspaper and television reports of individual and cluster suicides do not usually include adequate education on the topic, and because many films have unrealistically presented or romanticized the act of suicide, it is important for schools to address the problem in a way that provides information and encourages young people to reach out for help prior to reaching the point of despair.

A carefully prepared and well-presented classroom presentation made by a member of the school's core team (or another presenter who has expertise on the topic) is essential. Such a presentation should include information on causes, myths, and symptoms as well as information about how to obtain help through the school. *Under no circumstances should media be used in which adolescents are shown a suicide plan.* In addition, on the elementary level, school faculty should not present programs on the topic of suicide prevention; their efforts are better focused on developmental counseling and classroom presentations directed at helping children overcome traits (such as low self-esteem or poor communication skills) that may put them at risk for suicidal behavior at a later time. Although these efforts should be continued through secondary education, middle and high school students are better served through presentations that address adolescent suicide directly. (Middle and high school students almost always have direct or indirect experience with suicide and appreciate the opportunity to obtain information and ask questions.)

Legal Considerations

Prior to discussing intervention strategies in the next section of this chapter, it seems appropriate to comment about some legal aspects of suicide prevention and intervention efforts in schools. In an excellent review of the results of school violence litigation against schools, Hermann and Remley (2000) noted that, even though those who are employed by school districts are expected to exert reasonable care to prevent harm to students, the courts have been reluctant to find educators liable for injuries related to violence or self-harm. State law claims usually fail because much of today's school violence (and suicide attempts and completions are components of school violence) results from what can be termed *spontaneous acts of violence*. This fact should not, however, lull school personnel into a false sense of security or complacency. A growing number of legal opinions have indicated that an unanticipated act of violence can be predictable and, thus, actionable under state law. Therefore, counselors, teachers, administrators, and other members of school staffs can protect themselves, as well as the youth they serve, by writing and implementing suicide prevention, crisis management, and postvention policy and procedures. These policy and procedures documents should mandate staff development for all school personnel so that all adults in the school setting recognize risk factors, possible behavioral, verbal, cognitive, and personality indicators, as well as role responsibilities and limitations. What we view as best practices are more likely to be followed if schools take a proactive rather than a reactive stance to this growing epidemic in our country's youth.

INTERVENTION STRATEGIES

Individual and Family

There are times that adolescents at risk for suicide are not identified until a crisis state has been reached. In such circumstances, it is important for all concerned to initiate action for the purpose of assessing lethality and determining appropriate follow-up. Because many professionals who are not counselors lack experience with adolescents who are in the midst of a personal crisis, the following guidelines may prove helpful. Note that these guidelines can be read in the context of working with Jim, the student in the case study. The assumption that one would have to make, however, is that all the adults traveling with Jim and his peers would have participated in staff development efforts and would include a counselor or other professional who could assess suicidal risk. An additional assumption is that families would be supportive of the use of these guidelines, either because they realized that the situation had escalated beyond their capacity to handle the situation or because they had participated in a school-sponsored presentation to the community on the topic of adolescent suicide prevention and intervention.

1. *Remember the meaning of the term* **crisis management.** When thinking of crisis management, it is important to understand the meaning of the word *crisis* as well as the word *management*. The word *crisis* means that the situation is not usual, normal, or average; circumstances are such that a suicidal adolescent is highly stressed and in considerable emotional discomfort. Adolescents in crisis usually feel vulnerable, hopeless, angry, low in self-esteem, and at a loss for how to cope. The word *management* means that the professional involved must be prepared to apply skills that are different from those required for preventive or postvention counseling. An adolescent in crisis must be assessed, directed, monitored, and guided for the purpose of preventing an act of self-destruction. Because adolescents who are experiencing a suicidal crisis may be quite volatile and impulsive, the need for decisive, rapid decision making on the part of the intervener is extremely important.

2. *Be calm and supportive.* A calm, supportive manner on the part of the intervener conveys respect for the perceptions and internal pain of an adolescent preoccupied with suicidal thoughts. Remember that such an adolescent usually feels hopeless and highly stressed. The demeanor and attitude of the helping person are pivotal in the process of offering assistance.

3. *Be nonjudgmental.* Statements such as "You can't be thinking of suicide; it is against the teachings of your church" or "I had a similar problem when I was your age and I didn't consider suicide" are totally inappropriate during a crisis situation. An adolescent's perception of a situation is, at least temporarily, reality and that reality must be respected. The same caution can be applied to the necessity of respecting a suicidal adolescent's expression of feelings whether

these feelings are those of depression, frustration, fear, or helplessness. Judgmental, unaccepting responses and comments only serve to further damage an already impaired sense of self-esteem and decrease willingness to communicate. Adolescents could sink further into depression or increase their resolve to carry through with a suicide plan if others are critical and unwilling to acknowledge what appear, to the adolescent, to be unsurmountable obstacles.

4. *Encourage self-disclosure.* The very act of talking about painful emotions and difficult circumstances is the first step in what can become a long-term healing process. A professional helper may be the first person with whom such a suicidal adolescent has shared and trusted in months or even years, and it may be difficult to do simply because of lack of experience with communicating thoughts and feelings. It is important to support and encourage self-disclosure so that an assessment of lethality can be made early in the intervention process.

5. *Acknowledge the reality of suicide as a choice but do not normalize suicide as a choice.* It is important for practitioners to let adolescents know that they are not alone and isolated with respect to suicidal preoccupation. It is also important to communicate the idea that suicide is a choice, a problem-solving option, and that there are other choices and options. This may be difficult to do in a way that does not make such an adolescent feel judged or put down. An example of what could be said to an adolescent in crisis is "It is not unusual for adolescents to be so upset with relationships or circumstances that thoughts of suicide occur more and more frequently; this does not mean that you are weird or a freak. I am really glad you have chosen to talk to me about how you're feeling and what you are thinking. You have made a good choice since, now, you can begin exploring other ways to solve the problems you described."

6. *Actively listen and positively reinforce.* It is important, during the initial stages of the crisis management process, to let the adolescent at risk for suicide know you are listening carefully and really understanding how difficult life has been. Not only will such careful listening and communicating, on the part of the professional, make it easier for the adolescent to share, but also it will provide the basis for a growing sense of self-respect. Being listened to, heard, and respected are powerful and empowering experiences for anyone who is feeling at a loss for how to cope.

7. *Do not attempt in-depth counseling.* Although it is very important for a suicidal adolescent to begin to overcome feelings of despair and to develop a sense of control as soon as possible, the emotional turmoil and stress experienced during a crisis usually make in-depth counseling impossible. Developing a plan to begin lessening the sense of crisis an adolescent may be experiencing is extremely important, however, and should be accomplished as soon as possible. Crisis management necessitates the development of a plan to lessen the crisis; this plan should be shared with the adolescent so that it is clear that circumstances will improve. Counseling/therapy cannot really take place during the height of a suicidal crisis.

8. *Contact another professional.* It is a good idea to enlist the assistance of another professional, trained in crisis management, when an adolescent thought to be at risk for suicide is brought to your attention. School and mental health counselors should ask a colleague to come into the office and assist with assessment. It is always a good idea to have the support of a colleague who understands the dynamics of a suicidal crisis; in addition, the observations made by two professionals are likely to be more comprehensive. Because suicidal adolescents may

present a situation that, if misjudged or mismanaged, could result in a subsequent attempt or completion, it is in the best interests of both the professional and the client for professionals to work collaboratively whenever possible. It should also be noted that liability questions are less likely to become issues and professional judgment is less likely to be questioned if assessment of the severity of a suicidal crisis and associated recommendations for crisis management have been made on a collaborative basis. *No matter what the circumstances, document all that is done on behalf of the youth through keeping careful case notes.*

9. *Ask questions to assess lethality.* A number of dimensions must be explored to assess lethality. This assessment can be accomplished through an interview format (a crisis situation is not conducive to the administration of a written appraisal instrument). The following questions help determine the degree of risk in a suicidal crisis; all of them do not need to be asked if the interview results in the spontaneous disclosure of the information:

- *"What has happened to make life so difficult?"* The more an adolescent describes the circumstances that have contributed to feelings of despair and hopelessness, the better the opportunity for effective crisis management. The process of describing stress-producing interpersonal situations and circumstances may begin to lower feelings of stress and reduce risk. It is not unusual for an adolescent in the midst of a suicidal crisis to describe a multifaceted set of problems with family, peers, school, drugs, and so on. The more problems an adolescent describes as stress-producing and the more complicated the scenario, the higher the lethality or risk.

- *"Are you thinking of suicide?"* Although this may not be the second question asked during an assessment of risk (ask it when you think the timing is right), it is listed here because it is the second most important question to ask. Adolescents who have been preoccupied with suicidal thoughts may experience a sense of relief to know there is someone who is able to discuss suicide in a straightforward manner. Using the word *suicide* will convey that the helping professional is listening and is willing to be involved; using the word *suicide* will not put the idea of suicide in the mind of a nonsuicidal adolescent. This particular question need not be asked until such time the assessor has developed the rapport and trust of the adolescent; timing is important in this regard so that relief rather than resistance is experienced on the part of the adolescent.

- *"How long have you been thinking about suicide?"* Adolescents who have been preoccupied with suicide for a period of several weeks are more lethal than those who have only fleeting thoughts. One way to explore several components of this question is to remember the acronym FID: When asking about suicidal thoughts, ask about *frequency* or how often they occur, *intensity* or how dysfunctional the preoccupation is making the adolescent ("Can you go on with your daily routine as usual?"), and *duration* or how long the periods of preoccupation last. Obviously, an adolescent who reports frequent periods of preoccupation so intense that it is difficult or impossible to go to school, to work, or to see friends, and for increasingly longer periods of time so that periods of preoccupation and dysfunction are merging, is more lethal than an adolescent who describes a different set of circumstances.

- *"Do you have a suicide plan?"* When an adolescent is able to be specific about the method, the time, the place, and who will or will not be nearby, the risk is higher. (If the use of a gun, knife, medication or other means is described, ask if that item is in a pocket or purse and request that the item be left with you. Never, however, enter into a struggle with an adolescent to remove a firearm. Call the police or local suicide or crisis center.) Most adolescents will cooperate with you by telling you about the plan and allowing you to separate them from the means. Remember, most suicidal adolescents are other-directed; such a trait should be taken advantage of during a crisis management situation. Later, when the crisis has subsided and counseling is initiated, the adolescent's internal locus of control can be strengthened.

- *"Do you know someone who has committed suicide?"* If the answer to this question is yes, the adolescent may be of higher risk, especially if this incident occurred within the family or a close network of friends. Such an adolescent may have come to believe that suicide is a legitimate problem-solving option.

- *"How much do you want to live?"* An adolescent who can provide only a few reasons for wishing to continue with life is of higher risk than an adolescent who can enumerate a number of reasons for continuing to live.

- *"How much do you want to die?"* The response to this question provides the opposite view of the one above. An adolescent who gives a variety of reasons for wishing to die is more lethal than an adolescent who cannot provide justification for ending life. It may be unnecessary to ask this question if the previous question provided adequate data.

- *"What do you think death is like?"* This question can be an excellent tool for assessment purposes. Adolescents who do not seem to realize that death is permanent, that there is no reversal possible, and that they cannot physically return are at higher risk for an actual attempt. Also, adolescents who have the idea that death will be "romantic," "nurturing," or "the solution to current problems" are at high risk.

- *"Have you attempted suicide in the past?"* If the answer to this question is yes, then the adolescent is more lethal. Another attempt may occur that could be successful because a previous attempter has the memory of prior efforts and the fact that he or she conceptualized and carried through with a suicide plan. An additional attempt may correct deficits in the original plan and result in death.

- *"How long ago was this previous attempt?"* is a question that should be asked of any adolescent who answers yes to the previous question. The more recent the previous attempt, the more lethal the adolescent and the more critical the crisis management process.

- *"Have you been feeling depressed?"* Because a high percentage of adolescents who attempt or complete suicide are depressed, this is an important question. Using the acronym FID to remember to ask about frequency, intensity, and duration is also helpful in the context of exploring an adolescent's response to this question. As previously discussed, a determination needs to be made about the existence of clinical depression if such a condition is suspected. Adolescents who report frequent, intense, and lengthy periods of depression resulting in dysfunctional episodes that are becoming closer and closer together, or are continuously experienced, are at high risk.

- *"Is there anyone to stop you?"* This is an extremely important question. If an adolescent has a difficult time identifying a friend, family member, or significant adult who is worth living for, the probability of a suicide attempt is high. Whomever the adolescent can identify should be specifically named; addresses, phone numbers, and the relationship to the adolescent should also be obtained. (If the adolescent cannot remember phone numbers and addresses, look up the information, together, in a phone book.) In the event it is decided that a suicide watch should be initiated, the people in the network of the adolescent can be contacted and asked to participate.

- *"On a scale of 1 to 10, with 1 being low and 10 being high, what is the number that depicts the probability that you will attempt suicide?"* The higher the number, the higher the lethality.
- *"Do you use alcohol or other drugs?"* If the answer to this question is yes, the lethality is higher because use of a substance further distorts cognition and weakens impulse control. An affirmative response should also be followed by an exploration of the degree of drug involvement and identification of specific drugs.
- *"Have you experienced significant losses during the past year or earlier losses you've never discussed?"* Adolescents who have lost friends because of moving, vitality because of illness, their family of origin because of a divorce, and so on are vulnerable to stress and confusion and are usually at higher risk for attempting or completing suicide if they have been preoccupied with such thoughts.
- *"Have you been concerned, in any way, with your sexuality?"* This may be a difficult question to explore, even briefly, during a peaking suicidal crisis. Generally, adolescents who are, or think they may be, gay or lesbian are at higher risk for suicide. It is quite difficult for adolescents to deal with the issue of sexual orientation because of fear about being ridiculed or rejected. They may have experienced related guilt and stress for a number of years, never daring to discuss their feelings with anyone.
- *"When you think about yourself and the future, what do you visualize?"* A high-risk adolescent will probably have difficulty visualizing a future scenario and will describe feeling too hopeless and depressed to even imagine a future life.

As noted at the beginning of this discussion, it is not necessary to ask all of these questions if the answers to them are shared during the course of the discussion. Also, it is appropriate to ask additional questions after a response to any of the above when it seems constructive to do so. It should be noted that the interviewing team must make judgments about the truthfulness of a specific response by considering the response in the total context of the interview.

10. *Make crisis management decisions.* If, as a result of an assessment made by at least two professionals, the adolescent is at risk for suicide, a number of crisis management interventions can be considered. They may be used singly or in combination; the actual combination will depend on the lethality determination, resources and people available, and professional judgment. It is the responsibility of the professionals involved, however, to develop a crisis management plan to be followed until the crisis subsides and long-term counseling or therapy can be initiated.

- *Notify parent/legal guardians.* Parents of minors must be notified and asked for assistance when an adolescent is determined to be at risk for a suicide attempt. Often, adolescents may attempt to elicit a promise of confidentiality from a school or mental health counselor who learns about suicidal intent. Such confidentiality is not possible; the welfare of the adolescent is the most important consideration, and parents should be contacted as soon as possible.

  Sometimes parents do not believe that their child is suicidal and refuse to leave home or work and meet with their son or daughter and members of the assessment team. At times, parents may be adamant in their demands that the school or mental health professional withdraw their involvement. Although such attitudes are not conducive to the management of a suicidal crisis, they are understandable because parents may respond to such information with denial or anger to mask true emotions and cope with apprehensions that perhaps their child's situation reflects their personal inadequacies as people and parents. Because an adolescent at risk for a suicide attempt cannot be left unmonitored, this provides a dilemma for a school or a mental health agency. Because conforming to the wishes of uncooperative parents places the adolescent at even greater risk, steps must be taken despite parental protests. Although some professionals worry about liability issues in such circumstances, liability is higher if such an adolescent is allowed to leave unmonitored and with no provision for follow-up assistance. It may be necessary to refer the youth to protective services for children and families when parents or guardians refuse to cooperate. Schools and mental health centers should confer with legal counsel to understand liability issues and to make sure that the best practices are followed in such circumstances.

- *Consider hospitalization.* Hospitalization can be the option of choice during a suicidal crisis (even if the parents are cooperating) when the risk is high. An adolescent who has not been sleeping or eating, for example, may be totally exhausted or highly agitated. The care and safety that can be offered in a psychiatric unit of a hospital are often needed until the adolescent can experience a lowered level of stress, obtain food and rest, and realize that others consider the circumstances painful and worthy of attention. In many hospital settings, multidisciplinary teams (physicians, psychiatrists, counselors, social workers, nurses, nurse practitioners, teachers) work to individualize a treatment plan and provide for outpatient help as soon as the need for assistance on an inpatient basis subsides.

- *Write contracts.* At times, professionals may decide that developing a contract with the adolescent may be enough to support the adolescent through a period of crisis and into a more positive frame of mind after which the adolescent would be more receptive to long-term counseling or therapy. Such a contract should be written out and signed and dated by the adolescent and the counselor. The contract can also be witnessed and signed by other professionals, friends, or family members.

  Contracts should require the adolescent to
  1. Agree to stay safe.
  2. Obtain enough food and sleep.
  3. Discard items that could be used in a suicide attempt (guns, weapons, medications, etc.).
  4. Specify the time span of the contract.
  5. Call a counselor, crisis center, and so on if there is a temptation to break the contract or attempt suicide.
  6. Write down the phone numbers of people to contact if the feeling of crisis escalates.
  7. Specify ways time will be structured (walks, talks, movies, etc.).

- *Organize suicide watches.* If hospital psychiatric services on an inpatient basis are not available in a given community and those doing the assessment believe the suicide risk is high, a suicide watch should be organized by contacting the individuals whom the adolescent has identified in response to the question, "Is there anyone to stop you?" After receiving instruction and orientation from the professional, family members and friends should take turns staying with the adolescent until the crisis has subsided and long-term counseling or therapy has begun. In our opinion, it is never a good idea to depend on a family member alone to carry out a suicide watch; it is usually too difficult for family members to retain perspective. Friends should be contacted and included in a suicide watch even though confidentiality, as discussed earlier, cannot be maintained.

- *Refuse to allow the youth to return to school without an assessment by a mental health counselor, psychologist, psychiatrist, or other qualified professional.* An increasing number of school districts are adopting this policy. Although it could be argued that preventing a suicidal youth from returning to school might exacerbate suicidal ideation and intent, this policy increases the probability that the youth will receive mental health counseling and provides the school with support in the process of preventing the youth from engaging in self-harm.

School and Community

When an adolescent has attempted or completed a suicide, it is imperative, particularly in a school setting, to be aware of the impact of such an event on the "system." Usually, within just a few hours, the fact that an adolescent has attempted or completed suicide has been chronicled through the peer group. This could present a problem to the faculty and staff in a given school building because not answering questions raised by students can engender the sharing of misinformation or rumors and encouraging open discussion could embarrass an attempter on his or her return.

The following guidelines should prove helpful. Had Jim been in the regular school program when he made his attempt, these guidelines would have been put into effect immediately.

1. The principal of the building in which a student has attempted or completed suicide (even though such an incident most likely occurred off the school campus) should organize a telephone network to notify all faculty and staff that a mandatory meeting will take place prior to school the next morning. (Prior to the meeting, the principal should confirm the death through the coroner's office or through the student's family.) The principal should share information and answer questions about what happened during such a meeting. In the case of a suicide completion, it is recommended that the principal provide all faculty and staff with an announcement that can be read, in each class rather than over a public address system, so that everyone in the school receives the same information. The announcement should confirm the loss and emphasize the services the school and community will be providing during the day and subsequent days. Details about the circumstances or the family of the deceased should not be given so that confidentiality is maintained in that regard.
2. Faculty and staff should be instructed to answer student questions that spontaneously arise but should be told not to initiate a discussion of suicide in general.
3. Faculty and staff should be told to excuse students from class if they are upset and need to spend time in the office of the building counselor or another member of a core or crisis team.
4. Parents who are upset by the suicidal incident should be directed to a designated individual to have questions answered. Parents should also be provided with options for counseling, whether this counseling is provided by school personnel or referred to members of the mental health community.

5. At times, newspaper and television journalists contact the school for information about both the suicide attempt or the completion and the school's response to the aftermath. Again, it is important to direct all such inquiries to a designated individual to avoid the problems created by inconsistency or sharing inaccurate information.

6. If a suicidal attempt occurs prior to the initiation of prevention and crisis management efforts in a given building, it is not a good idea to immediately initiate classroom mental health education even if faculty, staff, and core teams have been prepared and a written policy has been developed. Allow sufficient time to pass to prevent embarrassment to the returning student and his or her family.

7. Be alert to delayed or enhanced grief responses on the part of students prior to the anniversary of a suicide completion. Often students will need opportunity to participate in a support group with peers or individual counseling prior to and, perhaps, beyond the anniversary date.

8. Do not conduct a memorial service on the school campus after a suicide because doing so may provide reinforcement to other students preoccupied with suicidal ideation. This means that it is unwise to conduct an on-campus memorial service after a death for any reason—it is difficult to explain why a student who has committed suicide is not being remembered when another student, faculty, or staff has been memorialized previously. Excuse students to attend the off-campus memorial or funeral. Do the same thing after deaths for other reasons.

9. Early in the sequence of events, as listed above, one or two individuals from the school should contact the family and ask if there is any support they might need that the school can provide. It is a good idea to offer such assistance periodically, as time passes, because so many families are left alone with their grief once the memorial or funeral has taken place.

ADAPTATIONS FOR DIVERSITY

It is important to note that the information contained in the introductory section of this chapter suggests a number of adaptations for diversity, particularly with respect to prevention efforts. Because data suggest that Caucasian adolescent males are the highest risk group for suicide, extra efforts should be made to involve those young men who may be vulnerable in early prevention efforts. Individual and group counseling, focused on some of the personality traits described earlier, could and should be initiated in the elementary school years. Such early prevention efforts are preferable to waiting until suicidal preoccupation develops and observations about behavior can be observed. Because Native Americans have the highest adolescent suicide rates of any ethnic group in the United States, teachers, counselors, and parents should be alerted to early signs so that efforts can be made to avert the development of at-risk behaviors.

The etiology of suicide is something that all adults should be made aware of so that young people experiencing psychiatric illness, abuse, confusion about sexual identity, chronic or terminal physical illness, and so on (see discussion earlier in the chapter) can be monitored, supported, and referred for counseling/therapy when needed. Staffing sessions should be routinely conducted in elementary, middle, and high school settings so that young people who may be at risk for suicide attempts or completions could be routinely monitored and assisted. Because we know that adolescents who experience what they interpret as shameful or humiliating experiences with peers and with family members may, at times, be at high risk, these young people should also be the focus of observation and action should the need for prevention or intervention efforts be identified. In general, the more adults can be made aware of both risk factors and the suicidal profile, the earlier and more effective the prevention or intervention efforts.

SUMMARY

We believe that individuals who are interested in working with suicidal youth must obtain more extensive information than that provided in this chapter. In addition, such individuals should obtain supervision from professionals qualified to provide such supervision after observing actual assessment interview and counseling/therapy sessions. Generally, neither assessment nor preventive or postvention sessions should be attempted by anyone who has graduated from a graduate program with *less than* a 2-year coursework and practicum/internship requirement. (In the case of counselors, such a graduate program should follow the standard set by the Council for the Accreditation of Counseling and Related Educational Programs.) In addition, membership in the American Association of Suicidology, participation in workshops and conferences focused on the topic of adolescent suicide, and consistent reading of the journal *Suicide and Life-Threatening Behavior* and other related books and journals are imperative.

Readers should also be cautioned not to use the material in this chapter as the sole basis for mental health education on the topic of adolescent suicide prevention or faculty/staff development in schools. This chapter provides an overview and an excellent starting point for professionals. Those without expertise on the topic or graduate preparation as a counselor, social worker, psychologist, psychiatric nurse, or other helping professions will not be able to answer questions of clients, families, and other professionals on the basis of reading a single chapter on this topic. Finally, anyone reading this chapter should be cautioned against initiating an adolescent suicide prevention, crisis management, and postvention program without writing a description of the various components so it can be checked by other professionals (including attorneys) and followed by all those involved in such an initiative.

An adolescent who becomes suicidal is communicating the fact that he or she is experiencing difficulty with problem solving, managing stress, expressing feelings, and so on. It is important for us to respond in constructive, safe, informed ways because the future of our communities (whether local, national, or international) is dependent on individuals who are positive, functional, and able to cope with the complex demands of life. As research and clinical experience provide additional and more sophisticated information about adolescent suicide, it will be necessary to incorporate this information into prevention, crisis management, and postvention efforts. To abdicate our responsibility to do so would communicate a lack of interest in the youth of today and a lack of concern about the future of society.

REFERENCES

Adelman, H. S., & Taylor, L. (2000). Moving prevention from the fringes into the fabric of school improvement. *Journal of Educational and Psychological Consultation, 11,* 7–36.

American Psychiatric Association. (2000). *Diagnostic and statistical manual of mental disorders* (4th ed., text revision). Washington, DC: Author.

Beautrais, A. L., Joyce, P. R., & Mulder, R. T. (1999). Personality traits and cognitive styles as risk factors for serious suicide attempts among young people. *Suicide and Life-Threatening Behavior, 29*, 37–47.

Berlin, I. N. (1987). Suicide among American Indian adolescents: An overview. *Suicide and Life-Threatening Behavior, 17*, 218–232.

Berman, A. L., & Jobes, D. A. (1991). *Adolescent suicide: Assessment and intervention*. Washington DC: American Psychological Association.

Blumenthal, S. J. (1991). Letter to the editor. *Journal of the American Medical Association, 265*, 2806–2807.

Borowsky, I. W., Ireland, M., & Resnick, M. D. (2001). Adolescent suicide attempts: Risks and protectors. *Pediatrics, 107*, 485–493.

Brent, D. A., Perper, J. A., Moritz, G., Baugher, M., Schweers, J., & Roth, C. (1993). Firearms and adolescent suicide: A community case-control study. *American Journal of Diseases in Children, 147*, 1066–1071.

Bush, J. A. (1976). Suicide and Blacks. *Suicide and Life-Threatening Behavior, 6*, 216–222.

Canetto, S. S., & Sakinofsky, I. (1998). The gender paradox in suicide. *Suicide and Life-Threatening Behavior, 28*, 1–23.

Cantor, P. (1976). Personality characteristics found among youthful female suicide attempters. *Journal of Abnormal Psychology, 85*, 324–329.

Capuzzi, D. (1988). *Counseling and intervention strategies for adolescent suicide prevention* (Contract No. 400-86-0014). Ann Arbor, MI: ERIC Counseling and Personnel Services Clearinghouse.

Capuzzi, D. (1994). *Suicide prevention in the schools: Guidelines for middle and high school settings*. Alexandria, VA: American Counseling Association.

Capuzzi, D., & Golden, L. (Eds.). (1988). *Preventing adolescent suicide*. Muncie, IN: Accelerated Development.

Capuzzi, D., & Gross, D. (2000). "I don't want to live": The adolescent at risk for suicidal behavior. In D. Capuzzi, & D. Gross (Eds.), *Youth at risk: A prevention resource for counselors, teachers, and parents* (3rd ed., pp. 319–352). Alexandria, VA: American Counseling Association.

Cavaiola, A. A., & Lavender, N. (1999). Suicidal behavior in chemically dependent adolescents. *Adolescence, 34*, 735–744.

Centers for Disease Control and Prevention. (2000). CDC Surveillance Summaries (No. SS-5). *MMWR, 49*, 10.

Cohen, E. M. (2000). Suicidal ideation among adolescents in relation to recalled exposure to violence. *Current Psychology, 19*, 46–56.

Committee on Adolescence. (2000). Suicide and suicide attempts in adolescence. *Pediatrics, 105*, 871–874.

Coy, D. R. (1995).The need for a school suicide prevention policy. *National Association of Student Services Professionals Bulletin, 79*, 1–9.

Cull, J., & Gill, W. (1982). *Suicide probability scale manual*. Los Angeles: Western Psychological Services.

Curran, D. F. (1987). *Adolescent suicidal behavior*. Washington, DC: Hemisphere.

Davidson, M. W., & Range, L. M. (1999). Are teachers of children and young adolescents responsive to suicide prevention training modules? Yes. *Death Studies, 23*, 61–71.

Davis, P. A. (1983). *Suicidal adolescents*. Springfield, IL: Charles C Thomas.

Diekstra, R. F. (1989). Suicidal behavior in adolescents and young adults: The international picture. *Crisis, 10*, 16–35.

Faigel, H. (1966). Suicide among young persons: A review of its incidence and causes, and methods for its prevention. *Clinical Pediatrics, 5*, 187–190.

Fernquist, R. M. (2000). Problem drinking in the family and youth suicide. *Adolescent Psychology, 35*, 551–558.

Freese, A. (1979). *Adolescent suicide: Mental health challenge*. New York: Public Affairs Committee.

Garland, A. F., & Zigler, E. (1993). Adolescent suicide prevention: Current research and social policy implications. *American Psychologist, 43*, 169–182.

Gibbs, J. T. (1988). Conceptual, methodological, and sociocultural issues in Black youth suicide: Implications for assessment and early intervention. *Suicide and Life-Threatening Behavior, 18,* 73–79.

Gust-Brey, K., & Cross, T. (1999). An examination of the literature base on the suicidal behaviors of gifted students. *Roeper Review, 22,* 28–35.

Hafen, B. Q. (Ed.). (1972). *Self-destructive behavior.* Minneapolis, MN: Burgess.

Hafen, B. Q., & Frandsen, K. J. (1986). *Youth suicide: Depression and loneliness.* Provo, UT: Behavioral Health Associates.

Harry, J. (1989). *Sexual identity issues: Report of the Secretary's Task Force on Youth Suicide: Vol. 2. Risk factors for youth suicide* (DHHS Publication No. ADM 89-1622). Washington, DC: Government Printing Office.

Henry, A. F., & Short, J. F. (1954). *Suicide and homicide.* Glencoe, IL: Free Press.

Hermann, M. A., & Remley, T. P., Jr. (2000). Guns, violence, and schools. The results of school violence litigation against educators and students shedding more constitutional rights at the school house gate. *Loyola Law Review, 46,* 389–439.

Hoberman, H. M., & Garfinkel, B. D. (1988). Completed suicide in children and adolescents. *Journal of the American Academy of Child and Adolescent Psychiatry, 27,* 688–695.

Hussain, S. A., & Vandiver, K. T. (1984). *Suicide in children and adolescents.* New York: SP Medical and Scientific Books.

Jacobs, J. (1971). *Adolescent suicide.* New York: Wiley-Interscience.

Johnson, S. W., & Maile, L. J. (1987). *Suicide and the schools: A handbook for prevention, intervention, and rehabilitation.* Springfield, IL: Charles C Thomas.

Kiev, A. (1977). *The suicidal patient.* Chicago: Nelson-Hall.

King, K. A. (1999). Fifteen prevalent myths concerning adolescent suicide. *Journal of School Health, 69,* 159–161.

King, K. A. (2000). Preventing adolescent suicide: Do high school counselors know the risk factors? *Professional School Counseling, 3,* 255–263.

King, K. A. (2001a). Developing a comprehensive school suicide prevention program. *Journal of School Health, 71,* 132–137.

King, K. A. (2001b). Tri-level suicide prevention covers it all. *Education Digest, 67,* 55–61.

Kirchner, J. E., Yoder, M. C., Kramer, T. L., Lindsey, M. S., & Thrush, C. (2000). Development of an educational program to increase school personnel's awareness about child and adolescent depression. *Education, 121,* 235–246.

Kovacs, M., Beck, A., & Weissman, A. (1975). The use of suicidal motives in the psychotherapy of attempted suicides. *American Journal of Psychotherapy, 29,* 363–368.

Lyon, M. E., Benoit, M., O'Donnell, R. M., Getson, P. R., Silber, T., & Walsh, T. (2000). Assessing African American adolescents' risk for suicide attempts. *Adolescence, 35,* 121–134.

Mazza, J. J., & Reynolds, W. M. (1998). A longitudinal investigation of depression, hopelessness, social support, and major and minor life events and their relation to suicidal ideation in adolescents. *Suicide and Life-Threatening Behavior, 28,* 358–374.

McWhirter, J. J., & Kigin, T. J. (1988). Depression. In D. Capuzzi & L. Golden (Eds.), *Preventing adolescent suicide* (pp. 149–186). Muncie, IN: Accelerated Development.

Metha, A., Weber, B., & Webb, L. D. (1998). Youth suicide prevention: A survey and analysis of policies and efforts in the 50 states. *Suicide and Life-Threatening Behavior, 28,* 150–164.

National Center for Health Statistics. (2002). Deaths: Leading causes for 2000. *National Vital Statistics Reports, 50,* 16.

National Institute of Mental Health. (2002). *Suicide facts.* Retrieved November 21, 2002, from http://www.nimh.nih.gov/research/suifact.htm

Orbach, I. (2001). Therapeutic empathy with the suicidal wish: Principles of therapy with suicidal individuals. *American Journal of Psychotherapy, 55,* 166–184.

Peck, D. (1983). The last moments of life: Learning to cope. *Deviant Behavior, 4,* 313–342.

Price, J. H., Dake, J. A., & Kucharewski, R. (2001). Assets as predictors of suicide attempts in African American inner-city youths. *American Journal of Health Behavior, 25,* 367–375.

Rohde, P., Lewinsohn, P., & Seeley, J. R. (1991). Comorbidity of unipolar depression: Comorbidity with other mental disorders in adolescents and adults. *Journal of Abnormal Psychology, 100,* 214–222.

Ross, C. (1980). Mobilizing schools for suicide prevention. *Suicide and Life-Threatening Behavior, 10,* 239–243.

Russell, S. T., & Joyner, K. (2001). Adolescent sexual orientation and suicide risk: Evidence from a natural study. *American Journal of Public Health, 91,* 1276–1281.

Satcher, D. (1999). *Remarks at the release of the Surgeon General's call to action to prevent suicide.* Retrieved November 21, 2002, from http://www.surgeongeneral.gov/library/callto action/remarks.htm

Schneidman, E., Farberow, N., & Litman, R. (1976). *The psychology of suicide.* New York: Jason Aronson.

Shaffer, D. (1988). The epidemiology of teen suicide: An examination of risk factors. *Journal of Clinical Psychiatry, 49,* 36–41.

Shaffer, D., & Craft, L. (1999). Methods of adolescent suicide prevention. *Journal of Clinical Psychiatry, 60,* 70–74.

Shaffer, D., Garland, A., Gould, M., Fisher, P., & Trautman, P. (1988). Preventing teenage suicide: A critical review. *Journal of the American Academy of Child and Adolescent Psychiatry, 27,* 675–687.

Sommes, B. (1984). The troubled teen: Suicide, drug use, and running away. *Women and Health, 9,* 117–141.

Speaker, K. M., & Petersen, G. J. (2000). School violence and adolescent suicide: Strategies for effective intervention. *Educational Review, 52,* 65–73.

Stanard, R. P. (2000). Assessment and treatment of adolescent suicidality. *Journal of Mental Health Counseling, 22,* 204–217.

Stein, M., & Davis, J. (1982). *Therapies for adolescents.* San Francisco: Jossey-Bass.

Stillion, J., McDowell, E., & Shamblin, J. (1984). The suicide attitude vignette experience: A method for measuring adolescent attitudes toward suicide. *Death Education, 8,* 65–81.

Sudak, H., Ford, A., & Rushforth, N. (1984). Adolescent suicide: An overview. *American Journal of Psychotherapy, 38,* 350–369.

Velkoff, P., & Huberty, T. J. (1988). Thinking patterns and motivation. In D. Capuzzi & L. Golden (Eds.), *Preventing adolescent suicide* (pp. 111–147). Muncie, IN: Accelerated Development.

Wyche, K., Obolensky, N., & Glood, E. (1990). American Indian, Black American, and Hispanic American youth. In M. J. Rotheram-Borus, J. Bradley, & N. Obolensky (Eds.), *Planning to live: Evaluating and treating suicidal teens in community settings* (pp. 355–389). Tulsa: University of Oklahoma Press.

Zenere, F. J., III, & Lazarus, P. J. (1997). The decline of youth suicidal behavior in an urban, multicultural public school system following the introduction of a suicide prevention and intervention program. *Suicide and Life-Threatening Behavior, 27,* 387–403.

12 | "I Am Somebody": Gang Membership

Sonja C. Burnham

Gangs have been present in history for centuries. Literature and music reveal the existence of groups that meet the criteria established by Jackson and McBride (1987): "A gang is a group of people that form an allegiance for the common purpose, and engage in unlawful or criminal activity" (p. 20). Spergel (1990) added to a clear definition of gang activity by stating that "the principal criterion currently used to define a *gang* may be the group's participation in illegal activity" (p. 179). Robin Hood and his Merry Men are most recognizable as a group that fits these definitions. Robin Hood's gang was using force and weapons to prey on the rich to provide for the poor. Literature and popular movies have romanticized their behavior, but they were still operating outside the law.

Gangs have existed in the United States since the Revolutionary War. One notable example was Jean Laffite, who led his buccaneers against the British in Louisiana in support of General Andrew Jackson. The days of the Wild West were notorious for gangs. The most notable of these may have been Jesse James and his brother Frank, who were legendary for their activities. In response to the early gangs, government officials offered rewards for the capture of these individuals (Jankowski, 1991).

Gangs are having an enormous impact on all of society, in all parts of the country. No geographical area, racial or cultural group, or school district is immune to problems that may be traced to some aspect of gang activity. Because the gang problem has become so extensive, approaches to prevention of increased gang activity and intervention of existing gang activity need to be undertaken simultaneously. Approaches to prevention of gang involvement concern not just gang members but families, schools, communities, and others who are involved with these groups.

This chapter first defines the problem by looking at gangs in the past; factors for gang involvement in the present, including characteristics of gangs and male and female gang members; and ethnic gangs. A case study profiles a young man involved in gangs as a way of understanding the reality of those factors. The chapter then considers approaches to prevention and intervention strategies at individual, family, school, and community levels and concludes with a discussion of adaptations for diversity.

PROBLEM DEFINITION

Youth gangs began emerging in America during the shift from an agrarian society to an industrialized one. During the 1920s cities that were becoming industrialized grew rapidly. Cities such as New York, Boston, and Chicago were becoming urbanized.

Large numbers of immigrants from varying cultures flocked to these cities seeking a better life for themselves and their children. They were not accepted into the mainstream culture, which was White, Anglo-Saxon, and Protestant. The parents worked at low-paying menial jobs that barely allowed them to earn a living while trying to assimilate into the culture; the youth banded together for socialization and protection as they experienced adolescence in an unfamiliar country that was frustrating and alien to them. Dozens of gangs made up of members from similar racial, ethnic, and cultural backgrounds emerged. These gangs began to become destructive and often to be well known by their gang names and unique clothing (Sachs, 1997). The youth tended to continue in these gangs throughout their adult life.

Thrasher (1926), an early investigator of gang activity during the late 1920s, viewed youth gangs as means to socialize young delinquents to organized crime, to turn the youth into gangsters, as the adult men were known. The large urban areas were the birthplace of many of the notorious Mafia gangs, and gang wars ensued over territory and other activities such as bookmaking, extortion, gunrunning, and liquor sales. Because southern cities experienced less rapid growth, and immigrants did not migrate to the South in as large numbers, economic growth as well as gang growth moved in that region at a slower pace.

During the 1930s and 1940s, a change occurred within the overall racial and cultural makeup of gangs. African American, Puerto Rican, and Mexican American gangs began to outnumber the previously predominant White gangs. Gang wars escalated with the use of handguns, knives, chains, and other self-made implements. Drug use as well as drug trafficking increased among gang members. Gang conflicts continued through the 1950s and saw a slight decrease during the 1960s, perhaps because of the Vietnam War.

Estimates of gang activity today vary. The U.S. Department of Justice has estimated that more than 16,000 different gangs, with more than 500,000 gang members, are active (Huff, 1998); estimates in the *American Bar Association Journal* have put the figures nearer to 23,338 different gangs and a membership of 665,000 (Gibeaut, 1998). Figure 12–1 shows the major gangs found in the United States and their major locations (Los Angeles and Chicago) as well as the various types of gangs throughout the country. As the figure indicates, the Crips and the Bloods, which were the two most powerful Black gangs during the first half of the 20th century, continue to dominate in Los Angeles. In Los Angeles, gang-related murder decreased in the mid 1990s but had a resurgence of 143% between 1999 and 2000 (T. McCarthy, 2001).

Factors for Gang Involvement

From the early 1990s researchers have continued to look at gang involvement, attempting to uncover the factors that underlie gang activity and explain the continued growth and spread of gangs in the United States. Miller (1958), for example, looked at gang members and how they had been reared and found that it was not unusual for gang members to come from a matriarchal environment. Gang members from these homes, Miller held, were often models for younger members who learned their sex role behavior from the more experienced gang members who were similar to them in ethnic and cultural background.

Some theorists viewed gangs as a subculture that is the result of lower-class male youth being unable to attain wealth and success through traditional and acceptable means (Cloward & Ohlin, 1960; Cohen, 1955). Because working-class youth often are not adequately trained to meet the requirements of middle-class society, gangs are the

Figure 12–1 | U.S. Gangs

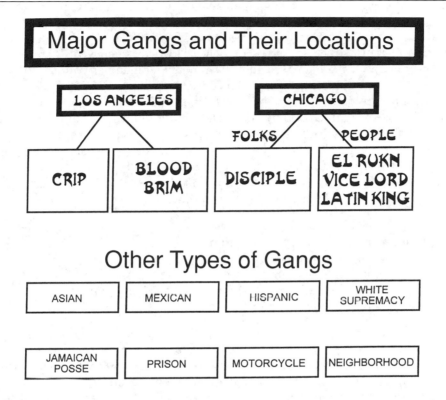

Various gangs and/or sects may join forces or war with other factions.

means of reacting to and making adjustments in their lives to find their own social status and acceptance. Further, gangs have an organizational structure that spells out rules concerning expected levels of aggressive behavior as well as the status and prestige earned as a result of adhering to these rules (Bernard, 1990). Matza (1964) disagreed with the subculture theory, instead viewing adolescents as being suspended between childhood and adulthood and seeing this time as a period of risk for males who are discovering their identities and trying to become aligned with a peer group. Because these youth fear losing status by not being accepted, they are easy targets for gangs that specify a rigid structure of behavior in those who want to become members.

For another example, Morales (1992) viewed the family as a crucial factor for putting youth at risk for gang involvement. Those families whose structure and functioning have disintegrated and broken down through poverty, alcoholism, drug addiction, chronic illnesses, and incarcerated family members put youth at great risk. Thus, according to Morales, adolescents who are involved with overwhelming family problems seek gang membership as a way to belong and gain recognition and protection.

Other factors linked by researchers to gang involvement include delinquency (Curry & Spergel, 1992), lower socioeconomic status (Hirschi, 1969), ethnic minority status and identity (Gray-Ray & Ray, 1990; Hagadorn, 1991; Vigil, 1988), and lack of influence by parents (Fagan, 1989; Fagan, Piper, & Moore, 1986). A research study completed by Dr. Chanequa Walker-Barnes collected data using structured family interviews (Hamilton, 2002). This researcher was looking for connections between familial criminality, drug use, and gang membership and youth involvement in these activities when it occurs in a youth's family of origin. Data analysis revealed that parental criminality and drug use are significant factors related to the increased risk of gang membership, drug use, and delinquency. However, there is little empirical evidence to show how gang members differ from nongang member youth.

The psychosocial control theory, which concerns the factor of delinquency and its relation to gang involvement, has been both influential and supported by research. Internal control was emphasized by Hirschi (1969), for example, as the mechanism for explaining conformity and delinquency, with such factors as poor family relations and failure in school being indicators of increased potential for delinquency. A new version of the theory (Gottfredson & Hirschi, 1990) presented six factors of adolescents who have high self-control that are thus factors inversely related to delinquency and, consequently, gang membership. These are the following:

1. ability to defer gratification
2. stamina to persist in a course of action
3. ability to be cognitive and verbal
4. ability to engage in long-term pursuits
5. ability to perceive the value of cognitive and academic skills
6. possession of sensitivity and feelings of altruism toward others.

Many factors for gang involvement already described were supported in a study by Dukes and Martinez (1994) that examined the precursors and consequences associated with gang membership in the United States. These researchers found that nearly 1 of every 20 youth in the study was an active gang member, and that those who were active gang members came from poor backgrounds and were living away from their parents. Findings also revealed that those youth who were gang members or wannabes had the lowest self-esteem and poorest psychosocial health and, in addition, were members of minority ethnic groups. Thus they also had less resistance to peer pressures.

Gang Characteristics
In the last decade, as researchers have worked with specific gangs in specific areas of the United States to identify factors that can be ameliorated, gang structures and characteristics have been described. Spergel (1995), for example, defined three major types of delinquent youth culture or gang activity that can be characterized by (a) racket activities, (b) violent conflict, and (c) theft. He further stated that without appropriate analysis of the particular community's gang activity, the intervention into and prevention of these activities will be extremely difficult. Klein, Maxson, and Miller (1995), for another example, studied Chicanos and Black gangs in Los Angeles for several decades and concluded that the leadership of these gangs is of paramount importance. However, this leadership is not a position but more a collection of functions, with the gang leader's duties varying with each function, such as fighting, athletics, or girls. Skolnick (1995), in yet another example, concluded that there are two types of gangs: entrepreneurial and cultural. He proposed that the more a gang is involved in the drug trade, the less it becomes a cultural phenomenon and the more it becomes a business enterprise, which presents great difficulty when intervention strategies are sought to decrease gang activity. A related finding, by Knox, Laske, and Tromanhauser (1992), who researched gangs over the last decade, is that there is a direct correlation between the presence of gangs in and around schools and increases in school violence.

Yablonsky (1997), after a review of the research available on gangs, reached the following conclusions about gang characteristics:

1. Gangs are fiercely involved with their territory, hood, or barrio and will fight ferociously to protect their turf.
2. There are different levels of participation in gangs, in part due to age, and these can be characterized by core or marginal participants.
3. Diverse patterns of leadership exist in gangs.
4. Many gangs are totally and intensely involved in the commerce of drugs.
5. Gangs, in part, are generated by their cultural milieu in response to a society that blocks opportunity to achieve the success goals of the larger society. (p. 184)

Gang Member Characteristics

A typical gang member is usually male, a poor student, or a school dropout. He is unemployed and often unemployable and has a police record. Because the gang provides identity, status, and a surrogate family, members develop complete loyalty. Some family members support their children's involvement in gangs to support their own drug habits. In general, gang members are from a lower economic background and are very prevalent in African American and Hispanic populations. However, Caucasians join gangs such as skinheads, Hell's Angels, and satanic groups. The gang members tend to stay on their turf and commit crimes against those who are unable to defend themselves. Their violent work has the advantage of being done during the nighttime hours, from speeding cars, through overpowering victims by their numbers, and by shooting from roofs and other familiar vantage points (C. McCarthy, 1998).

To characterize gang members fully, however, *gang member* needs to be defined. According to Yablonsky (1997), the word *member* as defined in the dictionary—"one of the individuals composing a group; a constituent part of a whole" (*Merriam-Webster's*, 1995, p. 724)—does not necessarily fit most gang members because gangs are neither distinct nor clearly delineated groups. In his research Yablonsky has instead observed three general but distinct statuses of gang membership:

1. *Wannabes (Wbs):* These are youth from about age 9 to age 13 who aggressively seek roles and status in a gang.
2. *Gangbangers (Gs):* These youth are ages 13 to 25 and already accepted as gang members. This group is considered the core—or soldiers—of a gang and comprises about 80% of members in the contemporary multipurpose violent gang.
3. *Older (or original) gangsters (OGs):* These youth are usually founders of the gang and have achieved permanent status in their gang. Many OGs are retired or semiretired but continue to maintain the permanent status of OG. Note that *gangster* is a term often used in place of *gang member*.

Wannabes in general seldom attend school and come from dysfunctional families in which their parents are often into drugs and alcohol and often abuse them sexually, physically, and emotionally. Wannabes work for older gangsters, often as mules for drugs, and their ultimate goal is to become a gangbanger. As wannabes work for gangbangers and older gangsters and commit violent acts to prove their worthiness to be a gangbanger, they are often promoted into the full status of a gangbanger. Generally, wannabes continue a life of crime and violence and serve time in prison.

The general public carries a misconception that all individuals involved with gangs participate to a similar degree. As just noted, some gang members are involved in gang activities only in a limited way, whereas others—primarily gangbangers and old gangsters—have daily involvement in gangs. The gangbangers and old gangsters not only are fully committed to their gang but also often live near each other. Generally the gang serves all their social needs. Marginal gang members are often designated as more active participants if they are seen with other core gang members, dress in a similar manner to those gang members, and are caught in activities associated with certain gangs. Police and other authorities will label such individuals as gang members, sometimes even after the gang affiliation has terminated (Yablonsky, 1997). For these individuals, shedding the gangster label is almost impossible because law enforcement agencies are slow to believe that a gang member at any level has disaffiliated with the gang. (About half of all active gang members in the United States today have tried to quit gang life [National Gang Crime Research Center, 1998].) Core gang members are totally involved with the activities of the gang and become vehemently encouraging and supportive of violent behavior. Many gangbangers are swept into a delusionary state of being persecuted by police, other gangs, or anyone who gets in their way. These gang members believe that self-esteem, status in the world, and pleasurable activities are all tied to the gang. They may be easier to recognize because they have 24-hour participation and involvement and live out the paranoid gangster code of ethics and lifestyle. No matter what the level of involvement may be, gang members share the beliefs and values that allow them to behave in ways that will gain them prestige, acceptance, and status in the gang world. Gang members often use graffiti to advertise what gangs control certain regions. These are often elaborate and symbolize various gang codes, slogans, or affiliations, as shown in Figure 12–2.

Gang members, because of their dysfunctional backgrounds, are almost always in some way emotionally on the edge. The sociopathic personality that some gang members exhibit contributes to the total involvement and commitment that they have to their gang. The attitudes these gang members have set them up for violence in all their interactions.

Figure 12–2 | Examples of Gang Graffiti in Memphis, Tennessee: Colors and Speech and Dress Codes

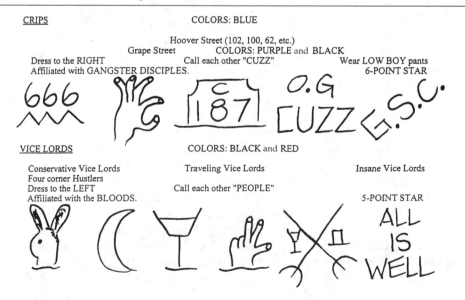

Gang members look at females as sex objects to be treated in any way they choose for their own pleasure. These attitudes can be clearly heard in much "gangsta" rap. Their attitude toward females in general is one of disdain, with gang members delineating their women as either whores or saints. The whores are only there to be used in any manner gang members choose, whereas the saints are there to mother their children and be idolized.

For young girls, their first introduction to gangs may be through rap music. As young females become drawn to rap and its forbidding lyrics, which repeat over and over racial epithets, violent acts, various forms of sexual abuse, and death, they begin to change. Because these changes may be accompanied by the usual adolescent hormonal changes, and probably myriad family problems, these girls begin to seek out the gang culture. Sooner or later a gang member will find these girls and bring them into the gang for their sexual use or as someone to rob, prostitute themselves, or commit violent acts at the command of gang leaders (Palango, 1997).

Often gang members are overtly homophobic and will present themselves with a macho image to dismiss the insecurities they may have about their own masculinity (Yablonsky, 1997). In prisons, aggressions toward homosexuals, or perceived homosexuals, can be brutal beatings, often leading to death.

While acting out irrational violent behavior, core sociopathic gang members tend to show little social conscience or real concern for others. Sympathy for others is not a primary concern for gangsters. Their only concern is for their own emotional and material comfort. In short, these individuals exhibit the following characteristics: "(a) limited feeling of guilt, (b) few feelings of compassion or empathy for others, (c) behavior which is dominated by egocentrism and satisfying their own goals, and (d) manipulation of others for immediate self gratification" (Yablonsky, 1997, p. 113).

It is the norm for gang members to have low self-esteem. Their violent behavior serves to allow them some means to stroke their egos. Violence often allows them to become enmeshed in a state of euphoria. They get their highs from the violent, brutal acts that they perpetrate to gain these feelings. Their ability to rationalize away this behavior is a function of gang involvement.

It is no wonder that gangs offer a seductive alternative to impoverished, unadventurous, or humdrum lives. Youth who see gang members wearing cool clothes and jewelry and buying sought-after material goods of the moment are lured into aspiring to be one of them. Joining a gang also gives members protection from other gangs, because protecting their own home boys is paramount for gang members.

Females in Gangs

Most research on gangs and gang membership has focused on males and their drug use, family dysfunction, peer pressure, and self-esteem. Even though females have committed crimes side by side with male gang members, females most often have been briefly discussed and perceived as playing secondary roles in most gangs. Their main role usually has been defined as one of providing sexual services to male gang members (Yablonsky, 1997).

Female gang members have become more independent and liberated through the 1980s and 1990s, however, and have taken on roles more comparable with those of male gang members. Serious crime by females has steadily increased over the past two decades (Campbell, 1987, 1992; Spergel, 1992; Taylor, 1993). Further, "since the 1980s females in gangs have become more violent and more and more oriented to male crime" (Fishman, 1992); "female gang members are hard core and deadly" (Taylor, 1993, p. 45); and females in gangs have committed serious crimes such as drive-by shootings, armed robberies, muggings, automobile thefts, and drug dealing (Covey, Menard, & Franzese, 1992; Molidor, 1996). The increased level of violence is often attributed to the availability of guns and other sophisticated weapons.

Despite substantiation of increased violent behaviors and criminal activities, female gang members are nevertheless usually not studied separately. This may be because most gang researchers have been male and most perceptions of females have come from male gang members. Research is particularly needed into the girl-only gangs that have gained some national attention, even though information on these gangs is not easily located (LeBinh, 1997).

In one of the few studies of female gang members, Molidor (1996) conducted interviews to learn about criminal behavior as well as the physical, sexual, and psychological abuses the females experienced as gang members. Factors for female gang involvement were found to be similar to those of male gang members (Molidor, 1996), with lack of education and severely dysfunctional family life as major factors (Covey et al., 1992). Many young females came from homes and neighborhoods in which alcohol and drug use and distribution were prevalent. Female initiations into gangs were also often severely painful and humiliating. However, once the females were part of a gang, they too felt they belonged to a family and acquired a sense of power.

In a comparative study of females involved in gangs and other adolescent females, Shulmire (1996) collected data focused on family demographics and family relationships, school functioning, psychosocial functioning, and level of contacts with gangs. Among the findings were the following:

- Mothers of gang-involved females had lower educational levels than mothers of the other females.
- Gang-involved females reported feeling mistreated at home more often than other females.
- Gang-involved females revealed problematic relationships with their fathers.
- The friendship patterns and social-structural considerations of gang-involved females were connected to gang membership.

Gang membership for females appears to be tied to personal self-esteem, relationships to members of their families of origin, and their environment, school, and neighborhood. These families will need to have their needs met in these areas if they are to choose an alternative lifestyle. In addition, even though current research into female gang members has revealed that their factors for gang involvement are similar to many of those observed for male gang members, prevention and intervention for females in gangs may need to be developed separately from those for males involved in gangs.

Ethnic Gangs

Because gangs fulfill needs that are traditionally fulfilled by an individual's home and school, it is logical to expect that disenfranchised youth of all races will participate in gang activities. Gang membership tends to reflect the local ethnic population and varies geographically. For example, Asian gangs are found in the Northwest and other locations with significant Asian populations. In Los Angeles, where Hispanics make up the largest minority group, Hispanic gang membership is significant. Any organized response to gang activity must include knowledge of the culture and its influence on members of the gang. The brief descriptions of Asian, African American,

Hispanic, and White supremacist gangs that follow illustrate the commonalities and ethnic influences (Palmer, 1992).

Asian Gangs

Most Asian gang members arrived in the United States as minors or young adults. These adolescents and young adults, with no support system and often without knowledge of the majority language, are at high risk to associate with gang members who are of their race and speak the same language. This bond increases their alienation from the mainstream culture. Because of experiences in their homelands, many Asians do not trust the police and rely on gangs for protection and problem solving. Unemployment and lack of marketable skills make Asian gang members look to extortion, physical assaults, residential robbery, and burglary as means to get money.

Palmer (1992) described three levels of the Asian gangs. A *casual gang* is a group of friends who operate together in committing crime by consensus with no leadership; these members participate in the most violent of crimes. The *informal gang* is headed by a charismatic leader, but gang membership fluctuates and is transient in nature. The *formal gang* has an even more defined administrative structure with a defined chain of command.

Extortion is acknowledged to be the most prevalent form of crime committed by Chinese gang members and their primary source of income. Through extortion, the gangs exert their control on the Chinese community. Police estimate that more than 90% of Chinese business owners regularly pay one or more gangs. When retail businesses refuse to pay, their shops may be vandalized, burglarized, or set on fire. Asian gangs were once thought of as being exclusively ethnic Chinese. However, with the migration of Southeast Asians into the United States, gang membership presently includes Cambodian and Vietnamese youth. Organized crime is the thrust of much of the literature on Asian gangs (Palmer, 1992).

African American Gangs

African American gangs often exist in neighborhoods where household heads are single females and gang affiliations regularly occur. Gangs tend to form in sets based on a locality. Gang names include surnames, such as Crips or Bloods, with the full name being, for example, the Rolling 70s Crips or the Insane Gangsta Bloods. Black gangs exist in the same territory as other ethnic gangs but typically do not fight across ethnic boundaries. Little formal administrative structure exists (unlike the Asian gangs). Gang members frequently sell crack cocaine and heroin, but it is unusual for gang members to use these drugs. Most Black gang members drink beer and smoke marijuana. Gang members are totally opposed to authority. Teenage parents teach their children gang signs and dress them in gang colors. Gang members frequently recruit their siblings. Dress and color are important symbols of some types of African American gangs, and gang members may adopt certain items of clothing that are worn in designated colors or in specific ways. For example, members of the Los Angeles-based African American gang, the Crips, wear blue clothing to display their loyalty (as they do in Memphis; see Figure 12–2). Their rival gang, the Bloods, wear red clothing. Although the colors differ, the articles of clothing that identify an individual as a gang member are often the same. Examples include bandannas, colored shoelaces, or a particular style of trousers. These gangs have their own brand of violence and revenge. Drive-by shootings can result from disagreement over turf. Other activities include robberies and assaults, prostitution, and sale of sophisticated weapons (Jackson & McBride, 1987).

Hispanic Gangs

Hispanic gangs were recorded in southern California in the early 1890s and grew in strength after the Zoot Suit Riots of 1943. These riots involved off-duty military and Hispanic males who were not involved in World War II because of their immigrant status. The discrimination and prejudice of this incident caused Latinos to band together. Soon the Hispanic criminal element took the opportunity to engage in more unlawful pursuits (Allender, 2001). Hispanic immigrants from various sections of Mexico formed gangs to defend their newly acquired territory. Then, as now, Hispanic gangs form alliances for purposes of strength. Their belief that the gang is more important than the individual reflects a value in their culture (Morales, 1982).

Hispanic gangs are generational and primarily male. Young males are known as PeeWees or lil Winos. An individual gang member who live to age 22 becomes a *veterano*. Veteranos act as advisors to younger gang members, and they also hide members, dispose of weapons, and arrange meeting places. Gangs are usually named after the street, housing project, or barrio from which the gang originates. Members identify closely with their neighborhood (or hood), and it is this name they tattoo on themselves and write on walls throughout the city. Gangs are composed of divisions roughly based on age cohort. In a sense, the gang is similar to an army, with the divisions operating with some autonomy while still loyal to the hood. These gangs ostensibly operate to protect the hood but actually are operating to promote prized violent behaviors. The size of the gang roughly correlates to the size of the barrio in which the gang lives. Gangs range in size from 30 members to 300 members. Gang boundaries are dynamic, changing as members move in and out, often in response to a specific situation. For core members, the gang becomes a total institution, much like a commune or a military unit, completely absorbing the individual into the subculture. Core members of the gang interact with one another according to established patterns that bind them as gang members and that are clearly identifiable, both by other gang members and by others not involved in the gang. Interaction within the gang is specific and ritualistic in form, with sanctions applied whenever someone does not adapt to the patterned form of behavior. Members from rival gangs challenge each other to test group fidelity and to establish membership. The challenge is one of the rituals that clearly identifies gang membership and intensifies the sense of belongingness to the group (Morales, 1992).

White Supremacist Groups

White supremacists are often referred to as skinheads because of their closely cropped hair or shaved heads. The movement began in England in 1968 and moved formally into the United States in 1984. In 1986, the Skinheads of America formed an alliance with the Aryan Nation, an existing White supremacist organization. This group believes that the White race is superior to all others. They do not believe in mixing the races. Skinheads promote racial hatred and violence by distributing literature targeting people of color, gays, lesbians, and Jews. They seek to intimidate and harass individuals through physical attacks and through racial slurs. Disenfranchised adolescents who are experiencing academic problems or drug and alcohol abuse, or who have been physically or sexually abused are especially at risk. At-risk youth are recruited through school activities, literature, and the Internet. The goal of the gang is to gain superiority and power through intimidation. Gang members dress in military-style clothes, steel-toed boots, and T-shirts with White Pride logos. Symbols used by skinheads include the circled swastika, an upside-down two-sided ax, a circled A, and a rifle sight (Palmer, 1992). A 1988 nationwide survey of neo-Nazi skinheads indicated continued membership growth and persistent propensity for engaging in violence—mainly against racial and religious minorities. The gangs are composed overwhelmingly of teenagers, many as young as 13 and 14 years of age. It is alarming to note that the skinheads provide a recruitment pool for other White supremacy groups, such as the Order, the Nationalist Socialist Vanguard, and the White Aryan Resistance. White supremacy groups draw from skinhead gangs in the effort to recruit "soldiers dedicated to the cause" (Palmer, 1992).

CASE STUDY

Anthony, a 13-year-old New York youth, lives in Brooklyn's dangerous, gang-infested Bedford Stuyvesant section. It is one of the oldest Black ghettos in the United States. He lives on the fourth floor of a crumbling tenement with his aunt and sleeps on a mattress in a room he shares with his cousins. His mother is a 31-year-old crack addict who is in and out of jail. His father, with whom he has had little contact except when he was being beaten by him, is also an addict and is in prison doing time for dealing drugs. Anthony carries a .25 automatic for protection like most of his homeboys. He seldom attends school and is therefore unable to read or write well. He smokes marijuana and drinks heavily. He wears designer jeans, a T-shirt, and a $45 pair of Pumas with starched shoelaces.

By the time Anthony was around 9 or 10 years old, he was exhibiting pregang behaviors in elementary school. In fact, he was usually found during recess playing "gangs" with others who were from similar backgrounds. As Anthony became old enough to move closer to gang members, he did so at first by volunteering to do simple errands, such as running money or drugs between members. This was almost inevitable because both his parents modeled violent behavior and were heavy drug users.

Anthony continued his move toward gangs by being willing to do any errand or activity that brought him closer to an actual gang member. He isolated himself from any friends who were not interested in gangs, and soon he was a loner on the streets. He quit attending school regularly. In effect, he had no parents to monitor his activities or other relatives to model more acceptable behaviors and to encourage him to stay in school.

As he grew older, Anthony began to wear the colors of his chosen gang and became involved in wannabe gang behaviors that broke the law and involved violence. The police labeled him as a gang member even though he was still only an apprentice. Anthony was on his way to becoming fully involved in gang activities.

APPROACHES TO PREVENTION

The emergence and spread of gang activity have no geographical boundaries. Gangs in the United States, which started in largely urban areas, have now spread to small town U.S.A. Even rural areas are feeling the impact of some gang activity. Often gang-like activities are perpetrated by gang wannabes instead of hard-core gangsters. The presence of individuals willing to strive for the gang lifestyle in any location sends a message to all. Those who are concerned with trying to reclaim these individuals from gangs and redirect them into socially acceptable lifestyles know that a variety of interventions must be used. It is also clear that even with some successful interventions, the social system that promotes and tolerates injustice and encourages gang activity must be changed. Disintegrated families, drugs, lack of economic opportunities, unacceptable ways to gain social status, and poor social support structures such as schools and community agencies are all areas that need to be addressed. Because the problem is large and spreading, strategies must be undertaken concurrently to make any successful impact. Programs that offer the best hope for success are those that lead these youth back from lives of crime and violence to a society that can offer them an attainable social status and social programs that help them to realize the need for change while offering a clear path to follow.

Individual

The initial approach to lessening the number of youth joining and remaining in gangs has to be a one-to-one approach. To prevent young boys and girls from meeting their needs by affiliating with gangs, as Anthony did, the individual within the family is the first line of attack. Youth need to know and value themselves so that they are able to value others. There must be a new route available to these at-risk youth that invites them to value themselves.

The following list of critical ages and activities describes life span development of gang members and illustrates how early these young gang wannabes begin to develop and how young boys and girls may begin their journey to violence and often death:

Average Age	Activity
8.9 years	First heard anything about gangs
9.2 years	First bullied by someone in a gang
9.2 years	First met someone in a gang
10.4 years	First bullied someone else in school
11.3 years	First fired a pistol or revolver
11.3 years	First saw trauma (killing or injury) from gang violence
12.0 years	First joined the gang
12.0 years	First arrested for a criminal offense
12.3 years	First got his or her own gun
13.0 years	First got a permanent tattoo
16.5 years	Age of typical current gang member
24.1 years	Age they expect to get married
26.1 years	Age they expect to quit the gang
59.5 years	Age they expect to die

Children can make better choices about their behavior when they have adequate information and are given skills to control their behavior. The following points may help youth to know what to do when it concerns gangs:

1. Know how gang members recruit others. Wanting to belong may make children accept intimidation by gang members.
2. Know how to respond to gang member invitations to join their gang.
3. Take fears seriously about being around gang members and talk with trusted adults about these fears.
4. Know what your goals are and don't let joining a gang deter you from what it is that you really want out of life.
5. Surround yourself with positive individuals.
6. Use common sense. If being around gang members is uncomfortable, make plans that will keep you safely involved in other activities (Ezarik, 2002).

Note that even though gang members think they will leave their gang and live until at least 60, the grim reality is that many die very young (Knox, 1998).

To combat this scenario of events, young people must desire to resist gangs. Adults who work with youth, like Anthony in the case study, must find ways to help them meet their needs through ways that are both nonviolent and acceptable. If the family is not available, other youth often are ready to assist at-risk youth.

Peer helping programs have been developed across the country, and because it is peer groups interacting in these programs, they often have more chance of being successful. Peer pressure, which can negatively affect the choices youth make, can also be a powerful positive prevention tool.

One-to-one mentoring programs have also been developed based on positive role modeling. Youth who are at risk for gang involvement are particularly receptive to the positive effects of being mentored by a successful role model, and research has demonstrated that at-risk minority youth paired with successful role model minorities benefit greatly (Landre, Miller, & Porter, 1997). One such program is Big Brother/Big Sister, a well-recognized, long-established program that pairs a child with an adult for the purpose of guidance and friendship. Other programs, sponsored by local agencies, community groups, and business and industry, are additionally available in most communities. When at-risk youth experience one-to-one mentoring and interact with a positive mentor similar to themselves, they often become able to look toward a gang-free future.

Family

According to many surveys and task forces, the number one tool for fighting gang involvement is parent involvement. Strong families are a major asset. A recent study of 300 participants from a high school in Miami, Florida, gives the family an antigang strength that generally was not thought present previously (Black, 2002). The majority of the participants were from single-parent families. Over half of the students were Latino, about 25% were African American, and the rest were White or other. The researcher was looking for a parenting style that seemed to have some effect on behavior. When individual ethnic group results were extracted from the data, the African American kids resulted in better behavior over time. Another interesting finding was that the level of gang involvement decreased over the course of the first year of high school, which might indicate that being in a gang was perhaps a temporary behavior for many students that would wane after the first year of high school. In other words, parenting does matter, and the ethnic group one belongs to may have a big impact on which kids become gang members and stay with it through to adulthood.

Some states have enacted strong laws that hold parents accountable for the actions of their children, especially in school. Even single-parent families can begin very early to instill in their children a sense of worth and respect for themselves and others.

Many antigang programs are in operation across the nation. Those that are successful (a) provide more leisure-time activities with youngsters; (b) support a tougher law enforcement against gang activities in the community; (c) increase efforts to dry up sources of gang revenue, such as drugs and narcotics; and (d) increase parental supervision of children, including their activities and their friends (Moore, 1998).

Parents can also fight gangs by becoming better parents, that is, by improving their skills and taking more serious responsibility for their children. Parents who become effective gang fighters

- monitor the company their children keep
- monitor their children's whereabouts
- keep their children busy with positive activities at school, at church, or in organized recreational activities
- model good behavior for their children and let them know how they are valued as individuals
- spend time with their children and include them in family activities often
- watch for signs of pregang behavior, and at the first sign, intervene quickly and seek help from school, community groups, and law enforcement. Police officials are willing to help deter youth from gang involvement (C. McCarthy, 1998).

School

In recent years, youth have become anxious about their safety because of increased violence in the schools, and research has clearly illustrated that increased violence in communities and school comes with gang involvement. Although not all school violence is gang related, there is enough gang-related violence to cause many schools to adopt a dress code with zero tolerance for gang paraphernalia, such as gold chains, baggy pants, and bandannas (see Figure 12–2). Special drug and gang prevention officers often are seen patrolling the halls of many urban schools. Metal detectors are commonplace, and a sense of being under siege often pervades the school setting. Strong schools, however, are a major asset in blocking gang activity. The school is a perfect place to identify and work closely with troubled students such as gang wannabes. Schools can also help make sure that parents are involved with their children at school every step of the way, even if it means trying unconventional things such as having parents' night on a Saturday morning when parents can attend and providing day care for younger children in the family. School counselors, teachers, and administrators must all take an active role in finding more appropriate ways of dealing with all the issues underlying drug activity. They must work closely with law enforcement and with social service agencies that can provide services that may shore up a disintegrating family (Lieutenant W. Hissong, Southaven, Mississippi, police force gang specialist, personal communication, March 22, 1999). For example, creative scheduling of school instruction and atypical school hours might serve to meet the needs of students who come from homes where the eldest become parents to younger siblings. Many law enforcement personnel state that in schools "teachers are naturally the first line of defense." Partnering with school personnel, police can make significant progress in preventing violence in the schools. Police are providing training in the schools so teachers can recognize gang signs, language, dress, and other gang paraphernalia. Many teachers are flabbergasted with the kinds of weapons that gang members use as well as their level of commitment to violent behavior. A significant impact is made when jailed gang members agree to come to talk at school about their lives of crime. Because of the increasing number of gangs throughout the country, "gang training" needs to be an ongoing activity (Steindorf, 2002).

Gang members are often bright and resourceful. They belong to organizations that have elaborate social and organizational structures that must be known and remembered. The systems of codes and symbols of typical gangs attest to the fact that many gang members possess exceptional cognitive abilities. For example, gangs use alphabets that are individualized for their own gang (see Figure 12–3 for partial alphabets), and they communicate using these alphabets so other gangs or law enforcement will not detect their plans. Gangs are dynamic groups that change over time and are influ-

Figure 12–3 | Gang Alphabets

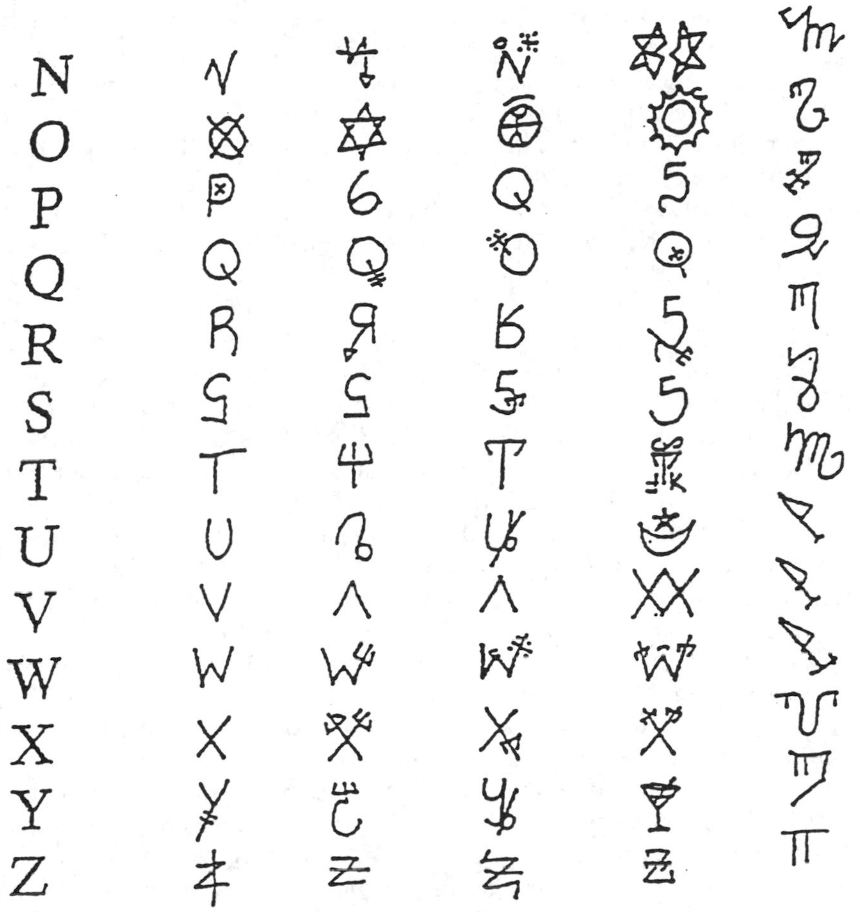

enced by their environment. For example, some gangs that previously used symbols such as bandannas, hats, or baggy clothes to identify themselves have now gone to more public symbols, such as apparel from the NFL and NBA.

Schools are recognizing and changing their approach to academic accountability. With academic competence also comes a measure of social prestige. This can go a long way in keeping marginal gang wannabes in the mainstream of the school culture (Dunston, 1993; Meeks, Heit, & Page, 1995).

Gang prevention programs must emphasize increasing the self-esteem of at-risk youth. Interventions to build self-esteem rest on the assumption that if a person likes himself or herself, he or she will be less likely to engage in activities that are harmful to self or others (Wilson-Brewer & Jacklin, 1990). Self-esteem enhancement is a long-term process. It must begin with healthy parenting practices, be nourished by the community, and be consistently enhanced by schools through activities that give adolescents a feeling of belonging and accomplishment. Juarez (1992) has suggested that self-esteem activities target male youth because of their dominant role in gang activities. Alternative community support systems that enhance self-esteem development should focus on manhood development with emphasis on rites-of-passage programs to assist male teens in the move from adolescence into adulthood.

Among effective approaches to prevention that can be used in school settings are two techniques that have been demonstrated to be successful: conflict resolution education and dispute mediation training. One of the first conflict resolution curricula for adolescents was developed by Prothrow-Smith (1987). Participants learn how to communicate in such a way as to not escalate the conflict, to utilize problem-solving skills, and to maintain self-control through anger management. Conflict resolution education focuses on the use of peers as dispute mediators. Selected students are trained in communication, leadership, problem solving, and assertiveness. In middle schools, peer mediators resolve playground conflicts. In high schools, they may resolve disputes in interpersonal relationships. Teachers, security personnel, and others may receive dispute mediation training so they can help to resolve problems that are inherent in their work.

The ultimate goal of gang awareness and prevention activities is to provide safe and secure school campuses where students can learn and teachers can teach effectively (Elder, Fisher, & Forthman, 1994). If successful prevention of gang involvement is the goal, students must be involved in school-based programs from an early age (Landre et al., 1997). One definitive way to accomplish this is to invest as much money in hiring elementary school counselors as school systems do in hiring high school counselors (Peep, 1996). Additionally, all school staff, including auxiliary personnel, need to be educated in gang awareness and prevention (Trump, 1993a).

Children who are economically deprived need to be provided with choices at school that will make dropping out less likely. Teaching methods and materials need to be evaluated for appropriateness to real-life situations. Youth grow up today in an MTV fast-paced world. Much of what happens at school is not relevant or presented in a palatable way. Instructional methods such as cooperative learning, cross-age tutoring, and team building can all help increase students' involvement and interaction with teachers (Bodinger-deUriate, 1993). Changes in the power structure in school also help drive children away. Children need to be respected no matter what their socioeconomic status is or from what cultural background they have come (Lal, Lal, & Achilles, 1993). School needs to be a caring and nurturing environment that encourages students to be involved and connected with their peers and teachers.

School programs with the best chance for preventing gang involvement offer gang prevention topics such as (a) consequences of gang membership, (b) gang resistance skills and assertiveness training skills (Elder et al., 1994; Meeks et al., 1995), (c) coping and stress management skills, (d) decision-making skills, (e) conflict prevention/peer mediation, (f) character development and responsibility, and (g) drug and substance abuse prevention (Meeks et al., 1995; Miars, 1996; Trump, 1993a). One program that presents a number of these gang prevention skills in Gang Resistance and Education Training (GREAT), which has been presented to eighth graders. Preliminary results have suggested that students who complete this program report more prosocial behavior than their peers who do not complete the program or who do not participate in the program (Esbersen & Osgood, 1997).

Another program that offers students training in coping skills is the Improving Social Awareness—Social Problem-Solving (ISA) Project. This program includes instruction in critical thinking skills and problem solving at the elementary level and targets topics such as substance abuse or gang resistance at the secondary level.

Drug abuse training and abuse prevention are essential components of school-based gang prevention programs (Trump, 1993b) because drug abuse is closely related to gang activity. One program containing these components is the Drug Abuse Resistance Education (DARE) program, which is widely used in school settings and is highly supported by law enforcement.

Other school (and community) programs that provide students with alternatives in learning and playing that have great promise include using sports and field trips, which provide students with opportunities they might never have otherwise because of their financial and family circumstances, and incorporating opportunities for vocational training and job placement into the curriculum (Bodinger-deUriate, 1993). Research has suggested that youth who are in gangs will select reputable employment over crime if given that option. Job placement and job tryouts need to be funded for at-risk youth so that they will aspire toward long-term employment once they finish school (Taylor, 1990). The School-to-Work Opportunities Act, signed into law in 1994, provides for funding to support a comprehensive, high-quality, school-to-careers transition system to enable all students to successfully enter the workplace. A major component of this initiative is to ensure that all students, even those with academic deficiencies or disabilities, are provided adequate training that will lead to jobs offering livable wages and advancement (Moore, 1998).

Community

Taylor (1990) suggested that what is necessary for the control or reduction of gangs is the availability of jobs and the larger world of business and industry. Gang members often get involved in gangs via involvement in drug trafficking. All youth want to have a certain level of material goods. We see this in advertisements that play to the wants and peer pressures of our youth. When youth get involved in gangs, even in a minor way, they make a lot more money than can be made at a fast food restaurant or car wash. Many more jobs must be developed for youth that pay more than minimum wage. Communities must make a concerted effort to contribute to this concept through local business and industry.

Many communities have struggled with youth violence and gang development. A number of programs have been developed and implemented at local levels, and some have produced positive results. No one program, no set of strategies, can be considered the answer to the multifaceted and complex problem of gang involvement, however. As the 21st century arrives, Americans need to be ready to take back the youth of our society from gangs. To do this, there must be dramatic changes in families, schools, communities, and this nation. No one group is able to do the work alone. Individual groups and programs need to form coalitions and collaborative groups that tie programs together and make them successful as well as cost- and time-effective. An example is the 100-man march several years ago that began an active involvement of minority men with each other, their children, and youth in their communities. It is grassroots efforts like this that help to reduce gang violence.

INTERVENTION STRATEGIES

Individual

Two strategies for dealing with individual gang members, especially those still on the fringes, are counseling and the use of psychodrama. Both of these intervention strategies have an effective therapeutic component and can be easily incorporated with other programs in schools, through community agencies, or in prisons. Counseling is most effective with marginal gang members or wannabes because it teaches new behavioral alternatives that allow these youth to become involved in constructive activities. Group counseling can provide opportunities for members to help each other gain insights and see their faulty thinking and behavior patterns. Group counseling is like a gang interaction. Members are more comfortable and able to participate fully in the activity. Positive changes often occur through working in this type of group because all the members are working from a similar family and community background (Yablonsky, 1997).

Psychodrama differs from counseling because the primary activity is for the individual to work through his or her personal, home, and community problems by acting them out using an alter ego. The success of this intervention is rooted in the fact that if gang members are able to take a minute and work through some of their reactionary behavior in reality, chances are greater that the negative behavior can be thwarted. If, for example, a male gang member has reacted to a minor threat from one of his own gang by vowing to kill him, he can instead role-play through the drama in his head, work through some of the anger, and particularly work on what consequences await him if he goes through with this threat. Often, after psychodrama occurs, underlying causes may surface that have triggered an inappropriate reaction to a relatively minor problem. Counseling and psychodrama have great value when working with gangsters. They provide direct training to those involved, allow opportunities for individuals to vent their anger and rage in a controlled environment, and slow down events so that gangsters can take time to see and understand what is actually taking place.

Gangsters live in the moment and react to whatever stimuli are affecting them. They need a mechanism by which they are given a chance to think through their behavior or make changes in their initial behavioral reaction to the stimuli. Psychodrama and group counseling allow gangsters to learn from each other in an open environment that what causes their violent impulses is often based on the emotional, physical, or sexual abuse they may have received as young children in a dysfunctional family system (Yablonsky, 1997).

Family

Today, many families are headed by a single parent, usually the mother, who is the only wage earner and, therefore, is unable to monitor the children. For these families, after-school and weekend programs often provide a safe haven for latchkey youngsters as well as give parents peace of mind while they are at work. For example, the Family Network Partnership is a program jointly sponsored by a university and community agency to help support families by providing recreation, tutoring, and peer helping (Moore, 1998). Most low-income families are unable to afford recreational activities or pay for tutoring.

School

Schools are also beginning to be more of a clearinghouse for family resources by sending home information to parents via school newsletters and other community publications. The intervention most needed in schools usually is during the hours of 3:00 p.m. until 7:00 p.m., which is often referred to by law enforcement as the prime time for crime. With good after-school programs, youth can be kept busy and will not have to spend time engaged in unproductive or unlawful activities (Moore, 1998). Many parent–teacher groups are beginning to see this need, and parent volunteers are investing their time with groups of youth after school by providing them with interesting and enjoyable activities.

Many schools are also used in the summer for remedial and recreational activities. Youth whose parents are unable to afford camps and sports activities need alternatives that provide safe and constructive programming.

Community

One of the earliest interventions was begun by the New York City Youth Board in 1946. It was known as the *detached worker project*. This project had the following goals: (a) reduced antisocial behavior, particularly street fighting; (b) friendly interactions with other street gangs; (c) increased democratic participation within the gangs; (d) broadened social horizons; (e) responsibility for self-direction; (f) improved personal and social adjustment of the individual; and (g) improved community relations. In this model a professional, such as a social worker or police officer, works directly with a gang on its own turf. Each professional is assigned to a particular gang. Even though this approach has some success, the project worker often cannot provide the proper interventions commensurate with the level of gang involvement. Marginal gang members can often be helped by getting them to counseling groups, providing recreation to fill some of their time and connect them with more wholesome male role models, and providing job opportunities for them. Core gang members require a more intense level of intervention. Problems occur when project workers make incorrect diagnoses of gang structure and makeup. These programs also require an effective police presence in the community (Yablonsky, 1997).

The detached worker project model takes apart a gang's structure. It deals first with the marginal gang members or wannabes to help redirect their energies by providing constructive activities that will utilize their time as well as supply acceptable social interaction, thereby drawing them more into the mainstream of society.

Another early program that emerged in cities like New York, Chicago, and Boston during the 1930s was known as the Adult Youth Association (AYA) approach. Settlement houses or community recreation centers were developed to deal with youth in these areas, where boredom, low economic status, and cultural differences were all contributing to the alienation of young men.

The AYA approach is primarily based on the premise that male youth, in particular, need good role models to learn basic acceptable socialization skills and that the role models can be provided by community volunteers working with at-risk youth in recreational endeavors and other social activities. It is also based on the knowledge that even in ghetto areas it is not unusual to see known gang members involved in a pickup game of basketball. The success of this approach is based on the fact that community volunteers can better know and serve the needs of the community's youth because they are members of the same community (Yablonsky, 1997). This type of program often draws on its own success stories for future volunteers. Those at-risk individuals who were able to turn their lives around often return to their own neighborhoods to become the youth leaders and role models for the next generation.

Because the AYA is well integrated into each community, and the workers are members or returning members of that community, the chance of successful outcomes is raised. The fact that AYAs use recreation as a focus often leads to teams and leagues developing in one or more sports. Those at-risk youth who belong to these leagues often replace the idea of being in a gang with the idea of joining an athletic league and derive the positive aspects of this organization. Marginal gang members, who may disengage more easily because of their low level of gang involvement, may replace the benefits of gangs with those of a sports league. The most important aspect of any AYA is to allow the recreational and social activities to evolve naturally through the inter-action of the local community volunteers and the youth. If communities bring already developed programs to neighborhoods without allowing for local youth to participate in the planning, the chance for success is diminished.

Throughout the 1990s gangs continued to grow in numbers and strength and became more violent. Many communities have attempted to fight back against gang proliferation and expansion. According to Miller (1990), success requires a nationwide program that can give communities a framework and process by which local organi-zations could be informed of current methods and tools and supported financially.

A Presidential Committee on Juvenile Delinquency and Youth Crime developed such a program during the administration of President John Kennedy. To deter gang violence, federal offices were to be established to oversee the national antigang effort, to provide remedial programs to needy areas of the country, and to follow the effects through research and evaluation. When President Kennedy was assassinated, program funding ceased.

Many major cities have responded to the increased proliferation and intensity of violence, choosing methods that fit their city's needs. Austin, Texas, long plagued with gangs, experienced several acutely violent and savage murders in 1990 that alerted the entire city to the need for action. All elected officials made controlling gang activity their number one priority. A task force of elected officials, schools, social services, and citizens worked from a multidisciplinary approach to find ways to control gang activ-ity. City officials felt the Austin police force should have a special unit devoted to gangs. The criminal intelligence unit started publishing bulletins about gang activi-ties. Police were given special training on how to recognize and report gang activity, and local prosecutors were committed to making gang-related crime the top prosecu-tion priority. In addition, a public service media campaign was developed, and gang unit efforts were complemented by beefed-up budgets to social service, health, and child-care agencies. As a result, Austin now has several programs that work toward controlling and eliminating the level of gang crime that was apparent in 1990.

A study completed in 1996 by the Police Executive Research Forum (PERF) exam-ined the history and nature of gangs as well as the responses of public agencies to gangs from 1991 to 1996 in five major cities: Austin, Chicago, Kansas City (Kansas), Metro-Dade (Florida), and San Francisco (Painter & Weisel, 1997). The study also reviewed how individual police responded to particular local gang problems. Each city worked to find solutions that fit its particular needs because no one antigang pro-gram works for all cities, given the diversity of region, race, and culture. This study, for example, suggested that all gang activity is not necessarily tied to heavy drug activity, that the city's geographical location may influence the amount of drug activ-ity. From the PERF study's highlights of what each of the five cities has done to respond to gangs and their affiliated activities, it seems clear that each community will have to find its own most appropriate ways to respond to local gang activity. This will require a collaborative community approach, carried out by a well-informed, trained police force and supported by governmental leadership.

Taylor (1990) suggested strategies that should be incorporated in any community team effort. One is that the community needs to put up a strong fight against the neg-ative effects of drugs, and this fight needs to start at home at an early age. Another is to get parents talking with their children. Being a good role model is paramount, but parents must be explicit in their zero tolerance for any drug activity. Yet another is to encourage strong homes. Whether they are in a Chicago ghetto or in a more rural area of Colorado, such homes form the foundation for antidrug, gang-free communities. Even poor families or single-parent homes can be strong against the issues that support gang activity.

In Milwaukee, Wisconsin, where a high level of gang activity exists, including violent crime, a former Jesuit priest who has had previous experience in the business sector developed what he called the Homeboyz Interactive (www.homeboyz.com). It is a nonprofit training business that takes gang-involved and drug-addicted youth off the streets, puts them through a treatment program, supports them through high school until they graduate, and guides them to full-time employment. About one fourth of these individuals choose to become a computer programmer while the rest are given technical training and move to a variety of jobs. Of the 150 participants who completed this program, none has ever been fired (Grennan, Schlumpf, & Schorn, 2002).

With the advent of easily accessible technology, gangs have found an avenue to get their messages out locally, nationally, and internationally. One such Web site known as Glock3 was established in January 1996 in Detroit and is used by local gangs to seek out other gangs for the purpose of creating national alliances. The Internet provider discovered the nature of this site and deleted it from its service; however, it was picked up by an Internet provider in New Zealand. This site has a great deal of instructional information, which it shares with other gangs throughout cyberspace. Subjects such as how to obtain better weapons, the best way to traffic drugs, and in particular how to hook gang wannabees into a gang are discussed on this site. Many of these Web sites are in English and Spanish so it is easy for many ethnic groups to communicate. Many gang members use this and other sites to brag about their activities and justify what they do (Smith, 1997). There are a variety of Web sites that parents, teachers, and law enforcement can refer to that may be helpful when learning about gangs. One Web site, www.Gangsta.com, brags that it is the best site for reaching an estimated 700,000 gang members in 700 cities in the United States. Other sites are listed in the Appendix at the end of this chapter.

To be successful in preventing gang activity in communities, programs need a strong theoretical framework. However, this is an area that is extremely complex and not easily researched (Miller, 1990). The lack of systematic evaluation plans to determine long-term effectiveness of prevention and intervention strategies is one major reason why promising programs are scrapped before they are fully implemented. The only data collected and used to judge success or failure are often increases or decreases in crime statistics during new-program implementation. Community programs also need a two-pronged program of prevention as well as intervention (Regini, 1998).

The American gang policy, developed by the National Gang Crime Research Center in Chicago, adopted a zero tolerance to gangs and gang activity in the 1980s. Its slogan was "Say no to gangs." There was funding to fight the drug aspect of gangs, but not enough. For the 21st century, the center's gang policy is adopting a negative tolerance toward gangs. This policy's slogan is "Say goodbye to gangs." This policy states that the cost is high for doing gang business. Money will be available to use civil, administrative, and criminal sanctions to prevent new recruits and target hardcore gang members for stiff sentences. All economic incentives must be removed from gang involvement. New and smarter laws will need to be passed to deal with gangs. The message must be sent to gangs in a strong and consistent way that gang terror is over (National Gang Crime Research Center, 1998).

ADAPTATIONS FOR DIVERSITY

Prevention and intervention strategies will be of little value to those who work to block gang involvement if there is not a basic understanding of the ethnic and cultural factors that influence individuals. People have always clustered together in groups for social interaction, protection, self-development, and simply because of their proximity to each other. Basic social expressions such as language, norms, sanctions, and values reveal valuable information (Axelson, 1999). This information is critical when developing the best approaches to diverse gangs.

All individuals come from their own particular ethnic and cultural group. Ethnic characteristics can be traced back to national origins or geographic regions. Culture is learned from experiences in the environment. Because the United States is a pluralistic society in terms of culture, there are a variety of ethnic groups to address. There are also subcultures that are racial, ethnic, regional, economic, or social communities that are distinctly different from other dominant groups in society. Gangs can be considered a subculture (Baruth & Manning, 1991).

Knowing that gangs represent diverse ethnic and cultural groups is of great importance when choosing approaches to block their influence and spread, as the earlier discussion of ethnic gangs has suggested. In the case of Anthony, whose ethnic root is African American, his cultural roots or learned experiences are steeped in the drug-infested and extreme poverty of his ghetto and place him at extremely high risk of joining a gang. It is easy to recognize that Anthony views the gang as a way of meeting his need to be part of a culture that offers him friends for social interaction, a unique language, a set of values, and codes to live and work by, even though the work is crime related.

For those who work with gangs, it is imperative that the ethnic and cultural backgrounds of specific gangs are reviewed as prevention programs are planned or interventions are undertaken. Uninformed assumptions about how gangs view the world or what norms or values they adhere to will not lead to successful outcomes. Providing opportunities that offer gang members a chance to reclaim ethnic pride or learn to function in an acceptable cultural milieu will enhance the likelihood of a successful outcome.

SUMMARY

Gangs have been around for decades. Their influence on society is felt by all Americans. The financial and individual losses to communities and families can be seen in towns, large and small. Gang members are a diverse group, but they all seek to have their individual social and emotional needs met through gang involvement. Being part of a gang organization allows members to feel protected and affirmed by those who matter to them and to have a sense of belonging in an environment that alienates them from mainstream culture. Many factors in families, schools, and communities influence gang wannabes to become gang members. Thus it is important to intervene very early with potential gang members, with interventions developed to combat the causes that are individual to each community while providing ongoing prevention activities. Effective laws and law enforcement are also needed. Diversity issues in gangs need to be addressed to find ways to solve the problems specific to a geographical region, large city, or small town in America. It is only when communities work collaboratively with all the resources they have toward strong prevention programs and effective intervention activities that progress will be achieved.

REFERENCES

Allender, D. (2001, December). Gangs in middle America. *Law Enforcement Bulletin, 70*(12).

Axelson, J. (1999). *Counseling and development in a multicultural society* (3rd ed.). New York: Brooks/Cole.

Baruth, L. G., & Manning, M. L. (1991). *Multicultural counseling and psychotherapy: A life-span perspective.* New York: Macmillan.

Bernard, T. J. (1990). Angry aggression among the truly disadvantaged. *Criminology, 28,* 73–75.

Bodinger-deUriate, C. (1993). *Membership in violent gangs fed by suspicions.* Los Alamitos, CA: Southwest Regional Laboratory. (ERIC Document Reproduction Service No. ED358 399)

Campbell, A. (1987). Self-definition by rejection: The case of gang girls. *Social Problems, 34,* 451–456.

Campbell, A. (1992). *The girls in the gang.* Malden, MA: Blackwell.

Cloward, R. A., & Ohlin, L. E. (1960). *Delinquency and opportunity: A theory of delinquent gangs.* New York: Free Press.

Cohen, A. K. (1955). *Delinquent boys: The culture of the gang.* New York: Free Press.

Covey, H. C., Menard, S., & Franzese, R. J. (1992). *Juvenile gangs.* Springfield, IL: Charles C Thomas.

Curry, G. D., & Spergel, I. A. (1992). Gang involvement and delinquency among Hispanic and African American adolescent males. *Journal of Research in Crime and Delinquency, 29,* 273–291.

Dukes, R. I., & Martinez, R. (1994). The impact of ethgender on self-esteem among adolescents. *Adolescence, 29,* 105–115.

Dunston, M. S. (1993, March/April). Signs of the times: Gangs and their symbols. *Police Marksman,* pp. 16–38.

Elder, R., Fisher, C., & Forthman, J. A. (1994). *On alert! Gang prevention school inservice guidelines.* Sacramento: California Department of Education. (ERIC Document Reproduction Service No. ED 370 170)

Esbersen, F. A., & Osgood, D. W. (1997, November). *National evaluation of G.R.E.A.T.* (National Institute of Justice research in brief). Washington, DC: U.S. Department of Justice, Office of Justice Programs.

Ezarik, M. (2002, March). How to avoid gangs. *Current Health, 28*(7), 20.

Fagan, J. A. (1989). The social organization of drug use and drug dealing among urban gangs. *Criminology, 27,* 633–669.

Fagan, J. A., Piper, E. S., & Moore, M. (1986). Violent delinquents and urban youth. *Criminology, 23,* 439–466.

Fishman, L. T. (1992, March). *The Vice Queens: An ethnographic study of Black female gang behavior.* Paper presented at the annual meeting of the American Society of Criminology, Chicago.

Gibeaut, J. (1998). Gang busters. *American Bar Association Journal, 84,* 64–69.

Gottfredson, M., & Hirschi, T. (1990). *A general theory of crime.* Stanford, CA: Stanford University Press.

Gray-Ray, P., & Ray, M. C. (1990). Juvenile delinquency in the Black community. *Youth and Society, 22,* 67–84.

Grennan, H., Schlumpf, H., & Schorn, J. (2002, March). Good news. *U.S. Catholic, 67*(3), 11.

Hagadorn, J. M. (1991). Gangs, neighborhoods, and public policy. *Social Problems, 38,* 529–541.

Hamilton, K. (2002, July 4). Gangbusters: Parents still play key role in saving kids from the streets. *Black Issues in Higher Education, 19*(10), 27.

Hirschi, T. (1969). *Causes of delinquency.* Berkeley: University of California Press.

Huff, C. R. (1998, March). *Criminal behavior of gang members and at-risk youths* (National Institute of Justice research review). Washington, DC: U.S. Department of Justice, Office of Justice Programs.

Jackson, R., & McBride, D. (1987). *Understanding street gangs.* Sacramento, CA: Custom.

Jankowski, M. S. (1991). *Islands in the street: Gangs and American urban society.* Berkeley: University of California Press.

Juarez, P. D. (1992). The public health model and violence prevention. In R. C. Cervantes (Ed.), *Substance abuse and gang violence* (pp. 43–59). Newbury Park, CA: Sage.

Klein, M., Maxson, C., & Miller, J. (Eds.). (1995). *The modern gang reader.* Los Angeles: Roxbury.

Knox, G. (1998). What do we know about the gang problem in America today? *Official Proceedings of the 1998 Second International Gang Specialist Training Conference, 1,* 419.

Knox, G., Laske, D., & Tromanhauser, E. (1992). *Schools under siege.* Dubuque, IA: Kendal/Hunt.

Lal, S. R., Lal, D., & Achilles, C. M. (1993). *Handbook on gangs in schools: Strategies to reduce gang-related activities.* Newbury Park, CA: Corwin Press.

Landre, R., Miller, M., & Porter, D. (1997). *Gangs: A handbook for community awareness.* New York: Facts on File.

LeBinh, P. (1997). *Girl-only gangs: A bibliography.* (ERIC Document Reproduction Service No. ED 413 275)

Matza, D. (1964). *Delinquency and drift.* New York: Wiley.

McCarthy, C. (1998). What are gang characteristics? *Official Proceedings of the 1998 Second International Gang Specialist Training Conference, 1,* 443.

McCarthy, T. (2001, September 3). L. A. gangs are back. *Time, 158,* 46.

Meeks, L., Heit, P., & Page, R. (1995). *Violence prevention: Totally awesome teaching strategies for safe and drug free schools.* Blacklick, OH: Meeks Heit.

Merriam-Webster's collegiate dictionary. (10th ed.). (1995). Springfield, MA: Merriam-Webster.

Miars, R. D. (1996). Stress and coping in today's society. In D. Capuzzi & D. Gross (Eds.), *Youth at risk: A prevention for counselors, teachers, and parents* (2nd ed., pp. 129–147). Alexandria, VA: American Counseling Association.

Miller, W. (1958). Lower class culture as a generating milieu of gang delinquency. *Journal of Social Issues, 14,* 5–19.

Miller, W. B. (1990). Why the United States has failed to solve its youth gang problem. In C. R. Huff (Ed.), *Gangs in America* (pp. 263–287). Newbury Park, CA: Sage.

Molidor, C. E. (1996). *Female gang members: A profile of aggression and victimization.* (ERIC Document Reproduction Service No. EJ 530 433)

Moore, M. (1998). Investing in our children: Report on youth violence and school safety. *Official Proceedings of the 1998 Second International Gang Specialist Training Conference, 1.*

Morales, A. (1982). The Mexican American gang member: Evaluation and treatment. In R. M. Becerra, M. Karno, & J. Escobar (Eds.), *Mental health and Hispanic Americans: Clinical perspectives.* New York: Grune & Stratton.

Morales, A. (1992). A clinical model for the prevention of gang violence and homicide. In R. C. Cervantes (Ed.), *Substance abuse and gang violence* (pp. 105–120). Newbury Park, CA: Sage.

National Gang Crime Research Center. (1998). A message from the National Gang Crime Research Center: Understanding the "negative tolerance" policy on and about gangs. *Journal of Gang Research, 5*(3), 76.

Painter, E., & Weisel, D. (1997). Crafting local response to gang problems: Case studies from five cities. *Public Management, 79*(7), 75.

Palango, P. (1997, December 8). Danger signs. *Maclean's, 110*(49).

Palmer, M. (1992). *Gang profiles.* Portland, OR: Northeast Coalition of Neighborhoods.

Peep, B. B. (1996). Lessons from the gang: What gang members think about their schools suggests new direction for classroom reform. *The Social Administrator, 53,* 26–31.

Prothrow-Smith, D. (1987). *Violence prevention curriculum for adolescents.* Newton, MA: Education Development Center.

Regini, L. A. (1998). Combating gangs. *F.B.I. Law Enforcement Bulletin, 67,* 1–5.

Sachs, S. L. (1997). *Street gangs awareness: A resource guide for parents and professionals.* Minneapolis, MN: Fairview Press.

Shulmire, S. R. (1996). *A comparative study of gang-involved and other adolescent women.* (ERIC Document Reproduction Service No. ED 412 477)

Skolnick, J. (1995). Gangs and crime as old as time: But drugs change gang culture. In M. Klein, C. Maxson, & J. Miller (Eds.), *The modern gang reader.* Los Angeles: Roxbury.

Smith, G. (1997, March). Cyber thugs. *Popular Science, 250,* 32.

Spergel, I. A. (1990). Youth gangs: Continuity and change. In M. Tonry & N. Morros (Eds.), *Crime and justice: A review of research* (pp. 171–275). Chicago: University of Chicago Press.

Spergel, I. A. (1992). Youth gangs: An essay review. *Social Service Review, 6,* 121–140.

Spergel, I. A. (1995). *The youth problem.* New York: Oxford University Press.

Steindorf, S. (2002, June 25). Police give teachers a primer on gangs. *Christian Science Monitor, 94*(148).

Taylor, C. S. (1990). *Dangerous society.* East Lansing: Michigan State University Press.

Taylor, C. S. (1993). Female gangs: A historical perspective. In C. S. Taylor (Ed.), *Girls, gangs, women, and drugs* (pp. 13–47). East Lansing: Michigan State University Press.

Thrasher, T. (1926). *The gang: Study of 1,313 gangs.* Chicago: University of Chicago Press.

Trump, K. S. (1993a). Tell teen gangs: School's out. *American School Board Journal,* 39–42.

Trump, K. S. (1993b). *Youth gangs and schools: The need for intervention and prevention strategies.* Cleveland, OH: Cleveland State University. (ERIC Document Reproduction Service No. ED 361 457)

Vigil, D. (1988). *Barrio gangs: Street life and identity in southern California.* Austin: University of Texas Press.

Wilson-Brewer, R., & Jacklin, B. (1990, December). *Violence prevention strategies targeted at the general population of minority youth.* Paper presented at the Forum on Youth Violence in Minority Communities: Setting the Agenda for Prevention, Atlanta, GA.

Yablonsky, L. (1997). *Gangsters: Fifty years of madness, drugs, and death on the streets of America.* New York: New York University Press.

APPENDIX

Web Sites

About.Com's Guide to Juvenile Gangs and Crime
http://about.com/newsissues/law/library/weekly/aa110397

American Gang Graffiti
http://members.tripod.com/~Carl815/amergraf.html

Asian Gangs: A Bibliography
http://www.communitypolicing.org/publications/iag/asian_gngs/index.html

Bajito Onda
www.BajitoOnda.org/bajito.html

Bibliography of Gang Literature
http:/www.ncjrs.org/pdffiles/fs-9640.pdf.html

A Comprehensive Response to America's Youth Gang Problem
http://www.ifpinc.com/Gangs/gangfaq.html

The Gang Awareness Page
http://www.novagate.com/novasurf/gang.html

Gang Crime Prevention Center
http://www.gcpc.state.il.us/

Gang Education and Training Resource Guide
http://www.gwcinc.com/gguide.html

Gang Information Resource Guide for Parents and Teachers
http://www.upsd.wednet.edu/UPSD/CHSganghand.html

Gangs 2000
http://www.hitech.com/cgia/gangs2000/menu.html

Gangs and Security Threat Group Awareness
http://www.dc.state.fl.us/pub/gangs/index.html

Gangs OR Us
http://www.gangsorus.com/

National Gang Crime Research Center
http://www.ecgia.com/gangdigest/journal.html

National Youth Gang Center
http://www.iir.com/nygc/

Skinhead Street Gangs
http://www.aracnet.com/~1wc123/skinhead.html

Street Gang Dynamics
http://www.gangwar.com/dynamics.html

What's a Parent to Do About Gangs
http://www/ncpc.org/10ad2.html

13 | Counseling Queer* Youth: Preventing Another Matthew Shepard Story

Fernando J. Gutiérrez

Queer adolescents are the least visible of the adolescent minority groups. This invisibility is a significant problem for them because they have to live hidden lives, and clinicians have difficulty identifying struggles these youth may be having as a result of their sexual orientation (O'Connor, 1992). The focus in working with queer adolescents has generally been on assisting these adolescents to cope with and adjust to their sexual orientation, which makes the adolescent the identified "client."

However, to continue addressing only the psychological maladjustment is like treating the symptom rather than the cause. Many of the issues troubling queer youth are the result of living in a society that stigmatizes and marginalizes them (Hershberger & D'Augelli, 2000). Hershberger and D'Augelli attributed the source of this stigmatization and marginalization to a motive by some members of society to force queer youth to internalize this disdain so as to force them to rid themselves of their queer feelings and identity and replace them with socially acceptable heterosexuality. Hershberger and D'Augelli concluded that, in counseling queer youth, it is not the queer identity that needs to be repaired but the hostility expressed against it.

The purpose of this chapter is to discuss the prevention needs of queer youth and the interventions that counselors can make at the individual, organizational, and societal levels to change the cultural context of queer youth to prevent more deaths of innocent persons, such as Matthew Shepard, who are victimized because of ignorance and intolerance just for being who they are. (Matthew Shepard, a queer youth from Laramie, Wyoming, was killed by two young assailants because of his sexual orientation. He was taken to a remote location, tied to a fence, beaten and bludgeoned, and left to die.)

Queer teenagers face several problems: deterioration of academic performance, homelessness, substance abuse, arrests for criminal activity, sexual victimization, sexually transmitted diseases, and attempted suicides (Herr, 1997; Remafedi, 1987). As counselors we need to treat these adolescents; however, the problems these adolescents face do not stem from an intrapsychic psychopathology but from adjustment reactions and responses to victimization by society (Hershberger & D'Augelli, 1995; Savin-Williams, 1994).

---

* The term *queer* is used in this chapter as an acceptable term within the sexual minority communities who have reowned the label that society has placed on these minorities. Reowning the label is a coping mechanism to remove the sting from the attempted insult by society. The term includes lesbian, gay, bisexual, and transgendered persons.

Other stressors for queer youth are the assumptions of others, such as society, family, and friends, that queer youth are defective; these assumptions result in stigmatization because of perceived deviance (Herdt, 1989). A study of queer youth in a sample from 14 metropolitan communities in the United States found that 80% of queer youth had been victims of verbal insults, 44% had received threats of attack, 23% had property damaged, 33% had objects thrown at them, 30% were chased or followed, 22% had been sexually assaulted, 17% had been physically assaulted, 13% were spat on, and 10% had been assaulted with a deadly weapon (Hershberger & D'Augelli, 1995). Queer youth are also vulnerable to forced or encouraged sexual conduct prior to age 19 (Doll et al., 1992).

In a sample of 1,925 lesbians, 24% had been beaten or physically abused as they were growing up, 19% were survivors of incest, and 21% were victims of rape or sexual molestation during childhood (Bradford, Ryan, & Rothblum, 1994). In a study of gay and bisexual male youth, almost 60% of the youth interviewed were abusing substances at the time of the interview, and their substance abuse pattern met the clinical criteria for substance abuse. Of these participants, 17% had participated in a chemical dependency treatment program.

Heterosexual adolescents have other visible heterosexual adolescents from whom to learn and emulate, whereas queer youth must remain invisible and, therefore, have become very isolated in navigating the complex adolescent stage of development. Plummer (1989) pointed to the heterosexist and homophobic peer adolescent culture as a contributor in the development of the negative self among queer youth. Coleman and Remafedi (1989) suggested that in addition to positive affirmations of these adolescents' sexual orientation, the counselor must address the following psychological problems resulting from stigmatization: psychological maladjustment, impaired psychosocial development, family alienation, inadequate interpersonal relationships, alcohol and drug abuse, depression and suicidal ideation, and concerns about HIV infection and other sexually transmitted diseases (Coleman, 1988).

Treatment issues should no longer focus on assisting gender-dysphoric individuals in adjusting to their new gender but to reaffirm a new transgendered identity (Carroll, Gilroy, & Ryan, 2002). Carroll et al. suggested that a shift needs to occur from a focus on transforming transgendered clients to a focus on transforming the cultural context in which these clients live. Other counselors have made similar suggestions regarding queer individuals. Dworkin and Gutiérrez (1992) advocated a shift in priorities toward a community counseling approach to the issue of addressing queer issues. Dworkin and Gutiérrez recommended delivering services to the community and not just responding to the onset of pathology. They identified counselor activities recommended by the Boston Conference on the Education of Psychologists for Community Mental Health Committee in 1966, such as active participation in community affairs, preventive intervention at the community level, collaboration with responsible laypeople to reduce community tensions, promoting research that supports sexual minority status as a difference rather than a pathology, working with lawmakers in developing public policy, and educating the public about erroneous queer stereotypes.

PROBLEM DEFINITION

An Underinformed Public

The public at large holds a heterosexual bias based on myths and stereotypes about queer youth. Dworkin and Gutiérrez (1989) stated that "because we do not know the process by which sexual orientation develops, we cope by using methods that are familiar though not always relevant. In the past, when we didn't understand something, we labeled it as a sin or illness" (p. 6).

Money (1987) addressed heterosexual bias when he stated that *sexual preference* is a moral and political term rather than a scientific term, one that implies a voluntary choice. Money pointed out the danger of this heterosexual bias because holding this view gives biased individuals justification to impose heterosexuality on others. If it is a preference, then queer folk could be legally forced to choose heterosexuality or experience punishment.

However, there is legal precedent that such pressure is unconstitutional. In *Skinner v. Oklahoma* (1942), a case in which the state wanted to sterilize habitual criminals, Justice Jackson stated, "There are limits to the extent which a legislatively represented majority may conduct biological experiments at the expense of the dignity and personality and natural powers of a minority—even those who have been guilty of what the majority define as crimes" (p. 541).

Gutiérrez (1994, p. 245) stated, "To force a gay, or lesbian, to behave heterosexually is such an abhorrent experiment conducted by the current legislatively represented majority, which is conducting this experiment at the expense of the dignity and personality of gays and lesbians." Imagine the psychological damage if the reverse were to happen—that heterosexuals be forced to live gay and lesbian lives because a group in power decides that it is the law of the land for everyone to behave homosexually (Hally, 1993).

Why Do We Feel This Way?

There is evidence that sexual orientation and gender variation are biological processes; therefore, to answer the question, we need to understand the biological process of sexual differentiation. Sexual differentiation proceeds as a result of the influence of the following subsystems: "chromosomal sex, H-Y antigenic sex, gonadal sex, prenatal hormonal sex, internal genital sex, external genital sex, pubertal hormonal sex and rearing, and gender identity/role formation" (Money, 1987, p. 389). These subsystems create sexual differentiation in three major biological systems of the human body: the reproductive tract, the external genitalia, and the brain and central nervous system (Money, 1987).

Reproductive Tract

Money (1987) stated that the human embryo during the first 8 weeks after conception is actually female. The embryo continues to develop as female unless masculinizing hormones are introduced as a result of the messages sent from the x-y (male) chromosome. The reproductive tract is formed by the differentiation of the gonads into either testes or ovaries. The male hormones prevent the mullerian ducts from developing into the uterus and fallopian tubes, according to Money. Testosterone then allows the wolffian ducts to develop into the prostate gland and seminal vesicles. Sometimes, a male embryo will experience an undescended testicle, for example. This seems to occur because of interference in the message sent to the gonads to differentiate into either a testicle or an ovary.

External Genitalia

The external genitalia in the fetus forms the labia minora in the female and the clitoris and hood. If the fetus is to be a male, according to Money (1987), the tissues that are the labia minora in the female fuse along the midline of the underside to form the tubular urethra of the penis in the male. The clitoris differentiates into the head of the penis, and the clitoral hood differentiates into the foreskin of the penis. The tissues that would form the labia majora of the vagina in the female fuse along the midline and form the scrotum in the male (Money, 1987). Sometimes, a mutation occurs in the fusing of the tissue of the penis, creating differences in penile formation. For example, in some fetuses that differentiate to male, the opening of the urethra, instead of being at the end and center of the head of the penis, will be underneath the head of the penis along the shaft.

Brain and Central Nervous System

Money (1987) explained that hormonalization of the brain is ambitypic, meaning that there are two processes going on. If the brain differentiates into a male, the hormones are masculinizing the brain. The converse of this process is not feminization, but demasculinization. At the same time, another process is going on in which the brain, which is differentiating as male, is being defeminized. The converse of this process, according to Money, is feminization of the brain. Money explains that this ambitypic differentiation allows for the coexistence of both feminine and masculine "nuclei and pathways, and the behavior they govern, in some, if not all parts of the brain"(p. 387). Money further explained,

> There are alternative ways in which one side [of the brain] could be rendered masculine and the other feminine to a sufficient degree to constitute bisexuality. Likewise, there are alternative ways in which the brain may be masculinized when the genitals are feminized, or vice versa, so as to constitute homosexuality. (p. 388)

Sexual differentiation generally proceeds in the same direction at every stage; that is, a person develops internal genitalia of the same sex as the external genitalia and the same sex as the brain/central nervous system (Lips, 1978). Lips explained variations in the differentiation process that allow for a person to differentiate as male in one stage and as female in the other stages. A person can have the internal and external genitalia of one sex and the brain formation of the other or both sexes. Thus, a gay man can be clear as to his gender, male, but perceive the world from a more feminine perspective and be sexually attracted to other males because of the specific development of the brain/central nervous system toward this direction.

Sexual orientation is akin to the concept of language formation:

> You do not choose your native language as a preference, even though you are born without it. You assimilate it into a brain prenatally made to receive a native language . . . once assimilated . . . into the brain, a native language becomes securely locked in—as securely as if it had been phylogenetically preordained to be locked in prenatally by a process of genetic determinism or by the determinism of fetal hormonal or other brain chemistries. (Money, 1987, p. 385)

Money (1987) concluded that

> the only scholarly position is to allow that prenatal and postnatal determinants are not mutually exclusive. . . . When nature and nurture interact at critical developmental periods, the residual products may persist immutably. . . . The postnatal determinants that enter the brain through the senses by way of social communication and learning also are biological, for there is biology of learning and remembering. (p. 398)

We have just seen the many steps and complexity of events that create sexual differentiation. In any of these steps, variations can occur to explain differentiations in sexual orientation and gender variations.

Heterosexist Assumptions

Because heterosexuals are a majority in society, there is a tendency to view the world strictly from a heterosexual perspective. The United States is a pluralistic society. A characteristic of a pluralistic society is that it respects the rights and differences of the minority groups in the society and does not impose a "majority view." Levine and Padilla (1980, p. 3) defined pluralistic counseling as "therapy that recognizes the client's culturally based beliefs, values, and behaviors that is concerned with the client's adaptation to his or her particular cultural milieu . . . [and] considers all facets of the client's personal history, family history, and social and cultural orientation." To this definition, sexual orientation and gender variation should be added.

Levine and Padilla (1980) suggested that a pluralistic counselor will be knowledgeable about majority and minority cultures, the points of impact between cultures, and the processes by which cultural elements influence individuals. Counselors can be effective only if their own attitudes toward homosexuality are positive and congruous with the current scientific knowledge about sexual orientation and transgender issues, that is, that these are variations of sexual expression (Coleman & Remafedi, 1989).

For example, Erikson (1968) developed a psychosocial/psychosexual stage of identity development. During the adolescent period, according to Erikson, adolescents must deal with the nuclear conflict between identity and identity confusion. Erikson identified further part conflicts related to this stage, which he defined as the conflict between sexual polarization and bisexual confusion. Erikson made a heterosexual assumption when he described this psychosocial/sexual stage. A queer affirmative interpretation of this stage would view the resolution of the conflict as sexual identity versus sexual identity confusion, without creating a heterosexual bias and assumption that heterosexuality is the preferred mode of resolving the conflict or that bisexuality is a confused state. Erikson's theory, however, acknowledges different potentialities for sexual orientation. His mistake was in assuming that heterosexuality is the ultimate outcome in the resolution of this conflict.

CASE STUDY

Juan is an 18-year-old college freshman dealing with coming out to himself. Juan is a first-generation Hispanic male who immigrated with his parents when he was 11 years old. Juan was born with an undescended testicle, and when he was 8 years old, he received shots to assist the descent of the testicle. At the age of 6, he began to become aware of sexual feelings. Juan would play doctor with a female classmate of his at school. He also learned to masturbate by placing his penis between his legs and squeezing.

When Juan came to the United States, his parents became friends with other people from their country. One of these friends was a body builder who had a picture of himself in a brief bikini-type bathing suit sitting on his nightstand in the bedroom. One day Juan had to go into the bedroom to get something for this friend and saw the picture. Juan became very aroused on seeing the picture.

The next year, Juan entered sixth grade. He had a male teacher who was an attractive, tall, black-haired, sensitive Italian man. Juan developed a secret crush on his sixth-grade teacher. Juan had all these feelings that confused him. He remembered that the school counselor had visited his class, inviting students to speak to him if they needed to talk about anything. Juan also remembered the admonition that his father had given him at the age of 7. His dad had commented in front of Juan that he hoped he would never have a gay son. Having a gay son in the Hispanic culture would mean shame on the family. Juan did not go see the school counselor and continued carrying the confusing feelings with him as he was growing up.

At age 15, Juan had a friend, Carlos, of the same age, from his country, living nearby. This friend was much more sexually sophisticated than Juan and had access to his father's X-rated magazines. Carlos invited Juan to view the X-rated magazines in Carlos's bedroom. They both unbuttoned their pants and began masturbating themselves while looking at the photos. Juan and Carlos did not view this as a homosexual experience, despite the fact that, after a while, the sexual play changed focus from looking at the photos to looking at each other masturbate. Carlos's sister came home shortly after Juan and Carlos were finished. Juan felt a lot of guilt, and when Carlos invited him to do it again on another occasion, Juan declined. Juan gave the excuse that his religious beliefs did not allow him to focus on sex. Juan was still an altar boy at this age.

Juan attended a college preparatory high school for boys. When Juan was in high school, two of his classmates in his homeroom, who appeared quite effeminate, befriended him. One day they made a surprise visit to Juan's house. Juan's mother greeted them. These friends did not know exactly where Juan lived so they stopped at the neighbor's house to ask where Juan's house was. Juan's mother was embarrassed that the neighbors saw these effeminate classmates looking for Juan and that somehow the family would be shamed by the association. Juan himself was not effeminate. When they left, Juan's mother angrily confronted Juan about these friends and forbade Juan to see these friends again or to have them come to the house again.

Juan went through high school having crushes on male teachers and classmates. He felt lonely because he could not talk about his feelings with anyone. He thought about talking to a priest during confession, but he felt attracted to the priest to whom he would confess his sins. Also, giving these feelings a voice would mean that Juan would have to own these homosexual feelings, and he wasn't ready to do that. During his high school years, Juan would deny his gay feelings. He felt much pressure to like girls, so he would fantasize about them with the hopes that he would "straighten out."

Juan did not have much contact with girls because he went to an all boys school. He had to study a lot so he did not have much time for dating anyway. This was a good excuse for Juan to avoid the issue of dating during high school. He did go to the high school prom with the daughter of the family at whose house his two effeminate friends had stopped to ask for directions a couple of years back. Juan felt good that he was somehow covering up that incident by showing interest in the daughter.

Juan felt lonely and isolated during high school. Note that these years are the years for an adolescent to resolve the developmental nuclear conflict of intimacy versus isolation (Erikson, 1968). Juan would cry himself to sleep on many occasions because of the pain he felt about hurting his parents and family if they found out he was gay.

After graduating from high school, Juan went away to college. His decision to go away to school was an unconscious desire to create some psychological distance between him and his family so that he could explore his identity without their intrusion.

Juan did very well during his first semester in college; however, during his second semester, his grades began to slip. He became depressed and lost interest in his extracurricular activities. He decided to go to the counseling center for help. During the counseling sessions, Juan talked about several issues. The counselor noticed that Juan avoided issues of dating and intimacy. The counselor suggested to Juan that Juan might want to talk about his social life for the next session.

When Juan came to his next session, instead of coming into the office from the front door, Juan decided to enter the office on that day from the back door. The counselor opened the session by reminding Juan that they had agreed to discuss Juan's social life. Juan made attempts to talk about prior heterosexual dates. Juan sensed that his counselor knew that he was not being honest. Juan's defense mechanism of denial was no longer working for him. Juan told the counselor, "I know you know. Now somebody else knows." Juan's fear that the counselor would reject him overwhelmed him and he ran out the door. The counselor followed Juan and saw him go into the campus chapel. The counselor called Juan at home later to ensure he was going to be alright.

Juan wrote the counselor the following letter:

> Your words have not left my mind since you called. You're right—it is very painful for me (and always has been). But you're wrong. I'm not "O.K."; I am in essence a *freak*! (God, how I wish to be normal . . . why doesn't *He* help me?)! I found out in your office the truth—it was then, that someone *else* knew too!! I don't want it known!—ever!! Ever since my life has collapsed. I'm gripped with the constant fear of my family finding out. (I'm sick.) *Never*, never have I entered a church for help; never have I felt so vacant, so cheap, so hollow, so VULGAR!; and help never came—well *screw you* GOD!
>
> My greatest wish (and has been) to love and be loved, and to love as nature *meant* it to be; all I feel is bitter, apathetic . . . nothing matters any more (school nor music nor myself).
>
> Thank you for caring.
>
> I hurt.
>
> I wish to be alone . . . forever.
>
> J.
>
> P.S. I need time to think.

Bracciale, Sanabria, and Updyke (2003) pointed out that it is important for the counselor not to hurry the client in examining and owning his or her sexual orientation. In Juan's case, Juan felt overwhelmed even at the thought of talking about his social life. Perhaps a better approach by the counselor would have been to ask Juan if he wanted to talk about his social life on the day that they had agreed to talk about it as opposed to reminding Juan that they had agreed to talk about it. This would have given Juan a choice as to whether he wanted to talk about it. By reminding Juan that they had agreed to talk about it, it did not give Juan a choice as to whether to pursue the exploration of his sexual orientation. Juan felt trapped in the situation, and it created a crisis for him that caused him to flee the anxiety-producing situation. Bracciale et al. emphasized the need for the client to set his or her own pace in figuring out his or her sexual orientation. Sometimes the counselor, in his or her eagerness to help the client get there, can push a little too soon.

APPROACHES TO PREVENTION

Individual

The case of Juan illustrates the loneliness and isolation that many queer youth feel. According to Uribe and Harbeck (1992), members of minority groups receive support and acculturation by and from other family members and community resources regarding their status as a member of that minority group. However, the queer teenager is often alone and isolated while dealing with the awareness of his or her newly acquired minority status as queer. "While many minority groups are the target of prejudice (beliefs) and discrimination (actions) in our society, few persons face this hostility without the support and acceptance of their family as do many gay, lesbian, and bisexual youth" (Uribe & Harbeck, 1992, p. 13).

Because a support group did not exist on Juan's high school campus, Juan had to put his developmental growth on hold until he reached college, where there was a program that could assist him in his exploration. Juan had to put on hold the resolution of his part conflict of sexual identity and sexual identity confusion, which, in turn, affected his ability to move on to the next nuclear conflict of intimacy versus isolation. Heterosexual students, however, get to experiment with dating and sexual attraction and behavior in high school, building their psychosocial/sexual skills necessary to move to this next stage of development.

Family

Another approach to prevention for the benefit of queer youth is educating the parents. In general, parental reactions consist of two facets: (a) The parents apply their negative perceptions of homosexual identity to their child and reject the child as a stranger, and (b) the parents feel guilt and failure for fear that somehow they caused their child to become homosexual (Strommen, 1989, p. 40).

For the parent, and members of society at large, a subjective perception is developed that the homosexual is "a member of another species, someone whose essential wants are unrecognizable and different" (Weinberg, 1972, p. 97). This subjective perception turns into prejudice. Sometimes, this prejudice can in turn create hatred, such as the hatred that allowed two individuals to terrorize, torture, and take the life of Matthew Shepard. Therefore, any approach to prevention with the queer community needs to involve the dissemination of state-of-the-art scientific information regarding this population.

School

Uribe and Harbeck (1992) described the formation of Project 10, an in-school counseling program at Fairfax High School in Los Angeles, California, with two purposes: (a) to provide emotional support, information, resources, and referrals to queer youth or individuals who wanted accurate information on the subject of sexual orientation zand (b) to heighten the school community's acceptance and sensitivity to queer issues. This project has grown in impact to the national level as a forum for the expression of the needs of queer teenagers.

In forming Project 10, Uribe and Harbeck (1992) identified three steps that needed to be taken to create a receptive environment to the project:

- break through the wall of silence surrounding the topic of homosexuality to reach the target group
- provide a safe and supportive atmosphere so youth could discuss their sexuality in a nonthreatening way
- develop a nonjudgmental posture to serve as a guideline in dealing with queer youth.

Project 10 provided not only counseling support groups for queer students but also education and educational materials, school safety measures, faculty and staff training, human rights advocacy, dropout prevention strategies, and use of community resources.

At the college level, Gutiérrez (1987) discussed the formation of a campus program at a Catholic college based on a campus ecology model. A campus ecology model shifts the focus away from the individual and toward the creation of an environment that facilitates the personal growth and development of the queer students. To do so, the academic institution must examine its implicit and explicit attitudes, rules and regulations, and factors that affect queer youth on campus (Gutiérrez, 1987). The focus is on the individual growth of the queer student, as well as the growth of heterosexual students, faculty, staff, administrators, and the community at large so that they can reach acceptance, not just tolerance, of sexual orientation and gender variational differences.

This college campus program, like Project 10, encouraged counselors, faculty, and staff to deal with their own internalized homophobia because of fear of being seen as homosexual or being discovered as a homosexual. Uribe and Harbeck (1992) pointed out that most minorities cannot hide their status as a member of that minority group. Queer individuals, however, can often hide their homosexuality, giving rise to a socialization process that requires learning to hide (Uribe & Harbeck, 1992). One cannot fight the fight while remaining in the closet.

Community

Approaches to prevention must target different levels of audiences. One must target the affected group (i.e., the queer youth), but one must also target the environment and community that impact this group.

Addressing the needs of queer youth within the schools can be a very political process. For programs to be effective, school districts must work with the community to involve them in the process so that the school districts can obtain the backing of the community. Education must begin with the parents and community leaders to make them aware of the need for the intervention strategies within the school systems.

Other approaches to prevention involve participation in professional organizations that provide the leadership to mold the agenda of the profession to address the needs of queer youth (Dworkin & Gutiérrez, 1992). Research funding to generate studies on issues affecting queer youth is essential, according to Dworkin and Gutiérrez (1992) who stated, "The best weapon to counteract the oppression by specific interest groups is research" (p. 337). Dworkin and Gutiérrez also encouraged counselors to stand up and take action to inform lawmakers and government officials involved in setting public policy regarding the reality of the queer population to avoid decisions from being made on the basis of fears and erroneous stereotypes.

INTERVENTION STRATEGIES

Rappaport (1977, as cited in Banning, 1980, p. 214) identified four intervention strategies from an ecological perspective: individual strategies, group strategies, associational strategies, and institutional strategies. Individual strategies include advising, counseling, or psychotherapy. Group strategies focus on particular groups, such as couples counseling and sensitivity groups. Associational strategies focus on the aspects of an organization that do not adapt to the needs of its members or whose structure impedes the developmental growth of members within the organization. The focus is on organizational dynamics or the operational system of the organization; these include consultation, organizational development, or social organization consultation. Institutional strategies include working to effect change in the attitudes of the organizational administration, faculty, and staff toward the students, as well as the organization's value orientation, policies, and other factors that contribute to a poor ecology for student growth and development (Gutiérrez, 1987).

Individual

Individual strategies, according to Gutiérrez (1987), focus on the coming-out process of queer youth. Recognition of same-sex sexual attraction often occurs at around age 10 (McClintock & Herdt, 1996). For Juan, his awareness to same-sex sexual attraction came even earlier, at age 6. Self-labeling as queer typically occurs at about age 15 (Hershberger & D'Augelli, 1995). This self-labeling can be quite traumatic to individuals. Once a person self-labels as queer, he or she is at the point of no return; the person owns the label and cannot take it back. This awareness can be very frightening to an individual and is the cause of many suicide attempts by queer youth. It is estimated that approximately 30% of suicides among young adults are related to sexual orientation issues (National Center for Health Statistics, 1986).

For Juan, his admission to the counselor that he felt same-sex sexual attraction was the point of no return. Sharing this information with others is even more frightening than admitting it to oneself because to admit it to oneself can be changed by defense mechanisms such as intellectualization, rationalization, and denial, but admitting it to another is harder to deny or take back. Many times, the client will beat around the bush with the counselor. They will say things like "I'm really afraid to say this to you," "I don't know how you will take it," or "I think you will be shocked." A response to these statements can be, "Did you kill somebody?" This response often works to alleviate the anxiety the client feels because the client knows that what he or she is about to reveal is not as serious as murdering somebody and it reduces his or her anxiety level to a more manageable level.

Troiden (1989) described the coming-out process as consisting of four stages:

- *sensitization*, in which the youth develops an awareness of being different from others
- *identity confusion*, in which the youth begins to recognize behaviors and feelings that could be labeled queer
- *identity assumption*, in which the youth begins to own this queer identity
- *commitment*, in which queer becomes a way of being as opposed to a way of behaving.

Juan felt this identity confusion. He needed support in sorting out his feelings and seeing how the queer label fit him. For a client to go through these stages, he or she needs an affirming counselor who can reframe all the negative messages that the client has received about queer orientations. Once these messages have been neutralized and the client receives positive messages, the client can learn to accept who he or she is. For gay youth, it is not a matter of choosing the lifestyle but of accepting who they are without societal value judgments about who they are. When they met again, Juan's counselor talked to Juan about his letter. The counselor pointed out to Juan that, perhaps, God put the counselor in Juan's path, thereby gently challenging Juan's perception of abandonment by God. The counselor assured Juan that he did not perceive Juan as a freak. The counselor pointed out to Juan that his yearning to love and be loved as nature meant it to be can be different for different people. In Juan's case, nature meant him to love and be loved by another man.

For Juan, this acceptance by the counselor was a reenactment of the nuclear conflict of trust versus mistrust (Erikson, 1968). During this nuclear conflict, the child learns to trust himself, his world, and his sense of self in relationship to his parents and significant others. To incorporate this new information into his self-identity, Juan needed to revisit this nuclear conflict and resolve it so that he could learn to trust himself and his world again as a queer person.

After coming out to oneself, the next step is to come out to share this new discovery with a significant other. D'Augelli, Hershberger, and Pilkington (1998) conducted a study with queer youth and found that three quarters of these youth chose a close friend to share this first disclosure. Only 9% chose a parent as the first person to whom to disclose this new identity, and all of these were to their mothers.

Once clients accept their own same-sex attraction, they are now ready to face other people like themselves. Juan asked to meet other students on campus who were going through the same process. The counselor arranged to introduce him to another student on campus, Paul. It was safe for Juan to meet with just another student rather than to join a group. Dealing with the individual differences of another student is not as overwhelming. It also does not involve the peer pressure of being like the other members of the group. This way Juan could compare his situation with that of the other student and could evaluate similarities and differences without the pressure of having to be "politically correct" in his identity.

This stage for Juan was similar to Erikson's (1968) nuclear conflict of autonomy versus shame and doubt. In this stage, children learn that they are separate from their parents and begin to explore their world and assert their own individuality. Juan and Paul could further evaluate the norms and values of the queer world without having to commit to it and accept everything about this world. As in any other culture, there are variations within the queer culture (Gutiérrez, 1994), and Juan and Paul needed to figure out where they fit in relationship to these variations. As Juan and Paul developed their queer identity, eventually they were ready to join a support group of other students who were dealing with these issues.

Family

Individual strategies can also assist the parents of these youth. On learning of their son's or daughter's queer status, parents often go through similar feelings of shock and isolation (Boxer, Cook, & Herdt, 1995). They go through stages of loss similar to those of someone who experiences a death in the family: denial, anger, bargaining, depression, and acceptance (Kubler-Ross, 1969). Parents may feel that their son or daughter is just going through a phase. They may be angry at whomever "exposed" their son or daughter to this lifestyle. They may become angry at themselves and blame themselves for "causing" their son's or daughter's "queerness." They may even become angry at God, like Juan did in his letter to the counselor.

The queer youth and their parents may go through a bargaining stage, where they bargain with God that if God changes the youth back to "normal" they promise to do x, y, or z. When they see that bargaining is not working for them, they become depressed, and, as they receive more information about the situation, they gradually learn to accept what is going on within themselves or their children and are able to accept themselves or their children as queer.

Robinson, Walters, and Skeen (1989) identified three factors that contribute to a sense of grief by the parents on finding out that their child is queer: (a) an assumption that the child is part of the accepted heterosexual majority and the loss of the dreams of the child's traditional marriage and generation of grandchildren for these parents, (b) the realization that the child is part of a minority group, and (c) the fact that the minority group to which their child belongs has a long history of persecution.

D'Augelli et al. (1998) found that 51% of mothers were accepting of their child's revelation of queer status, 30% were tolerant, 9% were intolerant, and 10% were rejecting. D'Augelli et al. also found that 27% of fathers were accepting of their child's revelation of queer status, 32% were tolerant, 16% were intolerant, and 29% were rejecting. This same study found that 57% of siblings were accepting of their sibling's revelation of queer status, 19% were tolerant, 9% were intolerant, and 15% rejecting.

Although the above figures are encouraging for most queer youth, too many other youth who disclose their queer status to family members risk doing so. D'Augelli et al. (1998) found that mothers verbally abused 38% of daughters and 24% of sons after they revealed their status, 10% of mothers of lesbian daughters and 3% of mothers of gay sons physically threatened their children when they revealed their status, and 10% of mothers of lesbian daughters and 3% of mothers of gay sons physically attacked their children when they revealed their status. In contrast, 19% of fathers abused their revealing daughters and sons, 10% of fathers physically threatened their revealing daughters while only 2% of fathers physically threatened their revealing sons, and 5% of fathers actually physically attacked their revealing daughters while 2% of fathers actually physically attacked their revealing sons. These figures suggest that lesbian youth are more likely to be rejected by both parents and to be victimized by them.

D'Augelli et al. (1998) found that, among revealing lesbians, 19% of brothers and 10% of sisters verbally abused them, 5% of brothers and 14% of sisters physically threatened them, and 0% of brothers and 7% of sisters physically attacked their lesbian sisters. Among revealing gay youth, 22% of brothers and 13% of sisters verbally abused their gay brother, 14% of brothers and 0% of sisters physically threatened them after the revelation, and 7% of brothers and 2% of sisters physically attacked the gay youth after the revelation of their queer status. These figures indicate that lesbian and gay youth receive rejection and are victimized by same-sex siblings more than by opposite-sex siblings.

The grief process for heterosexual parents and family members appears to take 2 years to work through and fully accept the child's sexual orientation (Borhek, 1983), which seems to be the same amount of time associated with the resolution of grief from a divorce or death of a loved one (Robinson et al., 1989).

Although in the majority of the cases, the families of queer youth were either accepting or tolerant, the incidents of abuse, even if verbal, were sufficiently high as to make a queer youth question the risk of revealing their queer status to their families. In Juan's case, the counselor suggested to Juan that he might want to first test his family's reactions to homosexuality in general. Juan might want to have a discussion with his family about Rosie O'Donnell's coming out, for example, to see how receptive or supportive his parents are to learning that someone with whom they are familiar is queer.

Because Juan is away at college, he does not get home very often. The counselor recommended to Juan to wait until the summer break before bringing the subject up with his family. Holidays, which tend to be emotionally charged times of the year when all kinds of issues for families arise, may not be the best time to bring up the subject. Waiting until the summer also gave Juan enough time to continue exploring his sexual orientation in a group and to learn from other members of the group who had already come out to their parents how they approached it, what worked for them, and what didn't.

Another intervention for Juan's parents included the referral of Juan's parents to their local priest. The counselor identified a priest in Juan's family's Catholic parish who was supportive of sexual orientation issues. He then referred Juan's parents to speak to this priest so the priest could provide pastoral guidance around sexual orientation issues. Many religions support pastoral programs that affirm a person's sexual orientation (Gutiérrez, 1987).

School

Group Strategies

Group strategies can consist of counselor-led support groups for queer youth or for their parents. Groups can also be self-help, such as those led by Parents and Friends of Lesbians and Gays (PFLAG). Given the above statistics of family responses to queer youth's disclosures of their queer status, it is imperative that schools, queer youth community centers, and community mental health centers establish programs for family members to be able to explore their reactions to their queer family members' revelations and to educate these family members about the biological as well as psychosocial aspects of queer status.

Counselors need to be aware of the culture of the group with whom they are working. In Juan's case, the counselor must be aware of not only the gay culture but also the Hispanic culture (the ethnic issues are addressed below, in the Adaptations for Diversity section). Juan's counselor could refer Juan to the local lesbian/gay community center and to social groups in which Juan could meet others like himself, such as the local gay/lesbian chorus, bicycle club, runners' group, and so on. Meeting other queer youth in these contexts can give these youth a different picture of who they are as queer youth and what life can be like for them. This process is similar to Erikson's (1968) nuclear conflict of identity versus identity confusion. Of course, certain oppressive elements of society would like queer youth to think that their life is doomed if they continue to live this lifestyle.

With individual and group counseling support, Juan was able to understand the biological basis for his feelings. His parents were able to stop blaming Juan for being who he is and also stopped blaming themselves for causing Juan's queerness. They learned that they had no control over Juan's status and were able to stop feeling guilty about themselves as parents. For many queer youth, however, there is a sense of a foreshortened future. Feeling that their life is doomed, they turn to the immediate pleasures of life because they do not know what tomorrow will bring. Time perspective for adolescents is very short term. Because adolescents are forced to go underground for their social network, they have very few positive role models and little adult supervision. This situation creates an environment in which substance abuse and high-risk behaviors can flourish. Because the adolescents do not see a future for themselves, why sacrifice and delay gratification?

Paul was able to develop his queer identity; however, unlike Juan, he chose a different path. He did not have the same support from his family that Juan was able to receive from his family. Paul was a strikingly handsome, Swedish-looking, blonde young man. He became unsure of his identity, so he sought validation from other gays by becoming promiscuous. Paul's parents were extremely religious and rejected him after he came out to them. They went as far as throwing him out of the house and cutting off his tuition assistance. Erikson (1968) stated that the counterpart of intimacy is distantiation, or the readiness to repudiate those forces or people whose essence seems dangerous to one's own. Paul's reaction to his parents' religiosity and rejection of him was to reject those forces whose essence was dangerous to his own, his gayness. Erikson warned that youth who are not sure of their identity shy away from interpersonal intimacy and throw themselves into acts that are promiscuous or with self-abandon. These youth develop what Erikson called the negative identity. Although parents of queer youth are not responsible for their child's queer status, they do influence the child's ability to develop a healthy sense of identity. Paul would go to the local gay bar, and because he was not yet of age to enter the bar, he would hang out in the bar's parking lot, offering free oral sex indiscriminately to patrons entering the bar. Paul felt validated for being popular with the bar patrons. Even though he was in college, Paul had no sense of a positive future for himself, so he behaved in a manner that exposed him to sexually transmitted diseases. Paul chose to become a porn movie actor in same-sex pornographic movies. Because of his high-risk behaviors, Paul contracted AIDS and died from it. Because queer youth are vulnerable to substance abuse and high-risk sexual behaviors as a coping mechanism for stressors as a result of their queer status, it is imperative that these youth receive information and support regarding these issues to prevent deaths, such as Paul's, from happening.

Associational Strategies

Hershberger and D'Augelli (1995) cited a study by Gross, Aurand, and Adessa (1988) that showed that in a sample of gay men, 50% of the sample reported victimization in junior high school and 59% in high school; lesbians in the sample reported that 12% of them were victimized in junior high school and 21% in high school. Savin-Williams (1994) cited studies by Remafedi (1987) that showed that over two thirds of gay and bisexual youth had school-related problems; nearly 40% were truant, and 28% dropped out of school. These statistics indicate that schools are not safe places for queer youth.

Uribe and Harbeck (1992) discussed various associational strategies that they implemented at the beginning of Project 10 at Fairfax High School, such as developing an informational brochure that was distributed throughout the community regarding the project and training a core group of teachers, administrators, and counselors. As an organization, the high school was not meeting the needs of gay and lesbian students. The structure of the services in place did not address the needs of these students because the faculty and staff did not have the proper knowledge and training to address these issues. There was a lack of awareness that this was even a problem within the organization. The brochure that was designed and circulated provided a context for the program and educated the high school, the Board of Education, and the community at large as to the problem and the need for the Project 10 program. A training program for staff and faculty bridged the gap of services that were being provided to heterosexual students by training the faculty and staff on the issues facing queer youth and providing these faculty and staff with the skills they needed to address not only the needs of the queer youth but also the heterosexual students' needs in adjusting to the reality of sharing a campus with queer youth. The initial reaction to the program was very positive, according to Uribe and Harbeck. Only 10 negative phone calls were recorded initially.

Gutiérrez (1987) implemented several associational strategies at the college level. He met with his director at the counseling center to obtain approval for the outreach to queer youth on campus. Prior to this point, the counseling center had not made any affirmative efforts to communicate to queer youth that they were welcome in the counseling center and that the staff of the counseling center was knowledgeable, able, and willing to serve the specific needs of queer youth on campus.

The counseling center and the campus ministry office began to explicitly list sexual orientation issues among the issues addressed by the centers, thereby giving sexual orientation visibility as an issue to be addressed on campus. This was done in a queer affirmative way to prevent the wrong impression that these offices were there to "cure" students of their queerness.

The counselor then enlisted the assistance of the Campus Ministry Office and the Women's Center to cosponsor the showing of the movie *Word Is Out* on campus, followed by a discussion afterward. Eighty students attended this showing. The average attendance for workshops sponsored by the counseling center had been 5–8 students. This response was indicative of the yearning for these services by students on campus, queer and heterosexual alike, who were searching for information and support around these issues.

A training workshop was also conducted for resident assistants and hall directors on how to conduct conflict resolution when problems arose in the residence halls regarding sexual orientation. Issues addressed in these trainings could include how to counsel a resident who finds out that his or her roommate is queer, how to counsel a queer resident who is feeling attraction toward his or her roommate who does not reciprocate the feelings, how to diffuse animosity on the floor regarding the presence of a queer student in the residential community, how to conduct educational programming for residents around queer issues, and discussions of safe sex that include queer issues.

The university received two negative phone calls from parents who had found out about the university's new program. These phone calls were fielded to the counselor, who was able to educate the parents regarding the importance of a university education in creating awareness about diversity in our society, which includes queer individuals. The parents were satisfied with the counselor's response, and there were no further complaints.

Institutional Strategies

Any change in an institution must have the involvement of the policy and decision makers within the institution if effective change is to take place. A study of Oberlin College by Norris (1992) regarding the institutional culture of the college revealed that, although the college has a progressive tradition and was one of the first institutions of higher learning to adopt a nondiscrimination clause based on sexual orientation in 1973, the implementation of the clause has been lacking. Norris suggested that the paradox results from two competing sets of values, one focused on equal rights and the other on a heterosexual orthodoxy. Norris concluded that the inability of the institution to legitimate discussion of sexuality and the concerns of queers on its campus prevents an open airing of issues and concerns.

Gutiérrez (1987) described how the president of Santa Clara University, a Catholic Jesuit institution, obtained the backing of the Board of Trustees before the issue of sexual orientation was addressed on this campus. The president then legitimized the discussion of the issue of sexual orientation by making the issue part of a university-wide Institute on the Family, which was open to the public.

For Project 10, Uribe and Harbeck (1992) obtained the backing of the school board members, administrators, teachers, and students, both queer and heterosexual, as well as members of the community. For example, the City of West Hollywood became involved in providing the funding for library materials, a hotline, incidental costs of publicity, awards, and scholarships sponsored by Project 10. Having such a united front prevents scapegoating of the staff attempting to implement the program as well as shared pride in the success of the program. It also insulates the institution from attacks from opposing groups, because opposing groups can see how much support from the community there is for the program.

The institution must also ground whatever it is doing in research and scholarly rationale. At Santa Clara University, for example, the success of the program was the result of a solid grounding in a theological and pastoral context that was congruous with and not adverse to the religious values of the institution.

When mainstream institutions fail to meet the needs of queer youth, institutions must be formed to meet these needs. Such was the case of the Harvey Milk School in New York City. Most of the students attending this school had dropped out of other New York City public schools primarily because of peer harassment (Martin & Hetrick, 1988). However, this type of institutional strategy should be utilized sparingly, lest we create a world of separate but equal institutions.

The separate but equal method was tried with African Americans in the 1950s, and *Brown v. Board of Education* (1954) held this type of arrangement to be unconstitutional. Other precedents that discourage the separation of individuals who are different from the mainstream are seen in the Individuals With Disabilities Education Act Amendments of 1997. This act prohibits the separation of students with disabilities and requires school districts to mainstream these students and provide a least restrictive environment and a free and appropriate education. So too, queer youth are entitled to a free and appropriate public education free of harassment and free of a hostile environment.

Community

To avoid community criticism and feelings of alienation, the president of Santa Clara University decided to include gays and lesbians in an Institute on the Family that the university was sponsoring during that semester. The institute workshop was open to the community. The counselor assisted with the makeup of the panel, which consisted of a graduate student from a local university, the founders of the local chapter of PFLAG, and a gay male couple from Dignity/San Francisco who were raising one of the partners' 6- and 8-year-old girls. The two girls were also on the panel, and they were the most powerful panelists as they talked about the love they felt from both male parents and the positive experience in their household.

ADAPTATIONS FOR DIVERSITY

Individual Strategies

In working with ethnic minority queer youth, the counselor must be aware that these students are dealing not only with their queer identity but their ethnic identity as well as their personal identity. These identities must be integrated. Therefore, the counselor must become aware of not only the theories of queer identity (Cass, 1979; Troiden, 1989) but also models of minority identity development (Atkinson, Morten, & Sue, 1979; Gutiérrez, 1985; Loiacano, 1989; Parham, 1989).

Chan (1992) identified several factors to look at in the family background of ethnic minority individuals. These include the following: (a) Is the client an immigrant or American born? (b) What is the client's ethnic group? (c) What are the specific values of the ethnic group, the client's family, and the client? (d) How closely does the client follow traditional ethnic customs? (e) What is the client's socioeconomic status? and (f) What is the client's level of bilingualism?

Latinos and Latinas represent a variety of nations, races, and cultures; therefore, they belong to no one group (Morales, 1992). Generally, however, Latinos/Latinas hold the cultural values of familismo, machismo, simpatía, personalismo, and respeto, according to Morales. These values need to be explored as to how they are affected by the superimposed queer context. Ethnic minority groups such as African Americans experience the same racism in the queer culture that they experience in mainstream heterosexual White society, so they are forced to go back to their African American community for support, where they encounter the homophobia that also exists in the White heterosexual mainstream society (Gutiérrez & Dworkin, 1992).

Juan was very transculturated; he was bilingual and bicultural. Juan's ethnic identity was really not an issue for him, but his sexual identity was. Juan held all the internalized homophobic perceptions of seeing himself as a freak and that in order to love as nature meant it to be, he had to love heterosexually. These homophobic values are further magnified in his Hispanic culture, where machismo and Catholicism are so strong. Juan needs to explore how machismo, familismo, respeto, and Catholicism fit into his life as a gay individual.

Juan needs the validation of other Hispanic gays. In many major cities there are gay and lesbian Hispanic organizations that provide emotional and social support within a cultural context. These queer ethnic minority organizations are crucial in preventing the split identified by Gutiérrez and Dworkin (1992) between the racist queer community and the homophobic ethnic minority community. Counselors need to become familiar with these organizations to be able to provide the information to their clients.

Family Strategies

Juan's parents were predominantly Spanish speaking, so they needed referrals to support services that were bilingual and bicultural. For example, earlier, I mentioned that Juan's parents could be referred to a priest who is gay affirming. It would be important for the counselor to investigate a referral for the family with the parish priest who ministers to the Hispanic community. Juan could be helpful to the counselor in identifying this priest.

Another resource for families can be the Metropolitan Community Churches. These churches exist in most major cities in the United States and around the world. The services in these churches are quite similar to a Catholic Mass, except that women are allowed to participate at the altar table. At these churches, queer people often bring family members so that the families can experience the love shared for queer people by these churches. In Fort Lauderdale, for example, attendance at the Sunshine Cathedral reaches over 700 individuals on any given Sunday (although this is an unusually high number, given that Fort Lauderdale is in the Bible Belt and even queer people go to church on Sunday).

Many communities now have PFLAG chapters offering assistance and support in Spanish. Otherwise, PFLAG can assist the counselor in finding an appropriate support network for the family, depending on the family's ethnic or racial background. A support group such as PFLAG can be invaluable in providing families with guidance and role modeling from other parents and family members of the family's ethnic/racial background. It is important to send out the message to all racial/ethnic groups that queer youth exist in all cultures and races.

As family members grow in their acceptance of their children and the issues that their sexual orientation raised for the family, eventually, they could be encouraged to take a leadership role in PFLAG or in the school system or community to advocate for the needs of queer youth and their families for those families who are members of the same ethnic/racial background.

School Strategies

Unless the school holds the value of diversity to begin with, it will be difficult for institutional strategies to be implemented. This is why the involvement of individuals identified under the Community Strategies subsection below is crucial. When school organizers have the group backing of key individuals in the various organizations that make up the community, the task becomes simpler. The more groups the program organizers have behind them, the easier it will be to convince the less supportive members of the community to participate in the project. These leaders can then approach the decision makers of the school to bring them on board to back the programs and to give their blessings to strategies to change the institutional attitudes and values.

Ethnic communities have become accustomed to the White majority making the decisions and excluding ethnic group voices. Therefore, ethnic minorities have become accustomed to the exclusion, and they stay away from the decision-making process. Ethnic minority leaders must be identified and given the power and authority to initiate the dialogue with their communities.

In one recent example, a gay Hispanic leader was invited to attend a meeting of a local politician running for office by the White gay/lesbian campaign committee supporting this politician. A meeting was called to invite Hispanic politicians to attend a meeting with the gay/lesbian community. The gay Hispanic community leader was not asked to contact the Hispanic politicians, many whom he knew. When the gay Hispanic leader got to the home where the meeting was to be held, he was told that the meeting had been canceled because of lack of response. The organizers had not called him to let him know the meeting had been canceled. The mistake by the White gay/lesbian campaign committee was not to utilize the gay Hispanic leader as a bridge to the two communities. This occurred because of lack of diversity awareness from the political organizers and the gay/lesbian leaders on how to approach ethnic minority communities.

Community Strategies

Uribe and Harbeck (1992) pointed out that the implementation of Project 10 was not successful in predominantly Black and Hispanic schools, suggesting that particular strategies need to be developed to address these populations. What is essential in working with specific groups is that the program designer involve the members of the population one is attempting to reach in the planning of the program. To make Project 10 work in the African American and Hispanic communities, for example, the program organizers need to meet with each community individually.

The organizers can involve queer leaders of the ethnic minority community as bridges to the leaders of the ethnic minority heterosexual communities. It is important that the organizers identify the following from the various groups: the leaders in the ethnic minority churches, both lay and clergy; the leaders of the ethnic minority PTA groups; the political leaders; the ethnic minority members of the school board; the ethnic minority student leaders from the heterosexual community; and the queer ethnic minority student leaders.

Additionally, because machismo tends to be more highly held in the ethnic minority communities, perhaps involvement of athletes who can be seen as leaders and role models who can legitimize the discussion of queerness within ethnic minority schools. Once these group leaders have been identified, they must be trained and sensitized to the issues of queer youth, so that, in turn, they can join the struggle of institutionalizing the programs.

A while back, I was invited by the Cristina Show, the Hispanic Oprah Winfrey, to be the professional guest on a show on gay and lesbian adolescents coming out to their parents. This show is seen by millions of Spanish-speaking television viewers around the world. It was my opportunity to educate millions of Hispanic viewers around sexual orientation. The studio audience was filled with teenagers from various schools who had been bused to be in the audience. When we left the television studio, the audience was waiting for us outside. We were not pelted with stones or insults. Instead we were treated as one would treat a movie star leaving the entertainment venue. We knew that we had done our job of educating these students.

Another powerful community strategy occurred in the recent Miss America Pageant for 2003. Teresa Benitez, Miss Nevada, offered a declamation as her talent portion of the competition. Her declamation consisted of the words of Matthew Shepard's mother during the sentencing phase of Matthew's assailants. It was such an impactful contribution toward the education of millions of television viewers about people who are "different," which was the context of Ms. Benitez's declamation. The Miss America Pageant is a conservative organization, and there were many messages and references to Christianity and "My Savior Jesus Christ" among the contestants. Ms. Benitez's message rang loud and clear within these messages. Ms. Benitez came in as third runner-up in the Miss America competition. She intends to become a U.S. Senator some day. As a Hispanic gay person, I was moved by Ms. Benitez's courage. This is the type of community education that needs to happen.

SUMMARY

According to Uribe and Harbeck (1992),

> Cultural taboos, fear of controversy, and deeply rooted, pervasive homophobia have kept the educational system in the United States blind-folded and mute on the subject of childhood and adolescent homosexuality. The paucity of literature and understanding in this area is a national disgrace. Young men and women struggling with their sexual orientation during a time of intense physical, social, and developmental change are failed by physicians, educators, mental health professionals, and clergy who breach their ethical and professional obligations by being uninformed and unresponsive to the special problems and need of these youth. (p. 11)

In this chapter, I have defined the problem as the public's lack of scientific knowledge regarding sexual differentiation and the heterosexist assumptions that do not embrace the pluralistic society that forms the fiber of American culture. I have explored the many stressors that queer youth face, such as invisibility, isolation, victimization, suicide potential, substance abuse, and exposure to sexually transmitted diseases because of high-risk behaviors. These unique stressors call for affirmative counseling interventions by culturally sensitive and queer-affirming counselors.

The point was made that while queer youth need to address these stressors, counselors need to shift the focus of treatment to the true client, the community at large, to transform the cultural context in which queer youth live. To create this transformation, an ecological approach needs to be undertaken that would include individual, group, associational, and institutional strategies to effect the societal changes.

We experienced slices of the lives of Juan and Paul with differing outcomes. Both had an affirming counselor who was able to move these individuals toward acceptance of their sexual identity; however, queer youth do not live in a vacuum. They need the love and support of significant others, especially family. Ironically, Paul's family was the more "religious" of the two families. However, being religious does not necessarily translate to the values that many religions profess—love of one's neighbor as one loves oneself. The case of Juan shows how a loving family can go a long way toward a person's self-acceptance and successful resolution of identity crisis. The case of Paul was tragic and could have been averted by the loving guidance of parents who could accept their son as nature made him.

How many more Matthew Shepards must die before society replaces hatred toward queers with understanding and acceptance? Uribe and Harbeck (1992, p. 27) said it best, "The pain and hardship suffered by adolescent, gay, lesbian, and bisexual [and transgendered] youth is no longer invisible, and our lack of action is no longer professionally or ethically acceptable."

REFERENCES

Atkinson, D., Morten, G., & Sue, D. (1979). *Counseling American minorities*. Dubuque, IA: Brown.

Banning, J. (1980). The campus ecology manager role. In U. Delworth & G. Hanson (Eds.), *Student services: A handbook for the profession* (pp. 209–227). San Francisco: Jossey-Bass.

Borhek, M. (1983). *Coming out to parents: A two-way survival guide for lesbians and gay men and their parents*. New York: Praeger.

Boxer, A., Cook, J., & Herdt, G. (1995). Double jeopardy: Identity transitions and parent child relations among gay and lesbian youth. In A. D'Augelli & C. Patterson (Eds.), *Lesbian, gay and bisexual identities over the lifespan*. New York: Oxford University Press.

Bracciale, M., Sanabria, S., & Updyke, J. (2003). *Assisting parents of gay and lesbian youth*. Workshop presented at the annual convention of the American Counseling Association, Anaheim, CA.

Bradford, J., Ryan, C., & Rothblum, E. (1994). National lesbian health care survey: Implications for mental health care. *Journal of Consulting and Clinical Psychology, 62*, 228–242.

Brown v. Board of Educ. 347 U.S. 483 (1954).

Carroll, L., Gilroy, P., & Ryan, J. (2002). Counseling transgendered, transexual, and gender-variant clients. *Journal of Counseling & Development, 80*, 131–139.

Cass, V. (1979). Homosexuality identity formation: A theoretical model. *Journal of Homosexuality, 4*, 219–235.

Chan, C. (1992) Cultural considerations in counseling Asian American lesbians and gay men. In S. Dworkin & F. Gutiérrez (Eds.), *Counseling gay men and lesbians: Journey to the end of the rainbow* (pp. 115–124). Alexandria, VA: American Counseling Association.

Coleman, E. (Ed.). (1988). *Psychotherapy with homosexual men and women*. New York: Haworth.

Coleman, E., & Remafedi, G. (1989). Gay, lesbian, and bisexual adolescents: A critical challenge to counselors. *Journal of Counseling & Development, 68*, 36–40.

D'Augelli, A., Hershberger, S., & Pilkington, N. (1998). Lesbian, gay, and bisexual youth and their families: Disclosure of sexual orientation and its consequences. *American Journal of Orthopsychiatry, 68*, 361–371.

Doll, L., Joy, D., Bartholow, B., Harrison, J., Bolan, G., Douglas, J., et al. (1992). Self-reported childhood and adolescent sexual abuse among adult homosexual and bisexual men. *Child Abuse and Neglect, 16*, 855–864.

Dworkin, S., & Gutiérrez, F. (1989). Counselors be aware: Clients come in every size, shape, color, and sexual orientation. *Journal of Counseling & Development, 68*, 6–15.

Dworkin, S., & Gutiérrez, F. (1992). *Epilogue: Where do we go from here?* In S. Dworkin & F. Gutiérrez (Eds.), *Counseling gay men and lesbians: Journey to the end of the rainbow* (pp. 335–339). Alexandria, VA: American Counseling Association.

Erikson, E. (1968). *Identity youth and crisis*. New York: Norton.

Gutiérrez, F. (1985). Bicultural personality development: A process model. In E. Garcia & R. Padilla (Eds.), *Advances in bilingual education research* (pp. 96–124). Tucson: University of Arizona Press.

Gutiérrez, F. (1987). *Managing the campus ecology of gay/lesbian students on Catholic college campuses.* (ERIC Document Reproduction Service No. ED324612).

Gutiérrez, F. (1994). Gay and lesbian: An ethnic identity deserving equal protection. *Law and Sexuality: A Review of Lesbian and Gay Legal Issues, 4,* 195–247.

Gutiérrez, F., & Dworkin, S. (1992). Gay, lesbian, and African American: Managing the integration of identities. In S. Dworkin & F. Gutiérrez (Eds.), *Counseling gay men and lesbians: Journey to the end of the rainbow* (pp. 141–156). Alexandria, VA: American Counseling Association.

Hally, J. E. (1993). *The construction of heterosexuality, fear of a queer planet: Queer politics and social theory.* Minneapolis: University of Minnesota Press.

Herdt, G. (1989). Gay and lesbian youth: Emergent identities and cultural scenes at home and abroad. *Journal of Homosexuality, 17,* 1–42.

Herr, K. (1997). Learning lessons from school: Homophobia, heterosexism and the construction of failure. *Journal of Gay and Lesbian Social Services, 7*(4), 51–64.

Hershberger, S., & D'Augelli, A. (1995). The impact of victimization on the mental health and suicidality of lesbian, gay, and bisexual youths. *Developmental Psychology, 31,* 65–74.

Hershberger, S., & D'Augelli, A. (2000). Issues in counseling lesbian, gay, and bisexual adolescents. In R. M. Perez, K. De Bord, & K. Bieschke (Eds.), *Handbook of counseling and psychotherapy with lesbian, gay, and bisexual clients* (pp. 225–248). Washington, DC: American Psychological Association.

Individuals With Disabilities Education Act Amendments of 1997, 20 U.S.C. § 1400 *et seq.* (Lexis 1998).

Kubler-Ross, E. (1969). *On death and dying.* New York: MacMillan.

Levine, E., & Padilla, A. (1980). *Crossing cultures in therapy: Pluralistic counseling for the Hispanic.* Monterey, CA: Brooks/Cole.

Lips, H. (1978). Sexual differentiation and gender identity. In H. Lips & N. Colwill (Eds.), *The psychology of sex differences* (pp. 52–79). Englewood Cliffs, NJ: Prentice-Hall.

Loiacano, D. (1989). Gay identity issues among Black Americans: Racism, homophobia, and the need for validation. *Journal of Counseling & Development, 68,* 21–25.

Martin, A., & Hetrick, E. (1988). The stigmatization of the gay and lesbian adolescent. *Journal of Homosexuality, 15,* 163–183.

McClintock, M., & Herdt, G. (1996). Rethinking puberty: The development of sexual attraction. *Current Directions in Psychological Science, 5,* 178–183.

Money, J. (1987). Sin, sickness, or status? Homosexual gender identity and psychoneuroendocrinology. *American Psychologist, 42,* 384–399.

Morales, E. (1992). Counseling Latino gays and Latina lesbians. In S. Dworkin & F. Gutiérrez (Eds.), *Counseling gay men and lesbians: Journey to the end of the rainbow* (pp. 125–139). Alexandria, VA: American Counseling Association.

National Center for Health Statistics. (1986). *Vital statistics of the United States: Vol. 2. Mortality, Part A.* Hyattsville, MD: Author.

Norris, W. (1992). Liberal attitudes and homophobic acts: The paradoxes of homosexual experience in a liberal institution. In K. Harbeck (Ed.), *Coming out of the classroom closet* (pp. 81–120). New York: Harrington Park Press.

O'Connor, M. (1992). Psychotherapy with gay and lesbian adolescents. In S. Dworkin & F. Gutiérrez (Eds.), *Counseling gay men and lesbians: Journey to the end of the rainbow* (pp. 3–21). Alexandria, VA: American Counseling Association.

Parham, T. (1989). Cycles of psychological nigrescence. *The Counseling Psychologist, 17,* 187–226.

Plummer, K. (1989). Lesbian and gay youth in England. *Journal of Homosexuality, 17,* 195–223.

Remafedi, G. (1987). Adolescent homosexuality: Medical and psychological implications. *Pediatrics, 79,* 331–337.

Robinson, B., Walters, L., & Skeen, P. (1989). Response of parents to learning that their child is homosexual and concern over AIDS: A national study. *Journal of Homosexuality, 18,* 59–80.

Savin-Williams, R. (1994). Verbal and physical abuse as stressors in the lives of lesbian, gay male, and bisexual youths: Associations with school problems, running away, substance abuse, prostitution, and suicide. *Journal of Consulting and Clinical Psychology, 62,* 261–269.

Skinner v. Oklahoma, 316 U.S. 535 (1942).

Strommen, E. (1989). You're a what?: Family member reaction to the disclosure of homosexuality. *Journal of Homosexuality, 18*, 37–57.

Troiden, R. (1989). The formation of homosexual identities. *Journal of Homosexuality, 17*(1/2), 43–73.

Uribe, V., & Harbeck, K. (1992). Addressing the needs of lesbian, gay, and bisexual youth: The origins of Project 10 and school-based intervention. In K. Harbeck (Ed.), *Coming out of the classroom closet: Gay and lesbian students, teachers, and curricula* (pp. 9–28). New York: Harrington Park Press.

Weinberg, G. (1972). *Society and the healthy homosexual.* New York: St. Martin's Press.

14 | Death in the Classroom: Violence in Schools

Abbé Finn

In the years from 1983 to 1993, there was an alarming increase in life-threatening youth violence (Cook & Laub, 1998). This violence crossed all socio-economic boundaries, and the consequences were felt throughout the United States (Center for the Prevention of Handgun Violence, 1990). There has been a sudden increase in school violence (Furlong & Morrison, 2001), and national policy has been revised to address the causes of the problem. Many intervention programs have been implemented, and some have been shown to be effective and others have not (U.S. Department of Health and Human Services [USDHHS], 2001a). Many have been implemented without scientific investigation or any demonstration of efficacy (Elliott, 1998; Skiba & Knesting, 2002), and some have been shown to be harmful (Mendel, 2000).

Issues contributing to the problem of youth violence are multidimensional and caused by many factors working together (USDHHS, 2001a). Some of these factors are explored in this chapter. *Violence* is defined as any action or threat of action that would result in intimidation, coercion, physical harm, or personal injury. The topic is examined from the perspective of the various types of prevention and intervention programs with special attention paid to describe programs that have been evaluated and have demonstrated effectiveness.

The alarming rate of violence has raised national awareness and concern, resulting in great public demand for the development and implementation of prevention and intervention programs to eliminate the bloodshed. Remedies include increased school security, zero tolerance, psychosocial profiling, school climate reform, social skills training, and peer mediation programs. To be effective, the prevention and intervention programs should be based on the theoretical causes of youth violence.

PROBLEM DEFINITION

The decade from 1983 to 1993 marked a period of time described as a "violence epidemic" (Cook & Laub, 1998). No social class, neighborhood, or community in the United States was immune from the widespread consequences. Lasting physical and emotional scars were left on individuals, families, schools, and communities. Many children were killed or maimed during this time period (USDHHS, 2001a). Twenty-five percent of inner-city youth have been victims of or witnesses to extreme forms of violence. Community hostilities and violence often bleed into the school environment (Mulvey & Cauffman, 2001). This is why many prevention and intervention programs coordinate their efforts across the school and community domains.

During this same period, the rate of violent crime committed by youth rose by 1,000%. It has been estimated that violence costs the United States $508 billion a year: $90 billion is spent on the criminal justice system, $65 billion on security, $5 billion on the treatment of victims, $170 billion on lost productivity, with $178 billion in expenses to the victims (Illinois Center for Violence Prevention, 1998). It is estimated that persons under the age of 20 committed one third of the murders in the United States. Among African American adolescent males, murder was the second leading cause of death (Center for the Prevention of Handgun Violence, 1990; James & Gilliland, 2000). Between 1985 and 1994, the rate of incarceration and arrest increased by 67% for young males and by 125% for young females (Dahlberg, 1998). Suicide, another extreme form of violence, was the third leading cause of death (Flannery, Singer, & Wester, 2001). Adolescent suicide and murder are highly correlated. Vossekuil, Reddy, Fein, Borum, and Modzeleski (2000) studied the student assailants in 37 school shootings and found that approximately 75% of the perpetrators had threatened or attempted suicide prior to committing the school shootings.

Schools, usually perceived as safe havens from violence, became part of the battleground. During the 1986–1987 academic year the school crime report from the School Safety Council (1989) indicated that 3 million faculty, staff, students, and visitors were victims of crime while at school in the United States. From 1986 to 1990, 71 people were killed at schools in the United States. Of these, 65 were students and 6 were school employees. An additional 242 were held hostage at gunpoint and 201 were seriously wounded (Center for the Prevention of Handgun Violence, 1990). For every hour school was in session in the United States, 900 teachers were threatened, and approximately 40 teachers and more than 2,000 students were physically assaulted (Futrell, 1996; Shafii & Shafii, 2001). In a 1996 survey, 47% of teens responded that they thought violence was increasing in schools, with 10% reporting that they feared a classmate would shoot them. From February 1997 to April 1999, there were eight incidents of mass school shootings with at least 32 deaths (Chandras, 1999; Gibbs & Roche, 1999; King & Murr, 1998).

Most of the violence occurring in schools was not as extreme as school shootings. The majority of school violence occurs in undersupervised areas (Astor, Mayer, & Behre, 1999). Fearing victimization, 20% of the surveyed students reported that they were too intimidated to use the school restrooms and avoided particular hallways, locker rooms, and stairwells (Children's Institute International, 1996; Elliott, Hamburg, & Williams, 1998).

Fortunately, there has been a slight but steady decline in violent crime among adolescents since this violence epidemic. However, the Report of the Surgeon General cautions against complaisance. Although the rate of arrests of youthful offenders has declined, confidential self-reports indicate that the rate of potentially lethal acts of violence has remained unchanged. Despite the decline in violence, the rates of arrests are still 70% higher than they were before 1983 (USDHHS, 2001b), and the number of mass murders or suicide paired with homicide at schools has increased, averaging five per year from 1994 to 1999 (USDHHS, 2001a). According to the National Center for Educational Statistics and the Bureau of Justice Statistics, students reporting that they were victims of crime at school decreased from 10% to 8% between 1995 and 1999 (Kaufman et al., 2001). In addition, fewer students are carrying weapons to school. Kann et al. (2000) reported that approximately 7% of high school students carried a weapon to school in 1999 compared with 12% in 1993 (Kann et al., 1995). Although this is an improvement, it continues to cause concern for schools and communities because these statistics mean that in a school of 2,000 students, 140 students (on one or more occasions) carried weapons to school in a year. Therefore, on any given day there could be several students at school carrying weapons (Hermann & Finn, 2002).

Students, educational professionals, parents, and community leaders are very concerned with school safety and greatly distressed with the outbreak of youth violence. Most prevention programs follow the public health prevention model of primary, secondary, or tertiary prevention. Primary prevention programs identify characteristics that increase the risk of the public health problem and intervene with large heterogeneous groups through education or behavioral change. For example, with underage alcohol abuse, teens are encouraged through public service announcements not to drink and drive. Secondary prevention programs identify individuals or groups of people at risk for the specific problem and target them for intervention. As an example of secondary prevention, drug-using teens are targeted to receive counseling. Tertiary prevention programs attempt to limit the reoccurrence of a problem or further deterioration of people exhibiting symptoms of a public health problem (Lawler, 2000). Some call these postvention programs. In our example, community drug rehabilitation clinics are opened to treat drug-abusing teens and to provide counseling.

CASE STUDY

The day began at Thurston High in a deceptively normal way. Some students were arriving in a rush fearing they would be late, others were early and eating their breakfast while finishing their homework. No one had a premonition about the disaster that was about to strike. At about 7:50 a.m. on May 21, 1998, 15-year-old Kip Kinkle arrived at school armed with a .22-caliber semiautomatic rifle concealed in the folds of his trench coat and two pistols and a hunting knife tucked into the waistband of his pants. On his way down the hall, he encountered a student who had teased him for public display of affection at school. Without breaking stride, Kip shot him in the head. Seconds later Kip passed another student, one he didn't even know, and shot him in the face. Moments before the first period bell rang, Kip strode into the cafeteria filled with approximately 400 students. Striding from the doorway he opened fire, emptying the rifle's 50-round clip. He shot into the crowd but sometimes aimed at specific students firing point blank. When the chamber was empty, four boys tackled Kip in an attempt to halt the carnage. One of these boys had been shot in the chest and had a collapsed lung. Kip continued to struggle and was able to reach one of the handguns and shot several of the children who were restraining him. While on the ground, Kip begged the other students to shoot him. Later the students, who had moments before been his targeted victims, said that shooting Kip had never crossed their minds even though they were holding Kip's guns. By the end of the day, Kip had killed four people and injured 20.

After his arrest, Kip was handcuffed and placed in an interrogation room. While in the cell, he wriggled out of the handcuffs, removed a knife he had taped to his leg, and attacked a police officer. The officer escaped injury by subduing him with pepper spray. During the attack, Kip begged the officer to shoot him.

The killing spree had actually begun the afternoon before, when Kip killed his father and then his mother. Earlier that day, Kip had been arrested for buying a stolen gun and was suspended from school for storing it in his locker. He was detained by police and released to his father's custody. In the aftermath of these horrible events, people wondered how this could happen in a sleepy, all-American small town like Springfield, Oregon. However, on closer examination, Kip gave many signals that he was in serious trouble.

Physically, Kip was small, standing 5 feet 5 inches, weighing 125 pounds, with red hair and freckles. He was emotionally immature, socially isolated, targeted for teasing by the bigger boys, and scholastically challenged. Both of his parents were very respected educators, and his older sister was an excellent student. In contrast, Kip struggled in school. Even though his parents were loving and caring, there was not a good fit between Kip and his family. They were intellectual and athletic, whereas he was a poor student who was awkward and clumsy. Kip was diagnosed with learning disabilities and was also suffering from depression. For a short time, he was treated by a psychologist and had been prescribed antidepressants, which he stopped taking. Adding to his depression, Kip had recently endured the breakup of a romantic relationship. After the shootings, Kip disclosed that he was hearing voices. Unfortunately, he failed to report to his psychologist that he was having auditory hallucinations. He had developed a fascination with the suicide pact in *Romeo and Juliet*. When the police arrived at his home to investigate his confessed murder of his parents, the soundtrack was blasting from Kip's stereo.

After the fact, students came forward with other information foreshadowing Kip's future violence. For example, Kip had reportedly bragged about skinning a live cat, and he also bragged about making bombs. He made bombs and exploded them in an abandoned stone quarry. After the killings, police discovered 20 live bombs set to go off. Some were large enough to cause collateral damage to the neighborhood, resulting in the evacuation of 15 nearby houses. Kip nurtured a deep fascination with weapons and explosives. He persuaded his parents to buy him several guns. Over the years, he acquired an arsenal, which he kept hidden in the attic over his bedroom. On May 20th, Kip's father brought him home from jail and told him that he was confiscating all of his guns. Kip later reported to the police that he felt compelled to kill his father rather than surrender his weapons. When interviewed by the police, Kip repeated over and over again that he believed that he had no other choice but to kill his parents (Dowling & Johnson, 1998; Kesey, 1998; Sullivan, 1998).

APPROACHES TO PREVENTION

Effective violence prevention programs share several common characteristics. Nine elements have been identified as necessary in order for the program to work:

- specific norms
- skills training
- comprehensive multimodal approaches
- coordination among programs within and outside of the school
- changes to the physical plant
- at least 10 to 20 sessions
- training for the entire school staff, parents, and community
- multiple teaching methods
- a sensitivity to the school and community culture (Lawler, 2000).

These nine elements can best be illustrated using a school-based example.

The first necessary component of an effective prevention or intervention program is a specific, clear, and consistent school policy. Schools should promote peaceful resolution to problems and discourage violence. The teachers, counselors, coaches, administrators, parents, and community members should be in agreement on the value of peaceful resolution to problems. The second necessary component for the program are skills training for students, faculty, and parents. The skills training curriculum should include anger management, conflict resolution, taking the social perspective of others, problem solving, peer negotiations, and active listening skills. Part of the peer negotiations training includes ways to resist peer pressure and techniques for making new friends. The third characteristic of successful programs is that they are comprehensive, integrated, and multimodal in nature. They involve the community leaders, law enforcement, school personnel, and members of the press. A consistent message of peaceful resolution and antiviolence is encouraged and is infused into all forms of communication. The fourth element is the coordination of all of the prevention programs. For example, the drug abuse prevention program is coordinated with the violence prevention program that is in concordance with the suicide prevention program and the teen pregnancy program. All share common elements of decision-making skills, peer refusal skills, social competency, and self-esteem. These skills are infused into the curriculum for subjects such as social sciences, health, physical science, and English composition. When learning is reinforced across the curriculum, more of the information is retained and it is more likely to become part of the students' daily lives.

The fifth element concerns the physical design and administrative policies of the school. In effect, an assessment is made regarding security risks that are present in the school and these are remedied. For example, fences might be built surrounding the school to control the access to school grounds, and outdoor lighting might be installed to improve the security for people attending school functions after dark. Administrative policy decisions are made to reduce congestion and increase adult supervision. Another example of administrative policy is the decision to require school uniforms to reduce the showing of gang colors, thereby reducing the influence of gangs at school.

The sixth characteristic of programs that work is the amount of exposure that students have to the training program. Students need to have between 10 and 20 sessions the first year followed by repeated exposures (5 to 10 sessions) in the following years. Schools that have a high rate of new admissions to the school should include all new students in the prevention program in their first year. The seventh characteristic involves training for the teachers, students, parents, and community. The program should begin with teacher and administrative in-service training before school starts in the early fall to set the stage for the entire year. Key student leaders should be identified and trained in the summer, with the rest of the student population exposed to the program as soon as school begins. The program should be integrated into the curriculum across all grades. The normative education should begin in kindergarten and continue throughout the entire school career.

The eighth characteristic of an effective program concerns multimodal approaches to learning. The students are exposed to the curriculum through a variety of teaching approaches, including role-plays, literature, quizzes, discussions, group projects, and current events. The ninth element necessary for an effective program is related to the cultural sensitivity of the program and intervention procedures to the needs of the community. All methods and principles of the program must be consistent with the ethnic and cultural makeup of the school and community (Lawler, 2000), including input of community and school members during the design phase of the program.

Many of the effective youth violence prevention programs are shown to be cost beneficial. They can save taxpayers from the expenses of the criminal justice system, medical care of crime victims, social service costs for children supported while the parents are incarcerated, and increased work productivity of people who would otherwise spend their lives in jail (USDHHS, 2001b). The youth violence prevention programs that targeted specific populations of youthful offenders were most cost-effective. These are secondary prevention programs because they target the people most likely to offend again and come under the supervision of the legal system (Washington State Institute for Public Policy, 1999). Some of the prevention programs reduce violence through indirect means by preventing some of the conditions, such as child abuse, known to give rise to violence later on. The prevention programs can be organized by the emphasis on the individual, family, school, and community levels.

Individual

Psychosocial profiling is the most controversial individual youth violence prevention strategy. This is because although most young violent perpetrators fit some of the profile, many more will fit the profile but never become violent (Mulvey & Cauffman, 2001). Relying on the psychosocial profiles alone would result in many young people being falsely labeled as violent who would never commit a violent act (Vossekuil, Reddy, & Fein, 2001). Even the report by the Federal Bureau of Investigation recommending the use of "threat assessment teams" through psychosocial profiles states that there are no reliable profiles or distinguishing characteristics that reliably discriminate between people who commit violence and those who do not (O'Toole & The Critical Incident Response Group, 2000; USDHHS, 2001a). Consequently, in the worst case scenario, overreliance on a checklist of characteristics can overlook some violent youth if the checklist is not accurate or can falsely identify as dangerous some youth who are not, if the checklist is too sensitive (Baily, 2001; Finn & Remley, 2002).

On the side of the debate favoring profiling, violent youth and school shooters share some of the same characteristics. To overlook psychosocial profiling as one of many tools to prevent violence may increase risk of harm by ignoring what is known about violent students. Many educators fear that ignoring warning signs outlined by the psychosocial profile increases the school's liability (Lumsden, 2000). Theoretically, the greater the number of severe characteristics the youth presents, the higher the likelihood for violence (Finn & Remley, 2002; USDHHS, 2001b). The best use of psychosocial profiling is in the identification of students in need of counseling or some other form of supportive intervention (Baily, 2001; Finn & Remley, 2002; Hermann & Finn, 2002). It is hoped that if students get the appropriate intervention in a timely fashion, violence can be averted. Dwyer, Osher, and Warger (1998) identified early warning signs.

The following characteristics describe the perpetrators of the multiple school shootings. Almost all of the shooters were European American males. The students who perpetrated the most severe acts of violence at schools planned them in advance. They planned the attacks for at least 2 weeks. They had multiple reasons for their attacks and believed that they were justified in their actions. Seventy-five percent of the attackers held grievances against students, teachers, or administrators. They could not keep their violent plans to themselves and told others. Among the school shooters, 75% told friends or classmates. One school-shooting perpetrator told a total of 24 acquaintances (Vossekuil et al., 2001). Certainly, the majority of people making threats never carry them out; however, most people who harm others have made threatening remarks. Some make clearly threatening statements listing time, place, targeted victims, and choice of weapons. For example, the shooters at Columbine High School presented a video in their media arts class describing their plan of attack. They also threatened and indeed shot another student they had specifically named on their

Internet Web site (Gibbs & Roche, 1999). Sometimes the students make obscure statements. On the other hand, youth may make obscure threats through poetry, artwork, or journal writing (Dwyer et al., 1998).

Students who commit the most violent crimes show a fascination with weapons and ultraviolent films, video games, and music (Dwyer et al., 1998). Sometimes they mimic the dress, posture, and behavior of main characters from films. The school shooters at Moses Lake, Oregon, and Littleton, Colorado, wore trench coats, modeling their clothing after antagonists in their favorite movies.

Violent youth are socially withdrawn or belong to a socially rejected, antisocial group (Borduin & Schaeffer, 1998; Kashani, Jones, Bumby, & Thomas, 1999; USDHHS, 2001a). Many also show symptoms of severe psychiatric disorders (Dwyer et al., 1998), with some hearing voices commanding them to commit the violent crimes. For example, the school shooters from Pearl, Mississippi, and Springfield, Oregon, had hallucinations. Both began their killing spree by shooting their parent(s). Many violent young people did not receive the appropriate level of psychiatric treatment or stopped taking their medication on purpose to increase their level of violence (James & Gilliland, 2001). Many engaged in angry outbursts at school and other public places or assaulted others with little provocation (Vossekuil et al., 2001), with the level of violence escalating rapidly.

Revenge was a common motive for the school shootings (Vossekuil et al., 2001). The perpetrators express a belief that their actions are justified because of previous histories of having been bullied by other students (Ross, 2003) or having had a failed romance. The shooters in Jonesboro, Arkansas; Pearl, Mississippi; and Springfield, Oregon, specifically targeted the girls they believed had wronged them.

There are several ways to classify the factors associated with youth violence. The Surgeon General Report categorized the youth violence risk factors according to the size of the effect on the statistical outcome. Their research showed that a history of criminal offenses, substance abuse, weak social connections, antisocial delinquent peers, and belonging to a gang had the largest statistical impact on the outcome (USDHHS, 2001a). The factors associated with youth violence were further subcategorized by domain. Late-onset individual characteristics include all of the above plus risk-taking behaviors, commission of crimes, and violent acts toward others. However, the report also identified protective factors. These include tolerance toward social differences, having a high IQ, having prosocial values, and believing that there are negative consequences for antisocial actions (USDHHS, 2001a).

Early-onset violence risk factors in the family domain include living in poverty, having parents who demonstrate antisocial behaviors, having a poor parent–child relationship, growing up with poor parental supervision and discipline, living in a single-parent home, and having abusive or neglectful parents. Late onset factors include having low parental involvement and family conflict. Protective factors in the family domain include having warm, supportive, and involved parents who like their child's friends (USDHHS, 2001a).

Early-onset factors in the school domain include having poor school performance and having a poor attitude toward school and learning. In addition to the previous factors, late-onset factors contributing to violence include grade failure and retention. Factors that protect children from violence in the school domain include the student's involvement in school activities, having a commitment to school, and getting recognition at school for success.

Factors in the peer group domain, correlated with an early onset of violence, are having a weak connection with friends and having friends who behave in an antisocial manner. Late-onset factors also include gang membership. The mitigating factor in the peer group domain is having friends with conventional values. In the community domain, only late-onset factors were identified. These included living in drug-infested, high-crime neighborhoods that are poorly organized and fail to meet the needs of the community (USDHHS, 2001a). Characteristics in the individual domain with early onset that increase the likelihood of violence include legal offenses, substance use, being of male gender, acting out aggressively, hyperactivity, having a psychological disorder, exposure to violence in the media, an expression of antisocial behavior (individual, family, school, peer group, or community), and age of onset (USDHHS, 2001a).

Family

Lasting changes with children can be made only if changes are also made in the family system. The earlier interventions are made, the better the outcome is for the child. Early intervention can improve prenatal care, reduce maternal drug use, and protect the developing fetus from the many negative consequences of these behaviors. One of the programs demonstrated to be effective is the Home Visitation by Nurses Program. It begins before the child is born and continues through the child's 2nd birthday. The purpose of this program is to improve the health outcomes by supporting and guiding young, often single, women through the prenatal and postnatal period to the toddler years. In this program, the same nurse visits the young woman and her family twice monthly during the pregnancy and weekly following childbirth. The nurse gets to know the family and is able to train the mother in parenting skills. By taking this program to the mother's home, the nurse circumvents the problems young mothers encounter due to lack of transportation and other difficulties keeping appointments. Depending on the needs of the family, the nurse may visit once monthly after the child is 6 weeks old. The nurse advises the mother and monitors her health during the pregnancy and the child's health and development following delivery. The visits usually last between 1 and 1.5 hours. With low-income women, the program has demonstrated effectiveness through a 15-year follow-up. The women's behavior was healthier during pregnancy because of the intervention. This was especially true for the cessation of smoking and drinking while pregnant. There were fewer complications such as hypertension and kidney infections. There were significantly fewer cases of child abuse, neglect, and injuries to the children. The women participants also took more responsibility for their lives, including planning future pregnancies, reduction in welfare dependence, and reduction in substance abuse and illegal behavior. In a 16-year follow-up, the children whose mothers participated in this program had significantly fewer arrests, convictions, and alcohol consumption. This program has been shown to be cost beneficial at a rate of at least four to one. The cost of the program is recovered by the time the child reaches age 4. The future benefits extend to other children born to these mothers in later years (Lawler, 2000; Olds, Hill, Mihalic, & O'Brien, 1998; USDHHS, 2001a).

School

The earliest attempts to prevent school violence focused on improving school security. These security precautions included mandated use of school uniforms, controlled access to schools, increased presence of uniformed security guards or police, the removal of hall lockers, and the installation of metal detectors. Some students and parents have questioned the right of administrators to search students and their belongings, but courts have consistently found that schools have this right in order to keep schools safe. They are granted this prerogative through the concept that teachers and administrator act in the role of the students' parents (in loco parentis). School personnel have an obligation to protect the children from others and themselves. The duty to protect students takes precedence over the students' right to privacy (Yell & Rozalski, 2000).

Many school districts have spent a great deal of their resources on the installation of metal detectors to halt the influx of weapons onto school campuses. For example, in 1 year, New York City spent over $28 million for this purpose (Kemper, 1993). At least 25% of the largest urban school districts use metal detectors (National School Safety Center, 1990). The cost of security and detection devices goes way beyond the initial investment in equipment. There is a continuous need for training, manpower, and maintenance of the detection devices. Trump (1997) warned that the school must react at a level consistent with the security threat in that school and community. He also stated that the security force must be trained in working with adolescents, de-escalation, and conflict resolution. If not, a poorly trained security force can decrease rather than increase safety.

With so many resources devoted to security, it is important to ask whether these measures are effective in reducing violence at schools. The Centers for Disease Control and Prevention (1991) found that these devices were effective in reducing the number of students carrying weapons at school but had no effect on the number of students carrying weapons outside of school. Because the majority of the most serious acts of violence and injuries occur off of school property, these measures do not have an appreciable impact on the overall safety of children. Mercy and Rosenberg (1998) concluded that they could not find any studies investigating if these measures decrease the incidence of gun violence at schools. However, it is reasonable to conclude that fewer weapons at school equal safer schools. Some communities have adopted community-policing policies to increase the safety of students walking to school. "Safe School Routes" are designated and community volunteers are on duty observing the children as they pass twice daily. This program has been shown to increase the children's perception of safety with a minimal cost to the community (Mercy & Rosenberg, 1998).

The Bullying Prevention Program specifically addresses the most common form of violence occurring in schools (Batsche & Knoff, 1994). Bullying can include coercive verbal comments, physical intimidation, or a combination of the two. It is sometimes more similar to chronic, systematic terrorism carried out by one or more people targeting a specific person (Furlong, Sharma, & Rhee, 2000). As a result, the child becomes a social outcast with a drastic reduction of self-esteem.

Victims of bullying tend to share certain physical characteristics, such as being overweight, being small in stature, being underweight, or projecting general weakness. Victims of bullying share certain personality characteristics, such as shyness, passivity, or effeminacy (for males) (Furlong et al., 2000; Olweus, 1997; Olweus, Limber, Mihalic, 1999). Universally, the bully has much more power than the victim. Olweus (1997) described two types of victims: passive or provocative. The passive types of victims are more anxious, insecure, introverted, shy, and quiet; demonstrate low self-esteem; and feel lonely and abandoned at school. Provocative victims show many characteristics of hyperactive attention deficit disorder. In contrast to the passive victims, the provocative victims aggravate and annoy their attackers, leading to the harassment. This in no way justifies the bullying that later takes place.

There are gender differences between the ways boys and girls bully. When boys bully they tend to use physical intimidation, abuse, and humiliating pranks. The pattern of behavior for girls is not so obvious but just as emotionally damaging. Girls tend to tease and exclude girls who are targeted for bullying. In the United States, 23% of middle school children reported that they had been the targets of bullies on several occasions in the past 3 months (Olweus et al., 1999). The negative consequences of bullying are not limited to childhood. Many adults report lasting effects from their childhood bullying (Olweus, 1994). The bully also suffers negative consequences. Bullies, especially males, are more likely to break rules, act in other antisocial ways, use and abuse drugs, and commit crimes. Permitting bullies to act out also has a negative impact on the general classroom and school climate. Tolerance of bullying behavior creates a more hostile atmosphere (Olweus et al., 1999). In order for bullies to operate, there must be support by other classmates with tacit approval by teachers and administrators.

The Bullying Prevention Program confronts these behaviors by addressing the issues at the school, classroom, and individual levels. Intervention at the school level begins with an anonymous survey of the students regarding the nature, severity, and prevalence of bullying at the school. The school then holds a daylong meeting to discuss the results and plan the schoolwide intervention. The schoolwide plan targets areas on the school grounds requiring higher supervision. At the classroom level, rules are established that discourage bullying and intimidation. Classroom meetings are held with open discussions defining bullying behavior and describing the negative outcomes from bullying. Students are given an opportunity to discuss alternatives to bullying behavior. At the individual intervention level, children identified as bullies are given individual and group counseling to learn other more appropriate behavior. Children identified as victims are also given an opportunity for counseling. All of the parents of children receiving counseling are invited to participate in family counseling at the school. The counselors also act as consultants to the teachers who have students identified as bullies or victims of the bullies. The outcomes of the program showed a large and statistically significant reduction in the number of students reporting victimization by bullies. Other antisocial behaviors such as vandalism, violence, theft, and truancy were also significantly reduced. Students and teachers reported a significant improvement in school climate. There were significantly fewer discipline problems, improved attitude toward scholastic activities, and an improvement in the social relationships among students (Lawler, 2000; Olweus et al., 1999; USDHHS, 2001a). Other violence prevention programs target the members of the community.

Community

The Midwestern Prevention Project (MPP) is a primary prevention program and is an example of a broad-based community intervention program. It incorporates the mass media, educational systems, families, community, health care providers, and peer groups. The goal is to interrupt the pattern of addiction starting with tobacco use and progressing to alcohol use and abuse of other illegal substances. This prevention approach is multimodal, targeting students, parents, and community leaders in various domains. The drug abuse prevention message is transmitted in print and electronic media at least 31 times per year. The mass media campaign ranges from 15-second public service announcements to hour-long talk shows and continues for 5 years. Educational programs are offered to parents throughout the life of the program.

The program relies on support from the community to maintain the goal of drug use abstinence by youth. Communities support the ideals by refusing to sell drugs and alcohol to minors and offering activities that compete with the drug culture. The community also takes a lead in supporting community mental health centers for the treatment of drug abuse to decrease the demand for drugs. Law enforcement contributes to the program by controlling the supply side of the problem, diligently prosecuting merchants selling alcohol to underage children and drug dealers. Judges can mandate offenders to diversionary programs in which they get treatment, maintain abstinence, or go to jail.

When Willie Sutton, a famous gangster, was asked why he robbed banks he answered, "because that's where the money is." Schools are the appropriate location for drug prevention programs because that's where the children are. The school portion of the MPP begins in the sixth or seventh grade. Teachers, counselors, and peer mediators are trained and take leadership roles in the program. The students participate in 10 to 13 class sessions in the first year with at least 5 booster sessions the following year. The sessions focus on peer pressure, drug refusal, and decision-making skills. At school the message is supported by taking every opportunity across the curriculum to educate students about the risks of drug abuse.

Families support the program by modeling responsible behavior and refusing to serve alcohol to minors on any occasion. Parents also learn to recognize the early warning signs of drug use among their children and ways to confront their children when they begin experimentation. The parents refuse to tolerate any substance use. They are encouraged to model responsible alcohol use. To learn these skills, parents participate in parenting classes twice a year focusing on discipline and communication skills.

The MPP was an effective prevention program for children and also had an impact on the behavior of the parents. It resulted in a 40% drop in daily cigarette smoking among the student participants and a similar reduction in parental drug use. This resulted in more positive parent–child communications and relations. The program also resulted in a reduction in the demand for drug treatment because fewer people in the community initiated drug use to begin with (Lawler, 2000; Pentz, Mihalic, & Grotpeter, 1998; USDHHS, 2001a). The MPP had an impact on individuals and the entire community.

INTERVENTION PROGRAMS

Intervention programs are synonymous with secondary prevention programs from the public health model previously discussed in this chapter. They are intended to interrupt behaviors that have already begun. They usually target particular groups of people who are either exhibiting the behavior or at risk for this dangerous behavior. There is a price paid by individuals participating in intervention rather than prevention programs because they are already in trouble. Some damage may already have been done. However, because intervention programs target specific individuals, families, students in school, and community members, they are more cost-effective. Only the people in need of care participate in the program.

Individual

Some programs focus on the school environment, others on family functioning, and others on internal and interpersonal processes. The Promoting Alternative Thinking

Strategies (PATHS) program is an example of the last. This program is designed for implementation in schools for children in kindergarten to fifth grade. The goal of the program is to reduce violence and high-risk behaviors while increasing prosocial behaviors and improving peer relationships. The curriculum contains developmentally appropriate activities promoting emotional competency and increasing understanding of self and others.

The teacher gets support from the project staff and coordinator in teaching the PATHS curriculum in general and special education classrooms. It is integrated into the daily assignments. The materials, consisting of an instructor's manual and six volumes of lessons in three major units, are shared with the parents in parent meetings. The first unit teaches self-control covered in 12 lessons. The second unit focuses on feelings and interpersonal relationships taught in 56 lessons. The third unit concentrates on teaching the 11 steps to problem solving in 33 lessons. A supplementary unit reviews the principles of the program in 30 additional lessons. There are five themes in the PATHS program: self-control, emotional understanding, positive self-esteem, interpersonal relationships, and problem-solving skills. One hundred thirty-one lessons are introduced over 5 years. Each lesson can last for up to five class meetings. The curriculum is based on a multimodal approach using direct instruction, pictures, role-plays, supplemental reading, and classroom discussions. Parents are notified about their child's progress through the mail. Homework assignments are designed to keep the parents involved with the curriculum and program goals. As a result of the program, participants significantly increased their ability to recognize and understand emotions and were better able to solve social problems and develop solutions. They also decreased aggressive or violent behavior. Teachers reported increased frustration tolerance and successful conflict resolution. In a 1-year follow-up study, the teachers reported that participants showed decreased sadness, increased self-esteem, decreased angry outbursts, decreased violence, and fewer conduct problems. The average cost of implementation of the program over a 3-year period was $15 to $45 per year per student (Greenberg, Kusche, & Mihalic, 1998; Lawler, 2000; USDHHS, 2001a).

Family

The Functional Family Therapy (FFT) program targets young people who have demonstrated delinquent, substance-abusing, or violent behavior. Other participants have been diagnosed with oppositional defiant disorder, conduct disorder, or other disruptive behaviors. The program aspires to change the participants' behavior by increasing protective factors and reducing risk factors. One or two therapists (counselors, nurses, social workers, or physicians) are assigned to the youth and their families. They deliver counseling and other services to the children and their families in their homes, schools, and clinics. There are five phases to the program: engagement, motivation, assessment, behavior change, and generalization. In the engagement phase, the therapists establish a relationship with the youth and their families and are on the lookout for signs of premature termination. During the motivation phase, the therapists design interventions targeting maladaptive behaviors, emotions, and beliefs. They work to build a strong therapeutic alliance, trust, hope, and the change agenda. In the assessment phase, the mental health professionals observe the family interactions and analyze the strengths and weaknesses in the family system. During the behavior change phase, the therapists focus on communication training, basic parenting skills, contracting for behavior change, and recognition of behavior costs and consequences. The final phase is the generalization phase, in which newly acquired skills are implemented into other domains of their lives. The therapeutic team individualizes the program to meet the needs of each family and maintains the goal to make long-term positive gains.

The FFT program has been shown to make positive changes with children diagnosed with conduct, oppositional defiant, disruptive, and other behavior disorders. There was a significant reduction of substance abuse and violent delinquent behavior by the termination of the program. The participants were much less likely to commit crimes and need further contact with social service organizations. Younger children in the family also benefited from the counseling services, with significant reduction of delinquent and substance abuse behaviors. The program costs approximately $1,350 to $3,750 for an average of 12 home visits. The costs are quickly offset when compared with the expense once a person enters the criminal justice system and with the loss of future income. The FFT model has been used for over 28 years with thousands of families (Alexander et al., 1998; Lawler, 2000; USDHHS, 2001a).

School

The theoretical basis for school violence prevention programs assumes that violence occurs in a cultural context. Therefore, to decrease violence in schools, there must be changes in the school environment. It is presumed that there are characteristics of the culture that promote the use of violence to meet the wants and needs of students. These can include an attitude that is permissive and encouraging of the use of force to achieve goals. Just think for a moment of the cheers heard at football games. Words such as *fight*, *beat*, and *hit* predominate. This attitude does not exist only at schools. Many children are instructed by their parents to hit back if someone hits them first. Because of the rise in concern over school violence, schools have adopted a zero tolerance for violence. The driving force of zero tolerance is the belief that school violence occurs because the schools and communities have ignored warning signs that violence is imminent. There is a great deal of evidence demonstrating that this is the case. For example, the student perpetrators gave many clues regarding their intention to cause grievous harm but the signs were overlooked in Columbine, Colorado; Pearl, Mississippi; Paducah, Kentucky; and Springfield, Oregon.

Zero tolerance is a concept that became popular during "the war on drugs." This get-tough policy implies that strict rules will be applied without any excuses for major as well as minor infractions. Overapplication of the policy with resulting negative consequences to individuals is considered an acceptable price to pay for safety (Skiba & Knesting, 2002). Under this policy students are suspended or expelled for any weapons violation, threat to others, or use or sale of drugs at school. The Gun-Free Schools Act of 1994 made zero tolerance national policy. It has been applied in districts to include any object that may be used as a weapon. Students and their parents are informed of the consequences of violating school policy. Many parents believe that this policy is carried to an extreme. For example, as a result of this policy, a 5-year-old child was expelled for wearing a toy ax as part of a fireman's costume at a Halloween party at school (Skiba & Knesting, 2002).

States have also enacted laws making it a crime to bring weapons to school, resulting in suspension, expulsion, and arrest of offending students. Following the carnage of the 1980s and 1990s, this policy makes sense. Schools are caught in the dilemma of preventing violence through hypervigilance or repeating mistakes of the past by ignoring student threats. The courts have consistently upheld administrators' decisions to expel and discipline students bringing weapons to school, dealing or using drugs, or threatening other people (Skiba & Knesting, 2002; Yell & Rozalski, 2000). The controversy arises when administrators expel and suspend students for trivial offenses. An important research question is: Does zero tolerance reduce the risk of violence? Skiba and Knesting (2002) concluded that it does not. They believe that it might exacerbate student misbehavior and reduce student morale. This is supported by evidence in the case of Kip Kinkle, the school shooter near Springfield, Oregon. The day before he killed his parents and shot 24 people at school, Kip Kinkle was suspended and arrested for bringing a gun to school.

In many schools, the administrators ignore a certain amount of bullying and teasing because they perceive it as normal and harmless. In reality, experiencing bullying can have lasting negative effects on children. The person who was bullied may in turn become a bully, or it may have a lasting impact on his or her self-confidence and self-esteem (Ross, 2003). The Secret Service National Threat Assessment Center identified a past history of having been the victim of bullying, persecution, threats, and injury from peers with school shooting perpetrators. They associated a past history of bullying with 66% of the school shooting incidents (Vossekuil et al., 2001). In addition, schools that promote antisocial behavior over prosocial behavior increase the risk of violence and other antisocial activities. In contrast, rewarding and recognizing prosocial actions increases the occurrence of these behaviors and decreases antisocial activities (Mattaini & Lowery, 2000). Behaviorists have long been encouraging parents and teachers to catch children in the act of doing something right. However, children are often admonished, corrected, and punished as the main means of behavior control. Consequently, children can recite a litany of things that they are not supposed to do but are challenged to come up with things that they are *encouraged* to do. By changing the focus from punishment to praise, the focus changes from the negative to the positive. Mayer, Butterworth, Nafpaktitis, and Sulzer-Azaroff (1983) recommended written praise over spoken praise. They suggested that written notes praising students and parents are far more effective than spoken recognition. They used praise boards to recognize students' accomplishments on a daily or weekly basis. They found that merchants were willing to contribute to the program by issuing gift certificates as rewards for the students' accomplishments. This further builds a bridge from the school to the community. Community involvement has consistently been associated with effective school violence prevention and intervention programs (Lawler, 2000).

The Quantum Opportunities Program (QOP) is another example of a school-based violence intervention program. QOP addresses the problem of violence intervention by increasing economic and educational opportunities for participants. QOP targets specific groups of students. The goal of the QOP is to provide educational, social, and vocational opportunities to disadvantaged youth from the 9th through the 12th grades. QOP provides an opportunity for 750 hours of education (computer instruction, tutoring for basic academic skills), service (community service, volunteering with agencies), and personal development activities (exposure to cultural activities, training in life skills, college planning, job preparation, and assistance with applications for scholarships). Approximately 20 students met in each group with one adult throughout the year; the adult functioned as a mentor, teacher, counselor, disciplinarian, and problem solver. Financial incentives were offered to the children for participating in the program. There were substantial benefits for the participants. For example, they were more likely than the control group to graduate from high school (63% vs. 42%), more likely to attend college (42% vs. 16%), less likely to have children while they were teenagers (24% vs. 38%), and somewhat less likely to have been arrested (19% vs. 23%). The program costs $10,600 per participant over the 4 years and is considered cost beneficial because of reduced expenses for the criminal justice system and because of increased lifetime earnings by the participants, who increased earning power as a result of their increased rate of high school graduation and secondary education (Lattimore, Mihalic, Grotpeter, & Taggart, 1998; Lawler, 2000; USDHHS, 2001a).

Community

The Multisystemic Therapy (MST) program is a community intervention program that has demonstrated effectiveness. It focuses on families, schools, and the community targeting violent, substance-abusing juvenile offenders from the ages of 12 to 17. The causes of the problems are viewed as stemming from the family, school, and individual factors; therefore, the interventions encompass all of these domains. The strengths that naturally occur within these areas are assessed and supported to encourage positive change. The MST program addresses the issues faced by families raising adolescents and empowers the participating youth to deal with problems in the schools, families, and community. The purpose is to improve parental disciplinary practices, improve family communication and family relationships, and decrease the power of deviant peer relationships while improving the participants' social skills and social relationships. Another goal is to improve the participants' school and vocational performance. The program mobilizes the support networks within the extended family, neighbors, and friends to back up the goals of the family. The MST program is another home-based program. The therapists focus on skill building for parenting, family therapy, and cognitive–behavioral approaches. Special attention is paid to the social networks that contribute to delinquency and drug abuse. The therapists work to remove the barriers to support services. Each family receives in-home support every week. The program usually includes 60 hours of therapeutic contact over 4 months. The length of involvement is determined by the needs of the family and client.

The MST program has been shown to be effective with serious juvenile offenders with whom many other interventions have failed. The program has shown long-term results, including 25% to 70% reduction in rearrest, improvement in family functioning, and decreased problems associated with mental health disorders. The average cost of the intervention per participant was $4,500. This program was determined to be the most cost-effective intervention for juvenile offenders (Henggler, Mihalic, Rone, Thomas, & Timmons-Mitchell, 1998).

ADAPTATIONS FOR DIVERSITY

Children living in large, inner-city neighborhoods characterized by high-density, high-poverty homes that are dilapidated and generally in run-down conditions, with ethnically heterogeneous populations are more likely to live surrounded by crime (Smith & Jarjoura, 1988). This describes most children attending large, inner-city schools. Interestingly, ethnic heterogeneity is believed to cause an increase in crime because residents of diverse backgrounds are less likely to get to know each other and, therefore, are less likely to watch out for each other and their property (Taylor & Gottfredson, 1986). Children living in high-crime neighborhoods are at increased risk for victimization and for observation of crimes. Over 60% of inner-city youth have directly witnessed a shooting, and 50% have observed stabbings with 60% of these resulting in deaths (Jenkins & Bell, 1994). The violent criminal activity in childhood is increased when children grow up in communities in which the gangsters are the only ones with money and crime seems to pay. Children attending schools where they represent the ethnic minority are at much greater risk for violent victimization (U.S. Department of Justice, 1991). Therefore, school leaders should be sensitive to the need to protect children from each other. Administrators and teachers should be knowledgeable about diverse cultures and be sensitive to the needs of these children and their families. Schools must represent a safe haven for children from violence. Teachers and administrators must welcome students representing diverse backgrounds into the schools.

Each of the prevention and intervention programs described in this chapter was developed with the diverse ethnic, socioeconomic, and cultural makeup of the participants in mind. They were designed to include the input from the students, their families, faculty, administrators, and community members. Many began with a needs assessment. This is an important element because school violence has occurred at schools representing every type of community. Contrary to public expectations, the worst mass shootings have occurred at schools where there seemed to be few individual, family, or community indications of violence. Columbine, Pearl, Jonesboro, and Thurston are suburban, affluent schools. The perpetrators were apparently affluent, White, male students. Because school violence perpetrators defy stereotypes, each violence prevention or intervention program must be designed with the diverse population of the school and community in mind.

SUMMARY

In the years from 1983 until 1993, America was rocked by youth violence. The murder and suicide rates increased dramatically. In the years that followed, the unthinkable happened: Young men terrorized and murdered their classmates and teachers at school. Some of them began their killing sprees by murdering their parents. This explosion of violence caused students to fear for their lives while at school. These concerns have brought about many changes in the ways that schools operate.

Several programs have been initiated to prevent violence in the communities, homes, and schools. Schools have taken new security measures in an effort to help students feel safe. Administrators have also initiated zero-tolerance policies to discourage students from making threats in and outside of school and have a plan to intervene when they do.

Experts on violence prevention have studied young violent offenders and have compiled lists of characteristics shared by the most violent. Unfortunately, overreliance on these lists can result in false positives. Many prevention and intervention programs have been designed to address maladaptive behaviors. These programs address school climate, community environment, family issues, interpersonal relationships, and career and educational opportunities. All of the reviewed prevention/intervention programs demonstrated their effectiveness and were cost beneficial.

Youth violence is a complicated problem. Although there are no easy solutions to youth violence, there are prevention and intervention programs that work. Effective programs are comprehensive, coordinating school, family, community, and individual services. The programs are designed to last for an extended period of time. The implementation of these programs requires commitment from the youth, families, schools, and communities.

To help students with their myriad problems, schools should have full-service counseling centers. Here, students in need of intervention can be assessed, treated, and, when necessary, referred to other mental health professionals for the appropriate level of care. Parents and teachers should see themselves as partners, with similar goals to help every child achieve his or her full potential. Americans should never again mourn the loss of children to school violence.

REFERENCES

Alexander, J., Barton, C., Gordon, D., Grotpeter, J., Hansson, K., Harrison, R., et al. (1998). *Blueprints for violence prevention: Book 3. Functional family therapy.* Boulder, CO: Center for the Study and Prevention of Violence.

Astor, R., Mayer, H., & Behre, W. (1999). Unowned places and times: Maps and interviews about violence in high schools. *American Educational Research Journal, 36,* 3–42.

Baily, K. (2001). Legal implications of profiling students for violence. *Psychology in the Schools, 38,* 141–155.

Batsche, G. M., & Knoff, H. M. (1994). Bullies and their victims: Understanding a pervasive problem in the schools. *School Psychology Review, 23,* 165–174.

Borduin, C. M., & Schaeffer, C. M. (1998). Violent offending in adolescence: Epidemiology, correlates, outcomes, and treatment. In T. P. Guillotta, G. R. Adams, & R. Montemayor (Eds.), *Delinquent violent youth: Theory and interventions* (pp. 144–174). Newbury Park, CA: Sage.

Centers for Disease Control and Prevention. (1991). *Attempted suicide among high school students—United States 1990.* Atlanta, GA: U.S. Department of Health and Human Services, Public Health Service.

Center for the Prevention of Handgun Violence. (1990). *Caught in the crossfire: A report on gun violence in our nations schools.* Washington, DC: Author.

Chandras, K. (1999). Coping with adolescent school violence: Implications for counselors. *College Student Journal, 33,* 302–311.

Children's Institute International. (1996). *Armed and ready for school.* Los Angeles: Pacific Visions International.

Cook, P., & Laub, J. H. (1998). The unprecedented epidemic in youth violence. In M. Yonry & M. H. Moore (Eds.), *Youth violence, crime and justice: A review of research* (Vol. 24, pp. 27–64). Chicago: University of Chicago Press.

Dahlberg, L. L. (1998). Youth violence in the United States: Major trends, risk factors, and prevention approaches. *American Journal of Preventive Medicine, 14,* 259–272.

Dowling, C., & Johnson, L. (1998, July). High school heroes. *Life, 21*(8), 52–62.

Dwyer, K., Osher, D., & Warger, C. (1998). *Early warning, timely response: A guide to safe schools.* Washington, DC: U.S. Department of Education.

Elliott, D. S. (1998). Editor's introduction. In D. S. Elliott (Ed.), *Blueprints for violence prevention: Book 8. Multisensorial treatment foster care.* Boulder, CO: Center for the Study and Prevention of Violence.

Elliott, D., Hamburg, B., & Williams, K. (1998). *Violence in American schools.* Cambridge, England: Cambridge University Press.

Finn, A., & Remley, T. P. (2002). Prevention of school violence: A school and community response. In D. Rea & J. Bergin (Eds.), *Safeguarding our youth: Successful school and community programs* (pp. 19–27). New York: McGraw-Hill.

Flannery, D., Singer, M., & Wester, K. (2001). Violence exposure, psychological trauma, and suicide risk in a community sample of dangerously violent adolescents. *Journal of the American Academy of Child and Adolescent Psychiatry, 40,* 435–442.

Furlong, M., & Morrison, G. (2001). The school in school violence: Definitions and facts. In H. Walker & M. Epstein (Eds.), *Making schools safer and violence free: Critical issues, solutions, and recommended practices* (pp. 5–16). Austin, TX: PRO-ED.

Furlong, M., Sharma, B., & Rhee, S. (2000). Defining school violence victim subtypes: A step toward adapting prevention and intervention programs to match student needs. In D. Sandhu & C. Aspy (Eds.), *Violence in American schools: A practical guide for counselors* (pp. 67–87). Alexandria, VA: American Counseling Association.

Futrell, M. (1996). Violence in the classroom: A teacher's perspective. In A. Hoffman (Ed.), *Schools, violence, and society* (pp. 3–19). Westport, CT: Praeger.

Gibbs, N., & Roche, T. (1999, December 20). The Columbine tapes. *Time*, 40–60.

Greenberg, M. T., Kusche, C., & Mihalic, S. F. (1998). *Blueprints for violence prevention: Book 10. Promoting alternative thinking strategies (PATHS)*. Boulder, CO: Center for the Study and Prevention of Violence.

Henggler, S. W., Mihalic, S. F., Rone, L., Thomas, C., & Timmons-Mitchell, J. (1998). *Blueprints for violence prevention: Book 6. Multisystemic therapy*. Boulder, CO: Center for the Study and Prevention of Violence.

Hermann, M., & Finn, A. (2002). An ethical and legal perspective on the role of school counselors in preventing violence in schools. *Professional School Counseling, 6*, 46–54.

Illinois Center for Violence Prevention. (1998). *Fact sheets: Cost of violence*. Chicago: Author.

James, R., & Gilliland, B. (2000). Crisis in schools. *Crisis intervention strategies* (4th ed.). Belmont, CA: Brooks/Cole.

Jenkins, E. J., & Bell, C. C. (1994). Violence among inner city high school students and post-traumatic stress disorder. In S. Freidman (Ed.), *Anxiety disorders in African Americans* (pp. 76–78). New York: Springer.

Kann, L., Kinchen, S. A., Williams, B. I., Ross, J. G., Lowry, R., Grunbaum, J. A., et al. (2000). Youth risk behavior surveillance—United States, 1999. *Morbidity and Mortality Weekly Report CDC Surveillance Summary, 49*, 1–96.

Kann, L., Warren, C. W., Harris, W. A., Collins, J. L., Douglas, K. A., Collins, M. E., et al. (1995). Youth risk behavior surveillance—United States, 1993. *Morbidity and Mortality Weekly Report CDC Surveillance Summary, 44*, 1–56.

Kashani, J., Jones, M., Bumby, K., & Thomas, L. (1999). Youth violence: Psychosocial risk factors, treatment, prevention, and recommendations. *Journal of Emotional and Behavioral Disorders, 7*, 200–211.

Kaufman, P., Chen, X., Choy, S. P., Peter, K., Ruddy, S. A., Miller, A. K., et al. (2001). *Indicators of school crime and safety: 2001* (NCES 2002-113/NCJ-190075). Washington, DC: U.S. Departments of Education and Justice.

Kemper, P. (1993, Fall). Disarming youth. *California School Boards Journal*, 25–33.

Kesey, K. (1998, July 9). Land of the free, home of the bullets. *Rolling Stone*, 51–55.

King, P., & Murr, A. (1998, June 1). A son who spun out of control. *Newsweek*, 32–33.

Lattimore, C. B., Mihalic, S. F., Grotpeter, J. K., & Taggart, R. (1998). *Blueprints for violence prevention: Book 4. The Quantum Opportunities Program*. Boulder, CO: Center for the Study and Prevention of Violence.

Lawler, M. (2000). School-based violence prevention programs: What works? In D. Sandhu & C. Aspy (Eds.), *Violence in American schools: A practical guide for counselors* (pp. 247–266). Alexandria, VA: American Counseling Association.

Lumsden, L. (2000, September). Profiling students for violence. *ERIC Digest 139*. (ERIC Document Reproduction Service No. ED 446 344)

Mattaini, M., & Lowery, C. (2000). Constructing cultures of peace and nonviolence: The PEACE POWER! Toolkit. In D. Sandhu & C. Aspy (Eds.), *Violence in American schools: A practical guide for counselors* (pp. 123–138). Alexandria, VA: American Counseling Association.

Mayer, G. R., Butterworth, T., Nafpaktitis, M., & Sulzer-Azaroff, B. (1983). Preventing school vandalism and improving school discipline. A three year study. *Journal of Applied Behavior Analysis, 16*, 135–146.

Mendel, R. A. (2000). *Less hype, more help: Reducing juvenile crime. What works—and what doesn't*. Washington, DC: American Youth Policy Forum.

Mercy, J., & Rosenberg, M. (1998). Preventing firearm violence in and around schools. In D. Elliott, B. Hamburg, & K. Williams (Eds.), *Violence in American schools* (pp. 159–187). Cambridge, England: Cambridge University Press.

Mulvey, E., & Cauffman, E. (2001). The inherent limits of predicting school violence. *American Psychologist, 56,* 797–802.

National School Safety Center. (1990). *Weapons in schools* (NSSC Resource Paper). Malibu, CA: Author.

Olds, D., Hill, P., Mihalic, S., & O'Brien, R. (1998). *Blueprints for violence prevention: Book 7. Prenatal and home visitation by nurses.* Boulder, CO: Center for the Study and Prevention of Violence.

Olweus, D. (1994). Bullying at school: Long term outcomes for the victims and an effective school based intervention program. In H. Rowell (Ed.), *Aggressive behavior: Current behavior* (pp. 97–130). New York: Plenum Press.

Olweus, D. (1997). Tackling peer victimization. In D. P. Fry & K. Bjoerkqvist (Eds.), *Cultural variation in conflict resolution: Alternatives to violence* (pp. 215–231). Mahwah, NJ: Erlbaum.

Olweus, D., Limber, S., & Mihalic, S.F. (1999). *Blueprints for violence prevention: Book 9. Bullying prevention program.* Boulder, CO: Center for the Study and Prevention of Violence.

O'Toole, M. E., & The Critical Incident Response Group. (2000). *The school shooter: A threat assessment prospective.* Quantico, VA: Federal Bureau of Investigation. Retrieved from www.fbi.gov/library/school2.pdf

Pentz, M. A., Mihalic, S. F., & Grotpeter, J. K. (1998). *Blueprints for violence prevention: Book 1: The Midwestern Prevention Project.* Boulder, CO: Center for the Study and Prevention of Violence.

Ross, D. (2003). *Childhood bullying, teasing, and violence: What school personnel, other professionals, and parents can do* (2nd ed.). Alexandria, VA: American Counseling Association.

School Safety Council. (1989). *Weapons in schools.* Washington, DC: U.S. Department of Justice.

Shafii, M., & Shafii, S. L. (2001). *School violence: Assessment, management, and prevention.* Washington, DC: American Psychiatric Association.

Skiba, R., & Knesting, K. (2002). Zero tolerance, zero evidence: An analysis of school disciplinary practice. In R. Skiba & G. Noam (Eds.), *Zero tolerance: Can suspension and expulsion keep schools safe?* New York: Jossey-Bass.

Smith, D., & Jarjoura, G. R. (1988). Social structure and criminal victimization. *Journal of Research in Crime and Delinquency, 25,* 27–52.

Sullivan, R. (1998, October 1). A boy's life. *Rolling Stone,* 46–54.

Taylor, R., & Gottfredson, J. (1986). Environmental design, crime, and prevention: An examination of community dynamics. In A. J. Reiss Jr. & M. Tony (Eds.), *Communities and crime* (pp. 244–262). Chicago: University of Chicago Press.

Trump, K. (1997). Security policy, personnel, and operations. In A. Goldstein & J. Close (Eds.), *School violence intervention: A practical handbook* (pp. 265–289). New York: Guilford Press.

U.S. Department of Health and Human Services. (2001a). *Youth violence: A report of the Surgeon General.* Rockville, MD: U.S. Department of Health and Human Services, Centers for Disease Control and Prevention, National Center for Injury Prevention and Control; Substance Abuse and Mental Health Services Administration, Center for Mental Health Services; and National Institutes of Health, National Institute of Mental Health.

U.S. Department of Health and Human Services. (2001b). Youth violence: A report of the Surgeon General: Executive summary. *American Journal of Health Education, 32,* 169–174.

U.S. Department of Justice, Bureau of Justice Statistics. (1991). *School crime: A national victimization survey report.* Washington, DC: U.S. Government Printing Office.

Vossekuil, B., Reddy, M., & Fein, R. (2001). The Secret Service safe school initiative. *Education Digest, 66*(6), 4–11.

Vossekuil, B., Reddy, M., Fein, R., Borum, R., & Modzeleski, W. (2000). *U.S.S.S. safe school initiative: An interim report on the prevention of targeted violence in schools.* Washington, DC: U.S. Secret Service, National Threat Assessment Center.

Washington State Institute for Public Policy. (1999). *The comparative costs and benefits of programs to reduce crime.* Olympia, WA: Author.

Yell, M., & Rozalski, M. (2000). Searching for safe schools: Legal issues in the prevention of school violence. *Journal of Emotional and Behavioral Disorders, 8,* 187–197.

15 | "I Can't Live Without It": Adolescent Substance Abuse

Camea J. Gagliardi, Alberta M. Gloria,
Sharon E. Robinson Kurpius, and
Christina Lambert

Although there is not a standard reason for adolescents using substances, the most common reasons are for excitement or thrill-seeking, consolation or escape, fitting in, and rebellion. Yet, adolescent drug use is associated with a variety of negative consequences, including increased risk of serious drug use later in life, school failure, poor judgment (which puts adolescents at increased risk for accidents), violence, unsafe sex, pregnancy, and suicide. Tobacco use, hazardous alcohol use, and most categories of illicit drug use have shown consistent increases in prevalence throughout much of the 1990s in most developed countries, suggesting that the substance use problem among adolescents remains unsolved. Interventions are not uniformly effective, although those focusing on the adolescents' social environment hold the most promise (Bauman & Phongsavan, 1999).

Current evidence suggests that self-report measures of substance use by adolescents from the general population are typically reliable and stable, with lifetime use being highest among alcohol users and lowest for cigarette and marijuana users (Shillington & Clapp, 2000). Since 1975, the National Institute on Drug Abuse (NIDA, 2002) has supported the Monitoring the Future (MTF) national survey. This national, school-based survey provides data on drug use among 8th, 10th, and 12th graders, as well as three attitudinal indicators related to drug use: perceived risk of harm, disapproval of others who take drugs, and perceived availability. NIDA reported the following trends: High rates of drug use continued at all grade levels, but illicit drug use among 8th, 10th, and 12th graders remained stable or decreased in some cases across a 4-year period. Since the 1999 MTF survey, small reductions in cigarette smoking occurred at all three grades, although marijuana use remained stable. The increases seen during the mid-1990s have leveled off or decreased, and among 8th graders use has decreased significantly. Past year marijuana use among 8th graders decreased from 18.3% in 1996 to 15.6% in 2000. The few significant increases from 1999 to 2000 were in the use of ecstasy at all three grade levels, anabolic-androgenic steroids among 10th graders, and heroin use among 12th graders, yet the recent increase in ecstasy use slowed down in 2001. The perceived availability of ecstasy increased among 12th graders, from 40.1% in 1999 to 51.4% in 2000.

Adolescent substance abuse often results in harm to youth, their families, communities, and society as a whole. According to recent U.S. Department of Health and Human Services (USDHHS, 2002) statistics, drug and alcohol abuse contributes to the death of more than 120,000 Americans and costs taxpayers more than $143 billion every year in preventable health care costs, lost productivity, automobile crashes, law enforcement, and crime. More specifically, alcohol use is associated with over half of all murders and rapes in the United States and is a factor in 40% of all violent crimes as about 20,000 crimes involve alcohol or other drugs (Inaba & Cohen, 2000). Most recently, President George W. Bush allocated $4.4 billion to provide treatment and services for substance abuse for the 2003 fiscal year (USDHHS, 2002). Although the yearly estimated costs of health care, lost productivity, and legal and social support systems are extreme, monetary amounts do not describe the emotional, social, and psychological costs to families and communities (Funkhouser & Denniston, 1992).

PROBLEM DEFINITION

In addressing the issue of adolescent substance use prevention and intervention, several questions are raised. First, what drugs are currently being used and abused? Second, what are the characteristics of adolescents who are most at risk for substance abuse? Third, what psychosociocultural factors influence adolescent substance use and abuse? Fourth, what types of prevention and intervention strategies can be implemented for adolescents and their families? Although relatively simple questions, they are not as easily answered.

To understand substance use and abuse issues, the first step is to contextualize the discussion of these concerns. As such, a historical and legal perspective of drug use is provided, followed by a description of physiological mechanisms of drug use. Second, a summary of drugs commonly used by adolescents and a discussion of psychosociocultural influences of drug use are presented. Finally, prevention and intervention strategies for educators, counselors, parents, and families are highlighted within the systemic contexts of schools, families, and communities.

ASSUMPTIONS ABOUT DRUGS AND DRUG USE AND ABUSE

In discussing drug use, several assumptions need to be made explicit. Specifically, drugs are not inherently good or bad. Instead, the attributes of who is taking drugs, for what purposes, when and where drugs are taken, and how much and how frequently drugs are taken are the factors that influence value judgments regarding certain chemical substances (Robinson, 1989). For example, if an adult were to have a glass of wine or beer after work, it would most likely be viewed differently from an adolescent who had a glass of wine or beer after school. Although the former scenario might be considered as relatively benign, the latter might be viewed as bad and the adolescent as at risk for substance abuse.

Another common assumption is that drug use is the same as drug abuse. Despite a plethora of literature differentiating "use" and "abuse" (Bukstein, 1995), such a distinction may be disputable given that *any* use by adolescents is considered illegal given age restrictions on tobacco and alcohol use. As such, it may be considered as a form of abuse. It is the premise of this chapter that historical and legal events, physiological perspectives, psychosocial factors, and cultural and contextual differences are helpful to understanding adolescent drug use and abuse.

CHRONOLOGY OF HISTORICAL AND LEGAL EVENTS

The United States has an extensive history of establishing laws in an attempt to regulate substances. To understand the historical context of drug use, a chronological timeline is presented.

1791	Whiskey first taxed.
1842	Opium taxed.
1914	An estimated 1 in every 400 Americans addicted to opium or its derivative.
1919–1929	Physicians and druggists arrested for prescribing drugs to addicts. Illegal drug trade flourished as they protected themselves by refusing to treat addicts.
1920	Prohibition laws regarding alcohol instituted—many continued to use alcohol illegally.
1932	Marijuana considered the "assassin of youth" by Federal Bureau of Narcotics (Mandel & Feldman, 1986).
1933	Eighteenth Amendment (i.e., Prohibition Amendment) repealed.
1937	Marijuana Tax Act legally controlled marijuana.
1956	Narcotics Drug Control Act mandated tough penalties for heroin-related offenses, including sanctioning the death penalty for anyone caught selling heroin to a minor.
1962	White House Conference on Drugs, convened by President John F. Kennedy, advocated medical treatment for drug abuse.
1964–1970	A time of drug consciousness with prodrug advocacy.
1970	Controlled Substances Act expanded role of community mental health centers and hospitals in drug abuse treatment; established maximum penalties for manufacturing, distributing, and possessing drugs; and supported drug education.
1973	President Richard Nixon proclaimed a War on Drugs, increasing the federal antidrug budget from $40 million in 1969 to $750 million in 1973 (Mandel & Feldman, 1986).
1980s	Decline in the use of marijuana, sedatives, tranquilizers, and hallucinogens. Cocaine and stimulant use steadily increased.
1982	*Hutto v. Davis:* Davis sentenced to 40 years for possession of 9 ounces of marijuana with the intent to sell. The U.S. Supreme Court ruled against Davis's appeal of cruel and unusual punishment (Inciardi, 1986).
1986	Anti-Drug Abuse Act developed to curb drug trafficking. The United States worked with international governments to monitor international borders (Public Law 99-570). Drug-Free Schools and Communities Act passed, providing the Department of Education with $200 million for drug abuse education in the schools (Business Research Publications, 1987).
1988	Anti-Drug Abuse Act appointed drug policy director and established a zero tolerance policy for those who manufacture, import, distribute, or use illicit drugs (Public Law 100-690).
1990s	Youth continued to believe in their invincibility, assuming that they would not become addicted to chemical substances. Drugs of the 1990s included heroin, methamphetamines, marijuana, alcohol, and cigarettes.

1992	Reorganization of the Alcohol, Drug Abuse, and Mental Health Administration into the Substance Abuse and Mental Health Services Administration (SAMHSA).
1995	U.S. Food and Drug Administration declared cigarettes to be "drug delivery devices." Restrictions proposed on marketing and sales to reduce smoking by young people.
2000	Use of "rave" drugs increased.
2001	USA Patriot's Act limited certain jobs to individuals who had never used drugs.

PSYCHOPHYSIOLOGY OF DRUGS

Drug Phases

The psychophysiology of different drugs varies from drug to drug and from individual to individual; however, *all* drugs go through a series of phases:

Phase 1: Absorption of the drug into the body (see Table 15–1).

Phase 2: Transport of the drug. The drug is transported via the bloodstream to the part of the body where it will exert its effect.

Phase 3: Action of the drug. An effect or action of the drug depends on the type, potency, and purity of the drug; the contaminant or ingredient (e.g., baby powder) used to cut the drug; the personality and physiology of the user; and the social environment in which the drug is taken.

Phase 4: Excretion of the drug. When the body metabolizes the drug, its action is stopped and the drug is excreted from the body.

The Nervous System

The nervous system is made up of the central nervous system (CNS) and the peripheral nervous system (PNS; see Figure 15–1). Composed of the brain and the spinal cord, the CNS is responsible for interpreting and acting on body sensations. The PNS

Table 15–1 | Absorption of a Drug Into the Body (Phase 1)

Method of drug ingestion	Entry into the bloodsteam	Examples of drugs
Swallowed or taken orally (the most common method)	Absorbed through the intestinal walls	Alcohol, tranquilizers, and stimulants
Smoked or inhaled	Absorbed through the lungs	Marijuana, nicotine, and inhalants
Snorted	Absorbed through the mucous membranes	Cocaine and crank
Injected into a vein (mainlining) or under the skin (skin-popping)	Shot directly into the blood stream	Heroin

Figure 15–1 | The Nervous System

Somatic nervous system	→	Controls *voluntary* muscular actions	→	Arm or leg movements
Autonomic nervous system	→	Controls *involuntary* body actions	→	Heart rate, digestion, breathing

comprises various nerve processes that connect the CNS with receptors, muscles, and glands. The PNS is often subdivided into the somatic nervous system and the autonomic nervous system.

The somatic nervous system interfaces with the CNS to control voluntary muscular actions such as arm and leg movements. In contrast, the autonomic nervous system controls involuntary body actions such as heart rate, digestion, and breathing. The autonomic nervous system is composed of the sympathetic and parasympathetic nervous systems that stimulate or inhibit an organ's activities.

Drugs influence specific structures of the brain that are responsible for particular thoughts and behaviors (see Figure 15–2). For instance, the cerebral cortex controls reasoning, language, and sensory discrimination, and the basal ganglia maintains good muscle tone. The hypothalamus is involved in eating, drinking, temperature, and sex drive, whereas the limbic system is involved in emotions, physical activity, and memory. Further, the medial forebrain bundle is known as the pleasure center, the brainstem controls respiration and vomiting, and the medulla oblongata is involved in aggression (Carlson, 2001).

Chemical messengers that carry information throughout the nervous system can be classified as either hormones or neurotransmitters. Although drugs can influence the release of hormones by a gland into the blood, their major impact is on neurotransmitters—chemicals released by nerve cells throughout the CNS. Neurotransmitters influence the transmission of nerve impulses from one nerve cell to another. The major neurotransmitters that interact with psychoactive substances are acetylcholine, dopamine, norepinephrine, serotonin, gamma-aminobutryic acid (more commonly referred to as GABA), and endorphins. The influence of different drugs on neurotransmitters varies, and the exact process of influence continues to be explored (Carlson, 2001).

Figure 15–2 | Brain's major structures. The amygdala and hippocampus are located deep within the brain, however, and are shown in the approximate areas in which they are located. From *Mind Over Matter: The Brain's Response to Drugs*, by the National Institute on Drug Abuse (2000a). In the public domain.

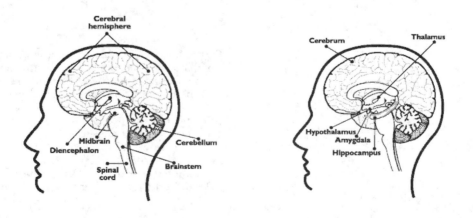

Behaviors are influenced when drugs excite, inhibit, or block the actions of neurotransmitters. For instance, cocaine is believed to block a nerve cell's reuptake of norepinephrine and dopamine in areas such as the medial forebrain bundle, resulting in a feeling of euphoria for an extended time (see Figure 15–3). In contrast, tranquilizers block the reuptake of dopamine in the basal ganglia, resulting in muscle relaxation. Tranquilizer abuse, however, can result in muscle rigidity. Influencing the neurotransmitters in the medulla oblongata, PCP or angel dust can result in violent and bizarre aggressive behaviors.

Although research on the interaction of neurotransmitters, drugs, and behavior is just beginning to uncover these complex relationships, it is clear that psychoactive drugs affect the body's chemical pathways. When drugs are abused, overused, or combined, the effects can be dangerous or even deadly. For example, combining alcohol with sedatives, barbiturates, or tranquilizers may result in respiratory failure. Drugs interfere with the normal functioning of the nervous system and other organs in the body. The decision to use drugs should thus be considered with caution and information. That is, all drug users, in particular adolescents, must be aware that research has not yet fully discovered the many physiological or psychological side effects of drug use.

UNDERSTANDING DRUGS AND THEIR EFFECTS

The best predictor of drug abuse in adolescents is early age of onset of experimental use. In a recent study, adolescents who used substances before sixth grade were found to have poorer decision-making skills, more susceptibility to peer pressure, more negative perceptions of school, and less confidence in their skills than adolescents who did not use by the end of sixth grade (Sobeck, Abbey, Agius, Clinton, & Harrison, 2000).

Adolescents report use of many illicit drugs, including amphetamines (e.g., black beauties and white bennies), methamphetamines (i.e., speed, crank, crystal, ice, fire, and glass), cocaine (i.e., coke, snow, nose candy, flake, blow, big C, lady, white, and snowbirds), heroin (i.e., smack, horse, brown sugar, junk, big H, and dope), phencyclidine (i.e., PCP, ozone, wack, and rocket fuel), lysergic acid diethylamide (LSD), and ecstasy. Reported use of these and other drugs has remained relatively stable with some significant changes. Use of cigarettes by American teenagers has continued to decrease since 1996, paralleling an attitudinal shift against smoking (NIDA, 2000b), and the increase in heroin and ecstasy use seen in recent years has begun to slow

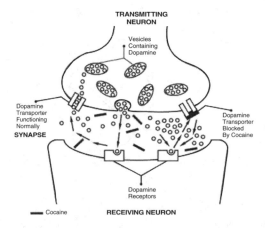

Figure 15–3. | A picture of cocaine in the synapses. The cocaine blocks the dopamine transporter from pumping dopamine back into the transmitting neuron. The synapse is flooded dopamine that intensifies and prolongs the stimulation of receiving neurons in the brain's pleasure circuits, resulting in a cocaine "high." From *Mind Over Matter: The Brain's Response to Drugs*, by the National Institute on Drug Abuse (2000a). In the public domain.

(Johnston, O'Malley, & Bachman, 2002). Although not illegal substances, adolescents can also easily access chemicals such as diet pills, over-the-counter stimulants (e.g., NoDoz), coffee, or buzz beans (i.e., chocolate-covered coffee beans). For purposes of this review, however, only alcohol, nicotine, marijuana, and inhalants are reviewed in depth.

Alcohol

An estimated 24 gallons of beer, 2 gallons of distilled spirits, and over 2 gallons of wine are sold each year for every man, woman, and child in the United States. The most commonly used drugs are beer and wine. The sweet, fruity taste of wine coolers often prevents adolescents from considering that wine coolers have a higher alcoholic content than a can of beer. According to NIDA (2000b), more than 70% of 8th graders perceive alcoholic beverages as "fairly easy" or "very easy" to get. Thirty percent of 12th graders, 26.2% of 10th graders, and 14.1% of 8th graders reported binge drinking (5+ drinks in a row) in the 2 weeks prior to the survey. Lifetime prevalence of alcohol use is 79.7% for high school seniors, 70.1% for 10th graders, and 50.5% for 8th graders (NIDA, 2000b). Research has shown that the earlier adolescents begin to drink, the heavier the alcohol use by their college years (Robinson, Gloria, Roth, & Schuetter, 1993).

Found in all alcoholic beverages, ethanol acts as a depressant on the CNS. When an individual's blood alcohol level (BAL) is .04% (usually after one or two alcoholic beverages), the cerebral cortex becomes less efficient such that the individual will have decreased alertness, relaxed inhibition, impaired judgment, increased heart rate, and a general sense of feeling good (Avis, 1990). As a person's BAL increases, judgment ability declines, reaction time is slowed, and both sensory and motor capabilities are impaired. Most states define drunkenness at a BAL of .10%, intoxication is officially reached at .20% BAL, a stupor is reached at .30% BAL, and .35% BAL is the minimal level that can result in respiratory failure and death. The vomiting reflex (controlled by the brainstem) can be activated at .12% BAL. Alcohol also causes a lower level of blood flow to the brain, decreasing oxygen levels as well as nutrient and waste removal. In addition, alcohol-related changes in cortical functions can also result in behavioral changes. The more rapid the intake of alcohol, the greater the behavioral changes as one becomes less inhibited. Physical damage due to alcohol use is rare in adolescents as they have probably not been abusing for a long enough period of time for damage to occur. Withdrawal symptoms for adolescents who have been heavy alcohol users include tremors, perspiring, agitation, disorientation, and brief seizures. With prolonged abuse, gastritis with hemorrhaging and inflammation of the pancreas can result. Bleeding, severe vomiting, and changes in the blood necessitate hospitalization. Chronic alcoholism in adults can result in chronic liver disease, inflammation of various nerves, and impaired memory (Inaba & Cohen, 2000).

Nicotine

Nicotine, the primary active ingredient in tobacco, is ingested through cigarettes, cigars, pipes, and smokeless tobacco (i.e., chew). The most popular method of ingesting nicotine is by smoking. Adolescent girls are more frequent users of cigarettes, whereas adolescent boys are more likely to use smokeless tobacco.

The pharmacological and behavioral processes that determine physiological tobacco addiction are complex as nicotine acts as both a stimulant and sedative to the CNS. Specifically, nicotine results in a rapid and evenly absorbed distribution or "kick" because of the sudden release of epinephrine. Epinephrine stimulates the CNS to release glucose for energy. After the glucose is used by the body, a period of low energy leads the user to use more nicotine (NIDA, 1998a). When nicotine is absorbed, it is carried on droplets of tar (Inaba & Cohen, 2000). The amount of tar in a cigarette varies from 7 mg for a low-tar cigarette to 15 mg for a regular cigarette. The half-life of nicotine is 2 hours; however, regular smoking results in an accumulation of nicotine in the body. Thus, daily smokers are exposed to the effects of nicotine 24 hours a day (NIDA, 1998a).

Smokers have increased heart rates because the carbon monoxide in cigarette smoke causes them to lose 15% of the oxygen-carrying capacity of their blood. Further, decreased blood flow (and oxygen) to the skin results in smokers appearing older than nonsmokers. Smoking also makes artery walls less flexible, increasing the risk and severity of hardening of the arteries. In addition, smokers have a higher expectancy rate of lung cancer, emphysema, and bronchial disorders (NIDA, 1998a). The negative health effects of second-hand or sidestream smoke are also a concern, particularly for nonsmokers. Research has shown that nonsmoking spouses of smokers have a higher rate of lung cancer than do spouses of nonsmokers. Further, young children and infants exposed to second-hand smoke also have more respiratory and asthma problems (Inaba & Cohen, 2000).

In 2000, NIDA reported that adolescent cigarette use had dropped. Daily smoking in the past month declined from 15.9% in 1999 to 14.0% in 2000 among 10th graders, and from 23.1% to 20.6% among 12th graders. This trend parallels an attitudinal shift. Adolescents' perceived risk of harm from smoking a pack or more of cigarettes per day increased among 8th, 10th, and 12th graders. Despite these trends and warning labels placed on cigarette packages and advertisements regarding the dangers of smoking, the prevalence rate of adolescents who smoke remains high. Adolescents who smoke have higher rates of alcohol use and other drug use, particularly marijuana.

Marijuana

Currently, there are over 200 slang terms for marijuana, a mind-altering or psychoactive weed (i.e., pot, reefer, herb, grass, dope, ganja, mary jane, and hash). Marijuana is generally smoked as a cigarette (i.e., joint or nail) or in a pipe or bong. More recently, blunts or cigars that have been emptied of tobacco and filled with marijuana are used. The most widely used illegal drug in the United States, marijuana is generally the first illegal drug that adolescents use. Consisting of dried, shredded flowers and leaves of the hemp plant, the psychoactive effect of marijuana is achieved from the chemical delta-9-tetrahydrocannabinol (THC). There are various grades or types of marijuana, including sensinilla, containing as much as 8% THC, and hashish, containing up to 50% THC. Marijuana sold on the street is estimated to contain between 2% and 5% THC. Although the general use of marijuana is below that of the late 1970s and early 1980s, adolescent use increased in the early 1990s. This upward trend in use seen during the mid-1990s has leveled off, and use among 8th graders has decreased. In 2000, marijuana use was 32.2% for 10th graders and 15.6% for 8th graders (NIDA, 2000b). Since 1999, marijuana use has remained stable for 8th, 10th, and 12th graders.

When marijuana is smoked, THC is rapidly absorbed into the blood. Although marijuana creates a sedative, dreamy high, it alters the metabolization of serotonin and dopamine. Further, the long half-life of marijuana means that daily smokers may be continually high as it is never out of the body's system. Schonberg and Schnoll (1986) cited considerable research on the negative effects of marijuana on brain, cardiovascular, pulmonary, endocrine, and psychological functioning. For instance, marijuana affects the transfer of information from short- to long-term memory, decreasing an individual's ability to learn (Kingery-McCabe & Campbell, 1991). Heavy marijuana smoking has also been linked to the amotivational syndrome of lethargy and decreased motivation in adolescents. In particular, adolescents who use marijuana before or during the school day impair their desire and ability to learn. According to the National Household Survey on Drug Abuse (Substance Abuse and Mental Health Services Administration, 2002), adolescents with an average grade of D or below were more than four times as likely to have used marijuana in the past year as adolescents who reported an average grade of A. Many of the effects of smoking marijuana are similar to those of drinking alcohol, including lowered secretions of sex hormones; impaired motor coordination, reaction time, and sensory perception; and decreased ability to follow moving objects. With poorer motor coordination and distorted time/distance perceptions, those who drive under the influence of marijuana have the same safety risks as those who drive under the influence of alcohol.

Although current research has not indicated whether or not physiological addiction to marijuana occurs, research on the effects of marijuana is still in its infancy. There is an increasing belief that marijuana smoke affects the lungs in a manner similar to tobacco smoke. Chronic smoking of marijuana impairs airflow in the lungs and is more likely to produce daily coughs, symptoms of bronchitis, and more frequent chest colds (NIDA, 1998c). As users inhale more deeply to hold marijuana smoke in their lungs, the amounts of tar and carbon monoxide are three to five times greater than for tobacco smokers (NIDA, 1998c). Only long-term research will be able to verify the relationship between marijuana smoking and cancer.

Inhalants

Inhalants are ordinary household products that are inhaled or sniffed by children to get high. Inhalants include solvents, gases, and nitrites. Solvents are household substances such as paint thinner, degreasers, gasoline, glue, and office supply substances such as correction fluids or felt-tip markers. Gases include butane lighters, whip cream dispensers (i.e., whippets), spray paint, hair spray, and medical anesthetic gases, such as ether, chloroform, and nitrous oxide. Adolescents between the ages of 11 and 15 are the primary users of inhalants, as inhalants are inexpensive and readily available and are perceived as a substitute for alcohol.

Inhalants contain volatile hydrocarbons that cause a strong, short-lived, euphoric high. Inhaled through the nose or mouth (i.e., huffing), inhalants can cause intoxicating effects that last only a few minutes or several hours if repeatedly ingested (NIDA, 1998b). Symptoms of inhalant use are similar to those of alcohol use, including lack of coordination, restlessness, confusion, disorientation, difficulty walking, and delirium. One-time use of inhalants can cause death by acute intoxication as oxygen is displaced in the lungs, which is a particular concern in light of the fact that one in five eighth-grade students reported using inhalants at least once in their lives (NIDA, 2000b). Further, sudden sniffing death can occur when excessive exercise and stress immediately follow inhalant abuse. Although adolescents may enjoy the giddy high associated with sniffing, chronic use of inhalants can result in hearing loss (from paint sprays and glues), limb spasms (from glues, gasoline, and whipping cream dispensers), brain damage (from paint sprays and glues), and bone marrow damage (from gasoline; NIDA, 2000b).

PSYCHOSOCIAL INFLUENCES OF SUBSTANCE USE

In addition to the physiological influences of drug use, scholars and researchers have identified psychological and sociocultural influences of adolescent substance use and abuse. In synthesizing the literature, we first provide a current model of substance use, followed by a brief review of contextual and cultural concerns that relate to adolescent substance use. The significance of cultural contexts in understanding adolescent substance is also discussed.

Continuum of Drug Use: A Psychosocial Perspective

Muisener (1994) created a drug use and experience continuum for adolescents, identified as the Adolescent Chemical Use Experience (ACUE) continuum (see Table 15–2). Likened to other psychosocial frameworks of drug use (e.g., Avis, 1990), the ACUE

Table 15–2 | Drug Use Continuum

	Stage 1	Stage 2	Stage 3	Stage 4
Type of use	Experimental	Social use with peers	Operational; also known as compensatory users (Nowinski, 1990)	Dependent
Reason for use	Bored, curious, seeking fun, responding to peer pressure	Seeks a mood swing of drugs with friends (Macdonald & Newton, 1981)	Preoccupation with the mood swing of drugs (Macdonald & Newton, 1981)	Use chemicals in order to feel normal
Characteristics of drug use	Aware of differences between having fun and getting into danger	Considered fairly adaptive and normative for many adolescents	Actively engage in the drug effects Two types of operational users: 1. Pleasure pursuant: those who seek the effects of the drug to feel good 2. Pain-avoidant: those who use drugs to avoid dealing with painful feelings or to cope with life events and concerns	Adolescents devote a great deal of time and energy to getting high Become experts or connoisseurs of street drugs Drugs are an escape or a means to avoid discomfort rather than experience pleasure (Avis, 1990) Sense of self and identity is often interwoven with drug use
Outcome of drug use	Adolescents typically do not develop serious drug problems	Adolescents who misuse or overindulge in substances are at risk for continued drug use	Adolescents at higher risk for drug abuse if they establish an unhealthy coping mechanism of using drugs to deal with issues	Adolescents at high risk for health concerns

continuum considers social and environmental factors that influence drug use. Although the stages of Muisener's model overlap and cutoff points are arbitrary, it provides a framework from which to distinguish the different substance use experiences of adolescents.

All adolescents will differ in their experiences across the ACUE continuum (Muisener, 1994). Of those adolescents who are experimental or social drug users, only a fraction will progress to dependency. When considered at a national level, however, this represents a staggering 1 million teenagers. Similarly, approximately 4% to 5% of teens between the ages of 15 and 19 use illicit drugs regularly. Muisener noted, however, that those who abuse substances can regress to less problematic stages of use at a later time.

Cultural and Contextual Considerations of Drug Use

Currently, what is known about adolescent substance use is primarily based on data from White adolescents (Rebach, 1992; Wang, Bahr, & Marcos, 1995). Although this research provides a starting point from which to address preliminary concerns and issues, contextual and cultural considerations need to be integrated to be relevant and appropriate for other populations. Typically, environmental contexts and constructs of race and ethnicity are generally not examined in relation to adolescent substance use (Jillson-Broostrom, 1993; Wang et al., 1995). However, because everyone has a culture and a cultural understanding of the world (i.e., worldview), it is necessary to delineate some of the different cultural and contextual issues that need to be considered in relation to adolescent substance use. Further, the large differences between and within racial and ethnic groups also warrant consideration such that aggregation of individuals or groups does not continue.

Differences in family composition are a potential influence on adolescents because the family is frequently the first and last source of support for individuals (J. Fields & Casper, 2001). In terms of family households, less than half (48%) of Black households were married-couple households in 2000. Latinos/Hispanics had a higher percentage, at 68%, and Asian/Pacific Islanders (80%) and Whites (83%) had substantially higher married-couple households (J. Fields & Casper, 2001). When family size is considered, however, more than half of Latino/Hispanic (52%) and American Indian/Alaskan Native (55%) children lived with two or more siblings. Less than half of Black (43%) and Asian/Pacific Islander (40%) children lived with two or more siblings, whereas White (24%) children were least likely to live with two or more siblings (J. Fields, 2001).

The demography of the United States is rapidly diversifying. Although Whites continue to comprise the largest percentage of the U.S. population (75.1%), almost one quarter of the population is considered a racial or ethnic minority. Currently, Latinos/Hispanics (12.5%) and Blacks (12.3%) have the largest proportion, whereas American Indians/Alaskan Natives (0.9%), Asians (3.6%), and Native Hawaiians and other Pacific Islanders (0.1%) make up a smaller proportion of the total U.S. population. Also, individuals having two or more races/ethnicities comprise 2.4% of the U.S. population (Grieco & Cassidy, 2001).

A closer examination of the different racial and ethnic groups reveals that the differences in family size often reflect the extended family in the home and need to be considered as potential influences. In terms of family structure, the average Black household contained 2.9 persons as compared with 2.5 for Whites, 3.6 for Hispanics, 3.4 for Asian Americans, and 3.1 for American Indians (O'Hare, 1992). American Indians are the youngest ethnic group, with 37.4% being 18 years of age or younger, followed by Hispanics (36.7%), African Americans (33.8%), Asian Americans (30.4%), and Whites (25.1%; U.S. Bureau of the Census, 2001). The Asian American population is estimated to be growing at the fastest rate of any U.S. ethnic group. Asian groups in the United States include Chinese (2.7 million), Filipino (2.4 million), and Asian Indian (1.9 million; U.S. Bureau of the Census, 2001).

Given the changing demography of the United States, programs need to address acculturative stress (Smart & Smart, 1994) and language barriers. These considerations are relevant for both Asian and Hispanic/Latino populations. Examining the Hispanic/Latino populations, Mexicans (58.5%) were the largest subgroup, followed by other Hispanics (17.3%), Puerto Ricans (9.6%), South and Central Americans (8.6%), and Cubans (3.5%; Guzmán, 2001). The American Indian and Alaskan Native population is also highly diverse, with more than 500 federally recognized tribal entities and 300 federal reservations (Klein, 1993). However, American Indians share the loss of tribal and individual decisions as a result of federal and governmental control (Thurman, Swaim, & Plested, 1995). Currently, the five largest American Indian tribal groups are Cherokee, Navajo, Latin American Indian, Choctaw, and Sioux (Ogunwole, 2002). Further, with the birth rate of biethnic or biracial children higher than for any other group, increased attention to identity concerns for these adolescents is warranted (Herring, 1997).

Ethnic Differences in Substance Use

In a review of the substance use research, Rebach (1992) found that White youth tend to use alcohol and most other drugs at higher rates than do Asian, Black, or Hispanic youth. This finding was confirmed in the most recent report by the National Household Survey on Drug Abuse (2001). American Indian students had the highest alcohol use rate, whereas Blacks had the highest abstention rate from alcohol. Black and Hispanic youth began marijuana use at a later age and were less likely to become heavy users compared with their White counterparts.

Rebach (1992) noted that health problems are a major consequence of racial/ethnic minority substance use. For example, esophageal cancer and cirrhosis of the liver are the most frequent health problems associated with alcohol use among racial/ethnic minorities (Herd, 1988). Alcohol-related health problems among American Indians occur two to five times more often than for the general population (Rebach, 1992). Another consequence of substance use among racial/ethnic minorities is a disproportionately high number of violent crimes and arrests (Rebach, 1992). As racial/ethnic minority adolescents are highly influenced by their families and extended families (Ho, 1992; Marín, 1991), effecting change by using the support of families is essential (Goddard, 1993). For this reason, prevention and intervention programs need to utilize the family systems to change drug use patterns.

Ultimately, there is no typical profile of an adolescent drug abuser. Factors that influence adolescent substance use vary and require comprehensive and multidimensional prevention and intervention approaches that are culturally congruent at the individual, familial, and community levels through the integration of psychological, social, and cultural contexts.

CASE STUDY

Julie is a White 15-year-old high school sophomore who lives with her family in a large urban city in the Midwest. Having lived in the city all her life, her father's company is in the process of downsizing, and there is an expected financial need for the family to move to a smaller and more affordable place of residence. Julie is the youngest of three children. Marlene is a high school senior (17 years old), and Camille is a junior in college (21 years old) at a school that is 2 hours away from home. Julie has few major responsibilities at home; however, one includes helping Marlene cook dinner and wash dishes. Julie is interested in joining an academically related club but has opted not to join the French and German language clubs like she did last year because it requires her mother to pick her up in the early evening.

In Julie's family, her father is the primary source of income as her mother has had an inconsistent work history. Although Julie's mother has a college degree in accounting, she has had difficulty maintaining employment given her alcohol use over the last 10 years and more recent marijuana use. With the possibility of moving, Julie's mother's drinking has escalated to the point of her passing out in the family room on a daily basis. When this occurs, Julie's father and older sister refer to her mother as "feeling sick" and "needing time to rest."

Julie has a tendency to lack self-confidence, has difficulty with unstructured settings, attempts to serve as caretaker for others (particularly her mother), and yearns for social recognition and attention. At school, she often goes along with others in order to be accepted. A B+ student, Julie's grades have dropped as she has consistently failed to turn in her homework assignments. Noting that she seems tired and easily distracted in class, several of her teachers have referred her to the school counselor, Ms. Latrice.

After becoming comfortable with Ms. Latrice, Julie admits that for the last 5 months she has been drinking alcohol before school as she "wants to know what my mom feels like during the day." Also, she also has found and smoked several of her mother's marijuana cigarettes after dinner when her father retreats to his home office to contend with financial issues and her mother has passed out from drinking. Julie claims to have made a new set of "cool" friends at school since she brought one of her mother's marijuana cigarettes to school.

APPROACHES TO PREVENTION

The primary question that frequently arises when dealing with adolescent drug use is, What can parents, educators, and counselors do to prevent or deter adolescents from using drugs? NIDA recently published a research-based guide titled *Preventing Drug Use Among Children and Adolescents* (Sloboda & David, 2001). This guide posits that the most crucial risk factors for drug abuse related to the family include the following:

- chaotic home environments, particularly in which parents abuse substances or suffer from mental illnesses
- ineffective parenting, especially with children with difficult temperaments and conduct disorders
- lack of mutual attachments and nurturing.

Other risk factors relate to children interacting with others outside of the family, specifically the school, peers, and the community, including

- inappropriate shy and aggressive behavior in the classroom
- failure in school performance
- poor social coping skills

- affiliations with deviant peers or peers around deviant behaviors
- perceptions of approval of drug-using behaviors in the school, peer, and community environments.

The NIDA guide also identifies certain protective factors, the most salient of which include

- strong bonds with family
- experience of parental monitoring with clear rules of conduct within the family unit and involvement of parents in the lives of their children
- success in school performance
- strong bonds with prosocial institutions such as the family, school, and religious organizations
- adoption of conventional norms about drug use.

Prevention factors can enhance protective factors and move toward reversing or reducing risk factors. The NIDA research-based guide also describes 10 prevention programs that have been tested in a family, school, or community setting with positive results: Project STAR, the Life Skills Training Program, Adolescent Alcohol Prevention Trial, Seattle Social Development Project, Adolescents Training and Learning to Avoid Steroids: The ATLAS, Project Family, Strengthening Families Program, Focus on Families, Reconnection Youth Program, and Adolescent Transitions Program. Prevention and education regarding substance abuse among children and adolescents are often targeted toward families and schools.

Family

Many of the psychosocial models explaining adolescent drug involvement support a complex etiology of substance use with multiple determining factors. Among these factors are biological factors, environmental factors, and societal and cultural influences (Swadi, 1999). Much of this research posits environment as a moderator of risk factors, stressing the importance for children to bond with peers, parents, and others with drug-resistant attitudes (Bauman & Phongsavan, 1999; McDonald & Towberman, 1993; Sobeck et al., 2000).

As families are the most essential socialization system for children (Oyemade & Washington, 1990), they must be an integral component of broad-based prevention methods. The literature indicates inconsistencies regarding the influence of family on adolescent drug use. Abusive, alcoholic, single-parent, and blended families, families with latch key children, families with inconsistent limit setting and rules for behavior, and families with low bonding have been related to adolescent drug use. Girls are more likely to engage in chemical use and risky sexual behavior when they lack attachment to their fathers and when they have older siblings who engage in risky behavior (Hart, Robinson Kurpius, & Kerr, 2001). Regardless of family difficulties, the role of the family in preventing adolescent substance use can be significant (Wang et al., 1995).

Although parents may be knowledgeable about alcohol and drug use, they may be unaware or may deny that their children have been exposed to or have used alcohol/drugs. Furthermore, it is often difficult for parents and families to acknowledge substance abuse, and their attitudes often deter them from acting against drug use (e.g., talking with their children about the dangers of drug use; Burns & Margarella, 1990). Recognizing and requesting help with the problem may trigger intense feelings of anger, hurt, betrayal, or failure for parents. Additional barriers to parents addressing substance use with their children include a lack of time, a misperception of their children's world, difficulty in communicating with their children regarding sensitive issues, not wanting to appear as if they mistrust their children, and lack of current information (Burns & Margarella,1990).

Family-based prevention for Julie. NIDA (Sloboda & David, 2001) offers five research-based prevention principles for family-based programs. Family-based programs should reach families of children at each stage of development. Research has shown that the highest risk periods for drug use among adolescents are during developmental transitions and during difficult life changes. Julie has already experienced many transitions from infancy to young adulthood, including leaving home to go to school for the first time, transitioning from elementary school to middle school, and experiencing the social and academic pressures associated with high school. Prevention programs should train parents in behavioral skills to reduce conduct problems in children, improve parent–child relations, provide consistent discipline and rulemaking, and monitor adolescents' activities. An educational component should provide parents with drug information for themselves and their children. Programs should be directed to families whose children are in kindergarten through 12th grade to enhance protective factors at all stages of development. Finally, they should provide access to counseling services for families at risk. A comprehensive family-based prevention program for Julie would need to involve her parents in skills-based training and drug use education and provide intervention for her alcoholic mother and possibly group counseling for her family.

School

Peer drug use has been identified as the single factor most likely to predict current drug use (Chassin, Curran, Hussong, & Colder, 1996; Iannotti, Bush, &Weinfurt, 1996). Hart et al. (2001) found that girls' risk behavior levels, in particular, were positively correlated with their perceptions of their peers' risk behavior levels for substance use, risky sexual behavior, and suicidality. Oetting's (Dinges & Oetting, 1993) peer cluster theory helps to explain the strong relationship between drug use and the drug involvement of peers. The basic premise is that adolescent drug use is a group activity that takes place in the social context of peer clusters who establish group norms for drug use. According to the theory, strong connections between family members provide a solid foundation for doing well in school and building friendships with other young people who share positive norms and ideals. When there are weak bonds with the family or school, when the family is dysfunctional, or when antisocial or prodrug norms are communicated, young people are more likely to be attracted to and associate with other problem youth. For example, Chassin et al. (1996) found that parental alcoholism encouraged adolescent substance use through impairment of parental monitoring and increased stress. According to peer cluster theory, this increases the likelihood that adolescents will associate with peers who support substance use. Experiences with family, school, religion, or other social factors all interact to determine an adolescent's likelihood of joining a drug-using friendship group (Dinges & Oetting, 1993).

School-based prevention for Julie. NIDA (Sloboda & David, 2001) offers eight research-based prevention principles for school-based programs. The school-based programs should reach children from kindergarten through high school, or at the very least during the critical middle school or junior high years. They should contain multiple years of intervention, should use well-tested standardized interventions with detailed lesson plans and student materials, should be facilitated by age-appropriate interactive teaching methods (i.e., modeling, role-playing, discussion, reinforcement), and should foster prosocial bonding to the school and community. School-based programs need to teach communication, self-efficacy, and assertiveness, as well as drug resistance skills that are culturally and developmentally appropriate; promote positive peer influence and antidrug social norms; emphasize skills-training teaching methods; and include 10 to 15 sessions in Year 1 and 10 to 15 follow-up sessions. They should adhere to the effective intervention core elements of structure, content, and delivery, and they should be periodically evaluated for effectiveness. A comprehensive school-based intervention would pay particular attention to Julie's need for prosocial bonding to her school and community and training in self-efficacy and assertiveness, given her need to be accepted and her tendency to lack self-confidence. Further, attention needs to be paid to helping her become more successful in school behavior and performance to increase the likelihood that she will form pro-social bonds with her peers and the school.

Community

According to the NIDA, "Prevention programs work at the community level with civic, religious, law enforcement, and governmental organizations to enhance anti-drug norms and prosocial behavior through changes in policy or regulation, mass media efforts, and community-wide awareness programs" (Sloboda & David, 2001, p. 5). According to Johnston et al. (2002), there has been a steady decline in inhalant use since 1995, as perceived risk has grown due, in part, to the active efforts of the Partnership for a Drug-Free America and other community organizations. Community-based prevention programs might include new laws and enforcement, advertising restrictions, and drug-free school zones.

Community-based prevention for Julie. Community-based prevention for Julie would provide the broader context of a cleaner, safer, more drug-free environment in which individually targeted family and school programs can function effectively. NIDA (Sloboda & David, 2001) offers six research-based prevention principles for community-based programs. A comprehensive community prevention program would have components for the individual, the family, the school, the media, community organizations, and health providers that are integrated in theme and content. It would use the media and community education strategies to increase public awareness, attract support, and reinforce family and school-based programs. Ideally, the program components would be coordinated with other community efforts to reinforce prevention messages. The prevention curricula should be carefully designed to reach different populations at risk and be of sufficient duration to have an impact. The program should include a needs assessment for that community, planning, implementation, and review for refinement, with feedback to and from the community at each stage. Finally, the community program's objectives and activities should be specific, time-limited, feasible, and integrated so that they can work together across program components and can be used to evaluate program progress and outcomes.

INTERVENTION STRATEGIES

If intervention rather than prevention is warranted for adolescent substance abuse, it often occurs in more structured settings, such as treatment programs targeted for individuals. Treatment programs vary by type, services, and setting. For example, settings include short-term inpatient crisis care, inpatient programs, day-care programs, residential treatment, halfway houses, and outpatient treatment programs. Although all programs make extensive use of group and individual therapy, they also require some parental or familial involvement and attempt to provide family counseling to focus on the underlying problems in the family milieu. The more actively involved and supportive the family, the greater the chance of recovery for the substance abuser. Community-level programs can provide either prevention or intervention.

Individual

When an adolescent is using alcohol and other chemical substances, individual counseling is often warranted. Individual counseling can be obtained from community mental health agencies, hospitals, managed health care organizations (HMOs), and private practice therapists. Some HMOs provide both inpatient and outpatient drug and alcohol counseling, although the number of sessions is often limited. An experienced counselor who is nonjudgmental and can provide a safe environment will most likely elicit the adolescent's willingness to participate.

Motivation is also critical for stopping alcohol and drug abuse. More successful youth recognize that they have a problem and want to change (Kusnetz, 1986). Those who are less likely to be successful are referred by the criminal justice system, have used drugs for a longer time, are more immersed in the drug culture, come from families in which the adults are substance abusers, and have histories of violence and gang involvement (Kusnetz, 1986). Regardless of the history of the abuser, self-motivation and family involvement are paramount for change to occur.

Exploring the adolescent's perceptions of home, school, and peers can help to identify the motives, beliefs, and behaviors that contribute to his or her substance use. Counseling should also address self-esteem, self-efficacy, anger, hopelessness (e.g., nothing is going to get better), and the need to belong. Issues of identity (e.g., cultural, racial, or sexual) also need to be considered as identity development is central to psychological adjustment (Phinney, Lochner, & Murphy, 1990). For some adolescents, acculturation also needs to be assessed. For instance, counselors must understand the environmental and internal stresses experienced by immigrant adolescents as they balance their native and host culture values (Gloria & Peregoy, 1996). This concern is particularly relevant for biracial adolescents (Herring, 1997). Similarly, addressing environmental concerns of racism and discrimination is needed, particularly as many racial/ethnic minority or gay/lesbian/bisexual adolescents feel hopeless, isolated, or alienated. For instance, in an exploratory study of 83 youth between the ages of 14 and 18, Freeman (1990) found that many White students (85%) indicated that conflicts with parents and peers or role model expectations were major contributors to their substance abuse, whereas almost all Hispanic youth (98%) discussed cultural identity concerns and used drugs to help minimize environmental stresses such as racism.

Individual interventions for Julie. Julie has been experimenting with alcohol and marijuana over the last several months. Therapeutic interventions would foster discussion of what is happening at home and at school and how this relates to her substance use. The counselor can discuss how her self-perceptions (e.g., low self-esteem and low self-efficacy) and her desire for peer recognition could be related to her at-risk behaviors. Involving Julie in group counseling with similar at-risk youth could foster her coping skills and her sense of self-worth while providing her with accurate information about potential consequences of her drug use. She would probably benefit from being in a group that included other adolescents, particularly girls, thus reinforcing her gender identity and increasing her overall sense of self-worth.

Family

If parents suspect that their child is using drugs, they are encouraged to talk with their child about their concerns and why drugs are harmful. Parents need to communicate that they are opposed to any drug use and that they intend to enforce that position. Parents are encouraged to be understanding ("I realize you're under a lot of pressure from friends to use drugs"), firm ("As your parent, I cannot allow you to engage in harmful activities"), and self-examining ("Are my own alcohol and drug habits exerting a bad influence on my child?"; NIDA, 1984). Sarcasm, accusations, and sympathy-seeking or self-blaming behaviors will only make a child defensive and inattentive to parents. Acknowledging that one's child is using drugs and the need for assistance does not imply parental failure but instead reflects caring and parental support.

A confrontation with a child regarding drugs can be charged with many emotions; however, parents need to remain calm, open, loving, and firm. Parents need to listen and not just give advice. It is essential to teach children how to make responsible decisions, to accept the consequences of their decisions, and to love themselves. Parents also need to know the differences between firmness and punishment. Children respect fair limits that take into consideration their age and maturity level. Consistency in setting limits helps a child understand acceptable parameters for behavior. Although adolescence is a time for seeking independence, autonomy, and self-identity (Bukstein, 1995), most adolescents need and want some parental direction. A balance between adolescent autonomy and family is needed, particularly as low family attachment and involvement are associated with increased risk of substance abuse (Hawkins, Catalano, & Miller, 1992; Wang et al., 1995). This balance is particularly relevant for adolescents and families who value familialism and interdependence (Gloria & Peregoy, 1996; Ho, 1992).

Parents and family play a critical role in adolescent substance abuse interventions as they are the single most important contributors to an adolescent's environment. Specifically, parents transmit cultural values and beliefs and provide support, encouragement, and acceptance within the family. As the adolescent's substance use and the family environment reciprocally affect one another, parents are instrumental in bringing the family to counseling or applying other intervention strategies.

Parents can look for changes in their child's mood, attitude, grades, peer group, extracurricular activities, and interpersonal interactions as indicators of possible substance use. When parental discipline designed to change substance use behaviors is not effective, a family systems approach is warranted. Within a family systems framework, counselors focus on both the adaptive and maladaptive exchanges among family members and between the adolescent and his or her environment (Ho, 1987). Emphasis is on improving the transactions that occur within the family, using the family as a natural support system, and applying the experiences of the family system.

A second recommended intervention focuses on communication dynamics within the parent–adolescent relationship. Adolescents often feel that parents criticize, make demands, control, rarely listen, and do not understand their pressures, concerns, or feelings. Effective communication is important in light of findings that weak family relations, low bonding, perceived lack of support, and high number of family conflicts are related to a higher frequency and severity of substance use (Rhodes & Jason, 1988). Although the content of what is being said is important, parents also need to listen for the feelings that accompany the message (Daroff, Marks, & Friedman, 1990). Hearing the underlying emotional message may be difficult or painful, and thus parents may find a third party, such as a counselor, helpful in facilitating, teaching, and modeling communication with their adolescents.

A good parent–child relationship serves as a buffer between the environment and the child (Hawkins et al., 1992; Rutter, 1987). Additional family factors that promote a positive outcome for adolescents include rewarding them for independence with moderate risk taking, encouraging them to assume responsibility, and modeling examples of helpfulness and caring (Werner, 1984). Further, as some cultures value interdependence of family members, counselors can create a balance of adolescent–parent involvement. Such a balance allows for culturally relevant and meaningful interventions (Thurman et al., 1995).

A third family-based intervention is based on a behavioral framework. The goal is to replace maladaptive substance use behaviors with healthy adaptive behaviors. For instance, behaviors that adolescents are more likely to engage in (e.g., participating in after-school activities, going out with friends, talking on the phone) can reinforce those behaviors that they are less likely to engage in (e.g., cleaning their room, making curfew, completing chores). The first step of a behavioral intervention is to determine what the adolescent considers to be positive reinforcements. Each positive reinforcement needs to be salient, available, and able to be allotted in graduated portions by parents.

Another behavioral intervention is applying logical consequences for adolescent behaviors. This approach challenges adolescents to take responsibility for their behaviors. As logical consequences are applied firmly and consistently, these behaviors must be accompanied by discussion and respect (Daroff et al., 1990). As with positive reinforcements, logical consequences will differ for each adolescent. Being grounded for a weekend may seem drastic and earth shattering for one adolescent but endurable or irrelevant for another. To prevent challenging of parental authority, parents must clearly define and specify inappropriate and unacceptable behaviors at the start of the behavioral intervention.

Behavioral contracting between parents and adolescents allows for the specific determination of rules and consequences while providing a catalyst for clear communication. Defining acceptable and unacceptable behaviors and identifying logical and feasible consequences (e.g., grounded for the weekend vs. forever) can help to ensure success of such interventions. A possible contract might include no drinking at parties, no ditching classes, and no mouthing off to teachers. Privileges such as telephone use, peer interactions, and dating need to be linked to specific acceptable behaviors, such as consistent school attendance and honoring curfews. As adolescents fulfill requirements, terms of the contract can be renegotiated, thereby increasing their self-efficacy and sense of responsibility.

Family interventions for Julie. Julie would benefit from her family being more aware of the impact family dynamics can have on her self-worth and behaviors. Unfortunately, Julie's mother is modeling maladaptive coping with life's problems by drinking alcohol and smoking marijuana. Family counseling not only would address Julie's behaviors but also would help her mother develop more effective strategies for dealing with her problems. In addition, more open and effective communication between Julie and her parents could be facilitated. The counselor can also explore how Julie's older sisters could help relieve some of the stresses resulting in Julie's drinking and smoking marijuana. Further, because Julie has relatively few responsibilities at home, perhaps a contract can be developed between Julie and her parents that would encourage her to join the French and German language clubs if she meets specific goals with respect to her school work and her alcohol and marijuana use behaviors.

School

The primary arena for substance abuse recognition, prevention/education, and intervention is the school system. Teachers and school counselors are often the first to recognize substance use behaviors. As early detection is central to decreasing adolescent drug use, they play critical roles in intervention efforts. Teachers and school counselors who provide nurturing and understanding learning environments often create a refuge from the home environment (Werner, 1984). A school counselor or teacher who is perceived as open and receptive is most likely to have success as adolescents struggle with developmental concerns of boundary, trust, and identity (R. Fields, 1992; McKim, 1991). These trusted relationships allow for disclosure of family, peer, or school difficulties as well as drug use.

During the 1960s and 1970s, educators fought drug abuse by focusing on knowledge and attitudes, with the assumption that changes in substance use would follow (Schinke, Botvin, & Orlandi, 1991). Single-dimension, information-only, and one-shot presentations (with no follow-up programming), however, have minimal impact on substance use (Gonet, 1998). Examining 143 adolescent drug prevention studies, Tobler (1986) identified five major prevention strategies: knowledge-oriented strategies only, affective strategies only, social influence and life skills approaches, knowledge plus affective strategies, and alternative strategies.

Prevention and intervention approaches can be both informal and formal. For instance, the Just Say No approach of telling adolescents to refuse drugs is an example of an informal, unidimensional, simplistic approach to a multidimensional, complex problem. Students are told to respond behaviorally without addressing the cognitions or feelings involved in making such a decision. More importantly, such programming is based on the premise that the inability to say no is due to one's deviance, rather than integrating sociocultural considerations into the program's premise. Specifically, substance use is often a coping response to factors beyond an individual's control, such as ignorance, poverty, racism, prejudice, sexual/physical abuse as a child, dysfunctional family life, or mental incompetence (Warheit & Gil, 1998).

Other informal approaches involve developing a working partnership with the parents to prevent drug use. Depending on parental cooperation and school counselor availability, workshops can occur after normal school hours for students and their parents. Information and skill-based training, such as assertiveness training and decision-making skills, can help students make informed decisions about substance use (McWhirter, McWhirter, McWhirter, & McWhirter, 1993). These workshops can help students identify situations and circumstances that promote and maintain their substance use. School counselors can apply innovative strategies in their workshops, such as talks by recovered abusers, movies, group outings, and drug-free parties. In addition to workshops, school counselors can serve as liaisons to parents regarding adolescents' behavior and academic performance. For changes to occur, students must perceive the counselor's role as an advocate, not as a narc or another adult who does not understand.

School counselors can also coordinate academic and vocational opportunities for students in the school system and the community. School programs such as early release for work-study programs and vocational school training may provide students with an avenue to continue their education in an environment receptive to their interests and needs. For instance, students can participate in alternative school programs such as early release or individually-paced programs.

Another informal school-based intervention targets naturally occurring peer groups. As most students trust and relate to their peers, peer support and education groups are effective ways of relaying information to adolescents (Robinson Kurpius, in press). Peer discussion groups allow students to discuss their experiences and difficulties with peer pressure and acceptance. Students can find validation in knowing they are not alone in their experiences and feelings. Similarly, finding out that not everyone is using drugs can help to dispel adolescent drug myths. Most importantly, the group can help foster healthy peer relationships that promote self-growth. Students Against Drunk Driving (SADD) is an example of this type of intervention. Involvement in extracurricular activities such as sports, clubs, or music programs can also serve as an informal source of adolescent support.

There exists a multitude of formal, structured programs for the prevention and intervention of adolescent substance use. Multicomponent programs are more effective than unidimensional approaches (Gonet, 1998). Similarly, prevention and intervention programs need to help adolescents to increase their sense of self-efficacy about making decisions through addressing the four senses of (a) belonging, (b) usefulness in life, (c) competency and being valued by others, and (d) self-empowerment (Kassebaum, 1990).

A widely used structured prevention and intervention program that utilizes multiple components is the Growing Healthy Program, which has been shown to reduce alcohol, drug, and cigarette use among adolescents (Dryfoos, 1990). Promoted by the National Center for Health Education (National Diffusion Network, 1986), this health education program for kindergartners through seventh graders combines general health issues with reading, arts, sciences, and physical education to address issues of body systems, safety, nutrition, hygiene, fitness, mental health, and healthy lifestyles. Using audiovisuals, models, workshops, and students' parents, this program integrates school, family, and community in prevention and intervention efforts. Girl Power!, sponsored by the USDHHS, is designed to serve girls between the ages of 9 and 14. Strong no-use messages are integrated into self-defined groups that address self-esteem, self-identity, and empowerment issues.

Other school-based, noncurricular programs include in-house psychoeducational programs and support services. Dryfoos (1990) reviewed the popular Student Assistance Program (SAP) that utilizes full-time professional counselors to provide alcohol and drug abuse prevention and intervention services to 11th and 12th graders. Services include (a) group, individual, and family counseling; (b) resources for students who are struggling academically; and (c) consultations with parents and community leaders. SAP counselors are typically employed by external organizations and are not under the same confidentiality and time constraints as school counselors. Evaluations of SAP approaches have indicated significant reductions in alcohol and marijuana use along with significant increases in school performance.

Another school-based program is the Talented At-Risk Girls: Encouragement and Training for Sophomores (TARGETS; Kerr & Robinson Kurpius, 1999) project that has been offered through Arizona State University since 1992. This project, funded by the National Science Foundation, focuses on the career aspirations and at-risk behaviors of teenage girls. Through activities such as future day fantasies, individual career counseling sessions, and group discussions of at-risk behaviors such as alcohol and drug use, sexuality, and suicide, adolescent girls are provided with self-care knowledge and encouragement to pursue their career dreams. Three- to 4-month follow-up with over 500 girls has revealed that this program enhanced career aspirations, job and future self-efficacy, and self-esteem while decreasing at-risk behaviors.

Unfortunately, most commercial curriculum packages are not supported by empirical research and have not been systematically evaluated (Bangert-Drowns, 1988;

Dryfoos, 1990). Some of these programs include Children Are People, All Stars, 8:30 Monday Morning, DARE, Lions/Quest Program—Skills for Adolescents, Project Pride, and Get High on Yourself. Although these programs address drug problems from multiple perspectives, objective and valid evaluation continues to be problematic.

Regardless of whether the school-based program is formal or informal, it should address the primary factors involved in the etiology of substance abuse. These factors include peer use of illicit substances (Kandel & Yamaguchi, 1985), peer pressure (Brook, Whiteman, Gordon, Nomura, & Brook, 1986), early antisocial behavior (Hawkins, Lishner & Catalano, 1985), familial relations (Wang et al., 1995), cultural influences (Gloria & Peregoy, 1996; Thurman et al., 1995; Trimble, Bolek, & Niemcryk, 1992), and media influences (Vega & Gil, 1998b). Also, as pointed out by Dryfoos (1990), incorporating behavioral, cognitive, and affective strategies is important in all prevention efforts. Wallack and Corbett (1990) called for a more comprehensive and multifaceted approach to prevention (intervention) that takes a variety of societal and cultural factors into account while also focusing on environmental factors.

School-based interventions for Julie. Perhaps the most appropriate school-based intervention for Julie is the TARGETS program. By participating in this research-based program, Julie would be exposed to both group and individual counseling that would support increased efforts at school and decreased substance use. The program also addresses self-esteem and self-efficacy issues. These are particularly relevant for Julie given her need to be liked, to use substances to escape, and to allow her peers to influence her behaviors. In addition to TARGETS, it would be helpful if Julie were involved in an ongoing school-based support group of peers who are struggling with similar problems. Given Julie's high need for approval and peer acceptance, she might do well in a peer-led group.

Community

Community interventions can be provided in a wide variety of ways. Popular media prevention strategies have questionable effects on drug use behaviors. In particular, information contained in these strategies may not effectively communicate the reality of drug use or abuse that is relevant and applicable to students. That is, if an adolescent experiments with drugs and does not experience adverse effects, the parallel of a "fried brain" may not seem applicable to him or her. This type of commercial fosters an information gap between the reality of drugs and the intended message. Less credence is also given to public service announcements made by movie stars and athletes when some of these same individuals are later found to be using substances.

McWhirter et al. (1993) identified five community-based programs available for adolescents: drug-free programs, residential treatment facilities, therapeutic communities, day-care programs, and aftercare programs. Drug-free programs are usually outpatient programs within a residential treatment program. Activities range from individual and group counseling to challenging experiential programs. Residential treatment facilities are inpatient and focus on long-term recovery. Requiring the adolescent to live on-site, these programs focus on resocializing youth by teaching new life skills. In particular to adolescents from racial/ethnic minority backgrounds, learning and applying bicultural skills to manage different cultures is necessary.

A similar residential type of treatment program is therapeutic communities, designed for adolescents who are recovering substance use offenders and who are referred from the juvenile court system. Focusing on extinguishing substance use, therapeutic communities rely on peer influence and group action to change attitudes and destructive behaviors. Day-care programs, on the other hand, typically are less structured than residential programs. Their services usually include academic learning and counseling as well as supervised social activities. Aftercare programs target the adolescent who has been discharged from treatment. The premise of these programs is that treatment is a life-long process.

Other community-based interventions often involve law enforcement systems that collaborate with the community. Police often talk with the parents of the adolescent arrested for a substance use offense. Police, parents, schools, and community task forces can work together effectively to design community-wide prevention and intervention programs to combat adolescent substance use. For instance, Boys and Girls Clubs and Community YMCAs provide alternative activities. Adult volunteers and recovered users often staff these programs, providing healthy, productive, and positive role models. Such organizations bring individuals, schools, and communities together to share responsibility for preventing and intervening in adolescent substance use and abuse.

Community-based interventions for Julie. Getting Julie involved with the school and local French and German language clubs would be beneficial. These interventions could foster a sense of belonging as well as pride in who she is as an emergent linguistic and female. She needs more positive experiences in her life, and these community interventions have the probability of providing her with the positive individual and group-member recognition she needs and wants.

ADAPTATIONS FOR DIVERSITY

Because many adolescent prevention and intervention programs do not include cultural or contextual issues, Wallack and Corbett (1990) called for a combination of approaches affecting the political, social, and cultural environment, in addition to the individual. Specifically, the environmental issues of discrimination and racism are of particular concern. Labouvie (1986) found that a sense of powerlessness or helplessness was related to heavy substance abuse. Substance use helped adolescents achieve a sense of emotional self-regulation. As approximately 10% of adolescents are lesbian, gay, or bisexual (Berk, 1993), same-sex interests often result in familial and internal conflict (Herring, 1997). Accordingly, these youth are vulnerable to alcohol and drug use as they often feel rejected by the self and the heterocentric values of the United States.

Underscoring the importance of integrating contextual and cultural considerations into prevention and intervention programming, Oetting, Beauvais, and Edwards (1988) identified ineffective strategies for working with American Indian adolescents. Programs with good ideas but identified as ineffective focused on improving self-esteem; viewed alcohol as a substitute for social acceptance; perceived depressed, anxious, or emotionally disturbed youth as alcohol users; and did not actively or completely exclude alcohol use. Although these preventive activities may be ineffective for one specific cultural group, the same activities may be effective with adolescents with other cultural backgrounds. Adolescent substance abuse is a serious issue; therefore, researchers, parents, school systems, and counselors cannot afford to administer a "one size fits all" prevention or intervention program.

In accessing information about substance use prevention and intervention, there are several alternatives from which to choose. First, the public library is an excellent source for information about state laws related to drugs. Learning about state laws and the legal rights of minors can be helpful in providing straight talk and accurate information about drugs. Second, if parents or adolescents are concerned about openly seeking information, a variety of free publications, pamphlets, posters, and other drug education information can be ordered by phone. For instance, the first research-based drug prevention guide for children and adolescents (*Preventing Drug Use Among Children and Adolescents*) is available through the National Clearinghouse for Alcohol and Drug Information (NCADI; toll-free telephone: 1-800-729-6686). Similarly, the publication *Keeping Youth Drug Free* is also available from NCADI. It is estimated that NCADI receives over 250,000 inquiries and distributes over 20 million information products each year.

The Internet is another rich source of information regarding substance use and abuse prevention. A variety of government and private agency Web sites are available and user-friendly. For families interested in surfing the Web to gain information about drugs, a few Internet addresses to visit include the following:

- www.health.org to access the Substance Abuse and Mental Health Services Administration
- www.nida.nih.gov to access the National Institute on Drug Abuse
- www.niaa.nih.gov to access the National Institute on Alcohol Abuse and Alcoholism

Within most Web sites, links (i.e., other sites of potential interest) and programs specifically target adolescents and different racial and ethnic minority groups. Most information is easy to read and presented in a fun and attention-getting fashion. Most sites also provide additional links and referral information. Addresses and phone numbers for different prevention and treatment organizations are also generally provided. The majority of information on Web sites can be downloaded for parents or adolescents to use in later discussions. Finally, the NIDA Infofax provides a 24-hour toll-free phone line from which drug information can be ordered via fax or mail. Audio information on topics such as the health effects of drugs, drug use and AIDS, and drug treatment and prevention can also be listened to in English or Spanish. The phone numbers are 1-888-644-6432 and 1-888-889-6432 (hearing-impaired).

SUMMARY

The most recent data from the NIDA (2000b) indicate that the substance use problem among adolescents remains unsolved. Adolescents, parents, teachers, counselors, and other community members must share responsibility in the prevention and intervention of adolescent drug use. Both prevention and intervention programs need to educate adolescents about the negative effects of drugs and provide opportunities for them to bond with peers, parents, and others who have drug-resistant attitudes (Bauman & Phongsavan, 1999; McDonald & Towberman, 1993; Sobeck et al., 2000). They should focus on adolescents' behaviors, feelings, and thoughts within a culturally and socially congruent environment (Gloria & Peregoy, 1996; Trimble et al., 1992). The manner in which programs focus on adolescents, however, must be informed by cultural values and beliefs specific to group and subgroup norms (Thurman et al., 1995; Trimble et al., 1992; Vega & Gil, 1998a). That is, prevention and intervention programs must be designed to be congruent with the values and worldview of the culture within which they are implemented. Although we may never totally stop substance use or abuse, one of our most important tasks is to prepare our youth to be wise decision makers and to draw on their cultural, social, and familial strengths and supports.

REFERENCES

Avis, H. (1990). *Drugs and life*. Dubuque, IA: Brown.

Bangert-Drowns, R. L. (1988). The effects of school-based substance abuse education: A meta-analysis. *Journal of Drug Education, 18*, 243–265.

Bauman, A., & Phongsavan, P. (1999). Epidemiology of substance use in adolescence: Prevalence, trends, and policy implications. *Drug and Alcohol Dependence, 55*, 187–207.

Berk, L. E. (1993). *Infants, children, and adolescents*. Boston: Allyn & Bacon.

Brook, J. S., Whiteman, M., Gordon, A. S., Nomura, C., & Brook, D. W. (1986). Onset of adolescent drinking: A longitudinal study of intrapersonal and interpersonal antecedents. *Advances in Alcohol and Substance Abuse, 5*, 91–110.

Bukstein, O. G. (1995). *Adolescent substance abuse: Assessment, prevention, and treatment*. New York: Wiley.

Burns, C., & Margarella, M. (1990). Reaching parents. In *Communicating about alcohol and other drugs: Strategies for reaching populations at risk* (U.S. Department of Health and Human Services Publication No. ADM 90-1665, Office for Substance Abuse Prevention Monograph B5, pp. 211–247). Washington, DC: U.S. Government Printing Office.

Business Research Publications. (1987, September). Education department starts school year with "Challenge" public service campaign. *Substance Abuse Reports, 18*, 3–4.

Carlson, N. R. (2001). *Physiology of behavior*. Needham Heights, MA: Allyn & Bacon.

Chassin, L., Curran, P. J., Hussong, A. M., & Colder, C. R. (1996). The relation of parent alcoholism to adolescent substance use: A longitudinal follow-up study. *Journal of Abnormal Psychology, 105*, 70–80.

Daroff, L. H., Marks, S. F., & Friedman, A. S. (1990). The parents' predicament. In A. S. Friedman & S. Granick (Eds.), *Family therapy for adolescent drug abuse* (pp. 85–108). Lexington, MA: Lexington Books.

Dinges, M. M., & Oetting, E. R. (1993). Similarity in drug use patterns between adolescents and their friends. *Adolescence, 28*, 253–267.

Dryfoos, J. G. (1990). *Adolescents at risk: Prevalence and prevention*. New York: Oxford University Press.

Fields, J. (2001). *Living arrangement for children: Household economic studies* (Current Population Reports, P70-74). Washington, DC: U.S. Department of Commerce.

Fields, J., & Casper, L. M. (2001). *America's families and living arrangements: Population characteristics* (Current Population Reports, P20-537). Washington, DC: U.S. Department of Commerce.

Fields, R. (1992). *Drugs and alcohol in perspective*. Dubuque, IA: Brown.

Freeman, E. M. (1990). Social competence as a framework for addressing ethnicity and teenage alcohol problems. In A. R. Stiffman & L. E. Davis (Eds.), *Ethnic issues in adolescent mental health* (pp. 247–266). Newbury Park, CA: Sage.

Funkhouser, J. E., & Denniston, R. W. (1992). Historical perspective. In *A promising future: Alcohol and other drug problem prevention services improvement* (U.S. Department of Health and Human Services, Publication No. ADM 92-1807, Office for Substance Abuse Prevention Monograph B10, pp. 5–15). Washington, DC: U.S. Government Printing Office.

Gloria, A. M., & Peregoy, J. J. (1996). Counseling Latino alcohol and other substance users/abusers: Cultural considerations for counselors. *Journal of Substance Abuse Treatment, 13*, 119–126.

Goddard, L. L. (1993). The role of the family in alcohol and other drug use prevention. In *The second national conference on preventing and treating alcohol and other drug abuse, HIV infection, and AIDS in Black communities: From advocacy to action* (Center for Substance Abuse Prevention Monograph 13, pp. 161–173). Washington DC: U.S. Department of Health and Human Services, Public Health Service.

Gonet, A. M. (1998). Groups for drug and alcohol abuse. In K. C. Stoiber & T. R. Kratochwill (Eds.), *Handbook of group intervention for children and families* (pp. 172–192). Needham Heights, MA: Allyn & Bacon.

Grieco, E. M., & Cassidy, R. C. (2001). *Overview of race and Hispanic origin* (Census 2000 Brief, C2KBR/01-1). Washington, DC: U.S. Department of Commerce.

Guzmán, B. (2001). *The Hispanic population* (Current Population Reports, C2KBR/01-3). Washington, DC: U.S. Census Bureau.

Hart, S., Robinson Kurpius, S. E., & Kerr, B. (2001, August). *Adolescent at-risk behaviors: Effects of parents, older siblings, and peers.* Paper presented at the annual convention of the American Psychological Association, San Francisco.

Hawkins, J. D., Catalano, R. F., & Miller, J. Y. (1992). Risks and protective factors for alcohol and other drug problems in adolescence and early adulthood: Implications for substance abuse prevention. *Psychological Bulletin, 112,* 64–105.

Hawkins, J. D., Lishner, D. M., & Catalano, R. F. (1985). Childhood predictors and the prevention of adolescent substance abuse. In C. L. Jones & R. J. Battejes (Eds.), *Etiology of drug abuse: Implications for prevention* (Research Monograph 56, pp. 75–126). Rockville, MD: National Institute on Drug Abuse.

Herd, D. (1988). Drinking by Black and White women: Results from a national survey. *Social Problems, 35,* 493–505.

Herring, R. D. (1997). *Counseling diverse ethnic youth: Synergetic strategies and interventions for school counselors.* Fort Worth, TX: Harcourt Brace College.

Ho, M. K. (1987). *Family therapy with ethnic minorities.* Newbury Park, CA: Sage.

Ho, M. K. (1992). *Minority children and adolescents in therapy.* Newbury Park, CA: Sage.

Iannotti, R. J., Bush, P. J., & Weinfurt, K. P. (1996). Perceptions of friends' use of alcohol, cigarettes, and marijuana among urban schoolchildren: A longitudinal analysis. *Addictive Behaviors, 21,* 615–632.

Inaba, D. S., & Cohen, W. (2000). *Uppers, downers, and all arounders: Physical and mental effects of psychoactive drugs.* Ashland, OR: CNS Publications.

Inciardi, J. A. (1986). Getting busted for drugs. In G. Beschner & A. S. Friedman (Eds.), *Teen drug use* (pp. 63–83). Lexington, MA: D. C. Heath.

Jillson-Broostrom, I. (1993). Health and related data for racial/ethnic populations in the United States: Realities and need. In *The second national conference on preventing and treating alcohol and other drug abuse, HIV infection, and AIDS in Black communities: From advocacy to action* (Center for Substance Abuse Prevention Monograph 13, pp. 247–264). Washington DC: U.S. Department of Health and Human Services, Public Health Service.

Johnston, L. D., O'Malley, P. M., & Bachman, J. G. (2002). *Monitoring the Future national results on adolescent drug use: Overview of key findings, 2001.* Bethesda, MD: National Institute on Drug Abuse.

Kandel, D. B., & Yamaguchi, K. (1985). Developmental patterns of the use of legal, illegal, and medically prescribed psychotropic drugs from adolescence to young adulthood. In C. L. Jones & R. J. Battejes (Eds.), *Etiology of drug abuse: Implications for prevention* (Research Monograph 56, pp. 193–235). Rockville, MD: National Institute on Drug Abuse.

Kassebaum, P. (1990). Reaching families and youth from high-risk environments. In *Communicating about alcohol and other drugs: Strategies for reaching populations at risk* (U.S. Department of Health and Human Services, Publication No. ADM 90-1665, Office for Substance Abuse Prevention Monograph B5, pp. 11–119). Washington, DC: U.S. Government Printing Office.

Kerr, B., & Robinson Kurpius, S. E. (1999). *Guiding girls in engineering, math, and sciences: A year-end report.* Arlington, VA: National Science Foundation.

Kingery-McCabe, L. G., & Campbell, F. A. (1991). Effects of addiction on the addict. In D. C. Daley & M. S. Raskin (Eds.), *Treating the chemically dependent and their families* (pp. 57– 78). Newbury Park, CA: Sage.

Klein, B. T. (Ed.). (1993). *Reference encyclopedia of the American Indian* (6th ed.). West Nyack, NY: Todd.

Kusnetz, S. (1986). Services for adolescent substance abusers. In G. Beschner & A. S. Friedman (Eds.), *Teen drug use* (pp. 123–153). Lexington, MA: D. C. Heath.

Labouvie, E. W. (1986). Alcohol and marijuana use in relation to adolescent stress. *International Journal of Addictions, 21,* 333–345.

Macdonald, D. I., & Newton, M. (1981). The clinical syndrome of adolescent drug abuse. *Advances in Pediatrics, 28,* 1–15.

Mandel, J., & Feldman, H. W. (1986). The social history of teenage drug use. In G. Beschner & A. S. Friedman (Eds.), *Teen drug use* (pp. 19–42). Lexington, MA: D. C. Heath.

Marín, G. (1991). Influence of acculturation on familialism and self-identification among Hispanics. In M. E. Bernal & G. P. Knight (Eds.), *Ethnic identity: Formation and transmission among Hispanics and other minorities* (pp. 181–196). Albany: State University of New York Press.

McDonald, R. M., & Towberman, D. B. (1993). Psychosocial correlates of adolescent drug involvement. *Adolescence, 28,* 925–937.

McKim, W. A. (1991). *Drugs and behavior: An introduction to behavioral pharmacology* (2nd ed.). Englewood Cliffs, NJ: Prentice Hall.

McWhirter, J. J., McWhirter, B. T., McWhirter, A. M., & McWhirter, E. H. (1993). *At-risk youth: A comprehensive response.* Pacific Grove, CA: Brooks/Cole.

Muisener, P. P. (1994). *Understanding and treating adolescent substance abuse.* Thousand Oaks, CA: Sage.

Myer, J. (2001). *Age: 2000* (Census 2000 Brief, C2KBR/01-12). Washington, DC: U.S. Department of Commerce.

National Diffusion Network. (1986). *Education programs that work* (12th ed.). Longmont, CO: Sophris.

National Household Survey on Drug Abuse (2001). *2001 National Household Survey on Drug Abuse.* Retrieved from http://www.samhsa.gov/oas/nhsda.htm#NHSDAinfo

National Institute on Drug Abuse. (1984). *Parents: What you can do about drug abuse* (DHHS Publication Number ADM-1267). Washington, DC: U.S. Government Printing Office.

National Institute on Drug Abuse. (1998a). *Cigarettes and other nicotine products.* Retrieved from http://www.nida.nih.gov/Infofax/tocacco.html

National Institute on Drug Abuse. (1998b). *Inhalants.* Retrieved from http://www.nida.nih.gov/Infofax/inhalants.html

National Institute on Drug Abuse. (1998c). *Marijuana.* Retrieved from http://www.nida.nih.gov/Infofax/marijuana.html

National Institute on Drug Abuse. (2000a). *Mind over matter: The brain's response to drugs.* Retrieved from http://www.drugabuse.gov/MOM/MOMIndex.html

National Institute on Drug Abuse. (2000b). *Monitoring the Future Study.* Retrieved from http://www.nida.nih.gov/infofax/HSYouthtrends.html

National Institute on Drug Abuse. (2002). *Monitoring the Future Study.* Retrieved from http://www.nida.nih.gov/

Nowinski, J. (1990). *Substance abuse in adolescent and young adults: A guide to treatment.* New York: Norton.

Oetting, E. R., Beauvais, R., & Edwards, R. (1988). Alcohol and Indian youth: Social and psychological correlates and prevention. *Journal of Drug Issues, 18,* 87–102.

Ogunwole, S. U. (2002). *The American Indian and Alaska Native population: 2000* (Census 2000 Brief, C2KBR/01-15). Washington, DC: U.S. Department of Commerce.

O'Hare, W. P. (1992). America's minorities: B. The demographics of diversity. *Population Bulletin, 47,* 1–47.

Oyemade, U. J., & Washington, V. (1990). The roles of family factors in the primary prevention of substance abuse among high risk Black youth. In A. R. Stiffman & L. E. Davis (Eds.), *Ethnic issues in adolescent mental health* (pp. 267– 284). Newbury Park, CA: Sage.

Phinney, J. S., Lochner, B. T., & Murphy, R. (1990). Ethnic identity development and psychological adjustment in adolescence. In A. R. Stiffman & L. E. Davis (Eds.), *Ethnic issues in adolescent mental health* (pp. 53–72). Newbury Park, CA: Sage.

Rebach, H. (1992). Alcohol and drug use among American minorities. In J. E. Trimble, C. S. Bolek, & S. J. Niemcryk (Eds.), *Ethnic and multicultural drug abuse: Perspectives on current research* (pp. 23–57). Binghamton, NY: Harrington Park Press.

Rhodes, J. E., & Jason, L. A. (1988). *Preventing substance abuse among children and adolescents.* New York: Pergamon Press.

Robinson, S. E. (1989). Preventing substance abuse among teenagers: A school and family responsibility. *Counseling and Human Development, 21,* 1–8.

Robinson, S. E., Gloria, A. M., Roth, S. L., & Schuetter, R. M. (1993). Patterns of drug use among male and female undergraduates. *Journal of College Student Development, 34,* 130–137.

Robinson Kurpius, S. E. (in press). Peer counseling. In A. E. Kazdin (Ed.), *Encyclopedia of psychology.* Washington, DC: American Psychological Association and Oxford University Press.

Rutter, M. (1987). Psychosocial resilience and protective mechanisms. *American Journal of Orthopsychiatry, 57,* 316–331.

Schinke, S. P., Botvin, G. J., & Orlandi, M. A. (1991). *Substance abuse in children and adolescents: Evaluation and intervention.* Newbury Park, CA: Sage.

Schonberg, S. K., & Schnoll, S. H. (1986). Drugs and their effects on adolescent users. In G. Beschner & A. S. Friedman (Eds.), *Teen drug use* (pp. 43–62). Lexington, MA: D. C. Heath.

Shillington, A. M., & Clapp, J. D. (2000). Self-report stability of adolescent substance use: Are there differences for gender, ethnicity and age? *Drug and Alcohol Dependence, 60,* 19–27.

Sloboda, Z., & David, S. L. (2001). *Preventing drug use among children and adolescents: A research-based guide* (NIH Publication No. 02-4212). Bethesda, MD: National Institute on Drug Abuse.

Smart, J. S., & Smart, D. W. (1994). The rehabilitation of Hispanics experiencing acculturative stress: Implications for practice. *Journal of Rehabilitation, 60,* 8–12.

Sobeck, J., Abbey, A., Agius, E., Clinton, M., & Harrison, K. (2000). Predicting early adolescent substance use: Do risk factors differ depending on age of onset? *Journal of Substance Abuse, 11,* 89–102.

Substance Abuse and Mental Health Services Administration. (2002). National Household Survey on Drug Abuse. *The NHSDA Report: Marijuana use among youths.* Retrieved from http://www.health.org/govstudy/shortreports/MJ&dependence/

Swadi, H. (1999). Individual risk factors for adolescent substance use. *Drug and Alcohol Dependence, 55,* 209–224.

Thurman, P. J., Swaim, R., & Plested, B. (1995). Intervention and treatment of ethnic minority substance abusers. In. J. F. Aponte, R. Y. Rivers, & J. Wohl (Eds.), *Psychological interventions and cultural diversity* (pp. 215–233). Boston: Allyn & Bacon.

Tobler, N. (1986). Meta-analysis of 143 adolescent drug prevention programs: Quantitative outcome results of program participant compared to a control or comparison group. *Journal of Drug Issues, 16,* 537–567.

Trimble, J. E., Bolek, C. S., & Niemcryk, S. J. (Eds.). (1992). *Ethnic and multicultural drug abuse: Perspectives on current research.* New York: Harrington Park Press.

U.S. Bureau of the Census. (2001). *Total population by age, race, and Hispanic or Latino origin for the United States: 2000* (Census 2000 PHC-T-9). Washington, DC: Author.

U.S. Department of Health and Human Services. (2002). *HHS fact sheet: Substance abuse—A national challenge: Prevention, treatment and research at HHS.* Retrieved from http://www.hhs.gov/news/press/2002pres/subabuse.html

Vega, W. A., & Gil, A. G. (Eds.). (1998a). *Drug use and ethnicity in early adolescence.* New York: Plenum.

Vega, W. A., & Gil, A. G. (1998b). Prevention implications and conclusions. In W. A. Vega & A. G. Gil (Eds.), *Drug use and ethnicity in early adolescence* (pp. 177–196). New York: Plenum.

Wallack, L., & Corbett, K. (1990). *Illicit drug, tobacco, and alcohol use among youth: Trends and promising approaches in prevention* (Office for Substance Abuse Prevention: Monograph 6). Washington, DC: U.S. Department of Health and Human Services, Public Health Service.

Wang, G. T., Bahr, S. J., & Marcos, A. C. (1995). Family bonds and adolescent substance use: An ethnic group comparison. In C. K. Jacobson (Ed.), *American families: Issues in race and ethnicity* (pp. 463–492). New York: Garland.

Warheit, G. J., & Gil, A. G. (1998). Substance use and other social deviance. In W. A. Vega & A. G. Gil (Eds.), *Drug use and ethnicity in early adolescence* (pp. 37–70). New York: Plenum.

Werner, E. E. (1984). Resilient children. *Young Children, 40,* 68–72.

16 | Nowhere to Turn: Homeless Youth

Melissa Stormont

The face of the homeless person has changed over the past several decades. Often now the face is that of a child: a child without a home. Families with small children now represent up to 43% of the U.S. homeless population (Dail, 1993; National Coalition for the Homeless, 1999c). Conservative estimates indicate that at least 500,000 youth are homeless in the United States (National Coalition for the Homeless, 1994b; Shane, 1996). Schools and communities need to extend outreach efforts to identify children who are homeless because they are entitled to the same free and appropriate education as their peers who have homes (Shane, 1996). To ensure their appropriate education, professionals who work with children need to be educated on homelessness in general and on the unique needs and characteristics of these children.

Children who are homeless are at great risk for academic and behavioral problems in school (Butler, 1989; Danseco & Holden, 1998; Lewis & Doorlag, 1987; Reeves, 1988). These children may look and act different from their same-age peers, and these differences demand sensitivity and understanding from teachers and other professionals who work with these youth. It is evident that the educational needs of children who are homeless warrant collaborative outreach efforts and interventions from teachers, counselors, administrators, and communities. Every professional involved needs to be aware of the resources available to assist these children. Schools must better prepare themselves to reach and to teach children who are homeless as, sadly, both schools and society consistently ignore such children.

This chapter first describes homelessness, both demographically and more descriptively using a case study. Next, the chapter delineates preventative measures for ending homelessness by presenting the causes of homelessness for individuals and families and then presenting ways that the community, the government, and other profit or not-for-profit agencies can provide outreach efforts. Following the prevention section is the intervention section, which includes a description of interventions that can be driven by the schools for individual students who are homeless and their families. The intervention section concludes with possible linkages from the school to the community to help meet the educational needs of these students. Adaptations for diversity are detailed next and include additional considerations for working with these children. The last section of this chapter deals with another prevention issue: ending the cycle of homelessness by conducting outreach efforts and supporting the development of life and job skills for street youth.

PROBLEM DEFINITION

Homelessness means having a primary residence that is a public or private shelter, emergency housing, hotel or motel, or any other public space including public parks, cars, abandoned buildings, or aqueducts (National Coalition for the Homeless, 1990). Other definitions of homelessness also include those individuals who have to double up in housing with friends and family members or live in overcrowded housing conditions (National Coalition for the Homeless, 1998b). The latter definition includes those individuals who are homeless and living in rural areas where there are more limited shelter facilities (National Coalition for the Homeless, 1999e). Regardless of how homelessness is defined, being homeless means more than not having a fixed place to sleep. Homeless people have nowhere to put the things they cherish, things that connect them to their past. They have often lost contact with their family and friends and may have to uproot their children from school. Homelessness means suffering the frustration and degradation of living hand to mouth, depending on the generosity of strangers or the efficiency of a government agency for survival.

At least 1 million families in the United States are homeless, with incidence rates increasing at a rate of 25% a year (National Coalition for the Homeless, 1990). According to research that has been conducted on increases in shelter capacity, homelessness has increased two to three times over the past two decades (National Coalition for the Homeless, 1999c). From the most recent statistics available, it is clear that the faces of the homeless have changed drastically since the days of the White, male alcoholic or "skid row bum." According to a survey by the U.S. Conference of Mayors (as cited in National Coalition for the Homeless, 1999c), 38% of the homeless in the United States are families and 25% are children. Within these families half of the children are under the age of 6 (National Coalition for the Homeless, 1998a). They may never go to school, or they may enter school for the first time at a late age.

Conservative estimates indicate that one in five homeless children are not currently in school (Cherey, 1995; National Coalition for the Homeless, 1994a). For children attending school, research has found that homeless children were significantly more likely than children who were poor but housed to have missed more than 3 weeks of school in the last 3 months (Wood, Valdez, Hayashi, & Shen, 1990). One reason given for missing school was that families were in transition. Homeless children may also miss school due to frequent sick days. Unfortunately, the problem of homelessness in children is not decreasing. In fact, children may be the fastest growing group of the homeless population (National Coalition for the Homeless, 1994a; Shane, 1996). Worestendiek's (as cited in Shane, 1996) research in Philadelphia found a 25% increase from 1988 to 1993 of children in homeless shelters.

Homeless children come from all geographical areas. Many state-level studies continue to support that homelessness is a problem present in nonmetropolitan areas (National Coalition for the Homeless, 1993). Children who are homeless also represent different ethnicities. However, a disproportionate number of minorities, especially African American, are represented in the homeless population (Shane, 1996). According to one report that described the percentage of the homeless by ethnicity, 58% of the population of homeless were African American, 29% were Caucasian, 10% were Hispanic, 2% were Native American, and 1% were Asian American (National Coalition for the Homeless, 1998b). Children may have different needs according to their different cultural backgrounds, which will need to be addressed in a culturally sensitive way. These adaptations for diversity are presented later in the chapter. Overall, most children who are homeless have different needs from children who are not homeless, and they may have extensive problems in school. The following case of a homeless family illustrates the problems that the children might face in school.

CASE STUDY

It was 3:00 a.m. At a local gas station, a man was trying to bum $5 worth of gas off the attendant as his family waited, shivering, in their junky car. The attendant obliged the family and called a local homeless shelter asking if they would let the family stay even though their doors were closed for the night. The children arrived at the shelter, hungry and cold. Their parents tucked them in and stayed up for awhile chatting with the volunteers. They were homeless because of one bill they could not pay—their electric bill. They tried to survive in their trailer without heat, lights, or hot water but it was too hard on their children.

The children woke up and ate breakfast. Their clothes were wrinkled. They were dirty and extremely tired. They went to school after less than 3 hours of sleep. What will their teachers think when they fall asleep in class? How will they get food for lunch? What will their peers think? They came to school dirty, wearing the same clothes as the day before. Contributing to the fact that these children will look different, another concern is what can these children talk about with their peers? They have had to grow up too fast. Their worries are not the same as other children's. They are worried about their next meal and where they will seek shelter. However, their needs are the same. They need a home and all of the securities that come with it. They also need an education.

CONSEQUENCES FOR CHILDREN

The case example reveals what the consequences of homelessness may be for youth in the classroom. In addition, these youth who attend school typically do not have school records, immunization records, a permanent address, transportation, school supplies, gym shoes, appropriate clothing, a full stomach, a neat appearance, or clean clothes (Gonzalez, 1990). One study found that 15% of homeless children had incomplete immunizations (Bass, Brennan, Mehta, & Kodzis, 1990). Redlener and Johnson (as cited in National Coalition for the Homeless, 1999b) conducted a study of children living in New York homeless shelters and found that 61% of children were deficient in immunizations. Homeless children also may have chronic health problems and typically do not get medical care (Bass et al., 1990; Burg, 1994; Shane, 1996). Health care problems appear to be more prevalent in children who are homeless than in children who are poor but have housing (Wood et al., 1990). Research has found that children who are homeless have more health problems and more barriers to obtaining adequate health care than children who are poor but live in low-income housing (Burg, 1994). Redlener and Johnson (as cited in National Coalition for the Homeless, 1999b) found that children who were homeless were at four times greater risk for asthma than other children their age.

These physical insufficiencies only begin to describe these children's lives. Children who are homeless may go home to a shelter where there is often noise, inconsistency in adult supervision (e.g., shelter rules vs. parents' rules), no place to do homework, no privacy, and no resources. Additionally, homeless children are at risk for having been exposed to domestic violence (Eddowes & Hranitz, 1989; Shane, 1996). According to Maslow's hierarchy of needs, shelter, security, and food must be obtained before reaching higher order needs such as psychological and self-actualization needs (Maslow, 1968). Thus, the additional problems associated with homelessness are profound for children (Harrington-Lueker, 1989). These children may experience numerous emotions related to their homelessness, including embarrassment, anxiousness, fear, low self-esteem, depression, suspiciousness, and feelings of helplessness (Bassuk & Rosenberg, 1988; Harrington-Lueker, 1989). Understandably, children who are homeless might not care about completing their homework.

APPROACHES TO PREVENTION

Obviously, the best way to prevent the problems of homeless youth is to prevent homelessness. Homelessness, however, is a complicated social issue that requires a multilevel approach. Providing permanent affordable housing is only part of the solution. Ending homelessness is a matter of providing people with opportunities for housing, decent wages, health insurance, treatment for health problems, and an education. It is also a matter of understanding the issues surrounding families who become homeless and respecting their needs. The solution for ending homelessness needs to be addressed at individual, family, school, and societal levels.

Individual

Poverty, Unemployment, Low Wages

Since 1970 there has been a substantial increase in the number of persons living in poverty; by 1996 the number of poor Americans exceeded 36.5 million (National Coalition for the Homeless, 1998a). In addition, there has been an increase in the number of Americans living in extreme poverty, with 40% of people who are poor living on incomes that are well below the poverty level. Some factors that contribute to poverty are falling wages and unemployment. The basis of employment in the United States has changed dramatically over the past 20 years from a highly paid manufacturing-based economy to a low-paid service-based structure. The result of this shift is reflected in the growing number of people who are made homeless due to underemployment. Nationally, the United States lost 882,000 manufacturing jobs between 1980 and 1988. Although new jobs were created during this time period, 88% were in retail and restaurant work (HomeBase, 1993).

Unemployment is also considered a leading cause of increased homelessness (National Coalition for the Homeless, 1998c). In June 1993, a 7% unemployment rate in the United States translated to 8.9 million workers out of work (National Coalition for the Homeless, 1993); 1.7 million people were considered as long-term unemployed in June 1993. Once people become homeless, it is increasingly difficult to find a job because, without a home, they do not have a permanent address or telephone number to include on job applications. Also, work alone does not mean that a family will be able to rise out of poverty. Jobs need to provide enough compensation for a family to survive. Overall, 60% of new jobs created since 1979 pay less than $7,000 a year (HomeBase, 1993). By the end of the 1980s, 49% of employed taxpayers (47.2 million people) had annual incomes below $20,000 (Bartlett & Steele, 1992). Under these low-wage conditions, after paying rent, a family is hard pressed to stretch their remaining dollars to pay for food, let alone insurance, telephone, medical expenses, clothing, and school. If there are preschool-age children in the home, it is often not economical for both parents to work because their wages are likely to be devoted entirely to child-care expenses. For a single parent, holding a job may not be an option unless the child attends school or free child care is available. In addition, most low-paying jobs do not include health care benefits. Accordingly, the serious illness of one family member can lead to tremendous financial hardship or homelessness.

Increased Costs of Housing/Lack of Low-Income Housing

Federal standards specify that housing should not exceed 30% of a household's income. However, almost two thirds of renters who are poor pay 50% or more of their income for housing (Dolbeare, 1991). In fact, rent for a one-bedroom apartment is unaffordable for at least one third of renters in all 50 states. More recent reports continue to stress that the lack of affordable housing is a major problem leading to homelessness (National Coalition for the Homeless, 1998c). Although federal, state, and local housing assistance programs are available to the low-income community, only one third of low-income renter households receive such assistance (Dolbeare, 1991). When the task of trying to obtain affordable housing interacts with the low wages that people who are impoverished receive, finding housing becomes almost impossible. The National Coalition for the Homeless (1998c) reported that "in the median state a minimum-wage worker would have to work 83 hours each week to afford a two-bedroom apartment at 30% of his or her income, which is the federal definition of affordable housing" (p. 2).

In 1968, housing legislation was passed to create 6 million units of federally subsidized low-income housing. By the late 1970s, only 2.7 million units had been built (National Coalition for the Homeless, 1990). The prospects of additional low-income housing in the future are dubious. It was estimated that a loss of 1 million units would occur over a 20-year period as a result of subsidy expirations, opt-out provisions in Section 8 contracts, and losses due to physical or financial collapses (HomeBase, 1993). Reports have documented that between 1993 and 1995 alone, 900,000 housing units were lost (National Coalition for the Homeless, 1998c).

Reductions in Federal and State Entitlement Programs

National and state policy changes since the Reagan era of the 1980s have greatly impacted people with low incomes. Federal housing programs designed to create or subsidize low-cost housing were cut as much as 75% under President Reagan's administration (National Coalition for the Homeless, 1990). As many states faced severe fiscal distress, they also made drastic cuts in programs that assist the poor. State programs such as Aid to Families With Dependent Children (AFDC), general assistance benefits, and Supplemental Security Income for the elderly poor and the differently abled were cut more sharply in 1990 and 1991 than in any year since the early 1980s (Center on Budget and Policy Priorities, 1992). In 1992, 44 states cut or froze their AFDC benefits. Similar reductions occurred in 40 states in 1991. These reductions were more than any decreases since 1981. Overall, over a 24-year period (1970–1994), AFDC benefits for families of three fell 47% (National Coalition for the Homeless, 1998c). A new program titled Temporary Assistance to Needy Families (TANF) was designed to replace AFDC; however, TANF typically only provides assistance to people who are 75% below the level of poverty. General assistance benefits were also reduced or eliminated in 22 states from 1991 to 1992. Twenty-six of 27 states either froze or cut Social Security benefits for poor elderly and disabled recipients during 1992 (Center on Budget and Policy Priorities, 1992). These cutbacks have left holes in the safety net. Without these benefits to fall back on, many people were and are destined for economic hardship and homelessness.

Failure of the Health Care System

The health care system in the United States is severely lacking. Over 40 million Americans have no health care insurance, and there is a shortage of substance abuse treatment programs and community facilities for people who are chronically mentally ill (National Coalition for the Homeless, 1993). Poor physical health is often cited as a contributing factor to becoming homeless. According to the U.S. Bureau of the Census, in 1997 approximately 33% of people living in poverty indicated that they had absolutely no health insurance (National Coalition for the Homeless, 1999b). This is particularly troublesome given the high rates of chronic and acute health problems in this population. For example, people who are homeless are more likely than people with housing to have tuberculosis, diabetes, hypertension, upper respiratory infections, frostbite, and addictive disorders (National Coalition for the Homeless, 1999b).

Given these risk factors it is difficult to provide consistent and ongoing treatment for health problems. Furthermore, for homeless people with addictions, the traditional substance abuse treatment methods are inadequate (National Coalition for the Homeless, 1999b). Issues of poverty, physical and mental illness, and remediating skill deficits are rarely included as a part of treatment but are blatant barriers to a homeless person's potential life of stability and self-sufficiency. The programs that do exist are unable to meet the service demands. In one 1991 study of local treatment programs for the homeless, results indicated that 80% of the local programs were forced to turn away homeless clients seeking help. In addition, there exists a lack of supportive, alcohol- and drug-free housing. In the state of Massachusetts, only 185 openings were available in drug-free housing for the 25,000 homeless people who received treatment annually. People with chronic mental illness also have a shortage in appropriate housing, relegating many to the streets. During the 1960s, deinstitutionalization became the treatment policy for serving the mentally ill. As a part of that policy, 2,000 federally supported community mental health centers were planned, but less than 800 were actually established (National Coalition for the Homeless, 1993). Although the increase of homeless people is often attributed to the deinstitutionalization of persons with mental illness during the 1970s, the federal government has established that this movement was not the primary cause of increased homelessness. In fact, the dramatic increases in the homeless population occurred much later than the 1970s. It was the decade of the 1980s, characterized by poverty and a lack of affordable housing, that resulted in growing numbers of people finding themselves on the street.

Families

To prevent homelessness for families, it is important to understand the unique needs of families who are homeless. Such families typically become homeless for the same reasons as other individuals with the exception of mothers who become homeless as a result of fleeing domestic violence. As the needs of single mothers are distinct, they are addressed in the section of this chapter on adaptations for diversity. The best way to prevent homelessness for families is to identify families at risk for homelessness and provide support services. It is more cost-effective to spend money preventing homelessness by preventing evictions (e.g., providing vouchers to landlords for past payments, legal assistance, cash assistance programs), keeping families in shared housing situations, and assisting families who are living in condemned buildings by providing them with transition help than it is to support families in shelters once they become homeless (Lindblom, 1996). More important than cost-effectiveness is the fact that once families are homeless, the road to reestablishing self-sufficiency is much more difficult and the effects of homelessness on children may be traumatizing, not only because of the lack of permanent housing but also because of the other risks that may accompany homelessness (Bassuk & Weinreb, 1994).

Families may experience great hardship when they become homeless, including the fact that, if there is a father present, he is oftentimes separated from the rest of the family. It is also not uncommon for children to be divided and placed in different shelters because of space requirements or possibly placed in foster care because of the families' homelessness (Bassuk & Weinreb, 1994; Shinn & Weitzman, 1996). For many families the way to end homelessness and secure a stable residence includes many important factors. Research on service providers' opinions toward what was important for homeless families to possess, secure, and keep affordable housing included mothers' motivation, financial and food assistance, employment opportunities, housing, coping skills, education, and training (Buckner, Bassuk, & Zima, 1993). What causes concern based on this research is that even though service providers recognized that most of the mothers are working and many suffer from depression, they still cited mothers' motivation and attitude (not the provision of support services) as the most important factor for obtaining and sustaining housing.

A better approach for service agencies working with families who are homeless is to not assume that mothers can "motivate themselves" or that families are not already motivated. In actuality, homeless families spend an inordinate amount of time, energy, and persistence trying to meet the basic needs of their family. On the average, a homeless family spends 37 hours a week trying to obtain food, clothing, shelter, child care, public assistance, and job training (HomeBase, 1993). Therefore, it is important for shelters and programs to support families in obtaining their basic needs. This idea was supported in a review of the literature, where it was stipulated that "residential programs meant for women with young children ought to consider all aspects of families and children" (Buckner et al., 1993, p. 395). To meet such a need, the Stewart B. McKinney Homeless Assistance Act of 1986 included family support centers to assist families in meeting their needs. Unfortunately, when funding was cut by 27% in 1996, the family support program was eliminated. Without such programs it will be more difficult to link families with information about programs that are available to them (National Coalition for the Homeless, 1999d).

School

It is very important that children who are homeless attend school and are provided the same quality education as their peers who are not homeless (Bassuk & Weinreb, 1994). It is also important to ensure that barriers that prevent students who are homeless from attending school are eliminated wherever possible (National Coalition for the Homeless, 1999a). Federal funds are provided to local and state agencies to review and change policies, practices, regulations, and laws if they serve as an obstacle to children who are homeless in terms of enrolling, attending, or succeeding in school. Barriers still exist that affect the enrollment of children who are homeless in school and include fees, transportation, and incomplete immunizations (National Coalition for the Homeless, 1999a). For a growing population of youth who are living on the streets, the fact that they do not have a legal guardian can serve as a barrier to school enrollment or attendance.

For students who have parents who are involved in their education, according to the Stewart B. McKinney Homeless Assistance Act of 1986, parents can keep their children in the same school or re-enroll them in the school district where they are living temporarily. However, some schools may report that parents' requests are not feasible because of the costs of transportation that schools would have to assume (National Coalition for the Homeless, 1999a). It is important that children who are homeless and attend school have teachers, principals, counselors, and communities who are willing to do their part to ensure that children are educationally successful. Part of this includes involving parents and respecting their desires regarding school placements that are in the best interest of their children (National Coalition for the Homeless, 1999a). The role of the school in supporting children and their families is addressed in detail in the intervention section.

Community

It is obvious that the prevention of homelessness will have to include a multifaceted effort that considers both the needs of the family (housing) and the needs of individuals within a family (mental health treatment). Many researchers group the causes of homelessness at the individual level (e.g., mental health problems, substance abuse) and the external/systemic level (e.g., lack of affordable housing, falling wages, cutbacks in federal programs; Buckner et al., 1993; Herron & Zabel, 1995; Tracy & Stoecker, 1993). As there are so many causes of homelessness, it is critical that, in addition to providing temporary or permanent housing, mental health and other supports are also provided on an individual basis for families (Buckner et al., 1993). It is also critical that community workers help remove barriers to ensure that children who are homeless receive adequate health care, including immunizations and wellness checkups. One study removed some of the barriers to adequate health care for families by providing transportation, including taxi vouchers or bus tokens, to health care facilities (Danseco & Holden, 1998). Communities can also help remove barriers by keeping children who are homeless in school and by helping to ensure that, once in school, children are receiving an appropriate education in a comfortable environment. Community involvement in the education of homeless children is covered in the intervention section.

In summary, even with the complexity of ending homelessness, the most frequently cited cause of and solution for ending homelessness is, not surprisingly, safe and affordable low-income housing (Tracy & Stoecker, 1993). Indeed, researchers have concluded that "until this country establishes a comprehensive housing policy, there is little hope that our other efforts on behalf of children can be sustaining" (Bassuk & Weinreb, 1994, p. 56).

INTERVENTION STRATEGIES

Hoping that the government will recognize these tragic problems and change inadequate policies is unrealistic. The sad truth is that thousands of families are destined for homelessness. Thus, individual parents and professionals need to work with families and communities to design and implement effective interventions that will ensure that homeless youth are receiving the education that they need and deserve.

Individuals: Parents

To ensure that their children are receiving an appropriate education, parents need to know their rights within the educational system, including their children's right to receive an appropriate education as stated in the Stewart B. McKinney Homeless Assistance Act of 1986 and recent amendments (Foscarinis, 1996). Parents could contact a local shelter, social service agency, or church for assistance in obtaining the information related to their rights. Parents could also work as an advocate for other homeless families and inform them of their educational rights.

The former suggestions may be idealistic considering the magnitude of the problems that parents who are homeless are typically experiencing. Therefore, schools must take a leadership role in bridging the gap between homeless shelters and the schools. Schools are an important socializing agent, second only to the family (Kauffman, 1993). As such, school personnel need to consider what effect they will or can have on every individual student's future success in life. Counselors, teachers, and administrators may not be able to influence the quality of a student's life outside of school. However, they can influence a student's life once that child is seated in a classroom, which is of major importance as Kauffman (1993) wrote, "In our culture, success or failure at school is tantamount to success or failure as a person" (p. 225). Furthermore, without an education, children who are poor are unlikely to acquire the skills to become adults who do not live in poverty (National Coalition for the Homeless, 1999a).

Individuals: School Counselors

School counselors' knowledge and sensitivity to serving homeless children in the schools make them the best coordinator of resources for these individuals. The complex emotional and educational needs of homeless children match the training and work of school counselors. In addition, it is mandated by the 1994 amendments to the Stewart B. McKinney Act that local and state educational agencies communicate and coordinate services with local and state housing authorities (Foscarinis, 1996). School counselors could coordinate efforts to educate teachers and administrators on the characteristics and educational needs of children who are homeless. One guide for the selection of interventions is to conduct research on child characteristics that may help buffer homeless children under extreme stress from experiencing major trauma from their experience. Counselors can coordinate school and community efforts to address some of these protective factors, including developing strong physical health, high self-esteem, positive social skills, planning abilities, success in school, strong support systems, family closeness, and positive school experiences (Garmezy and Rutter, as cited in Wagner, Schmitz, & Menke, 1996).

To help children who are homeless succeed in school, counselors also need to help teachers modify their classroom to accommodate behavioral and social difficulties by being aware of models that have been effective for children (Gonzalez, 1990). It is important to note that each child will be different and some children who are homeless may not need any additional interventions. However, it is important for teachers to be prepared to use modifications and interventions if and when they are needed. Counselors also need to be knowledgeable of the services (state and local) available for homeless children and help coordinate community efforts to advocate for the educational needs of these children. Counselors could also work with administrators to develop or institute programs such as programs to increase retention of students (HomeBase, 1993). Further, counselors could help arrange for independent study options and other special adaptations for students who are homeless that will possibly increase their opportunities for success in school.

Individuals: Teachers

Teachers should have in-service training, which could be organized by school counselors and administrators, on general information related to homelessness, children's characteristics, suggested classroom modifications, and ways to facilitate positive self-esteem and success in school (Eddowes & Hranitz, 1989; Wagner et al., 1996). Children who are homeless are more likely than their peers to be doing poorly or failing in school (Bassuk & Rosenberg, 1988) and to have repeated a grade in school (Wood et al., 1990). It is, therefore, particularly important that teachers are aware of the diverse needs of these children and can create individualized interventions for them. This individualization requires that teachers be cognizant of what constitutes success in school. For example, two studies have documented what elementary (Hersh & Walker, 1983) and secondary (Kerr & Zigmond, 1986) teachers believe are important student characteristics or skills for school success. The following are critical skills that students need for success in school: follow established classroom rules; listen to teacher instructions; comply with teacher commands; do in-class assignments as directed; produce work of acceptable quality given his or her skill level; have good work habits (e.g., make efficient use of class time, be organized, stay on task); make her or his needs known in an appropriate manner; express anger appropriately; and behave appropriately in nonclassroom settings and respect the property and the rights of others.

If we consider the children from the case example described earlier, it is easy to discern that achieving these competencies may be problematic. Thus, the following suggestions for teacher interventions are focused on academic adaptations for achieving success, behavioral management, emotional well-being and self-esteem, and educating other students on the characteristics and problems faced by children who are homeless. Some of the interventions are relatively easy and require only a small time commitment from teachers. Others, however, may be too demanding for some teachers. Counselors should help teachers decide which of these suggestions are feasible for them. Counselors could then use some of the modifications themselves (e.g., teaching social skills 1 day a week).

Academic Adaptations

Teachers should administer quick, informal assessments to students who are homeless. Teachers also need to develop an assessment and work folder for the student that can be easily transferred to another school. To do adaptations, a teacher needs to analyze informal assessment data and begin instruction in various areas accordingly. Teachers should begin instruction in content areas at a place where the child can succeed. Teachers should also be very systematic and not assume that children have gone through the curriculum with the same consistency as their peers. That is, children who have been chronically homeless may have moved schools or been absent from school during times that certain basic prerequisite skills were taught. It is, therefore, important that teachers never assume that a student will have all of the foundation skills because he or she is at a certain grade level. Criterion-based assessments can help teachers determine skills that have been mastered and where there are deficits in knowledge that need to be remedied.

In addition, there are many small changes a teacher can make in terms of homework assignments. If students have difficulty completing written work, a teacher can adjust the amount of work required by students or change the output requirements (e.g., a child could recite a story into a tape recorder instead of writing it out). Teachers should modify homework assignments for a child who has no place to work after school (Eddowes & Hranitz, 1989). A teacher can also help promote organizational abilities for students who are homeless by having a private area in the classroom that is the students' place to keep their work. Students should be allowed to post their work in a special place to help them take pride in what they have done.

Behavioral Management

Children who are homeless often live in a hectic environment outside of school. Therefore, these children should be provided with a positive, supportive classroom in school. Teachers should always set up conditions in which children can succeed academically and socially and then praise them accordingly. In addition, teachers should give clear, concise rules and be consistent when enforcing them (Eddowes & Hranitz, 1989). Teachers should also take the time to explain to the children why the rules are necessary. Teachers then need to inform shelter officials and parents of all rules and assignments. Special rewards and contingency plans can be arranged for children who need encouragement to complete their homework.

Emotional Well-Being

Counselors should make sure that teachers are sensitive to homeless children's well-being at all times. Teachers should be aware of the physical as well as emotional risk factors associated with homelessness. They should make such accommodations as the following simple modifications within the classroom that can promote social and emotional well-being. For example, to eliminate embarrassing situations for homeless children, teachers should make other arrangements if children usually celebrate their birthdays by bringing treats to school (Indiana Department of Education, 1988). Social growth can be facilitated by establishing a buddy system for homeless children; the teacher could state that the child is new in the school and then praise peers for making the child feel comfortable (Gonzalez, 1990). Other interventions teachers can implement that may help include the following: emphasizing classroom survival skills such as listening, asking for help, and following classroom rules (Indiana Department of Education, 1988; Wagner et al., 1996); using social skills training with the entire class from simple skills (saying please and thank you) to more complex skills (inappropriate comments; Indiana Department of Education, 1988; Wagner et al., 1996); and relieving anxiety through having a supportive, noncompetitive classroom (Wagner et al., 1996). Above all, teachers with students who are homeless should make school a safe place where the children can learn and see hope for their futures.

Educating Other Students

Unfortunately, many adults still have some misconceptions regarding the homeless population. A large sample of the general population reported that they thought more than half of the homeless population were drug addicts, and 37% reported that they thought that being homeless was freeing in that people would not have the same worries that other adults have (Link et al., 1996). It is clear that all students should be educated on factors related to homelessness. When they learn about the factors of homelessness, other students may become more compassionate to children who are in this situation. Hopefully, this process will aid in the successful social integration of students who are homeless into our schools.

HomeBase, a project in San Francisco, has developed an information packet that includes classroom activities a teacher can use to introduce homelessness, to look at its causes and effects, and to explore taking action on homelessness. The lesson plans are detailed and varied for age appropriateness (Grades K–3, 4–8, and 9–12). For example, in the K–3 lesson on introducing students to homelessness, students are asked to discuss the importance of homes. Students then use a picture of a house to answer open-ended questions on, for example, what they like to do in their home, why their home is important to them, and what people do in their homes (HomeBase, 1993). This information packet could be an excellent resource for any school. Teachers could use this packet as a base from which to make their own unique lesson plans in similar formats.

Individuals: Principals

Principals also need to get involved with homeless children's education when the children initially arrive at school, while they are enrolled, and when they leave. Upon arrival to a new school, children should be met and closely monitored by the principal (Gonzalez, 1990). This may help a child feel welcome and important. Once children are attending school, counselors and principals should initiate immediate academic assessments, particularly if the children have been out of school for a long period of time (Indiana Department of Education, 1988). Medical, counseling, and nutritional consultations for these children should be arranged through the school system. Schools could also be opened earlier and closed later to serve these children food and give them adequate shelter (most homeless shelters make families leave before school begins and do not open until late evening; Eddowes & Hranitz, 1989).

When homeless children are leaving school, the principal should give them a transfer card and possibly contact the next school the child will be attending (Indiana Department of Education, 1988). It is important to minimize the stress of moving from school to school (Bassuk & Weinreb, 1994). Making the transition to a new school smooth for children helps to ensure that they feel welcome and that parents do not have to worry about obtaining appropriate documentation.

Empowering Families

There are many ways that families need support from community agencies and schools. Therefore, researchers have suggested that the needs of children and their families be addressed through an interdisciplinary team headed by a case manager (Wagner et al., 1996). As indicated previously, law mandates the coordination of these agencies, and the school counselor or a social worker can coordinate this team.

First, when coordinating services for families, it is important that families and children are provided a safe and secure shelter facility that has a consistent routine and structure (Bassuk & Weinreb, 1994). There are also many programmatic changes that shelters can make to help encourage the restabilization of families. First, shelters can allow families to stay for 24 hours (Bassuk & Weinreb, 1994). This would enable one family member to work while the other family members are in a safe environment. Research has shown that most parents who are homeless have full- or part-time jobs, and eliminating the stress of worrying about their families' safety may help more parents maintain their jobs (Danseco & Holden, 1998).

Providing parent education and job training, encouraging problem-solving skills, and building support networks are other critical aspects of a program designed to help reestablish families into affordable housing and sustain them (Bassuk & Weinreb, 1994; Wagner et al., 1996). The need for these programs has been supported in research where service providers cited preventative solutions for homelessness, including affordable housing, job training, education in daily living skills, rebuilding self-esteem, substance dependency treatment, and providing mental health services (Tracy & Stoecker, 1993).

Other goals of the interdisciplinary team could be to support families in meeting the physical needs of their children and, as indicated in the community outreach section on prevention, to remove barriers to receiving adequate health care. The team should also assist parents and children in managing the emotional distress associated with being homeless and help families achieve renewed hope and build on existing or create new social support systems (Wagner et al., 1996). These interdisciplinary goals are very similar to a framework provided by other professionals for empowering families of children with special needs (Turnbull & Turnbull, 1997). These professionals emphasize the importance of treating each family individually, understanding family factors that will affect empowerment (family members' knowledge, skills, motivation), and the importance of professionals using certain guidelines for collaborating with families. These guidelines, referred to as the eight necessary obligations for professionals to recognize, work on, and attend to in order to achieve reliable alliances with families, include "knowing yourself, knowing families, honoring cultural diversity, affirming family strengths, promoting family choices, envisioning great expectations, communicating positively, and warranting trust and respect" (Turnbull & Turnbull, 1997, p. 47).

Community Outreach: Counselor or Home-School Coordinator

Teachers and principals are busy with the demands of school that already extend their work beyond an 8-hour school day, and asking them to become advocates for homeless children may appear beyond their call of duty. However, there are successful outreach strategies to aid in fulfilling these responsibilities that, again, can be coordinated by a community outreach representative, such as the school counselor or home-school coordinator. Community outreach representatives could begin by setting up networks with local shelters and emergency housing facilities. This would allow the representative to visit shelters on a monthly basis to meet with homeless families and keep them informed about their children's progress.

Communities need to be aware of the prevalence of homelessness and the need for volunteers to help homeless families. Identifying homeless students who need help getting to school is a first step in terms of outreach. Community advocates are needed to help identify those students who are not currently receiving an education. This could be done through posting flyers in hotels/motels and in other places people without homes may be living (e.g., bus depots, drop-in centers, bridges; HomeBase, 1993). Outreach to those students who have not accessed educational services is critical. It is also important to have continuous lines of open communication with local shelters and churches that house students currently in school. Volunteers should be recruited to get homeless parents involved and interested in their children's education. Community help is critical for ensuring that the lines of communication remain open among schools, parents, and shelters (Eddowes & Hranitz, 1989).

Counselors can be key agents in initiating community assistance, which may be provided in various forms. For example, communities could help make sure that these children have transportation to and from school (Gonzalez, 1990). Schools could collaborate with day-care centers to establish free care before and after school and to arrange transportation (Gonzalez, 1990). Another transportation option is for parents who live near a homeless shelter to volunteer to pick up children from the shelter and take them to school. This could also provide good opportunities for social interactions with other children if the children were transported in a group.

Parents in the community could be assigned a child who is homeless for whom they could provide, for example, birthday treats, school supplies, or clothing (Gonzalez,

1990). If the child moves but is in the same area, the family that originally sponsored the homeless child should remain the same, thus providing valuable continuity. People in the community could also be encouraged to interact with homeless youth before or after school or to volunteer time to tutor or assist them once or twice a week (Gonzalez, 1990).

Lastly, state residency laws cannot be used to ban homeless children from schools. The Stewart B. McKinney Homeless Assistance Act was amended in 1994 and specifically states that all homeless children, including preschool children, are entitled to a free and appropriate education (National Coalition for the Homeless, 1999d). However, there are no laws requiring in-depth identification of such children so that they can be educated in the schools based on their unique needs. Thus, it is up to communities and, more specifically, to shelters and social services to work together as a coalition to protect the rights of these children to a free and appropriate education. Furthermore, community programs need to provide support for families in terms of linking them with the information they need regarding services they can access. For example, outreach programs, such as Healthcare for the Homeless, are available to provide health care for the uninsured person (National Coalition for the Homeless, 1999b). Information on community resources for free immunizations can also be provided to families through outreach efforts.

ADAPTATIONS FOR DIVERSITY

Within homeless families there are many additional factors for professionals to consider, including diverse needs of these children, single mothers, and cultural diversity. Understanding the characteristics of these diverse subpopulations will help further outreach efforts and attempts to design more appropriate intervention options.

Risk for Academic and Emotional Problems

Unfortunately, many homeless youth are faced with other needs that require intervention in addition to those already described. Given that impoverished children are at increased risk for academic and emotional problems (Lewis & Doorlag, 1987), it is not surprising that children who are poor and without homes will also be at risk. Research has indeed documented that homeless children experience academic, behavioral, and emotional problems and that these problems manifest themselves at all ages (Bassuk & Rubin, 1987; Whitman, Accardo, Boyert, & Kendagor, 1990; Wood et al., 1990). Specifically, research has found that children who are homeless have significantly more behavioral problems than children who are poor but housed (Wood et al., 1990). A particular characteristic that is important to consider for school-age children who are homeless is their increased risk for depression. Research has found that the vast majority of these children have depressive symptomatology, with up to 66% of these children showing symptoms at a level severe enough to warrant a clinical evaluation (Bassuk & Rubin, 1987; Wagner et al., 1996).

Depression in children has been linked to decreased academic performance (Schmitz, 1993, as cited in Wagner et al., 1996). Some support for a depression–academic performance link within the population of homeless children has been found in one study that reported that 30% of children had repeated a grade in school (Danseco & Holden, 1998). Whether this is because of depression, academic skill deficiencies, or failure due to not completing assignments needs to be addressed so teachers and other professionals can better tailor interventions to students.

It is understandable that children living in extremely stressful conditions will suffer emotionally. Being aware of the high risk for depression in this population can help direct the screening of homeless children at an early age for both behavioral and academic problems and individualized interventions. It is also important to recognize that homeless children may manifest temporary behavior problems that are related to the anxiety that they are experiencing from their situation. For example, a homeless child may display classic symptoms of hyperactivity (e.g., difficulty attending to tasks), but it may be because this student is preoccupied with his or her family's difficulties and more pressing problems. Thus, differential diagnosis of problems that will be ameliorated by providing permanent shelter to a child and assisting his or her family should be differentiated from more permanent problems related to extreme levels of depression, anxiety, and learning difficulties.

It is also important to assess students and determine what is the main cause of school difficulties, because children who are homeless are at risk for academic problems, developmental delays, learning disabilities, and mild mental retardation (Bassuk & Rubin, 1987; Whitman et al., 1990; Wood et al., 1990). Research has documented that 9% of homeless preschoolers failed two sections of the Denver Developmental Screening Test and 15% failed one (Wood et al., 1990). Other research found that 35% of school-age homeless youth scored one standard deviation below the mean on an intelligence test (Whitman et al., 1990). Explanations for high rates of mild disabilities include the following: Homeless children are at high risk for lead exposure (Burg, 1994), which has been linked to higher incidence of learning disabilities (Lerner, Lowenthal, & Lerner, 1995); mothers of homeless children have inadequate prenatal care and are at greater risk for drug use; and homeless children lack postnatal health care, which places such children at risk for mild disabilities.

Single Mothers

Research has shown that a large percentage of homeless families are headed by a single female. It is clear from an extensive review of the literature in this area that single mothers with children are a distinct subgroup within the population of the homeless and have different psychological and demographic characteristics. The needs of mothers with small children are also very different from the needs of other homeless people (Buckner et al., 1993). Research by Burt and Cohen (as cited in Buckner et al., 1993) found that, when compared with single women who were homeless but not caring for children, homeless mothers caring for children were younger, were less educated, and had been homeless for shorter periods of time. Mothers who were homeless were less likely than unaccompanied single women to be alcoholics and less likely to suffer from mental illnesses or substance dependency that required hospitalization. However, mothers were more likely to report greater degrees of psychological distress than single women.

The psychological distress for homeless mothers appears to be much greater than the distress of poverty alone. Thus, even though mothers caring for dependent children appear to have less major substance abuse and mental health problems than other homeless people, research has found that mothers living in shelters have more substance abuse problems than mothers who live in low-income housing (Wood et al., 1990), which may be related to the psychological distress homeless mothers report. The psychological distress related to being a homeless mother may be due to the precipitating events to homelessness and the lack of outside support available once homeless. That is, many women with children are homeless because they are fleeing domestic violence (Dail, 1993). According to the National Coalition for the Homeless

(1998c), studies have found that up to 50% of women are homeless because they are fleeing domestic abuse. Sadly, the stress related to being homeless with children may ultimately drive many mothers back to their abusers as they lack support from immediate family and friends.

The lack of support that homeless mothers report is another major consideration for working with this diverse population. Research has found that 26% of homeless women reported no consistent support (Dail, 1993). Related research documented that 43% of mothers who were homeless reported minimal or limited support from other people (Bassuk & Rubin, 1987). The lack of support is much more profound for mothers who are homeless when compared with mothers who are poor but living in low-income housing. In one study that predominantly included African American mothers, researchers documented that mothers in low-income housing saw or talked to more friends and relatives on a weekly basis than mothers who were homeless (Letiecq, Anderson, & Koblinsky, 1998). Furthermore, mothers who were homeless reported there were fewer people that they could count on in times of need and less family support in the last 6 months than mothers in low-income housing. One study found that 22% of homeless mothers could not name one person who was a support to them, whereas the majority of housed mothers could name three or more sources of support (Bassuk & Rosenberg, 1988). Mothers who were homeless reported twice the rate of domestic abuse as mothers who were housed. Lastly, almost one third of these mothers cited their child as a main source of support, and another study similarly found that 24% of mothers who were homeless reported that their child was their major source of support (Bassuk & Rubin, 1987).

Another factor to consider for mothers who are not receiving much support from relatives and friends is that they may face a major child-care dilemma. They cannot leave their children in shelters or temporary housing situations where they are oftentimes not separated from other homeless populations who are possibly substance abusers, mentally ill, or violent (Dail, 1993). The following quote eloquently describes the plight of single mothers with children:

> It is obvious that these mothers are extraordinarily stressed and are facing almost insurmountable problems of single parenting under the difficult circumstances of poverty, lack of extended family support, lack of affordable child care available to them if they could work, and are without a home. In reality, any smaller combination of these circumstances could render almost anyone immobilized, and it is highly unlikely that any improvement can occur without ongoing social assistance and interpersonal support. (Dail, 1993, p. 59)

Cultural Diversity

In addition to cultural differences related to marital status and gender, ethnicity and geographical location need to be considered when working with children who are homeless. There is extreme disparity between the percentage of minorities in the general population and the percentage of minorities who are homeless. In fact, researchers have documented percentages of homeless minorities as high as 85% in certain areas (Danseco & Holden, 1998). More conservative estimates indicate that at least half of mothers who are the heads of homeless families are ethnic minorities (Dail, 1993). Thus, when implementing preventative and secondary interventions, it is important to recognize that the homeless population is different from the general population. With this knowledge, preventative outreach approaches should target community and state-run services that serve minority groups, particularly African Americans, and support families who are teetering on the brink of homelessness. Once African American mothers become homeless, it is very important to provide linkages with social service organizations and other sources of support. Research has shown that, once homeless, this group may be particularly at risk for alienation or a lack of support from family and friends (Letiecq et al., 1998).

There is also a misconception in the general public that homelessness is an urban problem. Rural homelessness may be increasing at a faster rate than urban homelessness, and the demographic characteristics of the rural homeless appear to be different from the urban homeless (Herron & Zabel, 1995). Specifically, rural people who are homeless are more likely to be Caucasian than their urban counterparts (Herron & Zabel, 1995; National Coalition for the Homeless, 1998a). Other reports have documented that homeless people in rural areas may be more likely to be homeless because of domestic violence (Aron & Fitchen, 1996). Another important consideration for working with homeless populations in rural areas is that it may be more difficult to identify rural families who are homeless because they may have a stronger support network and may be living in temporary residences with family and friends or because they may be living in wooded camp areas or other remote areas (Aron & Fitchen, 1996). Outreach efforts in rural areas should consider research by Vissing (as cited in National Coalition for the Homeless, 1999d) that has found that families represent the majority of people who are homeless in rural areas.

It is very important to remember to honor cultural diversity when working with all families and to always be culturally sensitive without being stereotypic (Turnbull & Turnbull, 1997). To be culturally sensitive, professionals need to understand the impact that culture has on how individuals perceive the world (Watson, 1996). To provide services to families who are homeless, professionals can make some culturally sensitive arrangements, for example, by ensuring that the provider and the family have a language or cultural match, by having flexible hours and accepting walk-ins, and by using clergy or respected members of cultures (e.g., healers) in interventions (Watson, 1996).

PREVENTION: BREAKING THE CYCLE OF HOMELESSNESS

The last area of importance to be addressed in this chapter includes information on a group of homeless youth who are beginning to receive a lot of well-needed research: homeless youth living on the streets without parents. It is prudent to conclude this chapter with a discussion of homeless adolescents as they are at risk for many negative outcomes, and if left without resources and assistance, they will most likely re-create the cycle of homelessness for their children.

The number of adolescents (under 18 years of age) who are considered homeless street youth is from 250,000 to 1,000,000 according to Robertson (as cited in Unger et al., 1998). Homeless adolescents are a difficult population to identify as 85% may not use homeless shelters (Greenblatt & Robertson, 1993). Once adolescents arrive at shelters, it is important that shelters have a place for them to stay. One report documented the efforts of one city to establish more shelters for homeless adolescents and stressed the importance of coordinating services for adolescents once they are in emergency housing facilities (Yates, Pennbridge, Swofford, & Mackenzie, 1991). These services include providing transportation to health care services or providing access for mobile teams to provide services within shelters and supporting youth in acquiring independent living skills.

The need for interventions and outreach programs for this population is clear. Research has consistently found that many street youth report psychological problems, including depression, low self-esteem, and suicidality (Greenblatt & Robertson, 1993; Kennedy, 1991; Unger, Kipke, Simon, Montgomery, & Johnson, 1997). One study reported that the prevalence of psychological disorders in homeless adolescents was three times higher than in adolescents who were not homeless, and rates of drug and alcohol abuse were five to eight times higher in adolescents who were homeless (Greenblatt & Robertson, 1993). It is also important to note that adolescents who are homeless may have had a major family crisis leading to their situation that may make them even more vulnerable to having psychological problems once living on the streets or in temporary housing situations (Greenblatt & Robertson, 1993; Kennedy, 1991).

In addition, homeless youth engage in high-risk behavior, possibly to physically or psychologically survive on the street, including drug use, unprotected sex, and unprotected sex with intravenous drug users (Greenblatt & Robertson, 1993; Kipke, O'Connor, Palmer, & Mackenzie, 1995; Rotheram-Borus, Parra, Cantwell, Gwadz, & Murphy, 1996). The repercussions for such high-risk behaviors include contracting sexually transmitted diseases including AIDS (Sweeney, Lindegren, Buehler, Onorato, & Janssen, 1995). According to their study, 4% of teenagers who were homeless had tested positive for HIV, with rates as high as 17% for teenage boys who engaged in sex with men (Sweeney et al., 1995).

To work effectively with homeless adolescents, professionals must understand the barriers to providing services to this population and the needs of this population. The immediate needs of adolescents include their physical needs for shelter, clothing, and food and their medical needs, which include education on behaviors that will place them at risk for HIV infection (Greenblatt & Robertson, 1993; Shane, 1996). When educators and service providers attempt to reach out to street youth, it is important to understand the day-to-day lifestyle of adolescents who are living on the streets (Lloyd & Kuszelewicz, 1995). In addition, many adolescents may distrust adults and therefore will not access services. So the question is, How can professionals work with this population of homeless youth?

There have been successful programs documented in the literature, including storefront services for youth to drop in and pick up information about AIDS (Lloyd & Kuszelewicz, 1995). Focus groups that are led by adults who have similar demographic characteristics, and who have possibly been homeless themselves, are another intervention option. One study used a comprehensive intervention program that included small-group sessions facilitated by a trained leader with a similar demographic background and included individual counseling when needed. The interventions included information on (a) general knowledge of HIV and AIDS, (b) the importance of using coping skills effectively, and (c) resources available to adolescents (Rotheram-Borus, Koopman, Haignere, & Davies, 1991). Findings from this study were that the number of sessions that adolescents participated in was associated with a reduction in high-risk behavior and an increase in consistent condom use.

Thus, a consistent and sensitive outreach approach that provides ongoing information in many different formats on the risks of certain behaviors may be the best option. Fear tactics should not be used as they may alienate the youth who need the information the most (Lloyd & Kuszelewicz, 1995). It is also important that educators and professionals understand that this group of youth may be very challenging to reach. Youth who are homeless take risks every day just to survive.

Another important factor to consider in outreach efforts for adolescents is that not all street youth or potential street youth are so hard to find. Research has documented that younger adolescents (12–15 years old) have different characteristics when compared with older adolescents (16–23 years old), with the most important difference for school-based services being that two thirds of homeless younger adolescents have attended school in the past month compared with only 27% of homeless older adolescents (Unger et al., 1998). Thus, schools can provide early assistance to the younger population of homeless adolescents to attempt to get them off the streets as quickly as possible. One important preventative measure is to target youth who are having problems in school and provide appropriate services. In fact, many adolescents who are runaway youth report recent school stresses, including failing a grade, being expelled, or having particular problems with teachers (Rotheram-Borus et al., 1996).

Other characteristics of younger adolescents that have been documented include the following: They are more likely to be female, more likely to have been homeless for shorter periods of time, more likely to have stayed in a residence in the past year, and more likely to rely on other people for shelter and money and to cite gang affiliations as their peer group when compared with older adolescents. Both groups of adolescents report that they have engaged in illegal activities at rates of 40%–45% to get money. Overall, younger adolescents may be in a better position for professionals to assist them and help get them off the streets. They rely more on other people and are more at risk for gang affiliations possibly because they have difficulty making it alone on the streets (Unger et al., 1998). Early intervention is very important with young adolescents who are living on the streets because the risk of drug and alcohol abuse and depression is higher for adolescents who have been on the street for more than 1 year (Unger et al., 1997).

Another subgroup of the homeless population that is easy to find are those who are in foster care. About 20% to 25% of youth who are released from foster care when they are 18 go directly to homeless shelters (Azar, 1995; Nazario, 1993). Not only are youth not linked with a place to stay, but also they are not transitioned into the workforce. It is important that adolescents are provided with life skills, including how to select and prepare for future employment. Although emancipation plans are required for foster youth over 16 years of age, many teens in foster care do not receive life skills, and many youth who were in foster care do not have a high school diploma (Nazario, 1993). If adolescents do not achieve a high school education, then their job prospects are even worse. Thus, educators and community organizations need to work with social services to support the provision of life and job skills to adolescents in foster care.

The need to support life and job skills is especially important for adolescent females who are on the street or in foster care. In a report for the Children's Defense Fund, Mihaly (as cited in Shane, 1996) found that many young mothers who became homeless were in foster care or on the street as teenagers. Other researchers in the field also stipulate that many homeless adolescents grew up in homeless families (Campbell & Peck, 1995). Thus, if adolescents are left to the streets and unprepared for self-sufficiency and have their own children on the street, then the task of supporting the individual is compounded and another life becomes subjected to the hard life on the streets.

In an effort to prevent homelessness in youth, professionals must understand life conditions that are also associated with the onset of homelessness. For professionals who work with individuals in community support agencies, it is important to consider such risk factors. In an investigation of characteristics that were associated with the onset of homelessness in a group of homeless and nonhomeless adults, research found that alcohol abuse was associated with and a possible contributing factor for the onset of homelessness (North, Pollio, Smith, & Spitznagel, 1998). Alcohol abuse was the only characteristic that occurred in the group that became homeless earlier than in the group that did not become homeless. Other psychiatric diagnoses of the participants (e.g., major depression, anxiety disorders) were not associated with the onset of homelessness. In the group of participants who became homeless, early onset of homelessness was predicted by the level of family risk variables and maternal psychiatric illness; level of education was a protective characteristic.

Another group of youth who are at risk for becoming homeless are those who have serious psychiatric problems. In an investigation of the level and predictors of homelessness in youth, researchers followed adolescents who had been treated in a residential program for 5 years postdischarge (Embry, Stoep, Evens, Ryan, & Pollock, 2000). A large percentage (33%) had experienced homelessness at least once after being discharged, with half of the youth who experienced homelessness having an episode within a year after being discharged. Characteristics of youth who were more likely to experience homelessness included a history of physical and drug and alcohol abuse. Thus, it is critical to support follow-up outreach and intervention efforts for youth who are included in treatment programs, especially if these risk factors are present on their entry into the program. If youth have a history of physical abuse in their families, then they may be less likely to seek or to receive support from their families on release and may continue a destructive pattern of substance abuse.

Other research has investigated more specific family factors that may contribute to alcohol abuse and homelessness in teenage youth (McMorris, Tyler, Whitbeck, & Hoyt, 2002). The approach used to frame the relationships among family and youth characteristics was a risk amplification model. Youth who were homeless and abused alcohol had a history of parental alcohol abuse, parental rejection, and physical and sexual abuse. The homeless youth who reported higher rates of alcohol use had spent more time on the streets, had spent more time with deviant peers, and had engaged in antisocial or self-deprecating acts to survive on the street. The importance of family characteristics of homeless youth was further underscored in another study on youth who were homeless and sought assistance from an outreach program (Rew, Taylor-Seehafer, Thomas, & Yockey, 2001). Characteristics of this group included that half reported being asked to leave their homes by their parents, and almost half (47%) reported being sexually abused. Other research with a large sample of homeless youth found that 50% of youth reported being sexually abused at some point in their life (Rew, Fouladi, & Yockey, 2002). Research has also investigated characteristics that were associated with resilience in youth (Rew et al., 2001). Youth who were more likely to believe in their own competence and were more accepting of themselves (i.e., high ratings of resilience) were less likely to report feeling lonely and hopeless and to engage in risky behaviors. Thus, outreach and other intervention programs for youth at risk should also include enhancing individuals' perceptions of self-worth and self-efficacy.

SUMMARY

It is clear that children who are homeless suffer physically, psychologically, socially, and academically. It is unconscionable that many of these children are not being served when a portion of this population could be readily identified through homeless shelters and other social agencies. Given a problem of this magnitude, who will advocate appropriate education for homeless children? Homeless families may not be aware of the educational rights of their children or may feel powerless to change the status quo. Thus, not only must there be provisions for homeless children in the classroom, but also their parents must be informed and involved. Counselors, teachers, administrators, and communities need to take the initiative for both passing laws and educating parents about their rights.

Research on homeless children is growing but still scarce despite the large numbers of homeless children in the United States. More information regarding homeless children and the barriers they face within and outside of the school system is needed. Similarly, future research should document successful classroom models that meet the needs of homeless children. Additionally, state departments of education must recognize the prevalence of homelessness and homeless children's needs. Once educational departments have a clear picture of homelessness in their state, they should apply for federal grants to fund their interventions.

The implications of not identifying and intervening with children who are homeless include thousands of children growing up uneducated and bitter. How can children be involved in a society they do not understand or respect? How can they find empowerment and break the cycle of homelessness if no program has identified them and provided opportunities? It is devastating and unconscionable that homeless children even exist in this country. Our society is destined for an even greater tragedy if the educational rights and opportunities for homeless children are not mandated and vigorously upheld. The suggestions presented in this chapter combined with a collaborative effort among counselors, teachers, administrators, and communities are one part of a strategy for ensuring an educational home in every child's future.

REFERENCES

Aron, L. Y., & Fitchen, J. M. (1996). Rural homelessness: A synopsis. In J. Baumchi (Ed.), *Homelessness in America* (pp. 81–85). Phoenix, AZ: Oryx Press.

Azar, B. (1995, November). Foster care has bleak history. *APA Monitor, 26*, 8.

Bartlett, D. L., & Steele, J. B. (1992). *America: What went wrong*. Kansas City, KS: Andrews & Micheal.

Bass, J. L., Brennan, P., Mehta, K. A., & Kodzis, S. (1990). Pediatric problems in a suburban shelter for homeless families. *Pediatrics, 85*, 33–38.

Bassuk, E., & Rosenberg, L. (1988). Why does family homelessness occur? A case-control study. *American Journal of Public Health, 78*, 783–788.

Bassuk, E., & Rubin, L. (1987). Homeless children: A neglected population. *American Journal of Orthopsychiatry, 57*, 279–286.

Bassuk, E. L., & Weinreb, L. (1994). The plight of homeless children. In J. Blacher (Ed.), *When there's no place like home: Options for children living apart from their natural families* (pp. 37–62). Baltimore: Brookes.

Buckner, J. C., Bassuk, E. L., & Zima, B. T. (1993). Mental health issues affecting homeless women: Implications for intervention. *American Journal of Orthopsychiatry, 63*, 385–399.

Burg, M. A. (1994). Health problems of sheltered homeless women and their dependent children. *Health and Social Work, 19*, 125–131.

Butler, O. B. (1989). Early help for kids at risk: Our nation's best investment. *NEA Today, 7*(6), 50–53.

Campbell, C. A., & Peck, M. D. (1995). Issues in HIV/AIDS service delivery to high risk youth. In G. A. Lloyd & M. A. Kuszelewicz (Eds.), *HIV disease: Lesbians, gays, and the social services* (pp. 159–178). New York: Haworth Press.

Center on Budget and Policy Priorities. (1992). *The states and the poor*. Washington, DC: Author.

Cherey, D. (1995). The homeless. In N. L. Herron & D. Zabel (Eds.), *Bridging the gap: Examining polarity in America* (pp. 167–195). Englewood, CO: Libraries Unlimited.

Dail, P. W. (1993). Homelessness in America: Involuntary family migration. *Marriage and Family Review, 19*(1–2), 55–75.

Danseco, E. R., & Holden, E. W. (1998). Are there different types of homeless families? A typology of homeless families based on cluster analysis. *Family Relations, 47*, 159–165.

Dolbeare, C. (1991). *Out of reach: Why every day people can't find affordable housing.* Washington, DC: Low-Income Housing Information Service.

Eddowes, E. A., & Hranitz, J. R. (1989). Educating children of the homeless. *Educational Digest, 55*, 15–17.

Embry, L. E., Stoep, A. V., Evens, C., Ryan, K., & Pollock, A. (2000). Risk factors for homelessness in adolescents released from psychiatric residential treatment. *Journal of the American Academy of Child and Adolescent Psychiatry, 39*, 1293–1299.

Foscarinis, M. (1996). The federal response: The Stewart B. McKinney Homeless Assistance Act. In J. Baumohl (Ed.), *Homelessness in America* (pp. 160–171). Phoenix, AZ: Oryx Press.

Gonzales, M. L. (1990, June). School + home = a program of reeducating homeless students. *Phi Delta Kappan*, 785–787.

Greenblatt, M., & Robertson, M. J. (1993). Lifestyles, adaptive strategies, and sexual behaviors of homeless adolescents. *Hospital and Community Psychiatry, 44*, 1177–1183.

Harrington-Lueker, D. (1989, July). What kind of school board member would help homeless children? *American School Board Journal* 12–19.

Herron, N. L., & Zabel, D. (1995). *Bridging the gap: Examining polarity in America.* Englewood, CO: Libraries Unlimited.

Hersh, R. H., & Walker, H. M. (1983). Great expectations: Making schools effective for all students. *Policy Studies Review, 2*, 147–188.

HomeBase. (1993). *Reaching and teaching children without housing: Improving educational opportunities for homeless children and youth.* San Francisco: Author.

Indiana Department of Education. (1988). *Education of homeless youth.* Indianapolis, IN: Author.

Kauffman, J. M. (1993). *Characteristics of emotional and behavioral disorders of children an youth* (5th ed.). New York: Merrill.

Kennedy, M. R. (1991). Homeless and runaway youth mental health issues: No access to the system. *Journal of Adolescent Health, 12*, 576–579.

Kerr, M. M., & Zigmond, N. (1986). What do high school teachers want? A study of expectations and standards. *Education and Treatment of Children, 9*, 239–249.

Kipke, M. D., O'Connor, S., Palmer, R., & Mackenzie, R. G. (1995). Street youth in Los Angeles: Profile of a group at high risk for human immunodeficiency virus infection. *Archives in Pediatric Adolescent Medicine, 149*, 513–519.

Lerner, J. W., Lowenthal, B., & Lerner, S. R. (1995). *Attention deficit disorders: Assessment and teaching.* Pacific Grove, CA: Brooks/Cole.

Letiecq, B. L., Anderson, E. A., & Koblinsky, S. A. (1998). Social support of homeless and housed mothers: A comparison of temporary and permanent housing arrangements. *Family Relations, 47*, 415–421.

Lewis, R. B., & Doorlag, D. H. (1987). *Teaching special students in the mainstream.* New York: Merrill.

Lindblom, E. N. (1996). Preventing homelessness. In J. Baumohl (Ed.), *Homelessness in America* (pp. 187–200). Phoenix, AZ: Oryx Press.

Link, B. G., Phelan, J. C., Stueve, A., Moore, R. E., Bresnahan, M., & Struening, E. L. (1996). Public attitudes and beliefs about homeless people. In J. Baumohl (Ed.), *Homelessness in America* (pp. 143–148). Phoenix, AZ: Oryx Press.

Lloyd, G. A., & Kuszelewicz, M. A. (Eds.). (1995). *HIV disease: Lesbians, gays, and the social services.* New York: Haworth Press.

Maslow, A. H. (1968). *Toward a psychology of being* (2nd ed.). New York: Van Nostrand.

McMorris, B. J., Tyler, K. A., Whitbeck, L. B., & Hoyt, D. R. (2002). Familial and "on-the-street" risk factors associated with alcohol use among homeless and runaway adolescents. *Journal of Studies on Alcohol, 63*, 34–44.

National Coalition for the Homeless. (1990). *Homelessness in America: A summary.* Washington, DC: Author.

National Coalition for the Homeless. (1993). *The problems of homelessness: Causes and trends.* Washington, DC: Author.

National Coalition for the Homeless. (1994a). *Education of homeless children and youth.* Washington, DC: Author.

National Coalition for the Homeless. (1994b). *How many people are homeless in the U.S. and recent increases in homelessness.* Washington, DC: Author.

National Coalition for the Homeless. (1998a, May). *How many people experience homelessness?* (NCH Fact Sheet #2). Retrieved from http://nch.ari.net/numbers.html

National Coalition for the Homeless. (1998b, May). *Who is homeless?* (NCH Fact Sheet #3). Retrieved from http://nch.ari.net/who.html

National Coalition for the Homeless. (1998c, May). *Why are people homeless?* (NCH Fact Sheet #1). Retrieved from http://nch.ari.net/causes.html

National Coalition for the Homeless. (1999a). *Education of homeless children and youth* (NCH Fact Sheet #10). Retrieved from http://nch.ari.net/edchild.html

National Coalition for the Homeless. (1999b). *Health care and homelessness* (NCH Fact Sheet #8). Retrieved from http://nch.ari.net/health.html

National Coalition for the Homeless. (1999c). *How many people experience homelessness?* (NCH Fact Sheet #2). Retrieved from http://nch.ari.net/numbers.html

National Coalition for the Homeless. (1999d). *The McKinney Act* (NCH Fact Sheet #18). Retrieved from http://nch.ari.net/mckinneyfacts.html

National Coalition for the Homeless. (1999e). *Who is homeless?* (NCH Fact Sheet #3). Retrieved from http://nch.ari.net/who.html

Nazario, S. (1993, December 12). Sex, drugs, and no place to go. *Los Angeles Times*, p. A1.

North, C. S., Pollio, D. E., Smith, E. M., & Spitznagel, E. L. (1998). Correlates and early onset and chronicity of homelessness in a large urban homeless population. *Journal of Nervous and Mental Disorders, 186*, 393–400.

Reeves, M. S. (1988, April). Self-interest and the common weal: Focusing on the bottom half. *Education Week*, 14–21.

Rew, L., Fouladi, R. T., & Yockey, R. D. (2002). Sexual health practices of homeless youth. *Journal of Nursing Scholarship, 34*, 139–145.

Rew, L., Taylor-Seehafer, M., Thomas, N. Y., & Yockey, R. D. (2001). Correlates of resilience in homeless adolescents. *Journal of Nursing Scholarship, 33*, 33–40.

Rotheram-Borus, M. J., Koopman, C., Haignere, C., & Davies, M. (1991). Reducing HIV sexual risk behaviors among runaway adolescents. *Journal of the American Medical Association, 266*, 1237–1241.

Rotheram-Borus, M. J., Parra, M., Cantwell, C., Gwadz, M., & Murphy, D. A. (1996). Runaway and homeless youths. In R. J. DiClemente, W. B. Hansen, & L. E. Ponton (Eds.), *Handbook of adolescent health risk behavior* (pp. 369–391). New York: Plenum Press.

Shane, P. G. (1996). *What about America's homeless children?* Thousand Oaks, CA: Sage.

Shinn, M., & Weitzman, B. C. (1996). Homeless families are different. In J. Baumohl (Ed.), *Homeless in America* (pp. 109–122). Phoenix, AZ: Oryx Press.

Stewart B. McKinney Homeless Assistance Act of 1986, Pub. L. No. 100-77 & 11301 *et seq.*, 101 Stat. 482 (1987).

Sweeney, P., Lindegren, M. L., Buehler, J. W., Onorato, I. M., & Janssen, R. S. (1995). Teenagers at risk of human immunodeficiency virus Type 1 infection. *Archives in Pediatric Adolescent Medicine, 149*, 521–528.

Tracy, E., & Stoecker, R. (1993). Homelessness: The service providers' perspective on blaming the victim. *Journal of Sociology and Social Welfare, 20*(3), 43–59.

Turnbull, A. P., & Turnbull, H. R. (1997). *Families; professionals and exceptionality: A special partnership* (3rd ed.). Upper Saddle River, NJ: Merrill.

Unger, J. B., Kipke, M. D., Simon, T. R., Montgomery, S. B., & Johnson, C. J. (1997). Homeless youths and young adults in Los Angeles: Prevalence of mental health problems and the relationship between mental health problems and substance abuse disorders. *American Journal of Community Psychology, 25*, 371–394.

Unger, J. B., Simon, T. R., Newman, T. L., Montgomery, S. B., Kipke, M. D., & Albornoz, M. (1998). Early adolescent street youth: An overlooked population with unique problems and service needs. *Journal of Early Adolescence, 18,* 325–348.

Wagner, J., Schmitz, C. L., & Menke, E. (1996). Homelessness and depression in children: Implications for intervention. In *The Hatherieigh guide to child and adolescent therapy* (pp. 79–102). New York: Hatherleigh Press.

Watson, V. (1996). Responses by the states to homelessness. In J. Baumohl (Ed.), *Homelessness in America* (pp. 172–178). Phoenix, AZ: Oryx Press.

Whitman, B. Y., Accardo, P., Boyert, M., & Kendagor, R. (1990). Homelessness and cognitive performance in children: A possible link. *Social Work, 35,* 516–519.

Wood, D. L., Valdez, R. B., Hayashi, T., & Shen, A. (1990). Health of homeless children and housed, poor children. *Pediatrics, 86,* 858–866.

Yates, G. L., Pennbridge, J., Swofford, A., & Mackenzie, R. G. (1991). The Los Angeles system of care for runaway/homeless youth. *Journal of Adolescent Health, 12,* 555–560.

17 | "This Isn't the Place for Me": School Dropout

*Mary A. Hermann**

The incidence of school dropout is reaching epidemic proportions. As of October 2000, 3.8 million young people between the ages of 16 and 24 had dropped out of school (National Center for Education Statistics [NCES], 2002). This figure represents almost 11% of that age group. The incidence of school dropout seems to be worsening. In 2002, the NCES reported that 5% of students enrolled in high school in October 1999 had dropped out of school by October 2000.

Society suffers when students do not finish high school. Dropping out of school has been associated with substance abuse and other delinquent behaviors (Jimerson, 1999; Swaim, Beauvais, Chavez, & Oetting, 1997). Students who drop out of school are more likely to spend time in prison, earn low wages, and depend on public assistance (Dynarski & Gleason, 2002). Mortenson (1997) explained that since 1973, "the labor market has been brutally redistributing income among workers according to their educational attainment". Mortenson found a strong positive correlation between formal education and high income. People with the least formal education have experienced substantial declines in income and standard of living. Mortenson stated that this redistribution "clearly signals the end of the high wage–low skill labor economy." Thus, dropouts negatively impact the economy because they have limited resources and generally are not well-trained workers or lucrative consumers (Velez & Saenz, 2001).

The underlying causes of school dropout are complex and multidimensional (Christenson, Sinclair, Lehr, & Godber, 2001). Although the label *dropout* has been applied to large numbers of students who do not finish school, such a label fails to adequately represent the fact that youth who drop out of school are a diverse group who leave school for many different reasons. Bickel, Bond, and LeMahieu (1988) noted that the term *dropout* is potentially misleading because it implies that school dropout is an event instead of a process and that the student is the sole decision maker in the process. In actuality, some students do not drop out but merely fade out after a period of feeling alienated from school. Other students can be subtly or not so subtly pushed out of school by school personnel who do not want to deal with them any longer. Still other students are pulled out by more important demands on their time such as parenting or having to work. Yet, regardless of the reasons for school dropout, school personnel and counselors who work with youth cannot afford to passively watch school attrition increase.

*The author wishes to acknowledge the contribution of James W. Kushman, Conrad Sieber, and Paula Heariold-Kinney, authors of this chapter in the previous edition of this book.

PROBLEM DEFINITION

There is not one single cause of student dropout. Numerous individual, family, and structural factors contribute to students' decisions to leave school (Newcomb et al., 2002; Velez & Saenz, 2001; Wayman, 2002b). Rumberger (1993) defined individual factors as factors that refer to the individual student's attributes, attitudes, and behaviors and family factors as the social, human, and cultural resources and experiences provided by the family. Structural factors range from school practices to economic and prevalent social conditions. Rumberger further explained that the individual, family, and structural factors that contribute to school dropout are interrelated.

Ethnicity

Students' ethnic background has been correlated with risk for dropping out of school. The NCES (2002) reported that the dropout rates for African American youth were higher than for Caucasian youth. Although the difference between these two groups decreased in the 1970s and 1980s, this difference remained relatively constant in the 1990s. In 2000, the dropout rate for Asian/Pacific Islanders was 3.8%, the rate for Hispanics was 27.8%, the rate for African Americans was 13.1%, and the rate for Caucasians was 6.9%. In the same year, 44.2% of Hispanic youth who were born outside of the United States dropped out of school. Although the dropout rate was lower for Hispanic youth born in the United States, these youth were still more likely to drop out than any other ethnic group. These findings are consistent with the findings of McMillen, Kaufman, Hausken, and Bradby (1993), who reported that among Hispanics who speak English well the dropout rate was 17%, compared with a dropout rate of 83% for Hispanics who speak no English at all. Rumberger (1993) hypothesized that such statistics may be due to the understandably high correlation between language proficiency and both academic achievement and grade retention, variables that have been directly correlated with higher dropout rates. Additionally, Velez and Saenz (2001) explained that Latino families move frequently because of economic opportunities, and thus Latino students often have to continually adapt to new school environments. This weakens the connection between the students and the school and teachers and contributes to the risk of school dropout.

In their qualitative study on Chicano/Latino students who dropped out of school, Avilés, Guerrero, Howarth, and Thomas (1999) reported the participants expressed that they believed school staff had low expectations of them and exhibited negative attitudes toward them. Furthermore, these students believed that they were disciplined more harshly than other students. Participants stated they were placed in English as a Second Language classes seemingly on the basis of appearance or name, even if they were fluent in English. Being placed in special programs was a source of embarrassment for these participants. Participants also explained they were not encouraged and were often discouraged from participating in extracurricular activities. Themes that ran through the participants' perceptions of the school environment were marginalization, alienation, and discrimination.

Wayman (2002a) also found that some students perceived differential treatment by teachers based on ethnic background. He noted school dropouts held this perception more than other students. Wayman explained that whether or not such bias existed, the perceptions of teacher bias based on ethnicity were real for the students who held these perceptions. Moreover, even if the bias was not directed at them, students' belief that these perceptions existed contributed to student disengagement and alienation, both of which hinder academic achievement.

Socioeconomic Status

Socioeconomic status has been correlated with school dropout (Alexander, Entwisle, & Kabbani, 2001; Rumberger, 1993; Vitaro, Larocque, Janosz, & Tremblay, 2001). Alexander et al. found that socioeconomic status had the strongest correlation to school dropout. Furthermore, Rumberger completed an extensive review of the literature and noted that when socioeconomic status was held constant, much of the difference in dropout rates among various racial/ethnic groups disappeared or was greatly diminished.

Educational researchers have concluded that urban youth from low-income families are at high risk for dropping out (Alexander et al., 2001; Rumberger, 1993). The NCES (2002) reported that in 2000, teenagers living in families with incomes in the lowest 20% of reported family incomes were six times as likely as teenagers living in families in the highest 20% to drop out of school. Velez and Saenz (2001) explained that socioeconomic status is related to quality of life and schools in the neighborhood. Students living in neighborhoods in poor areas may have to deal with inadequate housing and high crime rates. Schools in impoverished neighborhoods often have fewer resources and larger class sizes. Velez and Saenz found that in schools with a high student-to-teacher ratio, teachers cannot provide the individualized attention necessary to facilitate learning for all students.

School

Baker et al. (2001) found that schools contribute to student failure and to student dropout by negatively affecting student motivation and engagement in school. Students who are engaged in school are less likely to drop out (Alexander et al., 2001). Dropping out of school often results from a gradual disengagement from school activities, a process that begins in childhood (Garnier, Stein, & Jacobs, 1997). Alexander et al. noted that even at-risk youth start school with enthusiasm, optimism, and an eagerness to learn. Yet, students who experience failure in the school environment gradually disengage from the learning process.

Alexander et al. (2001) found that for most dropouts, school was not a comfortable environment, and thus the students' attachment to school was weak. Dropouts often find life outside of school more enjoyable than life in school. Consequently, when students have conflicting demands on their time from work opportunities or other responsibilities, school becomes less important.

Vitaro et al. (2001) reported that poor academic performance was predictive of dropping out. Furthermore, Newcomb et al. (2002) found that academic competence had the strongest correlation to completing high school. Students with higher grades are less likely to drop out of school (Keith & Schartzer, 1995; Velez & Saenz, 2001). Chinien and Boutin (2001–2002) concluded that some students drop out of school because of the difficulties they encounter with schoolwork. They noted that these learning difficulties are exacerbated by a strong sense of rejection. The consequences of these feelings of rejection by the school environment include students eventually disengaging from the learning process.

Jimerson, Anderson, and Whipple (2002) reviewed the literature and found that retaining students in a grade is one of the strongest predictors of school dropout. In their study of Baltimore school children, Alexander et al. (2001) found that 80% of students who repeated more than one grade dropped out of school, and 94% of students who repeated a grade in both elementary and middle school eventually dropped out. Students retained in early elementary school were at a much higher risk of dropping out than students who were promoted, and retention in any grade prior to high school increased the risk of student dropout. Alexander et al. also reported that even when socioeconomic status was held constant, significant differences were found based on whether the student was retained. These researchers reported that 75% of students from higher socioeconomic backgrounds dropped out when they were retained in middle school as opposed to 11% of students from higher socioeconomic backgrounds who were not retained.

Jimerson (1999) found that retained students were 20% to 25% more likely to drop out of school than low-achieving students who were socially promoted. He noted that any short-term benefits related to retention soon dissipated, and the overall effect of this remediation strategy was school withdrawal. Jimerson et al. (2002) clarified that retention is not the single event leading to dropout. However, children who have been exposed to risk factors such as low socioeconomic status and low parental level of education are put at greater risk for retention, and after a student is retained, the student is at much higher risk for school dropout. Thus, Jimerson concluded that student retention is not effective as a remediation strategy and strongly suggested that other, more effective remedial strategies be utilized.

Alexander et al. (2001) hypothesized that being retained in the same grade may promote difficulties in terms of social relationships. Gleason and Dynarski (2002) noted that students who have been retained are often 2 or more years older than classmates. Being older than one's classmates is particularly detrimental in middle school when self-consciousness is heightened and peer acceptance is so important. Resulting feelings of alienation from peers increase risk of school dropout.

The transition to high school is challenging for many students and can result in feelings of alienation and disengagement from school. High schools are usually larger, more impersonal, and more academically challenging than middle schools. Even students who have experienced success in school can have difficulties with this transition. The transition for at-risk students, particularly students who have experienced failure in school, can be even more difficult.

Vitaro et al. (2001) found that disruptive behavior, even in early grades, was predictive of dropping out. Students who followed school rules were less likely to drop out (Alexander et al., 2001). Velez and Saenz (2001) posited that not accepting societal goals and the resulting disruptive behaviors could be associated with an attempt to restore self-esteem that had been damaged by rejection from teachers and the educational system as a whole.

School factors associated with high dropout rates also include high absenteeism (Avilés et al., 1999; Gleason & Dynarski, 2002; Scanlon & Mellard, 2002). Avilés et al. conducted a qualitative study in which they interviewed 33 female and 39 male Chicanos/Latinos who had dropped out of high school in the last 5 years. Participants' reasons for dropping out included receiving failing grades as a consequence of missing numerous days of school. Not completing makeup work and poor communication between the school and home were also cited by the participants. The participants explained that the reasons for frequent absences from school included work schedules and lack of interest in schoolwork. Participants indicated that if the school had been more flexible in terms of accommodating their work schedules, they would have stayed in school. Participants also stated that they were often bewildered by regulations related to attendance and found that school personnel lacked sensitivity to their needs. Furthermore, the participants reported that there was a discrepancy in what they and their parents believed to be legitimate absences and what the school recorded as excused absences.

Family

Family variables related to school dropout include parental support for education and stress levels in the family system. Alexander et al. (2001) found that almost 56% of students with low levels of emotional support from parents dropped out of school compared with 27% of students with high levels of parental support. Alexander et al. also found that the risk of dropout is increased by high levels of stress in the family.

Multicultural variables have been linked to family variables in the study of school dropout. Keith and Schartzer (1995) examined family–school involvement factors of Mexican American students in the 8th grade for their predictive value in determining dropouts at the 10th-grade level. In terms of family involvement, Mexican American students whose parents discussed school activities with their children, expressed high aspirations for children, and were proficient in English were less likely to drop out.

Parenting styles also seem to influence dropout behaviors. Rumberger, Ghatak, Poulos, and Ritter (1990) found that an engaged, authoritative, and participatory parenting style seemed to be related to high school graduation. Parents of students who completed high school were more likely to provide support for their child's academic activities. These parents used encouragement, praise, and other positive responses to school and academic work completed by their children. Students were more likely to drop out of school if they had overly permissive parents, especially if the parents were not involved in their child's education and did not provide guidance and support for their child's decision making. Rumberger et al. found that parenting that was too permissive also seemed to lead to increased influence by the student's peer group. If students were involved with other students at risk for dropout, this effect could be particularly detrimental.

Peers

Mazza and Eggert (2001) found that adolescents at risk for school dropout were likely to engage in more social activities and less likely to do homework. Vitaro et al. (2001) noted that both association with deviant peers and rejection from conventional peers have been linked to dropping out of school. Lack of friendships with conventional peers can increase the possibility of disengagement from school. Thus, association with peers who do not value education has been understandably linked to school dropout.

Stress

Stress has been correlated with student dropout. Hess and Copeland (2001) found that ninth graders who eventually dropped out reported significantly more severe stress-related life events. Similarly, Velez and Saenz (2001) found that students who take on adult roles such as parenthood experience increased stress and are more likely to drop out of school.

CASE STUDY

Emelio is a 15-year-old freshman in an inner-city high school in Houston, Texas. He entered high school with reading and math achievement scores around a 7th-grade level. He reports that teachers treat him differently from other students. As soon as he does the slightest thing wrong, he says his teachers are "all over" him. He states that his teachers don't care about him. He also says that a lot of times he tunes out in class because he doesn't understand the lectures anyway.

Emelio's school is in an impoverished neighborhood. It has a disproportionate share of low-achieving students, insufficient resources, and overcrowded classrooms.

The teachers and administrators are predominantly Caucasian, and the students are predominantly Hispanic.

Emelio lives in a two-bedroom apartment in a high-crime neighborhood with his mother and two younger brothers. His mother has been divorced for 8 years. She works two part-time, minimum-wage jobs. She wants a better job, but she is so busy with her current jobs and taking care of three children, she has little time to engage in a job search. She also feels unqualified for many jobs because she dropped out of school when she was 16 and she doesn't believe she has any marketable skills.

Emelio's mother tries to help her sons with their homework. She wants them to complete high school so that they can "make something of their lives." She even missed work once so she could attend a PTA meeting at the high school. However, she was uncomfortable at the meeting because she felt that the teachers treated her as if she was insignificant.

Emelio is the oldest son and wants to help his mom. He was 7 years old when his dad walked out, and since then he has described himself as "the man of the house." He helps around the house and takes care of his brothers when his mom goes to her night job. His father has not contacted anyone in the family. Emelio doesn't mind not having any contact with his father because his dad drank a lot and had a "really bad temper." Emelio's father provides no financial assistance to the family. Emelio plans to get a job soon so he can help out financially.

APPROACHES TO PREVENTION

Individual

Consideration of students' attributes, attitudes, and behaviors is critical in designing prevention activities to reduce school dropout. Students' attributes include ethnicity, socioeconomic status, and IQ. Relevant attitudes are motivation and optimism. Behaviors linked to school dropout include students' classroom behaviors.

Although some student attributes such as ethnicity and socioeconomic status cannot be altered, the impact of these variables can be diminished. Counselors can be at the forefront of prevention efforts aimed at reducing the impact of these variables. For example, one risk factor associated with ethnicity is language proficiency. If students are not proficient in English, counselors can help link students with appropriate services in the school setting and in the community. Another risk factor associated with ethnicity is alienation. By establishing caring relationships with students and fostering the creation of a school environment that promotes inclusion for all ethnic groups, counselors also help minimize the potential negative impact of students' ethnicity.

Attitudes such as enthusiasm, optimism, and eagerness to learn are associated with academic success. All students need to be provided with an opportunity to learn. Yet, simply having students spend more time on learning activities will not suffice if students are not motivated to learn. If students are to become motivated, they need to believe that they can succeed in school and perceive some present and future value for their hard work.

Students' classroom behaviors have also been associated with academic success. School counselors have a unique role in the promotion of appropriate classroom behaviors. In their position statement, *The Professional School Counselor and Discipline,* the American School Counselor Association (ASCA, 2001) takes the position that the school counselor acts as a resource person with expertise in developing discipline plans for prevention and intervention purposes. Yet, ASCA clarifies that the role of the school counselor is not that of a disciplinarian, and thus the school counselor's role is not to give out punishment. The school counselor's role is to help create behavior changes by participating in the establishment and maintenance of school policies that encourage appropriate classroom behavior. According to ASCA, the school counselor is also expected to remain cognizant of students' diverse cultural, developmental, and emotional needs as the counselor acts as a liaison and a mediator in creating effective learning environments.

ASCA states that professional school counselors make indispensable contributions to helping prevent school dropout (ASCA [2001] position statement, *The Professional School Counselor and Dropout Prevention/Students-at-Risk*). ASCA recognizes that the underlying reasons for students dropping out of school include personal and social problems such as low self-esteem, family problems, neglect, and abuse. School counselors can help students with these issues. School counselors can facilitate students' belief in their abilities through individual and group counseling. School counselors can help students learn to manage stress effectively. School counselors can also assist students in finding sources of support in school personnel, family, peers, and the community. Furthermore, school counselors can work closely with students to help them understand the lifelong, devastating effects of dropping out of school (ASCA [2001] position statement, *The Professional School Counselor and Dropout Prevention/ Students-at-Risk*).

Counselors' efforts can help lessen the likelihood that students, like the student in our case study, will drop out of school. Emelio seems to have low self-esteem. He struggles academically, gets into trouble with his teachers, and does not believe school personnel care about him. Experiencing a caring relationship with a school counselor and participating in guidance programming that includes self-esteem building activities may help Emelio feel better about himself and the school experience. Discipline interventions with a school counselor's input in developing a discipline plan that considers Emelio's cultural, developmental, and emotional needs may be beneficial to Emelio as well. A counselor could help locate the additional support Emelio needs to overcome learning challenges he is experiencing. Finally, activities highlighting the value of schoolwork may increase Emelio's motivation to perform well in school.

Family

Rumberger (1995) found that academic support from parents through activities like attending PTA meetings and volunteering at school events was strongly associated with students completing school. He also concluded that students were more likely to stay in school if parents talked with their children about school, helped them with their homework, and held high academic expectations. However, even when dealing with supportive families, school personnel need to reach out to parents and involve them in school activities. Children benefit when parents feel that the school is a partner in educating their children.

Lopez, Ehly, and Garcia-Vazquez (2002) explained that programs for parents can provide parents with support and ideas to assist them in advocating for their children in the school setting. Counselors can be at the forefront of the effort to provide these programs as well as workshops on parenting styles that are associated with children's school success. Counselors can also encourage parents to communicate with teachers, administrators, and other school personnel. Furthermore, counselors can help link families experiencing stress with community resources.

When parents do attend school events, it is imperative that they do not feel marginalized. In our case study, Emelio's mother missed work so that she could attend a PTA meeting. Clearly, she is a mother who is concerned about her son's experience in school. Yet, she felt uncomfortable in the school setting and will probably not return. Counselors can help parents like Emelio's mother feel more empowered in the school environment and become active participants in the school community.

School

Schools are partially responsible for the failure of their students (Baker et al., 2001). In a commentary on the current accountability trend in schools, Alexander et al. (2001) stated that if school policies do not address the learning needs of all children, these policies can lead to students dropping out of school. Of particular concern is the policy of student retention. Marcus and Sanders-Reio (2001) explained that school personnel need to be made aware of the high correlation between retention and school dropout.

To prevent school dropout, schools need to engage all students in the learning process and foster the enthusiasm that students have when they first start school. Teachers should include meaningful activities as well as activities that challenge students academically in curricula. School personnel also need to promote attendance and make special efforts to bridge detrimental cultural, language, and procedural barriers related to attendance.

The statistics on minority students' high dropout rates are indicative of a school system that has been slow to respond to cultural diversity. The failure of schools to respond to cultural diversity can also be viewed as a failure of schools to capitalize on the dynamic resources and opportunities for learning created by cultural pluralism. Our society is becoming increasingly culturally diverse. Wayman (2002a) explained that schools can respond to the reality of a pluralistic society by developing curricula that are more inclusive of minorities and promote cultural sensitivity within the school climate. Not only will these types of interventions help minority students, but they can benefit all students by promoting tolerance for differences.

Counselors working with students can help create school environments that promote inclusion for all cultural groups. For example, counselors can play a role in raising the consciousness of teachers and administrators about cultural dynamics, and they can be proactive in helping schools create practices, procedures, and organizational structures that promote inclusion of all students. Furthermore, it is vital that school staff be trained in working with students who are ethnically and linguistically diverse (Lopez et al., 2002; Wayman, 2002a). Counselors can be at the forefront of this effort. Counselors can also help ensure that students with language barriers are receiving the services they need to succeed academically.

Counselors can assist students in building positive peer relationships. Lopez et al. (2002) postulated that social support is associated with academic achievement and prevention of dropout. Students who drop out often have a weak peer network or a peer network that includes peers who are disengaged from school and thus also at high risk for dropout (Marcus & Sanders-Reio, 2001). Marcus and Sanders-Reio suggested that the likelihood of school completion could be increased by fostering students' healthy attachment to other students. These authors advised school personnel to promote positive peer relationships and intervene against peer abuse and rejection, particularly in elementary and middle school. Counselors can also enhance social support for minority students by implementing multicultural support groups (Lopez et al., 2002). These groups could provide opportunities for students to meet with other students and to discuss issues related to peers, the school, and the community.

Fostering the development of a sense of community at school includes advocating for smaller schools and structuring school activities to include ample opportunity for students to bond with adults and peers at school (Marcus & Sanders-Reio, 2001). Schools with low teacher/student ratios retain students until graduation more than schools with higher ratios (Baker et al., 2001). Large teacher/student ratios limit the ability of teachers to monitor student outcomes carefully and minimize the opportunity for the development of supportive teacher/student relationships. Counselors need to remain cognizant of the benefits of low teacher/student ratios and promote small class sizes.

Moving to larger, unfamiliar school environments can disrupt relationships and social support (Baker et al., 2001). Middle school students who move to high school experience increased academic demands as well as the developmental transitions associated with adolescence. Counselors can help improve children's and parents' adjustment to new schools by interventions such as facilitating the building of positive relationships and fostering mutual respect among parents, teachers, and students.

Newcomb et al. (2002) found that deviant behavior was associated with high school dropout. Interestingly, these authors found that tobacco use was the deviant behavior most highly correlated to school failure. The correlation between school failure and tobacco use was even higher than the correlation between school failure and students' use of alcohol or other drugs. Thus, although developmental guidance programming aimed at preventing alcohol and drug use is beneficial to students, Newcomb et al. also advised early efforts in terms of the prevention of tobacco use.

ASCA takes the position that school counselors are to provide comprehensive developmental counseling programs for all students, including students at risk for dropping out of school (ASCA [2001] position statement, *The Professional School Counselor and Dropout Prevention/Students-at-Risk*). Thus, programming designed to help keep students in school should be part of developmental guidance curricula. School counselors are also expected to work with other professionals such as social workers, psychologists, and other school personnel to help meet the needs of all students. Furthermore, ASCA reiterates that school counselors need to work with parents to help foster each child's development.

In the case study, Emelio struggles academically. He is a year older than most other ninth-grade students, so he was probably retained in at least one grade. He functions at about a seventh-grade level and has difficulty understanding what is going on in classes. Based on these factors, his low socioeconomic status, and his Hispanic background, he may be considered at risk for dropping out of school. Prevention efforts to minimize his risk for dropout could have included counselors working to make sure that his academic needs were addressed more adequately and fostering positive relationships between Emelio and his teachers and Emelio and his peers. A counselor could have helped Emelio deal with any adjustment issues he had when he moved into high school. A school environment that embraced diversity and promoted multicultural activities could have been beneficial as well.

Community

In the community, counselors can be advocates for schools and students. Counselors can promote the value of providing all students with a quality education. Counselors can also assist schools in obtaining human and financial resources from the community. For example, counselors can engage in collaborative relationships with community social service agencies so that appropriate referrals can be provided to students.

Counselors can encourage school and community collaboration by providing students access to community members. This task can be accomplished through activities like inviting professionals from the community to the school to talk to students about political issues or career opportunities in the community. Furthermore, counselors can help create job shadowing and other student volunteer programs.

Activities involving community members can help students see the value of staying in school. Emelio would probably benefit from school activities featuring community members. Hearing members of the community discuss job opportunities and the importance of staying in school may be helpful to Emelio, especially if some of the guest speakers were Hispanic. Having opportunities such as job shadowing could also help Emelio see a purpose for staying in school.

INTERVENTION STRATEGIES

Wang, Haertel, and Walberg (1994) studied resilience in terms of academic achievement and defined *educational resilience* as "the heightened likelihood of educational success despite personal vulnerabilities and adversities brought about by environmental conditions and experiences" (p. 46). Educational researchers examining resilience in at-risk student populations have identified factors that moderate the effects of students' individual and environmental vulnerabilities (Wayman, 2002b). Wayman described personal resilient factors as student attributes and attitudes that buffer the negative effects of a student's adverse situation. These attributes include positive self-concept and motivation. Developing a positive self-concept and optimistic attitude is particularly critical for minority students (Wayman, 2002b).

Wang, Haertel, and Walberg (1997) explained that educational resilience is the result of continual interaction between students and their environment. Wayman (2002b) described environmental factors that contribute to resilience as external influences that protect against negative influences facing at-risk youth. Wayman identified adult support as a factor that enables students to develop trust and learn from their challenges. Educational resilience has also been associated with both family commitment to education and peer support (Gonzalez & Padilla, 1997; Horn & Chen, 1998).

Although Wayman's (2002a) work on educational resilience looked primarily at degree attainment after students drop out of school, his findings are relevant to intervention efforts with students at risk for dropping out of school. For example, protective factors identified in the educational resilience framework included students' self-confidence and positive attitudes about finishing school. Wayman argued that these factors are easier to change than socioeconomic status and students' academic capabilities, prevalent factors identified in previous research on school dropout. Furthermore, Wayman found that some of the negative effects from risk factors such as socioeconomic status became insignificant after the introduction of educational resilience factors. Thus, Wayman suggested that school personnel implement resilience-building strategies in their schools. Counselors can utilize resilience-building strategies in their work with students. Counselors can also provide training to teachers on effective resilience-building strategies.

Individual

Dynarski and Gleason (2002) studied the effectiveness of various dropout reduction interventions. They described current interventions aimed at counteracting the numerous negative school experiences at-risk students face. These interventions included activities aimed at building students' self-esteem and increasing students' coping skills. Additionally, Dynarski and Gleason advocated for providing students with greater access to counselors to help students deal with challenges, including personal and family difficulties that are affecting success in school.

Hess and Copeland (2001) stated, "It is critical that we develop intervention programs that help students cope effectively with high levels of stress and create more extensive support systems to assist them with their emotional, social, and educational needs" (p. 403). These authors suggested providing interventions that focus on increasing students' engagement in school, improving students' problem-solving skills, strengthening family support systems, and helping students make good choices about friendships. Counselors can play a key role in these interventions.

Marcus and Sanders-Reio (2001) noted that attachment to peers promotes student achievement and engagement in school. Both association with deviant peers and rejection from conventional peers have been linked to dropping out of school (Vitaro et al., 2001). Lack of friendships can increase the possibility of disengagement from school. Thus, Vitaro et al. suggested that school personnel foster students' association with conventional peers.

Gleason and Dynarski (2002) suggested that the degree to which students persevere when they experience difficulties and optimism about the future may influence dropout. Similarly, Worrell and Hale (2001) found hope in the future to be a protective factor for students at risk for dropping out of school. Counselors can help create a school environment that promotes optimism in schools.

In the case study, Emelio may already be at risk for dropping out of school. Counselors' interventions related to building self-esteem, enhancing his support system, and improving stress management skills could help Emelio overcome his academic challenges as well as effectively manage any stress he is experiencing because of his responsibilities at home. Counselors could also help Emelio see how staying in school relates to success in the future. These interventions could help keep him in school.

Family

According to ASCA, school counselors are expected to consult with and support parents of at-risk students (ASCA [2001] position statement, *The Professional School Counselor and Dropout Prevention/Students-at-Risk*). Family members can play a role in intervening to prevent students from dropping out of school. For example, Hess and Copeland (2001) found students who graduated from high school relied more on family members when experiencing stress. Counselors can reach out to parents and provide guidance for family members who want to offer more emotional and academic support to students.

In the case study, Emelio's mother tries to help her sons with their homework and stresses the value of an education. However, when she attempted to participate in a school/parent function, she felt uncomfortable. Counselors can assist parents like Emelio's mother who want to be supportive of their children's education but may not know how to best achieve that goal.

School

Educational researchers have noted the importance of providing interventions to keep students engaged in learning (Baker et al., 2001; Dynarski & Gleason, 2002; Worrell & Hale, 2001). Engaging students who are at risk for dropping out is particularly important. Dynarski and Gleason found that successful school programs also provided students with appropriate academic challenges. Furthermore, teachers in successful programs connected lessons with real-life applications and experiences.

Newcomb et al. (2002) reiterated the critical role that academic remediation and support play in preventing school dropout. They advised teachers to promote high school graduation as an achievable goal. Pianta (1999) advocated for providing students showing difficulties in school adjustment or performance with support services before they fail. From an attachment perspective, these support services should be provided in a manner that preserves students' attachment to teachers and peers.

Commenting that educational reform is influenced more by politicians than educational researchers, Jimerson et al. (2002) suggested using great caution in using retention as an academic intervention for students experiencing academic difficulties. Unfortunately, teachers are often unaware of the research on the negative implications associated with retention (Haberman & Dill, 1993). Thus, Jimerson et al. stated that research on intervention strategies for low-achieving students, particularly alternative strategies to retention, need to be disseminated to school personnel to influence intervention strategies aimed at facilitating the success of students at risk of educational failure. Furthermore, this information should also be disseminated to the public.

Another ineffective remedial approach is ability grouping. This approach involves placing low-achieving students in classrooms with other students struggling academically. Research has shown that placing low-achieving students together in the same classroom does not improve student achievement (Kulik, 1993; Lesters & McDill, 1995). In fact, ability grouping may worsen the situation because such placement negatively stigmatizes lower achieving students. Thus, students in these classrooms may experience shame and lowered self-esteem. Conversely, when lower achieving students are mixed with average and high-ability students, negative stereotypes are avoided and students struggling academically often show more academic success.

Alternatives to retention and ability grouping need to be promoted. These alternatives include providing individualized instruction within the classroom so that all students can succeed. Dynarski and Gleason (2002) also advocated for smaller schools and scheduling time during school for students who are struggling academically to meet in small groups and work on academic skills with tutors or mentors. Students tutoring other students and cooperative learning are other strategies found to be effective when working with students who are struggling academically.

Another model addressing the needs of at-risk students is Henry Levin's Accelerated Schools (Levin, 1987; Levin & Chasin, 1994). At the heart of Levin's model is the belief that even students who are at risk possess strengths. These strengths include students' experiences, culture, language, and learning styles. School personnel can take students' strengths into consideration when designing instructional programs. This model also stresses parental involvement and empowering school staff and parents to be a part of the school decision-making process. Thus, in this model, school personnel, parents, and other community members participate in the educational process in meaningful ways.

Velez and Saenz (2001) stated that "policy makers and educational leaders need to promote efforts aggressively to ensure today's Latino students do not turn into a lost generation whose future is abandoned due to short-sighted political and fiscal concerns" (p. 462). Avilés et al. (1999) suggested advocating for Latino students, helping educate others in the school system about how to help these students and educating school personnel about multicultural issues. They also suggested including elements of Chicano/Latino culture in school settings and encouraging students to take pride in their heritage. Christenson et al. (2001) explained that successful interventions help students who feel marginalized by the school culture, school personnel, and other students become members of the school community.

In their position statement, ASCA (2001, *The Professional School Counselor and Dropout Prevention/Students-at-Risk*) explains that one of the roles of school counselors is to work with other school personnel in identifying potential dropouts. The goal of the school counselor in this instance is to identify these students and intervene before the students engage in self-destructive behaviors such as dropping out of school. The school counselor is expected to work closely with these at-risk students and encourage them to stay in school. ASCA explains that this task can be accomplished through providing responsive programs. These programs include components such as building self-esteem and improving decision-making skills. The school counselor is also expected to provide individual, group, family, and crisis counseling services to meet students' educational and career counseling needs. The school counselor may even need to help students find alternative means of completing their education (ASCA, 2001).

In the case study, Emelio could benefit from academic remediation and support services. Individualized instruction and peer tutoring could also help. Emelio would probably respond favorably to school personnel showing care and concern for him. Multicultural activities that promote pride in his ethnic heritage may help bolster his self-esteem and increase his engagement in school as well.

Community

Alexander et al. (2001) noted that academic success and positive personal and family resources somewhat buffer at-risk students who live in impoverished communities, but these students are still extremely vulnerable. Avilés et al. (1999) stated that school counselors can help students use inherent cultural strengths to overcome obstacles preventing academic success. These authors explained that counselors can also assist students in taking advantage of home and community resources. School counselors can act as a liaison between schools and the community. For example, Velez and Saenz (2001) suggested that the business community provide training opportunities for Latino youth and thus engender hope in the future. School counselors can help schools engage community members in this type of program. Such an intervention could help buffer the effects of poverty on students like Emelio.

ADAPTATIONS FOR DIVERSITY

Culture, ethnicity, students' learning differences, and family socioeconomic status can be considered risk factors for student dropout. However, these factors can also be viewed as attributes to the learning community. For example, fostering pride in students' cultural heritage can lead to increased self-esteem and tolerance for differences. Furthermore, utilizing the resources and social support inherent in many communities can benefit all students.

Counselors can help make school a comfortable place for every student. Workshops for school personnel on multicultural issues seem to be indicated. Counselors can also sponsor activities and clubs related to pride in diversity. Counselors can help make sure that students who need English as a Second Language classes or other academic support receive the services they need. Finally, counselors can take an active role in promoting communication between the student's family and school and increasing parents' involvement in school.

SUMMARY

School dropout is a serious social problem. Large numbers of dropouts place a burden on unemployment and welfare services as well as the criminal justice system. The correlation between ethnicity and student dropout is particularly disturbing, considering that the Hispanic population is the largest minority population and remains one of the fastest growing populations in the United States (Velez & Saenz, 2001). The trend of increased school dropout is likely to continue. Thus, school systems need to work harder to address the needs of all students.

Counselors can be instrumental in providing successful prevention and intervention efforts for students at risk for school dropout. Counselors can advocate for all students, facilitate the development of self-esteem in students, help school personnel see the negative implications of current policies such as retention, encourage positive teacher/student interactions, foster family support and healthy peer relationships, and engage members of the community in school activities. Counselors can also help schools create environments that promote inclusion for all ethnic groups and academic success for all students. Furthermore, counselors can help students become more educationally resilient by providing interventions such as promoting optimism, teaching students how to effectively manage stress, and helping students learn from the challenges they encounter. Through counselors' efforts, school dropout rates can be significantly reduced.

REFERENCES

Alexander, K. L., Entwisle, D. R., & Kabbani, N. S. (2001). The dropout process in life course perspective: Early risk factors at home and school. *Teachers College Record, 103*, 760–822.

American School Counselor Association. (2001). *Position statements*. Retrieved October 30, 2002, from http://www.schoolcounselor.org

Avilés, R. D., Guerrero, M. P., Howarth, H. B., & Thomas, G. (1999). Perceptions of Chicano/Latino students who have dropped out of school. *Journal of Counseling & Development, 77*, 465–473.

Baker, J. A., Derrer, R. D., Davis, S. M., Dinklage-Travis, H. E., Linder, D. S., & Nicholson, M. D. (2001). The flip side of the coin: Understanding the school's contribution to dropout and completion. *School Psychology Quarterly, 16*, 406–426.

Bickel, W. E., Bond, L., & LeMahieu, P. G. (1988). *Students at risk of not completing high school*. Unpublished manuscript, University of Pittsburgh.

Chinien, C., & Boutin, F. (2001–2002, December/January). Qualitative assessment of cognitive-based dropout prevention strategy. *The High School Journal*, 1–11.

Christenson, S. L., Sinclair, M. F., Lehr, C. A., & Godber, Y. (2001). Promoting successful school completion: Critical conceptual and methodological guidelines. *School Psychology Quarterly, 16*, 468–484.

Dynarski, M., & Gleason, P. (2002). How can we help? What we have learned from recent federal dropout prevention evaluations. *Journal of Education for Students Placed at Risk, 7*, 43–69.

Garnier, H. E., Stein, J. A., & Jacobs, J. K. (1997). The process of dropping out of high school: A 19-year perspective. *American Educational Research Journal, 34*, 395–419.

Gleason, P., & Dynarski, M. (2002). Do we know whom to serve? Issues in using risk factors to identify dropouts. *Journal of Education for Students Placed at Risk, 7*, 25–41.

Gonzalez, R., & Padilla, A. M. (1997). The academic resilience of Mexican American high school students. *Hispanic Journal of Behavioral Sciences, 19*, 301–317.

Haberman, M., & Dill, V. (1993). The knowledge base on retention vs. teacher ideology: Implications for teacher preparation. *Journal of Teacher Education, 44*, 352–360.

Hess, R. S., & Copeland, E. P. (2001). Students' stress, coping strategies, and school completion: A longitudinal perspective. *School Psychology Quarterly, 16*, 389–405.

Horn, L. J., & Chen, X. (1998). *Toward resiliency: At-risk students who make it to college* (OERI Publication No. PLLI-98-8056). Washington, DC: U.S. Government Printing Office. (ERIC Document Reproduction Service No. ED 419 463)

Jimerson, S. R. (1999). On the failure of failure: Examining the association between early grade retention and education and employment outcomes during late adolescence. *Journal of School Psychology, 37*, 243–272.

Jimerson, S. R., Anderson, G. E., & Whipple, A. D. (2002). Winning the battle and losing the war: Examining the relation between grade retention and dropping out of school. *Psychology in the Schools, 39*, 441–457.

Keith, P. B., & Schartzer, C. L. (1995). *What is the influence of Mexican American parental involvement on school attendance patterns?* (ERIC Document Reproduction Service No. ED 415 450)

Kulik, J. A. (1993, Spring). An analysis of the research on ability grouping. *National Research Center on the Gifted and Talented Newsletter,* 8–9. (ERIC Document Reproduction Service No. ED 367 095)

Lesters, N., & McDill, E. L. (1995). *Rising to the challenge: Emerging strategies for educating youth at risk.* (Urban Monograph Series). Oak Brook, IL: North Central Regional Education Lab. (ERIC Document Reproduction Service No. ED 397 202)

Levin, H. M. (1987). Accelerated schools for disadvantaged students. *Educational Leadership, 44*(6), 19–21.

Levin, H. M., & Chasin, G. (1994). *Thomas Edison accelerated elementary school.* Stanford, CA: Center for Educational Research at Stanford. (ERIC Document Reproduction Service No. ED 375 502)

Lopez, E. J., Ehly, S., & Garcia-Vazquez, E. (2002). Acculturation, social support, and academic achievement of Mexican and Mexican American high school students: An exploratory study. *Psychology in the Schools, 39*, 245–257.

Marcus, R. F., & Sanders-Reio, J. (2001). The influence of attachment on school completion. *School Psychology Quarterly, 16*, 427–444.

Mazza, J. J., & Eggert, L. L. (2001). Activity involvement among suicidal and nonsuicidal high-risk and typical adolescents. *Suicide and Life-Threatening Behavior, 31*, 265–281.

McMillen, M. M., Kaufman, P., Hausken, E. G., & Bradby, D. (1993). *Dropout rates in the United States: 1992.* Washington, DC: National Center for Education Statistics, U.S. Department of Education.

Mortenson, T. G. (1997). Postsecondary education opportunities: The Mortenson research seminar on public policy analysis of opportunity for postsecondary education, 1997. *Postsecondary Education Opportunity,* 55–66. (ERIC Document Reproduction Service No. ED 416 754)

National Center for Education Statistics. (2002). *Dropout rates in the United States: 2000.* Retrieved September 12, 2002, from http://nces.ed.gov/pubs2002/droppub_2001/

Newcomb, M. D., Abbott, R. D., Catalano, R. F., Hawkins, J. D., Battin-Pearson, S., & Hill, K. (2002). Mediational and deviance theories of late high school failure: Process roles of structural strains, academic competence, and general versus specific problem behaviors. *Journal of Counseling Psychology, 49*, 172–186.

Pianta, R. C. (1999). *Enhancing relationships between children and teachers.* Washington, DC: American Psychological Association.

Rumberger, R. W. (1993). Chicano dropouts: A review of research and policy issues. In R. Valencia (Ed.), *Chicano school failure and success: Research and policy agendas for the 1990's* (pp. 64–89). London: Falmer Press.

Rumberger, R. W. (1995). Dropping out of middle school: A multilevel analysis of students and schools. *American Educational Research Journal, 32*, 583–625.

Rumberger, R. W., Ghatak, R., Poulos, G., & Ritter, P. L. (1990). Family influences on dropout behavior in one California high school. *Sociology of Education, 63*, 283–299.

Scanlon, D., & Mellard, D. F. (2002). Academic and participation profiles of school-age dropouts with and without disabilities. *Exceptional Children, 68*, 239–258.

Swaim, R. C., Beauvais, F., Chavez, E. L., & Oetting, E. R. (1997). The effect of school dropout rates on estimates of adolescent substance abuse among three racial/ethnic groups. *American Journal of Public Health, 87*, 51–55.

Velez, W., & Saenz, R. (2001). Toward a comprehensive model of the school leaving process among Latinos. *School Psychology Quarterly, 16*, 445–467.

Vitaro, F., Larocque, D., Janosz, M., & Tremblay, R. E. (2001). Negative social experiences and dropping out of school. *Educational Psychology, 21*, 401–415.

Wang, M. C., Haertel, G. D., & Walberg, H. J. (1994). Educational resilience in inner cities. In M. C. Wang & E. W. Gorden (Eds.), *Educational resilience in inner-city America: Challenges and prospects* (pp. 42–72). Hillsdale, NJ: Erlbaum.

Wang, M. C., Haertel, G. D., & Walberg, H. J. (1997). Fostering educational resilience in inner-city schools. In M. C. Wang, G. D. Haertel, & H. J. Walberg (Eds.), *Children and youth* (pp. 119–140). Newbury Park, CA: Sage.

Wayman, J. C. (2002a, February/March). Student perceptions of teacher ethnic bias: A comparison of Mexican American and non-Latino White dropouts and students. *The High School Journal*, 27–37.

Wayman, J. C. (2002b). The utility of educational resilience for studying degree attainment in school dropouts. *Journal of Educational Research, 95*, 167–178.

Worrell, F. C., & Hale, R. L. (2001). The relationship of hope in the future and perceived school climate to school completion. *School Psychology Quarterly, 16*, 370–388.

Index